The New S Language

A Programming Environment for Data Analysis and Graphics

The Wadsworth & Brooks/Cole Statistics/Probability Series

Series Editors

O. E. Barndorff-Nielsen, Aarhus University
Peter J. Bickel, University of California, Berkeley
William S. Cleveland, AT&T Bell Laboratories
Richard M. Dudley, Massachusetts Institute of Technology

R. Becker, J. Chambers, A. Wilks, *The New S Language: A Programming Environment for Data Analysis and Graphics*
S. M. Berman, *Sojourns and Extremes of Stochastic Processes*
P. Bickel, K. Doksum, J. Hodges, Jr., *A Festschrift for Erich L. Lehmann*
G. Box, *The Collected Works of George E. P. Box, Volumes I and II*, G. Tiao, editor-in-chief
L. Breiman, J. Friedman, R. Olshen, C. Stone, *Classification and Regression Trees*
G. Casella, R. Berger, *Statistical Inference*
J. Chambers, W. S. Cleveland, B. Kleiner, P. Tukey, *Graphical Methods for Data Analysis*
J. Chambers, T. Hastie, *Statistical Models in S*
W. S. Cleveland, M. McGill, *Dynamic Graphics for Statistics*
K. Dehnad, *Quality Control, Robust Design, and the Taguchi Method*
R. Durrett, *Lecture Notes on Particle Systems and Percolation*
R. Durrett, *Probability: Theory and Examples*
F. Graybill, *Matrices with Applications in Statistics, Second Edition*
L. Le Cam, R. Olshen, *Proceedings of the Berkeley Conference in Honor of Jerzy Neyman and Jack Kiefer, Volumes I and II*
E. Lehmann, *Testing Statistical Hypotheses, Second Edition*
E. Lehmann, *Theory of Point Estimation*
P. Lewis, E. Orav, *Simulation Methodology for Statisticians, Operations Analysts, and Engineers*
H. J. Newton, *TIMESLAB*
J. Rawlings, *Applied Regression Analysis*
J. Rice, *Mathematical Statistics and Data Analysis*
J. Romano, A. Siegel, *Counterexamples in Probability and Statistics*
J. Tanur, F. Mosteller, W. Kruskal, E. Lehmann, R. Link, R. Pieters, G. Rising, *Statistics: A Guide to the Unknown, Third Edition*
J. Tukey, *The Collected Works of J. W. Tukey*, W. S. Cleveland, editor-in-chief
    Volume I: *Time Series: 1949-1964*, edited by D. Brillinger
    Volume II: *Time Series: 1965-1984*, edited by D. Brillinger
    Volume III: *Philosophy and Principles of Data Analysis: 1949-1964*, edited by L. Jones
    Volume IV: *Philosophy and Principles of Data Analysis: 1965-1986*, edited by L. Jones
    Volume V: *Graphics 1965-1985*, edited by W. S. Cleveland
    Volume VI: *More Mathematical, 1938-1984*, edited by C. Mallows

The New S Language

A Programming Environment for Data Analysis and Graphics

Richard A. Becker
John M. Chambers
Allan R. Wilks

AT&T Bell Laboratories

Wadsworth & Brooks/Cole Advanced Books & Software
Pacific Grove, California

Printed in the United States of America

10 9 8 7 6 5 4

Library of Congress Cataloging-in-Publication Data

Becker, Richard A.
    The new S language.

    Bibliography: p.
    Includes Index.
    1. S (Computer program language) I. Chambers, John M.
II. Wilks, Allan Reeve. III. Title.
QA76.73.S15B43 1988   519.5'028'55133   88-5656
ISBN 0-534-09192-X

This book was typeset by the authors, using a PostScript-based phototypesetter. Figures were generated in PostScript by S and directly incorporated into the typeset document. The text was formatted using *troff* on a computer running the 9th Edition of the UNIX operating system.

Sponsoring Editor: John Kimmel
Editorial Assistant: Maria Tarantino
Production Editor: Dorothy Bell
Cover Design: Vernon T. Boes
Printing and Binding: The Maple-Vail Book Manufacturing Group,
    Manchester, Pennsylvania

To Eloise, Bea, and Fiona

Preface

S is a language and an interactive programming environment for data analysis and graphics. The S *language* is a very high-level language for specifying computations. The language is part of an *interactive environment*: S encourages you to compute, look at data, and program interactively, with quick feedback to enable you to learn and understand.

The primary goal of the S environment is to enable and encourage good data analysis. The facilities in S are directed toward this goal.

- S is about *data*: it provides general and easy-to-use facilities for organizing, storing, and retrieving all sorts of data.
- S is about *analysis*: that is, computations you need to understand and use data. S provides numerical methods and other computational techniques.
- S is about *programming*: you can write functions in the S language itself. These functions can build on the power and simplicity of the S language. Because S is highly interactive, new functions can be designed and tried out much faster than with most languages. S also provides simple interfaces to other kinds of computing, such as to commands from the UNIX system or to C or Fortran routines.
- Especially, S is about *graphics*: interactive, informative, flexible ways of looking at data. The graphics capabilities of S are designed to encourage you to create new tools and try out new ideas.

A wide range of people are presently using S in diverse areas—financial analysis, statistics research, management, academia—for analytical computing, graphics, and data analysis. Join them and learn the power of working with S.

How to Read This Book

This book describes the S language and environment. When you read it, we recommend combining reading with doing. Have a computer terminal handy, preferably with graphics, and start S running. Read a little, then try out some of the examples or exercises, and experiment with variations or with your own data. A good way to review or supplement the discussion of a particular S function, say `plot`, is to look at the on-line documentation by typing

```
> help(plot)
```

In particular, whenever the book suggests looking up something in Appendix 1, you can use the on-line documentation instead.

We have tried to organize the book to facilitate self-teaching. Most chapters contain exercises that review and sometimes extend the material. Answers to many of the exercises appear at the end of the chapter.

As you read through the book, you may notice a gradual transition. Early chapters focus on using S informally for your own analysis. Later on, the emphasis shifts to more ambitious use of S as a programming environment for applications. This shift reflects the experience of many S users, who find that S leads them gently into the world of software design.

The book begins with three introductory chapters that should be helpful to all users: a case study that shows S without trying to explain it; a tutorial chapter covering material in an informal way; and a more formal treatment of the basic techniques in the language. You should be able to get through this material with a few hours of work. At this point, you will be able to use S productively.

The next three chapters introduce many more capabilities and help you understand the philosophy behind S. Chapter 4 gives an introduction to graphics within S, ranging from high-level plotting commands to detailed control of plots. The emphasis is on analytical displays: those that are valuable during data analysis. Chapter 5 describes data in S, explaining how S organizes matrices, arrays, and other kinds of data and introducing techniques to help you organize data for your applications. Chapter 6 discusses how to write S functions, including editing, debugging, and using the interface to the UNIX system. When you have finished the first six chapters, you should be able to create new facilities in S and use it creatively in your data analysis.

Chapters 7 and 8 provide advanced material that will be of interest if you intend to develop applications within S that will be used by others. Function writing is the topic of chapter 7; it introduces the interface to C and Fortran plus powerful techniques for controlling how S works and for symbolic computation. Chapter 8 ties together the organization of data with the design of functions; the combination of these ideas will often be the key to effective use of S in your own major applications.

Chapter 9 is for everyone. It brings together ideas from other chapters in the book, providing case studies and examples of using S for a variety of tasks, from data organization to solving numerical problems to a computer game. It also discusses matters of style and strategy in the use of S. It is a repository for important concepts, general ways of attacking problems, and advice on how best to use S. Advanced graphics material follows in chapter 10, which shows how to use the capabilities of S to implement new graphics functions. Chapter 11 gives a compact description of the syntax and semantics of the S language, and will be of most interest to those of you who want to know how S really works. Finally, we end with an annotated bibliography listing some books that may be of interest to you as you use S.

The narrative material ends midway through the book. Most of the remainder is devoted to detailed documentation of the S functions and datasets. Documentation for S functions is presented in Appendix 1. Appendix 2 describes the datasets that are available in the system data directory. The material in Appendices 1 and 2 is also available on-line for the S user. Appendix 3 provides one-line descriptions of S functions, broken down by various topics. It can help you to find functions when you can't remember their names. Appendix 4 gives people who have used an earlier version of S a description of what has changed. An extensive index at the end of the book can be used for quick access to the places in the text where specific topics are discussed.

The Software

S is a software system that runs under the UNIX operating system on a variety of hardware configurations. S is designed to take advantage of other tools and languages provided by the operating system. As this book is being written, S runs on many different computers, from supermicros to large mainframe machines. Work is continually under way to implement S on new hardware.

For information on obtaining source code for S, contact:

AT&T Software Licensing Manager
Room 3A36
10 Independence Blvd.
Warren, NJ 07060-9824
(800) 462-8146

(908) 580-6355 *Fax*
(908) 580-5388 *International*

There are also a number of independent vendors selling binary-only versions of S. The binary versions are adapted to specific computers and, sometimes, to other operating systems. A list of the vendors is available from AT&T.

S and Statistics

S grew out of the interests and needs of people doing statistics research, and it is used extensively by statisticians. However, it is a language and environment for *data analysis*; a background in statistics is not needed to use S. This book, in fact, describes S for a general computing audience and does not present the statistical use of S. We and our colleagues are planning another book on statistical software in S. The present book is designed to be useful to anyone who has an interest in looking at data.

What's New

After looking at the title of this book, *The New S Language*, you might be wondering what the *old* S language was like. The old S language was described in two books, by Richard A. Becker and John M. Chambers: *S: An Interactive Environment for Data Analysis and Graphics*, published by Wadsworth in 1984, and *Extending the S System* in 1985. Since that time, S has changed in many ways.

For those of you who never knew the old version of S, don't worry—all that you need to know is contained in this book. For those of you who are familiar with old-S, new S is a more complete programming environment and occasionally does things differently than they were done before. Appendix 4 gives a summary of what has changed.

Acknowledgments

In writing this book, and generally in our research on S, we owe perhaps our largest debt to our users, who have provided hundreds of comments, questions, and complaints. In preparing this version of S, we owe a special debt to our colleagues at AT&T Bell Laboratories who have been using the new S language, for their many ideas and comments and for their patience as S evolved under their keyboards. We have also benefited greatly from feedback provided by a network of beta test sites inside and outside AT&T. A partial list of individuals to whom we owe thanks includes Doug Bates, Marilyn Becker, Bill Cleveland, Lorraine Denby, Anne Freeny, Bill Gale, Colin Goodall, Michael Greenacre, Trevor Hastie, Richard Heiberger, Don Kretsch, Diane Lambert, David Lubinsky, John Macdonald, Colin Mallows, Peter Nelson, Daryl Pregibon, Judy Schilling, Ritei Shibata, Bill Shugard, Masaaki Sibuya, Kishore Singhal, Irma Terpenning, Rob Tibshirani, Luke Tierney, and Alan Zaslavsky.

Ritei Shibata and Masaaki Sibuya, who translated the 1984 book into Japanese, gave us many useful comments. We are also grateful to John Kimmel and the staff at Wadsworth & Brooks/Cole for their support and encouragement. Last, but not least, thanks to Virginia Penn for helping to prepare the book for publication.

Richard A. Becker
John M. Chambers
Allan R. Wilks

Contents

1

How to Beat the Lottery

One of the best ways of getting acquainted with S is to use it to help you understand a particular set of data. Let's look at a situation where you might be motivated to perform data analysis.

1.1 Using S to Understand Data

The lottery is a common feature of modern life. Lotteries range from the Irish Sweepstakes, with its yearly large drawings and enormous payoffs, to daily numbers games run by state governments (as well as illegal games run by bookies).

You might wonder why we are presenting lottery data here. There are several answers. First, there is the traditional association between probability theory and gambling—the foundations of statistics go back to studies of games of chance. Lotteries raise many interesting questions. In fact, data analysis may be the only practical way of answering questions such as "Is the lottery fair?" A second reason is that the ubiquity of gambling and lotteries has acquainted almost everyone with the basic concepts involved. A third reason is that a scientific look at lottery data may provide answers to the important questions: "Should I play, and if so, how should I play?"

1.2 New Jersey Pick-It Lottery Data

The specific data we will look at concerns the New Jersey Pick-It Lottery, a daily numbers game run by the state of New Jersey to aid education and institutions. Our data is for 254 drawings just after the lottery was started, from May, 1975 to March, 1976. Pick-It is a parimutuel game, meaning that the winners share a fraction of the money taken in for the particular drawing. Each ticket costs fifty cents and at the time of purchase the player picks a three-digit number ranging from 000 to 999. Half of the money bet during the day is placed in a prize pool (the state takes the other half) and anyone who picked the winning number shares equally in the pool.

      The data available from the NJ Lottery Commission gives for each drawing the winning number and the payoff for a winning ticket. The winning numbers are:[†]

```
> lottery.number    # print the winning numbers
  [1] 810 156 140 542 507 972 431 981 865 499  20 123 356
 [14]  15  11 160 507 779 286 268 698 640 136 854  69 199
 [27] 413 192 602 987 112 245 174 913 828 539 434 357 178
 [40] 198 406  79  34  89 257 662 524 809 527 257   8 446
 [53] 440 781 615 231 580 987 391 267 808 258 479 516 964
 [66] 742 537 275 112 230 310 335 238 294 854 309  26 960
 [79] 200 604 841 659 735 105 254 117 751 781 937  20 348
 [92] 653 410 468  77 921 314 683   0 963 122  18 827 661
[105] 918 110 767 761 305 485   8 808 648 508 684 879  67
[118] 282 928 733 518 441 661 219 310 771 906 235 396 223
[131] 695 499  42 230 623 300 380 646 553 182 158 744 894
[144] 689 978 314 337 226 106 299 947 896 863 239 180 764
[157] 849  87 975  92 701 402   1 884 750 236 395 999 744
[170] 714 253 711 863 496 214 430 107 781 954 941 416 243
[183] 480 111  47 691 616 253 477  11 114 133 293 812 197
[196] 358   7 996 842 255 374 693 383  99 474 333 467 515
[209] 357 694 919 424 274 913 919 245 964 472 935 434 170
[222] 300 476 528 403 677 559 187 652 319 582 541  16 981
[235] 158 945  72 167  77 185 209 893 346 515 555 858 434
[248] 541 411 109 761 767 597 479
```

The corresponding payoffs are:

```
> lottery.payoff   # print the payoffs
 [1] 190.0 120.5 285.5 184.0 384.5 324.5 114.0 506.5 290.0
[10] 869.5 668.5  83.0 188.0 449.0 289.5 212.0 466.0 548.5
[19] 260.0 300.5 556.5 371.5 112.5 254.5 368.0 510.0 102.0
[28] 206.5 261.5 361.0 167.5 187.0 146.5 205.0 348.5 283.5
```

[†]At this point, don't worry about understanding the italic typewriter-font S expression `> lottery.number`—that is what the S user types to produce the output that follows the expression. The ">" is the S prompt character and the text following the "#" is an S comment.

```
 [37]  447.0 102.5 219.0 292.5 343.0 332.5 532.5 445.5 127.0
 [46]  557.5 203.5 373.5 142.0 230.5 482.5 512.5 330.0 273.0
 [55]  171.0 178.0 463.5 476.0 290.0 176.0 195.0 159.5 296.0
 [64]  177.5 406.0 182.0 164.5 137.0 191.0 298.0 110.0 353.0
 [73]  192.5 308.5 287.0 203.5 377.5 211.5 342.0 259.0 231.0
 [82]  348.0 159.0 130.5 176.0 128.5 159.0 290.0 335.0 514.0
 [91]  191.0 304.5 167.0 257.0 640.0 142.0 146.0 356.0  96.0
[100]  295.0 237.0 312.5 215.0 442.5 127.0 127.0 756.0 228.5
[109]  132.0 256.0 374.5 262.5 286.5 264.0 380.5 357.5 478.5
[118]  511.5 218.0 353.0 162.5 184.0 548.0 166.5 147.5 240.0
[127]  386.0 130.5 287.5 230.0 480.5 247.5 380.0 238.5 237.5
[136]  214.5 394.5 416.5 392.5 244.5 202.0 371.5 553.0 293.5
[145]  295.0 178.0 334.5 226.0 194.0 388.5 353.0 404.0 348.0
[154]  163.5 216.5 283.0 388.5 567.5 250.5 478.0 267.5 326.5
[163]  369.0 512.5 341.0 188.5 386.0 239.0 480.5 105.0 227.0
[172]  130.5 384.5 294.5 154.0 324.0 116.0 229.0 301.5 334.0
[181]  143.5 212.0 448.0 126.5 417.5 276.5 303.0 211.0 373.0
[190]  209.5 207.5 195.0 317.0 170.5 230.0 143.0 361.0 452.0
[199]  260.5 308.5 206.0 256.5 291.0 421.5 295.5 119.5 268.5
[208]  221.0 151.5 314.5 313.5 323.5 204.0 241.0 637.0 214.0
[217]  348.0 191.5 384.0 220.0 285.5 335.0 251.5 131.5 328.0
[226]  392.0 509.0 235.5 249.5 129.5 303.0 201.5 365.0 346.5
[235]  210.5 334.0 376.5 215.5 312.0 239.5 221.0 388.0 154.5
[244]  268.5 127.0 537.5 427.5 272.0 197.0 167.5 292.0 170.0
[253]  486.5 262.0
```

Thus, for the first drawing, the winning number was 810 and it paid $190.00 to each winning ticket holder. Streams of numbers like this are both difficult to use and boring. One of the best ways to understand the data is to look at it graphically. Before doing any plots, however, we should think of the questions we might want to ask of the data. For example, there have been notorious cases of fraud in lotteries (see Figure 1.1).

Although a single rigged drawing is something that we could not detect with our data, we may be able to detect long-term irregularities. Let's look at the winning numbers to see if they appear to be chosen at random.

```
> hist(lottery.number)    # Figure 1.2
```

The histogram looks fairly flat—no need to inform a grand jury.

Of course, most of our attention will probably be directed at the payoffs. Elementary probabilistic reasoning tells us that, unless we can predict the future or rig the lottery, a single number that we pick has a 1 in 1000 chance of winning. If we play many times, we expect about 1 winning number per 1000 plays. Since a ticket costs fifty cents, 1000 plays will cost $500, so we hope to win at least $500 each time we win, otherwise we will lose money in the long run.

6 Named in Rigged $1 Million Pennsylvania Lottery

Special to The New York Times

HARRISBURG, Pa., Sept. 19 — The television announcer who conducts Pennsylvania's daily lottery, a lottery official and four other persons conspired to rig a lottery drawing and fraudulently won more than $1 million, a grand jury said today.

The grand jury said the six would have won even more money through the illegal numbers game in Pittsburgh, which uses the same three-digit number as the legal game, had the bookmakers who accepted their bets not refused to pay off.

The bookmakers refused because the heavy betting on the group's number, 666, led them to suspect that the April 24 drawing had been rigged. It was the bookmakers' suspicions that led to the investigation.

The grand jury recommended the indictment of the announcer, Nick Perry; four of his friends and Edward Plevel, the Bureau of State Lotteries official in charge of security that day, on charges of criminal solicitation, criminal conspiracy, theft by deception and rigging a publicly exhibited contest. It recommended that Mr. Perry and Mr. Plevel also be charged with perjury.

Under Pennsylvania law, the Attorney General makes specific, formal charges based on grand jury presentments. Attorney General Harvey Bartle 3d said today that the charges would be filed after the jury's report was received. Those named in the presentment could not be reached for comment immediately.

At a news conference today at which he announced the grand jury action, Gov. Dick Thornburgh also announced the resignation, effective Nov. 30, of State Revenue Secretary Howard Cohen. Mr.

Continued on Page 6, Column 3

HAPPY ANNIVERSARY MR. & MRS. EDWARD F. McCARTHY
THANKS FOR EVERYTHING LOVE. YOUR FAMILY—ADVT

Happy Half-Century, Good Doctor Norma. Care to try for another? Love. Bob, Mark. Susan—ADVT

Associated Press

In the April 24 lottery drawing, the 6 ball popped up three times

Figure 1.1. A case of lottery fraud in September, 1980. (© 1980 by The New York Times Company. Reprinted by permission. Wide World Photos.)

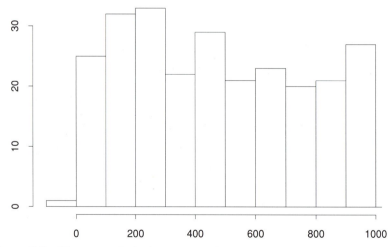

Figure 1.2. Histogram of winning numbers from 254 lottery drawings. Since there are 10 bars, the count should be approximately 25 in each bar, if the winning numbers are drawn at random. The small bar at the left represents the one time that 000 was the winning number.

Let's make a histogram of the payoffs.

```
> hist(lottery.payoff)    # Figure 1.3
```

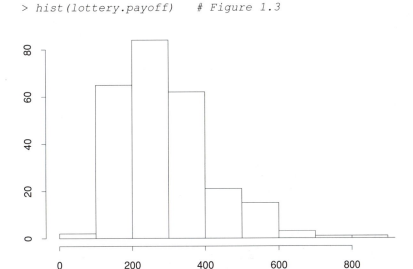

Figure 1.3. A histogram of the lottery payoffs shows that payoffs range from less than $100 to more than $800, although the bulk of the payoffs are between $100 and $400.

In our set of data there were a number of payoffs larger than $500—perhaps we have a chance. The widely varying payoffs are primarily due to the par-imutuel betting in the lottery; if you win when few others win, you will get a large payoff. If you are *unlucky* enough to win along with lots of others, the payoff may be relatively small. Let's see what the largest and smallest payoffs and corresponding winning numbers were:

```
> max(lottery.payoff)    # the largest payoff
[1] 869.5
> lottery.number[ lottery.payoff==max(lottery.payoff) ]
[1] 499
> min(lottery.payoff)    # the smallest payoff
[1] 83
> lottery.number[ lottery.payoff==min(lottery.payoff) ]
[1] 123
```

Winners who bet on "123" must have been disappointed; $83 is not a very large payoff. On the other hand, $869.50 is very nice.

Since the winning numbers and the payoffs come in pairs, a number and a payoff for each drawing, we can produce a scatterplot of the data to see if there is any relationship between the payoff and the winning number.

```
> plot(lottery.number, lottery.payoff)    # Figure 1.4
```

What do you see in the picture? Does the payoff seem to depend on the position of the winning number? Perhaps it would help to add a "middle"

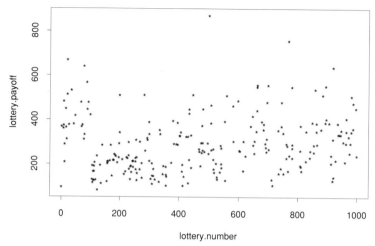

Figure 1.4. Scatterplot of winning number and payoff for the 254 different lottery drawings.

line that follows the overall pattern of the data:

```
> lines( lowess(lottery.number, lottery.payoff, f=.2) )
> # Figure 1.5
```

Can you see the interesting characteristics now in Figure 1.5? There are substantially higher payoffs for numbers with a leading zero, meaning fewer people bet on these numbers. Perhaps that reflects people's reluctance to think of numbers with leading zeros. After all, no one writes $010 on a ten dollar check! Also note that, except for the numbers with leading zeros, payoffs seem to increase as the winning number increases.

It would be interesting to see exactly what numbers correspond to the large payoffs. Fortunately, with an interactive graphical input device, we can do that by simply pointing at the "outliers":

```
> identify(lottery.number, lottery.payoff, lottery.number)
> # Figure 1.6
```

Can you see the pattern in the numbers with very high payoffs? Spend some time thinking before looking at the footnote, which contains the explanation.[†] Did you find the pattern? If so, you have accomplished something very important—you learned something new by looking at the data, and afterwards

---

[†]Most of the numbers with high payoffs have duplicate digits. The lottery has a mode of betting, called "combination bets" where players win if the digits in their number appear in any order. Ticket 123 would win on 321, 231, etc. The combination bet provides six ways to win and pays a one-sixth share. However, combination bettors must pick numbers with three different digits. Payoffs for the numbers with duplicate digits are not shared with combination bettors, and thus are higher.

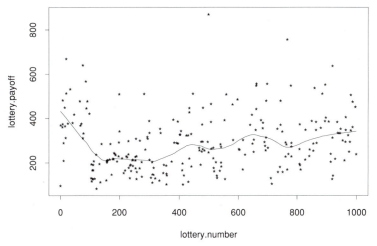

Figure 1.5. A smooth curve is superimposed on the winning number and payoff scatterplot.

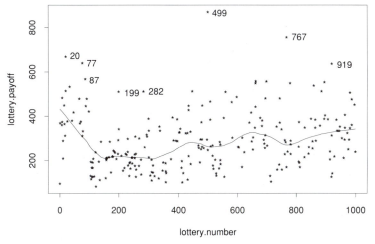

Figure 1.6. Outliers on the scatterplot are labelled with the actual winning number.

found that it could be explained by the rules of the game. Much of data analysis consists of detecting clues from patterns in the data and then following up on the clues to better understand the data.

If you are now ready to put down this book and place your bet on 088, wait just a moment. By looking at similar data from two later periods in the Pick-It lottery, beginning November, 1976 and December, 1980, we can see if the payoffs changed over time.

```
> boxplot(lottery.payoff, lottery2.payoff, lottery3.payoff)
> abline(h=500)  # horizontal line at 500, Figure 1.7
```

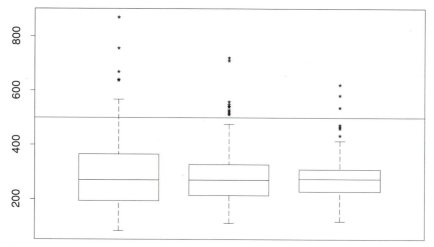

Figure 1.7. Boxplots show lottery payoffs for three different time periods: 1975, 1976, and 1980.

The box in a boxplot contains the middle half of the data; the whiskers extending from the box reach to the most extreme non-outlier; outlying points are plotted individually. Clearly, we are not the only people to have seen the patterns in payoffs. Over the period of years for which we have data, the payoffs settle down and it is now rare for a payoff to exceed $500.

1.3 A Comment

Throughout this chapter we have presented, without explanation, a number of S expressions and the resulting output. The reason for this was to concentrate on the data analysis as well as demonstrate that S is an unobtrusive tool; it doesn't force you to think like a programmer when you want to think about your data. You should have seen that the S expressions needed to analyze the lottery data were simple (you may want to go back and look at them). You should also have noticed the power of interactive data analysis combined with well-chosen graphical displays.

In the next section, we will again analyze some data. However, besides looking at the data, we will also turn more attention to explaining a number of basic features of S.

You now know that the title of this chapter is somewhat misleading; perhaps it should be "How to Lose Less in the Lottery." Place your bet if you enjoy gambling. Do not expect to win.

1.4 Related Reading

Irwin W. Kabak and Jeffrey S. Simonoff, "A Look at Daily Lotteries," *The American Statistician,* Vol. 37, No. 1, pp. 49-52, 1983.

Herman Chernoff, "An Analysis of the Massachusetts Numbers Game," *Statistics and Related Topics,* M. Csorgo, D. A. Dawson, J. N. K. Rao, A. K. Md. E. Saleh (eds.), North-Holland, 1981.

Herman Chernoff, "How to Beat the Massachusetts Numbers Game: An Application of Some Basic Ideas in Probability and Statistics," *The Mathematical Intelligencer,* Vol. 3, No. 4, pp. 166-172, 1981.

Jagdish S. Rustagi, "Probabilistic Structures of Modern Lottery Games," Technical Report No. 236, Department of Statistics, Ohio State University, May 1981.

2
Tutorial Introduction to S

The use of S requires some basic familiarity with interactive computing: how to log into the UNIX system, what keys to use on the terminal to delete characters and lines and to send interrupts, etc. This elementary training is generally available through introductory UNIX system manuals and courses. (See, for example, the book *Introducing the UNIX System*, listed in the bibliography.)

2.1 Invoking S

Once you are able to log into the computer and have received the UNIX system prompt "$", type the capital letter

```
$ S
```

to start running S. When finished with an S session, type (after the S prompt ">")

```
> q()
```

to quit.

2.2 Expressions and Data

A good way to start thinking about S is to compare it to a very powerful calculator. In an interactive session with S, you type *expressions*, and S does computations and, like a calculator, prints the results.

```
> 3*(11.5 + 2.3)
[1] 41.4
```

(In this and later examples, the user's typing is shown in *italic type-writer font* following the S prompt character ">", and the results printed by S follow in typewriter font.) Unlike a calculator, however, S

- works on whole data objects at once, not just single numbers,
- has several hundred functions (and allows the user to define many more),
- can generate graphical displays and reports as well as print numbers.

To get a feeling for S, let's suppose we have come on some interesting data, such as the following fragment of a table:

	Population	Illiteracy	Murder
Alabama	3615	2.1	15.1
Alaska	365	1.5	11.3
Arizona	2212	1.8	7.8
Arkansas	2110	1.9	10.1
California	21198	1.1	10.3
Colorado	2541	0.7	6.8
Connecticut	3100	1.1	3.1
Delaware	579	0.9	6.2
Florida	8277	1.3	10.7
Georgia	4931	2.0	13.9

Table 2.1. Part of a table of statistical data on the states of the United States: population in thousands, percent illiteracy, and murders per 100,000 population.

The most basic kinds of data that S deals with are numbers such as 3615, 2.1, 3.615e6 (this notation means 3.615×10^6); logical values (TRUE and FALSE), and character strings such as "Georgia" and "Murder Rate". Results can always be kept around for further use by picking a name and *assigning* that name to the result of an expression:

```
> g ← 4931
```

creates an S *object* called g containing the single value, 4931. The sequence of characters "g ←" is normally read as "g gets". The left arrow is typed as the two characters "<" and "−". Once the assignment takes place, g can appear in another S expression, to stand for the object currently assigned the name g. In particular, just typing the name of an object by itself causes its value to be printed on the terminal:

```
> g
[1] 4931
```

Expressions are made up by combining object names and constants (numbers, TRUE and FALSE, character strings) with *operators* and *functions*. Operators include the usual arithmetic operations, comparisons, and a few special operators. Thus,

```
> g * 1000
[1] 4931000
```

is an expression that is evaluated to multiply the data value in g by 1000. This expression *does not* change the value of g, since no assignment was done.

Numerical, graphical, and other computations in S are done by functions, which are called by giving their name followed by their *arguments* in parentheses; e.g., the c function

```
> c(15.1, 11.3, 7.8)
[1] 15.1 11.3  7.8
```

collects its arguments to form an object (here with 3 data values). We often call a simple object, such as the three numbers here, a *vector*. As we said, S operates on whole vectors, not just single numbers. Observe what happens when an entire vector is multiplied by a number:

```
> c(15.1, 11.3, 7.8)*2.7
[1] 40.77 30.51 21.06
```

The c function is a good way to create small objects, like the data in the third column of Table 2.1:

```
> murder ← c(15.1, 11.3, 7.8, 10.1, 10.3,
+ 6.8, 3.1, 6.2, 10.7, 13.9)
```

We used a long enough name here to help us remember what data was assigned. Generally, names can contain letters, digits, and periods ("."), and must start with a letter. Although it is a good idea to use meaningful names for objects, a name need bear no relation to the contents of the object and names can be reused whenever desired. As the example shows, expressions can be spread over several lines, with blanks and tabs inserted between parts of the expression to make them more readable, if you like. S prompts for a continuation line by means of the "+" prompt character.

There are several hundred functions in S; to see them collected into related groups, look in Appendix 3. S functions can be used

- to compute summaries: mean(x), range(x), lsfit(x,y)
- to perform transformations: sin(x), log(x), sqrt(x)
- to manipulate data: sort(x), unique(x)
- to perform many specialized computations.

Some S functions, primarily those that deal with printed or graphical output, are useful for their *side effects* instead of their value. The functions hist and plot, introduced in the lottery example of chapter 1, produce graphical output;

we will look at more graphical functions in section 2.6. Another function, stem, computes and prints a summary of a collection of data—producing what looks like a histogram on its side:

```
> stem(murder)

N = 10    Median = 10.2
Quartiles = 6.8, 11.3

Decimal point is 1 place to the right of the colon

    0 : 3
    0 : 678
    1 : 00114
    1 : 5
```

Though $c(x1, x2, \ldots)$ is fine for generating small objects, for somewhat larger objects it is usually best to put the data values into a file, say with a text editor, and then use the S scan function. We can escape from S to an editor, say ed, and create a UNIX system file "illitdata" containing the data from the second column in Table 2.1:

```
> !ed
a
2.1    1.5    1.8    1.9    1.1
0.7    1.1    0.9    1.3    2
.
w illitdata
38
q
>
```

The "!" in front of ed tells S that we want the rest of the line sent as a command to the UNIX system. The lines beginning a, w, and q, are commands to *ed*; 38 is the number of characters that *ed* wrote to the file. We can then read these numbers and put them into an object with the S expression:

```
> illit ← scan("illitdata")
> illit
  [1] 2.1 1.5 1.8 1.9 1.1 0.7 1.1 0.9 1.3 2.0
```

S expressions can have character string values as well as numerical or logical ones. For example, suppose we have created a file "statecodes":

```
> !cat statecodes
AL AK AZ AR CA
CO CT DE FL GA
```

We can read it in just the same way:

```
> states ← scan ("statecodes",character())
```

The second argument, `character()`, tells `scan` that the data in the file consists of character strings. If any string contains blanks, we must tell `scan` that we don't want the individual words as separate items; one simple solution is to surround the items by quotes. We will use these three objects, `murder`, `illit`, and `states`, in the examples to follow.

2.3 Arithmetic

S has the usual arithmetic operators:

```
    +      −      *      /      ^
```

(the last one raises to a power). Looking at how these operators work will help give the flavor of computations in S. Here are some examples:

```
> murder / illit    # murders per thousand illiterates
 [1]  7.190476 7.533333 4.333333 5.315789 9.363636
 [6]  9.714286 2.818182 6.888889 8.230769 6.950000
> abs (murder − mean (murder))   # absolute residual from mean
 [1]  5.5700003 1.7700003 1.7299997 0.5700003
 [5]  0.7700003 2.7299997 6.4299997 3.3299997
 [9]  1.1700003 4.3700003
> 2^c (5,8,3)    # some powers of two
 [1]   32 256    8
```

The text beginning with # and going to the end of the line is a comment: we can type comments like this anywhere in S expressions. Such comments are a good way to record what has been found during an analysis. Also, you can now see the purpose for the `[1]`, `[6]`, etc. that are at the start of the lines of printed output—they show which element of the vector begins each line.

The first expression divided two vectors of the same length, element-by-element (`7.190476` is `15.1` divided by `2.1`, and so on). The two vectors don't need to be of the same length; in the second example, `mean (murder)` is a single number. In the subtraction, the single number is in effect replicated 10 times, to match the length of the vector `murder`. In general, the shorter vector is replicated until it is as long as the longer vector.

S has a very convenient special operator, "`:`", in addition to the standard arithmetic operators. The "`:`" operator creates the sequence between any two numbers in steps of `1` or `−1`:

```
> 0:10
 [1]   0  1  2  3  4  5  6  7  8  9 10
> 3:−7
 [1]   3  2  1  0 −1 −2 −3 −4 −5 −6 −7
```

Try the following exercises yourself. They introduce some more S functions.

Exercises

2.1   Invoke S and create the objects `murder`, `illit`, and `states` with the same data we showed in section 2.2. You can create files with a text editor, and read them in with `scan`, or use the c function. Be careful to check that your data agrees with ours. Now create another object, `population`, that has the data from the first column of Table 2.1.

2.2   Compute the mean of the illiteracy data, and its residuals from the mean value.

2.3   S also has the function `median` as an alternative to `mean`. Compute the medians of `murder` and `illit`. Are the medians different than the means?

2.4   The function `sort(x)` returns all the values in x, sorted smallest to largest. Look at sorted values for `murder` and compare those to `median(murder)`.

2.5   Convert the murder rate data to the number of murders in each of the 10 states.

2.6   S has all the usual mathematical functions. For example, `log10` transforms the data in its argument to their common logarithms. Compute the logarithms of the population data, and compare the result to `population`, say by using the `stem` function. What do you notice?

2.7   Suppose we create the numbers from 1 to 10:

```
x ← 1:10
```

The following expressions all produce ten zeros, in principle.

```
(x + 100) - 100 - x
(x + pi) - pi - x
((x * 10) / 10) - x
((x / 10) * 10) - x
```

Which ones do you think will turn out to be exactly zero? Play around with the expressions experimentally and try to see what is happening.

2.4 Comparison Operators

Just as S has *arithmetic* operators for addition, subtraction, etc., it also has *comparison* operators to compare data values: these compare two expressions and return logical values. For example, `x > y` returns a vector with TRUE wherever an element cf x was larger than the corresponding element of y and FALSE everywhere else.

```
> murder > 12
 [1] T F F F F F F F F T
```

The printed values, T and F, are alternate forms for the logical constants TRUE and FALSE. The other comparison operators are available as well: "<", ">=", "<=". Equality and inequality tests are "==" and "!=". Notice that the "==" is two characters long; the single character "=" is used to supply arguments to functions by name; we will see some examples in section 2.6.

Exercises

2.8   Why might it be a bad idea to use the equality operator when operating with numbers that are non-integers?

2.5 Extracting Data: Subscripts

Data can be extracted from an object by using an expression in square brackets following the name of the object. To get the first three values from the object murder:

```
> murder[1:3]
 [1] 15.1 11.3  7.8
```

As in the example, if the expression in square brackets produces positive integers, the result is the corresponding elements of the object (counting from 1 for the first element). Another frequently useful expression extracts all the data corresponding to TRUE values of some logical condition. In S this is done by enclosing in square brackets any logical expression of the same length as the object; e.g.,

```
> murder[murder>12]
 [1] 15.1 13.9
```

The logical expression often involves the object itself, as in this example, but doesn't need to. To find which states had high murder rates, for example:

```
> states[murder>12]
 [1] "AL" "GA"
```

Or, to find the illiteracy rate for California:

```
> illit[states == "CA"]
 [1] 1.1
```

Finally, we can choose some elements to *exclude* and get all the remaining data by negating the indices of the elements to exclude; for example,

```
> murder[-1]
[1] 11.3  7.8 10.1 10.3  6.8  3.1  6.2 10.7 13.9
```

gives all but the first element. This is an easy way to exclude outliers or special cases.

Subsets can be applied to any expression, not just to names of objects. To find which indices in `murder` correspond to high rates, we can type:

```
> which ← (1:10)[murder>12]
> which
[1]  1 10
```

This sort of expression is nice if we want to select repeatedly a few elements from a large object, since `which` will only be as large as the subscript, not as large as the whole object.

In the previous example, we had to know that there were ten numbers in `murder`. To avoid needing to know offhand how long an object is, we can use the `length(x)` function to return the number of elements in its argument. In the previous example, `1:length(murder)` would give the sequence of indices corresponding to `murder`.

Exercises

2.9   Summarize three different kinds of subscript expressions used to extract data.

2.10   Print the elements of `illit` in reverse order.

2.11   Print the elements of `illit` that are greater than the median illiteracy. Print the elements of `murder` for which illiteracy is greater than its median.

2.12   Notice the parentheses in the expression that computed `which`. Why do you think they are there? Experiment a little.

2.13* (This exercise is a little harder than the others, which is why it is marked with a star.)

Suppose we want to compute the *interquartile range*, the difference between the third quartile and the first quartile. (Quartiles are defined so that one-quarter of the data is smaller than the first quartile, and three-quarters of the data is smaller than the third quartile.) Find the interquartile range of `murder` and of `illit`. There are several ways to compute this in S. Try to follow both of these hints to get two different ways:

(i)   Use the elements of the sorted data that correspond to the first and third quartiles (the function `sort` is helpful);

(ii)   Use the idea that the first quartile is essentially the median of the smaller half of the data, and that this in turn is the part of the data less than the overall median.

2.6 Graphics

Up to this point, we obtained information from S by printing numerical values or by the specialized printout of the `stem` function. Printed output is useful, but graphics, such as scatterplots, provide much more information in an easy-to-comprehend form. S has extensive graphical capabilities which can be used with a variety of plotting devices. We will next look at some of these capabilities.

The first step in doing graphics in S is to call a *device function* that tells S what graphics device you intend to use. The device function only needs to be called once per session. This function often corresponds to the name of the terminal or workstation you are using, if that terminal has graphics capabilities. The device function may also specify that we want graphics to be done by some other software; for example,

```
> postscript ()
```

says that plots should be produced for printing on a laser printer or typesetter that understands the PostScript language. The plots shown in this book were produced with the `postscript` device function. Consult `Devices` in Appendix 1 to find a graphics device that S supports and to which you have access.

Once the device function has been called, we can produce a plot; for example:

```
> plot (illit, murder)    # Figure 2.1
```

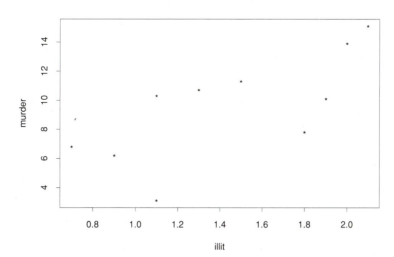

Figure 2.1. Scatterplot of murder versus illiteracy: 10 states.

One advantage of plots is that we can look at more data than would be possible with printed output, so let's expand our objects to include data from all 50 states. The data comes from objects in the S system data directory, objects that are available to all users: `state` in Appendix 2 describes this data.

```
> murder ← state.x77[, 5]   # 5th column is murder
> illit ← state.x77[, 3]   #3rd column is illiteracy
> states ← state.abb  # state abbreviations
```

These assignments have redefined the three objects `murder`, `illit`, and `states`. Their previous contents are replaced by the current assignment. Now we can redo the plot of Figure 2.1.

```
> plot(illit, murder)    # Figure 2.2
```

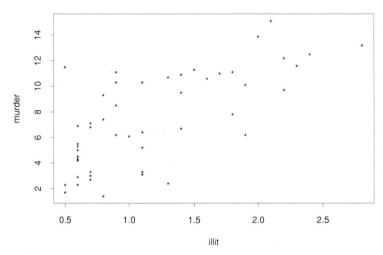

Figure 2.2. Scatterplot of murder versus illiteracy: 50 states.

The full 50-state data produces a more suggestive picture. When looking at this plot, some new questions about the data come to mind. Indeed, the great power of interactive graphics in data analysis is its ability to reveal unexpected features in the data. We will explore some of the features in the next set of exercises. The points appear to fall in a loose pattern, with murder rate rising with illiteracy. Points that have particularly large values of either variable or that lie on the edge of the overall pattern attract our attention. The S function `identify` can be used to label these points interactively (look up your graphics device in Appendix 1 to see how to use its graphical input capability). In this case we use:

```
> identify(illit, murder, states)   # Figure 2.3
[1] 18 10   1
```

to point at and label three states with large values on both variables. The first two arguments to `identify` should be the same data as was used to make the plot. The third argument says what to plot at each identified point; if you omit it, the indices of the identified points are used. The term *indices* refers to the

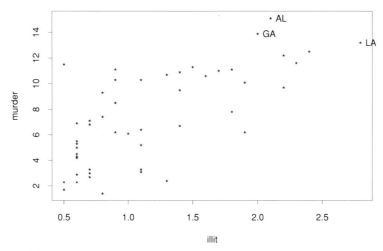

Figure 2.3. Scatterplot of illiteracy and murder rates with several extreme points identified.

integer positions of the points in the x and y vectors. These indices are returned in any case as the value of identify.

There are several other ways to add information to a scatterplot or to other plots in S. The expression points(x,y) plots an asterisk at the points defined by x and y. Suppose we want to mark the points for which murder rates are high, say greater than 10:

> *nasty ← murder>10*

defines the indices of the states we want. Since points overlays the previous plot, we need to distinguish the new points somehow, say by plotting a different character this time. This is accomplished by using an optional argument to points specifying the plotting character.

> *points(illit[nasty], murder[nasty], pch="O")   # Figure 2.4*

The optional argument, pch="O" changes the plotting character from the default "∗" to "o". Notice that we preceded this argument by the name pch, followed by a single "=" character. This is a useful way of providing arguments, by *name*, to S functions. In fact, points and other graphical functions recognize many optional arguments, known as *graphical parameters*, that control the plotting. Depending on what a particular graphics device can do, we could also change character size (cex=1.5) or color (col=2).

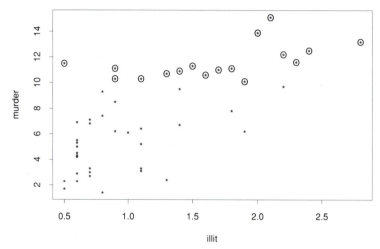

Figure 2.4. Scatterplot of illiteracy and murder rates. Points where the murder rate is larger than 10 are emphasized.

The expression

```
text(x,y,label)
```

plots labels, either character strings or numerical values, at the specified points. Instead of overstriking the previous points, we can plot the state abbreviations, as in Figure 2.5:

```
> text(illit[nasty], murder[nasty], states[nasty], adj=0)
```

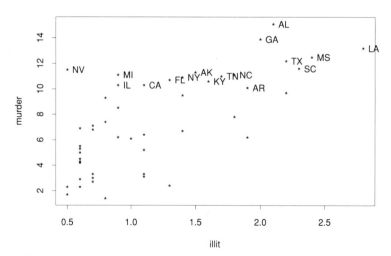

Figure 2.5. Scatterplot of illiteracy and murder rates. Points with murder rate larger than 10 are labelled with the state abbreviation.

We left-justified the text by using a graphical parameter adj=0 so that the labels would not overwrite the points. One of the exercises in the next set requires you to use `text` *instead* of a scatter of points.

Scatterplots are particularly useful because they can be applied to so many different analyses. S has functions for a number of other graphical displays, and many more can be created from the basic graphical functions, such as `points`, `lines`, and `text`. One kind of specialized plot is a map; for example

```
> usa(states=FALSE)
```

plots a map of the United States. By default, it also plots the state boundaries; we left these off (by `states=FALSE`) to have more room to add other information to the map. If you look up `state` in Appendix 2, you may notice that `state.center` is an object with components `x` and `y` giving the coordinates for the state centers. These components can be extracted as follows:

```
> state.x ← state.center$x
> state.y ← state.center$y
```

(The `o$x` operation returns the component named `x` from the object `o`.) Now we can indicate the states with high murder rate suitably on the map:

```
> text(state.x[nasty], state.y[nasty], "HIGH")   # Figure 2.6
```

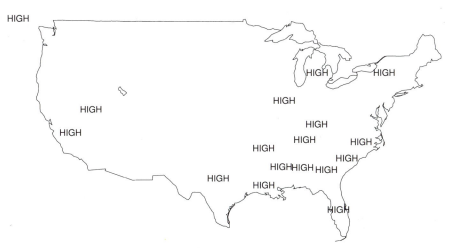

Figure 2.6. A map of the United States with the word "HIGH" plotted at the center of each state with a high murder rate.

Notice the geographical relationships amongst the states with high murder rates. Could you see this in the earlier figures?

Exercises

2.14   Use the value returned by `identify` to produce a new scatterplot of illiteracy and murder rates with any "outliers" omitted.

2.15   The `plot` function has an optional argument, `type`, that controls what type of plot is made (points, lines, etc.). In particular, `type="n"` plots nothing, but sets up the plot and draws axes and axis labels. Use this to generate a scatterplot of illiteracy and murder, but with the *state abbreviations* labelling the points, instead of the default plotting character.

2.16   Per capita income is available for the states, also:

```
> income ← state.x77[ , 2 ]
```

Make a plot that shows states with (1) high and (2) low per capita income, on a scatterplot of illiteracy and murder. Play around with different versions of the techniques used so far, until you get a plot you find insightful.

2.17   Look at Figure 2.2. Why do the points on the plot appear to line up in vertical columns?

2.18   The function `symbols` is a useful function for drawing circles, rectangles, and other symbols on plots. Look up the documentation for `symbols` and use this function to plot a scatter as in exercise 2.16, but with circles at each of the points. The radius of the circles should be proportional to income. What would you do to make the *area* proportional to income? Would it be better to use `income - 3000`?

2.19*   Let's make a plot to show the geographic distribution of income. Draw the USA map. Choose four text strings for very low, low, high and very high values of income. Plot the first string at the coordinates of states with less than the first quartile of income, the second at states above the first quartile but below the second (i.e., the median), and so on.

2.20*   The text strings in the previous exercise can all be plotted in one call to `text`. How? (Hint: when subscripting, an element from the data can appear in the subset as often as desired.)

2.7 Writing Functions

So far, we have used functions that were supplied as part of the S environment. Appendix 3 contains a list of the S functions, organized by topics; if you have a specific task in mind, you can look there to find out if a function exists for that computation. Suppose, however, that none of the functions is exactly what you want. What should you do? You can *create* a function of your own; for example, the expression

```
square ← function(x) x^2
```

creates a function object named `square`, that, when called with any S expression as its argument, returns the square of the data in that argument `x`. We can now use `square` just like any supplied function:

```
> square(1:5)
[1]  1  4  9 16 25
```

As another example, suppose we wanted to know which elements in a vector had the minimum value. Looking in Appendix 3, we find the related function `min`, which finds the smallest value in its argument. Given `min`, a good way to accomplish our task is:

```
is.min ← function(x) x==min(x)
```

Now we can just remember the name of the function, rather than having to figure out again how the calculation was done, and we can incorporate a call to the function in any other computation; for example,

```
> state.name[is.min(illit)]
[1] "Iowa"          "Nevada"          "South Dakota"
```

Exercises

2.21 Section 2.5 suggested the calculation

```
(1:length(murder))[murder > 12]
```

be used to find the numerical indices for which the condition was true. This is just the kind of computation that would be clearer if we could use a function call, `which(murder>12)`, instead. Write a definition for `which`.

2.22 The function `is.min` returns a logical vector identifying the minimum values. Write a function (call it `mins`) that calls `is.min` and returns the numerical indices of the minimum values; for example,

```
> mins(state.illit)
[1] 15 28 41
```

2.23 To come up with a good definition for a function, it helps to consider different approaches to the computation. In the previous exercise, we used `is.min` to define `mins`. But the S function `order` also seems related. It returns the indices that would order a vector; so that the first element of `order(x)` says which element of `x` is smallest, and so on. This suggests the alternative definition, perhaps simpler, for `mins`:

```
mins ← function(x) order(x)[1]
```

Do the two definitions produce different results for the `illit` data? Which version do you prefer?

You can look at the definition of any function by typing its name:

```
> square
function(x)x ^ 2
```

This same technique allows you to examine any of the functions that you created or that were supplied as part of the S environment! Don't confuse printing the value of a function object with calling a function with no arguments. For example,

```
> postscript
```

prints the definition of the `postscript` function while

```
> postscript()
```

calls the function. Remember, a function call must always include the parentheses.

What do you do if your first version of a function doesn't work properly? If you decide how to fix it, do you need to retype the entire function? No. There are several ways in S to edit functions. For example, if you want to use the *vi* screen editor to revise the function `square` and put the new version in `newsquare`:

```
> newsquare ← vi(square)
```

The `vi` function puts you in the *vi* text editor, working on a (temporary) file that contains the definition of `square`. When the changes are completed, write the file and quit from the editor. The `vi` function will return the edited version of the function as its value. This means that there will be a new function `newsquare`: `square` will be unaltered. Remember that you must assign a name to the object returned by the `vi` function. Otherwise, as always, S will simply print the value returned by `vi` without changing anything.

Functions can help organize user interactions. For example, here is a function that quizzes the user to answer a number of questions. It prints out the question, reads a line from standard input and compares that line to the supplied answer. To print the question in a nice form, we use a low-level printing function, `cat`. This function takes any number of arguments and prints them out, with a blank separating data items. Also, we call a function `readline` to read the line from the terminal.

```
quiz ← function(questions,answers)
    for(i in 1:length(questions)){
        cat(questions[i],"? ")
        if(readline()==answers[i])cat("Right!\n")
        else cat("No, the answer is:",answers[i],"\n")
    }
```

A session with `quiz` would look like:

```
> dumb.q ← c("Number of planets",
+ "Number of angels on the head of a pin")
> dumb.a ← c(9,"Lots")
> quiz(dumb.q,dumb.a)
Number of planets ? 9
Right!
Number of angels on the head of a pin ? 1e20
No, the answer is: Lots
```

The function `cat` does not automatically put a newline at the end of its print-ing. We took advantage of this to put the user's reply on the same line as the question. Newlines are put explicitly in the text as "\n".

Exercises

2.24 Write a definition for the function `square.root`. Compare your answer to the function `sqrt` already in S.

2.25 You can use the `vi` editor function to edit all sorts of S objects. Try editing a function and then try to edit a numeric vector.

2.26 Modify `quiz` to return a vector specifying which questions the user got wrong. You should set up a vector, say by

```
scores ← logical(length(questions))
```

and fill it in.

2.27 When functions call themselves, the process is called *recursion*. This is often the cleanest way to organize a complicated calculation. Modify `quiz` so that it calls itself recursively on the questions that the user got wrong. It should use the vector computed in the previous exercise to select the set of questions and answers for the new call to `quiz`. Make sure the function doesn't loop forever if the user gets all the questions right.

2.28 Now add to the previous version a little dialogue that asks the user whether `quiz` should requiz on the errors. You should print out a message, read a line in response and check whether the reply was "y" or "n".

The philosophy of good programming emphasizes using existing software to do specialized tasks. Chapters 6 and 7 will present interfaces from S to tools of various kinds, including subroutines written in low-level languages like C and Fortran. However, the most frequently useful interface, and the easiest to use, is to *commands* in the UNIX system. These commands operate on text, usually separated into lines. The S function `unix` takes a char-acter string containing a command, executes the command, and returns a char-acter vector with one element per line of output from the command. For exam-ple, suppose we want the current date and time, as a character string, perhaps to use in a title for a plot or printout. The command, `date`, prints exactly this information. So we can define a function

```
date ← function()unix("date")
```

to return the information we want.

Using `unix` is simple. Section 6.3 gives a number of specific examples that provide models for applications.

Exercises

2.29   Calling `unix` is the way to define the function `readline` used in `quiz`. We
want to read one line typed by the user (on the standard input) and echo that
line to the standard output. Convince yourself that this can be done in the
shell by executing the commands:

```
read h; echo $h
```

and then typing any single line of text. Use this command to write the function `readline`.

2.30   Functions don't have to have *any* arguments. Write a horoscope function,
`horoscope()`, that selects from some suitable comments, such as

```
c("Business affairs need careful attention",
    "New romantic attachments are in prospect",
    "Beware of mysterious strangers")
```

by using the function `sample(x,1)` to sample one element from a vector `x`.

2.31   Revise the `quiz` function so that it presents the questions in a random order.
Hint: `sample(x)` produces a random permutation of the items in `x`.

2.8 Wrap-up

At this point, you may well feel that this tutorial introduction to S has gone on
long enough. The antidote for this feeling is to actually practice some of the
things mentioned here. In particular, do at least some of the exercises and then
try to use S on some (simple) data of your own. Even though later chapters
will go into more detail and introduce more functions, you should already be
able to analyze some data with what you now know about S.

Answers to Selected Exercises

2.2   (page 16)

```
> mean(illit)
[1] 1.44
> illit-mean(illit)
```

```
            [1]   0.66  0.06  0.36  0.46 -0.34 -0.74 -0.34 -0.54
            [9]  -0.14  0.56
```

2.3   (page 16)
```
            median(murder); median(illit)
```

2.5   (page 16)
```
            > (murder / 100) * population
            [1]   545.865   41.245  172.536  213.110 2183.394
            [6]   172.788   96.100   35.898  885.639  685.409
```

2.6   (page 16)
```
            > stem(population)

            N = 10    Median = 2820.5
            Quartiles = 2110, 4931

            Decimal point is 3 places to the right of the colon

               0 : 46
               1 :
               2 : 125
               3 : 16
               4 : 9
               5 :
               6 :
               7 :
               8 : 3

            High:  21198

            > stem(log10(population))

            N = 10    Median = 3.448183
            Quartiles = 3.324282, 3.692935

            Decimal point is at the colon

            Low:   2.562293

               2 : 8
               3 : 334
               3 : 5679
               4 : 3
```

The population data is more strung out, with one large value. The logs look smoother, more "bell-shaped".

2.7   (page 16)   The machine uses "floating point" arithmetic to store fractional numbers and can only store a finite number of bits of precision. Because the machine arithmetic cannot exactly represent tenths, there is a small discrepancy between (3/10)*10 and 3, for example.

2.8   (page 17)   See the previous exercise—equality testing of floating point numbers is generally a bad idea because the answers are usually not exact.

2.9   (page 18)   Numeric: positive integers tell which positions in the data should be returned.

Logical: the values corresponding to TRUE subscripts are selected.

Negative: negative integers tell which positions in the data should NOT be returned.

2.10   (page 18)
```
illit[ length(illit):1 ]
```
There is also a function `rev(x)` that reverses a vector, but it has not yet been introduced.

2.11   (page 18)
```
illit[ illit>median(illit) ]
murder[ illit>median(illit) ]
```

2.13   (page 18)   Using hint (i), since there are 10 values in `illit`, we can find the lower quartile halfway between the 2nd and 3rd sorted values and the upper quartile halfway between the 8th and 9th sorted values. Hence:
```
sorted ← sort(illit)
lower.quartile ← mean(sorted[2:3])
upper.quartile ← mean(sorted[8:9])
iqr ← upper.quartile - lower.quartile
```
Using hint (ii),
```
bottom.half ← murder[ murder<median(murder) ]
top.half ← murder[ murder>median(murder) ]
iqr ← median(top.half)-median(bottom.half)
```
Of course, you could also look in the index and find the function `quantile` to compute the quartiles.

2.14   (page 24)
```
i ← identify(illit,murder)   # find outliers
plot(illit[-i],murder[-i])   # new plot with no outliers
```

2.15   (page 24)
```
plot(murder,illit,type="n")
text(murder,illit,state.abb)
```

2.16   (page 24)
```
plot(illit,murder,type="n")
text(illit[income<4000], murder[income<4000], "L")
text(illit[income>5000], murder[income>5000], "H")
others ← income >= 4000 & income <= 5000
points(illit[others],murder[others])
```

2.17   (page 24)   The illiteracy values are accurate to only one decimal place.

2.18   (page 24)   To encode `income` in the areas of the circles, use `sqrt(income)` as the circle radius:
```
symbols(illit,murder,circles=sqrt(income))
```
Subtracting 3000 from `income` helps to emphasize the differences between the income levels.

2.19   (page 24)   Compute quartiles as in exercise 2.13. Then use statements such as
```
text(state.x[income<lower.quartile],
      state.y[income<lower.quartile], "very low")
```

2.20   (page 24)   Construct a vector `group` that tells for each observation which of the four income groups (1, 2, 3, or 4) it is in. (This is still hard: see functions `quantile` and `cut` for a quick and general way of doing this.) Another possibility is to interactively look at a stem-and-leaf display to find appropriate cut points. Yet another alternative is to use
```
group ← trunc((rank(income)-1)/length(income)*4)
```
Also, construct a character vector `symbol` that gives the four symbols you

want plotted. Then, simply use

```
text(state.center, symbol[group])
```

to add the symbols.

2.21   (page 25)

```
which ← function(x)
    (1:length(x))[x]
```

Note how the expression `(1:length(x))` is subscripted. Also notice that the argument `x` serves two purposes—it tells which values are TRUE and also gives, by its length, the set of possible integers in the result. Another, perhaps better, definition for `which` would be

```
which ← function(x)
    seq(along=x)[x]
```

Why is it better? What would happen if `length(x)` were zero?

2.22   (page 25)

```
mins ← function(x)
    (1:length(x))[is.min(x)]
```

or

```
mins ← function(x)
    (1:length(x))[x==min(x)]
```

2.23   (page 25)   The two functions differ when there are several places in the vector with the minimum value. The solution using `order` is incapable of telling this and also is slower than the other version (because sorting or ordering is a computation that takes time proportional to *n log n* where *n* is the length of its input, but finding the minimum takes time proportional to *n*.)

2.26   (page 27)

```
quiz ← function(questions,answers)
{
    scores ← logical(length(questions))
    for(i in 1:length(questions)){
        cat(questions[i],"? ")
        scores[i] ← readline()==answers[i]
        if(scores[i]) cat("Right!\n")
        else cat("No, the answer is:",answers[i],"\n")
    }
    scores
}
```

2.27   (page 27)

```
quiz ← function(questions,answers)
{
    if(length(questions)<1) return()
    right ← logical(length(questions))
    for(i in 1:length(questions)){
        cat(questions[i],"? ")
        right[i] ← readline()==answers[i]
        if(right[i]) cat("Right!\n")
        else cat("No, the answer is:",answers[i],"\n")
    }
    quiz(questions[!right],answers[!right])
}
```

2.29   (page 28)

```
readline ← function()
    unix("read h; echo $h")
```

2.30   (page 28)

```
advice ← c("Business affairs need careful attention",
    "New romantic attachments are in prospect",
    "Beware of mysterious strangers")
horoscope ← function() sample(advice,1)
```

2.31   (page 28)

```
quiz ← function(questions,answers)
{
    if(length(questions)<1) return()
    right ← logical(length(questions))
    for(i in sample(1:length(questions))){
        cat(questions[i],"? ")
        right[i] ← readline()==answers[i]
        if(right[i]) cat("Right!\n")
        else cat("No, the answer is:",answers[i],"\n")
    }
    quiz(questions[!right],answers[!right])
}
```

3

Using the S Language

This chapter presents some key concepts and the basic techniques needed in order to use S; understanding them will lead quickly to good use of S. The chapter discusses the S language, functions, and the S environment, in a more systematic way than chapter 2.

> *You are encouraged to read this chapter thoroughly. This material is essential to making good use of S.*

3.1 Basic Concepts: Expressions and Data

When you use S, you type *expressions* that are interpreted and evaluated by the S system. The expressions include, but are not limited to, conventional algebraic and functional expressions:

```
$ S
> mean(ship)   # monthly US manufacturing shipments
[1] 59273.98
> median(abs(ship-median(ship)))
[1] 6090
> range(rnorm(1000))
[1] -3.241352  3.707867
> pnorm(3.707867)
[1] 0.9998955
> sqrt(sum((ship-mean(ship))^2)/(length(ship)-1))
[1] 11637.03
```

S prompts with the characters "> " when it is ready for you to type input just as the shell prompts with "$." You type expressions to the S system; it evaluates the expressions and prints the results. S expressions are composed from operators (plus, minus), from other special characters (parentheses, etc.), from functions (`abs` and `mean`, e.g.), and from data (constants and named objects).

Data in S are organized into named, self-describing *objects*. Objects are persistent—they remain from one S session to the next. S objects are stored by S (as UNIX system files) and are retrieved automatically when named in an expression. They may be vectors of data values (numbers, logical values, or character strings), more complicated data structures (such as arrays or lists), or functions or expressions in the S language. Commonly occurring classes of objects, for example, *matrices, arrays* and *time-series,* are recognized by many S functions.

Fundamental to the philosophy of S is the uniformity of expressions and data objects. The value of any expression, however complicated, is an object. This includes anything from simple arithmetic expressions to high-level statistical functions. So far as the language is concerned, any expression can appear as an argument to an operator or function. Of course, a particular function may generate an error if it cannot interpret the argument sensibly. As we proceed, examples will show how this uniformity leads to flexible, general computation.

S is a *case sensitive* language: corresponding upper- and lower-case letters are distinct in the names of functions and objects. Thus the name `ABC` is not the same as the name `abc`.

One important suggestion: it's good to be adventurous. If it isn't clear what S will do in response to a particular expression, try it. You are encouraged to try for yourself the S expressions given as examples.

3.2 The S Language

S provides an integrated environment for data analysis, numerical calculations, graphics and related computations. The S *language* is the medium through which all user computations and programming take place. It provides a way of interacting directly with S and also allows users to extend S.

3.2.1 *Expressions and Operators*

The S language includes *operators* for the usual arithmetic and logical operations. These compute on all the data values in their operands. Thus,

```
y + 1
```

computes its result by adding `1` to each data value in `y`. The arithmetic operators for add, subtract, multiply, and divide are:

    +   –   *   /

The operator "^" raises to a power, e.g. 2^3 is 8.

    There are *comparison* operators, which compare values and produce TRUE or FALSE:

    <   >   <=   >=   ==   !=

for *less-than*, *greater-than*, *less-than-or-equal-to*, *greater-than-or-equal-to*, *equal-to*, and *not-equal-to*. There are also *logical* operators

    & | !

which are used for the operations *and*, *or*, and *not*. Similar to the logical operators are the *control* operators

    && ||

which expect a single value for their first operand. If this value is TRUE, then && evaluates, and returns as its value, the second operand; otherwise, it returns FALSE without evaluating its second operand. Similarly, if the first operand of || is FALSE, then the second argument is evaluated and returned; otherwise, it returns TRUE without evaluating its second operand. For example,

```
if(all(x>0) && sum(log(x))>100) big ← T
```

would not evaluate the logarithms unless all the values in x were positive.

    The S operator ":" creates the sequence between any two numbers in steps of ±1:

```
> 9:23
[1]  9 10 11 12 13 14 15 16 17 18 19 20 21 22 23
> 12.5:8.5
[1] 12.5 11.5 10.5  9.5  8.5
```

Two other numeric operators are:

    %/%   %%

The operator "%/%" is integer divide; it divides and then converts the quotient to an integer by taking its *floor*, the greatest integer not greater than the quotient. The operator "%%" is a remainder or modulo operator: it gives the remainder when its first operand is divided by its second. S has a few other operators which will be introduced at appropriate times. You can write your own operators, too; see section 7.3.3.

3.2.2 *Assignment*

The operation of naming an object is called *assignment*. Assignment is performed by an operator that appears as an arrow, "←" in this book. The arrow may be typed as an underline character "_" or as the two characters "<-" (less-than, minus).[†] On the left of the arrow is a name, on the right any expression. It is helpful to think of S evaluating the expression to produce a data object and then moving the object in the direction of the arrow into a named place. Names may contain letters, digits, and periods, and should start with a letter. Users can choose names for their convenience and can re-use names arbitrarily. A common convention is to use lower-case letters and dot for names, leaving other characters for special purposes.

      The object that is the value of the expression on the right of the arrow is stored with the given name; e.g.,

```
>   x ← 9:23
```

gives the name x to an object containing the integers from 9 to 23. The sequence of characters "x ←" is conventionally read as "x gets". An assignment returns as its value the right-hand side of the expression. This means that multiple assignments

```
> y ← x ← 0
```

work as you would expect. Unlike other expressions, the result of an assignment is not printed automatically.

3.2.3 *Subscripts*

Data can be extracted from an object by:

```
x[ subscript ]
```

The value of `subscript` commonly has one of four forms:

1. positive integers: the corresponding elements of x will appear in the result; for example, x[1] to extract the first value from x, or x[1:5] for the first 5 values.

[†]The two characters must be adjacent—no space is allowed between the "<" and the "−". Thus, the expression typed x <- 3 is different from the expression typed x < -3; the first is an assignment, the other a comparison.

2. logical values: the elements of x for which the logical expression is true will be selected; for example, `x[ x>0 ]` or

   ```
   name[ height>72 & age<31 ]
   ```

3. negative integers: all elements except those specified will be selected; for example, `x[-1]` gives all but the first element of x.

4. character strings; this form of subscript will be discussed in section 5.1.3.

Subset expressions can also be assigned to, with the effect of replacing the corresponding elements of the vector:

```
x[ x<0 ] ← 0
```

replaces all negative elements with 0.

3.2.4 *Functions*

All the computations in S are done by *functions*[†]; e.g.,

```
mean(x)    # arithmetic mean
plot(x,y) # scatterplot of y versus x
c(1,-2.1,3.2,5.78)  # combine data values to make a vector
runif(5)  # 5 random numbers between 0 and 1
```

In general, functions are called by typing the name of the function followed by function *arguments* in parentheses:

```
fun.name(arg1, arg2, ...)
```

Here `fun.name` is the name of the function, and `arg1`, `arg2`, ..., etc. are expressions, to be taken as arguments to the function. For example, `mean(x)` calls the function `mean` to compute the arithmetic mean of the elements of x. Arguments may be either required or optional. Typically, functions will have a few required arguments, supplying the data on which the function operates—these must always be supplied. Optional arguments give special features or options to control the function in more detail. These may be omitted, with the function taking some default action.

When a function is defined, each argument is given a name, called its *formal name*. Formal argument names for each S function are listed in Appendix 1 under the function name. When calling the function, optional arguments are often supplied as the formal argument name, an =, and its value: `name=value`, where `value` is any expression. This means that you need only supply the arguments of interest, in any order, since the name uniquely identifies the argument. To make it easier to use named arguments, the name can be

---

[†]Even the operators we discussed before are actually functions with names like "+" or "<=".

abbreviated to its first few characters, as long as it can be distinguished from other argument names for the same function. As an example of the use of named arguments, one of many optional arguments to `plot` is `ylab`, specifying a label for the y-axis of the plot:

```
plot(x, log(y), ylab="Logged response values")
```

Note the distinction between naming arguments with "=" and assigning data with "←". The equal sign associates an argument name with an expression. The assignment operator assigns a name to an object. (And, of course, the operator "==" has nothing to do with assignment at all.) Here is an example showing all three notations in one expression.

```
> # compute the base 2 logarithm of salaries of
> #   people aged 35
> log.salary ← log( salary[age==35], base=2 )
```

S also has functions that take an arbitrary number of arguments. For example, the combine function,

```
c(arg1, ..., argn)
```

combines all the data in an arbitrary number of arguments to form one vector.

There are over 500 functions in S, described in detail in Appendix 1. Appendix 3 categorizes the functions so that you can easily look for a desired function. If S does not already supply what you want, you can easily define new functions, simply by writing a function definition in the language, and assigning a name to that definition (see section 2.7 and chapters 6 and 7). Such user-defined functions are used in exactly the same way as functions supplied with S.

3.2.5 *Continuation*

To improve readability in S expressions, you can use white space (blanks and tabs) freely to separate names, numbers, and other symbols. Long expressions can be continued over any number of lines, so long as it is clear that the end of the expression cannot have occurred yet. This can be ensured by ending the line with an operator or by not supplying enough right parentheses to close the expression; e.g.,

```
> z ← x+3.14159*(y-      # this line continued
+   mean(y,trim=.1))
```

The first line was doubly sure of being continued since it ended with the operator "−", and also had an unmatched left parenthesis. As shown above, S prompts with "+ " for continuation lines, and comments can be inserted in expressions, from the character "#" to the end of the line.

You can put several expressions on one line by separating them with semicolons "*;*". This is handy for short expressions:

```
> x ← sqrt(y); z ← log(y)
```

3.2.6 *Operators: Replication, Coercion, and Precedence*

In evaluating arithmetic comparison, or logical expressions, S occasionally runs across an anomalous situation, such as two operands of unequal lengths. When this occurs, S tries to produce a meaningful result. For example, if two operands are of unequal length, values from the shorter will be reused cyclically to make the result the same length as the longer. We already saw the most common case of this, when one argument is a vector and the other has only a single value, as in x+1.

Another anomalous case is when the modes of the operands do not match. For example, one operand may be logical and the other numeric. In this case, S always *coerces* the two operands to the mode that can hold the most information. When logical values are added to numeric values:

```
1 + (sex == "M")
```

the logical values computed from sex == "M" would be coerced to be numeric values with TRUE converted to 1 and FALSE converted to 0.

When several operators appear in an expression, as in 1:7 * 1:2, some uncertainty may exist in your mind as to which operation is done first. In this case, both occurrences of ":" are evaluated first, and the results then given to "*". This is usually described by saying that ":" has *higher precedence* than "*". Similar questions concerning the evaluation of other expressions involving S operators can be answered by Table 3.1. Operators higher in the table are evaluated before operators lower in the table. Operators with the same precedence are listed on the same line, and are evaluated left-to-right (except that assignment is evaluated right-to-left), as they appear in the expression.

Remember that parentheses can and should be used to make explicit the order of evaluation desired when you want to override the precedence of the operators (or when you can't remember the precedence):

```
x+(x>5)
(1:7)*(1:2)
n:(m-1)
(y-mean(y))*.01
```

Operator	Name	Precedence
$	component selection	**HIGH**
[[[	subscripts, elements	
^	exponentiation	
−	unary minus	
:	sequence operator	
%*name*%	special operator	
* /	multiply, divide	
+ −	add, subtract	
< > <= >= == !=	comparison	
!	not	
& | && ||	and, or	
← _ →	assignment	**LOW**

Table 3.1. Precedence rules for operators in S. Operators higher in the table "bind tighter" than operators below them.

Exercises

3.1 For the numbers

```
7.3, 6.8, .005, 9, 12, 2.4, 18.9, .9
```

a)   Find their mean.
b)   Subtract the mean from each number.
c)   Print the square roots of the numbers.
d)   Print those numbers that are larger than their square roots.
e)   Print the square roots of the numbers, rounded to 2 decimal places. Hint: there is a function named `round`.
f)   How much do the squares of the rounded roots differ from the original numbers?

3.2 One dollar invested at an annual rate of r percent compounded monthly for m months is worth

```
(1 + r/1200) ^ m
```

dollars. How much will one dollar be worth at the end of each of six years at 6%? What about 17%?

3.3 What is the value of the expression

```
1:7 * 1:2
```

Explain how this particular result is computed.

3.4 The expression

```
x ← y + 1
```

means that the values in y should have 1 added to them and the resulting object should be assigned the name x. What would you expect the expression

```
y + 1 -> x
```

to mean? When might it be useful?

3.5 How can you use %% to compute the units-digit of an integer, x? Use %/% to return all but the units digit. For example, given the number 123, the units digit is 3 and the other digits are 12.

3.6˜ Is the value of −1 %% 3 positive or is it negative? Does the value of the expression

```
(5:-5) %% 3
```

help to explain why?

3.3 Some Common S Functions

This section presents often-used S functions, collected into related groups. The first group contains data manipulation functions that create and rearrange data objects. The second group contains summaries: they take an object and produce a shorter object (often a single number) summarizing their input. The third group of functions is numerical transformations. These functions operate element-by-element on their input. Finally, we describe random number generation functions and other functions related to various statistical distributions.

3.3.1 *Data Manipulation*

The data manipulation functions introduced here include functions that combine objects, that create objects from "patterns", that rearrange the elements, find order, or match patterns in their input.

The function c combines all its arguments (treated as vectors) into a single vector. It is the usual way of combining a few values to create vectors inside expressions, or of entering small sets of data.

```
> small.primes ← c(1:3, 5, 7, 11)
> small.primes
[1]  1  2  3  5  7 11
> 2^c(1, 12, 19)
[1]      2   4096 524288
```

One special data value that you should know is NA; it means "Not Available" or "missing." You can insert NAs in the data yourself, or they may arise as the result of computations, for example in division by zero. Normally, the result of operating on an NA is another NA, hence:

```
> values ← c(1,NA,27.5)
> values
[1]   1.0    NA 27.5
> sqrt(values)
[1] 1.000000      NA 5.244044
```

There are many other characteristics of NAs that you will encounter in section 5.1.1.

The function `rep` replicates its first argument as many times as specified by its second argument:

```
> rep(1:3,2)
[1] 1 2 3 1 2 3
```

The second argument is either one number, or it has the same length as the first argument, in which case each element in the second says how many times to repeat the corresponding element of the first. Typically, this is used as follows:

```
rep(c("Low","Mid","High"),rep(5,3))
```

makes a character vector with 5 repetitions of each `"Low"`, `"Mid"`, and `"High"`.

The function `seq` is a general form of the ":" operator introduced earlier. The expression `seq(m,n)` is equivalent to `m:n`, but there are also one-argument and multi-argument forms. The expression `seq(x)` returns the vector `1:x` if `x` is a vector of length one. Using `seq(along=x)` returns the vector `1:length(x)` that goes along with `x` (it even returns an empty sequence if `length(x)` is zero). This is convenient for manipulating subsets of vectors; for example, an expression to determine which elements of `x` are negative would be:

```
seq(along=x)[ x<0 ]
```

Another argument, `by`, allows `seq` to step by something other than one in producing the sequence going from the first argument to the second.

```
> seq(-1, 1, by=.1)
 [1] -1.0 -0.9 -0.8 -0.7 -0.6 -0.5 -0.4 -0.3 -0.2
[10] -0.1  0.0  0.1  0.2  0.3  0.4  0.5  0.6  0.7
[19]  0.8  0.9  1.0
```

As an alternative, the argument `length` allows specification of the length of the resulting vector:

```
> seq(-pi, pi, length=10)
 [1] -3.1415927 -2.4434610 -1.7453293 -1.0471976
 [5] -0.3490659  0.3490659  1.0471976  1.7453293
 [9]  2.4434610  3.1415927
```

The function `sort` sorts the data elements of its argument; `sort(x)` returns the values of x in ascending numerical or alphabetical order. (Note: S sorts using the ASCII character set; hence, all numbers sort before all upper-case letters which sort before all lower-case letters.)

```
> x ← c(2, 6, 4, 5, 5, 8, 8, 1, 3, 0)
> sort(x)
 [1] 0 1 2 3 4 5 5 6 8 8
> sort(month.name)
 [1] "April"    "August"    "December"  "February"
 [5] "January"  "July"      "June"      "March"
 [9] "May"      "November"  "October"   "September"
```

The `order` function is closely related to `sort`. It returns the ordering permutation, i.e.,

```
x [ order(x) ]     # is the same as   sort(x)
```

Functions `sort` and `order` are helpful in doing data analysis that depends on sorting or on finding large or small values. The `order` function is used most frequently to permute other data consistently with the result of sorting one set of data.

```
> xorder ← order(x)
> xorder
 [1] 10  8  1  9  3  4  5  2  6  7
> a ← x[xorder]         #sorted version of x
> b ← y[xorder]         #y in the same order
```

Another capability of `order` is sorting on several fields. For example,

```
o ← order(name, salary)
```

gives an ordering that is alphabetical by name. If two names are identical, the salary determines the ordering.

The sorting routines sort in ascending order. To get sorts or orderings in *descending* order, use the reversing function `rev`; for example, `rev(sort(x))` returns x in descending order.

As illustrated by the example using `order`, the subset operation can rearrange a vector. It can also be used to replicate data values.

```
x[ c(1:5,4:1) ]
```

is the first through fifth values of x followed by the fourth through first values.

The function `rank` returns the positions of the original elements in the sorted data and takes account of ties.

```
> rank(x)
[1] 3.0 8.0 5.0 6.5 6.5 9.5 9.5 2.0 4.0 1.0
```

The `diff(x)` function produces a vector of the differences between successive elements of x. In simple cases, `diff(x)` is equivalent to

```
x[-1] - x[-length(x)]
```

Note that the result of `diff` is one element shorter than its input.

The function `match(x,y)` tries to find each element of x in y (a table of unique values). The *i*-th value in the result is the position of `x[i]` in y (or NA if `x[i]` was not found in y). Suppose, for example, that the data in x was coded "L", "M", or "H" for low, medium or high. For analysis, we prefer numerical values. Then,

```
match(x,c("L","M","H"))
```

is a vector that codes the characters as 1, 2, and 3. This is very similar to the operation carried out by the function `category`, described in section 5.3.3.

Of related interest is the function `unique(x)`, which returns each value that occurs in x, but makes sure that each value appears in the result only once. The function `duplicated` returns a logical vector telling which are the duplicated values.

Exercises

3.7   Data from the New Jersey Pick-it Lottery are in the system data directory under the names `lottery.number` and `lottery.payoff`.

a)   Find which winning numbers had payoffs of more than $500.

b)   Find the 10 smallest payoffs and the corresponding "unlucky" numbers. Hint: the function `order` is helpful.

3.8   Explain the behavior of the following S expressions:

```
> x ← 5; seq(x)
> x ← 2:5; seq(x)
```

Why might it be better to use `seq(along=x)` rather than `seq(x)` when writing a function?

3.9   Try the expression

```
> seq(-10,10,by=.1)
```

Can you explain why the printed result has as many decimal places as it does?

3.10   How would you sort some numeric data, say `salary`, in *decreasing* order? Given data on `name` and `salary` for the same individuals, how could you produce a list in alphabetic order by name, but sorting identical names by decreasing salary?

3.11 Given a vector `name` of names, a corresponding vector `salary` of salaries, and another list of names `promotion.list`, find the salaries of the people in `promotion.list`. What happens if "Smith" is in `promotion.list` but not in `name`?

3.3.2 *Summaries*

Summary functions typically compute a short summary of some data. For example, there are functions to add and multiply together all the elements of one or more vectors, `sum` and `prod`, which return a single number giving the sum or product. The functions `max` and `min` give the largest and smallest values in their arguments. These functions can have an arbitrary number of arguments. The function `range` returns a vector with two numbers which are the max and min of all its arguments. That is, `range(x,y)` is equivalent to `c(min(x,y),max(x,y))`.

Functions `all` and `any` take logical vectors and return a single `TRUE` or `FALSE` according to whether any or all of the values are `TRUE`. For example,

```
all(x>=0)
any(x<0)
```

return `TRUE` and `FALSE`, respectively, if there are no negative values in `x`.

Summaries that look for a "middle" value in a vector are:

```
mean(x);  median(x)
```

for arithmetic mean and median. The mean can be extended to trim a fraction of the largest and smallest values by the optional argument `trim`.

The expression `quantile(x,quantiles)` constructs the requested sample quantiles for a set of data `x`. For example,

```
> quantile(lottery.payoff,c(.25,.75))
[1] 194 365
```

returns a vector giving the `.25` and `.75` quantiles of the data in `lottery.payoff`. This means that `25%` of the values in the vector `lottery.payoff` are less than `194`, and `75%` of the payoffs are less than `365`.

Sample variances, covariances, and correlations are given by:

```
var(x);  var(x,y);  cor(x,y)
```

If the arguments are matrices, the results are covariance and correlation matrices, treating the columns of `x` and `y` as variables.

Exercises

3.12 The formula for computing a sample variance of a numeric vector x of length n can be written as:

$$\frac{1}{n-1} \sum (x - xbar)^2$$

where $xbar$ is the mean of x. The formula can also be written:

$$\frac{1}{n-1} \left(\sum x^2 - \frac{(\sum x)^2}{n} \right)$$

(the "desk calculator" formula). Write an S expression (or better, a function) that evaluates the variance according to the desk calculator formula. Given the set of data

```
x ← c(1.5, 17, 2.5, 12, 19.3)
```

Compute the variances of $x + 10\hat{}2$, $x + 10\hat{}3$, and so forth. When do the results start to change? Do the same test with the S function var.

3.3.3 *Numerical Transformations*

The S language includes the mathematical functions:

Name	Operation
sqrt	square root
abs	absolute value
sin cos tan	trigonometric functions (radians)
asin acos atan	inverse trigonometric functions
sinh cosh tanh	hyperbolic functions
asinh acosh atanh	inverse hyperbolic functions
exp log	exponential and natural logarithm
log10	common logarithm
gamma lgamma	gamma function and its natural log

Each of these functions returns a result identical to its argument, but with data values transformed by the mathematical function. In particular, operations on matrices and time-series yield matrices and time-series as values. For positive integer values, gamma (x+1) is the same as x-factorial. The lgamma function is needed because the gamma function grows so rapidly.

Here are five functions that compute elementary numerical results:

```
ceiling   floor   trunc   round   signif
```

ceiling and floor find the closest integer values not less than and not greater than the corresponding values in their arguments. The function trunc truncates values toward zero, while round rounds values to the nearest integral value. Optionally, round can take a second argument, giving the number of digits after the decimal to which rounding takes place. The function signif rounds data to the specified number of *significant* digits. Some examples:

```
> x
[1] -1.90691   0.76018 -0.26556 -1.89828   0.08571
> ceiling(x)
[1] -1   1   0 -1   1
> floor(x)
[1] -2   0 -1 -2   0
> trunc(x)
[1] -1   0   0 -1   0
> round(x)
[1] -2   1   0 -2   0
> round(x,1)
[1] -1.9   0.8 -0.3 -1.9   0.1
> signif(x,2)
[1] -1.900   0.760 -0.270 -1.900   0.086
```

You have already met one common S function, print. The print function is invoked automatically to print the results of an S expression. However, if you invoke print directly, it has the capability of controlling the number of significant digits printed.

```
> sqrt(1:10)
 [1] 1.000000 1.414214 1.732051 2.000000 2.236068
 [6] 2.449490 2.645751 2.828427 3.000000 3.162278
> print(sqrt(1:10),digits=3)
 [1] 1.00 1.41 1.73 2.00 2.24 2.45 2.65 2.83 3.00
[10] 3.16
```

You may also want to print more than the default number of digits in some circumstances, for example, when you want to get precise answers. Most S computations produce about 14 decimal digits, so to see them all:

```
> print(sqrt(1:10),digits=14)
 [1] 1.0000000000000 1.4142135623731 1.7320508075689
 [4] 2.0000000000000 2.2360679774998 2.4494897427832
 [7] 2.6457513110646 2.8284271247462 3.0000000000000
[10] 3.1622776601684
```

There is also a global option that controls the default number of digits printed; see section 3.4.6.

The function `cumsum` is almost the inverse of the differencing function `diff` (see section 3.3.1); that is, the *i*-th element of `cumsum(x)` is the sum of the first *i* elements of x. For example, if x ← 1:10, then `diff(x)` is a vector of 9 ones and x is equal to `cumsum(rep(1,10))`. In general, x is the same as `cumsum(c(x[1],diff(x)))`.

Exercises

3.13   Show that `cumsum(c(x[1],diff(x)))` gives x. What if `length(x)` is 1?

3.14   The *geometric mean* of a set of n numbers is the n-th root of the product of the numbers. Show how to compute this in S. Now suppose you have some data that might have very large or very small numbers. You still want to find the geometric mean, but the product of the numbers might be too big or too small for the machine to represent. How would you get the answer?

3.15   Write the factorial function

   (a)   using `gamma`.

   (b)   without using `gamma`.

3.3.4 *Generation of Random Numbers*

The function `runif` is a uniform random number generator (a combination linear-congruential and shift-register generator, for details see `.Random.seed` in Appendix 2). The expression `runif(n)` generates n pseudorandom numbers uniformly distributed between 0 and 1. Such numbers can be used, for example, as test data

```
mean(runif(100))
```

or to perform an operation with a specific probability;

```
if(runif(1)<.8) foo()
```

has probability `.8` of calling `foo`.

Even though uniformly distributed random numbers are convenient, pseudorandom values from other statistical distributions are often needed; e.g., as tests for some analysis or for simulations. S contains random number generators for a dozen distributions. They all have names consisting of the letter "r" followed by a code for the distribution, such as "norm" for the normal, "unif" for the uniform, and "t" for Student's t-distribution. The first argument is the sample size desired. Other arguments, if any, are the parameters of the distribution.

The expressions

```
> xn ← rnorm(100)
> xt ← rt(75,2)
```

store in xn a sample of size 100 from the standard normal distribution and in xt a sample of size 75 from the t-distribution with parameter (degrees of freedom) equal to 2. The codes for the distributions are:

Code	Distribution	Parameters	Defaults
beta	beta	shape1, shape2	-, -
cauchy	Cauchy	loc, scale	0, 1
chisq	chi-square	df	-
exp	exponential	-	-
f	F	df1, df2	-, -
gamma	Gamma	shape	-
lnorm	log-normal	mean, sd (of log)	0, 1
logis	logistic	loc, scale	0, 1
norm	normal	mean, sd	0, 1
stab	stable	index, skew	-, 0
t	Student's t	df	-
unif	uniform	min, max	0, 1

For information about the parameters of the distributions (including default values), see Appendix 1 under the corresponding code name.

In addition to random number generators for these distributions, there are also probability, quantile, and density functions named by placing the letter "p", "q", or "d" before the distribution code. (The exception is the stable family, for which only the random number function is available.) As an example, pnorm(x) gives the probability that a value from a standard normal distribution is less than x.

```
> pnorm(2.5)
[1] 0.9937903
```

Also, the expression qt(x,df) gives the quantile from the t-distribution on df degrees of freedom such that the probability is x that a number from this distribution is less than the computed quantile.

```
> qt(.95,7)
[1] 1.89508
```

says that 95% of numbers drawn from a t-distribution on 7 degrees of freedom will be less than 1.89508. Finally, the expression dgamma(x,shape) gives the density at x of a gamma distribution with shape parameter shape. The density functions can be plotted:

```
> draw.gamma ← function(shape){
+   x ← qgamma(seq(.001,.999,length=100) ,shape)
+   plot(x, dgamma(x,shape), type="l", xlab="", ylab="")
+ }
> draw.gamma(1.5)     # Figure 3.1
```

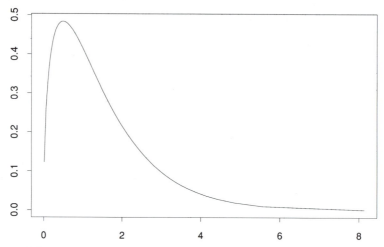

Figure 3.1. The shape of a gamma(1.5) distribution, drawn by the draw.gamma function.

The random number generator functions in S are special in that they have a *side effect*. Unlike most functions that always produce the same answer when given the same input, random number generators keep giving new sequences of random numbers. They do this by silently modifying a data object named .Random.seed in order to keep track of which random numbers have been generated so far. You can make use of this object in order to reset the random number generators to reproduce previous results.

```
> save.seed ← .Random.seed
> runif(10)
 [1] 0.5900458 0.8465232 0.6810173 0.5984296 0.4307826
 [6] 0.2572028 0.2853697 0.1123940 0.5360330 0.6622505
> .Random.seed ← save.seed
> runif(10)
 [1] 0.5900458 0.8465232 0.6810173 0.5984296 0.4307826
 [6] 0.2572028 0.2853697 0.1123940 0.5360330 0.6622505
```

You can also start the random number generator in a place of your choosing by the call

```
set.seed(i)
```

where i is an integer. Different values of i start the generator in different places. Use this function to ensure that two different simulations do not contain a common stretch of random numbers.

Exercises

3.16   Random number generators can create lots of numbers for you with a minimal amount of typing. How might you use `runif` to create a vector with numbers similar to

```
7.3, 6.8, 9, 12, 2.4, 18.9
```

3.17   The `runif` function has optional second and third arguments that tell the minimum and maximum values that it should produce. Produce a vector of 15 numbers uniformly distributed between –pi and pi. What do you expect the mean of these numbers to be? Check by computing the mean. Is your answer reasonable?

3.18   Use the function `draw.gamma` to plot several gamma distributions with different `shape` values.

3.19   Generate samples of size `100` from a gamma distribution with shape parameters `1`, `2`, `4`, `6`, and `10`. How does the sample mean vary with the shape parameter?

3.4 The S Environment

Expressions in the S language are evaluated in an environment providing facilities for editing, debugging, looking for information, and controlling the way S runs. The following subsections describe some features of this environment.

3.4.1 *Errors and Interrupts*

In general, you should not be afraid to experiment with a new kind of S expression. The language and the individual functions are designed to allow as much flexibility as possible. The effect of errors when they do occur is not usually serious. In interactive computing, errors tend to be detected quickly, and the corrections can be made directly.

Errors may be less likely, particularly when first using S, if complicated expressions are evaluated in a sequence of simpler steps, where the intermediate results are assigned names and reused. This has the added advantage that the intermediate results are available for examination, to see that they were computed as intended. As you become more accustomed to S, complicated expressions will grow more natural. Complicated expressions can be turned into functions so that only a simple function call is actually typed.

You may encounter two different kinds of errors in using S: those caused by "expressions" that S cannot understand and those detected by one of the functions during evaluation. The first type of error (a *syntax* error, so named because the input does not follow the syntactic rules for forming expressions), will be reported by typing back the offending expression, with the apparent location of the error marked:

```
>   x+7,5            # I meant 7.5
Syntax error: ","  used illegally at this point:
x+7,
```

The second type of error (an *evaluation* error), is reported by the function that could not compute the desired result:

```
>   1+"abc"
Error: Non-numeric second operand: e1 + e2
```

In this example, the "+" operator could not work with character data. Whenever you encounter a syntax or an evaluation error, a message will be printed to describe the error, execution of the current expression will terminate, and S will prompt for further expressions. When you encounter an evaluation error, S may also print Dumped after the error message. This means that other information is available to help you determine just where the error occurred. Typically, you can type:

```
traceback()
```

to see which function calls produced the error. Section 6.4.3 gives further ways to use the dumped information.

     You can interrupt execution of any expression by hitting the "del" key or "break" key (just which key depends on the terminal you are using and on the options you may have given to the UNIX system). For example, you may wish to interrupt long printouts or the execution of an expression that was incorrect.

     When a function wants to warn you about possible erroneous results, it issues a warning message. For example:

```
> 1:4 + 3:7
[1]  4  6  8 10  8
Warning messages:
   Length of longer object is not a multiple
   of the length of the shorter object in: e1 + e2
```

Here, S replicated the first vector to match the length of the second, but generated a warning message.[†] If there are more than 5 warning messages from one expression, S will not print them automatically since they may be repetitive and uninteresting. Instead, S will instruct you to call the warnings function if you wish to print them.

[†]This length test is a heuristic S uses to help you detect errors in arithmetic. If you want to avoid the warning, use the rep function to make the lengths match before doing the arithmetic.

3.4.2 *Editing and Error Correction*

The functions `vi` and `ed` invoke the corresponding text editors to allow changes to the data objects. The functions write a representation of the object to a file; you change the file using the editor, write the changed file, and quit from the editor. The changed object is returned as the value of the function. For example, to use the vi text editor to create an edited version of the function `draw.gamma` and assign it the name `new.draw.gamma`:

> new.draw.gamma ← vi(draw.gamma)

Remember that you should assign a name to the value of the function.

3.4.3 *On-Line Documentation; Help*

S comes with many functions and data objects, and it is likely that you will generate many of your own. To help you learn precisely what each function does and what each data object contains, S provides an on-line `help` function. The expression

> *help(plot)*

causes the documentation (as in Appendix 1) for the function `plot` to be printed on the terminal. Invoking `help()` without arguments produces documentation for `help` itself. You must enclose the argument in quotes if it contains characters other than letters, digits, or periods:

> *help("+")*

A short form of the on-line documentation can be obtained through the `args` function:

> *args(plot)*

will print a one-line description of `plot` with a full list of its arguments.

The `help` function can also print documentation for data objects. The expression

> *help(iris)*

will cause documentation to be printed for the system dataset `iris`. As you start creating your own functions or other objects, you can create your own documentation for them; see Appendix 1 under `prompt`.

Since the S system will continue to evolve, the printed documentation in Appendix 1 can, at best, be correct at the time of publication. However, the on-line documentation is updated whenever S functions change. Thus, the information given by the `help` function should be regarded as the true documentation for the objects in the system.

3.4.4 *UNIX System Interaction*

You can escape to the operating system to execute any command; alternatively, you can call the `unix` interface function to get back some values computed by a command. Any line that begins with the character "!" is passed, untouched, to the operating system for execution. This facility can be used to list files, to enter the text editor, etc. UNIX system commands that interact with the user return to the S environment when that interaction is complete.[†]

```
> !mail
... examine your mail,reply,etc ...
q
> # ready for next S expression
```

Section 2.7 introduced the use of the `unix` function, which causes the output of a command to be returned as a character vector in S. This interface allows all the power of commands in the UNIX system to be used in S functions.

As an example, consider the problem of reading character data from a file, one character string per line of the file. All this needs is:

```
my.text ← unix("cat myfile")
```

See section 6.3 for more examples.

Exercises

3.20   Suppose you have a file named `states` that contains 4 lines:

```
Alabama
New York
South Carolina
Wyoming
```

After evaluating the two expressions

```
state1 ← scan("states",character())
state2 ← unix("cat states")
```

what is the difference between the objects `state1` and `state2`?

[†]One caution: each line beginning with "!" starts a new shell. This means that commands that change directories or set environment variables will not affect a command in a later "!" escape.

3.4.5 *Interacting with S: History*

S keeps track of your sessions in an *audit* file, recording the expressions you type as well as the names of local objects that were read and written. The audit file is the mechanism S uses to provide you with a history of previously typed S expressions. The `history` function provides access to previous expressions, usually in order to re-evaluate one of them.

For example, suppose you wanted to re-evaluate a recent call to the `plot`, function:

```
> history(plot)
1: plot(log(population))
2: plot(murder)
3: title("Scatterplot example")
4: plot(illit, murder)
Selection: 1
```

In this case, there had been 4 expressions with the pattern "`plot`" appearing in them. The `history` function uses `menu` to present these expressions to you, with the most recent expression first. Selecting one of the expressions causes it to be re-evaluated; in this case, we redo the last plot.

If `history` gets no arguments, it displays the 10 most recent expressions. To change the maximum number of expressions that `history` will display, use the argument `max`; for example,

```
history("plot",max=1)
```

says to redo the last expression containing "`plot`". A related, simpler use of the auditing information is

```
again()
```

which re-evaluates the last expression (but not counting uses of `history` or `again` themselves).

S can also perform an analysis of the audit file, allowing you to track the complete history of a data analysis project. See AUDIT in Appendix 1 for more information.

3.4.6 *Options*

Various options that control the way that S works are set and examined by the `options` function. In general, `options` is executed by

```
options(option.name=option.value, ...)
```

where *option.name* and *option.value* are arbitrary pairings of names and values.

To see the complete set of options, execute

```
help(options)
```

Two of the available options are `prompt` and `continue`:

```
options(prompt="what? ", continue="more? ")
```

changes the standard S ">" prompt and "+" continuation prompt into "`what?`" and "`more?`". The `options` function also has arguments to control printed output;

```
options(width=80, length=20, digits=4)
```

announces that your output device has a width of 80 characters, has 20 lines on a page, and that results should be printed with 4 significant digits.

The current option settings can be viewed by executing `options()` with no arguments. Options that are set remain in effect through your current session with S. If you quit and re-enter S, the standard options will be restored. If you *always* want some nonstandard options, the best approach is to invoke `options` from a `.First` function (see section 3.4.9).

3.4.7 *Source and Sink Files*

There are times when work performed with S must be carried out repeatedly; for example, applying some computations to different data. By writing a function, as illustrated in section 2.7 and earlier in this chapter, you can turn the computations into a convenient, reusable form. A related technique is to use a text editor to put the computations into a file, in exactly the form you would type them to S. Suppose `cmdfile` is a file consisting of some S expressions. The expression

```
source("cmdfile")
```

causes S to read all the expressions on the file, and evaluate them as if they had been typed by the user. When the whole of the file has been read and the expressions evaluated, S resumes reading expressions from your terminal. An error or interrupt will also terminate reading from the source file. If the `source` function is interrupted or has an error, no assignments contained in the source file will be committed. This means that expressions executed inside a source file must *all* execute correctly or *none of the assignments done inside the file will be effective*. Source files may themselves contain `source` expressions.

Until you are sure the expressions in a source file are correct, it is advisable to have S echo the expressions to the terminal before it evaluates them. The logical argument `echo` to the function `options` controls this.

```
> options(echo=T)    # echo expressions from source file
```

The `source` function allows S input to come from a file; the `sink` function allows output that would ordinarily appear on your terminal to be diverted to a file. The expression

```
sink("my.output")
```

sends all subsequent printing that would have been done on your terminal, aside from prompts and error messages, to file `my.output` instead. To cancel this,

```
sink()
```

returns output to the terminal.

3.4.8 *Batch Execution of S*

There are occasions when interaction with S is unnecessary, e.g., when a large computation is to be carried out from a source file. At these times, *batch* execution of S is desirable since it frees the terminal for other interactive tasks. The command, executed *outside* of S,

```
$ S BATCH infile outfile
```

initiates execution of S with all input expressions coming from `infile` and all output placed on `outfile`. The output file contains a listing of the expressions from `infile` along with the printed output that results from evaluating those expressions. Any objects created or modified during batch execution are available for use in subsequent S sessions. The BATCH command should be invoked in the same directory in which you would run S interactively. Remember, too, that the "batch" job executes immediately; it merely runs at lower priority without an interactive terminal.

The `source` function is a good way of interactively testing an input file of expressions before using BATCH. A BATCH input file is not quite equivalent to a source file if errors are encountered. In batch execution, errors cause the offending statements to be ignored and the rest of the file is executed. Also, expressions are executed one at a time and assignments take effect immediately after the expression that created them.

3.4.9 *Controlling the S Session:* `.First`, `.Last`

S can carry out any computations you choose to start off your session. Define a function, `.First`, with no arguments. When you invoke S, it will automatically call this function. This is a convenient place to put standard startup actions:

```
.First ← function() cat("Welcome to S\n")
```

will cause S to print the message `Welcome to S` whenever it is first started. The `.First` function is a good place to attach data directories, to invoke graphics device functions, or to set preferred options.

```
.First ← function(){
    options(prompt="S: ",continue="\t")
    postscript()
    attach("/usr/einstein/.Data")
}
```

The `attach` function specifies the name of a directory that you would like to be searched for data objects. See section 5.4 for more details.

    Now that you know about `.First`, you probably can guess what `.Last` does. You can use the same technique to define a `.Last` function to wrap up on exit from S.

```
.Last ← function() cat("Goodbye\n")
```

For example, depending on your local conditions, you might use `.Last` to send graphics output from `postscript` to a printer. Generally, however, there is no need to close down a graphics device or to detach directories when you quit from S.

3.4.10 *S Library*

The S `library` function provides a way to access groups of S functions and datasets. The S library is a central repository in which any such material can be kept and made available to all local users of S.

    When you call `library` without arguments it prints a description of the available sections:

```
> library()
The following sections are available in the library:

SECTION   BRIEF DESCRIPTION

examples  Functions and objects from the S book
semantics The semantic model in chapter 11 of the S book
  ...
```

You can also ask for a description of the contents of a section by using the help argument:

```
> library(help=examples)
This section contains example functions and data objects
introduced in the S book.
    ...
```

If you would like to attach a particular section, give library a section name as an argument.

```
> library(examples)
```

The section name must correspond to one of the library sections installed on your computer system. The section "examples" contains most of the interesting functions that appear as examples in this book. The examples section of the library is supplied with S itself. Other sections may also be supplied, either with S or by the owners of S at your local site. Check your local library to see what is there. It should help you explore the material in this book and perhaps provide you with functions that have been contributed by others at your site.

Answers to Selected Exercises

3.1 (page 40)
```
x ← c(7.3, 6.8, .005, 9, 12, 2.4, 18.9, .9)
mean(x)
x - mean(x)
x^.5
x[x>x^.5]
round(x^.5,2)
x-round(x^.5,2)^2
```

3.2 (page 40)
```
(1+6/(12*100))^(6*12)   # end of 6 years
(1+6/(12*100))^((1:6)*12)   # end of each of 6 years
(1+c(6,17)/(12*100))^(6*12)   # 6 and 17 percent, 6 years
```
or perhaps a function
```
worth ← function(percent,years,compound=12)
        (1+percent/(compound*100))^(years*compound)
```

3.3 (page 40) The precedence rules say that the ":" operations will occur first. After these operations are carried out, we have two objects (with lengths 7 and 2, respectively) to multiply. The shorter object is replicated until it is 7 long, and then corresponding elements of the two length-7 objects are multiplied.

3.4 (page 40) The right-hand assignment arrow means the same thing as the left-hand arrow. When you type a long expression only to remember at the end that it would be a good idea to save the result, a right-hand arrow allows you to perform an assignment without retyping the line.

3.5 (page 41)

```
x %% 10
x %/% 10
```

3.6   (page 41)   Notice how the `%%` operator continues in sequence as the first argument crosses zero.

3.7   (page 44)

```
lottery.number[lottery.payoff>500]
o ← order(lottery.payoff)[1:10]
lottery.number[o]; lottery.payoff[o]
```

3.10   (page 44)

```
rev(sort(x))   # works for any data mode
- sort(-x)     # sorts in reverse order (only for numbers)
name[ order(name, -salary) ]
```

3.11   (page 44)

```
salaries[ match(promotion.list,names) ]
```

If "Smith" is in `promotion.list` but not in `names`, `match` will produce an NA which will turn into another NA in the subset expression.

3.12   (page 46)

```
desk.calculator ← function(x)
    (sum(x^2)-sum(x)^2/length(x))/(length(x)-1)
```

3.14   (page 48)

```
geometric.mean1 ← function(x)
    prod(x)^(1/length(x))

geometric.mean2 ← function(x)
    exp(sum(log(x))/length(x))
```

3.15   (page 48)

```
factorial ← function(x) gamma(x+1)

factorial2 ← function(x) prod(seq(x))
```

3.16   (page 51)   Since `runif` produces numbers uniformly distributed between 0 and 1, we could use

```
runif(6)*20
```

and get in the right ballpark. If we combined this with `round`, to round the resulting numbers to one decimal place, we have it.

3.17   (page 51)

```
x ← runif(15,-pi,pi)
mean(x)
```

3.20   (page 54)   Object `state1` contains a character object of length 6; `state2` has length 4. The `scan` function reads individual items separated by white space, but the `unix` function returns each line of the output as a separate character element.

4

Graphical Methods in S

The combination of interactive computing and graphics in S provides a powerful environment for understanding data. Plots can be used to look at data in a variety of ways and also to study the results of analyses, such as the fitting of models and various statistical summaries. Plots can be made using high-level plotting functions that produce an entire plot in one expression. Beyond this, graphical methods can be extensively revised, and new graphical methods constructed, by use of the S facilities for writing functions. Plots can be built up from a wide range of lower-level graphical functions. The graphical functions provided with S also share a collection of special arguments, known as *graphical parameters*, that provide detailed control over aspects of the graphics such as character size, line style, etc.

This chapter gives a quick introduction to graphics in section 4.1. Next, section 4.2 shows how to use S to plot various kinds of data. Section 4.3 discusses interacting with plots, and section 4.4 introduces a variety of specialized plots, including some plots traditionally used for "presentation graphics", such as barplots and pie charts.

The material in this chapter presents the basic notions of graphics within S, and should be sufficient for many applications. Those users wishing to exert detailed control over graphical output should read the advanced graphics material in chapter 10. The case studies in chapter 9, and particularly section 9.5 on presentation graphics, give additional examples.

4.1 Introduction to Graphics

S provides many high-level plotting functions, as well as facilities for adding to plots and controlling their appearance in detail.

A device function must be called before doing any plotting. S is a device-independent graphics system—after S knows the device type, all graphical output is tailored to that device. Thus, for S to know how to produce plots, you must call a function that specifies the type of graphics terminal or device to be used for plotting. The interactive terminals supported by S and the S functions that specify the devices are listed under `Devices` in Appendix 1. Device functions also exist to produce off-line plots, such as `postscript`. These functions typically send output to a file or process to be turned into plots on a laser printer or other hardcopy device. There is also a `printer` device function that works on any terminal, but gives considerably less attractive plots than true graphics terminals.

The device may be changed at any time during the S session (for example, changing between a graphics terminal and an off-line graphics device) by calling another device function. This automatically closes down the previous device, if any. Only one graphics device can be active at a time.

S graphics is based on functions that produce *graphics objects* These objects describe a plot and can be assigned or operated upon by other S functions. Graphics objects are automatically plotted, just as numerical objects are automatically printed. However, if you are doing "immediate" graphics, with the plots displayed as a direct result of the S expression, you do not need to worry about graphics objects. The rest of this chapter deals only with immediate graphics. We defer further discussion of graphics objects to section 10.2.2.

The most used high-level plotting routine is

```
plot(x,y)
```

which produces a scatterplot of the two sets of data.[†] For example

```
> plot(corn.rain, corn.yield)
```

produces the plot in Figure 4.1.

The function `plot` has an optional argument, `type`, which can be used to produce various other styles of plot; for example, for a plot with lines connecting the points in sequence, rather than characters plotted at the points:

[†]All S functions follow the convention of expecting the arguments x,y to specify data to plot, even though one might say "Plot *y* vs *x*." The convention (which is shared with model-fitting functions like `lsfit`) is convenient and easy to remember.

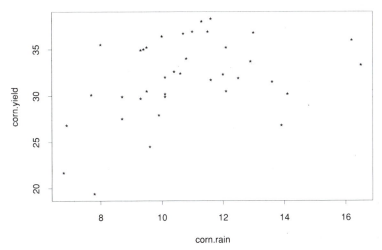

Figure 4.1. Yield of corn in bushels per acre as a function of rainfall in inches in six states, 1890 to 1927.

```
plot(x,y,type="l")
```

(The character inside the quotes is the letter *ell* standing for "lines", and not the digit one.) The default value is `"p"` (points), for a scatter of points. Other values for `type` are `"b"` (both) to plot both points and lines and `"n"` to draw axes but plot nothing.

Logarithmic transformations (to base 10) of either or both axes may be done automatically:

```
> plot(corn.rain,corn.yield,log="y")
```

will use a log scale for y. This differs from

```
> plot(corn.rain,log10(corn.yield))
```

in that the *y*-tick labels are on the original, not the log scale. Similarly, `log="x"` gives a log scale for the *x*-axis, and `log="xy"` or `log="yx"` gives a log scale for both.

The `plot` function will produce a time-series plot, if only one argument is given. In this case, the *x*-axis will show time, and the *y*-axis the data values. If the argument is not a time-series, the *x*-variable will be `1:length(x)`.

The `hist` high-level plotting function plots a histogram of a single set of data:

```
hist(x)
```

Arguments are available to control the number of bars, scaling, shading, etc.; see Appendix 1.

Once you have a plot, it can be titled by

```
title(main,sub,xlab,ylab)
```

which places a main title at the top, a subtitle at the bottom, and labels on the axes. (Any of the arguments may be omitted.) For example:

```
> title("Iris Data Analysis",
+     xlab="Sepal Length", ylab="Petal Length")
```

Many of the high-level functions will automatically generate x and y labels from the names of the plotted objects. In this case, simply omit `xlab` and `ylab` from `title`. You can also specify `main`, `sub`, `xlab`, and `ylab` as arguments in `name=value` form to any high-level plotting function.

Points, lines and text may be added to an existing plot through the functions `points`, `lines`, and `text`. For example, to plot a time-series and add a smoothed curve to the plot:

```
> plot(co2)
> lines(smooth(co2),col=2,lty=2) # Figure 4.2
```

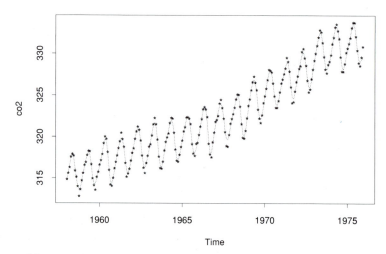

Figure 4.2. Plot of carbon dioxide data along with smoothed curve.

We specified values for the graphical parameters `col` and `lty` to control the color and line-type for the plotted curve. (Unfortunately, we cannot show color changes very well in this book). In using the `points` function, parameter `pch` may be used to specify an alternative plotting character; for example,

```
points(x,y,pch="+")
```

For making plots containing many points, either with `points` or with one of the high-level functions, you may prefer a plotting dot to a character. For a centered plotting dot, use `pch="."`. Also, specifying numeric values for the `pch=` argument uses a set of plotting symbols rather than characters; see `lines` in Appendix 1 for the set of symbols available. For a further description of graphical parameters, see section 10.3.

Exercises

4.1 Produce the plots of `corn.rain` and `log(corn.yield)` by the two expressions:

```
> plot(corn.rain,corn.yield,log="y")
> plot(corn.rain,log10(corn.yield))
```

Look at the difference in their appearance.

4.2 Plot a curve showing the function `sin` over the range $-\pi$ to π. Plot both `sin` and `cos` together on this range.

4.3 The expression

```
plot(corn.rain,corn.yield)
```

produces a plot with axis labels that could be improved upon. How would you produce the plot to make the *x*-axis label "Rainfall in Inches" and the *y*-axis label "Corn Yield, Bushels per Acre"?

4.2 Looking at Data

To understand the scope of graphics in interactive data analysis, it will help to organize our thinking along the lines of *what* we want to see in our plots. Summarization is an important goal of understanding data; we can use a graph, instead of numbers, to summarize the data. Plots have the advantage that much information can be presented; the human eye and brain can perceive patterns, and exceptions to patterns, in a very sophisticated way. Further, in an interactive setting, we can respond to these perceptions by doing new analysis, leading to new plots.

In this section we will examine the most common plotting situations and say briefly how S provides for such plots. Of course, the "data" need not be original observations; just as often, they will be the results of earlier analysis. Readers interested in more background are referred to the books *Graphical Methods for Data Analysis* and *The Elements of Graphing Data* mentioned in the bibliography. Sections 4.2.1 through 4.2.4 correspond roughly to chapters with similar names in the first book.

4.2.1 *Plotting Two-Dimensional Data*

The most frequently useful way of looking at the joint patterns of two variables, x and y, is through the *scatterplot*. S can produce a wide variety of scatterplots, adapted to different kinds of data. Let's look at some examples.

The objects stack.loss and stack.x in the S data directory record 21 experimental measurements of exhaust stack loss and of three related variables (the three columns of stack.x): air flow, water temperature and acid concentration. See stack in Appendix 2. To produce a scatterplot of airflow and stack.loss:

```
> airflow ← stack.x[,1]
> plot(airflow,stack.loss)     # Figure 4.3
```

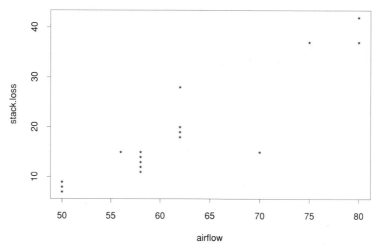

Figure 4.3. Scatterplot of airflow and stack loss.

A *time-series plot* is a scatterplot that displays a single object y against 1, 2, ... (or against the observation time, if y is a time-series). It is produced by giving plot just the one argument. For example, to see the stack loss in the successive experiments:

```
> plot(stack.loss)   # Figure 4.4
```

Although plot can be used to show one time-series, the function tsplot is able to plot any number of time-series arguments. If the time domains of the arguments are not identical, the time-series plot will use a large enough time domain to include all the data. For example

```
> tsplot(hstart,smooth(hstart),type="pl")   # Figure 4.5
```

will plot the time-series hstart as a set of points and a smoothed version of this data as a connected set of lines.

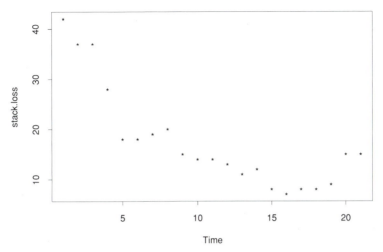

Figure 4.4. Time-series plot of stack loss.

As Figure 4.5 shows, `tsplot` uses different plotting characters, line styles, and colors, if they are available on the graphic device.

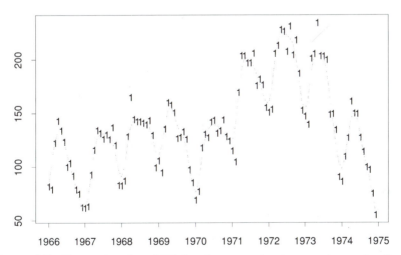

Figure 4.5. Time-series plot of US housing starts showing raw data and a fitted, smooth line.

The `matplot` function produces a scatterplot of several sets of data at once, plotting columns of one matrix against columns of another. By default, the sets of data are plotted as scatters using plotting characters "1", "2", ..., but the type of plot can be controlled by the `type=` argument as shown above with `tsplot`. As an example, suppose we want to make a plot of the sepal length and width for three varieties of iris. We form a 50 by 3 matrix for each of the two variables, which are part of the 50 by 4 by 3 array `iris`. Sepal length

and width correspond to values of 1 and 2 for the second subscript, so we can
create the matrices and plot by:

```
> Length ← iris[,1,]
> width ← iris[,2,]
> matplot(width,Length)      # Figure 4.6
```

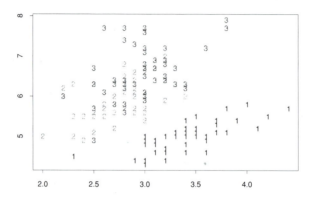

Figure 4.6. Sepal width and length for three varieties of Iris.

Here, the expression `iris[,1,]` generates a 50 by 3 matrix.

Many of the plotting functions try to make sense of missing values
(NAs) in the data. The general philosophy is that no point will be plotted if
one or more of its coordinates is NA, and no line segment will be drawn if
either of the end points contains an NA. This applies to `plot`, `tsplot`, and
`matplot`, as well as to the lower-level functions `points`, `lines`, and `text`.

Exercises

4.4   Figure 4.3 shows that there are only a few discrete values for `airflow`.
Make a *jittered* plot by adding enough random noise to the `airflow` values
to prevent them from overlapping.

4.5*   Write a function `jitter` so that

```
plot(jitter(airflow),stack.loss)
```

is a jittered scatterplot. Remember that you do not want to jitter too much—it
should still be possible to distinguish the various discrete values of `airflow`.
What is a good general algorithm for determining how much jitter to use?

4.6   Produce a jittered `matplot` of width and Length (see exercise 4.4). How
does your plot compare to Figure 4.6?

4.7 Produce a `matplot` as in Figure 4.6, but use the plotting characters "S", "V", and "G" to represent the species Setosa, Versicolor, and Virginica.

4.2.2 *Studying the Distribution of a Set of Data*

Plots can replace single-number summaries of data, like the mean or the standard deviation, by portraying the *entire distribution* of the data. A very common way of doing this is with the histogram; in S, the function `hist(x)` plots a histogram of the object x. There is also `stem(x)`, a semigraphical form of the histogram, which prints the histogram on its side, and which allows the viewer to read the (rounded) values of the data. See Chapter 2 of *Graphical Methods for Data Analysis* for more discussion of histograms and stem-and-leaf plots.

To emphasize that plots are important when applied to the results of analysis, as well as to the original data, let's suppose that we decided to fit a linear model to the `stack.loss` data discussed in section 4.2.1. The function `lsfit` will fit a linear model and return an object that contains, among other things, the residuals from that fit.

```
> stack.reg ← lsfit(stack.x, stack.loss)    # fit the model
> resids ← stack.reg$resid
```

Graphical displays are a good way to look at the residuals, see whether there are any suspicious values in them, and decide whether the residuals have the distribution you expected. The expression

```
hist(resids)
```

will produce a histogram of the residuals. In this case, particularly since there are only 21 observations, we may also use a semi-graphic display, produced by the function `stem`. While it takes more explaining than the histogram, it has the advantage that individual data values can be seen.

```
> stem(resids)   # display the residuals

N = 21    Median = -0.4550927
Quartiles = -1.711654, 2.36142

Decimal point is at the colon

  -7 : 2
  -6 :
  -5 :
  -4 :
  -3 : 10
  -2 : 4
  -1 : 97544
```

```
       -0 :  651
        0 :  9
        1 :  34
        2 :  468
        3 :  2
        4 :  6
        5 :  7
```

To show how the stem-and-leaf works, we can print the residuals, rounded and sorted:

```
> sort(round(resids,1))
        -7.2   -3.1   -3.0   -2.4   -1.9   -1.7   -1.5   -1.4
[ 9]    -1.4   -0.6   -0.5   -0.1    0.9    1.3    1.4    2.4
[17]     2.6    2.8    3.2    4.6    5.7
```

Notice that −7.2 appears as −7 in the stem (left of ":") and 2 in the leaf (on the right). Similarly, −3.1 and −3.0 appear as a stem of −3 and two leaves of 1 and 0.

Another alternative to plotting a histogram is to construct an explicit approximation to a probability density function that might have produced the data, and then plot that function as a curve. The function density produces the approximation, so that

```
       plot(density(resids),type="l")
```

would plot an approximate density for the residuals. Other simple ways of showing a distribution are the *one-dimensional scatterplot* and the *boxplot*. The one-dimensional scatterplot simply plots all the values in x against a constant. It hides too much information to be adequate on its own, but can contribute information when displayed in conjunction with other plots. We will show some uses of it in section 10.5.1 and in the exercises at the end of this section. The boxplot represents the data by a box showing the median and quartiles and by "whiskers" out from the box to show the range of the data. The function boxplot(x) will draw such a symbol. We will show some boxplots in section 4.2.3 for *comparing* distributions, which is the boxplot's strong point.

A special kind of plot for comparing a set of data with a probability distribution is the *probability* or *Q-Q* plot (*Graphical Methods for Data Analysis*, chapter 6). For example, statistical model-fitting techniques often assume that the errors in the model are distributed according to the normal (Gaussian) distribution. Naturally, one should always check that this assumption is reasonable. A good way to do so is to use the normal Q-Q plot. In S, qqnorm(x) sorts the data x and plots it against the corresponding quantiles of the normal distribution. If the points in this plot are approximately straight, the assumption is supported; various kinds of non-straightness indicate possible departures from normality in the data. We could examine the residuals from the linear model we fit to the stack loss data by:

```
> qqnorm(resids)    # Figure 4.7
```

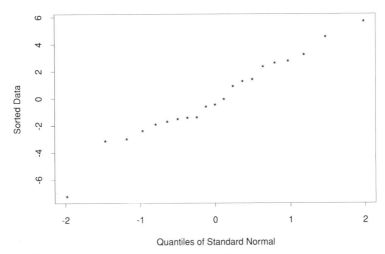

Figure 4.7. Normal quantile-quantile plot of residuals.

The points look reasonably straight; however we ought to wonder about the residual near $(-2,-7)$.

The normal distribution is certainly the most common reference distribution for probability plots, but the same kind of plot can be made against other distributions as well. The function `theoretical.plot` (shown below) does a probability plot against a specified distribution. The function takes the object to be plotted, a quantile function for the distribution and whatever other parameters must be supplied to define the distribution, such as shape or degrees-of-freedom. (By the nature of probability plots, location and scale parameters do not need to be given.) For example, suppose we have a set of data, `t.stats`, that are thought to be independent observations from a *t* distribution with 9 degrees of freedom. A plot to test that assumption is generated by:

```
> theoretical.plot(t.stats,qt,9)
```

The quantile function, `qt` in this case, and the definition of the other parameters must be consistent with the way quantiles are computed for that distribution. (See the table of distribution names in section 3.3.4.) Here's the definition for `theoretical.plot`:

```
theoretical.plot ← function(x, quantile.function, ...)
    plot(quantile.function(ppoints(x), ...), sort(x))
```

The argument `...` allows any number of extra arguments to be passed through to the quantile function (see section 6.1.3).

Exercises

4.8 Use `hist` and `density` to produce a histogram and a density plot of the `resids` data given in this section. How do the density plot, histogram, and stem-and-leaf display differ for this example?

4.9 The dataset `iris` contains 3 sets of 50 observations for 4 variables. Look at the distribution of the 150 values of sepal length (`iris[,1,]`) and sepal width (`iris[,2,]`) to see if they look normally distributed.

4.10 Do a stem-and-leaf display and a histogram of the iris sepal width data. Compare them. Which do you like better? Why?

4.11 Use `rnorm` to generate some data from the normal distribution, and plot it against the *t* distribution with various degrees of freedom, using `theoretical.plot`.

4.12 Write a function to produce a 1-dimensional scatterplot. Have the function take a vector of data and plot the values along a horizontal line.

4.13 A plot known variously as an *ecdf plot* or *quantile plot* plots the fraction of the data along the *x*-axis and the sorted data values on the *y*-axis. The expression

```
ppoints(x)
```

produces a vector of fractions corresponding to the data in `x`. Write a function to make a quantile plot of a vector `x`.

4.14 Create a set of data from the standard normal distribution by the expression

```
x ← rnorm(100)
```

Produce a density plot for this data and superimpose a line showing the theoretical density. Hint: use `lines(ppoints(x),dnorm(ppoints(x)))`. How close is the density estimate to the underlying density? What happens if you use various values of the `width` argument to `density`? What happens if you use a larger or smaller sample size?

4.2.3 *Comparing Data Distributions*

Given two separate sets of data (of the same or different lengths), we can compare the distributions graphically by the *empirical Q-Q plot*. This compares the distribution of `y` to that of another object, `x`, rather than to a theoretical distribution. In S, `qqplot(x,y)` plots a scatter of the sorted values of the two data sets. If `x` and `y` have different numbers of data values, points are interpolated in the larger set and plotted against the data in the smaller set. If the data have similar distributions (up to arbitrary location and scale parameters) the resulting plot will be roughly linear. Again, discrepancies from linearity can be analyzed to show how the two distributions differ. As an example, we can consider the lottery data used as a case study in chapter 1. Since we have several sets of data from the New Jersey lottery on the system data directory, we may want to compare the distributions of payoffs from the earliest and the latest sets of data:

```
> qqplot(lottery.payoff, lottery3.payoff)    # Figure 4.8
```

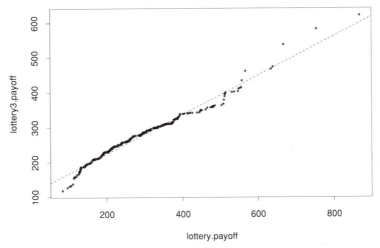

Figure 4.8. Empirical quantile-quantile plot of lottery payoffs for two different time periods.

The pattern of the plot is fairly linear over most of the range, with some deviation in the tails, suggesting a basically similar distribution for the two sets of data. We also show on the figure a line, fitted roughly to the pattern of the data. This could be done by eye, but can also be done numerically. (The technique is presented in exercise 4.20.) Once plotted, the line is helpful for seeing departures from linearity. In addition, the intercept and slope of the line tells how the two distributions differ in location and scale.

Empirical Q-Q plots compare two distributions and point out their differences. Another way to compare two or more distributions is to use a *boxplot*, with a schematic box for each set of data. A horizontal line is drawn through the box at the median of the data, the upper and lower ends of the box are at the upper and lower quartiles, and vertical lines ("whiskers") go up and down from the box to the extremes of the data. Points that are very extreme are plotted by themselves. While the boxplot shows less information than the Q-Q plot, it is an easy summary to look at and has the great advantage of applying to more than two sets of data. For example, we can compare the three sets of lottery payoffs by

```
> boxplot(lottery.payoff, lottery2.payoff, lottery3.payoff)
> # Figure 4.9
```

You can see that each successive set of lottery data is less spread out.

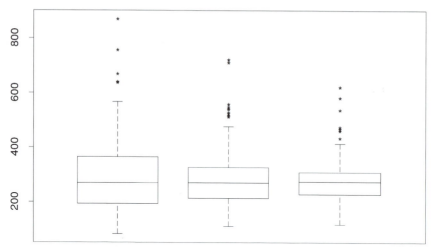

Figure 4.9. Boxplots showing distribution of lottery payoffs for three different time periods.

Sometimes the sets of data we want to compare are subsets of one object grouped by values of some other variable. In the analysis of the lottery data, for example, we noticed that the payoffs seemed to depend on the first digit of the winning number. We can draw boxes for the ten subsets of payoffs in a single plot to study this phenomenon graphically. Rather than extracting each set separately, we use the S function split to create a list, where each element of the list gives all of the payoffs that correspond to a particular first digit of the winning number. The boxplot function will draw a box for each element in the list.

```
> digit ← trunc(lottery.number/100)
> boxplot( split(lottery.payoff, digit) )    # Figure 4.10
> title(xlab="First Digit of Winning Number",ylab="Payoff")
```

Exercises

4.15 In chapter 1, we noticed that the distribution of payoffs for winning numbers with a leading zero digit was different from the rest of the payoffs. Use a Q-Q plot to investigate this difference.

4.16 Compare the iris sepal lengths and widths using two boxplots.

4.17 For the iris data in exercise 4.6, compare the distributions of sepal length among the three groups. Do the same for sepal width.

4.18 In Figure 4.10, what produces the labels under the boxes? Hint: look at the value returned by split(lottery.payoff,digit).

4.19 In Figure 4.10, there appears to be an upward trend in payoff as the leading digit of the winning number increases from 1 through 9. Produce a similar

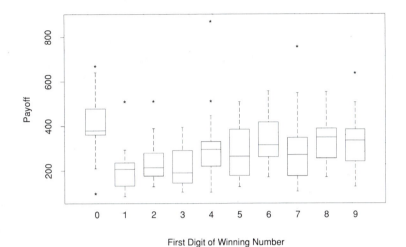

Figure 4.10. Boxplot of payoffs grouped by leading digit of the winning number. Notice the high payoffs for the first box.

figure, but move the box representing leading zero to the right of the box representing leading nine. Does it appear to fit in with the trend?

4.20 The line fit to Figure 4.8 was computed by the function lsfit. The lsfit function can take as arguments two vectors that give the *x*- and *y*-coordinates for the points. It will return a list with a component named coef giving the intercept and slope. The trick is that function qqplot has an argument plot=FALSE that tells it not to plot but instead to return a list with components named x and y that give the *x*- and *y*-coordinates of the points. Using this knowledge, explain how the following expressions produce Figure 4.8:

```
qqplot(lottery.payoff, lottery3.payoff)
xy ← qqplot(lottery.payoff, lottery3.payoff, plot=F)
r ← lsfit(xy$x, xy$y)
abline(r, lty=3)
```

4.2.4 *Plotting Multivariate Data*

Plotting two variables in a scatterplot is natural: a viewer can easily understand data represented by horizontal and vertical positions. For three or more variables there is no equally obvious way to plot data, although we believe that the scatterplot matrix display is usually the best static plot in this situation. The case of three variables is special, in that we are used to visualizing the real world in three dimensions. Some modern graphics workstations are capable, for example, of simulating three dimensions by real-time motion of two-dimensional projections of three variables. There are also techniques, some of which have been developed within the S environment, for applying high-interaction graphics to multidimensional data. For the purposes of this book, however, we will stay with static, two-dimensional plots.

Three-dimensional data can be represented in several ways with static plots. A simple approach is to do all three scatterplots of pairs of variables and lay these out on a page, in the style of the draftsman's drawing of an object. We often draw the transposed versions of those three plots, too, generating a *scatterplot matrix* display. The function `pairs(x)` does just this, assuming that `x` is a matrix with three columns, corresponding to the three variables to be plotted. The data set `stack.x` is such a set of data. The argument `full=T` says that we want both the upper and lower triangles of the display to appear.

```
> pairs(stack.x, full=T)    # Figure 4.11
```

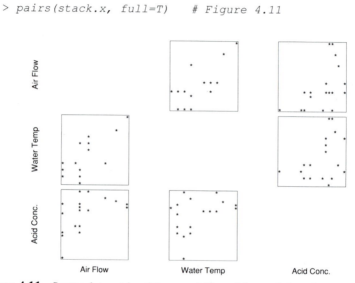

Figure 4.11. Scatterplot matrix of three variables of the stack loss data.

The `pairs` function can be used for any number of variables; if `x` is a matrix with p columns, $p(p-1)/2$ scatterplots will be drawn if `full=FALSE`, and $p(p-1)$ plots will be drawn if `full=TRUE`. However, as the number of variables goes up, it becomes harder to interpret the set of plots and get an overall sense of the data configuration.

Other graphical methods for multivariate data abandon the scatterplot and instead represent each observation with some graphical symbol. One then plots the symbols for all the observations. Such plots let you see clustering effects and overall trends (if the observations are ordered). Our experience is that they are usually less helpful for seeing patterns among the variables. The S functions `stars` and `faces` are examples of such plotting techniques.

One can, of course, combine a scatterplot showing two variables with the symbolic representation of other variables. The function `symbols` takes two sets of data for a scatterplot, just like `plot`, and then one of several arguments to define a set of symbols to plot at the coordinates defined by the first two objects. For example,

```
> symbols(airflow,stack.loss,circles=abs(resids))
> # Figure 4.12
```

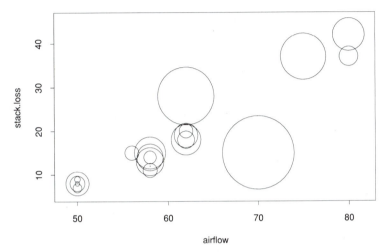

Figure 4.12. Size of residuals from stack loss regression is encoded in circle radius. Circle centers are determined by value of airflow and stack loss.

plots circles whose radius is proportional to the absolute value of the residuals from the stack loss regression.

Exercises

4.21 Extract the 50 by 4 matrix corresponding to the first group of iris flowers. Plot all four variables.

4.22 Construct data which lie on the surface of a sphere in 3 dimensions:

```
random.sphere ← function(n) {
    x ← rnorm(n)
    y ← rnorm(n)
    z ← rnorm(n)
    s ← sqrt(x^2+y^2+z^2)
    cbind(x/s, y/s, z/s)
}
```

Try using the `pairs` function on data generated by `random.sphere`. What can you see? What would happen if `rnorm` were replaced by `runif` in `random.sphere`? Try doing the same in 4 dimensions.

4.3 Interacting with Plots

Much of the value of interactive graphics lies in your ability to see a plot, react to it, and potentially to ask for more information or to augment the plot. This section describes some simple ways to identify information on a scatterplot or to add additional information to the plot. To use these techniques you need an interactive graphics device—one that lets you point at a place on the plot. We have found such devices an essential tool for data analysis. Later, it is possible to transfer the techniques developed on interactive devices to produce hardcopy on off-line plotters or laser printers.

Frequently, we would like to identify unusual points in a scatterplot, mark them in some way, and perhaps find out which data values produced them. This can be done interactively in S by:

```
> plot(x,y)
> identify(x,y)
```

The function `identify` causes the graphics device to prompt you to point at the objects of interest. (To point, you might use a mouse, cursor buttons, or a joystick; see Appendix 1 under the name of your graphics device function.) The selected points are marked on the plot by their indices in the data. When you finish pointing (how to signal this is also described in the device documentation), `identify` returns the indices of the identified points as its value. The indices can be used, for example, to select unusual data points, which will then be treated specially in a model or other analysis. In Figure 4.13, we plot absolute residuals from the regression model in section 4.2.2. We notice a few unusual points in the plot, and identify some of them interactively.

```
> plot(stack.loss, abs(resids))
> i←identify(stack.loss,abs(resids))    # Figure 4.13
> i
[1] 21  4  3  1  2
```

In this example, points were labelled with their position in the data vector— this is the default action of `identify`. Optionally, identified points can be marked on the plot with any label, by giving `identify` a character vector of the same length as x. To suppress marking on the plot, the optional argument `plot=F` can be supplied to `identify`. Once i has been computed as above, you could, for example, use `stack.loss[-i]` to look at the remaining data.

Another graphical technique for linear regression and other model-fitting situations is to plot a fitted lline on the data from which it was derived. This is done by the function `abline(a,b)`, which plots the line whose equation is $y = a + bx$.

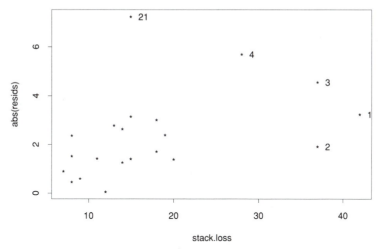

Figure 4.13. The result of interactive point identifications on a plot of absolute residuals against stack loss.

Function `abline` also recognizes the object returned by the model-fitting functions (like `lsfit`) and draws the line defined by the coefficients of a simple regression; for example,

```
> reg1 ← lsfit(airflow, stack.loss)
> plot(airflow, stack.loss)    # Figure 4.14
> abline(reg1)
```

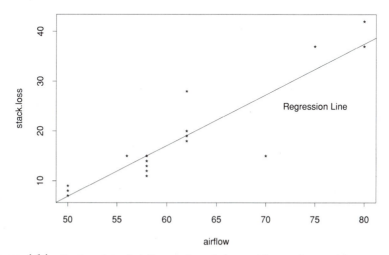

Figure 4.14. Scatter plot of airflow and stack loss, with superimposed least-squares regression line.

To add an annotation to a region of the plot where there is empty space, we can use `locator`, which returns the coordinates of the location(s) on the plot at which we point. The result returned by this function can be given as plotting coordinates to any S function; in particular, the function `text` will plot text on the current plot centered at the coordinates.

```
> text(locator(1),"Regression Line")
```

With `locator` you can ensure that the label does not overwrite anything else on the plot.

Exercises

4.23   The residuals from the smoothed housing start data are computed by

```
hstart - smooth(hstart)
```

    Produce a scatterplot of the residuals against the raw data.

4.24   Use `identify` to point at outliers on the residuals vs. `hstart` plot from the previous exercise.

4.25   Why might you want to use the `plot=F` argument to `identify`?

4.26   Construct a line plot of `sin(x)` for x ranging from $-\pi$ to π. Use `locator` to look graphically for the values of x that maximize the function. How close did you get to the actual value?

4.27   Use `locator` to digitize a simple shape. Hint: use the `type=` argument.

4.28   How might you use `locator` to help annotate a plot that is to be produced on an off-line device such as a laser printer?

4.4 Specialized Plots

This section deals with presentation graphics, maps, and with graphical methods tied to specialized forms of data (e.g., surfaces in three dimensions).

4.4.1 *Presentation Graphics: Bars, Pies, and VuGraphs*

This chapter is primarily concerned with how to produce graphs to analyze and understand data. However, analysis and understanding are seldom the final operations; a data analyst must communicate the results to others. Simplicity, attractiveness, and familiarity in the presentation are important to good communication, particularly to non-specialist audiences. While S is primarily intended as an *analytic* system, this section shows how to construct graphs that are attractive and effective. Section 9.5 contains further examples of presentation graphics.

Many of the analytic plots described earlier in this chapter may be used for presentation as well. Naturally, for presentation you may want to choose a graphics device that generates high-quality graphics, perhaps with color. For example, pen plotters with drafting-quality pens drawing on coated paper or on special transparency material can give good results. Laser printers provide high-quality graphics and text, and software can allow them to integrate graphics and text. A high-resolution raster terminal with a hardcopy device may also be valuable, particularly if it can generate 35mm slides directly.

Getting attractive plots for presentation may also involve you in special choices of graphical parameters; for example, choosing character sizes, line textures, colors or plotting symbols that carry your message vividly. Such choices depend on local conventions, your own aesthetic judgments and the characteristics of the graphics device being used. We suggest that you do some experimenting and write functions that provide the plotting styles you find pleasing.

The *barplot* or *bar graph* is perhaps the most common form of presentation graph. A barplot represents a measurement or count by the length of a bar. Many bars can be displayed on a single plot to represent different groups of data, and bars can be subdivided to reflect subgroups. The function

```
barplot(height)
```

is given a vector of bar heights. The argument `height` can also be a matrix, each column corresponding to one bar and the values in the column representing the sizes of the pieces into which the bar is subdivided.

The `barplot` function has several optional arguments. Giving `names` as a character vector argument labels the bars with the elements of the character vector. Other arguments, `density`, `angle`, and `col` combine to describe the way in which bars (or bar segments) should be shaded. These arguments are also used in other functions that can produce filled areas. If either `angle` or `density` is specified, the bars are shaded with lines at the specified `angle` and with `density` lines per inch. If `col` is specified in conjunction with `angle` or `density`, it controls the color of the shading lines. If `col` is specified alone, and if the graphic device has area-filling capabilities, the bars are filled with solid colors. (To get solidly filled bars on a pen-plotter, use a large value of density and be prepared to wait a long time!) Other arguments to `barplot` control details such as bar spacing; see Appendix 1.

Often, a barplot encodes grouping information in the colors or shading of bars or bar segments. The argument `legend` allows you to specify a character vector of names corresponding to the various levels of `angle`, `density`, and `col`. The legend is placed in the upper right-hand corner of the barplot. When more control over legend placement is desired, use the function `legend`. Not only can `legend` provide legends for barplots, but since it also allows specifications of line styles (parameter `lty`), and plotting characters (`pch`), it can appear on scatterplots, time-series plots, and other displays.

The following example uses fictitious data about the percent expenditures in three communities for five charitable services. The 15 data items are typed to a file, "perc.data":

```
5.4   3.1   3.5
5.7   8.6   25.0
20.4  26.0  22.0
36.3  34.1  28.0
14.4  11.4  4.5
```

and then are read in. We create the character vectors for community and services directly:

```
> percent ← matrix( scan("perc.data"),
+    ncol=3, byrow=T)
15 items read
> community ← c("Old Suburb", "Coast County", "New Suburb")
> service ← c("Child Care", "Health Services",
+    "Community Centers", "Family & Youth", "Other")
```

In Figure 4.15 we use a vector of angles for shading the bars, going from 45 degrees to 135 degrees, and plot divided bars for the three communities. Having set up extra lines of margin on the top to ensure enough room, before doing the barplot, we can use the `legend` function (see Appendix 1) to draw a legend box defining the angles in terms of the services.

```
> angles ← seq(45, 135, length=5)
> par(mar=c(4,4,8,1))
> barplot(percent, names=community, angle=angles)
> legend(locator(1), service, angle=angles)# Figure 4.15
```

Notice that we used the ability to read a point interactively in order to position the upper left-hand corner of the legend in an aesthetically pleasing spot on the graph.

When dealing with a category (section 5.5.3), the function `bartable` (shown below) will produce a barplot of the counts corresponding to the different levels of the category and will also produce the appropriate bar labels.

```
bartable ← function(category)
{
    tbl ← table(category)
    barplot(tbl,names=dimnames(tbl)[[1]])
}
```

For example, the following computations produce a category of national income by thousands of dollars, from the system dataset `saving.x` and then plot a barplot of the corresponding counts:

```
> income ← saving.x[,3] #national income data
> bartable(cut(income/1000,0:5))# Figure 4.16
> title("National Income",ylab="Number of Countries",
+    xlab="Income (Thousands of Dollars)")
```

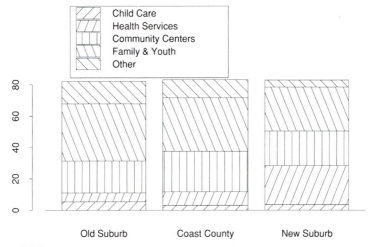

Figure 4.15. Barplot showing charitable contributions by percent in three communities to five services.

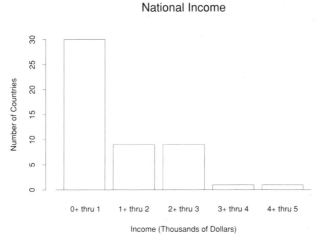

Figure 4.16. Bar graph of counts of national income in the `saving` data, using the `bartable` function.

The function `dotchart` produces a *dot chart*—a plot that conveys information similar to a barplot, using the horizontal position of dots, possibly with lines leading to them. The dot chart is a more effective tool for making quantitative judgements than the conventional barplot (see section 3.3 of *The Elements of Graphing Data*). Suppose we want to produce a dot chart of the community data. First, note that each percentage is attached to a specific service and community. Let us first create categorical variables reflecting this:

```
> serv ← category(row(percent),lab=service)
> com ← category(col(percent),lab=community)
```

Now, we construct our dot chart by

```
> dotchart(percent,levels(com)[com],group=serv)
>       # Figure 4.17
```

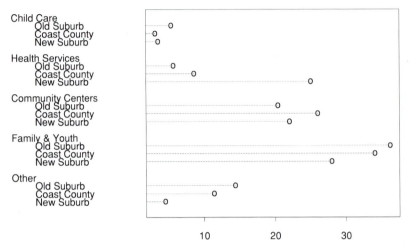

Figure 4.17. A dot chart of the charitable contribution data.

This allows us to judge how various communities differ in the percentages used for various services. We could have turned the expression around to see how the various components contribute to the total for each community:

```
> dotchart(percent,levels(serv)[serv],group=com)
>       # Figure 4.18
```

A common, although analytically ineffective, plot is the *pie chart*, a disc divided up into segments whose angles represent portions of a total given to different components. S provides a function for creating pie charts.

```
pie(x, label)
```

draws a circle and divides it into labelled parts with the x vector specifying relative areas, i.e., the *i*th slice takes up a fraction x[i]/sum(x) of the pie. Arguments density, angle, and col also work as they do with barplot to control hatching or filling of pie segments. Using the charity data,

```
> par(mar=c(4,4,4,14))
> pie(percent[,1], main=community[1], col=1:5, explode=1)
> legend(locator(1), legend=service, fill=1:5)
```

puts up a pie chart with an "exploded" segment and a legend, shown in Figure 4.19.

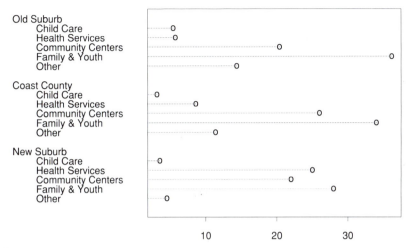

Figure 4.18. Another dot chart giving a different view of the charitable contribution data.

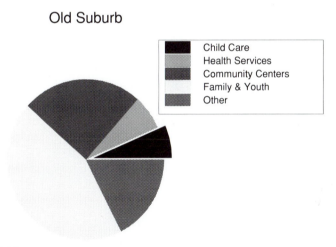

Figure 4.19. Pie chart for fraction of contribution to various services.

A graphics device with hardcopy capability, especially one that plots in color, can be used conveniently to generate slides or transparencies, even if these contain only simple text. The S function vu generates a plot of text information on the current graphics device, choosing appropriate character sizes, providing layouts for lists, changing colors and fonts, etc. The expression

```
vu(text)
```

takes a character vector and plots the individual character strings as lines of text. Character strings that start with a period ("."), are interpreted as layout commands, controlling aspects such as character size (.S), color (.C), and font (.F) in a style analogous to macro systems for the `troff` command.

When the material to be presented by `vu` is in the form of lists of items, the function `quickvu` generates the character vector suitable as the argument to `vu` without the user having to know any of the layout commands. `quickvu` prompts the user for lines for a title. An empty line signals the end of the title; then, the user is prompted for list items (by default, one line per item). Again, an empty line signals the end of the input, upon which `quickvu` returns a character vector complete with layout commands.

```
> my.text ← quickvu()
Title line: Computing for
Title line: Good Data Analysis
Title line:
List item: Interaction, Graphics
List item: Flexibility
List item: Extensibility
List item:
> vu(my.text,font="sr")
```

Computing for

Good Data Analysis

● Interaction, Graphics

● Flexibility

● Extensibility

Figure 4.20. Example of output created by the `vu` function.

If you want to have full control over formatting, you can use one of the editor functions (for example, `vi` or `ed`) to modify the details of `my.text`. For example, we could use

```
> my.text ← ed(my.text)
```

to produce the following:

```
.S 2
.CE
Computing for
Good Data Analysis
.S 1
.BL
.C 2
.LI
Interaction, Graphics
.LI
Flexibility
.LI
Extensibility
.LE
```

If this modified version of my.text were given to vu, it would produce a centered title and a bullet list (.BL) of three items. The title would be twice the size of the list items and in the standard color (color 1). The list items would be in color 2.

The actual size of the characters is chosen by vu to fill the plotting surface to the width and height desired (7 inches square by default).

Exercises

4.29   Given the data in the first 5 rows of dataset telsam.response (see Appendix 2 for details), display the percentage of respondents giving each of the four answers for each of the 5 interviewers. Try both pie charts and barplots. Which do you prefer? Why?

4.30   Suppose the three communities in Figure 4.15 had total charitable collections of

```
> total ← c(1104, 626, 2531)
```

in thousands of dollars. Redo the barplot in Figure 4.15, but in terms of money rather than percent.

4.31   With the data above, draw a pie chart for the total expenditures for each of the three communities, including the five services and also the remaining money (representing overhead).

4.32   Experiment with quickvu and vu to create vugraphs with various fonts. You can find the names of fonts by looking under font in Appendix 2.

4.4.2 *Maps*

A rather specialized high-level plotting function is `usa`, which produces maps of the United States. Just typing `usa()` gives a map of the coastline and state boundaries. The argument `states=FALSE` will omit the state boundaries; `coast=FALSE` omits the coastline. In addition, it is possible to specify a vector giving lower and upper limits for latitude (`ylim`) and longitude (`xlim`) to get a rectangular section of the map, e.g.,

```
usa(xlim=c(65,100),ylim=c(35,50))
```

for the Northeast. The resolution of the map does not increase as smaller regions are displayed, so maps of small areas are likely to look coarse. The coordinate system for the map places latitude on the *y*-axis and *negative* longitude on the *x*-axis (so that coordinates increase from left to right). The system data directory contains several objects, whose names begin with `"state."`, that contain coordinates appropriate for the map. For example, the object `state.center` is a plot structure, giving coordinates near the center of each state, so

```
usa()
text(state.center,state.abb)# Figure 4.21
```

produces a map with states identified by their 2-letter abbreviations.

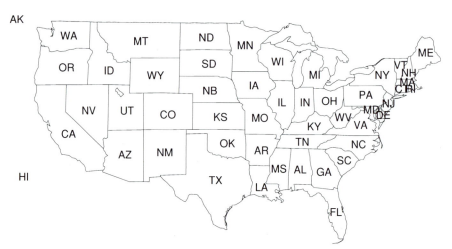

Figure 4.21. Map of the United States showing state abbreviations.

4.4.3 *Plotting Surfaces in Three Dimensions*

Two S functions, `contour` and `persp`, make contour plots and perspective plots of surfaces defined as a function of two variables. The expression

```
contour(x, y, z, v)
```

produces a *contour plot* of the surface that shows lines of constant height. The vectors `x` and `y` give positions along the *x*- and *y*-axes and the matrix `z` gives the height of the surface at the corresponding points. That is, `z[i,j]` is the surface height at `(x[i],y[j])`. Contours are drawn at the heights given by `v`, and if `v` is omitted, approximately 5 equally spaced contours are drawn. The expression

```
persp(z, eye)
```

provides a 3-dimensional perspective view of a surface with hidden line removal. The matrix `z` is assumed to have come from an underlying regular grid of equally spaced `x` and `y` values. It is also assumed to be centered at the origin and to extend ±1 in the *x* and *y* directions. The vector `eye` gives the (*x,y,z*) coordinates of the viewpoint in this coordinate system. The default viewpoint is `(-6,-8,5)`. Because of the implied coordinate system and because the surface is considered as a 3-dimensional object with comparable *x*-, *y*-, and *z*-coordinates, values in `z` should ordinarily be less than one in absolute value.

Other S functions can generate the data needed by `persp` and `contour`. The expression

```
interp(x, y, z)
```

creates the grid of surface heights `persp` from irregularly spaced (*x,y,z*) data points. The surface is approximated by triangular patches joining groups of 3 data points, and the regular grid of surface values is interpolated. The output structure contains components `x`, `y`, and `z`. The first two are vectors defining the *x-y* grid, and the last is the matrix of interpolated values. Since `interp` produces NAs rather than extrapolating, `contour` will not draw lines outside the convex hull of the data; no segment of a contour line will be drawn to an edge if either of the vertices of the edge is NA in the `z` matrix.

Let us now tie together the functions `interp`, `persp`, `contour`, and `usa` by means of an example. We can display the results of the 1976 United States presidential election, first on a map with contour lines, and next as a perspective view. First, let's extract the data from the `votes.repub` matrix, omitting Alaska and Hawaii:

```
> forty.eight ← seq(50) [
+   is.na(match(state.abb,c("AK","HI"))) ]
> vote.1976 ← votes.repub[forty.eight,"1976"]
```

The data is irregularly spaced, therefore we will need to use `interp` to generate a grid of data. Let's assume that by plotting the percent vote at the state center, we will get an adequate map.

```
> x ← state.center$x[forty.eight]
> y ← state.center$y[forty.eight]
> i ← interp(x,y,vote.1976)
```

Now plot a map and superimpose the contours (Figure 4.22).

```
> usa(state=F)
> text(x,y,round(vote.1976))      # the actual data
> contour(i$x,i$y,i$z,add=T,labex=0,col=3)
> # contour plot with unlabelled contour lines
```

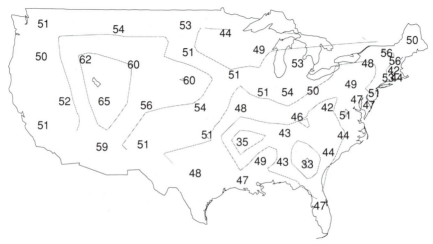

Figure 4.22. Percent vote for Republican candidate in the 1976 presidential election, with contours.

The `add=` argument causes the contour plot to be added to the underlying map, and `labex=0` causes the contour lines to be unlabelled.

We can show the election results in a perspective plot, too. However, we must first eliminate the missing values generated by `interp`.

```
> p ← i$z
> p[is.na(p)] ← min(p[!is.na(p)])   # replace NAs
> p ← p/max(p)    # scale
> persp(p)
```

The result is shown in Figure 4.23.

Notice that it was necessary to decide on a replacement value for the missing values, and that the `i$z` values were scaled to make a surface with an appropriate range of values. (Think of the height matrix as a physical object with sides measured from -1 to 1. The heights should also be scaled between -1 and 1 to get a realistic look.)

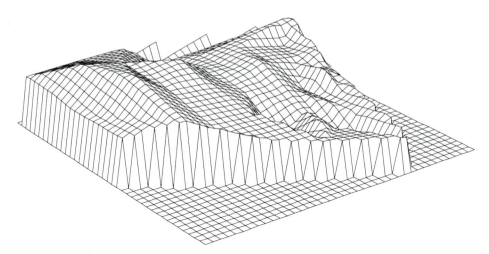

Figure 4.23. Percent vote for Republican candidate in the 1976 presidential election, shown by height in a perspective grid plot.

Exercises

4.33   Create a function that will take a 3-column matrix representing points on a surface in 3-space and produce a contour plot of the surface. Have the function superimpose the raw data values on the plot. Test your function on the data in akima.x, akima.y, and akima.z. Why would it be a good idea to round the superimposed data values to 2 or 3 significant digits?

4.34   Write a function to return a matrix of heights suitable for drawing a perspective plot. Make sure you do something about missing values and scale the result. Why is it better to return a matrix of heights rather than to call persp explicitly?

4.35   Suppose you are given a matrix of heights and you would like to draw a 3-dimensional barplot. How might you accomplish this with persp?

4.36   Data that represents mixtures of three components is basically two-dimensional, since the sum of the fractions must equal one. The function mixplot produces a plot appropriate to such data.

```
mixplot ← function(x,y,z,
        xlab="",ylab="",zlab="",largest=1){
    frame()
    par(pty="s",usr=c(0,1,0,1))
    lines(c(0,1,.5,0),c(0,0,.866,0))
    size ← x+y+z
    xx ← (y+.5*z)/size
    yy ← .866*z/size
    size ← sqrt(size/max(size))
    symbols(xx,yy,circles=size,inch=largest,add=T,err=-1,
        xlab="",ylab="")
    mtext(xlab,side=1,line=1,adj=0)
```

```
        mtext(ylab,side=4,line=1,adj=0)
        mtext(zlab,side=3,line=1,adj=.5)
    }
```

Apply it to the `telsam` data, showing the fractions of "excellent", "good", and "fair/poor" responses obtained by each interviewer.

Answers to Selected Exercises

4.3 (page 65)
```
plot(corn.rain,corn.yield,
    xlab="Rainfall in Inches",
    ylab="Corn Yield, Bushels per Acre")
```
4.5 (page 68)   Here is a workable `jitter` function.
```
jitter ← function(x,amount=NULL) {
    if(is.null(amount)){
        diffs ← diff(sort(x))
        amount ← min(diffs[diffs>0])/2
    }
    x+runif(length(x),-amount,amount)
}
```
4.6 (page 68)
```
matplot(jitter(Length),jitter(width))
```
4.7 (page 68)
```
matplot(Length,width,pch=c("S","V","G"))
```
4.10 (page 72)   The stem-and-leaf display shows better the discrete nature of the iris data (notice that the values have only one decimal place). The histogram does not show this level of detail.

4.12 (page 72)
```
one.dim ← function(x)
    plot(x,x*0)
```
4.13 (page 72)
```
quantile.plot ← function(x)
    plot(ppoints(x), sort(x),
        xlab="fraction of data",
        ylab="sorted values of data")
```
4.15 (page 74)
```
zero.digit ← lottery.number<100
qqplot(lottery.payoff[zero.digit],
    lottery.payoff[!zero.digit])
```
4.16 (page 74)
```
boxplot(iris[,1,],iris[,2,])
```
4.17 (page 74)
```
# iris is 50 samples by 4 variables by 3 groups
# sepal length is the first variable (second subscript)
boxplot(iris[,1,1],iris[,1,2],iris[,1,3])
# sepal width is the second variable
boxplot(iris[,2,1],iris[,2,2],iris[,2,3])
```
4.19 (page 74)
```
digit ← trunc(lottery.number/100)
```

```
            digit[digit<1] ← 10
            boxplot( split(lottery.payoff, digit) )
```
or we could have used
```
            digit ← trunc((lottery.number+
                ifelse(lottery.number<100,1000,0))/100)
```

4.23   (page 80)
```
            plot(hstart,hstart-smooth(hstart))
```

4.26   (page 80)
```
            x ← seq(-pi,pi,len=100)
            y ← sin(x)
            plot(x,y,type="l")
            locator()
```

4.28   (page 80)   Use an interactive device to preview the plot and use the `locator` function to get coordinates from that plot that are appropriate for putting on the annotation.

4.33   (page 91)
```
            contour.xyz ← function(x, y, z) {
                i ← interp(x, y, z)
                contour(i$x, i$y, i$z, labex = 0)
                text(x, y, signif(z,2))
            }
```

4.34   (page 91)   It is better to return the matrix of heights so that `persp` can be called repeatedly with various eye points.
```
            persp.xyz ← function(x, y, z, bottom = 0) {
                i ← interp(x, y, z)$z
                r ← range(i)    # scale to 0,1
                i ← ((i - r[1])/(r[2] - r[1]))
                i[is.na(i)] ← bottom
                i
            }
```

4.35   (page 91)   You might construct a function that will replicate the data values in the matrix a specified number of times. Once the data values have been replicated enough, they will produce a flat area which, when rendered by `persp`, will look like a 3-dimensional bar. For example
```
            bivariate.barplot ← function(x, k = 3) {
                n ← nrow(x)
                p ← ncol(x)
                rbind(0, cbind(0, x[rep(1:n, rep(k, n)),
                            rep(1:p, rep(k, p))], 0),
                    0)
            }
```
returns a matrix that replicates each value in its input `k` times, and borders the entire matrix with zeroes. This matrix can then be given to `persp` for actual rendering.

5

Data in S

Chapters 2 and 3 described expressions and functions, the language you use to communicate with the S system. This chapter describes the data that the language operates on: what kinds of data are provided, and what functions can be used to create and compute with such data.

Up to now we have been fairly informal in describing data in S. The objects used by various functions were assumed to be of the appropriate form, and the results of the functions were also assumed to "come out right" without any specific effort on your part. This is how it should be for most calculations. Objects in S are self-describing, so that you do not need to tell a function what sort of data you are providing.

This chapter begins by describing simple objects and the functions that create them, test for them, and coerce them to have specific modes. It presents character and complex data and then introduces non-atomic data. We then review two other important aspects of handling data: getting data into S, and organizing S objects into data directories. Finally, we discuss the classes of data available in S: matrices, arrays, categories and time-series, along with the attributes that define those classes.

5.1 Simple Objects

In the simplest view, objects in S are vectors that collect together some values or *elements*. The values can contain numeric, logical, or character data, or they can themselves be objects. In this chapter, we will occasionally use the term *vector*, rather than *object*, when we want to emphasize that we are talking about such simple objects. Objects that do not contain other objects as elements are called *atomic*. In this section, most of the discussion is restricted to atomic vectors. Examples of computations involving vectors are:

```
> 1:3
[1] 1 2 3
> month.name
 [1] "January"   "February"  "March"      "April"
 [5] "May"       "June"      "July"       "August"
 [9] "September" "October"   "November"   "December"
> month.length ← c(31,28,31,30,31,30,31,31,30,31,30,31)
> month.length > 30
[1] T F T F T F T T F T F T
```

Any object has two *attributes*: mode and length. The *mode* attribute is a character string that tells what kind of data is in the object. The atomic modes are "logical", "numeric", "complex", and "character". The *length* attribute tells how many data elements are in the object. Functions length(x) and mode(x) return the length and mode of any S object.

```
> mode(1:10)
[1] "numeric"
> length(weekdays)
[1] 5
```

These functions can also be used, in assignments, to change the mode or length:

```
mode(result) ← "character"
length(result) ← length(y)+2
```

S usually makes no special case out of objects of length 1: a value like 3.14 is a vector of length 1. If you use an object of length greater than one where only one element makes sense, S prints a warning message and just uses the first element of the object. It is also possible to have objects of length 0 — these have no data but they can have any of the modes above.

Objects can have attributes other than mode and length. For example, we can use the names attribute to assign a name to each element of a vector:

```
> names(month.length) ← month.name
> month.length
  January February March April May June July August
       31       28     31    30  31   30   31     31

  September October November December
        30       31       30       31
```

In what follows we will use the convention that a vector or simple object is one with no attributes other than its mode and length.

It is important to think of a vector as an entity, rather than as "built up" from single values. The philosophy underlying S is to organize computations in terms of whole data structures whenever possible, rather than as iterative calculations on single numbers or character strings. This is admittedly a view that comes with practice. Throughout the book we have tried to give examples that illustrate the benefits of thinking in terms of whole data objects rather than elements. Understanding thoroughly a few functions is particularly helpful; of these the most important is the subscripting function, "[". In section 5.1.3 and again in sections 5.5.1 and 5.5.2, we will discuss some of its uses.

5.1.1 *Data Values*

The elements in atomic vectors are numbers, complex numbers, logical values (TRUE or FALSE), or character strings. Explicit numerical values may be written in integer, decimal fraction, or scientific notation:

```
3    -5    6.272    3.4e10    7e3    4+6.7i
```

(The value 4+6.7i is a *complex number*: see section 5.1.6.) Internal blanks are *not* allowed in numbers. The internal representation of numeric data is generally irrelevant in S, except when interfacing to other languages such as C or Fortran (see section 7.2).

Logical constants are written as T or TRUE and F or FALSE.

Character strings may be specified by any string of characters, enclosed in matching quotes (") or apostrophes ('):

```
"Now is the time ..."
'Operators are: + - * /'
```

The enclosing quotes or apostrophes are only delimiters, not part of the string. A backslash character may be used to enter a character that would not otherwise be legal, typically a quote or apostrophe:

```
"You are reading the \"S user's guide\""  # or equivalently
'You are reading the "S user\'s guide"'
```

Newline characters in strings can be entered as \n. Other special characters in strings are \t (tab), \b (backspace), \r (carriage return) or \\ (backslash). Also, a 3-digit octal number following an escape character inserts the corresponding ASCII character; for example, the "bell" control character, with octal code 7:

```
> bell ← "\007"
> cat(bell)   # rings the bell on terminal
```

The special data value NA stands for Not Available. It may appear wherever a numeric, complex, or logical element is expected. Think of this as a placeholder to indicate missing data. An element of a numeric vector set to NA is marked as unknown or having no valid numeric value, for example.

There is an object named NA that can be used as a source for missing values:

```
c(1,NA,2)
```

creates a numeric vector of length 3 with its second element NA.

Operators (like arithmetic and comparison) that deal element-by-element return NA values wherever there are NAs in one of the arguments. Thus:

```
> c(1,NA,2) + c(7,8,NA)
[1]   8 NA NA
> c(1,NA,2) < c(7,8,NA)
[1]   T NA NA
```

In particular, the == operator follows the rule that operations on NAs produce NAs, so the value of x==NA is always a vector of NAs:

```
> c(1,NA,-2) == NA
[1] NA NA NA
```

(presumably not what was meant). The *only* valid test for missing values is the function is.na(x).

```
> is.na(c(1,NA,-2))
[1] F T F
```

Other functions that work element-by-element also usually reproduce missing values in their result where they existed in the input.

```
> abs(c(1,NA,-2))
[1]   1 NA   2
```

Some functions in S do not know how to handle missing values; if data with NAs is given to these functions, an error will result. Typically, functions that do more complicated numerical computations don't accept NAs:

```
> var(NA)
Error in call to .Fortran: subroutine dqr:
Missing values in argument 5
```

To prevent these errors, it is necessary to get rid of the missing values. Since the function is.na(x) returns a logical TRUE wherever x has a missing value,

```
x[!is.na(x)]
```

will return the data in x with missing values removed. There is no single generally valid mechanism for dealing with NAs, and in many cases the only reasonable answer is that the value of the function is not defined if there is missing data.

Exercises

5.1   With the definition

```
> x ← c(1, NA, -2)
```

what would you expect for the result of the expressions:

```
> 1 + NA - 2
> length(x)
> sum(x)
> mean(x)
> median(x)
```

How would you compute the sum of the non-NAs in x?

5.2   Experiment with the `bell` character string introduced earlier. How would you send a sequence of ten bells to the terminal? What happens when you try it?

5.3   Here is a function, `sleep`, that uses the corresponding command `sleep` to cause S to sleep for a specified number of seconds.

```
sleep ← function(seconds) unix(paste("sleep",seconds))
```

Given the `sleep` function and results from the previous exercise, write a function that rings the bell repeatedly for a specified duration with a specified time interval between rings. You might want to name the function `annoy` and give it an argument that tells how many times it should ring.

5.4   An exception to the rule that NAs in operators produce NAs is given by the `&` and `|` operators. What is the value of:

```
NA | TRUE
FALSE & NA
```

Why?

5.1.2 *Creating, Testing, and Coercing Simple Objects*

The following table lists commonly occurring modes in S, ordered by the amount of information they contain:

Mode	Meaning	Examples
`"null"`	the empty object	NULL
`"logical"`	truth values	TRUE, FALSE
`"numeric"`	numbers	1, -1.5, 3.77e-8
`"complex"`	complex numbers	3+4i
`"character"`	character strings	"abc", "New Jersey"
`"list"`	list of objects	list(1:10, "Hello")

In general, objects whose mode is mentioned earlier in the table can be turned into objects with a mode mentioned later without losing information. Whenever arithmetic or comparison operations are carried out on S objects, both operands are converted, usually without losing information, to have the same mode.

For example, whenever a logical object is used where the context requires numerical values, the logical values are *coerced* to numbers by the definition that TRUE is equivalent to 1 and FALSE to 0. This occurs not only in arithmetic, but in any function that expects numbers and gets logical values.

Suppose we have a logical expression age>65, and we would rather have a vector of character strings. One way to get this is to subscript two character strings, using the subscript 1 for people under age 65 and 2 for those over 65:

```
c("Young","Old")[ (age>65)+1 ]
```

(However, the function category gives a clearer way of doing the same thing; see section 5.5.3.) Conversely, if numerical values are coerced to logical, all zeros are FALSE, any nonzeros are TRUE, and NAs remain as NAs.

Another consequence of automatic coercion is that functions that expect character string data can be given data of *any* mode. For example, the function paste makes a character vector from the elements of all its arguments, pasted together as strings. To get the labels "Question 1" through "Question 20":

```
paste("Question",1:20)
```

The mode "null" is special: it implies an "empty" object. S provides an object, NULL, of mode "null". It plays a special role with components and attributes (sections 5.2 and 5.6).

Non-atomic modes like "list" describe vectors whose elements are themselves other S objects. The function list constructs a vector of mode "list" with one element in the result for each argument. Thus

```
x ← list(c(TRUE,FALSE), "Superman", c(1.75e14,33,9) )
```

generates a list of length 3. The first element of x is a logical vector of length 2, the second element is a character vector of length 1, and the third element is a numeric vector of length 3. We will discuss non-atomic modes in section 5.2.

For each mode, there are three functions: to create objects of that mode, to test for a simple object of that mode, and to coerce an object to that mode. The convention is that the function that creates objects has the same name as the mode:

```
logical(10)
```

returns an object of length 10 and mode `logical`. Similarly, functions `numeric` and `character` generate objects of given length and the corresponding mode. Not all generating functions will have this form; for example, the function `complex` for creating complex vectors has a more general set of arguments, since complex numbers can be specified in a variety of ways. There is also a "universal" generator function,

```
vector(mode, length)
```

which returns an object of the mode and length specified. If we wanted to generate a list of 10 elements, but didn't yet know what the elements were,

```
vector("list",10)
```

would do it. Remember that there may be zero-length objects of any mode.

A similar set of functions tests whether its argument is an object of a given mode; e.g.,

```
is.logical(x)
```

to test for a logical object. Functions `is.numeric`, `is.complex`, etc. test for other modes, and

```
is.vector(x, mode)
```

tests, typically, for a computed mode.

The corresponding explicit coercion can be accomplished by similar functions for each mode:

```
as.complex(1:10)
as.character(pi)
```

or by a function that takes the mode as an argument;

```
as.vector(x,mode)
```

The general definition of explicit coercion is that the value will be a simple object of the desired mode with the same length as the argument. In particular,

```
as.list(1:10)
```

creates a list of length 10 with each element a numeric vector of length 1.

Exercises

5.5   S allows the operands in arithmetic expressions or comparisons to be of different lengths. Experiment with one operand of length, say 10, and the other of lengths 1, 2, 5, and 7. Use several different operators such as "+", "^", and "!=". What is the general rule? What happens if one operand is of length 0?

5.6   What happens if you shorten a vector?

```
x ← 1:10
length(x) ← 5
```

What if you lengthen it?

```
length(x) ← 20
```

5.1.3 *Subscripting*

Subscripting is one of the most commonly used of all S operations, and is used
to extract and/or replicate values from objects. On the left side of an assignment, it forms the essential operation to *replace* values of elements. It has
special forms for matrix and array objects (see section 5.5). It is the operation
that is most intimately involved with attributes (see section 5.6). Subscripting
of simple objects in S is carried out by the syntax:

```
object [ subscript ]
```

This produces a new object that always has the same mode as the original
`object`. In particular, for non-atomic objects, it is often important to distinguish subscripting from extracting a single element; see section 5.2.

There are four forms of subscripts for general objects: numeric, negative, logical, and character. In addition, an *empty* subscript implies all the elements. Numeric subscripts specify the positions of the desired elements:

```
x[1:10]    # first 10 elements of x
x[c(1,3,5)]  # first, third, and fifth elements of x
x[c(1,5,1,10,1,20)] # six elements from x
```

In the third example, notice that the first element was picked up several times
by the subscript. The object returned by using positive subscripts is always
exactly as long as the subscript vector and can be any size relative to the subscripted object. For example, to create a vector with the elements of x
repeated four times, alternately in the original order and the reverse order:

```
> i ← seq(along=x)
> xrep ← x[c(i,rev(i),i,rev(i))]
```

This technique finds especially good applications with matrices and arrays (see
section 5.5.1).

Another form of subscript uses negative numbers. (Positive and negative numbers cannot be mixed in the same subscript.) Negative numbers mean
all but; thus,

```
x[-1]
```

is all of x except for the first element. Negative subscripts are often used to
exclude outliers:

```
x[-outliers]
```

gives all of the values in x that were not mentioned in outliers. Repeated negative values are ignored—you can only exclude any particular element of the object once.

There are several technical details. Non-integer subscripts are truncated toward zero. If a subscript is zero, nothing is returned for that subscript. If a subscript is NA, an NA is returned. If a subscript is larger than the length of the object being subscripted, then the result is an NA.

```
> x ← 1:5
> x[3.5]
[1] 3
> x[0]  # a 0-length vector
numeric(0)
> x[NA]
[1] NA
> x[10]
[1] NA
```

Of course, zero and NA subscripts are not likely to be used by themselves; more often they are used with positive subscripts.

Another form of subscript is the *logical* subscript, in which case the subscript vector should be of the same length as the subscripted object; any elements in the object corresponding to TRUE subscripts are returned in the result. Many powerful operations are possible with logical subscripts.

```
x[x>mean(x)] # the values in x larger than the mean
name[salary>30000]  # names of people whose salary
    # is more than 30,000
```

These expressions are much like queries in database management systems.

If an object has a names attribute, there is yet another way of referring to elements of the object—by name. To do this, we use character subscripts:

```
> x ← 1:3
> names(x) ← c("a","b","c")
> x["b"]
 b
 2
```

This form of subscripting is often used with lists, where names are often present. A closely related operation is

```
z$what
```

which extracts the *component* corresponding to name "what" (see section 5.2).

Any form of subscript can appear on the left of an assignment, with the meaning "replace all the elements that match this subscript," with values from the right side of the assignment. If the left and right sides have different modes, replacement is done so as not to lose information. Therefore, *either* the right or the left side may be coerced to give both sides the same mode. Then elements from the right side are successively substituted in the object on the left to correspond to the subscript expression. The right-side values are repeated cyclically as often as needed, as in arithmetic or comparison operations. As a special case, if the object on the right has length 0, there are no values for replacement, and the left-side object is unchanged.

More will be said about subscripting when we discuss classes of objects, such as arrays, for which the subscript function has special behavior. Also, there are special considerations for non-atomic data, which we have touched on here, but which will be covered in greater detail in section 5.2. The rules for subscripting are presented fully in section 11.4.

Exercises

5.7   How would you replace every third element (first, fourth, etc.) of an object with its negative value?

5.8   The expression

```
x[i] ← NULL
```

never changes any of the values in the object, regardless of `x` or `i`. Explain why.

5.1.4 *Character Vectors*

Many functions in S work with character data in a natural way: `sort` sorts character strings according to ASCII conventions, `==` tests for equality, `cat` prints strings. Remember, too, that any other mode can be coerced to character either implicitly by functions like `cat`, or explicitly.

For the most part, S functions that deal with character data treat each string as a single data value; a character string is not a vector of individual characters. On the other hand, there are endless possibilities for just such character manipulation by using the `unix` function to interface to the many tools in the UNIX system designed for this purpose. We will introduce functions that exploit this interface, beginning in section 6.3. For example, function `nchar`, introduced in section 6.3, counts the number of characters in each element of a character vector. Function `substring`, described in section 7.2, returns portions of the elements of character vectors.

The `paste` function is a flexible way of creating a character vector out of any combination of arguments. These character vectors can be used as commands for the `unix` function, or as labels for printing or plotting.

```
> paste(month.length, "days has", month.name)
 [1] "31 days has January"   "28 days has February"
 [3] "31 days has March"     "30 days has April"
 [5] "31 days has May"       "30 days has June"
 [7] "31 days has July"      "31 days has August"
 [9] "30 days has September" "31 days has October"
[11] "30 days has November"  "31 days has December"
```

The corresponding elements of all the arguments to `paste` are concatenated to form a single character string. The vector returned has as many character strings as the longest argument; shorter arguments are reused cyclically (as with the second argument in the example). Arguments that are not character strings are coerced to mode `"character"`. By default, a single blank is inserted between values from successive arguments. The special argument `sep=string` allows you to specify any separating string desired; for example, `sep=""` jams successive arguments together without blanks. Another argument, `collapse=string` allows you to specify a string that will be used between successive elements of the character vector as it is collapsed into one long string.

```
> paste(LETTERS,collapse="")
[1] "ABCDEFGHIJKLMNOPQRSTUVWXYZ"
> paste(letters,collapse=",")
[1] "a,b,c,d,e,f,g,h,i,j,k,l,m,n,o,p,q,r,s,t,u,v,w,x,y,z"
```

Two other functions related to `paste` are `cat` and `format`. The `cat` function converts all its arguments to character vectors and then prints them out, by default on the standard output. It is the key tool to print out information in a general, precise way, and is often used to construct specialized output. The `format` function takes a single vector as its argument and converts it to a character vector of the same length with the property that each element has the same number of characters. When the argument is numeric, `format` chooses one conversion format to represent all the elements:

```
> format(c(1, .005, 10.3))
[1] " 1.000" " 0.005" "10.300"
```

Exercises

5.9   Suppose the two vectors `value` and `cost` represent the results of several computations and the corresponding costs. You want to print some neat output of the form:

```
Run: 1 Result:  0.4077797 Cost: 85.16
Run: 2 Result:  0.5362221 Cost: 20.92
Run: 3 Result:  0.0759569 Cost: 69.31
Run: 4 Result:  0.3239556 Cost: 85.86
Run: 5 Result: -1.3531665 Cost: 14.94
```

```
Run: 6 Result: -2.4226151 Cost: 29.47
Run: 7 Result:  0.3441299 Cost: 34.75
```

You want all the numbers to line up above each other. Use the functions paste, format, and cat to generate the output.

5.10   When playing the game of Bingo, random combinations of a letter and a number are announced: "B13", "N35", etc. The way these letter-digit combinations are made is to draw an integer randomly from 1 to 75 and prefix it with one of the letters from "BINGO": "B" if the integer is between 1 and 15, "I" if it is between 16 and 30, etc. Write a function that will perform a Bingo drawing.

5.1.5 *Complex Numbers*

The mode complex in S is intended to represent the mathematical notion of complex numbers. Complex arithmetic is an important tool for some applications, but is irrelevant in many others. If you do not plan to use complex numbers, feel free to skim over or skip this section.

Complex numbers are usually understood as pairs of numbers, the *real* and *imaginary* parts, with arithmetic defined in a certain way. This is called the *rectangular* representation of complex numbers. A complex constant is a number followed by "+" or "−", followed by another number, followed by "i", with *no* internal blanks. If the real part of the number is 0, it can be omitted.

```
> z ← c(3+4i, 1i)
```

The rectangular representation is also used when complex data are printed:

```
> z
[1] 3+4i 0+1i
> 2*z
[1] 6+8i 0+2i
> z^2
[1] -7+24i -1+ 0i
> 1/z
[1] 0.12-0.16i 0.00-1.00i
```

As illustrated, the standard arithmetic operators obey the usual rules for complex arithmetic. Similarly, most of the element-by-element arithmetic functions and numeric summaries operate on complex data (we'll look at arithmetic functions in more detail later in this subsection). In particular the == and != operators work as expected. The other comparison operators, such as > and < could reasonably be expected to produce an error, since there is no natural ordering on the complex numbers. For convenience, however, they do work, comparing first the real parts, and when these are equal, the imaginary parts. This feature is used, for example, to give an unambiguous order to a vector of complex numbers using the sort function.

It is sometimes important to distinguish the use of "+" or "−" in complex constants from the arithmetic operators. If there are no intervening spaces, S will interpret anything that looks like a complex constant as a constant. You may need to force S to make the distinction by putting in blanks. For example,

```
> 1:10+1i
Error in call to :: Second argument isn't a number: e1:e2
```

invokes the ":" operator with arguments 1 and 10+1i (and, since ":" doesn't know how to work with complex numbers, results in an error). What you probably wanted was the sequence with real part 1:10 and imaginary part 1. To get that, use spaces to divorce the 10 from 1i:

```
> 1:10 + 1i
[1] 1+1i 2+1i 3+1i 4+1i 5+1i 6+1i 7+1i 8+1i 9+1i 10+1i
```

S does *not* automatically coerce numeric to complex because users without knowledge of complex arithmetic would find this confusing. So, although in complex analysis 0+1i is equivalent to sqrt(-1), in S:

```
> sqrt(-1)
[1] NA
```

There is an easy way to get the desired result, however.

```
> sqrt(as.complex(-1))
[1] 2.179918e-17+1i
```

All that is necessary is to make sure that you explicitly make the data mode "complex" before operating with complex arithmetic.

Try to think of complex numbers as single entities; specifying their real and imaginary parts is merely a notational convenience. A missing value of mode complex is a single NA; the real and imaginary parts cannot be NA separately. A complex vector of length 10 should be thought of as 10 complex values, not 20 numeric values arranged in pairs. However, when the real and imaginary parts are needed, there are functions Re and Im to compute them:

```
> cuberoot.1 ← (cos(2*pi/3) + sin(2*pi/3)*1i)^(0:2)
>        # cube roots of 1
> cuberoot.1
[1]  1.0+0.0000000i −0.5+0.8660254i −0.5−0.8660254i
> cuberoot.1^3
[1]  1+0i 1+0i 1+0i
> Re(cuberoot.1)
[1]  1.0 −0.5 −0.5
> sum(Im(cuberoot.1))
[1]  0
```

The other common form used to represent complex numbers is the *polar* representation, and there are S functions to compute the *modulus* (length) and *argument* (angle) of any complex number:

```
> Mod(cuberoot.1)
[1] 1 1 1
> Arg(cuberoot.1)/(2*pi)
[1]   0.0000000   0.3333333  -0.3333333
```

There is also a function `Conj` that will compute the complex conjugate:

```
> Im(Conj(cuberoot.1))
[1]   0.0000000  -0.8660254 0.8660254
> Arg(Conj(cuberoot.1))/(2*pi)
[1]   0.0000000   -0.3333333 +0.3333333
```

As with other modes, complex numbers may be generated by a standard function, `complex`. This takes optional arguments allowing the numbers to be specified in polar or rectangular form, and fills in default values when necessary:

```
> unit.square ← complex(real=runif(50), imag=runif(50))
>   #50 random complex numbers, uniform in the unit square
> unit.disk ← complex(arg=runif(50,-pi,pi))
>   #50 random complex numbers, uniform on the unit circle
```

In the second example the default value of 1 was used for the modulus. It is also possible to supply complex data as the initial values, or just to specify the length:

```
> z ← complex(length=20, data = 1i)
```

See `complex` in Appendix 1 for details. As another example of ways to generate complex data, the function

```
cis ← function(theta) exp(1i*theta)
```

returns a vector of complex numbers on the unit circle with the given complex arguments.

Complex numbers are plotted by interpreting their real and imaginary parts as the *x*- and *y*-coordinates of points. Hence

```
> plot(unit.disk)    # Figure 5.1
```

produces a plot of the random sample.

Most of the standard elementary functions work for complex numbers in S. In particular, the only functions in the table in section 3.3.3 that don't currently work on complex numbers are `gamma` and `lgamma`. Those who have some familiarity with complex numbers may want to know which branches of these functions are used in S. The following table summarizes this information.[†] The second column gives the branch choice for each function, and,

---

[†] S follows the same conventions as APL: see P. Penfield, *ACM SIGAPL*, pp. 248-256, 1981.

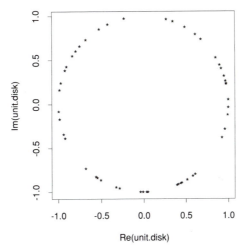

Figure 5.1. Numbers randomly distributed around the unit circle in the complex plane.

except for `Arg` and `log`, the expression given should be considered as a definition for the corresponding function. The third and fourth columns give the complements of the domains for each function, both for complex and non-complex (these are the regions where the function is undefined and produces an NA.) Numeric arguments are not automatically promoted to mode `complex`, even when they don't make sense for the real domain.

S Function	Branch Condition	Complement of Complex Domain	Complement of Real Domain
`Arg(z)`	$\text{Arg}(z) \ \varepsilon \ (-\pi, \pi]$	ϕ (see text)	n.a.
`exp(z)`		ϕ	ϕ
`log(z)`	$\text{Im}(\log(z)) = \text{Arg}(z)$	$\{0\}$	$(-\infty, 0]$
`z^w`	$\exp(w \log(z))$	ϕ (see text)	$\{z < 0, \ w \notin Z\}$
`sqrt(z)`	$z^{\frac{1}{2}}$	ϕ	$(-\infty, 0)$
`sin(z)`		ϕ	ϕ
`cos(z)`		ϕ	ϕ
`tan(z)`		$\{\frac{1}{2}n\pi : n \text{ odd}\}$	$\{\frac{1}{2}n\pi : n \text{ odd}\}$
`asin(z)`	$-i \log(iz + \sqrt{1-z^2})$	ϕ	$\lvert z \rvert > 1$
`acos(z)`	$-i \log(z + i\sqrt{1-z^2})$	ϕ	$\lvert z \rvert > 1$
`atan(z)`	$-i \log((1 + iz)\sqrt{1/(1+z^2)})$	$\{-i, i\}$	ϕ
`sinh(z)`		ϕ	ϕ
`cosh(z)`		ϕ	ϕ
`tanh(z)`		$\{\frac{1}{2}n\pi i/2 : n \text{ odd}\}$	$(-\infty, 1)$
`asinh(z)`	$\log(z + \sqrt{1+z^2})$	ϕ	ϕ
`acosh(z)`	$\log(z + (z+1)\sqrt{(z-1)/(z+1)})$	ϕ	$(-\infty, 1)$
`atanh(z)`	$\log((1+z)\sqrt{1-1/z^2})$	$\{-1, 1\}$	$\lvert z \rvert > 1$

Although complex numbers are rarely gathered as raw data, they have valuable computational properties. One of the most common uses is in the spectral analysis of time-series. The function `fft(z)` computes the (unnormalized) discrete Fourier transform of its argument, using the Fast Fourier Transform algorithm. This can be used to create a simple periodogram calculator as in:

```
pgram ← function(z) {
    n ← length(z)
    (Mod(fft(z))^2/(2 * pi * n))[1:(n %/% 2 + 1)]
    }
```

The expression in square brackets only takes the first half of the result, since if z is real, the periodogram is symmetric about the center. This function may be used with other S tools to analyze time-series.

Exercises

5.11   S does not automatically produce complex-valued numerical results from non-complex data. In particular, try some examples like `log(-1)` to see what happens. Suppose, however, that you *do* want logarithms of negative numbers to generate complex values. Write a function to do this, while still computing logarithms of positive numbers the way `log` does.

5.12   Try the `pgram` function on the `sunspots` dataset listed in Appendix 2. Can you discover the 11-year cycle?

5.13   The exponentiation operator for two length 1 complex arguments, `z^w`, yields a single value in S. Generically, however, z^w can have infinitely many values, depending on the choice of branch for $Arg(z)$. In fact, if

$$z = re^{i\theta} \quad \text{and} \quad w = a + ib$$

then $Arg(z)$ can be chosen to be $\theta + 2k\pi = \theta_k$, say, for any integer k. We then have:

$$|z^w| = r^a e^{-b\theta_k}$$

and

$$Arg(z^w) = b\log(r) + a\theta_k.$$

Write a function `pow(z,w,n=10)` that computes n values for `z^w`, using a range of n integers k that includes 0 (corresponding to the current definition of `z^w`). Try plotting the results of `pow(2,1i/50)` and `pow(2,5+1i/50,30)`.

5.14*   If you try `unique(pow(1,1/3))` with your answer to the previous exercise, you might expect to get just the three complex cube roots of 1. This does not happen, though, because of the small rounding errors that are inevitable in floating point computations. Design a version of `uniq` that takes a `tolerance` argument, saying that for `numeric` or `complex` arguments you are willing to believe that two values are the same if the relative difference between them is smaller than `tolerance`. This is easy for a `numeric` argument, but tricky for a `complex` one. Now incorporate your new version of `unique` into `pow` and try it out on the cube roots of 1.

5.15* It is generally true that `z^w` will have finitely many values precisely when `w` is a rational number, i.e., `Im(w)` is 0 and `Re(w)` is rational. In this case, the number of values of `z^w` is just the denominator of `w` when expressed as a fraction in lowest terms. Can you think of a way of detecting this case in `pow(z,w)`?

5.2 Non-Atomic Data; Components

In contrast to the atomic data discussed in section 5.1, many objects used in S contain other entire objects as elements. For example, the value returned to describe fairly complicated operations, as when fitting a linear model via the `lsfit` function, typically needs to be thought of as several component objects, organized together as a "`list`". This property is described in S by saying that the object returned is *recursive*. The two functions, `is.recursive(x)` and `is.atomic(x)`, may be used to identify recursive and atomic objects, respectively.

```
> is.atomic(letters)
[1] T
> is.atomic(list(1,2,3))
[1] F
> is.recursive(list(1,2,3))
[1] T
```

There are, in fact, many recursive modes. Three that can be used in a general way are "`list`", "`graphics`", and "`expression`". Of these, the first is the mode used for most recursive objects in computation. Graphics objects are produced by the graphics functions, and objects of mode `expression` are usually the result of parsing some text. We will use "`list`" as the paradigm for recursive data here, but the other two modes can be handled the same way. Other, specialized, modes arise, mostly in manipulating the S language itself. Their discussion is postponed to chapter 7.

Because of the recursive nature of lists, we must distinguish between subscripting a list and selecting a single element of a list. A subscripted list is always of mode "list"—any subscripted object always keeps the original mode. But a single element of a list could have any mode at all. For example, consider

```
a.little.list ← list(1:10, "Now is the time", 3+4i)
```

The first element of this list is of mode `"numeric"`, the second `"charac-ter"`, and the third `"complex"`.

```
a.little.list[3]
```

will be an object of mode `"list"` and length 1. But we need some way to get at that element itself; i.e., the vector of one complex number. There are three ways to do so. The expression using double square brackets:

```
a.little.list[[3]]
```

returns the third element, in this case as a complex vector. The expression

```
for(e in a.little.list)
    print(e)
```

executes `print(e)` with e successively set to each of the elements in the list.

The third method uses the `names` attribute of the list. It is often a good idea to construct lists with named elements. We call the elements in this case *components*, and typically extract or assign them by using the "$" opera-tor. Here we are working with a somewhat different model of the list object. Where before we were thinking of the elements of the list as more or less equivalent, now we imagine that each element has a special meaning, linked to the corresponding name for the component. It is the union of these com-ponents that "defines" the nature of the object. For example, a list with com-ponents named x and y, looks like something to plot; with components named `coef` and `resid`, a list appears to be the result of fitting a model.

Our little list has no names, but if we had constructed it a bit dif-ferently:

```
a.little.list ← list(a=1:10, b="Now is the time", c=3+4i)
```

we could get at the third element by using the element operator,

```
a.little.list[["c"]]
```

or through the component operator,

```
a.little.list$c
```

Either expression evaluates to the component named c of the object `a.little.list`. Components are never defined for atomic data: the value of x$c would always be `NULL` if x were atomic. On the other hand, elements of atomic objects are equivalent to the corresponding subscript expression.

Components can be deleted by assigning them the value `NULL`:

```
a.little.list$c ← NULL
```

deletes the component named c.

The design of data structures with well-chosen components to represent the result of a computation is one of the most powerful tools in organizing new computational facilities in S. This is the typical way in which S functions will return a result that has more structure than can be represented by a simple object, matrix, array, etc.

As we mentioned before, components of an object can be extracted by the "$" operator. For example, function `lsfit` fits a regression model and returns a regression object. If you assign the name `z` to a regression object,

```
z ← lsfit(x,y)
```

then the vector of coefficients is obtained as `z$coef`. The expression on the left of "$" is usually an object name, but it may be any expression:

```
allfits[[i]] $ resid
lsfit(x,y) $ coef
```

To plot the residuals from the regression in `z`:

```
plot(z$resid)
```

As in the case of named arguments to functions, it is only necessary to give enough characters of a component name to identify the component uniquely; for example, the following two expressions

```
lsfit(x,y)$res
lsfit(x,y)$residuals
```

are identical in effect, because the value of `lsfit` has only one component matching "res".

Many functions in S produce structures defined by components. Typically, several functions will be designed together to compute, plot and otherwise display a particular kind of analysis. The documentation in Appendix 1 describes, for each function, the components of the returned object. In addition to the functions specially designed for the specific class of objects, any other functions can be used on the objects as well, by extracting components as we did above to plot residuals from regression. The combination of functions specialized to particular classes with the use of general computation and plotting of components provides a crucial flexibility for handling non-trivial computing tasks.

You can design new classes of objects. This is an important part of using S as an application programming environment. Chapter 8 is largely devoted to that subject.

Exercises

5.16   Create an object `x` by executing

```
x ← as.list(1:10)
```

Before actually trying them, explain what the expressions

```
        x[3] + 7
```

and

```
        x[[3]] + 7
```

should produce. Try them.

5.17 A plot of the absolute value of the residuals against the fitted values can help detect changes in variability that are contrary to the assumptions of standard regression models. (The residuals are the difference between y and the fitted values.) Write a function that produces this plot.

5.18 The function `lapply` is designed to execute a function, given as an argument to `lapply`, on each element of a list. Construct a list with atomic components and use `lapply` to sort each component.

5.3 Data Input

Getting information *into* S is a key step in data analysis and other computing. The function `scan` is the general purpose function for reading fields containing atomic data from the terminal or from a file:

```
> x ← scan("myfile")
```

reads numeric values from the file named "myfile". It is important to keep clear the distinction between a *file* and an S *object, as generated by an assignment.* The files processed by `scan` are ordinary ASCII text files. S stores objects in special forms, for the sake of efficiency; permanent S objects are not text files.

The file read by `scan` should contain data items (numbers in this simple case), in a form that would be legal if the data were typed to S. The file (`myfile`) used in the expression above might contain, for example,

```
3.5   2.1
7.893   1.3e10   0   0   0
1
−37.892   80000
```

Then x would be of length 10, with the values shown.

Data items are separated by *white space* (that is, by blanks, tabs, or newlines). If the file argument is not given, `scan` will read items interactively from standard input. In interactive use, you will be prompted with the index of the next item to be read, and input will be terminated by an empty line.

```
> x ← scan()
1: 1 2.5 3.14159
4:
3 items read
```

Input can also be terminated by a line containing only the end-of-file character control-d.[†] Reading directly from the terminal is reasonable for small amounts of data. However, for larger amounts, most users will find it preferable to have the data items on a file, so that a text editor can be used to correct typing errors before input.

An item appearing as the two characters "NA" on input will generate a corresponding missing value in a numeric vector.

If you want to control the number of items read from the file, the optional argument n should be given:

```
scan("myfile",n=6)
```

reads only the first six items of the file shown.

The scan function needs to know what kind of data it is reading. By default it reads numbers. To read character strings, give it as a second argument any object of mode "character":

```
scan("myfile","")
```

(scan uses the mode of the argument to decide what mode the result should be). In the case of character data, we often want to allow internal blanks in fields. For this purpose, choose some separator character (a tab is a common choice), and arrange that fields be separated by a single separator character. Then the call

```
scan("myfile","",sep="\t")
```

replaces the default (white space) field separation rule and looks instead for tab characters as separators. Similarly,

```
scan("myfile","",sep="\n")
```

reads character data from a file a line at a time.

The most powerful use of scan is to read multiple fields simultaneously from a file. The model is that the file is a table of data; lines of the file are divided into fields (not necessarily of equal width). For example, here are the first few lines of a file containing two character fields, followed by four numeric fields:

```
Alabama       AL    3615   3624   15.1   41.3
Alaska        AK     365   6315   11.3   66.7
Arizona       AZ    2212   4530    7.8   58.1
Arkansas      AR    2110   3378   10.1   39.9
California    CA   21198   5114   10.3   62.6
```

[†]When we wish to denote a "control character" (that is, an ASCII character whose code is in the range 0-31), we will always use this "control-" notation. In this case, "control-d" signifies the ASCII character (code 4), which is typed by pressing "d" while the CONTROL or CTRL key is being held down.

```
Colorado        CO     2541    4884     6.8    63.9
Connecticut     CT     3100    5348     3.1    56
Delaware        DE      579    4809     6.2    54.6
Florida         FL     8277    4815    10.7    52.6
Georgia         GA     4931    4091    13.9    40.6
Hawaii          HI      868    4963     6.2    61.9
Idaho           ID      813    4119     5.3    59.5
Illinois        IL    11197    5107    10.3    52.6
Indiana         IN     5313    4458     7.1    52.9
Iowa            IA     2861    4628     2.3    59
```

(We've displayed the data neatly lined up here, but the actual file consists of fields separated by tabs, to allow the first field to have embedded blanks.) The style for reading such objects is to create a list, whose components correspond to the successive fields, and have the appropriate modes. The call to scan will return a list with all the data from the first field in the first component, all the data from the second field in the second component, and so on. In our example:

```
> z ← list(state="", abbr="", pop=0, income=0,
+   murder=0, 'hs grad'=0)
```

The control list may contain NULL values to tell scan to skip the corresponding field in the input; for example, if we didn't want to read the second field we could set abbr=NULL in the definition of z. The names of the components in the argument to scan are retained as the component names in the output. In particular, if you have an object resulting from scanning a previous file of the same form, this can be used as the argument.

```
> mydata ← scan("state.data",z,sep="\t")
```

This use of scan is the natural way to read text files containing tables of data.

There are a few circumstances when scan is not appropriate for reading data into S. When the data can be anything known to the rules of the S language, the function parse should be used. For example, this is how the source function reads in material. Also, if for some reason the data cannot be turned into any simple form of text file (or if there is some reason that a very efficient reading process is needed), it may be necessary to write special input routines, typically in C, and use the interface from S to C to create the S objects. The C interface is described in section 7.2.

Exercises

5.19   Use scan to read a data file that contains a mixture of character and numeric data.

5.20*   The file /usr/pub/ascii contains a table of the numerical code corresponding to each ASCII character (printing and nonprinting). Look at the file, make a suitably edited copy of it, and use `scan` to read it into S. (This exercise is a little harder than it sounds. Notice that the file has the character "|" surrounding items as well as separating them. Also remember that you will need to escape special characters, say by preceding them with a backslash.)

5.21* Suppose you have a file for input, but don't know what is in the fields. How would you find out, and read it with `scan`?

5.4 Data Directories and Frames

This section discusses how S organizes objects, both temporarily in *frames* and permanently in *data directories*. Section 5.4.1 explains how S searches for objects during the evaluation of a function call. Section 5.4.2 presents some functions that provide control over getting, assigning, and removing objects from specific places. Since the first subsection is more technical than the rest of this chapter, you may want to skim over it if your interest is more in how to get things done. You will need some understanding of it to use the functions in section 5.4.2, as well as for some of the more advanced programming techniques in later chapters, but you can understand the rest of this chapter without mastering section 5.4.1 in detail.

5.4.1 *Searching for Objects*

When S evaluates an expression, for example

```
sqrt(lottery.payoff)
```

it needs to find the objects used in the expression, in this case `sqrt` and `lottery.payoff`. S does this by searching through frames and data directories, stopping its search as soon as it has found the object it is looking for. Data access and storage in frames and directories happens automatically. However, it may help you to know what the rules are and what facilities are available to get or assign objects in nonstandard places.

A *directory* contains S objects, written to files by permanent assignments. A *frame* is a list of named S objects, maintained in memory by S. The important difference between frames and directories is that the objects stored in a frame are temporary—they will go away when the frame is destroyed. A frame can exist at the longest for the duration of an S session. Objects in directories persist until they are explicitly removed.

When you start an S session, S sets up a *search list*—a character vector giving the names of directories to be searched for objects. Normally, the search list contains:

- your S working data directory,
- the S functions directory, and
- the S datasets directory.

S also creates a *session frame* to hold objects for the duration of the S session and an *expression frame*, to hold objects for the duration of each top-level expression.

Let's follow the process of evaluating the expression

```
sqrt(lottery.payoff)
```

to illustrate how directories and frames are searched. The process is shown in a diagram in Figure 5.2.

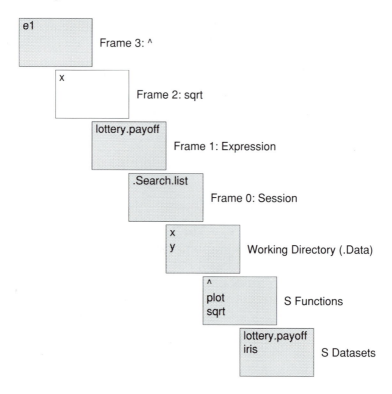

Figure 5.2. In this diagram, S is evaluating the expression `sqrt(lottery.payoff)`. S searches for objects in the shaded frames and data directories in order from left to right.

First, S has to find the function object named `sqrt`. It isn't in any of the frames, nor the working directory, but it is found in the S functions directory.

S sets up a new frame (frame 2 in the figure) for the call to sqrt. Since the value of sqrt is

```
function(x) x^.5
```

S next searches for function "^", finding it in the S function directory, also.

Frame 3 is now created for the call to function "^", and since it is an internally-defined function that requires evaluated arguments, its arguments, e1 and e2 are now evaluated. Argument e1 is matched to argument x in frame 2; x in turn is matched to lottery.payoff, and a search is instigated for that object. This time, the search terminates in the S datasets directory. After matching argument e2 to the value .5, function "^" is finally evaluated. Its value is passed back to frame 2, and frame 3 disappears. Evaluation of sqrt is now also complete, so its value is passed up to frame 1 and frame 2 disappears. Since the value of the expression was not assigned a name, S automatically prints the value.

As we saw in this example, S creates a frame for each function call, which persists until the function evaluation is complete. The frame for a function call is a list of objects available by name during the evaluation of the body of the function. The frame includes the arguments to the function and it will also include any new objects that are created by assignment inside the function.

The expression frame, known also as *frame 1*, corresponds to the expression you typed to S and persists through the complete evaluation of that expression. It contains copies of data objects used in the expression—in our example, it holds lottery.payoff—so that they are readily available if they are needed again in the expression. It can also be used by functions to share objects during expression evaluation. An example is given in section 9.6.

Objects in the session frame are retained throughout the current session with S but disappear when you quit from S. S functions use session objects for things that can reasonably be expected to start over from default values when a new session begins, like options and the search list. The session frame is also known as *frame 0*.

To save search time for frequently accessed functions, S provides an option, keep, that directs S to keep a copy of functions in memory, after they have been accessed or assigned. In our sqrt(lottery.payoff) example, the functions sqrt and "^" were initially found on the system function directory. If you repeated the same expression, however, the functions would be found in an internal "keep" frame, without needing to do any search. To turn off keeping of functions, use

```
options(keep=NULL)
```

You might want to do this if you were planning to access or assign a very large number of functions; for most applications, however, keeping functions is a reasonable strategy. The keep frame is handled so that its presence or absence does not affect the semantics of the search; i.e., if an object is found in the keep frame, the same object would have been found in the search of the data directories.

Now we can state the general rule for finding an S object. S looks for the object successively in:

- the local frame for the current function evaluation;
- frame 1 (the expression frame);
- frame 0 (the session frame);
- the keep frame;
- in turn, each of the directories named in the search list.

Notice that the search *does not* include all of the active frames. In particular, if S is evaluating a particular function, the search does not go through the frame of the calling function. That is why frame 2 (for sqrt) is not shaded in Figure 5.2 while we are evaluating the call from sqrt to ^. This means that objects are local to each function and are not accessible to functions it calls. Local assignments in sqrt cannot change the semantics of the call to ^. Consider these two function definitions:

```
foo ← function(){
    x ← 1:10
    bar()
}
bar ← function()
    1+x
```

Watch what happens when we call foo:

```
> x ← 7
> foo()
[1] 8
```

foo defines an object named x in its local frame and then calls bar. When bar tries to access object x, it does not look in foo's frame—it gets the value of x from the working data.

So far, we have described how S accesses data objects. How are data objects created in the first place? The rule for assignment or replacement expressions using the "<-" operator is simple: if the assignment occurs in frame 1, the object is assigned to the first directory on the search list, the S working directory. Assignments that take place in other frames—within the evaluation of some function call—are done in the frame of that function call, the *local* frame of the call. Assignments that use the double arrow operator, "<<-", always take place in the working directory.

As we mentioned earlier, the default search list contains three directories. The working data will be contained in a subdirectory named .Data under the current directory. If the local .Data directory does not exist, S looks for a subdirectory .Data of your login directory. This directory will be created if it does not exist. All that is needed to initialize S to work in any directory is to create a `.Data` subdirectory there, typically by the shell command

```
mkdir .Data
```

The second data directory in the default search list is the directory containing *system functions* such as `c`, `print`, and `sum`. The third data directory is the S *system data* directory, containing various data objects, including statistical examples and standard values (e.g., the lottery data, the names of the states, months, etc.).

Function `attach` is used to add more directories to the search list. By default, directories are attached right after the working data:

```
attach("/usr/joe/.Data")
```

will attach Joe's data directory in position 2 of the search list. Similarly, `detach` removes directories from the search list:

```
detach(2)
```

or

```
detach("/usr/joe/.Data")
```

takes Joe's data directory out of the search list. Since assignments are done in the first directory in the search list, it must always have write permission for the user. An attempt to create a search list that does not have this property generates an error.

The search list is kept in a character vector named `.Search.list`. The `attach` and `detach` functions update this vector, and assign the updated copy in frame 0, the session frame. (Assignment to frame 0 is accomplished by the `assign` function, described later in this section.) This means that any changes made to the search list persist for the duration of the S session.

Assignments to data directories (or to frame 0) do not actually take place until the completion of the entire expression containing the assignment, although the assigned version of the object is available to functions in the expression as soon as the assignment is evaluated. In database management terminology, S *commits* assignments on completion of the expression. The importance of this, aside from issues of efficiency, is that expressions which generate errors do not alter the permanent directories or frame 0. This helps S maintain a coherent database.

When S is searching for a function definition with a particular name, it will reject any object of the same name that is *not* a function. For example:

```
> sum ← sum(1:10)
> sum
[1]   55
> sum(1:10)
[1]   55
Warning messages:
   Looking for object "sum" of mode "function",
   ignored one of mode "numeric"
```

In this case, we created a local object named sum that almost hid the system function sum.

To obtain a list of the names of all objects in the working directory use the function ls.

```
> ls()    # working directory
[1] "i"   "tx"   "ty"   "tz"   "x1"   "y1"
```

The ls function can also be made to refer to any of the directories currently searched, by use of the optional argument pos. This specifies the position of the directory in the search list; by default, positions 1, 2, and 3 correspond to working, system function, and system data directories. For example:

```
> length(ls(pos=2)) #how many S functions?
[1] 482
```

When an object is no longer needed, it may be removed from the working directory by

```
rm(x)
```

Since S objects assigned in S expressions are stored as files in the .Data directory, it is possible to operate on the files using operating system commands. Commands can copy files, remove them, or utilize protection features of the file system. For example, you can use the chmod command to remove read permission for other users

```
> !chmod o-r .Data/x   # make x unreadable to others
```

or to make it unwritable by anyone:

```
> !chmod -w .Data/x
> x ← 3
Error: Assignment error: "x" exists without write permission
Error during wrapup
> rm(x)
Warning messages:
   "x" exists but doesn't have write permission
> x
[1]  3
```

This is a good mechanism to use to protect your data from yourself.

Because S keeps in-memory copies of certain objects, you must be careful when altering the contents of a file that contains an object. The function `synchronize` is designed to make sure that the S internal data structures and the contents of the data directories are consistent. For example:

```
synchronize()
```

causes all pending assignments to be committed and

```
synchronize(data=TRUE)
```

causes function definitions stored in the keep frame to be thrown away.

Exercises

5.22 What would be the effect of having the same directory appear twice in the search list?

5.23 Experiment with the effect of `attach` on the keep frame. Compute some expression of interest, use `ls.keep()`, to examine the contents of the keep frame, then attach some directory (by default, in position 2). Now look at `ls.keep()` again. Repeat the whole process, but attach the directory at the end of the search list (usually `pos=4`). Can you explain what is happening and why?

5.4.2 *Getting, Assigning, and Removing*

The discussion so far has concentrated on the ordinary process of access and assignment for S objects. The rest of the section presents some functions that give more control of the process of getting, testing, and assigning objects. Among the capabilities are:

- dealing with functions that have special characters in their names;
- testing for the existence of objects;
- dealing with objects on any chosen frame or directory.

The functions involved are closely related and can be considered together. They are:

```
get(name, directory, frame, mode)   #get an object
exists(name, directory, frame, mode) #does it exist?
assign(name, value, directory, frame) #assign an object
remove(names, directory, frame)   #remove objects
```

The function `exists` returns TRUE or FALSE according to whether an object exists that meets the requirements of the other arguments, whereas `get` returns the object but generates an error if the object does not exist. The argument `mode`, if supplied, specifies that the retrieved object must be of that mode.

```
exists("foo") # is there an object "foo" in the search path?
get("x",mode="function")  # get a function named "x"
get("^")         # get the exponent function
```

For all of these functions, `name` or `names` refers to character string(s) containing the names of objects. The argument `directory` refers to a data directory. If this argument is supplied, the function will look, assign or remove only from that directory. The directory can be supplied as a number, in which case it indicates an index in the current search list (for example, 1 for the working directory). It can also be supplied as a character string, which will be taken as the actual data directory in the file system—it is irrelevant whether the directory is currently on the search list.

Similarly, argument `frame` specifies one of the internal frames, possibly frames 0 or 1. If it is supplied, the functions operate in that frame. It is always an error to supply both `directory` and `frame`. The following loop creates 10 objects, x1, x2, ..., x10.

```
for(i in 1:10)
    assign(paste(x,i,sep=""),f(i))
```

To remove everything from your working directory:

```
remove(ls(),directory=1)
```

Suppose you want to get a copy of Joe's function `super.plot`:

```
super.plot ← get("super.plot",dir="/usr/joe/.Data")
```

will do the trick.

Exercises

5.24   Write a function `save(name,value)` that saves a backup copy of `value` under `name`. The idea is to have a subdirectory `.Ssave` under the user's login directory, in which the user saves important objects.

5.25   Write a function, `perm.assign(name,value)`, that works like the `<<-` operator, in that it always assigns to the working directory, but which is like `assign` in that it takes a character string argument for the name.

5.5 Classes of Objects in S

In section 5.1, we discussed simple objects, or *vectors*, of various modes. S also recognizes other classes of objects, in the sense that many functions in S handle such objects appropriately.

Class	Use
`vector`	simple objects
`matrix`	2-dimensional array (section 5.5.1)
`array`	multi-way array (section 5.5.2)
`category`	categorical data (section 5.5.3)
`time-series`	time oriented data (section 5.5.4)

The notion of a class is more general than that of a mode. For example, we can have a complex matrix, a logical array, or a character time-series. Functions exist to create, test for, and coerce to the various classes of objects. These are analogous to the functions for different modes of simple objects, discussed in section 5.1.2.

```
category(values,levels=1:max(values))
is.ts(hstart)
as.array(x)
```

One approach to such classes in S is to define extra properties, or *attributes*, which an object can possess, while still acting like a vector when the special properties are not relevant. Thus, while matrices are treated specially by many functions in S, they can also be used with functions which do *not* treat them specially. If `votes` is a matrix, one can produce a histogram plot of all the data in `votes` by

```
hist(votes)
```

because the `hist` function can treat the matrix as a simple vector. Depending on what the function does, the result may or may not retain the matrix properties of the argument. The same comments apply to the other classes of objects in S.

The rest of this section describes these classes and the special functions designed for them. Section 5.6 will go into a little more detail about attributes, and chapter 8 will show how you can define new classes of objects, to implement important applications in S.

5.5.1 *Matrices*

Matrices are defined by a `dim` attribute, a numeric vector of length 2 containing the number of rows and number of columns. Matrices are actually a special case of general multi-way arrays, but we begin with them because they are commonly used and more simple to describe than general arrays, which we will defer to section 5.5.2. Matrices can, but need not, have a second attribute, `dimnames`. If present, it provides character labels corresponding to the rows and/or columns of the matrix. Specifically, it is a list of two character vectors, either or both of which may be of length 0.

The matrix creation function, `matrix`, creates a matrix from information specifying the data, the number of rows, and/or the number of columns. By default, `matrix` expects data to come a column at a time. An optional argument, `byrow`, allows the data values to be interpreted as coming in a *row* at a time (as they would if data were being read from a printed table), and another optional argument, `dimnames`, specifies the list of character vectors giving the `dimnames` attribute. For example,

```
> m ← matrix(0,3,4) # a 3-row 4-col matrix of zeros
> matrix(1:12,3,4)
      [,1] [,2] [,3] [,4]
[1,]    1    4    7   10
[2,]    2    5    8   11
[3,]    3    6    9   12
> matrix(1:12,ncol=3,byrow=T,
+    dimnames=list(letters[1:4],LETTERS[1:3]))
   A  B  C
a  1  2  3
b  4  5  6
c  7  8  9
d 10 11 12
```

Notice the order in which the data elements are placed in the matrix: the `byrow=T` argument puts values in row-wise in the second example. S knows how to print matrices, and will use the `dimnames` attribute if present to label row and columns. If the matrix is too large to fit onto the display, the printing will break it into blocks that do fit, choosing as many columns as can fit on a line and then printing successive blocks of rows. (Arguments `width` and `height` to the `options` function provide control over what S considers the size of the display.) There is one special feature for *plotting* matrices as well: matrices with two columns will be interpreted as having the *x*-coordinates in the first column and the *y*-coordinates in the second column, in calls to functions like `plot`, `lines`, etc.

The functions

```
is.matrix(x)
as.matrix(x)
```

respectively test an object for being a matrix and coerce an object to be a matrix. Non-matrix objects are always coerced to a matrix with one column. Functions that expect matrices can usually be given vectors as arguments. These vectors will be coerced to matrices with one column. To force interpretation as a row matrix, use `matrix(x,nrow=1)`. It is possible to set the `dim` and `dimname` attributes by an assignment statement:

```
dim(m) ← c(6,2) #make m a 6 by 2 matrix
dimnames(m) ← list(LETTERS[1:6],NULL)
```

When assigning attributes this way, the object must be consistent with the assigned value; for example, the length must be the same as the product of the dimensions.

Many S functions treat matrices (and arrays) specially: subscripts and elements (`[..]` and `[[..]]`), arithmetic and comparison operators, and automatic printing, as well as a group of functions that exist solely to handle matrices.

The most important special treatment is probably that of subscripting. In the typical situation, two subscript expressions are supplied, in the form:

```
x[e1, e2]
```

`e1` and `e2` are treated as general subscript expressions, but applied respectively to rows and columns. In other words, all the specific uses of matrix subscripts follow from the general way subscripting is handled in S, but applied conceptually to all the rows of the matrix when interpreting `e1`, and to the columns when interpreting `e2`. Then the full subscript expression applies to the elements of the matrix that satisfy *both* the row and column conditions.

For example,

```
x[,c(1,3)]           # the first & third columns
votes[year<1900,]    # all rows i with year[i]<1900
x[1:3,-2]            # rows 1:3, of all columns but 2
```

Notice, in particular, that if the expression `e1` is empty, all rows of x are included; if `e2` is empty, all columns are included. Logical and negative subscripts have the same meaning for the rows and columns of matrices that they have for elements of vectors. Character subscripts also have the same meaning, in the sense that the first element of the `dimnames` attribute of the matrix defines names for the rows, and the second element defines names for the columns. Thus

```
> state.x77[c("Maine","Vermont"),]
        Population Income Illiteracy Life Exp Murder
   Maine      1058   3694        0.7    70.39    2.7
Vermont        472   3907        0.6    71.64    5.5
        HS Grad Frost   Area
   Maine    54.7   161 30920
Vermont    57.1   168  9267
```

creates a matrix with two rows, since the specified names occur among the row dimnames for the matrix. As with vector subscripts, it is possible to replicate rows and/or columns in subscripting matrices. In fact, this is a powerful technique (see the exercises below).

If the matrices resulting from subscripting end up with one row or one column, there is a choice to make. S can retain the matrix properties or it can drop one dimension to produce a vector. By default, S drops these redundant, or "dead," dimensions.

```
> m ← matrix(1:12,3,4)
> m[,2]
[1] 4 5 6
```

In most cases of interactive computing, that is the right choice since it tends to reduce complexity—why have a 1-column matrix when a vector will do. However, when you are writing functions, you may need to rely on a subscripted matrix remaining a matrix. In this case, add drop=F to the subscripts:

```
m[,which,drop=F]
```

This ensures that no dimensions will be dropped, and allows you to avoid surprises when one or the other subscript happens to leave only one element.

Exercises

5.26   Execute the following expressions:

```
as.vector(matrix(1:12,3,4))
as.vector(matrix(1:12,3,4,byrow=T))
```

Explain why the two results are different.

5.27   What would happen if we executed

```
> state.x77[c("Maine","Puerto Rico"),]
```

Why?

5.28   Suppose we have a function, coefs(x), that computes a vector of coefficients for each element in x, returning, say a length(x) by p matrix. We have a long vector, xbig, which has very many repeated values, and we want to compute coefs(xbig). But coefs is very slow and it seems a waste to recompute values. What would you do? (You *don't* need to do any iteration.)

5.29   Suppose you have a file, each line of which contains two numbers followed
by a name (no internal blanks). Use `scan` to read the data. Turn it into a
matrix with two columns, and give the matrix a `dimnames` attribute that uses
the names on the file as row names.

Notice that subscripting matrices with separate row and column subscripts can only extract regular (i.e., rectangular) subsets. Another special form
of subscript expression can extract irregular subsets. In this case there is a single subscript, which is itself a matrix. The subscripting matrix must have two
columns. Each row in the subscript matrix specifies the row and column of a
particular value to extract. To get the `[1,2]` and `[3,3]` elements from a
matrix, `m`, we build a matrix, `sub` that has the desired subscripts as its rows.

```
> m ← matrix(1:9,3,3)
> m
     [,1] [,2] [,3]
[1,]    1    4    7
[2,]    2    5    8
[3,]    3    6    9
> sub ← matrix(c(1,2,3,3),2,2,byrow=T)
> sub
     [,1] [,2]
[1,]    1    2
[2,]    3    3
> m[sub]
[1] 4 9
```

The more typical uses of such subscripts occur when the rows and columns to
be selected result from some other computational procedure.
    The following S functions create matrices, manipulate them, and give
their attributes.

Function	Purpose
`ncol(x)`	number of columns
`nrow(x)`	number of rows
`t(x)`	transpose
`cbind(...)`	combine columns
`rbind(...)`	combine rows
`diag(x)`	extract diagonal or create diagonal matrix
`col(x)`	matrix of column numbers
`row(x)`	matrix of row numbers
`apply(x,m,fun)`	apply a function to rows or columns
`sweep(a,m,stats,fun)`	sweep out row or column statistics
`outer(x,y,fun)`	outer product

The number of rows and the number of columns can be obtained from the
functions `nrow(x)` and `ncol(x)`. It is possible, as we saw, to create matrices

by extracting rows and columns from an existing matrix. In the other direction, vectors and matrices may be bound together as the rows or columns of a new matrix using `rbind` or `cbind`. For example, suppose `xold` is a matrix and `update` is a vector:

```
> xnew ← cbind(intercept=1, xold, update)
```

creates a new matrix with a first column of all ones, the next columns the same as the columns of `xold` and the last column taken as `update`. In general, `cbind` can have any number of arguments, any of which may be vectors or matrices. All matrices given to `cbind` must have the same number of rows. Notice that the single value, 1, was expanded to a vector of length equal to the number of rows of `xold`. The result has the same number of rows as the matrix arguments (or the length of the longest vector, if there were no matrix arguments). The function `rbind` works similarly with rows.

Both `cbind` and `rbind` automatically generate a `dimnames` attribute for their result when that makes sense. In particular, `cbind` uses `names` attribute of its arguments in order to determine row names; `rbind` uses the `names` attribute of its arguments in order to generate column names. If any arguments are matrices, their `dimnames` attributes are carried over. Any named arguments, such as `intercept=1`, use that name for a column or row name.

Functions that create new matrices or vectors from existing matrices are `t(x)` (the transpose of `x`), `row(x)` and `col(x)` (matrices of the same shape as `x`, but filled with the row number and the column number). The function `diag` extracts the diagonal of a matrix argument, and also creates matrices when given a vector of the desired diagonal elements and/or the desired dimensions for a diagonal matrix (the matrix will be an identity matrix if no data values are supplied).

The `apply` function provides a shorthand description for computations that operate iteratively on rows or columns of a matrix. For example, suppose we want to compute a vector of the means of all the columns of `xm`:

```
> col.means ← apply(xm,2,mean)
```

The first argument to `apply` is the matrix, the second says which dimension to apply the computations to (1 for rows, 2 for columns), and the third gives a function to apply. The above example is therefore equivalent to:

```
> col.means ← numeric()
> for(j in 1:ncol(xm))
+    col.means[j] ← mean(xm[,j])
```

If the function being applied takes additional arguments, these can be supplied as trailing arguments to `apply`. (These arguments will be the same on each call to the function from `apply`.) Frequently, one wants to follow up the computation of summaries like the column means above by operating on the original matrix with the marginal summaries. The function `sweep` provides an analogous shorthand for such computations. To compute residuals from the column means above:

```
> col.resid ← sweep(xm,2,col.means)
```

Conceptually, `sweep` expands `col.means` to the suitable matrix to look like `xm`, and then calls the "−" function to form the residuals. Any operator or function that works on two arguments can be given to `sweep`; subtraction is the default. The `outer` function will be described in section 5.5.2.

Another class of functions is specially designed to handle numerical computations involving matrices. Matrices can have any mode, even a non-atomic one, but most applications use numeric data. Ordinary arithmetic and comparison operations take special account of matrices. As with most classes of objects, operations in which one operand is a matrix and the other a vector will retain the matrix attributes. In addition, operations with two matrices having the *same* `dim` attribute will produce a result with the same `dim`. The operations will also try to retain `dimnames` attributes, if this makes sense. An attempt to operate on two matrices with inconsistent `dim` attributes generates an error.

Here are the numerical matrix functions that S provides:

Function	Purpose
x %*% y	matrix multiply
crossprod(x,y)	cross-products
lsfit(x,y)	linear regression
svd(x)	singular value decomposition
qr(x)	QR decomposition
solve(x,y)	solve equations or invert matrices
eigen(x)	eigenvalues
chol(x)	Choleski decomposition
cancor(x,y)	canonical correlations
discr(x,group)	discriminant analysis
backsolve(r,x)	back solve upper-triangular matrix

The multiplication operator, *, does ordinary element-by-element multiplication when used with matrices. Operator `%*%` performs matrix multiplication. The function `crossprod` computes the cross-product of two matrices or of a matrix with itself. The expression

```
> r ← lsfit(x,y)
```

does a linear least-squares regression of y on x and returns a *regression object*, as discussed at the end of section 5.2. Other functions implement the techniques of linear algebra on which the regression depends: for example, `qr` computes an orthogonal decomposition. A variety of functions with names beginning "qr." compute results using that decomposition. The function solve solves linear equation systems or inverts matrices. The functions svd, eigen, and chol implement singular value, eigenvalue, and Choleski decompositions, respectively. The functions cancor and discr compute the canonical correlation and multivariate discriminant summaries from multivariate statistical analysis.

Exercises

5.30 Given the matrix

```
> m ← matrix(1:12,3,4)
```

what would

```
diag(diag(m))
```

produce? Why?

5.31 Write a function that will produce a bingo card, a 5 by 5 matrix with columns labelled by the letters of BINGO filled with randomly selected numbers. The numbers in column 1 should be between 1 and 15, in col 2 between 16 and 30, etc. There should be no duplicate numbers on the card. Fill in the (3,3) element of the card with an NA, since that is a free square on a bingo card.

5.32* Write a function that "plays" bingo. It might, for example, take as its argument the names of the players. It could then generate a bingo card for each player and then draw numbers until one of the cards wins. You will probably want to use the results from exercises 5.10 and 5.31.

5.33 In the May, 1987 issue of *Comm. Assn. Comp. Mach.* (pp. 351-355), several computer programmers argued about the "right" way to write a program to solve the following problem: "find the first all-zero row of a matrix x".
1) How would you do it in S?
2) Locate all rows that are all-zero.
3) Compute the mean of the rows in which nonzero elements appear.
4) Compute the mean of the nonzero elements in each row.
5) Locate all rows for which the sum of the elements is odd.

5.34* Write a function that reads a matrix from a file by row, automatically setting nrow and ncol.

5.35 Given a 3 by 3 matrix m, what is the difference between the operations m * m and m %*% m?

5.36 Create a matrix of mode "list".

5.37 Use apply to sort each column of a matrix.

5.38* The match function allows us to join two matrices. Suppose we have a matrix, mydata, and want to cbind on some columns from a matrix update. The rows of the two matrices may be in different order, but we believe that the names of the rows given by the dimnames attribute are consistent. Use the match function to get the new columns in the right row order.

5.5.2 *Arrays*

The generalization of a matrix is a multi-way array. Where matrices have two subscripts, arrays may have one, two, three, or more. The array object is defined by the `dim` attribute. For example, a three-way array (like `iris`) with range `1:50` for its first subscript, `1:4` for its second subscript and `1:3` for its third subscript, could be created by the `array` function as follows:

```
> iris ← array(irisdata, c(50,4,3))
```

The data values should be ordered so that the first subscript varies fastest, then the second, etc. The first value becomes `iris[1,1,1]`, the second `iris[2,1,1]`, and so forth.

Arrays are printed as a series of matrices formed by fixing all but the first two dimensions. A heading for each matrix shows the values of the fixed dimensions:

```
> a ← array(1:24,c(2,4,3))
> a
, , 1
      [,1] [,2] [,3] [,4]
[1,]    1    3    5    7
[2,]    2    4    6    8

, , 2
      [,1] [,2] [,3] [,4]
[1,]    9   11   13   15
[2,]   10   12   14   16

, , 3
      [,1] [,2] [,3] [,4]
[1,]   17   19   21   23
[2,]   18   20   22   24
```

The special forms of subscripting described for matrices generalize to arrays. A 3-way array can be subscripted by expressions of the form

```
a[i1, i2, i3]
```

and similarly for arrays with other numbers of dimensions. Indexing with a matrix subscript can be applied to multi-way arrays: the subscript matrix should have k columns to index a k-way array. In fact, such subscripts are often used for indexing arrays whose number of dimensions is not known in advance.

Arrays can also have a `dimnames` attribute, either as an optional third argument to the `array` function, or by direct assignment of the `dimnames` attribute. For a k-way array, the `dimnames` should be a list of length k. The elements of the list will either be of length 0 (no names for that dimension) or of length equal to the corresponding element of the `dim` attribute. For example, a `dimnames` attribute for `iris` could be:

```
> dimnames(iris) ←
+    list(NULL,
+        c("Sepal L.", "Sepal W.", "Petal L.", "Petal W."),
+        c("Setosa", "Versicolor", "Virginica")
+        )
```

In this case, names are supplied for the second and third dimensions, but not the first.

Functions `is.array` and `as.array` test for and coerce to arrays. When a vector `x` is coerced to an array, it becomes a 1-way array with dimension `length(x)`.

As with matrices, there are functions that take general arrays as arguments and/or produce general arrays as results.

Function	Purpose
`apply(a,m,fun)`	apply a function to subarrays
`sweep(a,m,stats)`	sweep out marginal results
`outer(x,y,fun)`	general outer products
`aperm(a,i)`	permute dimensions
`table(...)`	generate multi-way tables
`loglin(table,...)`	loglinear models

The function `outer` takes two arrays and constructs an "outer product" by applying a function (by default "*"), to them. The simplest definition of outer product takes two vectors `x` and `y`, and produces the matrix containing

```
x[i] * y[j]
```

in its `[i, j]` element; in S this is `outer(x, y)`. The function `outer` can also take as a third argument the function to be applied.

When operating on two arrays, `outer` produces a new array by applying a function to all possible combinations of elements from the two arrays. Specifically, `outer(x, y)` makes two arrays, both with dimension vector

```
c(dim(x), dim(y))
```

The first has the data values from `x`, the second the data values from `y`, in each case replicated in the natural way to fill the bigger array. Then `outer` just executes the function with the two arrays as arguments. Aside from the default use of multiplication, there are many applications. For example, suppose we want to make character strings from all months for each year from 1990 to 1993:

```
outer(month.name,1990:1993,paste)
```

does it.

Arrays are often used as input to functions like `loglin`, which fits a loglinear model to an array, or to `apply`, which can apply S functions to subarrays. For example, suppose we want to create a matrix of all the means of the 50 observations for each variable and species of the `iris` data. The second and third subscript of `iris` correspond to variable and species. The function `apply` takes three arguments: the array, the list of which subscripts to *retain* in the result, and the function to be applied. In this example:

```
> apply(iris, c(2,3), mean)

         Setosa  Versicolor  Virginica
Sepal L.  5.006      5.936      6.588
Sepal W.  3.428      2.770      2.974
Petal L.  1.462      4.260      5.552
Petal W.  0.246      1.326      2.026
```

Similarly, the function `sweep` can be applied to multi-way arrays to operate on marginal statistics such as those computed by `apply`.

When subscripting arrays, it is important to remember that resulting dimensions of 1 are dropped. Hence,

```
iris[,1,]
```

is a 50 by 3 matrix. If you want this to retain its 3-dimensional array structure, use

```
iris[,1,,drop=F]
```

which produces a 50 by 1 by 3 array.

The function `aperm` permutes the subscripts of a multi-way array. The second argument to `aperm` tells how the original dimensions are to be permuted in the output. In the following example, the old third dimension (of length 3) comes first, followed by the old first and second dimensions.

```
> aa ← aperm(a,c(3,1,2))
> aa[,,1]
, , 1
      [,1] [,2]
[1,]     1    2
[2,]     9   10
[3,]    17   18
...
```

The operation carried out by `aperm` is a generalization of matrix transposition.

Exercises

5.39   Suppose we wanted labels for the first four weeks (1 through 4), for each month, for years 1990 to 1993. How would you produce that?

5.40   Use `apply` to produce a matrix containing the standard deviations (the square roots of the diagonal of the covariance matrices) for the 4 variables for each of the 3 groups of the iris data.

5.5.3 *Categorical Variables*

A *category* is an object used to represent data which is either qualitative, discrete-valued, or which is to be analyzed by breaking a quantitative variable into specified ranges. The key difference between a category and a simple vector is that the set of possible levels is given explicitly in a category, by the attribute `levels`, a character vector giving the levels. Not all possible levels need be present in a specific category. For example, a category for the age of children might have levels for each year from 1 to 10, but a specific group of children may have no eight-year-olds.

The creation function `category` forms categorical variables from discrete data values. For example, suppose `occupation` is a character vector with values like "statistician". Then

```
> category(occupation)
```

returns a category with an attribute `levels` containing an alphabetical list of the different occupations, and a data vector coding the values as 1, 2, ...

Additional arguments to `category` specify the set of values expected to occur in the data and corresponding character labels. Suppose `female` is a logical vector that contains `TRUE` for women and `FALSE` for men. You can construct a category `sex` by executing:

```
> sex ← category(female,c(FALSE,TRUE),c("Male","Female"))
```

While `female` and `sex` essentially convey the same information, the category has made the set of values more explicit, and provided additional labelling information that we will be able to use in further analysis. As with classes,

```
is.category(x)
as.category(x)
```

tests for, and coerces to objects of class `"category"`.

The `cut` function creates categories from continuous variables. For example, if `income` is a numeric vector,

```
cincome ← cut(income,4)
```

creates a category with 4 levels by cutting the range of `income` values into
four equal-length intervals. It is also possible to give `cut` an explicit set of
`breaks`; i.e., interval boundaries. Any values in the numeric vector outside
the range of the boundaries given will be coded as NA. One simple procedure
is

```
cut(income,pretty(income))
```

using a set of "pretty" numbers over the range of `income` to define the intervals. The simple break points generated by either of the above methods are
equally spaced numerically. If the distribution of the numeric values is highly
skewed, however, the resulting category may have most of its data in one or
two levels. To get approximately equal numbers in each level, a simple
method is to cut `rank(x)` instead of `x` itself. We will show an example
below.

Categories are treated specially in arithmetic. Since their values are
supposed to be legitimate indices into their `levels` attribute, the `levels` attribute is dropped during any arithmetic operations.

The real power of categories comes from having, or constructing,
several categories representing different kinds of information on the same set of
observational units. For example, the object `state.region` is a category that
defines where each state belongs, in four geographical regions. We can construct various other categories from qualitative or quantitative data defined on
the states, such as the columns of the matrices `state.x77` and `votes.repub`.
A category of 5 levels for the area of the states could be created by

```
> area ← cut(state.x77[, "Area"],5)
```

and similarly categories for other quantities can be defined. Several categories
on the same units are best thought of as an irregular multi-way array. All the
observations with the identical levels for all the categories fall into the same
"cell" of this array.

Two functions are used frequently in S to compute summaries and
derived values for such irregular arrays. The function `table` takes categories
as arguments and forms the table of counts;

```
table(state.region,area)
```

for example, produces a two-way array of counts corresponding to the two
arguments, which in general can be any categories corresponding to the same
set of observations. In this example:

	Range 1	Range 2	Range 3	Range 4	Range 5
Northeast	9	0	0	0	0
South	15	0	1	0	0
North Central	12	0	0	0	0
West	9	3	0	0	1

The distribution of values in the 5 area levels shows the problem with skew distribution mentioned above: 45 of the 50 states fall in the smallest range. We can either transform area, select some unequally spaced breaks by eye, or use the ranks, as for example:

```
> area ← cut(rank(state.x77[, "Area"]), 5,
+     c("Tiny", "Small", "Medium", "Large", "Huge"))
```

While we were at it, we chose nicer names for the levels. Now the table becomes

```
> table(state.region,area)
                Tiny Small Medium Large  Huge
     Northeast    6    2      1     0     0
         South    3    6      5     1     1
 North Central    0    2      4     6     0
          West    1    0      0     3     9
```

With a better choice of breaks, the geographic pattern in state size is easily seen in the table.

Another powerful function that can be used with categorical data is `tapply`. This function is analogous to the `apply` function for regular arrays, providing a shorthand for evaluating a function on the data values corresponding to each cell of a multi-way array. The multi-way array is defined in this case by a `list` of categories. We can form a vector of the state populations, parallel to the categories `state.region` and `area`:

```
> population ← state.x77[, "Pop"]
```

Then, to compute the mean population for each cell of the two-way table:

```
> tapply(population,list(state.region,area), mean)
                 Tiny Small  Medium    Large      Huge
     Northeast 3077.000  6459 18076.0       NA        NA
         South 2166.667  3584  4874.8 2715.000 12237.000
 North Central       NA  8024  6939.5 2305.000        NA
          West  868.000    NA      NA 1858.333  3495.111
```

Exercises

5.41   Which state in the `West` region is `Tiny`?

5.42   The system dataset `votes.repub` is an array whose columns are the percent vote for the Republican candidate for president in a number of elections. Form categories with two levels corresponding to whether the percent was greater than 50, for each of the 3 latest elections in the data. Make a table of counts for these categories.

5.43   Compute the minimum and maximum areas of the states in each of the five levels of `area`.

5.44 Look at the documentation for the `liver` data in Appendix 2. Form a coded category for the number of cells injected and compute tables describing the experimental design (how many observations were taken for each combination of cell number, experiment, and section).

5.45 Suppose you are given a character vector `occupation` which contains the occupations of a number of individuals. The expression

```
> occ ← category(occupation)
```

will create a category named `occ`. What would be the result of the expression:

```
> levels(occ)[occ]
```

5.46 A data entry task involves typing in a table of data, one column of which refers to branch offices of the ABC company. There are many rows in the table, and you would like to provide a function that highlights entries in which the office name was probably misspelled. How would you use categorical objects to do this: (i) given all the correct ABC branch office names; (ii) without knowing the correct names?

5.47 Given a category named `age` that was originally broken down into 10-year intervals, how could you recode it for 20-year intervals? Would it be easier or harder if the original (uncoded) data were available?

5.48 Suppose you are given two equal-length integer vectors, `current` and `new`, which describe how the current integer values of a category `old.cat` are to be mapped into new integer values of a recoded category `new.cat` with corresponding labels `new.lab`. Explain how the following expression carries out the recoding.

```
> new.cat ← category( new[match(old.cat,current)],
+     lab=new.lab )
```

Make up an example yourself and try it.

5.5.4 *Time-Series*

A vector of data is made into a time-series in S by associating with it a *time domain*; that is, a corresponding vector of the equally-spaced times with which the data is to be associated. The `tsp` attribute defines the time domain implicitly; it is composed of three numbers: the `start`, `end`, and `frequency` corresponding to the times at which the observations start, end, and to the number of observations per unit time period. It is assumed that the frequency is a positive integer.

For example, a monthly series starting in June of 1960 could be created from data on a file "co2data" by using the function `ts` as follows:

```
> co2 ← ts(scan("co2data"), start=c(1960,6), frequency=12)
```

Only two of the three time parameters (in this case `start` and `frequency`) need to be specified, since the other (`end`) can be computed from the number of data values. Also note that the vector `c(1960,6)` represents June 1960. The corresponding `tsp` value is actually stored as `1960.417`, computed as

```
1960 + (6-1)/12
```

The automatic printing of time-series includes labelling reflecting the time domain. In printing the series, the values of `1`, `4`, and `12` for `frequency` are treated specially, corresponding to the common occurrence of annual, quarterly, and monthly series.

```
> co2
        Jan    Feb    Mar    Apr    May    Jun    Jul
1958: 314.88 315.62 316.33 317.59 317.93 317.71 315.92
1959: 315.62 316.59 316.94 317.77 318.29 318.24 316.67
1960: 316.62 317.16 317.90 319.21 320.02 319.74 318.15
1961: 316.97 317.74 318.63 319.43 320.47 319.71 318.78
1962: 318.06 318.59 319.74 320.63 321.21 320.83 319.55
1963: 318.80 319.08 320.15 321.49 322.25 321.50 319.67
1964: 319.37 319.93 320.40 321.65 322.26 322.19 320.49
1965: 319.55 320.65 321.15 322.31 322.35 322.19 321.53
 . . .
```

As with matrices and arrays, time-series can have any mode. Many functions in S know how to operate on time-series; in particular, arithmetic operators operate on two time-series to produce a result defined on the intersection of the two time domains. For example, suppose we want to add 100 to the 1962 `co2` data:

```
> co2 + ts(100,start=1962,end=c(1962,12),frequency=12)
        Jan    Feb    Mar    Apr    May    Jun    Jul
1962: 418.06 418.59 419.74 420.63 421.21 420.83 419.55
        Aug    Sep    Oct    Nov    Dec
1962: 417.75 416.27 415.62 416.84 417.70
```

The subscript function reduces a time-series to a simple object (without a `tsp` attribute) since there is no guarantee that the result is equally spaced in time. However, notice that you can *replace* any subset of data values in a time-series and *not lose its attributes*. For example, if you had a newer version of the data values of `co2` in `new.data`, you could replace the data of `co2` with the newer data with:

```
> co2[] ← new.data
```

A good computing technique for time-series is to create one with the right time domain and then manipulate its contents. The function `window` is related to subscripting, and designed to take a time slice from a time-series.

```
window(x,start,end)      # sub-series
```

For example

```
> window(co2, 1965, c(1970,12))
          Jan    Feb    Mar    Apr    May    Jun    Jul
1965: 319.55 320.65 321.15 322.31 322.35 322.19 321.53
1966: 320.22 321.23 322.13 323.30 323.57 323.29 322.36
1967: 321.80 322.03 322.50 324.00 324.46 323.46 322.19
1968: 322.15 322.73 323.50 324.52 325.11 325.06 323.62
1969: 323.73 324.53 325.62 326.58 327.24 326.53 325.63
1970: 324.91 325.81 326.85 328.07 327.97 327.77 326.44
          Aug    Sep    Oct    Nov    Dec
1965: 319.13 317.99 317.70 319.15 319.27
1966: 319.17 317.89 317.54 319.36 320.51
1967: 320.57 318.91 318.81 320.24 321.59
1968: 321.55 319.89 319.80 320.73 322.25
1969: 323.28 322.21 321.67 322.61 324.07
1970: 324.92 323.49 323.50 324.34 325.39
```

Function `is.ts` tests its argument to see if it is a time-series; `as.ts` coerces its argument to be a time-series, with starting date 1 and frequency 1. Other return specific attributes of time-series. The functions `start(x)`, `end(x)`, `frequency(x)` return the corresponding elements of the `tsp` attribute of x. The function `time(x)` returns a time-series on the same domain as x, with values equal to the corresponding time. Similarly, the function `cycle(x)` returns a time-series whose values are the position of each observation within the cycle associated with the series. For example suppose x is a monthly series starting in February 1979 and ending in May 1980. The values in `cycle(x)` are

```
2, 3, 4, ..., 12, 1, 2, 3, 4, 5.
```

Special data-manipulation functions are also available for time-series.

```
diff(x)       # forward differences
lag(x,k)       # same data lagged k periods
aggregate(x,nf,fun)   # decrease periodicity by aggregation
```

The series `diff(x)` has the same starting date as x, but has length `length(x)-1`. The lagged series, in contrast, has the same number of data values as x with the starting and ending times altered. In aggregation, the idea is to change a series to a new series with a smaller frequency. For example, to compute quarterly concentrations from monthly `co2` data,

```
newco2 ← aggregate(co2,4,mean)
```

The second argument is the desired frequency, and the last argument is the function that performs the aggregation. Since `co2` is a measurement of concentration, we apply function `mean` to 3 monthly measurements to give the quarterly estimate.

For some applications (regression, for example) it is helpful to bind together time-series as columns of a matrix. The function `cbind` is not suitable if the series have different time domains, since it ignores the time-series nature of the arguments. The function

```
tsmatrix(x₁, x₂, ... )
```

binds its arguments as columns, but computes the intersection of all the time domains for time-series arguments.

Many useful operations can be defined on time-series by using the basic data manipulation operations. For example, suppose we want a function that smooths a time-series by computing the mean of 3 adjacent values. (There are many ways to smooth time-series; this is a simple, but not particularly good one. The function `smooth` gives a more robust smoothing method.)

```
mean3 ← function(y)
    (lag(y,-1) + y + lag(y,1))/3
```

The result of the sum is a time-series on the intersection of the time domains of `y` and the two lagged values; namely, a series that starts one observation later and terminates one observation sooner. In general, combinations of time-series manipulation, arithmetic and element-by-element functions will produce reasonable time domains for the result, but you should think carefully about the meaning of the computations. Does the time domain of the result correspond to what makes sense? (The exercises below give examples.)

Functions that expect time-series can be given vectors as arguments, which will be interpreted as yearly time-series starting at time 1. In arithmetic, two objects with `tsp` attributes are treated specially. The result always has a `tsp` attribute for the intersection of the time domains. If one series spans the time values of the other, the result retains all other attributes of the spanning series. If the series intersect in time, the result is a time-series with no other attributes. If both series have identical `tsp` attributes, then the result will have the union of their other attributes.

Exercises

5.49   In the definition of `mean3`, it would have seemed a little more natural to write

```
(y + lag(y,1) + lag(y,2))/3
```

Why is that wrong?

5.50   (i) Write a function that smooths by `k` adjacent means, where `k` is an argument to the function.

(ii)* Write the function without using iteration or `apply`.

5.51 It might be mildly annoying that mean3 has a smaller time domain than the original data. Rewrite it so that it has the same time domain. (The statistical question of what values to use to extend the smooth is nontrivial. Let's just use the original data.)

5.52 How could you write the tsmatrix function?

5.6 Data Attributes

In section 5.5, we discussed various data attributes in S that define classes of objects. In this section, we discuss the idea of attributes in general. Chapter 8 will go into the important technique of defining new classes.

To summarize, here is a table of the attributes that define the classes discussed in section 5.5. Functions like subscripting, arithmetic, and comparison recognize and treat these specially.

Attribute	Description
names	character names associated with data elements
dim	dimension of matrices and multi-way arrays
dimnames	list of character vectors; names for the levels of each dimension of an array
tsp	time-series parameters, start, end, frequency
levels	character vector giving levels for categorical data

In addition to the attributes listed in the table, each object in S has two *implicit* attributes, length and mode. Other attributes can be attached to the object to provide additional information. For example, the attribute names specifies a parallel character vector that gives a name to each element of the object. Remember the month.length example from section 5.1?

```
> month.length ← c(31,28,31,30,31,30,31,31,30,31,30,31)
> sum(month.length)
[1] 365
> names(month.length) ← month.name
> month.length
  January February March April May June July August
       31       28    31    30  31   30   31     31

September October November  December
       30      31       30        31
```

Why would we want to attach a names attribute to the month.length vector? First, it provides convenient labelling when month.length is printed. Second, the names attribute provides a mnemonic alternative to numeric subscripts:

```
> month.length["June"]
  June
    30
```

Not having to remember that June is the 6th month may not be very important, but in other cases it may be much easier to remember the identifier than its position in the list. Attribute `names` allows access to the components of lists, as we illustrated in section 5.2. Chapter 8 will go further into the design of new classes of objects by defining suitable components. Notice also that character subscripts can be used for the rows and columns of matrices, when the `dimnames` attribute of the matrix has been set. We used those to advantage in the examples of matrix computations in section 5.5.3.

Attributes affect the way certain S functions deal with objects, as `names` does for printing and subscripting. For each attribute, some set of functions may agree to recognize it and treat it in a meaningful way. The goal is usually to create a *class* of objects that can be treated as if they were built into S. For several such classes, enough functions share in knowledge of the class that we can say that S "recognizes" the class and its attributes. The `dim` attribute tells S that the object can be thought of as a multi-way array. The `tsp` attribute gives time-series parameters (starting date, end date, and frequency), so that the object can be thought of as equally spaced observations in time.

5.6.1 *Arithmetic and Comparison with Attributes*

What happens when operations are carried out on an object with attributes? If the operation takes an object as an argument, and returns a value by operating element-by-element on that object, then the value typically takes on all of the attributes of the argument. Hence, if `m` is a matrix, then `sqrt(m)` is also a matrix, since it retains its `dim` attribute.

Things get more complicated when we discuss binary arithmetic operators—there are more possibilities because they deal with two objects. We saw some special rules in the previous section for matrices, arrays, categories, and time-series:

- If both operands are matrices or arrays, then the `dim` attribute is retained if all dimensions match, and any other situation is an error.
- If both operands are time-series, the result has the intersection of the time domains.
- Categories always are coerced to simple objects.

In addition to these special situations, the following rules apply to both the classes of objects we have defined so far and to other, user-defined, attributes. If the two objects are of different lengths, then the result is identical to the longer object (except for the data values, of course). If the objects are of equal length, then the result has the union of the attributes of the two objects.

Functions are free to ignore attributes they don't understand and treat the objects as vectors. This simple concept brings a great deal of power to S: it means that new classes of objects can be added to S without changing functions that are not directly affected by that class.

For each attribute there is a function that retrieves the value of the attribute. The function names are the same as the attribute names. For example:

```
names(month.length)
levels(x) ← letters[1:10]
```

Each function can be used on the left-hand side of the assignment arrow to set the attribute.

When an attribute is not present, the function to access that attribute will return a NULL. Similarly, to get rid of an attribute, assign it the value NULL.

```
> dim(month.length)
NULL
> names(month.length) ← NULL    # get rid of names attribute
> month.length
 [1] 31 28 31 30 31 30 31 31 30 31 30 31
```

There is a function

```
attr(x,which)
```

to retrieve an arbitrary attribute which from object x. This function is used if the name of the attribute is the result of a computation, and for the new attributes we may want to define. The attr function can also be used on the left-hand side of an assignment:

```
attr(x,"dim") ← c(4,3)
```

As was the case with other attribute functions, attr will return NULL if a requested attribute is not present; to get rid of an attribute, assign it the value NULL.

The function attributes allows you to access or set *all* of the attributes of a particular object. It returns a list of attributes, named by the attribute names. Thus, the expression

```
names(attributes(x))
```

gives the character names of all attributes present in x. The attributes function can also be used on the left-hand side of an assignment:

```
attributes(y) ← attributes(x)
```

makes y have the same attributes as x. The implicit attributes mode and length are not returned or set by attributes.

5.6.2 *Throwing Away Attributes*

Certain functions ignore the structure implied by arrays, matrices, and time-series. For example, the function `sort` returns a vector of sorted data values. Even if the argument is a matrix or time-series, the result is no longer a similar structure. Similarly, subsets of matrices and time-series may be selected just as if they were vectors, in which case the result is a vector. For example,

```
co2[ co2>mean(co2) ]
```

produces the vector of all values in `co2` that are larger than the mean value. The general principle involved here is that functions that rearrange the elements of an object are likely to destroy the properties that make it an array or time-series. Therefore, these functions coerce their results to simple objects.

User-written functions that perform similar computations should also strip away attributes. Usually this happens automatically because the function is using sorting, subscripting, etc. To make sure that some object to be returned is just a simple vector, you only need to coerce it,

```
as.vector(x)
```

to remove any special attributes.

Functions that coerce to simple objects, like `as.numeric`, return an object with all special attributes stripped away. A matrix coerced will no longer be a matrix, for example. If you want to coerce data to a specific mode, without disturbing the other attributes, assign to the `mode` attribute itself. The function `mode(x)` on the left side of an assignment means that the mode of the argument should be set to the value on the right of the arrow, but that all other attributes of the object should be unchanged. For example, suppose data of mode "`logical`" should be promoted to "`numeric`", but all other modes, and any other attributes, should be unchanged.

```
if(is.logical(x)) mode(x) ← "numeric"
```

does the job. In contrast, `length(x)` appearing on the left of an assignment arrow to change explicitly the length of an object, does not retain the attributes. They normally would make no sense (if the length of a matrix is changed, its dimensions can no longer be valid).

Answers to Selected Exercises

5.1   (page 99)
```
> 1 + NA - 2
[1] NA
> length(x)
[1] 3
> sum(x)
[1] NA
```

```
> mean(x)
[1] NA
> median(x)
[1] NA
> sum(x)/length(x)
[1] NA
```

5.2   (page 99)
```
cat(rep("\007",10))   # send 10 bells
```
This will probably result in one long bell sound rather than ten individual rings of the bell.

5.3   (page 99)
```
annoy ← function(rings,duration,seconds)
    for(i in 1:rings){
        cat(rep("\007",duration))
        sleep(seconds)
    }
```

5.4   (page 99)   The "or" operation is TRUE whenever one operand is TRUE, regardless of the values of any other operand. Similarly, "and" is FALSE if either argument is FALSE.

5.5   (page 101)   Data values of the shorter operand are repeated, cyclically, to make the lengths equal, so that
```
1:10 + c(100,200)
```
adds 100 to all the odd values and 200 to all even values. If one operand is of length 0, it is implicitly replicated with NAs to the desired length; i.e, the result is all NA:
```
> numeric(0)+1:7
[1] NA NA NA NA NA NA NA
```

5.7   (page 104)
```
w ← seq(1, length(x), by=3)
x[w] ← -x[w]
```

5.8   (page 104)   NULL is an object of length 0 and mode null. The NULL is coerced to a 0-length object with the same mode as x. Therefore, no matter what object is on the left, and what elements the subscript specifies, nothing happens.

5.9   (page 105)
```
> lines ← paste("Run:",format(seq(along=value)),
+ "Result:",format(yy),
+ "Cost:",format(cost))
> cat(lines,sep="\n")
```
Note that the sequence numbers need to be formatted if there are more than 9 lines.

5.10   (page 106)
```
bingo ← function(){
    n ← trunc(runif(1) * 75)  # between 0 and 74
    paste(c("B", "I", "N", "G", "O")[n %/% 15 + 1],
        n + 1, sep = "")
}
```

5.11   (page 110)
```
mylog ← function(x){
    if(mode(x)!="complex" && any(x<=0)) mode(x) ← "complex"
    log(x)
}
```

Note that `mylog` retains attributes. You should not use `as.complex(x)` instead of setting the mode explicitly.

5.13   (page 110)

```
pow ← function(z, w, n = 10){
    if(w == 0) return(1+0i)
    if(z == 0) return(0+0i)
    r ← Mod(z)
    theta ← Arg(z) + 2*pi*( - floor((n - 1)/2):floor(n/2))
    a ← Re(w)
    b ← Im(w)
    complex(mod = r^a * exp(-b*theta),
        arg = b*log(r) + a*theta)
}
```

5.18   (page 114)   If `x` is a list,

```
lapply(x,sort)
```

will return a new list in which each element is sorted.

5.20   (page 116)   The simplest approach is to use an editor to remove the "|" at the beginning and end of the line and then to turn all the remaining "|"s into new lines (but *not* of course the line that codes "|" itself). It's then a good idea to clean up by removing trailing blanks. Having done that you can put a backslash in front of all characters other than alphanumerics at the end of the line. A suitable set of `ed` commands is:

```
1,$s/^|//
1,$s/|$//
1,$s/|/\
/g
1,$s/ *$//
1,$s/[^a-zA-Z0-9]$/\&/
```

That's the hard part. To read it in:

```
ascii.data ← scan("myfile",list(code=0,char=""))
```

5.21   (page 117)   By inspection, decide what the separator character is; let's say ":". You can get a good guess at the number of fields by:

```
table(nchar(unix("sed < myfile 's/[^:]//g'")))
```

which counts the number of separators per line (there may be a few separator characters hidden in strings, but the smallest value should dominate). That, plus 1, is the number of fields, say n. Then, read n character fields with `scan`, and try converting the resulting components to numeric. Those with 0 or very few NAs are likely numeric fields:

```
> z ← as.list(character(n))
> data ← scan("myfile",z,sep=":")
> nacounts ← numeric()
> for(i in 1:length(data))
+     nacounts[i] ← sum(is.na(as.numeric(data[[i]])))
```

5.22   (page 123)   Nothing (aside from slowing searches a little). Because the search process follows the same path for *every* name, anything that can be found in the directory will be found the first time it appears in the list.

5.26   (page 128)   The function `as.vector` drops the `dim` attribute of the matrix and shows the underlying vector. Matrices are always stored column by column as shown by these expressions.

5.28   (page 128)   Form the set of unique values in `xbig`, and compute the matrix of `coef` for that (smaller) vector:

```
> xsmall ← unique(xbig)
> msmall ← coef(xsmall)
```

Now this matrix can be efficiently expanded by using `match` to compute which element in `xsmall` corresponds to each element of `xbig`, and using this result to select rows of `msmall`:

```
> which ← match(xbig, xsmall)
> msmall[which, ]   # The answer
```

5.29   (page 129)

```
> data ← scan("myfile",list(0,0,""))
> x ← matrix(c(data[[1]],data[[2]]),ncol=2,
+    dimnames = list(data[[3]],NULL))
```

5.31   (page 132)

```
bingo.card ← function(){
    card ← matrix(0, 5, 5)
    for(i in 1:5) card[, i] ← sample(1:15, 5) + (i - 1) * 15
    card[3, 3] ← NA
    dimnames(card) ← list(rep("", 5),
        c("B", "I", "N", "G", "O"))
    card
}
```

5.33   (page 132)   Part 2 is probably easiest to answer first:

```
all.zero ← seq(nrow(x))[ apply(x==0,1,all) ]
```

Now, part 1 is easy:

```
all.zero[1]
```

or perhaps

```
ans ← NULL
for(i in 1:nrow(x)) if(all(x[i,]==0)) { ans ← i; break }
```

Which is faster? Where's the break-even point? Part 3:

```
apply(x,1,mean) [-all.zero]
```

Part 4 requires an auxiliary function:

```
non.zero.mean ← function(x) mean(x[x!=0])
apply(x[-all.zero,],1,non.zero.mean)
```

Now, for part 5:

```
row.sum ← apply(x,1,sum)
seq(row.sum)[row.sum %% 2 == 1]
```

5.34   (page 132)   The trick is to use the `unix` function to execute the command

```
sed 1q | wc -w
```

to look at the first line of the file and count the number of items there:

```
scan.matrix ← function(file){
    n ← as.numeric(unix(paste("sed 1q", file, "| wc -w")))
    matrix(scan(file), ncol=n, byrow = T)
}
```

5.35   (page 132)   The first multiplies `m` by itself element by element; the second does true matrix multiplication, where each element of the answer is the inner product of a row of `m` and a column of `m`.

5.36   (page 132)

```
matrix(list(1,2,3,4),2,2)
```

5.38   (page 132)   Suppose

```
> names ← dimnames(mydata)[[1]]
> newnames ← dimnames(update)[[1]]
```

The new columns of data can be put into the old order and appended to the old data by:

```
> mynewdata ← cbind(mydata,
+       update[ match(names,newnames), ])
```

Notice that `match` matches `names` to `newnames`. If there are observations in `names` that are not included in `newnames` the subset expression will contain `NA`s and hence `NA`s will be inserted in `mynewdata` at those positions.

5.39 (page 136)

```
> weeks ← paste("Week", 1:4)
> labels ← outer(outer(weeks,months,paste),
+ 1990:1993,paste)
> labels
[1] "Week 1 January 1990"   "Week 2 January 1990"
[3]   ...
```

5.40 (page 136) You first need a function to compute the standard deviations.

```
> sdev ← function(x)
+   diag(var(x)) ^ .5
```

Then:

```
> apply(iris,3,sdev)
         Setosa Versicolor Virginica
[1,] 0.3524897  0.5161711 0.6358796
[2,] 0.3790644  0.3137983 0.3224966
[3,] 0.1736640  0.4699110 0.5518947
[4,] 0.1053856  0.1977527 0.2746501
```

5.41 (page 138)

```
> state.name[state.region==4 & area==1]
[1] "Hawaii"
```

Note the use of `&`, not `&&`.

5.43 (page 138)

```
tapply(state.x77[,"Area"],list(area),range)
```

5.46 (page 139) First, read the relevant column via the `scan` function, into the object `branch`. In case (i), suppose `bnames` is the character vector of correct names:

```
> cat("Check the names in rows:\n")
> seq(along=branch)[ is.na(category(branch,bnames))]
```

in case (ii), the best we can do is point out names that appear infrequently:

```
> ttt ← table(branch)
> ttt[ ttt < max(3,length(branch)/100)]
```

5.49 (page 142) Look at the time domain. It has the same start date as `y`, but if there is any trend in the data, then the first element of the smooth is estimating the *second* element of the data. So the formula in the exercise will be off by one position, and systematically biased.

5.51 (page 143)

```
mean3 ← function(y){
    yy ← (lag(y, -1) + y + lag(y, 1))/3
    y[] ← c(y[1], yy, y[length(y)])
    y
}
```

5.52 (page 143) One approach would be to find the maximum of the `start` values and the minimum of the `end` values for each argument. Then simply use `window` with those values to chop each argument to the same time period, and glue the results together as columns of a matrix.

6
Writing Functions

Functions are the heart of S and writing or modifying them is the most important part of creating new capabilities based on S. This chapter discusses how to write functions. Section 2.7 introduced this topic; if you want a brief discussion of the important features, you should read that section first. This chapter picks up where section 2.7 left off, presenting new examples as well as a more complete description of functions, describing parts of the S language (such as looping expressions) that are used in writing functions, discussing the interface between S and commands in the UNIX operating system, and showing how functions can be edited and debugged.

6.1 Overview of Functions

First we give a description of the syntax of function definitions together with examples of functions. The section closes with a brief description of how to design functions.

6.1.1 *The General Form of Functions*

A function in S can have any number of arguments, and the computation that is done by it can be anything expressible in S. The general syntax of a function definition is

```
function( arguments )
    expression
```

where *arguments* gives the arguments separated by commas, and `expression` (referred to as the *body* of the function definition) is any legal S expression. For functions that do nontrivial calculations, the body is usually a sequence of expressions enclosed in braces and separated by semi-colons or newlines. The value of the last expression between the braces becomes the value of the whole expression, and therefore the value returned by the function. For example, here is a function, `larger`, that takes two arguments, `x` and `y`, and returns an object whose elements are the larger of the corresponding elements of the arguments:

```
larger ← function(x, y){
    y.is.bigger ← y > x
    x[y.is.bigger] ← y[y.is.bigger]
    x
}
```

The body of the function is a braced list of three expressions. The third expression will be returned as the value of the function.

Assignments executed inside a function take place in a *local data frame* created each time the function is called. (A frame, described in section 5.4, is a list of named objects. Frames are themselves objects in S; they can be examined during evaluation to help with debugging, as we will see in section 6.4.2.) These assignments inside the function are temporary, have no effect outside of the function, and disappear when the evaluation of the function is complete. In the example, an object named `x` in the working directory would not be altered by evaluating `larger`, nor would the data that was supplied as the argument to the function. Names of objects created in functions can therefore be chosen to be simple and informative.

The value of a function can be explicitly and immediately returned by using a `return` expression:

```
if(any(x < 0))return(NA)
```

You are never *required* to use a `return` expression; the same effect can be achieved by other expressions. However, use of `return` can improve readability.

If an error situation arises and the right action is to stop computation on the expression that led to this function call, the function `stop` will do that:

```
if(length(x) < 1) stop("No data")
```

S will print the argument to `stop` as the error message: `stop()` will stop silently, presumably because the error message already appeared. Unlike `return`, which returns a value to the calling function, `stop` aborts the entire expression being executed. After `stop`, S will parse and evaluate another expression.

If a function detects an anomalous situation that is not necessarily an error, it can execute `warning` with an appropriate error message:

```
if(any(x<0)){
    x[x<0] ← NA
    warning("NAs generated from negative input values")
    }
```

The warning messages occurring in any expression are printed after the entire expression has been evaluated.

6.1.2 *Missing Arguments; Defaults*

A call to an S function does not need to supply all the formal arguments in the function definition. Any subset of the formal arguments can be supplied, either by position or by name. The function can handle missing arguments two ways; either by providing a *default* expression in the argument list of the definition, or by testing explicitly for missing arguments. Here's a function, div.diff(x, n), that computes differences n times from a numeric vector, x. We want the user to be able to omit n, with the default value being 1.

```
div.diff ← function(x, n = 1){
    for(i in 1:n) x ← x[-1] - x[ - length(x)]
    x
}
```

The default expression for an argument can be any S expression.

S functions evaluate their arguments only when they are used; this is called *lazy evaluation*. For most functions, the time when the arguments are evaluated does not matter. However, there are exceptions. For example,

```
transform ← function(x,scale,...){
    if(!missing(scale))x ← x/scale
    ...
```

will rescale x only if scale was supplied. The function missing does not evaluate its argument, hence you need not supply a default value for scale.

Another consequence of lazy evaluation is that default values for an argument may refer to objects that will be defined inside the function before the specific argument has been evaluated.

```
mylsfit ← function(a, k = min(d)){
    a ← as.matrix(a)
    d ← dim(a)
    z ← lsfit(a[,1:k],yy)
    ...
```

The argument k will not be evaluated until 1:k is needed. Notice that lazy evaluation is needed here for two reasons: because d is not defined at first, but also because coercing a to be a matrix makes sure that dim(a) will not be NULL.

The function `missing` was shown in the `transform` example. It takes the name of one of the formal arguments in the function definition and returns `TRUE` if there was no corresponding actual argument in the current function call. Notice that no default expression needs to be given for the argument, so long as the body of the function tests for a missing argument before the actual argument is used. On the other hand, `missing` can be used even if the function definition *does* contain a default expression.

6.1.3 *Variable Number of Arguments*

Functions can be defined to take a variable number of arguments. The special argument name "`...`" in the function definition will match any number of arguments in the call. For example, a function that returns the mean of all the values in an arbitrary number of different vectors is:

```
mean.of.all ← function(...)
    mean(c(...))
```

so that

```
mean.of.all(us.sales, europe.sales, other.sales)
```

would concatenate the three objects and take the mean of all the data. The effect in this example is as if `c` were called with the same three arguments given to `mean.of.all`.

This use of "`...`", passing it as an argument in a call to another function, is its *only* legal use in the body of the function. This restriction does not get in the way. To loop over arguments, for example, we can create a list of the evaluated arguments,

```
list(...)
```

and then use a `for` loop to get at each in turn. The names, if any, attached to the actual arguments will also be passed down in the call to `list(...)`. In the previous example, to compute the mean of the individual means, instead of the mean of the concatenated data:

```
mean.of.means ← function(...){
    means ← numeric()
    for(x in list(...)) means ← c(means, mean(x))
    mean(means)
}
```

In evaluating

```
mean.of.means(us.sales, europe.sales, other.sales)
```

`x` is successively assigned the value of the first, second and third argument.

The function

```
nargs()
```

returns the number of arguments in the current call. An alternative definition of mean.of.means would be:

```
mean.of.means ← function(...){
    n ← nargs()
    means ← numeric(n)
    all.x ← list(...)
    for(j in 1:n) means[j] ← mean(all.x[[j]])
    mean(means)
}
```

The first way of looping over the arguments is clearly simpler in this case, but not always. Notice that the first line could *not* have been written

```
n ← length(...)
```

because length would then appear to get three arguments. This version,

```
all.x ← list(...)
n ← length(all.x)
```

would work.

It is important in using a list of all the argument values to keep the distinction clear between an *element* of the list as expressed by the double-brackets, all.x[[j]], and the list of length 1 containing that element, as expressed by single brackets, all.x[j]. The first version is what is nearly always wanted. See section 5.2 for a discussion of lists and elements.

The "..." mechanism is used when the function needs to process a collection of arguments. Often, some other arguments are needed in addition to this collection. In mean.of.means, for example, suppose we wanted to allow the optional argument trim to compute trimmed means. We add an argument trim to mean.of.means, and recognize this argument *only* when supplied by name. Such arguments are specified in the function definition *following* the "..." argument. In our example,

```
mean.of.means ← function(..., trim = 0.){
    means ← numeric()
    for(x in list(...))
        means ← c(means, mean(x,trim=trim))
    mean(means)
}
```

So, for example,

```
mean.of.means(trim=.1, us.sales, europe.sales, other.sales)
```

would take the mean of the 10% trimmed means on each object. It is important to remember that arguments following "..." in a function definition must be given by name when the function is called and the name *cannot* be abbreviated.

Exercises

6.1   Is there a difference between the values computed by `mean.of.all` and `mean.of.means`? Try it on some simple data.

6.2   The value of

```
mean.of.means(tr=.5,1:9)
```

is `2.75`. Explain.

6.3*   Is the expression `nargs()` equivalent to `length(list(...))`?

6.1.4 *Designing Functions*

We close this section with some brief thoughts on how to design a new S function. Thinking for a while before implementing a new function can produce a clearer, more easily implemented idea of what the function is intended to do and how the function can be written. The following simple steps are recommended.

- A function is characterized by the object it returns. Begin by understanding what information that object should provide. If there is some significant structure to this object, consider how to organize that structure (as discussed in section 5.2 and in chapter 8).
- Now organize the computations needed, proceeding from the top down; that is, by specifying the main steps in the computation, using the functions that are natural for this purpose, even if those functions themselves will need to be designed.
- Try to understand the important different cases. Where some circumstances make the function simpler to design, concentrate on those first. Often, more general cases can then be expressed in terms of simple cases.
- Expect the design process to be iterative: design a simple, perhaps limited, version first. Experiment with that, examine it critically, and develop better or more general versions.

Let's now use these four steps to design a function.

Suppose we want to plot a map of the United States, and superimpose on it symbols representing some other variable (murder rate, as in section 2.6, for example). We already have an S function, `usa`, to draw the map. For the symbols a first thought is to produce character strings coding various values of the added variable. The function `text` will produce the symbols, once we have coded the variable into character form. It's not entirely obvious how to do that, so to begin we will just assume the existence of a function, `text.code`, and define it later.

Here, then, is a function to produce the plot from the map positions, (x, y) and the corresponding values of z:

```
map.text ← function(x, y, z){
    usa(xlim=range(x), ylim=range(y))
    text(x, y, text.code(z))
    }
```

Suppose we decide to plot ".", "x", and "X" for the lower, middle, and upper third of the range of z. Then a definition of `text.code` would be:

```
text.code ← function(z){
    labels ← rep("x",length(z))
    r ← range(z)
    third ← (r[2]-r[1])/3
    labels[ z < r[1]+third ] ← "."
    labels[ z > r[2]-third ] ← "X"
    labels
}
```

Now, we can use the function.

```
> map.text(state.center$x, state.center$y,
+   state.x77[,"Murder"] )  # Figure 6.1
```

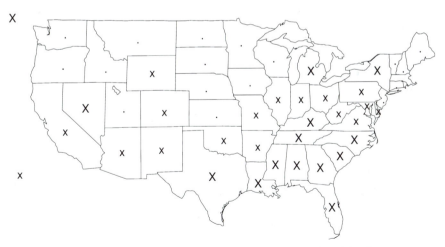

Figure 6.1. A plot of murder rates in the United States produced by the `map.text` function. The symbols ".", "x", and "X" represent murder rates in the lower, middle, and upper thirds of the range.

The process of refining this first version of the new function can now go on. We can ask how to generalize the coding, whether the computation is as natural or as efficient as we would like, and how different kinds of data might be handled. For example, our choice of three characters for coding z was rather arbitrary. Why not let the user specify the symbols, but provide our initial version as a default. That's easy:

```
map.text ← function(x, y, z, labels = c(".","x","X")){
    usa(xlim=range(x), ylim=range(y))
    text(x, y, text.code(z, labels))
    }
```

Of course, we will need to revise `text.code`, too (see exercises 6.6 and 6.7).

Exercises

6.4   A monthly loan payment is computed from the principal of the loan, p, the number of years of payments y, and the interest rate in percent i, according to the formula

$$payment = p\frac{(i/1200)(1+i/1200)^{12y}}{(1+i/1200)^{12y}-1}$$

Create an S function to carry out this computation. What would the monthly payment be for a $65,000 mortgage at 9.5% for 30 years?

6.5   Write a function that takes x- and y-coordinate data and a vector of labels, and produces a scatterplot with the labels at the points.

6.6   The first version of a function often can be improved, even if it works. Some questions to ask are: Does the function do a lot of work to get a result that should be simple? Does it depend on special circumstances that you might want to change? Our version of `text.code` is really rather messy: the calculations it uses to decide where to put low, medium and high labels are clumsy to look at, and depend entirely on dividing the range into 3 parts. Clean up `text.code` by assuming a function `range.code`, such that the call

```
        range.code(z,3)
```

returns a vector with 1, 2, or 3 where the corresponding element of z is in the lowest, middle, or highest third of the range of z. Now write the function `range.code` to take as arguments a vector z and an integer k. (Hint: use the S function `cut`.)

6.7   The second version of `map.text` passed the `labels` argument to `text.code`. Add a `labels` argument with a default value to `text.code`.

6.8   Combine the results of the previous two exercises to produce a more general version of `map.text`.

6.2 Organizing Computations

This section describes techniques in the S language for organizing the flow of computations: conditional evaluation of expressions, iteration, and recursion. All these can be important in expressing computations in a correct and natural way. S provides facilities that are similar to other languages you may have encountered, but typically more general.

You may wonder why these language features are described here, in a chapter on writing functions. The reason is that most non-trivial use of these statements is likely to occur inside functions.

6.2.1 *Conditional Computations:* if, switch, &&, ||

The if expression in S is similar to that of many other programming languages:

```
if( condition ) expr1
```

or

```
if( condition ) expr1 else expr2
```

In both cases, *condition* is first evaluated. If it evaluates to TRUE, then *expr1* is evaluated. If there is an else clause and if *condition* evaluates to FALSE, then *expr2* is evaluated. The value of the whole expression is the value of *expr1* or *expr2*, accordingly. If there is no else part and the condition is FALSE, the value of the whole expression is NULL. An else-less if is usually executed for its side effects, for example to do some assignment conditionally:

```
if(!missing(wt)) x ← x * wt
```

The *condition* should produce only a single logical value; if it does not, a warning message will be produced. Only the first element is used to decide which expression to evaluate.

When several if expressions are used together, an else is attached to the most recent else-less if. For example

```
if(a) if(b) 1 else 2
```

will evaluate to 1 if both a and b are TRUE, will evaluate to 2 if a is TRUE and b is FALSE, and will evaluate to NULL if a is FALSE.

S is very liberal about using expressions. An expression can be used nearly anywhere that it could possibly make sense. For example, an if expression can be used as an argument:

```
msg ← paste("There",if(n>1)"were" else "was",n,
    if(n>1)"outliers" else "outlier")
```

or on the right of an assignment

```
msg ← if(n>1) paste("There were",n,"outliers")
    else "There was 1 outlier"
```

Conditional values in this style often provide a natural way of expressing computations.

The `condition` part of an `if` expression may involve testing whether both or either of two requirements are met. These "and" and "or" control operators are written in S as "`&&`" and "`||`". The evaluation of

```
cond1 && cond2
```

is defined as follows: `cond1` is evaluated. If the first element is TRUE, `cond2` is evaluated and its value is the value of the whole expression. But if `cond1` is FALSE, then the whole expression evaluates to FALSE without evaluating the second condition. This helps avoid expressions that might produce errors; for example,

```
if(is.numeric(x) && min(x) > 0) ww ← log(x)
```

If the first condition is FALSE, evaluating the second condition would cause an error, and, of course, the entire `if` expression is designed to avoid errors in computing logarithms.

A similar rule applies for

```
cond1 || cond2
```

If `cond1` is TRUE, so is the expression, and `cond2` is not evaluated. Notice that there are related operators, "`&`" and "`|`", to express element-wise "and" and "or" operations. These work like most operators: they evaluate both operands and then return a logical vector containing TRUE where, respectively, both or either of the operands had a TRUE value. These operators are usually the right thing for computing vectors of logical values; "`&&`" and "`||`" should be used in `if` expressions.

When there are more than two possible situations, these can be expressed by a sequence of `if` expressions; for example,

```
if(command == "plot") do.plot()
else if(command == "print") do.print()
else stop("command should be plot or print")
```

Often, as in this example, we are testing different values of the same expression. In this case the function `switch` can be used to express the computation. A call to

```
switch(expr, ...)
```

proceeds by evaluating its first argument, `expr`, and using the result to select at most one of the following arguments to evaluate; the value of the selected argument is then the value of the call to the `switch` function.

The value of `expr` is expected to be a single character string or a single number. If `expr` is a character string, it is matched against the names of the remaining arguments in the call. A match causes that argument to be evaluated. If there is no match, an *unnamed* argument, if any, is taken to be the default expression and evaluated. If there is no match at all, the value of the call is NULL. For example:

```
switch(command,
    plot = do.plot(),
    print = do.print(),
    stop("Command should be plot or print"))
```

This expression calls `do.plot` if the value of `command` is `"plot"`, calls `do.print` if the value of `command` is `"print"`, and stops with an error message otherwise. The names that are given to arguments of `switch` don't have to be simple names; any string can be given, so long as it is quoted. For example,

```
switch(transformation,
    logarithm = take.logs(),
    "square root" = take.roots()
    )
```

The same action can correspond to several strings. If the actual argument with the matching string is missing, `switch` keeps on until it reaches the next available argument:

```
switch(log.option,
    YES = , yes = log(x),
    NO = , no = x,
    stop("Invalid form for log.option"))
```

If `expr` evaluates to a number, this number is interpreted as an integer. If it is in the range from 1 to one less than the number of arguments to `switch`, then the `(expr+1)`st argument is evaluated and returned as the value of the call to `switch`. If `expr` is a number outside of this range, NULL is returned. For example:

```
switch(length(x)+1,
    stop("x must contain 1 or 2 values"),
    plot(runif(x)),
    qqplot(runif(x[1]),runif(x[2])))
```

If the length of `x` is 0, an error is generated. If the length is 1 or 2, plotting functions are called.

Exercises

6.9   Write a function that checks the mode of its argument. If the mode is "`logical`", "`numeric`", or "`character`", return the sorted argument; otherwise, stop with an appropriate error message.

6.10   The `if` expression only takes a single logical value as its condition. How would you write a function that takes two (vector) arguments `x` and `power` and produces `x^power` if `power!=0` but produces `log(x)` if `power==0`? Hint: look up `ifelse` in Appendix 1.

6.11   Are the two expressions:

```
if(is.numeric(x) && min(x) > 0) ww ← log(x)
```

and

```
is.numeric(x) && min(x) > 0 && ( ww ← log(x) )
```

equivalent?

6.2.2 *Iteration:* `for, while, repeat`

This section describes the facilities for explicit iteration in S. You should be aware by now that S does most of its own iteration *implicitly*. For example, when you write `sqrt(x)` you automatically get the square-root operation applied to all elements of the vector `x`. In addition, there are S functions that automatically apply a function to sections of arrays (`apply`) or elements of a list (`lapply`).

Nevertheless, you will occasionally want to carry out your own explicit iterations. S provides several forms of expression for this purpose. The most common is the `for` loop:

```
for(name in values) expr
```

The evaluation proceeds by assigning `name` successively to each of the elements in `values` and evaluating `expr` once each time. Generally, `expr` uses `name` somewhere. The value of the entire `for` expression is the value of the last evaluation of `expr`. More often, the loop is used to construct some object by combining the values computed in the loop; for example,

```
for(el in list(...)) means ← c(means,mean(el))
```

The `for` expression automatically extracts elements from `values`, regardless of what kind of object is involved, hence one powerful use of the `for` loop is to apply a computation to a list of objects.

For computations more general than the example above, the usual approach is to generate a list of indices and loop over these:

```
for(i in seq(along=x)) z[[i]] ← g(x[[i]],y[[i]])
```

Note carefully the use of double square brackets in this example. Nearly always, the `for` loop implies that we want the *elements* of a list each time, not a list with one element in it, which is what `x[i]` would produce. (If `x` and `y` are numeric objects there is no distinction, but the `for` loop is often most powerful when used with lists.)

A second form of iteration, the `while` expression, keeps testing a condition and, so long as the condition is TRUE, evaluates the expression provided:

```
while(cond) expr
```

Execution begins by initially testing *cond*, and if its value is FALSE then *expr* is not evaluated at all. Loops using `while` are often used to iterate a numerical computation until some convergence criterion is met. For example, a simple model-fitting loop might be:

```
parameters ← initial.values
residuals ← get.resid(data, parameters)
while( ! converged(residuals) ){
    parameters ← new.fit(data,parameters)
    residuals ← get.resid(data, parameters)
    }
```

Finally, if the test for getting out of a loop is complicated, or does not naturally come at the top, a general `repeat` expression can be used:

```
repeat expr
```

simply keeps repeating *expr* forever.

```
parameters ← initial.values
repeat{
    residuals ← get.resid(data, parameters)
    if( converged(residuals) ) break
    parameters ← new.fit(data,parameters)
    }
```

In general, `repeat` is used when the condition for iteration doesn't fall easily into the simpler forms provided by `for` and `while`. In this case, the `repeat` loop was terminated by evaluating a `break` expression. When S evaluates a `break`, it exits the innermost enclosing `for`, `while`, or `repeat` loop.

The expression `next` is related to `break`. If `next` is evaluated from inside any loop, the next iteration of the loop is begun immediately, without finishing the computations in the current iteration.

```
for(el in list){
    if(is.atomic(el))next
    # some computations on sublists
}
```

Like the `return` expression in section 6.1.1, `next` is rarely required, but its use can make the function easier to read.

Exercises

6.12   Why is it important to use

```
for(i in seq(along=x)) ...
```

rather than

```
for(i in 1:length(x)) ...
```

when writing a loop? Hint: what happens when x has no data in it?

6.13*   Take the model-fitting paradigm illustrated above and turn it into a function that takes as arguments functions `get.resid`, `new.fit`, and `converged`, along with initial parameter estimates and data. Write the appropriate functions and apply your model-fit function to a particular problem.

6.2.3 *Recursion*

A *recursive* function is one that calls itself, either directly or indirectly. A familiar example is the recursive definition of the factorial function:

```
fact ← function(x)
    if(x<=1) 1 else x*fact(x-1)
```

This function, as written, works perfectly well in S. Of course, it is not very efficient, because it utilizes several function calls in order to compute a single number. A non-recursive version of this same factorial function might be written:

```
fact2 ← function(x)
    prod(1:x)
```

Although computing factorials recursively is a commonly used example, it is not necessarily a convincing demonstration of the utility of recursion in S. Let us try again.

    Consider the *check writing* problem: given a number n, we wish to express it in words as on a check. Why is recursion natural for this problem? Basically, because of the way we write numbers in English. If we know how to write numbers less than ten, we can (recursively) put this text in front of the word "hundred" for numbers less than one thousand, and so on. The idea is to call our function recursively to get the pieces needed and then paste all this together.

First, we construct two data objects that check.write will need.

```
numbers ← c("one","two","three","four","five","six",
    "seven","eight","nine","ten","eleven","twelve",
    "thirteen","fourteen","fifteen","sixteen","seventeen",
    "eighteen","nineteen")
tens ← c("ten","twenty","thirty","forty","fifty","sixty",
    "seventy","eighty","ninety")
```

Now we can write the operational part of the function:

```
cw ← function(n) {
    if(n == 0)
        character()
    else if(n < 20)
        numbers[n]
    else if(n < 100)
        c(tens[n %/% 10], cw(n %% 10))
    else if(n < 1000)
        c(numbers[n %/% 100], "hundred", cw(n %% 100))
    else if(n < 1000000)
        c(cw(n %/% 1000), "thousand", cw(n %% 1000))
    else if(n < 1000000000)
        c(cw(n %/% 1000000), "million", cw(n %% 1000000))
}
```

The function cw concatenates the various pieces of the written number. It does not handle zero and it returns a vector of the names rather than a single character string. We clean up these loose ends in the check.write function.

```
check.write ← function(n)
    if(n == 0) "zero" else paste(cw(n), collapse = " ")
```

Now, let's try a few amounts:

```
> check.write(73)
[1] "seventy three"
> check.write(12345)
[1] "twelve thousand three hundred forty five"
```

Notice how recursion is used in many places in the cw function.

Let us return to the factorial function. One objection to both the recursive and iterative versions was that they do not operate on whole vectors. If we can remedy this problem, then recursive functions will operate just like other S functions. The way we will do this is to continue the recursion on only the subset of the vector that requires more computation.

```
fact3 ← function(x){
    recurse ← x > 1
    x[!recurse] ← 1
    if(any(recurse)){
        y ← x[recurse]
        x[recurse] ← y * fact3(y - 1)
    }
    x
}
```

With `fact3`, we can compute factorials on entire vectors.

```
> fact3(1:10)
 [1]       1       2       6      24      120
 [6]     720    5040   40320  362880 3628800
```

This same model can be applied to many recursive computations to provide whole-vector operations.

Recursive functions are also very convenient for operating on S recursive data structures. The data mode `"list"` is typically used for such data, but the data structures representing the S language are recursive as well. In recursive data structures, the elements of a vector may be atomic data, such as numbers, or may themselves be vectors. Terminology in computer science sometimes refers to recursive data as *tree structures* and the elements, at whatever level, that contain atomic data as the *leaves*. S handles such structures in a more general way than most languages, particularly in that the vectors that form the leaves can be of arbitrary length.

Here is a function that illustrates how to organize computations on such data. Suppose we want to throw away all the recursive structure, retaining only a concatenated vector of all the atomic data in the leaves. Let's call the function `unlist`, since it essentially undoes the structuring effects of the `list` function. For example, suppose we have a list, z, containing 4 elements.

```
> lprint(z)
a = 1
b = c(2, 3, 4)
c = list(d = c(5, 6, 7), e = 8)
f = list(list(list(9)))
```

(See exercise 6.20 below for `lprint`). Then

```
> unlist(z)
 1  2  3  4  5  6  7  8  9
```

The key to an easy definition of `unlist` is to realize that it should call itself recursively to unlist any of the elements that are themselves recursive vectors. The function `c` will concatenate the data from successive elements. To decide whether a particular vector is recursive, we could enumerate the possible modes of recursive data. Instead, remember that S has a function `is.recursive` (introduced in section 5.2) that returns TRUE if its argument is a recursive vector. Then `unlist` can be defined as follows.

```
unlist ← function(data){
    if(!is.recursive(data)) return(data)
    y ← NULL
    for(x in data) y ← c(y, unlist(x))
    y
}
```

Notice the recursion inside the `for` expression.

Exercises

6.14 The function `logstar(x)` is defined as the minimum number of times to iterate the logarithm function so that

```
log(log(...(log(x))))
```

is less than 1. Implement the `logstar` function. Make it work for a vector of x values.

6.15 Write a recursive function that takes an integer as its argument and produces a vector of the digits in its base-10 representation. For example:

```
> digits(12345)
[1] 1 2 3 4 5
```

We will present a non-recursive version of the same function in section 9.2.3.

6.16 The `check.write` function is not sufficient for government use. Extend it to handle at least trillions. Can you extend it in a general way, so that large amounts are driven from a vector:

```
thousands ← c("thousand","million","billion","trillion",
          ...)
```

6.17 Suppose you prefer to see a number like 1776 written as

```
"seventeen hundred seventy six"
```

rather than

```
"one thousand seven hundred seventy six"
```

Change the `cw` function to work this way.

6.18 The greatest common divisor of two numbers can be computed through Euclid's algorithm:

```
gcd ← function(a,b)
    if(b==0) a else gcd(b, a%%b)
```

Revise `gcd` so that it will work when a and/or b have more than one element.

6.19 What happens if data of various modes (numeric, logical, character, etc.) are present in the leaves of the input to `unlist`?

6.20 Write the function `lprint`. You want to print the name of each element, "=", and the element. The functions `names` and `cat` will be helpful.

6.21* Revise your `lprint` function so that it operates recursively, i.e., when it encounters recursive data it reinvokes itself on each element of the recursive data. Make sure you show the levels of the data object.

6.22 In `unlist`, suppose you only wanted the atomic data at the top level of the list; if the element of the vector is recursive, ignore it. Write a function, `top.unlist`, that does this.

6.23 Instead of concatenating the data, suppose we want to produce a vector of some summary function of each of the leaves. For example

```
list.summary(z,mean)
 1 3 6 8 9
```

for the means of the leaves. Write `list.summary` in the style of `unlist`.

6.3 Using UNIX Commands

S has an interface to commands in the UNIX operating system, namely the function `unix`. Because commands have a very simple view of the world, the S interface is also very simple. Commands take a stream of characters as input, usually divided into lines by newline characters. They produce a similar stream of characters as output.

The S interface is:

```
unix(command, input, output)
```

The argument `command` is the command to be executed as if it had been typed to the shell. The argument `input`, if supplied, is the *standard input* to the command. Both `command` and `input` are interpreted as character vectors; when converted to streams of characters, elements of the vectors are separated by new-lines. The *standard output* from the command is returned by `unix` as a character vector, with one element for each line of the output of the command. However, the argument `output=F` causes the output *not* to be returned. In this case, and in the case that `input` is missing, the corresponding input or output for the command is the same as for S itself. This paragraph has given the entire definition of the `unix` interface. Because it matches the way commands are organized, however, this simple interface is very powerful. As examples here and in the rest of the book will illustrate, S takes advantage of many commands to solve "character-oriented" problems.

As a trivial example, the S function `date()` returns the current date and time as a character string; this string can be used to annotate plots and printed output. Its definition is:

```
date ← function()
        unix("date")
```

Another application is the function `readline` referred to in section 2.7. This function wants to return one line of input from the user. Figuring out how to do this in a shell command requires a little research on how the shell works. One solution is:

```
read h
```

which reads one line and sets a shell variable, h, to the result. Then

```
echo $h
```

prints the result. The definition of `readline` is then

```
readline ← function()
    unix("read h; echo $h")
```

Given the general model that commands in the UNIX system take streams of characters as input and produce streams of characters as output, one naturally finds many commands that operate on character data, doing string pattern matching, editing, text processing, and document formatting. S generally avoids duplicating these facilities and uses instead the `unix` interface. If you are familiar with commands like `sed`, `grep`, and `awk`, you should find it straightforward to use these to do pattern matching and text manipulation on S objects. The rest of this section gives examples.

One simple task is to count the number of characters present in each element of a character vector. The `nchar` function does this:

```
nchar ← function(s)
    as.numeric(unix("awk '{print length}'", input=s))
```

We can use it to count the number of characters in the names of the months:

```
> nchar(month.name)
 [1] 7 8 5 5 3 4 4 6 9 7 8 8
```

"January" has 7 characters, "February" 8, and so on.

Suppose we want to search for a string pattern in character data. A function, say `string.match(pattern,text)`, takes a character string in `pattern`, and returns a vector saying what elements in `text` contained the pattern as a substring. For example,

```
string.match("New",state.name)
```

identifies the state names containing the string "New". An S function to do this can be written using the command `fgrep`:

```
string.match ← function(pattern, text){
    command ← paste("fgrep -n -e '", pattern,
        "'|sed 's/:.*//'",sep = "")
    as.numeric(unix(command, text))
}
```

Notice that we enclosed the `pattern` inside apostrophes. This was to ensure that no characters of the pattern would conflict with the syntax of the UNIX system shell.

The use of commands in `string.match` is typical of similar functions: an S object, here `text`, is coerced to a character vector to become input to the command, one element per line. The command `fgrep` finds the patterns, and its `-n` option arranges to have the matching line numbers appear in the output along with the matched lines. (Ordinarily, `fgrep` just emits the matching lines from the input file.) Processing of the output of `fgrep` through the `sed` command strips off all but the line numbers. You can look up the `fgrep` command in the UNIX system manual to see in more detail what it does and how it is called. Finally, we turn the character result returned by `unix` into a vector of numbers by using `as.numeric`.

Functions that use `unix` are frequently valuable for studying and managing your working directory of S objects. By learning a few facts about how objects are stored, you can write new functions for such purposes. Objects assigned permanently become files, of the same name, in the S *working data* directory. The name of that directory is always the first element of the S vector `.Search.list`. Other elements of that vector are other directories that are searched in looking for data. So, for example, an S function to return the names of all objects in the working data directory is:

```
working.data ← function()
    unix(paste("ls",.Search.list[1]))
```

This is a very simple version of the function `ls`. See section 5.4 for much more detail on S data directories.

So far, `unix` has returned its output as a character vector in S. If the command being executed is itself *interactive*, it may use its output to communicate with the user. If so, the argument `output=FALSE` should be used to tell `unix` not to return the output to S. Examples are text editing functions, such as those we used for editing function definitions. Here is a simplified version of the `vi` function:

```
vi ← function(data){
    dput(data, "edit.data")
    unix("vi edit.data", out=F)
    source("edit.data")
}
```

The `out=F` argument to `unix` ensures that the `vi` command can use standard output to communicate to the user. (Whatever the value of `output`, the standard error file is untouched by the `unix` function, ensuring that error messages from commands will appear on the user's terminal.) With `output=F` there is still a mechanism by which the command can communicate back to S, although a limited one. When commands terminate, they do so with an *exit status*, which is normally 0 but which can be set by the command; for example the command

```
exit 1
```

sets the exit status to 1. The status of the command executed by `unix(...,` `output=F)` is returned as the value of the call to `unix`. The conventional use of exit status in commands is to indicate failure; the shell assumes that status 0 means success and a nonzero status means failure.

Exercises

6.24 Why does the expression

```
unix("cat myfile")
```

cause S to return a character vector, each element corresponding to one line of file `myfile`?

6.25 Another kind of pattern matching looks for *regular expressions*, which form a little language for describing string patterns. (See `grep` or `ed` in the UNIX system manual for a discussion of regular expressions.) The command `egrep` matches such patterns. Write a function `grep` that operates like `string.match` but which looks for a regular expression as a pattern. How does it compare to the `grep` function present in S?

6.26 As an alternative to the previous exercise, add an argument `regexp` to the `grep` function, such that if `regexp` is TRUE, the function looks for regular expressions; otherwise, it just matches plain strings. Should the default value for `regexp` be TRUE or FALSE?

6.27* Write a function that takes a vector of patterns and returns a logical matrix telling which patterns matched each element of the text argument. Label the rows of the matrix with the individual patterns and the columns with the text items.

6.28 The `ls` command allows you to supply patterns of file names, in which case `ls` returns only the file names matching the patterns. Make a second, optional, argument to `working.data` in which you can pass in a string that gives such a pattern, and include the pattern in pasting together the command for `unix`. What should the default value for the argument be?

6.29 There is an option, `-s`, to the `ls` command, which causes the output to contain the size of the corresponding files. Each line of output contains the size of a file (in blocks) followed by the name of the file; for example,

```
 1 last.debug
 1 last.warning
 1 linear.fit
 1 lk.norm
 1 mean.of.means
 1 mins
12 prof.1
12 prof.2
50 profl
```

Write a function that returns both the object names, as `working.data` does, and the corresponding sizes. You will need a command to strip off leading blanks and to turn the next blank into a newline. If you have used `sed`, go ahead and try it. Otherwise, use the following command, which should be `paste`'d onto the command used in `working.data`.

```
"|sed -e 's/^ *//' -e 's/ /\\n/'"
```

Note the two backslashes, so that `sed` will get "\n" since it can't handle actual newline characters. Why wouldn't the expression

```
unix("ls -s .Data")
```

produce the right result?

6.30   If you implemented the function in the previous exercise using the hints, you will see that it returns a character vector with *2n* elements, in pairs giving the size and name for each object. A nicer function might return the sizes, with the `names` attribute set to the object names. Modify your previous function to do this. (See the `string.match` example for converting the sizes to numbers.) You might want to use the fact that

```
x[seq(1,length(x),2)]
```

will select the odd-numbered elements of *x*.

6.31   The command

```
cmp -s file1 file2
```

compares the contents of two files and sets the return code to indicate whether the two files are identical or different. Write a function to check whether two S objects are identical based on `cmp`.

6.4 The Programming Environment

This section deals with S as a programming environment: with editing S functions, tracking down what's happening in the computations, or fixing problems that cause the functions to terminate with error messages.

6.4.1 *Editing*

Functions are S objects; they can be edited and reassigned by a variety of methods. Three approaches are the most commonly used:

- use `dump` to write one or more functions to a file, and `source` to get back the objects from the file after editing;
- use the S editing functions to invoke a text editor from within S;
- "cut and paste" directly on the screen of a terminal.

We will describe these methods briefly.

The function `dump` takes a vector of object names and the name of a file. Onto this file will be written some S expressions that when parsed will recreate the objects. For example, after evaluating

```
dump("larger","my.source")
```

the file "`my.source`" will contain an expression to define `larger`.

```
larger ← function(x, y){
    y.is.bigger ← y > x
    x[y.is.bigger] ← y[y.is.bigger]
    x
}
```

The inverse of this call to `dump` is `source("my.file")`, which will parse the contents of the file and carry out the assignment. In between the calls to `dump` and `source`, you can edit the file with any editor or any other commands you want. The `dump`/`source` mechanism is a good way to manage large collections of functions (or other objects).

For small editing jobs of single functions it may be simpler to call an editor directly from S. For example, there are functions `ed` and `vi`, corresponding to the standard text editors with the same names. These functions also operate by writing the object to be edited onto a file and then running the appropriate text editor with that file as input. When you finish editing, write the file, and quit from the editor, the edited version of the file is read back into S (in the case of functions, the edited file is parsed by the S parser), and returned as the value of the call to `ed` or `vi`. For example, if you want to use the screen editor `vi` to revise the function `larger` and put the revised version in `test.fun`:

```
test.fun ← vi(larger)
```

This expression *does not* change `larger`—the editor functions have no side effects. They return the edited version of the data as their value and do not have the side effect of changing any objects. If we had wanted the editing expression above to change the object `larger` right away, we could have used:

```
larger ← vi(larger)
```

If an error occurs (for example, if there is an error in parsing the revised function), you can resume editing the same file by invoking the editor function without an argument:

```
test.fun ← vi()
```

Finally, some terminals and workstations have a convenient "cut and paste" editor. In this case, function definitions and other S expressions can be edited right on the screen and then "sent" to S in their edited form, as if you had typed the changed expression.

Exercises

6.32   The functions `source` and `restore` both read back the files produced by `dump`. Look at their definitions. When would you prefer one or the other?

6.4.2 *Debugging*

Suppose you have written or modified a function and it fails to do what you want: either an S error message appears or the result of the function is not what it should be. The first thing to do, simple as it seems, is to print the function and look carefully at its definition. Ask yourself:

- Are you using some other functions that you aren't familiar with? If so, you should look up their definitions.
- Did you call the function with the correct arguments?
- Does the function assume something about an argument that is not true (e.g., does it assume that the argument is a matrix)?
- Does the function depend on something in the environment that isn't set correctly? For example, a graphics function can only be called after a device driver function has been called.

Suppose, however, that asking all of these questions does not point out any solution to the problem. The next step is to examine the function during evaluation, by editing into the function some *debugging expressions*. The simplest of these is a call to `browser`, which, when evaluated, prompts the user to enter S expressions. These are evaluated in the frame of the function that called `browser`, so you can examine the values of local objects.

Consider `larger`, again.

```
larger ← function(x, y){
   y.is.bigger ← y > x
   x[y.is.bigger] ← y[y.is.bigger]
   x
}
```

Here's an example of using the function:

```
> xxx
 [1]  -0.023 -31.957    4.218  -1.721  -2.070  -1.573
 [7]   2.404  -2.337    0.163   0.294
> yyy
 [1]  -4.432  -4.331    1.715  13.283  -1.781   2.113
 [7]  -0.328   0.839    3.267   4.413
> larger(xxx,yyy)
 [1]  -0.023  -4.331    4.218  13.283  -1.781   2.113
 [7]   2.404   0.839    3.267   4.413
> larger(xxx,-2)
 [1] -0.023     NA   4.218 -1.721     NA -1.573   2.404
 [8]     NA  0.163   0.294
```

The first result of the the function seems right, but the second one certainly isn't. What is wrong? Spending some time studying the definition of the function might well be all that's needed to find the error. (You might try it before reading on.)

Suppose, however, that thinking alone has not turned up anything. To look interactively at the computations in the function, we insert a call to browser when part, but not all of the computation is done:

```
larger ← function(x, y){
   y.is.bigger ← y > x
   browser()
   x[y.is.bigger] ← y[y.is.bigger]
   x
}
```

Now, when the call to browser occurs, a prompt is printed. Here, we answer "?" in order to get a menu of possible selections.

```
> larger(xxx,-2)
Browser called from: larger(xxx, -2)
Type number, ?, or expression (0 or return(...) to exit)
Selection: ?
1: y.is.bigger
2: x
3: y
```

The menu will contain only the arguments that have been evaluated at the time browser was called. (Recall that S uses *lazy evaluation* for its arguments and thus does not evaluate an argument until some expression requires its value.) You can respond to browser by making a selection from the menu:

```
Selection: 1
y.is.bigger:
 [1] F T F F T F F T F F
```

or by typing an arbitrary expression. Let's explore some subscript expressions to see what might be happening in our example:

```
Selection: x[y.is.bigger]
[1] -31.957  -2.070  -2.337
Selection: y[y.is.bigger]
[1] NA NA NA
```

Now we can see the problem: the two arguments are not of the same length, so when we select elements of the shorter one, we get NA, which is then substituted into the result.

The expressions typed to browser are evaluated in the frame of the function calling browser. In particular, assignment expressions will alter that environment. This allows us to try a little error correction interactively; in this case, we will replicate y to have the same length as x, and then return from browser, since the rest of the call to larger should now work.

```
Selection: y ← rep(y,length=10)
Selection: 0
 [1] -0.023 -2.000  4.218 -1.721 -2.000 -1.573  2.404
 [8] -2.000  0.163  0.294
```

That seemed to work. Now we can redefine larger to expand the shorter argument:

```
larger ← function(x, y){
    nx ← length(x)
    ny ← length(y)
    if(nx > ny) y ← rep(y, length = nx)
    else if(nx < ny) x ← rep(x, length = ny)
    which ← y > x
    x[which] ← y[which]
    x
}
```

The browser function takes over control of your interaction with S. In particular, errors and interrupts are caught by browser.

```
Selection: y[y.si.bigger]
Error in call to larger: Object "y.si.bigger" not found
Browser called from: larger(xxx, -2)
Type number, ?, or expression (0 or return(...) to exit)
Selection:
```

To exit browser, you type 0 or a return() expression. We haven't used the feature here, but any value inside the return will be the value of browser. You can use this returned value to alter the course of evaluation of the function interactively. For example, suppose that you want to investigate values in the function and then decide whether to use method 1 or method 2 in the remainder of the function. Insert the following into the function:

```
method ← browser()
```

Now, when you call your function you will interact with `browser`. If you evaluate `return(1)` from inside `browser`, the function will set `method` to 1 and continue using method 1. Responding with `return(2)` in `browser` will continue using method 2.

The quit signal (usually typed as control-backslash) provides a way to exit from `browser` and from the whole expression that generated the call to `browser`. Use a quit signal if you decide not to continue computing after browsing in the frame or if the function is in a loop, calling `browser` repeatedly. Since `browser` is catching all errors and ordinary interrupts, you cannot get out of it by calling `stop` or by hitting interrupt.

Occasionally, there is no need to browse interactively: some values just need to be printed during evaluation. Use the function `cat`. It prints anything—any number of arguments of any mode—in as simple a format as the data allows. In our `larger` function, we can look at the lengths of the arguments by inserting a call to `cat`:

```
larger ← function(x, y){
    nx ← length(x)
    ny ← length(y)
    if(nx > ny) y ← rep(y, length = nx)
    else if(nx < ny) x ← rep(x, length = ny)
    cat("Original and new lengths:",
        nx,ny,length(x),length(y),"\n")
    which ← y > x
    x[which] ← y[which]
    x
}
```

which would produce intermediate printing as follows:

```
> xx ← (1:4)/2
> larger(xx,1)
Original and new lengths: 4 1 4 4
[1] 1.0 1.0 1.5 2.0
```

Such messages can be placed at strategic points inside your functions during development to display the course of evaluation.

Another function that can be used in tracking down problems is `trace`. It causes messages to be printed whenever a specified function is invoked, and is especially helpful for functions that are called recursively.

Remember our recursive factorial function from section 6.2.3:

```
fact ← function(x)
    if(x<=1) 1 else x*fact(x-1)
```

Suppose we want to trace its evaluation.

```
> trace(fact)
> fact(4)
Entering frame 5 fact(4)
Entering frame 8 fact(x - 1)
Entering frame 11 fact(x - 1)
Entering frame 14 fact(x - 1)
Frame 14 value: 1
Frame 11 value: 2
Frame 8 value: 6
Frame 5 value: 24
[1] 24
```

The output shows `fact` as it is called recursively, with one line of output when the function is entered and another as it exits with a value. The frame number allows you to match the call with the corresponding returned value. You can trace as many functions as you like, by calling `trace` several times or by giving it a vector of function names as its argument. S keeps internally a list of the functions being traced. There are also several ways in which the function can be traced. See the documentation for `trace` and section 7.4.2 for more details.

The expression

```
untrace()
```

turns off all tracing, and

```
untrace(fact)
```

turns off tracing of function `fact`.

When errors are hard to track down or really strange things are happening, set the `check` option:

```
options(check=T)
```

causes the S evaluator to be fussier about various conditions and to check internally various assumptions that it normally takes for granted. Setting this option may cause a problem to show up earlier, or produce more informative error printing.

6.4.3 *Error Actions*

When an error or interrupt occurs, the S evaluator examines the current value of the option `error`. If this is not `NULL` (typically it is a function definition), the function will be called to carry out some wrap-up action. The default error option is the function `dump.calls`, which saves a copy of the nested function calls being evaluated when the error occurred and prints a message `Dumped`. By calling the function `traceback`, a printout of those calls can be obtained. For example:

```
> larger(yy,1)
Error: Object "yy" not found
Dumped
> traceback()
1: larger(yy, 1)
2: length(x)
```

The error (caused by misspelling the first argument to `larger`) actually occurred when the value of that argument was first needed; namely, in the computation of its length. (This is a consequence of the lazy evaluation used by S.)

The error action can be changed through the `options` function:

```
options(error=NULL)
```

will cause no action to be taken on errors. In the opposite direction,

```
options(error=dump.frames)
```

will cause a complete dump of all the local frames from the nested function calls in progress. With this error action in effect, `traceback` works as before, but function `debugger` can be invoked, as well. The `debugger` function presents a menu of the calls; if you select one of the menu items, you will be placed in a browser operating on the frame of that function. For example:

```
> options(error=dump.frames)
> larger(yy,1)
Error: Object "yy" not found
Dumped
> debugger()
1: larger(yy, 1)
2: y > x
Selection: 1
Browser called on data[[i]]
Type number, ?, or expression (0 or return(...) to exit)
Selection: ?
1: x
2: y
Selection:
```

(Caution: `dump.frames` can result in dumping a very large amount of data in complicated situations where many function calls have been nested. It should usually only be used temporarily, while stalking a pesky bug.)

As an example of browsing through dumped frames, consider the following case, in which an error has occurred in an unfamiliar function:

```
> lsfit(xx,yy)
Error in call to .Fortran: subroutine dqrls:
Missing values in argument 1
Dumped
```

Here our situation is that we understand roughly what `lsfit` is supposed to do, but not much about how it does it. The error message tells us that there were missing values somewhere, but it may not be easy to figure out where. By setting the error option to `dump.frames` and rerunning the expression, a dump of the local frames is saved. We can now invoke `debugger`:

```
> debugger()
1: lsfit(xx, yy)
2: .Fortran("dqrls",
    qr = x,
    as.integer(dx),
    pivot = as.integer(1:p),
    qraux = double(p),
    y,
    as.integer(dy),
    coef = double(p * q),
    residuals = y,
    qt = y,
    tol = as.double(tolerance),
    double(p),
    rank = as.integer(p))
Selection: 2
Browser called on data[[i]]
Type number, ?, or expression (0 or return(...) to exit)
Selection:
```

This may still be a little forbidding, given that we don't know much about `lsfit`, but since the problem was in the first argument to the Fortran routine `dqrls`, we can look in the traceback for the corresponding expression, and look for missing values:

```
Selection: is.na(x)
      [,1] [,2] [,3]
[1,]    F    T    F
[2,]    F    T    T
[3,]    F    T    T
  ...
```

There they are—we can now go back to see what we did wrong before calling `lsfit`.

Exercises

6.33 How does the `vi` function, when called with no arguments, remember the file that it was editing? Examine the `vi` function to find out.

6.34 What value does `browser` return if you evaluate `return()` or reply 0 as your selection?

6.35 Write a recursive function to compute Fibonacci numbers, based on the following facts:

```
Fib(0)==0
Fib(1)==1
```

and otherwise `Fib(n)` is

```
Fib(n-1)+Fib(n-2)
```

Trace its evaluation in computing `Fib(5)`.

Answers to Selected Exercises

6.1 (page 156) Yes, the difference is essentially in the weight that each observation gets. In the case of `mean.of.all`, each observation has equal weight; in the case of `mean.of.means`, each group of observations gets an equal weight.

6.2 (page 156) The `trim` argument of `mean.of.means` may not be abbreviated. In this case, `mean.of.means` computed the mean of `.5` and the mean of `1:9`.

6.3 (page 156) If the only argument to the function is `...`, the two expressions are equivalent. However, even then, `length(list(...))` causes all of the arguments to be evaluated, while `nargs()` does not. Also, `nargs` includes all arguments, not just those named in `...`.

6.4 (page 158)
```
> loan.payment ← function(principal, interest, years)
+ {
+    f ← interest/1200
+    k ← (1 + f)^(12 * years)
+    principal * (f * k)/(k - 1)
+ }
> loan.payment(65000,9.5,30)
[1] 546.555
```

6.5 (page 158)
```
labscat ← function(x,y,labels){
    plot(x,y,type="n")
    text(x,y,labels)
}
```

6.7 (page 158)
```
text.code ← function(x,labels=c(".","x","X"))
        labels[range.code(x,length(labels))]
```

6.9 (page 162)
```
switch(mode(x),
```

```
        logical=, numeric=, character= sort(x),
        stop("Invalid data mode")
        )
```

6.10 (page 162)
```
        transform ← function(x,power)
            ifelse(power==0,log(x),x^power)
```

6.11 (page 162) The value of the first expression is NULL or log(x). The value of the second is TRUE or FALSE. If the conditions are met, both have the same side effect of setting ww.

6.12 (page 164) If length(x) is 0, then the first loop will work correctly (the loop expression is not executed at all) but the second loop will execute two iterations, for i==1 and i==0.

6.14 (page 167)
```
        logstar ← function(x){
            recurse ← x > 1
            x[!recurse] ← 0
            if(any(recurse)){
                y ← x[recurse]
                x[recurse] ← 1 + logstar(log(y))
            }
            x
        }
```

6.15 (page 167)
```
        digits ← function(n, base = 10)
            if(n==0) 0 else dg(n,base)

        dg ← function(n, base = 10){
            if(n == 0) NULL
            else c(dg(n %/% base, base), n %% base)
        }
```

6.17 (page 167) To get full points for this exercise, you should have made only the one-character change from
```
        else if(n < 1000)
```
to
```
        else if(n < 2000)
```

6.18 (page 167)
```
        gcd ← function(a, b){
            a ← a + 0 * b # equalize lengths of a and b
            b ← b + 0 * a
            gcd2(a, b)
        }
        gcd2 ← function(a, b){
            recurse ← b!=0
            if(any(recurse)){
                tmp ← b[recurse]
                a[recurse] ← gcd(tmp, a[recurse] %% tmp)
            }
            a
        }
```

6.19 (page 167) At each stage they are coerced to match the most complicated mode encountered so far.

6.27 (page 171) The simplest method is to generate a separate match for each pattern, match the returned lines against the sequence of line numbers, and concatenate the results to form a matrix:

```
multi.match ← function(patterns, text){
    lines ← as.character(seq(along=text))
    output ← logical()
    for(p in patterns){
        command ← paste("egrep -n -e \"",
            p, "\" |sed 's/:.*//'", sep = "")
        found ← unix(command, text)
        output ← c(output, !is.na(match(lines,found)))
    }
    output ← matrix(output, length(patterns),
        length(text), byrow=T)
    dimnames(output) ← list(Patterns = patterns,
        Text = text)
    output
}
```

Less straightforward, but more efficient for a large number of patterns, would be to test all the patterns on each element of the text, by creating a program in the awk language. The for loop and the following line is then replaced by

```
cat("{",
    paste("if( $0   /", patterns, "/) print 1;
        else print \"\"",
    sep = ""),
    "}", sep = "\n", file = "...pgm")
output ← as.logical(unix(paste("awk -f ...pgm",file)))
```

6.31   (page 172)

```
identical ← function(a,b){
    dsname ← function(x)
        paste(.Search.list[1],"/",x,sep="")
    cmd ← paste("cmp -s",dsname(a),dsname(b))
    unix(cmd, output=F)
}
```

6.32   (page 174)   The restore function creates a completely new (non-interactive) S session to parse the dumped file, while source parses the file inside an expression. As a result, restore is better for big jobs, because it does not swell memory so much and can keep going after an error. For small jobs, source will be faster.

6.35   (page 181)

```
Fib ← function(n){
    if(n==0) 0
    else if(n==1) 1
    else Fib(n-1)+Fib(n-2)
}
```

7

More on Writing Functions

This chapter continues the discussion of programming in S begun in section 2.7 and chapter 6. The techniques described here are those needed mostly for more extensive, difficult, or specialized programming. These techniques are often important when writing functions for others to use. In this chapter, when we speak of "users", we mean the people who will use the functions you are writing.

Section 7.1 shows you how to organize interactions with users of your functions, by writing output to the user and reading responses, or by menu interactions. Section 7.2 describes the interfaces between S and subroutines written in the C and Fortran languages. This section also describes how to compile and load the C or Fortran routines for use with S, and how to call S from C.

Section 7.3 provides a few specialized programming techniques—how to handle files and how to clean up when errors or user interrupts occur. It also tells how you can define your own infix operators and replacement functions.

The remaining two sections are somewhat more advanced. Section 7.4 shows how control of the evaluation itself can be obtained by using special functions that give access to the S model of evaluation. As has been emphasized throughout this book, all S expressions and functions are themselves S objects. Section 7.5 presents techniques for manipulating these objects, that is, for using the S language as data.

7.1 Interacting with Users

Functions that need to communicate interactively with users must present some information *to* the user and then interpret the response *from* the user. For writing to the user, the function cat provides for precise control over the output, while print provides neatly formatted displays automatically. Word processing commands can also be used, through the unix interface.

For collecting and interpreting the user's response, an important consideration is whether we want to interpret the response as an expression in the S language. If so, we use the S parser parse. If not, we will likely use functions like scan or unix to read the responses.

Another input option is to use the menu function to display alternatives and get a response: it is easy to use and has the advantage, for some applications, of mapping directly into graphics menus on particular devices.

7.1.1 *Writing*

The functions cat and print are the basic tools for writing to users. The print function produces an attractive display of an arbitrary S object; it is the function used to automatically print the value of the S expression you type. It does not, however, allow detailed control over what appears in the output. For this purpose, cat is preferable.

The function cat takes any number of arguments, containing arbitrary expressions, and chooses the simplest adequate format to display each element of the first argument, followed by each element of the second argument, and so on. It is quite flexible for displaying information to users. It displays successive elements separated by a space and will not insert newline characters unless you explicitly use an argument containing the newline character, "\n", or use the optional argument fill.

For many applications, cat is the simplest way to display information. As an example, consider again the function quiz, discussed in section 2.7:

```
quiz ← function(questions,answers)
    for(i in 1:length(questions)){
        cat(questions[i],"? ")
        if(readline()==answers[i])cat("Right!\n")
        else cat("No, the answer is:",answers[i],"\n")
```

The first call to cat prints out one character string, followed by a question mark but *not* terminated with a newline. The user's response will then appear on the same line as the question. The other calls to cat write out a message terminated by an explicit newline.

Several special arguments to `cat` give additional control; for example, `sep` alters the separator character between successive elements. Two alternatives to the default single blank are

```
sep=""
```

to have no default separator, or

```
sep="\n"
```

to separate by newlines. The first call to `cat` in the example would have looked better without a blank before the question mark:

```
cat(questions[i],"? ",sep="")
```

Notice the explicit blank after the question mark. The separator character appears between elements (whether from the same argument or between one argument and the next), but does not appear after the last element.

To make `cat` write to a file, include the `file` argument, with the character string giving the file to be used. A related argument, `append=T`, allows successive calls to append to a file, rather than overwriting it. (We will talk about the recommended style for using files in section 7.3.1.) One other special argument, `fill=width`, causes output to be broken automatically with newlines, whenever printing the next element would cause the current line to exceed `width` characters. If you specify `fill=TRUE`, the width of the line is determined by the option named "`width`" (see `options` in Appendix 1). By default, `fill` is `FALSE`.

The main partner to `cat` is `paste`. An important distinction between the two functions is that `cat` is designed to write information to the terminal or to a file; `paste` creates S objects of mode `"character"`. Paste builds a character vector by concatenating the corresponding elements of each of its arguments, as character strings. Thus,

```
paste("(",pattern,")",sep="")
```

pastes parentheses around each of the elements of `pattern`. Like `cat`, `paste` has a `sep` argument defining what string should separate the concatenated elements. One way to think about what `paste` is doing is to imagine its arguments being written as parallel columns of character strings, extended by repetition, if necessary, so that all columns are the same length. The strings in a row are pasted together (with the specified separator) to form an element of the result, which is the vector of all these concatenated rows.

Having formed a single character vector, `paste` can also collapse this vector into a single string. If the argument `collapse` is supplied, collapsing takes place with the specified character string (perhaps empty) separating the collapsed elements:

```
paste(pattern,collapse="|")
```

creates a single string out of the elements of `pattern`, with a vertical bar separating the elements. These two forms can be combined, for example in

```
pattern ← paste("(", pattern, ")", sep = "", collapse = "|")
```

which would enclose all the elements of `pattern` in parentheses, with no blanks added, and then combine these with "|" in between.

Another function for generating user output is `format`. It takes a single argument and converts it to a character vector, with the property that each of the elements has the same number of characters. This is often used for getting output labels to line up. Together `cat` and `format` can be used to create almost any kind of display.

As you attempt to produce more sophisticated output, keep in mind the `unix` interface. All the display and word processing tools of the UNIX system are available from S. For interactive output to users, fancy word processing is unlikely to be worth the effort. However, the potential is there, and may be used for off-line output, such as report generation. S functions can create input to any commands for text processing, by merging computed results with the other information needed by the command. One example is the `tbl` function. This function takes a matrix and produces from it a file suitable for processing through the corresponding `tbl` *command*, which in turn is a preprocessor to the `troff` text processing command.

```
tbl ← function(x, file = "tbl.out"){
    d ← dim(x)
    if(length(d) != 2)stop("argument x must be a matrix")
    nfield ← d[2]
    table ← character(d[1])
    for(i in 1:d[1])
        table[i] ← paste(x[i,],collapse="\t")
    format ← rep(if(is.numeric(x))"n" else "l",nfield)
    seps ← c(rep("|",nfield-1),".")
    format ← paste(format,seps,collapse=" ")
    options ← "center, box;"
    cat(file=file,".TS",options,format,table,".TE",sep="\n")
}
```

If `x1` is a 4 by 3 matrix, `tbl(x1, "table1")` produces a file `table1` containing

```
.TS
center, box;
n | n | n .
-1.017        -1.883        -.02
-.132         .337          -1.012
-.36          0             .916
-.034         1.207         -1.383
.TE
```

The first and last lines are `troff` commands bracketing a table. The second and third lines specify options for the table and the form of the columns (the code n specifies that the data is numeric). The remainder of the file contains `nrow(x)` lines of data values, separated by tab characters.

The file written by `tbl`, in turn, can be used in a document prepared with `troff`. Incorporate the file into your `troff` input file `troff.in`, and process with the command

```
$ tbl troff.in | troff
```

and you will end up with the following table in your document:

−1.017	−1.883	−.02
−.132	.337	−1.012
−.36	0	.916
−.034	1.207	−1.383

Of course, this is only one of many ways in which output from S can use text processing and report generating tools.

7.1.2 *Reading User Input*

The choice of how to handle a user response depends on what the response means, that is, how does the function want to think about the incoming data? Data input was discussed in section 5.3. The techniques shown there can be used for reading user's responses, as well. For example,

```
cat("Enter values, empty line to terminate:\n")
n ← scan()
```

will prompt the user and read numbers from standard input.

In this section we will discuss some additional techniques specialized to reading user input. Two cases of interest are:

1. the data is just text, usually coming in a line at a time;
2. the data should make sense as an expression in the S language.

Our `quiz` example illustrates the first case: the user is to type a line of arbitrary text, to be compared to `answer[i]`. The general strategy in this case is to use the `unix` function to turn the data into lines of text, which it then reads and returns, one element per line, in a character vector. For example, the function `readline` reads one line and returns it as a character vector.

```
readline ← function()
    unix("read stuff; echo $stuff")
```

Essentially any kind of input can be read this way. All that is needed is to figure out how to turn the original input into one item per line, using the shell, editor, or other tools. For example, if `file` contains fields separated by tabs:

```
unix("tr '\t' '\n' <file")
```

turns each tab into a newline, reads the result line-by-line, and hence returns a character vector containing the fields. This could be combined with such niceties as eliminating empty fields or trailing blanks.

On the other hand, suppose the data has to make sense as an S expression. The general approach here is to use the S parser through the function `parse`. The argument `white=TRUE` allows `parse` to read successive expressions separated by arbitrary white space (blanks, tabs, or newlines). The call

```
parse()
```

will read one expression from standard input. The value of `parse` is always an unevaluated `expression` object:

```
> parse()
> sqrt(a)+9
expression(sqrt(a) + 9)
> parse()
> 3.14159
expression(3.14159)
```

If you want to evaluate the expression returned by `parse`, use the `eval` function:

```
> eval(parse())
> 3.14159
[1] 3.14159
```

Any number of items can be read in one call; in particular,

```
parse(-1)
```

will read from the standard input until an end of file (control-d character) is encountered. Input can also come either from a file by supplying the `file` argument, or directly from a character vector by giving the `text` argument.

7.1.3 *Menu Interactions*

Users of software built on S may know little, if anything, about writing S expressions. Such users may prefer a *menu interface* to the software, in which they respond to a question by selecting the menu item that best describes their answer. Menus are presented to users by printing the items and then reading the user's selection. For a character vector `choices`, the expression

```
menu(choices)
```

displays each element and returns `i` if the user picked `choices[i]`, or `0` if no valid choice was made.

Some graphics terminals and workstations provide a special menu-selection procedure; for example, a menu might pop up on the screen when the user presses a button on a mouse, or be pulled down by touching an appropriate icon. You then move the mouse to pick one of the menu items. If you have invoked a graphics device that includes a special menu facility, `menu` will automatically invoke that facility. If you want a printed menu regardless of the availability of a graphics menu, use

```
menu(choices,graphics=FALSE)
```

The returned value is the same whether a graphics or printed menu is used.

As an example, here is a simple menu-driven help facility for graphics functions.

```
graph.help ← function(){
    my.menu ← c(
        "Scatterplots",
        "Drawing lines",
        "Plotting text",
        "Titles and Legends")
    cat("Select a topic for help\n")
    pick ← menu(my.menu)
    switch(pick,
        help(plot),
        help(lines),
        help(text),
        {help(title); help(legend)}
    )
}
```

The function calling `menu` evaluates the `switch` function in response to the user's selection. The `switch` function is well matched to `menu`: `switch` is called with the value returned by `menu` as its first argument and an appropriate action expression in each of the remaining arguments. Nothing will happen if the user didn't make a selection, because `switch` does nothing if its first argument is out of range. A user might interact with `graph.help` as follows:

```
> graph.help()
Select a topic for help
1: Scatterplots
2: Drawing lines
3: Plotting text
4: Titles & Legends
Selection: 2
Add Lines or Points to Current Plot

USAGE:
        lines(x, y, type="l")
        points(x, y, type="p")
ARGUMENTS:
```

```
x,y:   coordinates of points.  The coordinates can  be
       given  by two  vector arguments  or by a single
   ...
```

A simple menu function like this will suffice for small-scale use, but several added features can improve the user interface. The exercises below explore extensions and alternatives to simple menu selection. As a general comment, the menu function is a good way to take the programming out of the user's hands for relatively simple situations. To go beyond menu interactions, for example by letting users supply S expressions in addition to simple selections, requires manipulating expressions. We will go into this in section 7.5.1.

Exercises

7.1 Modify graph.help to require the user to make a valid selection; that is, to repeatedly present the menu, followed by a message each time the user doesn't make a valid selection.

7.2 Study the following function and describe in words how it allows a user to make multiple choices from a menu:

```
multi.pick ← function(choice){
    picks ← NULL
    repeat{
        pick ← menu(choice)
        if(pick>0) picks ← c(picks,pick)
        else break
    }
    picks
}
```

7.3 An objection to the function in the previous exercise is that it doesn't explicitly allow the user to decide whether to exit or continue (using graphic input to select items, it may be easy to make a zero selection accidentally). Modify it, using the function cat to prompt the user with "More?[y/n]" and then read one item using the readline function. If the reply matches "n" break from the loop.

7.4 A different way to improve on multi.pick would be to add an extra choice, called "No more selections" to the menu, and break if the user picked this. Implement a version of multi.pick that uses this technique. Do you prefer this technique or the "More?[y/n]" prompt from the previous exercise?

7.2 Interface to C and Fortran

S functions can call routines written in C or Fortran. To make this work, you
must load the object code (i.e., the result of compiling the program using the C
or Fortran compiler) of the subroutine along with S. You must also write an S
function that uses the interface functions `.C` or `.Fortran` to invoke the subroutine. These steps involve a moderate amount of work, and before undertak-
ing it, you should ask yourself whether you really need to use special C or Fortran code. As an alternative, you can look for an equivalent way to solve your
problem using existing S functions. You might also be able to use the simpler
`unix` function to invoke a command. The C or Fortran interfaces are recommended if you have a well-tested, fairly complicated routine that would take
some time to rewrite as an S function, or if the computations are important and
will be much faster than an equivalent S function. And, of course, writing a
new subroutine may be your goal: in this case, dynamic loading and using S to
debug the routine often speeds up your work substantially.

   Loading Fortran or C routines with S may be done in two different
ways, dynamically or statically. For most applications, dynamic loading is preferred, but it is not currently available with all versions of the UNIX system.
Sections 7.2.1 and 7.2.2 are short descriptions of dynamic and static loading.
Section 7.2.3 follows up with a thorough discussion of the `.Fortran` and `.C`
functions.

7.2.1 *Dynamic Loading*

The easiest way to load your own routines written in C or Fortran with S is
use the `dyn.load` function.[†] For example, if you have a file `myfun.o` that
contains the object code for a routine you wish to call, use the expression

```
dyn.load("myfun.o")
```

The `dyn.load` function causes the object file to be loaded into the currently
running version of S, recognizes the routines that are defined inside `myfun.o`,
and resolves references between routines in `myfun.o` and routines in S (for
example, if a routine in `myfun.o` calls `printf` or another library routine that
is already present in S). Once `dyn.load` has been called, you can use functions `.C` and `.Fortran` to invoke routines loaded from `myfun.o`.

[†]The `dyn.load` function may not be available in all installations of S, depending on the
hardware and the version of the UNIX operating system.

To create an object file that can be used by `dyn.load`, follow these steps:

1. Use commands to create an object file. For example, if your source code is on the file `myfun.c`, then type

   ```
   $ make myfun.o
   ```

   or

   ```
   $ cc -c myfun.c
   ```

   In either case, you end up with an object file named `myfun.o`.

2. If there is only one routine, you can use the `dyn.load` function to load the object file directly:

   ```
   > dyn.load("myfun.o")
   ```

If you have several related routines (that call one another or that should be brought into S together) on several different source files, execute step 1 to produce an object file from each source file. Then execute

   ```
   $ ld -r -d -o all.o file1.o file2.o file3.o ...
   ```

This uses the loader, `ld`, to construct a single relocatable object file `all.o` by combining the individual object files `file1.o`, ... The specific name `all.o` is not important, although it must be different from any of the other file names. Use whatever name you feel is meaningful for the group of routines.

The `dyn.load` function returns an invisible character vector of the routines defined in the loaded object file.[†] Hence,

   ```
   print(dyn.load("all.o"))
   ```

is a way to find out exactly what routines are available in `all.o`.

Note that once the code is loaded, it is available for the remainder of the S session. You should not load the same version of the routines more than once per session, since it wastes space: see exercise 7.6 below. On the other hand, there are occasions when it is appropriate to reload object files. For example, if you are doing program development by modifying your Fortran or C routines and then trying out those routines in S, you can fix your source file, execute the `make`, `cc`, and `ld` commands while still running S, and then re-invoke `dyn.load`. The most recently loaded version of a routine is the one that is used when referred to in `.C` or `.Fortran` functions.

[†]Actually, the returned vector gives the external symbol names, which, on many systems, contain a leading underscore for C routines and a leading and trailing underscore for Fortran routines.

Exercises

7.5   Write a function to recompile and dynamically load the current version of a subroutine. You will want to make use of the `unix` function in doing this. Does your function do something appropriate if there were errors in the compilation process?

7.6   . If there were a way of checking to see if a particular routine had been loaded, then you could write a function like this:

```
foo ← function(x){
    do.load("/usr/joe/foo.o")
    .C("foo", x)
}
```

The `do.load` function would test to see if `"/usr/joe/foo.o"` had already been loaded, and if it had not, would `dyn.load` it. Write `do.load`.

7.2.2 *Static Loading: Private Copies of S*

Aside from `dyn.load`, there is another, less commonly used, process for loading subroutines with S, which constructs a local version of S in your current directory. Use this mechanism when your version of the operating system doesn't support `dyn.load`, when you have subroutines that will almost always be used, or when you have extensive sets of subroutines where `dyn.load` might prove too slow. The disadvantage here is that private copies of S take up lots of file space and must be recreated whenever changes are made to S.

If you find that having a local version of S is the proper approach in your situation, then invoke the command

```
$ S LOAD files ...
```

where *files* are the source files or libraries; e.g.,

```
$ S LOAD caps.c ppoint.r dchdc.f -lport
```

File names are expected to follow the convention that names ending in `.c`, `.f`, `.r`, and `.e` are C, Fortran, ratfor and efl source files respectively. Anything that does not follow this naming convention is assumed to be a library. The S LOAD command will make the object files corresponding to the source files and load these with S to form a local version of S in this directory. After this, when you run S in this directory, you will automatically get your local version including the subroutines in `caps.c`, etc.

7.2.3 *Using the* `.Fortran` *and* `.C` *Functions*

Once you have loaded the object code of your subroutine, the next step is to execute the subroutine. This is done by the interface functions `.Fortran` and `.C`. The C and Fortran interfaces to subroutines both work in essentially the same way. Consider a simple example. Suppose we have a Fortran routine that computes a set of plotting points for quantile-quantile plots. The first few lines of the subroutine are:

```
SUBROUTINE PPOINT(X,N)
REAL X(N)
INTEGER N
```

(the subroutine will overwrite the elements of X with suitable values in the range 0 to 1). In applications, N is known and the calling routine supplies a vector of N single-precision storage locations to hold the answer. The S expression to call this subroutine is:

```
.Fortran("ppoint", as.single(x), as.integer(n))
```

The interface call has one argument for each of the arguments to the Fortran subroutine, plus a first argument specifying the name of the subroutine. The arguments must have the *storage mode* expected by the Fortran routine; functions such as `as.single` should be used to assure this. To the Fortran routine, the argument will be an array of the corresponding Fortran data type. The value returned by `.Fortran` is a list, with one element for each of these Fortran arrays. Elements of this list may have names for easy reference. If the subroutine alters the data values in its arguments, as `ppoint` does, the corresponding element of the returned list will contain the altered values. This is the mechanism for transmitting data back from the Fortran subroutine.

The following S function uses the interface to Fortran to return a vector of plotting points:

```
ppoints ← function(x){
    n ← length(x)
    if(n<2){ n←x; x←single(n) }
    z ← .Fortran("ppoint", x=as.single(x), as.integer(n))
    z$x
}
```

The first element of the list returned by `.Fortran` is the vector of numbers computed by the subroutine; `ppoints` returns this as its value by using the name assigned to the argument.

To summarize, the interface to Fortran or C works as follows:

1. The first argument to `.C` or `.Fortran` is a character string naming the subroutine to be called.

2. Each of the remaining arguments must match the corresponding argument to the subroutine. Specifically, the data passed to the subroutine must have the correct `storage.mode`, and must have as many elements as the subroutine expects, since Fortran and C cannot find out either the kind of data or the length.

3. The name fields of these arguments can be specified to make it easier to extract those arguments from the returned list.

4. The value returned by `.C` or `.Fortran` is a list containing all the arguments passed to the subroutine.

5. The data in those arguments will reflect any changes made by the subroutine. Also, any attributes in the arguments will be retained, so that matrix arguments will come back as matrices, etc.

Point 2 is something new in S programming. The interface to C or Fortran depends on the way data is stored internally—this is the one place in S where you need to worry about *storage modes*. The S function calling `.C` or `.Fortran` must make sure that the arguments have storage modes equivalent to the data type declared for the corresponding argument in the C or Fortran routine. Storage modes are more detailed than the modes used elsewhere in S, in the sense that it is necessary to distinguish three storage modes, `double`, `single`, and `integer`, all of which correspond to the ordinary mode `numeric`. The storage modes and the corresponding data type declarations in C and Fortran are given in the following table.

S Storage Mode	C	Fortran
`"logical"`	`long *`	`LOGICAL`
`"integer"`	`long *`	`INTEGER`
`"single"`	`float *`	`REAL`
`"double"`	`double *`	`DOUBLE PRECISION`
`"character"`	`char **`	`CHARACTER(*)`
`"complex"`	`struct {`	`DOUBLE COMPLEX`†
	`double re, im; } *`	
`"list"`	`void **`	

Table 7.1. Storage modes in S, and corresponding data type declarations for subroutine arguments in C and Fortran.

The first column of the table gives the S storage mode; the second column shows how C programs should declare the corresponding arguments, and the third column shows the corresponding Fortran declarations. The last line is special; we will defer discussing it until section 7.2.4.

---

†Double complex is an extension to the Fortran 77 standard that is supplied by some versions of the `f77` compiler.

Once you have decided what storage mode a particular argument should have, there are two ways to get it. One is to use functions to generate or coerce an object to a vector with a given storage mode. These are functions like

```
double(n)
as.double(x)
```

which will generate an object of length n and coerce an object x to have storage mode "double". The functions character, complex, and list have already been encountered in sections 5.1 and 5.2, along with the corresponding coercing functions. The functions integer, single, and double, however, are specializations of numeric. They have no use other than in preparing vectors to pass to C or Fortran.

The functions above create vectors; that is, objects without special attributes. However, as mentioned in point 5 above, it is possible to retain attributes in the arguments. If this makes sense, you must still set the storage mode, in this case by assigning it directly:

```
storage.mode(x) ← "double"
```

The storage mode should be assigned immediately before the call to .C or .Fortran. Doing calculations on numeric objects may change the storage mode.

Let's look at a call to a C routine. The expression

```
.C("caps", as.character(x), as.integer(length(x)))
```

calls the interface .C to invoke a C subroutine named caps with two arguments. The first is coerced to be a vector of storage mode "character" and the second a vector of storage mode "integer". The S character vector corresponds to a data declaration of

```
char **
```

in C, that is, to a pointer to (a vector of) character pointers. The storage mode "integer" corresponds to a declaration

```
long *
```

Since the C language has a more general data-typing mechanism than Fortran, programming with the C interface requires more consideration of type matching. All the data types of the arguments to the C subroutines must be pointers, since they correspond to vectors in S, not to C scalars, and the data types must be among those shown in Table 7.1.

A subroutine `caps` corresponding to the `.C` call above is:

```
caps(strings, nstrings)
char **strings; long *nstrings;
{
    int c, diff = 'A' - 'a'; long n = *nstrings;
    while(n--){
        if((c=**strings)>='a' && c<='z')
            **strings = c + diff;
        strings++;
    }
}
```

Note that the second argument is a pointer, not a scalar as it more typically would be in writing C programs. You may need to change existing C routines to satisfy the data type requirements in Table 7.1. The changes are usually minor; for example, defining the local variable n in `caps` to hold the value pointed to by `nstrings`.

For both C and Fortran, function subprograms that normally return a (scalar) value need to be converted into subroutines that return the value through one of their arguments. This is usually easy, and is also an opportunity to return a vector of values in one call, to make the interface simpler and more efficient. Suppose, for example, we have a Fortran function that computes the Bessel function J_0:

```
DOUBLE PRECISION FUNCTION BESSJ0(X)
DOUBLE PRECISION X
...
```

To write an interface to `BESSJ0`, first define a subroutine that calls it:

```
SUBROUTINE SBESJ0(X, N)
DOUBLE PRECISION X(1)
INTEGER N

INTEGER I
DOUBLE PRECISION BESSJ0
DO I = 1, N
  X(I) = BESSJ0(X(I))
ENDDO

RETURN
END
```

A corresponding S function would be:

```
j0 ← function(x)
    .Fortran("sbesj0",x=as.double(x),
        as.integer(length(x)))$x
```

The subroutine is free to overwrite its argument, and is encouraged to do so for efficiency, rather than having a separate argument for the answers. The S interface ensures that no harmful side effects occur, since the arguments are copies.

Well-tested subroutine libraries are good sources for numerical algorithms, particularly Fortran algorithms for matrix operations. The subroutines in these libraries are usually designed for portability and generality. In addition, the subroutines normally are purely computational—they do not try to do any input or output. A restriction on Fortran routines called from S is that they cannot use Fortran input or output facilities. Fortran I/O must be eliminated from any subroutines before they can be used with S.

When using library subroutines from S, it is often possible to write an interface routine with a simpler calling sequence. For example, the algorithm DCHDC, from the LINPACK library,[†] computes a Choleski decomposition of a positive-definite matrix. The arguments to the routine are as follows:

```
SUBROUTINE DCHDC(A,LDA,P,WORK,JPVT,JOB,RANK)
INTEGER LDA,P,JPVT(P),JOB,RANK
DOUBLE PRECISION A(LDA,P),WORK(P)
```

The matrix A is square and symmetric of size P by P. On return, the upper triangle of the matrix contains the square root, computed by the Choleski decomposition. If JOB is nonzero, the algorithm will pivot variables in such a way as to handle semidefinite matrices. The vector JPVT is returned containing the pivoting of rows and columns performed; WORK is a work array. This algorithm is a typical example of a rather long, carefully constructed and tested subprogram that we would much rather not have to recode in S, even aside from efficiency considerations.

As usual, we must decide first what we really want in the result. We can start with the simplest version, in which no pivoting is done and the result is returned entirely in the matrix argument. For efficiency and to make the S function more readable, it is probably worth writing a new subroutine to call the LINPACK routine:

```
SUBROUTINE SDCHD(A,P,WORK,RANK)
INTEGER P,JPVT(1),RANK
DOUBLE PRECISION A(P,P),WORK(P)

CALL DCHDC(A,P,P,WORK,JPVT,0,RANK)
RETURN
END
```

This subroutine knows that S matrices have leading dimension equal to the actual number of rows, so that a separate LDA argument is not needed. An S Choleski function would then be:

[†]J. J. Dongarra, J. R. Bunch, C. B. Moler, G. W. Stewart, *LINPACK Users' Guide*, SIAM, 1979.

```
choleski ← function(a){
    p ← nrow(a)
    storage.mode(a) ← "double"
    z ← .Fortran("sdchd",a=a, p, double(p), rank=integer(1))
    if(z$rank<p) stop("Choleski decomposition is singular")
    z$a
}
```

Only the data values of a are passed to the Fortran routine; the changed values in a, along with all attributes of a, become part of the result of .Fortran. The assignment

```
storage.mode(a) ← "double"
```

makes sure that the data portion of the matrix a has storage mode "double", but does not cause it to lose its matrix nature as would be the case if

```
as.double(a)
```

were used.

The more general form of the LINPACK Choleski algorithm raises a question about what kind of S object should represent the result. The value of the function should be a matrix, (the decomposition itself) but also needs information describing the pivoting that was done. We can incorporate decompositions of singular matrices by returning the rank as part of the data structure. A convenient way to handle all this in S is to return the pivoting vector and the rank as further *attributes* of the result. The S expression

```
attr(a,"rank") ← z$rank
```

sets the attribute "rank" to the value of the expression on the right. (For a discussion of these ideas more generally, see chapter 8.) We now add an optional argument pivot to the S function, to allow pivoting to be done, and include attributes rank and pivot in the object returned when pivoting is allowed. We revert to using the original LINPACK subroutine (we could still have simplified the calling sequence slightly, but didn't bother).

```
choleski ← function(a,pivot=FALSE){
    if(!is.matrix(a))
        stop("choleski() needs a matrix")
    storage.mode(a) ← "double"
    p ← nrow(a).
    if(p != ncol(a))
        stop("choleski() needs a square matrix")
    z ← .Fortran("dchdc",a=a,p,p,double(p),
        pivot=as.integer(rep(0,p)),as.integer(pivot),
        rank=integer(1))
    a ← z$a
```

```
    if(pivot){
        attr(a,"pivot") ← z$pivot
        attr(a,"rank") ← z$rank
    }
    else if(z$rank<p)
        stop("Choleski decomposition is singular")
    a
}
```

We have also added a couple of checks on the matrix argument.

Let's look at another C example, which will lead to some additional design questions. Suppose we want an S function that returns substrings of the elements of a character vector; for example,

```
substring(text,2,6)
```

returns a character vector in which each element is the 2nd through the 6th character of the corresponding element in `text`. In case we need to know which state names begin with "New",

```
> state.name[substring(state.name,1,3) == "New"]
[1] "New Hampshire" "New Jersey"     "New Mexico"
[4] "New York"
```

A C subroutine to perform this computation would be

```
substrs(strings, nstrings, first, last)
char **strings; long *nstrings, *first, *last;
{
    char *p; long n, f, lst, slen;
    n = *nstrings; f = *first - 1; lst = *last - 1;
    while(n--) {
        p = *strings;
        slen = strlen(p);
        if(lst < slen) p[lst+1] = '\0';
        if(f > slen) *p = '\0';
        else p += f;
        *strings++ = p;
    }
}
```

For storage allocation in a C routine, invoke S_alloc, which is identical to the usual `calloc`, except that S automatically frees the space.

An S function to use the `substrs` subroutine would be:

```
substring ← function(text,first,last){
    storage.mode(text) ← "character"
    if(first>last) stop("must have first <= last")
    if(length(first)>1 || length(last)>1)
        stop("first and last must be single numbers")
    .C("substrs",text=text, length(text),as.integer(first),
        as.integer(last))$text
}
```

In substring, the condition first <= last is probably reasonable, but the second condition, that these two arguments be single numbers, is more for our convenience in designing the function than from logical necessity. The user might want to select different substrings from different elements in the text. We are now at a typical design decision: to balance increased generality in the S function against extra software design effort and, perhaps, reduced efficiency in handling simple cases.

Suppose we decide to allow arbitrary lengths for the three arguments to substring. A reasonable definition seems to be that we will extend first, last, and text to the same length by repeating shorter vectors cyclically. It might seem natural to pass all three lengths down to the C subroutine and let that routine do the cycling. But we have deliberately kept the interface to C simple by assuming that the C routine will *not* allocate any S data. We do not want to put the added complexity on the C level where programming, making changes, and debugging are relatively painful. A better principle is to keep the C and Fortran logic as simple as possible and do the manipulation in S, where it is usually easier. In this case, for example, the C code can be generalized simply by assuming that strings, first, and last all point to vectors of length n. The only change needed in the C routine is to add two statements inside the top of the while loop:

```
f = *first++ - 1;
l = *last++ - 1;
```

The S function must now generate appropriate vectors of elements (see exercise 7.10).

As unlikely as it seems when you write the code, there may occasionally be an error in the Fortran or C routines that you are executing from S. When that happens, the result may be a terse message and an abort from S:

```
> myfun ()
System terminating: bad address
$
```

Although S could print a message without aborting, the abort is done in the interest of safety. There is no protection between the S executive and the buggy routine—thus there may have been damage done to other parts of S. S aborts rather than execute with possibly corrupted data internal structures. Another safety feature is to use

```
options (check=TRUE)
```

while testing new Fortran and C algorithms. This causes S to perform extra consistency checks that can catch errors.

This leads to the next problem: when you have a problem, how do you diagnose what went wrong? In a C routine, your best bet is to insert calls to printf in order to determine what is happening at various stages of execution.

If the problem is in a Fortran routine, you must use one of the following debug print routines, since you cannot use any Fortran input or output routines.

```
SUBROUTINE DBLEPR(LABEL,NCHAR,DATA,NDATA)
SUBROUTINE  INTPR(LABEL,NCHAR,DATA,NDATA)
SUBROUTINE REALPR(LABEL,NCHAR,DATA,NDATA)
```

These routines can be called from Fortran and take as arguments a character string to label the output, the number of characters in LABEL, a data vector, and the number of elements in the data vector. For example, to print the WORK vector in subroutine SDCHD, insert

```
CALL DBLEPR("Work Vector",11,WORK,P)
```

in the appropriate place. See DBLEPR in Appendix 1 for more details.

Exercises

7.7   Implement a function to call the C caps routine. Implement a similar function using the unix function and the tr command. Do they produce the same answers? Which was easier to write?

7.8   Write a C routine that will capitalize the first letter of each word in its input arguments. The caps function should be a good place to start.

7.9   How would you modify the error message in the choleski routine to include the returned rank in the message "Choleski decomposition is singular"?

7.10   Modify the S function substring to make first, last, and text all of length equal to the maximum of the lengths of the three arguments. (The function rep will be useful.) Change the test first > last to check for failures anywhere in the two vectors.

7.11   The randu random number generator was an early linear-congruential algorithm for generating pseudorandom numbers on the interval 0 to 1. Here is a C routine that implements the generator (on a 32-bit machine).

```
randu(seed,n,output)
long *seed, *n; float *output;
{
    long i = *n, j = *seed;

    while(i--){
        j = j*65539 & 0x7fffffff;
        *output++ = j/2147483648.;
    }
}
```

The following function turns the C function into an S function:

```
randu ← function(n, seed=12345)
    .C("randu", as.integer(seed),
        as.integer(n),
        result=single(n))$result
```

Implement the `randu` function with your version of S, using either `dyn.load` or `S LOAD`. Try generating a matrix of numbers from `randu`:

```
m.from.randu ← matrix( randu(3000),1000,3,byrow=T )
```

Can you find the bad statistical properties of `randu` in `m.from.randu`?

Warning: This random number generator has bad statistical properties, and should *NEVER* be used for actual applications.

7.2.4 *Calling S from C*

So far, the assumption has been that the underlying data being passed to C or Fortran has been atomic; in particular, numeric or character. There are a few cases where you need to pass a pointer to C that corresponds to an entire S object. We won't discuss in this book C code that actually manipulates S objects internally—you rarely need to do this. However, there are some important applications where we would like to pass pointers to S objects *through* C and on to S again. The `list` line in Table 7.1 is designed to do just that. The elements in the list will correspond to pointers (to an undefined type, hence the `void *` declaration). The C code should not do anything to them (other than moving them around).

The application is to pass an S *function* to a C routine, which will then eventually arrange to have that function called, with data that will be determined in the C code. This technique is a flexible way to use subroutines to solve equations, do minimization, or fit nonlinear models. We want users to describe their functions or models in S, but we would like to use C or Fortran algorithms in many cases to solve the underlying numerical problem. The rest of this section describes how to organize such computations.

Figure 7.1 shows the relationships amongst the routines we will employ in this section. Refer back to it whenever you need an overview of what is going on.

S provides a C routine, `call_S`, which your C code can invoke to cause the evaluation of an S function call. Your C routine will provide a pointer to an S function definition and the necessary names, modes, lengths, and data values for the arguments in the function call. The `call_S` routine will communicate with S and return the number of results and pointers to the results. Thus, `call_S` is the inverse of the communication from S to C or Fortran.

Let's consider an example to make clearer the relationships among the pieces. The example will consider the problem of finding an approximate zero for a numeric function.

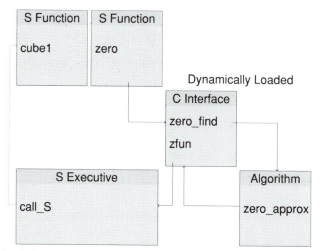

Figure 7.1. Organization of the `call_S` example. The arrows show function calls. The dotted arrow is an evaluation of `cube1` by the S executive. The routines in the bottom two rows are written in C; those in the top row are written in S. There are several sets of programmers involved: the ultimate user writes `cube1`, the S programmer writes `zero` and the C interface routines, and the S executive and algorithm are already written and are treated as black boxes.

We start with a subroutine implementing an algorithm for this problem, say a C function

```
double zero_approx(f,a,b,tol)
double a,b,tol;
double (*f)();
```

This C function takes two initial guesses, a and b, which bound the location of the zero, a tolerance `tol` saying how close to zero the user needs the result, and a pointer to the C function (of one argument), whose root or zero-crossing we want to find. Just to avoid confusing reuse of the word "function", let's call this the *curve*. We will call `zero_approx` the *algorithm*. This is what you have to start with: someone wrote the algorithm, not usually with any idea of calling it from S. You probably do not want to change it, except for minor details that don't involve the method itself. You do want to make it available, with your users able to define the curve in S, call your S function, and get back the root. So you want to end up with an S function

```
zero(f,guesses,tol)
```

that takes a function name or function definition, f, some initial guesses for the root, and an optional tolerance. The rest of this section shows how to build a bridge between your function and the algorithm.

The general technique, which applies to all such projects, is as follows. From S, your function will use .C to call a C routine, supplying the C routine with an S function definition, plus the guesses and tolerance. You will write this C routine. It will call the algorithm with the user's initial guesses and tolerance, but with a *fixed* C function that we will call zfun in our example. This C function, which you also need to write, will invoke call_S, giving it a (pointer to) the S function defining the curve, and a value in C (supplied by the algorithm) which will become the argument to the curve. Then call_S will return the value computed by the curve function to zfun, which will hand it back to the algorithm. In this way you have provided communication from S to the algorithm and back to S again. The algorithm can now iterate, happily unaware that S is involved, while your user can be equally unaware of the C code underlying the method.

Clearly, this is a subtler programming task than anything we have presented before, but it is not really difficult once you have practiced it a few times, and it opens up some very powerful iterative methods to use from S. Also, the approach outlined below keeps the C programming small and relatively simple. Let's complete the implementation of this example to see how it works. We will need a bit of extra C code to provide a subroutine suitable for the .C interface, and to hide away the pointer to the S function: let's assume this is a C routine called zero_find. Then an S function using zero_find could look like this:

```
zero ← function(f, guesses, tol = 1e-07){
    z ← .C("zero_find",
        list(f),
        ans=as.double(guesses),
        as.double(tol))
    z$ans[1]
}
```

The argument f is supposed to be a function definition. Notice the use of list to pass this to C. We expect zero_find to return the answer in the first element of the double vector passed to it. A suitable definition for zero_find is:

```
static void *func;

zero_find(ff, x, tol)
void **ff; double *x, *tol;
{
    double zfun(), zero();
    func = ff[0];
    x[0] = zero_approx(zfun,x[0],x[1],tol[0]);
}
```

The subroutine zero_find gets two initial guesses in x, and the tolerance for error. It stores in the static pointer func a pointer to an S function, calls the algorithm and returns the answer in x. Note the use of void ** for the pointer corresponding to mode list.

We are calling the algorithm with the function `zfun` for the curve. Now we have to write `zfun` to use `call_S`. Here is a description of the `call_S` aruguments.

```
call_S(func, nargs, arguments, modes,
        lengths, names, nres, results)
void *func;
void **arguments, **modes, **names, **results;
long nargs, *lengths, nres;
```

The first argument to `call_S` is the pointer to the S function. The next four describe what should go into the call to the S function: `nargs` is the number of arguments, and `modes`, `lengths`, and `names` are pointers to the modes (as character strings), the lengths and the names (again, character strings) for the arguments. In `arguments` we store pointers to data values. These pointers should follow the rules used in Table 7.1; for example, for `double` data, the corresponding element of `arguments` should be a pointer to double in C. However, we cast each of these to be a pointer to `void`. The last two arguments say how many results we want back from the S function and provide a vector of that size in which pointers to the results will be stuffed by `call_S`. Note that all of these C vectors must be allocated, of the right length, in `zfun`, and the vectors corresponding to arguments must be filled in before calling `call_S`. See `call_s` in Appendix 1 for details. After the return from `call_S`, we will extract the data we want from `results`.

In our example, there is only one argument, of type double and length 1. We don't care about its name, so we pass a 0 instead of that pointer. We expect a single result back, of storage mode `double`. Then `zfun` can be written as follows:

```
static double zfun(z)
double z;
{
    void *args[1], *values[1]; double zz[1], *result;
    char *mode[1]; long length[1];
    mode[0] = "double"; length[0] = 1;
    args[0] = (void *)(zz); zz[0] = z;
    call_S(func,1L,args,mode,length,(void **)0,1L,values);
    result = (double *)values[0];
    return( result[0] );
}
```

The first two lines of the body declare the arrays to hold the pointers needed, the next two stuff in the appropriate information about the arguments. Then we invoke `call_S`; we let it overwrite the pointer in `values[0]` with the result. We cast this pointer to the appropriate C type, and return the first element to the algorithm.

That's enough, in principle, to allow us to use our `zero` function in S. We will show an example, but then we want to strongly urge an extra

precaution in actual use. Let's define a cubic polynomial with one real root at
1.5:

```
cube1 ← function(x)
    (x^2 + 1) * (x - 1.5)
```

Our `zero` algorithm needs initial guesses at points where the curve has opposite sign. Figure 7.2 shows the curve; let's choose 0 and 5 as the guesses.

```
> x0 ← zero(cube1,c(0,5))
> x0
[1] 1.5
> print(x0,15)
[1] 1.49999999993834
```

(We printed the result to 15 significant figures to show we weren't cheating—
we didn't get the *exact* answer.)

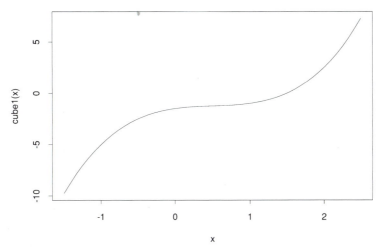

Figure 7.2. Cubic curve to test `zero`.

This looks fine, but there is a serious danger that needs to be handled
in our `zero` function; namely, that the user's curve function may not produce
the right kind of data to return to the C routine. While `call_s` can check for
some problems, it cannot verify that the storage mode is as asserted nor that
the lengths of the individual results are what the C code expects. For example,
suppose we wanted to test `zero` on a version of the cubic that truncated its
result to integer values. This works fine if we do it the usual way, but if we
happened to do something that set the storage mode to "`integer`" instead of
the expected "`double`", the numbers in `zero_find` are nonsense:

```
> cube2 ← function(x)
+     trunc((x^2 + 1) * (x - 1.5))
> zero(cube2,c(0,5)) #ok
[1] 1.445313
```

```
> cube3 ← function(x)
+    as.integer((x^2 + 1) * (x - 1.5))
> zero(cube3,c(0,5)) #NOT OK!
[1] 5
```

In other applications, where the length of one of the results is assumed in the C code, considerably worse disasters can occur. Just as, when using .C, we made sure the storage mode of the arguments was correct, so here we must make sure that the function invoked by `call_S` returns the right thing. There are several ways to do this, but the simplest in most applications is to assign the user's function, under a chosen name, in frame 1, where it will be available throughout the expression in which `zero` was called. Then we pass down to the algorithm, and thus back through `call_S`, a function of our own that calls the user's function, but that also can do some checking before and/or after.

Suppose we assign the user's function as "U" in frame 1 and create a function `f.check` that calls U, checks for a numeric result, and makes sure the storage mode is "double".

```
zero ← function(f, guesses, tol = 1e-07){
    f.check ← function(x){
        x ← U(x)
        if(!is.numeric(x))
            stop("Need a numeric result")
        as.double(x)
    }
    assign("U",f,frame=1)
    z ← .C("zero_find",
        list(f.check),
        ans = as.double(guesses),
        as.double(tol))
    z$ans[1]
}
```

Now the integer storage mode returned by `cube3` does no harm, and we can also check for ridiculous functions passed to `zero`:

```
> zero(cube3,c(0,5))
[1] 1.445313
> zero(paste,c(0,5))
Error: Need a numeric result
```

The key design point to keep in mind is that checks needed by the C code using `call_S` should be designed into the function that calls the corresponding algorithm. This is the stage at which the algorithm needs to be understood. Once a function like `zero` has been implemented, its users should be in as little danger as possible of coming to grief down in the C code.

Exercises

7.12   Are there other checks that `f.check` should make? What about the length of the result or the mode of the argument?

7.13   How would you implement an optional `trace` argument to `zero` that printed out the value of the argument and the result each time the curve function was called?

7.14*   Suppose the curve function could have other arguments, which were supplied as optional arguments to `zero`, using the "..." mechanism. How would you arrange for `zero` to make these available to the curve function?

7.3 Specialized Techniques

This section describes a few functions used in special situations. For example, we introduce functions to create files with unique names and to remove those files. We discuss the `on.exit` function, which provides a mechanism that allows cleanup actions to be performed when a function is exited, normally or because of an error. The section also describes techniques for writing functions that manipulate data of different modes and for writing your own infix and assignment operators.

7.3.1 *Making Files; Cleaning Up;* `on.exit`

In section 6.3, we described how the interface to commands could be used to perform tasks inside S functions. We used the `unix` function to execute the commands and to optionally send an S object to the standard input of the command. In this section, we will investigate how to use a command that expects two or more files as input.

Suppose we would like to see how two S functions differ from one another. Perhaps they carry out two slightly different versions of the same computation, and we would like to see only their differences. The `diff` command does precisely that when given two input files—it prints the differences between the two files. Hence, if we can get our two functions written to files and run the `diff` command, we can have what we desire.

Consider the following function:

```
function.diff ← function(f1, f2){
    file1 ← tempfile("diff1")
    file2 ← tempfile("diff2")
    on.exit(unlink(c(file1, file2)))
    cat(f1, sep = "\n", file = file1)
    cat(f2, sep = "\n", file = file2)
    if(!unix(paste("diff", file1, file2), output = F))
        cat("Identical\n")
}
```

The `function.diff` function illustrates three techniques:

- cleaning up on exit from the function;
- generating unique names for files or other things;
- using the return code from the `unix` function.

The style used in `function.diff` is recommended for any function with a temporary side effect that ought to be cleaned up before the function exits. In this case, `function.diff` creates two files, which should be unlinked after they are used. The call to `on.exit` does that, even if an error or interrupt occurs. The function `on.exit` takes a single S expression as its argument. It *does not evaluate the expression*, but saves it, associated with the local frame from which `on.exit` was called. When the function associated with the frame finishes execution, or when a `stop()` or other interrupt occurs before computations in that frame are finished, the expression given to `on.exit` will then be evaluated. So, in this case,

```
on.exit(unlink(c(file1,file2)))
```

ensures that the files go away. The expression to be evaluated can be changed by another call to `on.exit`; in particular, to delete an expression from the `on.exit` list, call it with an empty argument

```
on.exit()
```

This is the approach, for example, to specify an `on.exit` condition for errors, but not for normal completion.

```
function(...){
    on.exit(cat("Error occurred\n"))
    # do computations here ...
    on.exit() # no message for normal return
    value # to be returned from the function
}
```

Another use for `on.exit` is to cancel a change made by calling `options`. Suppose we use `options` to change a parameter, such as the number of digits in printing.

```
quick.print ← function(...){
    on.exit(options(old))
    old ← options(digits=2)
    for( el in list(...)){
        print(el)
        cat("\n")
    }
    invisible()
}
```

In addition to `on.exit` to reset the `digits` option, this function also uses `invisible` in order to return a nonprinting `NULL` value. This is to prevent the automatic printing of the value of the function. The function `quick.print` basically exists not for its value but for its *side effect*, that is, the primary purpose of the function is to produce printed output, not to return a value. There are several other S functions with side effects; they may modify a permanent S object, set a graphical parameter, or perform printing. Functions with *hidden* side effects are bad; they make your programming harder to understand—but side effects like printing and plotting are benign.

Another technique illustrated by `function.diff` is the generation of unique file names, so that one function's output won't accidentally overwrite that of another function. A call to `tempfile` generates a file name that should be unique, both for successive calls by the same user and also for calls by different users. This sounds like a difficult proposition, but the use of the `unix` interface makes it easy:

```
tempfile ← function(pattern = "file")
    unix(paste("echo /tmp/", pattern, "$$", sep = ""))
```

The command echoes back a string consisting of "/tmp/", the optional pattern (this is just to make the file name more informative) and the process number of the command itself. Since the operating system generates process numbers sequentially, it is highly unlikely that a duplicate will arise.

Finally, `function.diff` uses the value returned by the `unix` function to print a message if the two functions are identical. By default, `unix` returns the character vector produced by the command it invokes. However, when given argument `output=FALSE`, it returns the exit status of the command. The `diff` command has a zero exit status if there are no differences, and a nonzero status if differences were found.

Exercises

7.15   Fancy up the `quick.print` function to allow users to supply informative argument names that will be printed, on separate lines, before each argument. If there was no corresponding name, print the argument number.

7.3.2 *Functions for Data Manipulation*

Functions that manipulate data objects, rather than doing numerical calculations, should work cleanly regardless of whether the data involved are numbers, character strings or list-like data. A nice way to do this for some applications is to define the computation for integer data, and then use the subset operator to extend it to arbitrary data. The S function `rep` illustrates this technique. The `rep` function replicates the data in its first argument according to the pattern in the second argument. Either the whole vector is replicated or each element in turn is replicated, depending on the length of the second argument:

```
> labels ← c("HIGH","Med","low")
> rep(labels,3)
        "HIGH"   "Med"    "low"    "HIGH"   "Med"
[6]     "low"    "HIGH"   "Med"    "low"
> rep(labels,1:3)
        "HIGH"   "Med"    "Med"    "low"    "low"
[6]     "low"
```

Suppose this function is already defined for the special case that the data is stored as integers, say by the function `rep.int`. Then `rep` uses `rep.int` directly for integer data and uses `rep.int` to define the subset needed with other data:

```
rep ← function(x, pattern)
    if(storage.mode(x)=="integer")rep.int(x, pattern)
    else x[ rep.int(seq(along=x), pattern) ]
```

Now we can put our effort into designing `rep.int`, with the advantage that there is no worry about the kind of data being manipulated. Even implementing the computation in C (see section 7.2) is reasonable, assuming a real need for efficiency.

Exercises

7.16   How does `rep` work? For example, in executing

```
rep(labels,1:3)
```

what is the value of

```
rep.int(seq(x),pattern) ?
```

7.17   The function

```
sample(x, size)
```

produces a random sample of a specified `size`, from the arbitrary vector `x`. Suppose that a function `sample.index` exists, such that the call

```
sample.index(size,n)
```

returns a similar sample from the vector `1:n`. Write the general version of `sample` using `sample.index`. The designs of `sample.index` and `rep.int` are slightly different. In what way? Does it matter?

7.18 It would be nice to be able to generate a small sample from a very large population (say from the `5e9` people in the world) without having to generate the vector for the entire population first. Rewrite `sample` so that the user can give it a single number for the first argument and have the sample generated from a population of that size; for example

```
sample(5e9,100)
```

to get a sample of 100 from the set `1:5e9`.

7.19 The actual definition of `rep` allows a third argument, the desired length of the returned vector. If this argument is given, `pattern` is not used.

```
rep ← function(x, pattern, length.out=0){
    if(!missing(length.out))
        rep(x, ceiling(length.out/length(x)))[1:length.out]
    else if(storage.mode(x)=="integer") rep.int(x, pattern)
    else x[ rep.int(seq(x), pattern) ]
}
```

Explain how this works when `length.out` is supplied.

7.20 Why did we name the third argument of the `rep` function `length.out` rather than naming it `length`?

7.3.3 *User-Defined Operators*

In scientific work, it is natural to think of some functions as *operators*; e.g., we write addition as `x+y` rather than `"+"(x,y)`, even though the second form is a perfectly correct S expression. Along with the operators built into the S parser, you can define new operators using the convention explained here. The parser treats any set of characters delimited by `%` characters (and not containing a newline) as the name of an operator. Thus, an S expression, for matrix multiplication,

```
x %*% y
```

is equivalent to `"%*%"(x,y)`, and is evaluated by calling the function "`%*%`". These operators have precedence just below "`:`" (see section 3.2.6).

To create a special operator, we just need to define a function with the operator's name. For example, we might have a Fortran routine named `matmpy` to do matrix multiplication:

```
"%*%" ← function(x,y)
    .Fortran("matmpy",
        as.double(x),as.integer(dim(x)),
        as.double(y),as.integer(dim(y)),
        ans=matrix(0,nrow(x),ncol(y)))$ans
```

Defining new operators relies on being able to use "names" for objects that are not syntactically correct names in the language. In fact, nearly any string can appear, quoted, on the left of an assignment. To refer to this object, the expression `get("%*%")` will be needed, since `%*%` is not syntactically a name. Otherwise, there is nothing special about the object. To save typing, it may be convenient to develop such a function with an ordinary name, say `matmpy` in this case, just assigning it the special name `%*%` when it is ready to use.

Exercises

7.21   Define a multivariate comparison operator `%<%` to compare matrices `x` and `y` (assumed to have identical dimension attributes). The operator should return a vector of length `nrow(x)` whose elements should be TRUE if and only if *all* the elements in the corresponding row of `x` are less than those of `y`.

7.22*   The definition of `%<%` is not quite right. Logically, we would like to believe that

```
(x %<% y) %==% !(x %>=% y)
```

Design a set of comparison operators `%<%`, `%<=%`, `%==%`, etc., to make these relationships hold as much as possible. Hint: consider a three-valued logic: TRUE, FALSE, and NA.

7.23*   It is straightforward to redefine built-in operators (although it is not a very safe thing to do). Arrange for the operator `<` to be defined as `%<%` if the operands are lists and to have its old definition otherwise. You should install the new version in the session frame (see section 5.4) and use an object, say `.newcomp`, to mark the operators as overloaded.

7.3.4 *User-Defined Assignments*

We have shown assignment expressions with a variety of functions and operators on the left side, to replace some subset, element, or specific attribute of an object; for example,

```
x[1:length(x)/2] ← 0
dim(x) ← rev(dim(x))
```

Functions can be nested on the left side also:

```
dimnames(xmat) [[2]] [1] ← "Intercept"
```

So far, we have only used a limited set of left-side functions, but in fact S has a completely general method of evaluating assignments that makes it easy for you to arrange for any function to be used on the left side of an assignment, to replace any property of the object.

For an arbitrary function name, f, S evaluates the expression

```
f(x) ← value
```

as if it were the expression

```
x ← "f<-"(x,value)
```

The function named "f<-", which we will call the *replacement function* corresponding to f, is supposed to return the new version of x, after modifying whatever it is that f refers to, using the new data in value. To allow a new function on the left side of assignments, write a function that does the suitable replacement and give it the name to be used on the left side, followed by the two characters "<-". As an example, let's write a function to replace the diagonal elements of a matrix, so we can write expressions like

```
diag(r) ← diag(r) * 1.1
```

The function "diag<-" (call it "diag gets") could be defined as:

```
"diag<-" ← function(x, newdiag){
   x[row(x)==col(x)] ← newdiag
   x
}
```

Notice that "diag<-" returns the entire new object as its value. It does not worry at all about assignments as such—the S evaluator takes care of all that. It is necessary that there be a consistent right-side (i.e., ordinary) function corresponding to a left-side function. Otherwise, nested use of the left-side function will not work right (see section 11.2 if you want to know why). In other words, whatever property of the object is replaced by "f<-" must be extracted by the corresponding function "f".

Replacement functions can have any number of arguments, so long as they follow the convention that the *first* argument is the object in which the replacement is taking place. For example, the subset replacement function would be defined as

```
"[<-" ← function(object,...){
    ...
```

Actually, S provides internal definitions of this and the other replacement functions we presented earlier in the book, so that these very common assignments will be done more efficiently.

Exercises

7.24   Define a replacement function so that the assignment

```
row.labels(x) ← value
```

will replace the row labels of the given matrix with the new values. (Make sure it works whether or not x currently has row labels.) Define the appropriate right-side function as well. You would like to have it return a vector of empty character strings if x has no `dimnames` attribute. Why?

7.25   Generalize the previous exercise to allow extracting and replacing the labels for the i-th dimension of a multi-way array, a, via:

```
alabels(x,i) ← newlabels
```

Consider how you would allow i to be of length greater than 1.

7.26   The definition of "diag<-" in the text was an inefficient way to find the diagonal of the matrix. Write a version that does not generate intermediate matrices like `row(x)`.

Define functions that allow the time-series attributes `start(x)`, `end(x)`, and `frequency(x)` to appear on the left side of an assignment. You will need to decide how to change the other time-series parameters to keep consistency. Use a rule that says that changing the start or end date shifts the series, while changing `frequency` either selects from the current series or expands it. You can reasonably require that the old and new values of `frequency` are integer multiples, one way or the other.

7.3.5 *Efficiency: Time and Memory*

The efficiency of a particular computation usually depends in a complicated way on the local computing environment, including hardware, operating system peculiarities, and other computations competing for the machine. In most programming applications, it is unwise to worry about details of performance until the programs do what they are supposed to and are acceptable in design to their users. At that point, you may investigate the resources used by the computations and look for improvements. The idea is to look for the place where the computations use the most resources and then work at improving performance in that place. The two resources likely to become limiting factors for computations in S are the *time* taken to do the calculation and the amount of intermediate *memory* required.

For the people using the software, the most important resource is the "real" (that is, clock) time that the computation takes, but this measure is the most affected by other circumstances and the least reproducible. S provides this and two other measures of timing, as well as access to the pattern of memory used by the functions in a computation. The expression unix.time(expr) returns the time taken to evaluate expr. Time is returned as three numbers: user, system, and real time. All times are returned in seconds. The first of these measures the processor time used in S, the second the time used by the operating system in response to S's requests (e.g., disk reads and writes). As a simple example, let's look at the time taken to generate 10000 numbers from the uniform random generator. We will repeat the calculations 10 times.

```
> times ← numeric()
> for(i in 1:10)
+    times ← c(times,unix.time(runif(10000)))
> times ← matrix(times,3,
+    dimnames=list(c("User","System","Real"),NULL))
> times
            [,1]      [,2]       [,3]      [,4]       [,5]
   User 0.3500004 0.333334 0.3500004 0.333333 0.3500004
 System 0.0000000 0.000000 0.0000000 0.000000 0.0000000
   Real 1.0000000 0.000000 1.0000000 1.000000 0.0000000

            [,6]      [,7]       [,8]       [,9]       [,10]
   User 0.3499994 0.3166666 0.3499994 0.35000038 0.2833338
 System 0.0000000 0.0000000 0.0000000 0.01666665 0.0000000
   Real 2.0000000 0.0000000 0.0000000 2.00000000 2.0000000
```

When timing expressions that use the unix function to execute commands, you should consider the time taken by the child process executing the command. If any child process was involved, the function unix.time will return, as elements 4 and 5 of its value, the user and system time taken by child processes. For most purposes, these times could be added to the first two elements (occasionally, however, it may be important to contrast the time taken by two different commands, separately from the time taken by the main process). As an example, we time the ls function:

```
> times ← list()
> for(i in 1:3) times[[i]] ← unix.time(ls())
> times
[[1]]:
[1] 0.29999924 0.33333325 1.00000000 0.01666667 0.11666667
```

```
[[2]]:
[1] 0.08333397 0.16666675 2.00000000 0.06666667 0.08333333

[[3]]:
[1] 0.08333397 0.16666651 0.00000000 0.01666667 0.13333333
```

The times in these last two examples were for a large minicomputer.

The `unix.time` function gets its timing information from a simpler function, `proc.time`. This function returns a vector of cumulative times since the start of the S session, and can be used when the computations you want to time are not given by a single expression. Just save the value of `proc.time` before the computations and subtract it from the value of `proc.time` after the computations are complete.

Some practical issues should be kept in mind when timing computations.

- Try to time realistically large calculations. The overhead in the timing itself will affect estimates for small calculations, and the granularity in the timing mechanism becomes a problem. (User and system times are actually returned as multiples of $1/60$ or $1/50$ second; real time is in whole seconds.) Also, it is *not* a good idea to make a simple extrapolation from a very small problem to a similar large one.

- Where possible, parameterize the timings in terms of the size of the data used or other relevant variables. Try also to keep track of the conditions under which you time the calculations (e.g., the load on the computer).

- Be cautious in believing small timing differences. Many factors can alter the results: the load on the machine from other processes; computer hardware; the memory, disk, and other facilities on a particular machine; and the version of the operating system.

Serious performance studies of a computational method are essentially scientific experiments. They benefit from careful design and planning.

Memory for the frame associated with each S function call is allocated separately. The memory currently allocated in all S frames can be examined by the function `storage()`, which returns a list giving a complete description of the currently allocated storage (see Appendix 1 for details). A simpler summary is provided by the function `allocated()`. This returns a numeric vector, giving the total allocated memory for each of the currently open frames, ending with the function in which the call to `allocated` occurred. The `names` attribute of the vector returned gives the names of the corresponding functions. By calling `allocated` at certain times, one can see how the memory requirements depend on the computations used. For example, here is a version of the function `lapply` modified to show the storage allocated before and after the loop in which it does its calculations.

```
dbg.lapply ← function(X, FUN, ...){
    if(is.character(FUN)) FUN ← get(FUN)
    answer ← X
    alloc ← allocated()
    for(i in seq(along=X))answer[[i]] ← FUN(answer[[i]],...)
    new.alloc ← allocated()
    print(new.alloc - alloc)
    answer
}
```

It is important that the result returned by `allocated` be assigned a name—it should not be involved in other computations.

```
> dbg.lapply(as.list(1:3),sum)
# missing switch assign eval dbg.lapply
        0        0       0     0      4090
...
```

The display shows that there have been `4090` extra bytes allocated in the frame for `dbg.lapply` during execution of the loop.

Exercises

7.28   Time the expression

```
sort(runif(n))
```

for values of n ranging from 2^1 to 2^16. How does the execution time vary with n?

7.29   Section 6.2.3 introduced recursive functions. Carry out some timing tests to see how the recursive `fact` function compares to the non-recursive `fact2`.

7.30   Design a function that will take an expression, evaluate it a specified number of times, and return the execution times as the rows of a matrix.

7.31   What would happen if we changed `dbg.lapply` so that the lines

```
new.alloc ← allocated()
print(new.alloc - alloc)
```

were replaced with

```
print(allocated() - alloc)
```

Try it and explain what happens.

7.4 Control Over Evaluation

Up to now, we have spoken loosely of a "local data frame" as the list of the objects created during the evaluation of a call to an S function. In fact the local data frames are exactly lists in the S sense, and can themselves be accessed as S objects. Similarly, all the information that defines the *semantics* of S (that is, the meaning of evaluating expressions in S) may be encapsulated in a *model* for the S-language evaluator, together with some S objects in which that evaluator stores all the information needed during the evaluation. This model will be described in Chapter 11. In the present section, we will mention some aspects of the semantic model that can be used in writing functions. User-written S functions can examine the semantic model to get information about the current state of the evaluator: this is what the function `browser` does to provide a debugging tool. It is also possible to use the model to achieve special effects in evaluation, such as causing an expression to be evaluated in a specified local data frame.

7.4.1 *Objects Defining the Evaluator*

To clarify the role of the evaluator, consider what happens when the user interacts with S. An expression typed by a user, say:

```
> yy ← sqrt(w) * y
```

begins as a string of characters. This is read and parsed according to the S language by the S function `parse`. The value of `parse` is a vector representing the same expression, parsed but not evaluated. Another function, `eval`, takes this expression and evaluates it. For most purposes, this all happens automatically and the user is unaware of the separate steps.

All evaluation in S is under control of an expression object named `.Program`. By default, it is somewhat complicated, but a very basic version is

```
.Program ← expression(print(eval(parse(),local=F)))
```

S continues to evaluate the `.Program` expression throughout the S session. If an error or interrupt occurs, things are cleaned up and evaluation of `.Program` begins again.

As the evaluator proceeds, it examines the expression returned by the parser, evaluating each relevant part of the expression according to the definition of the S semantics. The elements of the expression are of different modes for different parts of the language; for example, there is a mode for assignment operations, for `if` statements, and so on. The most common and by far the most important part of the expression will be `calls` to S functions. As described in section 6.1, the evaluation of a call proceeds by matching the actual arguments to the supplied arguments. These matched arguments form the initial elements in a list, the *frame* for the function call. The body of the function definition is then evaluated, using that frame as local data. In the process, another call will typically be encountered. The evaluator then repeats the process, creating another frame for this call. The successive frames themselves form a list. The frames list is the fundamental object describing the current state of the evaluator. A few additional objects are required: the list of the calls themselves and a vector saying which frame was the *parent* of each frame, that is, the frame from which the call to this function came.

   While the model for S evaluation treats these objects as ordinary S objects, they are available to user functions only through special functions, for reasons of safety and efficiency. The following table describes the S functions that return objects describing the evaluation.

What	Function	Description
Call	`sys.call()`	The current function call
Calls	`sys.calls()`	The function calls that generated each frame
Frame	`sys.frame()`	The current frame; that is, the frame from which `sys.frame()` is called
Frames	`sys.frames()`	The local data frames for the currently open function calls
Frame Number	`sys.nframe()`	Which element of `frames` is the current frame
On Exit	`sys.on.exit()`	The expressions, if any, to be done to wrap up each frame
Parent Frame	`sys.parent(n)`	The frame number for the n-th generation caller of the current frame
Parent Frames	`sys.parents()`	Numbers of all parent frames of the current frame
Traced Functions	`sys.trace()`	A list of functions being traced. The names and values tell the traced functions and the corresponding tracer functions.

The frames are ordinary data of mode "`list`". They only exist during evaluation, and are accessible only via the S functions in the table above.

   The symbolic form of the call to the current function, given by `sys.call`, is often used to provide labels for printing or plotting.

   Section 6.4 showed how to use functions like `traceback` to examine the state of the evaluator after an error had occurred, and `browser` to evaluate and examine expressions, either in the middle of evaluation or after an error. Now we are in a position to examine how these functions work, and in the process see some examples of controlling evaluation.

Consider the browser, first. Like the evaluator itself, it parses an expression from the user:

```
expr ← parse(prompt="Selection: ")
```

The browser wants to evaluate the expression, but in the frame of the caller of the browser, *not* in the browser's own frame. This is accomplished by the use of an optional second argument to the `eval` function. This argument may be used to specify a frame in which to do the evaluation. The frame can be given either as a number or a list. Numbers are taken to be indices in the vector of current frames. In particular,

```
eval(expr,sys.parent(1))
```

evaluates `expr` in the frame of the function that called it, which is just what `browser` wants.

7.4.2 *Tracing Function Evaluation*

Section 6.4 introduced the `trace` function. Here, we will show how `trace` provides a flexible way of monitoring evaluation.

The call to `trace` can include two arguments: a character vector giving the names of functions to be traced, and a tracer function. In our earlier examples, we used a one-argument version of the `trace` function call which used the default tracer function, `std.trace`. In this section, we will show several tracer functions, and describe how you can write your own.

The way `trace` works is that a list of the functions to be traced and the corresponding tracer functions is kept internally. (The list is returned by the `sys.trace` function.) When the S evaluator is ready to evaluate a traced function, say `stem`, it actually invokes the tracer function, giving it, as its argument, the unevaluated call to `stem`. It is up to the tracer function to perform the desired trace actions and evaluate the call to the traced function.

Let's look at the standard tracer function, `std.trace`:

```
std.trace ← function(call){
    trace.on(F); on.exit(trace.on(T))
    n ← sys.nframe()
    cat("Entering frame", n, substitute(call), "\n")
    trace.on(T)
    x ← call
    trace.on(F)
    cat("Frame", n, "value:", deparse(x, short = 40), "\n")
    x
}
```

The first thing in `std.trace` is the expression `trace.on(F)`, which tells the S evaluator to turn off tracing. To see that this is necessary, imagine what would happen if a function inside the tracer function was itself traced. Once tracing is turned off, `std.trace` arranges to have it turned back on when it exits. It is important to do this via `on.exit` since the tracer will not regain control if the called function encounters an error.

Next, the tracer performs any actions it desires before evaluating the function call. Because of lazy evaluation, `call` has not yet been evaluated. Notice that `std.trace` uses `substitute` (section 7.5.2) to produce the actual call to the traced function.

The sequence

```
trace.on(T)
x ← call
```

actually carries out the call to the traced function and makes sure that tracing is turned on during its evaluation. Finally, tracing is turned off, the tracer performs any desired actions after the traced function is done, and the value, `x`, returned by the traced function, is returned by the tracer.

To summarize, a tracer function must

- Turn off tracing.
- Arrange for tracing to be turned back on when the tracer is exited.
- Perform any actions before the traced function is called.
- Turn on tracing.
- Evaluate the call to the traced function, and save its value.
- Turn off tracing.
- Perform any desired wrap-up actions.
- Return the value of the traced function call.

All of these steps must be carried out correctly or the tracer function may cause S to loop or terminate abnormally. Remember that the *quit* signal (control-backslash) will get you out of S in case of trouble.

In addition to `std.trace`, there are several other trace handlers supplied with S. The `browser.trace` function invokes the `browser` function just before evaluating the traced function. The `count.trace` function keeps track of the number of times each traced function has been called.

If you really must write a specialized tracer function, your best bet is to modify one of these tracer functions to suit your needs rather than starting from scratch.

Exercises

7.32   Ackermann's function is a highly recursive function defined as:

```
ackermann ← function(x,y){
    if(y==0)  0
    else if(x==0)  2*y
    else if(y==1)  2
    else ackermann(x-1,ackermann(x,y-1))
}
```

Use the `count.trace` tracer function to determine how many times `acker-mann` is called when evaluating `ackermann(0,4)`. Hint: read the documentation for `count.trace` before doing this, since it will tell you how to initialize the counter.

7.33   Suppose you wish to trace the evaluation of all of your own functions. What do you think of the following technique:

```
trace(ls())
```

Can you think of a better way to accomplish this goal?

7.4.3 *Taking Over Error-Handling:* `Restart`

When writing S functions for others to use you may want to give the user the ability to type arbitrary S expressions and yet have your function remain in control. Suppose you wanted to write a menu-based system to teach someone how to use S. At some points in the lesson, your function might have the student type an S expression to try out new material. What would happen if the student typed a syntactically incorrect S expression or one that generated an error in evaluation? Normally the error would cause the expression calling your teaching function to terminate.

     As an example, let's write a function that allows the student to type in an S expression that we will parse and evaluate. (This is much like the `.Program` example given in section 7.4.1.)

```
try.S ← function()
    print(eval(parse(),local=FALSE))
```

Now, let's try it:

```
> try.S()
> 1:10
 [1]  1  2  3  4  5  6  7  8  9 10
 [1]  1  2  3  4  5  6  7  8  9 10
```

The first line of printing is from the `try.S` function; the second line is S's automatic printing of the value of `try.S`. Our next step will be to use the value returned by `try.S` to determine if our student has accomplished the desired task.

Suppose we decide to write a function that presents a sample problem to our student.

```
seq.problem ← function(){
    cat("Type an S expression",
        "that creates the values 1, 2, ... 10\n")
    repeat{
        result ← try.S()
        if(all(result==1:10)) break
        cat("Sorry, that was incorrect, try again\n")
    }
    cat("Congratulations\n")
}
```

We do not check precisely *how* the student gets the answer, we just check that the expression has the right value. We keep presenting the problem until the student comes up with a correct response:

```
> seq.problem()
Type an S expression that creates the values 1, 2, ... 10
> c(1,10)
[1]   1 10
Sorry, that was incorrect, try again
> seq(10)
 [1]   1  2  3  4  5  6  7  8  9 10
Congratulations
```

This seems to work pretty well. Suppose, however, that our student was still having problems with syntax:

```
> seq.problem()
Type an S expression that creates the values 1, 2, ... 10
> 1,10
Syntax error: "," used illegally at this point
1,
Dumped
```

The error message is helpful to the student, but, unfortunately, we have been dumped out of our `seq.problem` function.

We would like to have `try.S` recover from syntax errors or evaluation errors, so the student has a chance to learn. The `restart` function is the key. If `restart(TRUE)` is evaluated, the current function will be restarted if an error occurs before the function returns.

```
try.S ← function(){
    restart(TRUE)
    print(eval(parse(),local=FALSE))
}
```

Now, let's see what happens when the student has problems:

```
> seq.problem()
Type an S expression that creates the values 1, 2, ... 10
> 1,10
Syntax error: "," used illegally at this point
1,
Dumped
Sorry, that was incorrect, try again
> 1:abc
Error: Object "abc" not found
Dumped
> 1:10
 [1]  1  2  3  4  5  6  7  8  9 10
Congratulations
```

Warning: `restart` is a dangerous tool. You can easily get into situations where an error occurring inside the `restart` domain will cause a loop. Once again, the *quit* signal, typed as control-backslash, is important. But be careful: one quit signal will terminate the `restart`. A second quit signal will terminate the S session.

Exercises

7.34   Why is it a good idea to check that the value returned by the user's expression was correct, rather than to check that it was the expected expression? Hint: how many different S expressions can you think of that would produce the vector 1, 2, ... 10?

7.35   Revise the `seq.problem` function so that the student is informed of a correct answer after 3 incorrect attempts.

7.36   Revise `seq.problem` so the user cannot get out by hitting interrupt.

7.37   What is causing the "`Dumped`" message when the student types a syntactically incorrect expression? How would you get rid of it?

7.38   Use `proc.time` to keep track of how long it takes the user to respond to a question and produce an appropriate message based on the timing. For example, if the user takes less than 2 seconds to answer, print "Wow, that was quick!", or for a response longer than a minute, print "Did you look it up in the book?"

7.39*   Devise a menu-driven S teaching program that uses `try.S` to allow the students to practice.

7.4.4 *Redefining* `.Program`

As mentioned earlier, all S evaluation is under control of the expression named `.Program`. You can print `.Program` to see what it does. A potentially very powerful (but also very dangerous) trick is to replace the standard `.Program` with one of your own. For example, you might want to work with a different parser, build a menu-oriented system into the inner workings of S, or restrict the user to certain kinds of expressions.

Of course, developing a new `.Program` is not quite as trivial as developing a new S function. The consequences of getting it wrong are much more serious, because once you create a nonworking `.Program`, S will slavishly use it and hence fail to work.

How, then, should you develop a new `.Program`, if you decide that is what you want to do? The idea is to give it a different name, say `My.program` and evaluate it by running

```
repeat eval(My.program,local=F)
```

Once you are convinced that your new version really works, you can assign it the name `.Program`.

```
> .Program ← My.program
```

Of course, even with these precautions, something may go wrong. Don't panic. Get out of S by sending a *quit* signal (type a control-backslash) and then execute

```
$ rm .Data/.Program
```

to remove the bad version of `.Program`.

Exercises

7.40 Try installing the following `.Program`:

```
.Program ← expression( print(eval(parse(),local=F)) )
```

How does this differ from the standard `.Program` from the user's point of view?

7.41 Why is there a second argument to `eval` in the `.Program` given in the previous exercise? What would happen if it were omitted?

7.5 Computing on the Language

In the normal course of an S session, the user types lines of text, which are converted by the `parse` function into parsed expressions. These expressions are then evaluated by the function `eval` and, when suitable, displayed automatically by the `print` function. But the parsed expressions are themselves perfectly valid S objects. You can save them after parsing without evaluating them, or arrange for functions to retrieve the parsed but unevaluated version of their arguments. Once you understand how the parsed expressions represent the S language, you can manipulate them to do essentially any symbolic computations you want. This section explores some of these techniques.

7.5.1 *Menu Actions*

As a simple example, consider again the menu-driven user interaction discussed in section 7.1.3. One desirable feature missing from the simplest use of the menu function is a close tie between the menu itself (that is, the character vector of choices presented to the user) and the actions that will be taken. The key to making this tie, and to developing a general menu facility, is to represent the actions explicitly as expressions in the S language, and to use the eval function to evaluate chosen expressions.

In the example of a graphics help facility, we defined a function graph.help that used menu to present the user with various topics and then switched on the user's choice to evaluate a corresponding expression. The text, the actions in response to the choices, and the call to menu were all combined in the graph.help function. However, the text and the actions alone completely define the specific part of this application; the rest of graph.help is just a standard use of menu.

A better design would construct the text and actions as a single S object, and pass this single object to a function that would handle both user interaction and evaluation of the chosen expression. The desired object in the graphics help example could be created by:

```
graph.help.menu ← expression(
    "Scatterplots" = help(plot),
    "Drawing lines" = help(lines),
    "Plotting text" = help(text),
    "Titles and Legends" = {help(title); help(legend)}
    )
```

The function expression returns a vector whose elements are the parsed but unevaluated expressions given as its arguments. Basically, expression lets the user enter arbitrary S expressions as literals, protected from evaluation. To carry out the menu selection and the resulting action, we can use a function like:

```
menu.action ← function(menu.data) {
    pick ← menu(names(menu.data))
    if(pick) eval(menu.data[pick])
}
```

The call

```
menu.action(graph.help.menu)
```

would produce the same user interaction as the function `graph.help` in section 7.1.3.

Exercises

7.42   Use the techniques presented in this section to rewrite `try.S` so that it takes an object composed of a target expression and text that tells the user what to do.

7.43   Would a version of `menu.action` that allowed multiple choices (for example, by calling the function `multi.pick` defined in exercise 7.2 instead of `menu`) differ from the definition above? To answer this, do some experimenting on the behavior of `eval` with `expression` objects of various lengths.

7.5.2 *Expressions as Symbolic Arguments*

Other applications that benefit from treating expressions as data involve using an expression, unevaluated, as the argument to a function. For example, a function that plots a smooth curve over a given range might want the *expression* for the curve, rather than the numeric values at a prechosen set of points. The plotting function could then choose the plotting points to give a good representation of the particular curve. A call to such a function might look like:

```
> curve.plot(cos(x)*sin(x)^.5,0,pi)
```

saying that the expression `sin(x)*cos(x)^.5` should be plotted for `x` ranging from `0` to `pi`, inclusive. Notice that the expression in the first argument is not to be evaluated immediately. Rather, we want `curve.plot` to choose a vector of suitable values for `x`, and then to plot the expression evaluated for this `x`. Our `curve.plot` will plot the curve at 50 equally spaced points over the range of `x`.

```
curve.plot ← function(expr,x1,x2){
    curve.expr ← substitute(expr)
    x ← seq(x1,x2,length=50)
    y ← eval(curve.expr)
    plot(x,y,type="l")
}
```

The function call

```
substitute(expr)
```

is the most important tool in symbolic computations in S. If any names appearing in `expr` correspond to objects in the local frame of the function calling `substitute`, the names are replaced by their local definitions. If a name corresponds to an argument, the appropriate actual or default expression for the name is substituted in `expr`. Then `substitute` returns the resulting expression *unevaluated*. (A second argument can be supplied to `substitute` to provide an explicit list in which to look for definitions, rather than using the local frame.)

In `curve.plot`, we create an object `curve.expr` containing the symbolic form of the actual argument associated with formal argument `expr`. Once `x` has been assigned, we explicitly force the evaluation of `curve.expr` in the local frame and assign its value the name `y`. This powerful notion of constructing an expression and later evaluating it explicitly will recur in many later examples. The expression

```
y ← eval(curve.expr)
```

evaluates the expression created in this way. The evaluation takes place in the local frame of `curve.plot`, where `x` now has the desired definition. Notice that the name `x` plays a special role: it is "free" (that is, not attached to any specific object), when `curve.plot` is called.

The effect of `curve.plot` can be obtained in a slightly different way, by assuming that the user provides a function definition for the curve:

```
curve.plot2 ← function(f,x1,x2){
    x ← seq(x1,x2,length=50)
    y ← f(x)
    plot(x,y,type="l")
}
```

The call to `curve.plot2` could either pass in the name of a function or an explicit function definition, such as

```
> curve.plot2(function(z)cos(z)*sin(z)^.5, 0, pi)
```

The caller has to do more work, but there is no longer a hidden requirement for the particular name `x`, and no explicit substitution and evaluation are needed. These two ways of passing symbolic expressions, function definitions and substitution, are complementary; often, both can be used together, as we will see in section 7.5.3.

Exercises

7.44   In `curve.plot`, it might appear that one could write

```
y ← expr
```

instead of

```
y ← eval(curve.expr)
```

Why not?

7.45   The function `deparse` is the inverse of parsing; that is, given an expression it generates a character string that would parse into that expression. In `curve.plot`, the value of

```
deparse(curve.expr)
```

would be the string `"cos(x) * sin(x)^0.5"`, for example. Use `deparse` and the function `title` to generate a *y*-axis label for the curve plot.

7.46   What is the difference between using `deparse(expr)` and `deparse(curve.expr)` in the previous problem? Experiment with them both and explain what is happening.

7.47   Write a function `surface.plot` that uses the S function `contour` to draw contours for a function of x and y, given an expression for the surface and ranges for x and y.

7.48   The function `contour` has several optional arguments that control the appearance of the plot. Use the "..." convention described in section 6.1.3 to let users of `surface.plot` supply these arguments.

7.5.3 *Constructing Expressions*

So far, we have passed expressions around and evaluated them, but have not needed to manipulate their contents. The expressions were assumed to come originally from parsing some input text. This is usually the case, but since the expressions are data, they can be constructed computationally, too. Consider the `curve.plot` function defined in the previous section. If we want to evaluate the expression for the curve repeatedly, for different vectors, `curve.plot` is clumsy. We would have to move the desired data into x each time. A better approach is to construct a function, inside `curve.plot`, whose body is the expression passed in by the user. This is how it can be done:

```
curve.plot3 ← function(curve, x1, x2){
    f ← function(x)NULL
    f[[length(f)]] ← substitute(curve)
    . . .
```

We first made a function, with formal argument x, and an arbitrary body, and assigned the function definition to a local object, f. Then we treated f as an ordinary vector and replaced the last element (which is the body of the function) by the expression for curve. Now f can be used as a local function to define the curve. Note the use of the double square brackets: we want to replace the last *element* of f with the entire right-hand side of the assignment. Most symbolic manipulation in S tends to involve altering individual elements of parsed expressions and should use double square brackets for replacement.

General use of this technique involves constructing vectors corresponding to expressions in the S language and then altering or examining parts of these vectors. To do this, we need to know what the vector corresponding to a particular expression looks like. The following table gives examples. In most cases, the elements appearing in the parsed expression are just strung out like a list in the natural way.

	Expression	Vector	Mode
Function Definition	`function(x,y=1)` `x+y`	`(x, y=1, x+y)`	`"function"`
Function Call	`abc(1:3, y[2])`	`(abc, 1:3, y[2])`	`"call"`
	`5+6`	`("+",5,6)`	`"call"`
Conditional	`if(test)x`	`(test, x)`	`"if"`
	`if(test)x else y`	`(test, x, y)`	`"if"`
Loops	`while(x>0)x ← y`	`(x>0, x ← y)`	`"while"`
	`for(i in e)cat(i)`	`(i, e, cat(i))`	`"for"`
	`repeat menu(z)`	`(menu(z))`	`"repeat"`
Braces	`{cat(x); x}`	`(cat(x), x)`	`"{"`
Assignments	`x ← runif(10)`	`(x, runif(10))`	`"<-"`
	`x[i] ← 0`	`(x[i], 0)`	`"<-"`

As a second example, suppose we want to construct a call to a given function, using as arguments the elements of a list. If the arguments are to be constructed from other information, the corresponding expressions can be inserted into the appropriate elements of a vector containing a call to the appropriate function. This operation is performed by the do.call function:

```
do.call ← function(what, args){
    this.call ← call(as.name(what), args)
    eval(this.call, local = sys.parent(1))
}
```

Suppose we would like to construct a function compose that takes as its arguments two other functions, f and g and returns as its value the function f(g(...)). The substitute function is essential here, too.

```
compose ← function(f, g)
substitute(function(x)f(g(x)))
```

For example, to construct a function that computes a product by taking the sum of logarithms:

```
> sum.of.logs ← compose(sum,log)
> myprod ← compose(exp,sum.of.logs)
> myprod
function(x)
exp(sum.of.logs(x))
> myprod(1:10)
[1] 3628800
```

That's one version of composition. Here is another:

```
compose2 ← function(f, g){
    gg ← substitute(g1(x))
    gg[[1]] ← g
    ff ← substitute(f1(y))
    ff[[1]] ← f
    ff[[2]] ← gg
    fun ← function(x)
        NULL
    fun[[2]] ← ff
    fun
}
```

What's the difference? Notice that, while the first definition actually substituted the unevaluated arguments f and g, this one creates calls with dummy names f1 and g1 that will *not* be substituted. Then it plugs in the actual, current definitions for the two functions. This uses the fact that calls in S can have either the name of a function or an actual function definition in them.

This is a subtle difference, but understanding it can be important. In the first case, if we redefined sum or log, then the effect of sum.of.logs would change too. If we had used the second version of compose, it would not, because sum.of.logs would contain the original definitions, not the function names. Another case in which the difference is important occurs when compose is called down several layers of function calls. Since substitute *always* does one level of substitution only, you would get the actual argument to compose and not the result of further substitution back up the chain of function calls. Play around with the two versions of composition in different situations, seeing whether the resulting functions have the same or different behavior. (By the way, once you understand the ideas in this discussion, congratulations! You have reached a high level of understanding S programming.)

Exercises

7.49 Why does function `myprod` contain `sum.of.logs` and not a composition of three functions? What would the expression

```
myprod ← compose(exp,compose(sum,log))
```

produce? Write a compose function that takes an arbitrary number of arguments.

7.50 How would you create a sum-of-squares function using `compose`? Can you figure out a way to use `get("^")` in the `compose` function to get a similar result?

7.51 Modify `curve.plot2` in section 7.5.2 so that it can put out a title consisting of the expression that is the body of its `f` argument.

7.52 Suppose we write a function, `trig.plot`, that calls the modified `curve.plot2` of the previous problem:

```
trig.plot ← function(fn)
    curve.plot2(fn,-pi,pi)
```

Try executing

```
trig.plot(sin)
```

to get a plot of a sine curve. What happens to the title? Why? (Difficult: can you fix it?)

Answers to Selected Exercises

7.1 (page 192)
```
graph.help ← function(){
    my.menu ← c(
        "Scatterplots",
        "Drawing lines",
        "Plotting text",
        "Titles and Legends")
    pick ← 0
    while(pick==0){
        cat("Select a topic for help\n")
        pick ← menu(my.menu)
        switch(pick,
            help(plot),
            help(lines),
            help(text),
            {help(title); help(legend)}
        )
    }
}
```

7.3 (page 192)
```
multi.pick ← function(choice){
```

```
                picks ← NULL
                repeat{
                    pick ← menu(choice)
                    if(pick>0) picks ← c(picks,pick)
                    else{
                        cat("More?[y/n] ")
                        if(readline()=="n") break
                    }
                }
                picks
            }
```

7.4 (page 192)

```
            multi.pick ← function(choice){
                choice ← c("No more selections", choice)
                picks ← NULL
                repeat{
                    pick ← menu(choice)
                    if(pick==0) next
                    if(pick==1) break
                    picks ← c(picks,pick)
                }
                picks
            }
```

7.5 (page 195)

```
            make ← function(x){
                object.file ← paste(x,".o",sep="")
                if(unix(paste("make",object.file),output=F)) stop()
                dyn.load(object.file)
            }
```

7.6 (page 195) The easiest way to write do.load is to create an object in frame 0 that tells if any particular object has been loaded previously.

```
            do.load ← function(name){
                dsname ← unix("tr '/' '.'", name)  # turn slash into dot
                if(!exists(dsname,frame=0)){
                    dyn.load(name)
                    assign("dsname",1,frame=0)  # session object
                }
            }
```

7.11 (page 204) Try looking at the results of a particular linear combination of columns of the matrix:

```
            stem( m.from.randu %*% c(9,-6,1) )
```

If you think of the rows of the matrix as specifying points in 3-space, the linear combination shows that all points in 3-space lie on one of only 15 different planes.

7.12 (page 211) If you experimented, you found that call_S itself can check for zero length in either the argument or the result. If the length of the result was greater than one, you might want to print a warning message. But checking for problems (like x being non-numeric) that would produce errors in the user's function itself is probably not worth the effort. Better to just let the error occur.

7.14 (page 211) The idea is to pass list(...) down to zero_find and have it squirrel-away a pointer to the list in a static variable. It can then pass that pointer to the curve function when zfun invokes call_S.

7.15   (page 213)

```
quick.print ← function(...){
    on.exit(options(old))
    old ← options(digits=2)
    z ← list(...)
    nn ← names(z)
    if(is.null(nn)) nn ← rep("",length(z))
    index ← seq(z)
    nn[nchar(nn)==0] ← index[nchar(nn)==0]
    for(i in index){
        cat(nn[i],":\n",sep="")
        print(z[[i]])
        cat("\n")
    }
    invisible()
}
```

7.19   (page 215)   The strategy is to calculate how many replications of `x` are needed, to call `rep` recursively to get this vector, and then to trim the result down to the length requested:

7.21   (page 216)

```
"%<%" ← function(x,y){
    x ← as.matrix(x); y ← as.matrix(y)
    if(any(dim(x)!=dim(y)))
        stop("x and y must have same dimensions")
    apply(x<y,1,"all")
}
```

7.22   (page 216)   The basic idea is to make `%<%` TRUE whenever all elements are less, FALSE when none are less, and NA otherwise.

7.23   (page 216)   You need to have the old operator around, say as function ".lt". The new version can be defined as

```
.new.lt ← function(x,y){
    if(!exists(".newcomp")).makenewcomp()
    if(is.list(x)) x %<% y
    else .lt(x,y)
}
```

The initialization goes like this

```
.makenewcomp ← function(){
    assign(".lt",get("<"),frame=0)
    assign("<",.new.lt,frame=0)
    assign(".newcomp",TRUE,frame=0)
}
```

The same technique, clearly, can be extended to the full set of operators.

7.24   (page 218)   The replacement function:

```
"row.labels<-" ← function(x, labels){
    x ← as.matrix(x)
    dn ← dimnames(x)
    nrow ← dim(x)[1]
    if(is.null(dn))
        dn ← list(character(nrow), NULL)
    else if(is.null(dn[[1]]))
        dn[[1]] ← character(nrow)
    dn[[1]][] ← labels
    dimnames(x) ← dn
    x
```

```
         }
```
Notice that we checked for both NULL dimnames and for the case that there were only column labels. Also, the replacement of labels in dn must have the [] to make sure that a short vector of labels gets replicated. For the right-side function:
```
      row.labels ← function(x){
         x ← as.matrix(x)
         ll ← dimnames(x)[[1]]
         if(is.null(ll))
             ll ← character(dim(x)[1])
         ll

      }
```
We want a vector of empty labels, rather than NULL, so that nested use of the assignment works right:
```
      row.labels(x)[1] ← "First try"
```

7.28   (page 221)   The time should be proportional to n*log(n), except for very small values of n.

7.31   (page 221)   The result is that allocated is called from within print and "−". This affects the length of the vector returned by allocated. Because the shorter vector is replicated to be as long as the longer one, the computed values are incorrect for these new frames, too.

7.33   (page 226)   The suggested technique should work, although it will cause a substantial amount of overhead inside S as all non-function objects will also be in the trace list. A better technique would be to write a function, lsfunction, that would return the names of the function objects in your working directory.

7.34   (page 228)   It is often too hard to check for reasonable expressions. For example, the following are all legitimate answers for the student to give:
```
      seq(10)
      1:10
      c(1,2,3,4,5,6,7,8,9,10)
```
and there are many other not-so-reasonable answers, too:
```
      rev(10:1)
      0:9+1
      . . .
```

7.37   (page 228)   The message is coming from dump.calls, the default function called when an error occurs. To get rid of the message, simply evaluate options(error=NULL).

7.40   (page 229)   This .Program does not check for top-level assignments—it always prints the value of the expression that it evaluates.

7.44   (page 233)   Since expr is an argument, it would ordinarily be evaluated in the caller's frame where x is not defined.

7.50   (page 236)   The easy way is to use
```
      > square ← function(x) x^2
      > sum.of.squares ← compose(sum,square)
```

7.52   (page 236)   The problem is that the substitute function only knows to go back one call to get the name of the function passed to curve.plot2, hence the plot is titled with "fn" rather than "sin". To solve the problem requires walking back up the chain of calls to find the function ultimately associated with the plot.

8

More about Data

When using S to deal with a substantial application, the best approach nearly always involves designing some S functions that work together, *and* a special class of S objects that represents the essential structure of the data involved in the application. For example, fitting linear models in S requires functions to compute the fitted model and to produce various summary statistics, diagnostics, and plots from the fit. These functions will communicate well with each other if they share knowledge about a class of objects that represent fitted linear models.

The power of this approach in attacking new computing applications comes from designing the functions and the class of objects together. Chapter 5 introduced the two mechanisms—*components* and *attributes*—that are needed to define the objects. Chapters 6 and 7 went into the necessary details about functions. In this chapter we will tie these ideas together and give some brief case studies illustrating the design process.

8.1 Classes of Objects in S

The process of defining a new class is an informal one. The idea is to establish a minimum set of components or attributes that objects in the new class must have, and to specify what those components or attributes must look like. Simultaneously, we will be designing the functions that will use the new objects. Of these functions, a few basic ones will create and manipulate the objects. These functions must agree on the components or attributes they expect.

241

Typically, one function will create objects from the new class. Just as `matrix` is a function that creates new objects in the matrix class, so you will probably write a function `thing` if you are calling objects in your new class `things`; this function will take some appropriate data and return a new `thing`. You will often also have a function `is.thing(x)` that will decide if `x` is a `thing`, and a function `as.thing(x)` that can coerce an object `x` into being a `thing`.

The degree to which the functions are natural and easy to implement is a good test of how well the class of objects has been designed. Beyond these basic functions, we will usually be designing others that implement whatever computations we need for our application. Also, we hope that our new class of objects will be used later for other related computations. The application functions should generally *not* refer directly to the components or attributes; instead, it should be possible to define these in terms of other functions. If so, you have made your application functions substantially independent of how the class of objects was implemented.

S provides a style and tools to let you design classes of objects. It does not enforce a specific discipline, however, and the discussion in this chapter is mainly aimed at showing how the style works in some examples. Therefore, we will mainly concentrate on examples, and defer to section 8.4 some general reflections. Detailed comparison of components versus attributes is also deferred to that section. Sections 8.2 and 8.3 respectively discuss the two mechanisms. The major distinction between the two is that attributes are aimed at defining new classes of objects that inherit the behavior of objects from an existing class, with respect to some important S functions. Other than that, you should read sections 8.2 and 8.3 mainly to see how defining new classes in S can help to implement substantial new applications.

8.2 Defining Classes by Components

A new class of objects can be specified by saying which components objects in the class should have. As an example, let's consider computations in S for linear least-squares models. The background is as follows. We begin with some *predictor* data—observations on one or more *variables*—usually stored as the columns of a matrix `x`. We want to fit another variable, `y`, to the `x` variables, using a linear model. This means finding a vector of coefficients `coef`, such that the *fit*:

```
x %*% coef
```

is close to `y` in the sense of least squares: the sum of the squares of the *residuals*:

```
y - x %*% coef
```

is as small as possible. After producing the fit, we are likely to want to study its properties, by producing statistical summaries indicating the significance of the coefficients, for example. We may want to look at the residuals in various kinds of plots or numerical summaries. There are also many specialized diagnostics that are more or less straightforward to compute from the coefficients, the residuals, and/or other numerical results. This suggests some functionality we will need:

```
z ← lsfit(x,y) #do the fit
ls.summary(z)    #some statistical summaries
residuals(z)     #get the residuals for plotting, etc
```

Even at this early stage, we can see that we want a new class of objects that will represent linear fits. These objects will be created by a fitting function and must include at least enough information to be able to compute summaries and residuals from the fit. For now, we will call this class the `lsfit` class, and observe that the `lsfit` function just mentioned is the creation function for `lsfit` objects, as outlined at the end of section 8.1.

Our first important consideration is how to fit the model, as this will have a direct bearing on what `lsfit` objects will look like. There have been for a long time some carefully worked-out numerical techniques for linear least-squares computations. In particular, the LINPACK library contains subroutines that use the *QR decomposition* of x to estimate the coefficients and other statistics.[†] We certainly want to take advantage of this work in our fitting. Since we expect to implement a number of numerical tasks in several functions, we decide early on to have the QR decomposition itself, in some form, as part of an `lsfit` object. We will call this the `qr` component. In fact, it turns out to be useful to consider QR decompositions as a class of objects themselves, useful not only for least-squares fitting, but also for other techniques involving multivariate data. So let us invent a second class—the `qr` objects. We will postpone looking at the details for the moment, and just note that the QR decomposition in LINPACK operates by taking a matrix and returning the decomposition. Thus we will want a function to create `qr` objects:

```
xqr ← qr(x)
```

whose definition we will give shortly. There is another LINPACK subroutine that takes the decomposition and some y data, and returns, for example, the coefficients or residuals from the fit. A natural way to handle this is to write functions that take a `qr` object and use it to compute other things; for example,

---

[†]J. J. Dongarra, J. R. Bunch, C. B. Moler, G. W. Stewart, *LINPACK Users' Guide*, SIAM, 1979. The QR decomposition of x finds an orthogonal matrix, Q, such that multiplying x by t(Q) produces an upper-triangular matrix.

```
qr.coef(xqr, y)
qr.resid(xqr, y)
```

to get the coefficients and the residuals.

So far, we have decided that an `lsfit` object should contain a `qr` component, itself a `qr` object, which describes the QR decomposition of the original `x` matrix. We also need at least one of: the original `y`, the residuals, or the fitted values, to be able to produce summaries and diagnostic plots. Of the three, the residuals seem the most frequently used (they also turn out to be the desirable choice from considerations of numerical accuracy), so we include them as a component of the `lsfit` object. We also include the coefficients from the fit, as these most directly describe the fit itself. The three components `coef`, `residuals`, and `qr` seem to be enough to do most of what we want. Our first version of the `lsfit` function can now be written:

```
lsfit ← function(x, y){
    xqr ← qr(x)
    list(coef = qr.coef(xqr,y),
        residuals = qr.resid(xqr,y),
        qr = xqr
    )
}
```

Using the datasets `longley.x` and `longley.y` in the S system data directory, we can use this `lsfit` to do a regression:

```
> xx ← cbind(Intercept=1, longley.x)
> reg1 ← lsfit(xx, longley.y)
> reg1$coef
 Intercept GNP deflator          GNP Unemployed Armed Forces
 -3482.259   0.01506187 -0.03581918 -0.0202023  -0.01033227

  Population       Year
 -0.05110411 1.829151
```

Having a simple working definition of the class of `lsfit` objects, and a function to generate them, we can now go on to write other functions to use the objects. We will also want to ask how we should make the whole capability better in various ways. In the case of `lsfit` there are two points that arise immediately. First, notice that we bound on a column of 1's to the `x` matrix; this was needed to get the intercept term in the regression. Since most linear models will include an intercept, the function should do it for us, optionally. Second, it is common to want to fit by *weighted* least squares, with the different observations getting different weights. Both these options are accommodated in a second version of the function:

```
lsfit ← function(x, y, intercept = T, wt){
    if(intercept)x ← cbind(Intercept=1,x)
    if(!missing(wt)) {
        ww ← wt ^ 0.5
        x ← x * ww
        y ← y * ww
    }
    xqr ← qr(x)
    z ← list(coef = qr.coef(xqr,y),
        residuals = qr.resid(xqr,y),
        qr = xqr
    )
    if(!missing(wt)) {
        z$residuals ← z$residuals / ww
        z$wt ← wt
    }
    z
}
```

The handling of `intercept` is trivial. The treatment of `wt` deserves some comment. We do three things if `wt` is included: we multiply the data by the square root of the weights before doing the calculations, we divide the residuals afterwards, and we include `wt` as an additional component of the object returned by `lsfit`.

Notice that all this happens *only* if the optional weights are included. We don't put any substantial extra calculations into the more typical case where weights are omitted. Further, other functions that might do some special calculations in this case (for example, `ls.summary`), can detect the special case equally easily:

```
ls.summary ← function(lsfit) {
    wt ← lsfit$wt
    if(!is.null(wt)) {
        # special calculations for weights
        ....
```

We can state this approach as a design goal:

> *If a special case will require substantial extra computation and/or generate a sizable extra component in the result, try to arrange that neither the computation nor the extra component are generated when the special case is not present.*

The approach works because the expressions

```
z$what
attr(z,"what")
```

both return `NULL` if `what` is not a component or attribute of `z`.

Exercises

8.1   The second version of `lsfit` implicitly assumed that the weights provided were positive. If any were zero, `NA`'s would result in the residuals. The right way to handle zero weights is to remove the corresponding rows of x and y from the `qr` calculation, and to compute the corresponding residuals from y − x%*%coef. Modify `lsfit` to do this.

8.2   Write a `polyfit` function, that takes a vector x, a vector or matrix y, and a chosen degree d, and fits a polynomial in x of this degree, using `lsfit`. How might you modify the class of `lsfit` objects to represent your new result?

Let's go back now to look at the class of `qr` objects generated by the QR decomposition. This will further illustrate the advantages of designing a set of functions and a class of objects together. There are subroutines in LIN-PACK that create and use the QR decomposition, and these constitute a fairly complete set of basic operations for fitting linear least-squares models. Using them in Fortran requires knowledge of their calling sequences, the way the decompositions are stored, and enough of the underlying numerical analysis to be sure the computation is done accurately. In S, we can hide all this in the `qr` class and in the functions that interface to the subroutines. Users of the functions only have to know what they want to do, not how things work internally. Even new applications should only require the developer to understand the numerical method itself, not the implementation.

First, we need to create the decomposition. This is done by a Fortran subroutine DQR. For our discussion in this book, we don't need to consider the details of what this subroutine does. It gives us back some Fortran arrays that encode the QR decomposition, in the Householder form (details can be found in chapter 9 of the LINPACK reference given earlier). These arrays must be made part of the `qr` objects. Specifically, DQR generates the decomposition as a matrix of the same dimensions as x, together with a vector of length `ncol(x)`. We will name these components `qr` and `qraux`. DQR also provides a means for detecting linear dependencies among the columns of x. To accommodate this information, we will provide additional components in the object for the estimated rank and a vector that in effect defines which columns were linearly dependent.

Here is the S function to generate the decomposition.

```
qr ← function(x, tol = 1e-07) {
    x ← as.matrix(x)
    storage.mode(x) ← "double"
    dx ← dim(x)
    p ← dx[2]
    z ← .Fortran("dqr",
        qr = x,
        as.integer(dx),
        pivot = as.integer(1:p),
        qraux = double(p),
        as.double(tol),
        double(p),
        rank = as.integer(p))
    z[c("qr", "qraux", "rank", "pivot")]
}
```

The `tol` argument is an optional cutoff for testing singularities.

The design of the `lsfit` objects was relatively unconstrained, and required us to decide which of several equivalent organizations seemed most attractive. The `qr` objects, on the other hand, have an internal structure that is much more constrained. The objects must have the information used by the Fortran routines to generate and use the decomposition. The other functions that call related Fortran routines, like `qr.resid`, get all the information they need from the four components shown above. In addition to `qr.resid` and `qr.coef`, functions `qr.fitted`, `qr.qy`, and `qr.qty` compute fitted values, transform `y` by Q and by the transpose of Q. (See `qr.coef` in Appendix 1 for details).

We mentioned earlier that the Fortran routines represent the QR decomposition as a matrix plus a vector. This is not a very natural representation, but rather a way to save a little space while encoding one upper-triangular matrix plus `ncol(x)` vectors. From the viewpoint of S programming, we don't care much since only the routines we are talking about here will ever see the internal details. There is even a serendipity: since the `qr` component is created as a result of making a copy of the original `x` in the call to `.Fortran`, it automatically retains all the attributes of `x`. In particular, it retains the `dim-names` attribute if this existed. Functions that use the `qr` object to compute other quantities are written to retain such information. For example, notice that the coefficients in the earlier sample of the use of `lsfit` came out with a `names` component, even though we did nothing special in `lsfit`. This happens because `qr.coef` transfers these to its value, as either row labels or names. This property of retaining attributes often happens naturally in creating new S objects. All you need to do in this and similar examples is to leave the data sufficiently alone not to destroy the attributes along the way; for instance, it was important to pass `x` itself along to `.Fortran`, rather than creating a new matrix. Of course, the opposite lesson applies as well: if you know you *don't* want to retain some attributes, you should check that they will disappear and explicitly set them to NULL if not. Getting them right numerically and making sure they retain appropriate names involved a moderate amount of fine-tuning (see exercise 8.5, for example). However, once that work is done, it pays off, because other functions get the benefits automatically, as in the case of lsfit. Let's look at one more application, a function called hat. This computes a result from a matrix x that in turn is useful in some statistical diagnostics. Here is the computation:

```
hat ← function(x) {
    x ← as.qr(x)
    d ← dim(x$qr)
    q ← qr.qy(x, diag(1, nrow = d[1], ncol=x$rank))
    ans ← numeric(d[1])
    for(i in seq(ans)) ans[i] ← sum(q[i,  ]^2)
    ans
}
```

What hat does numerically is not so much the point here (we will look at that in exercise 8.6 below). Two things are worth noting. First, all the computations can be done from the five functions that compute properties from the QR decomposition. There is no need to go back to the Fortran code, or even to know what the qr objects look like internally. Second, the hat function is designed to work right automatically with *either* a computed decomposition *or* the appropriate matrix of data. This is accomplished by the line

```
x ← as.qr(x)
```

which follows the custom mentioned in section 8.1 of having routines that coerce appropriate objects to belong to a special class. The coercion is trivial in this case:

```
as.qr ← function(x)
    if(is.qr(x)) x else qr(x)
```

Users of hat will not have to think about QR decompositions, but functions that have precomputed the decomposition can still use the same version of hat without extra computation.

Exercises

8.3   A useful diagnostic after fitting a linear model is to plot the quantiles of the residuals against the normal distribution, using the qqnorm function. Write a function, qqresid, to produce this plot, given an lsfit object. Label the plot so that your users do not need to know about lsfit objects. (How would it be labelled if you did nothing special about labels?)

8.4 Add to the function in the previous exercise the ability to identify interesting points on the plot, using the `identify` function. Try to find good labels for the identified points. Hint: look at the documentation for `qqnorm`.

8.5 Notice that the QR method we use does not produce an explicit Q matrix (for reasons of computational accuracy and efficiency). How would you compute Q?

8.6* (For readers with some background in linear algebra.) Given the answer to the previous question, what does the `hat` function compute?

8.3 Defining Classes by Attributes

We turn now to the second approach to defining classes of S objects: the technique of adding *attributes* to objects of some existing class. The starting class may be simple vectors, as in defining matrices, arrays, and time-series. Or we may start from objects that already belong to a more specialized class, as in our examples below.

The rest of this section presents two contrasting examples of the use of attributes. In the first, we build a new class of objects as a special kind of multi-way array, to represent a grid of observations in space and time. In the second, we extend the class of S function definitions in order to provide a basis for developing "smart" functions. Both applications would be major projects if we were to treat them in any depth. The discussion here just touches the surface, and is intended to suggest how defining suitable attributes can contribute to the development of such applications.

8.3.1 *Grids: An Extension of Arrays*

For our first example, we consider applications involving *spatial data*; data about the earth, its oceans, atmosphere, and nearby space. Scientific studies in meteorology, geology, oceanography, space sciences, and related disciplines depend on such data, which come (often in very large quantities) from satellite observations and ground, sea, and air monitoring equipment. We will define a class of objects to support analysis of this kind of data, which we will assume has three spatial coordinates relative to the earth, and one time coordinate. Thus, we are talking about 4-dimensional data, for four specific dimensions; say, latitude, longitude, altitude, and time. Particular instances of such data, however, can fail to vary along one or more of the dimensions and still be consistent with this view; for example, geologic data used in meteorology probably has no useful variation with time. While each of the four dimensions can be measured in many ways, there is sufficient scientific agreement that we can choose standard origins and units of measurement in the data objects being considered. The important consequence of this is that the data will be *commensurable*, so that arithmetic and comparison operations will be meaningful.

We will focus on *regular* grids of coordinates, for which the data is taken at regular intervals in each of the four dimensions. Much, if not most, spatial data does not start out in this form, and a full approach would need to deal with irregular grids as well. However, there are sufficient advantages to dealing with regular grids when doing analysis, modeling, and computations generally that interpolating irregular data to a regular form is likely to be an important preliminary step in analysis.

This class of objects has strong affinities to existing classes of data. It clearly acts like a 4-way array, with the first subscript varying with latitude, the second with longitude, the third with altitude, and the fourth with time. There is also a connection to time-series, in the sense that the origin and step length in each of the four dimensions will be given as part of the structure, and so will implicitly define parallel coordinates in each dimension, just as the time-series parameters implicitly define a parallel *time* for such objects. Still, the array analogy seems much stronger, particularly since S does not have a multivariate-time aspect to time-series. We will propose a new class of objects, to be constructed by starting with 4-way arrays and adding new attributes. Let's call them `grid` objects.

Our first proposal is very simple: we implement a `grid` as a 4-dimensional array, with an added attribute that defines the meaning of the four dimensions as actual positions in a standard coordinate system for latitude, longitude, altitude, and time. We shall call this the `coord` attribute of a `grid`. Because the grid is regular, two numbers are enough for each dimension: the origin and the distance from the origin to the next grid point. These are reminiscent of time-series parameters (section 5.5.4), but in this case the step can be any number, positive or negative. A simple implementation of the `coord` attribute is therefore a 2 by 4 matrix, the first row containing the origins and the second the steps for the four dimensions. Here is an example of accessing the `coord` attribute of a `grid` object named `temp1`:

```
> attr(temp1,"coord")
            [,1]          [,2]  [,3]    [,4]
[1,] 40.0000000   75.0000000 1235  158412
[2,]  0.1666667   -0.1666667   NA       1
> dim(temp1)
[1]  7  9  1 12
```

We are assuming specific units of measurement: degrees of north latitude, degrees of west longitude, meters above sea level and hours of universal time since 0:00 hours, January 1, 1970. Therefore, the data in `temp1` was taken starting at 75 degrees west longitude, stepping east by 1/6 degree, and starting at 40 degrees latitude, stepping north by 1/6 degree. The altitude was 1235 meters; the corresponding dimension element was 1, indicating that this data has only one altitude value. The stepsize for this dimension is therefore mean-ingless, and we have filled it in with NA. Finally, the measurements were taken at 1 hour intervals starting at 12:00 on January 27, 1988.

As we said in section 8.1, one of the first things we want to do with a new class of objects is to write functions that create an instance of the class and test whether an object is in the class. Following our conventions, we will call the generator function grid and we will model it on the array function, since our new class extends arrays. So:

```
grid(data, dim, coord)
```

should create a grid object with the given dimensions and coordinate system. Here is a definition; we will refine it a little in the exercises.

```
grid ← function(data, dim, coord){
    if(length(dim)!=4)
        stop("grid must have 4 dimensions")
    if(!(is.array(coord) && all(dim(coord)==c(2,4))))
        stop("coord must be a 2 by 4 matrix")
    value ← array(data, dim)
    attribute(value,"coord") ← coord
    value
}
```

is.grid is equally easy:

```
is.grid ← function(x){
    d ← dim(x)
    cd ← attr(x,"coord")
    length(d)==4 && is.array(cd) && all(dim(cd)==c(2,4))
}
```

Notice that since attr returns NULL for an undefined attribute, no special code is needed to check for the existence of a coord attribute before trying to access it. This is a generally useful fact to remember when writing functions that access attributes, but see exercise 8.8 for an example of the care that needs to be taken in using this feature.

Now we can create some functions that actually compute with grid objects. For each of the four dimensions of a grid, we can write a function that will generate a full vector of the coordinates for that dimension. For example, for the altitude:

```
altitudes ← function(y){
    d ← dim(y)[3]
    cd ← coord(y)
    if(d>1) seq(from=cd[1,3],length=d,by=cd[2,3])
    else cd[1,3]
}
```

Notice that we are assuming that there is a function coord to access the coord attribute. This is analogous to using the dim function to access the dim attribute of an array, rather than using the `attr` function. Besides looking cleaner, this style has the more important property that it does not explicitly depend on the implementation of the class, but only on the assertion that for any `grid` object, the information in `coord` can be computed somehow. Of course, since we are illustrating the use of attributes, the definition for `coord` is just:

```
coord ← function(x) attr(x, "coord")
```

For a slightly more extensive computation, we will consider part of the process of making one grid *conform* to another; that is, to approximate the values that the data from one grid would have at the coordinates in space and time defined by another grid. This is a key computation in using multiple sources of data. The most general form of this problem is a challenging numerical project. We will consider a special form of the problem; namely, when the approximation only involves one of the four dimensions. To begin, we specialize even further and consider only the first dimension, latitude. So we may state the simplified problem this way: we are given a `grid` object, and latitude information for a new grid, in the form of the starting coordinate, the step size, and the number of latitude values. We want to compute a new grid for these latitudes that otherwise looks as much as possible like the original grid.

The solution is fairly simple. For fixed values of the other dimensions (longitude, altitude, and time), we approximate the values in the new grid from the corresponding subset of values in the old grid. This is just a computation on vectors, and takes no account of the grid structure. Repeating this computation for all values of the other dimensions gives the new grid. Here is a solution, using the `spline` function for approximation:

```
fit.latitude ← function(g, start, step, n){
    d ← dim(g)
    cd ← coord(g)
    newd ← d; newd[1] ← n
    newc ← cd; newc[1,1] ← start; newc[2,1] ← step
    value ← grid(0,newd,newc) # the new grid object
    nin ← d[1]; iin ← 1:nin
    iout ← 1:n
    xin ← seq(from=cd[1,1],length=nin,by=cd[2,1])
    end ← start + step * (n-1)
    while(iin[1] < length(g)){
        value[iout] ← spline(xin, g[iin], n,
            xmin=start, xmax=end)$y
        iin ← iin + nin
        iout ← iout + n
    }
    value
}
```

The function creates the new `grid` object by replacing the latitude information from the old object with values implied by the arguments `start`, `step`, and `n`. Then it inserts the values approximated from `g` into the new grid. It should now be clear why we used the first dimension in our example. Arrays in S are stored with first dimension varying fastest. Therefore the first `nin` elements in `g` have the other 3 dimensions fixed, as do the first `n` elements in `value`. We approximate the latter, using the `spline` function, and replace them in `value`. Now we move on to the next `nin` elements in `g` and the next `n` elements in `value`, and do the same thing, continuing on until we have defined all the data in the new grid.

Exercises

8.7   We might want to create a grid object from a suitable 4-way array by supplying the coordinate information only. Modify the `grid` function to allow this.

8.8   Notice that, in `is.grid`, we explicitly tested whether the `coord` attribute was an array before testing the dimensions. Experiment with some objects that have no `coord` attribute, or one that is *not* an array to see what happens if this test is omitted.

8.9   Do you think there should be a nontrivial definition for `as.grid`, to coerce an arbitrary object to be a grid?

8.10   The `altitudes` function could be just a special case of a function, `coordinates(g,j)`, which would return coordinates for any of the four dimensions. (i) Write `coordinates` for the case that `j` is a single number. (ii) Extend it to the case that `j` is any subset of `1:4`.

8.11*   Write a function, say, `fit.time`, that works like `fit.latitude` but approximates one grid by another along the time dimension.

8.3.2 *Extended Function Definitions*

Let's turn now to a very different example, one that may look strange at first, but that turns out to be simple and powerful. S *functions* themselves form a class of S objects—a very important class, but one that is used in a highly specialized way. This class is identified by having the mode "`function`". While we have discussed functions throughout the book, we have only occasionally thought of them as objects to be themselves manipulated like other objects (section 7.5 had some examples). It turns out, however, that the special role of functions is highly localized. The evaluator looks for a function object when it needs to evaluate a call; once it has found the object, it uses its knowledge about the meaning of the elements of the function to match arguments and to evaluate the body of the function. The `deparse` function knows how to reproduce the form in which the function was originally written and the `parse` function knows how to create a suitable function object from the definition. The subscripting function knows just enough not to create an invalid function object. Otherwise, function objects are treated identically to any other object by nearly all computations.

It would be nice to have "smart" functions, which carried along with themselves such things as:

- their documentation, as found in Appendix 1 of this book;
- heuristics that tried to examine the arguments and/or the result of the function to catch possible errors;
- related functions, such as a special function to print the results of the function in an appealing way.

Any or all of these ideas could be implemented by defining suitable attributes for the function object.[†] Let's consider documentation. As you know, you can get documentation on an S function, say `lsfit`, by typing

```
help(lsfit)
```

The `help` function consults a file containing documentation text. We implement here an alternative approach, in which functions have an optional attribute (we'll call it `doc`) that contains similar information. The documentation then resides with the function; even better, we get to design the documentation as a class of S objects, leading to more flexible ways of using it.

Adding an attribute to a function definition does *not* change the current behavior of the function. Attributes do not affect the use of the function in evaluation; the evaluator simply ignores them. Printing a function definition will follow the general rule for printing objects with attributes. Functions are often written to a file with the `dump` function and later brought back via the `source` function. This will also work for functions with attributes.

In this respect, adding attributes to functions is somewhat simpler than the extension of numeric classes of objects, as in our previous `grid` example. For numeric classes we need to consider how arithmetic operations, for example, work on two objects from the class. Functions, on the other hand, have fewer specialized uses.

To see what happens, assume that a function, say `lsfit`, has the attribute `doc` containing a documentation object. Then

```
attr(lsfit,"doc")
```

will retrieve the documentation, and

[†]This example was originally suggested to us by Daryl Pregibon.

```
attr(lsfit,"doc") ← newdoc
```

will change it. However, as with the `grid` example, we probably want to avoid direct calls to `attr` by defining the functions `doc` and `doc<-` to get and set the attribute (replacement functions like `doc<-` are discussed in section 7.3.4).

What should the `doc` attribute contain? A simple idea is just to use a character vector that contains the text from the file that `help` currently retrieves. Another possibility is for the `doc` attribute to be a member of some new class of objects. If you look at any of the documentation in Appendix 1, you will see that there is a fairly regular structure to it. There are several sections: usage, arguments, value, examples, and other optional information. There is a title for the documentation. The sections on arguments and value may include subsections, labelled by the names of the arguments or the names of the components of the value. All of this lends itself to designing a documentation object. It can have components `usage`, `arguments`, `value`, and so on. These components may contain text or they may themselves have components.

Suppose the function `lsfit` has a `doc` attribute. Using the scheme we have just described,

```
doc(lsfit)$usage
```

gets us the usage information, and

```
doc(lsfit)$arguments$wt
```

gets documentation on the argument `wt`. We could then define specialized functions, if we wanted to hide the specific organization of the documentation objects. For example, a function `argdoc` could be defined to return the documentation for a particular argument:

```
argdoc ← function(f,which)
    doc(f)$arguments[[which]]
```

The `wt` documentation for `lsfit` could then be retrieved by `argdoc(lsfit, "wt")` Functions like `argdoc` tend to be rather trivial and clutter things up as they accumulate (though we will suggest how to make `argdoc` a little more useful in exercise 8.14 below). Balancing the goal of hiding the implementation details against the desire to not clutter things with many little functions will depend on the application and on the tastes of the implementer.

That is about all there is to the design process in this example. The real work, as usual with documentation, will be to generate the actual text, and then keep it up to date.

Exercises

8.12   Create a version of `lsfit` with documentation.

8.13   Implement the replacement function `doc<-` that allows users to assign the documentation attribute.

8.14   Extend the `argdoc` function in as many of the following ways as possible. Allow the user to supply 0, 1 or more argument names. With 0 names, return all the argument documentation, with 1 return documentation for one argument, with more than one return the list of the corresponding arguments' documentation.

8.15*   Write a function that prints out the documentation for a function in a nice format.

8.4 Attributes or Components?

We have seen examples of using both components and attributes in order to design a new class of objects in S. We have even seen a mix of the two approaches in the last example concerning function documentation. It is natural to ask which approach is best in a given application.

Components are convenient and natural if you are designing a new class of objects, as with `qr` and `lsfit` objects. By using attributes, on the other hand, we hope to retain the behavior of an existing class of objects as currently used by various functions in S, while we add new behavior triggered by the new attributes. Thus, the attributes approach emphasizes the *inheritance* of the behavior of objects from an existing class.

The two approaches are, in fact, equivalent, in the sense that any class defined by attributes is equivalent to one defined by components. We could imagine having each of the attributes as an equivalently named component, plus one more component called, say, `data`, that contained the object from the existing class. This would be inconvenient, however, because we would always have to use expressions like

```
x$data
```

rather than using simply `x`. Also, and more important in the long run, the attributes approach may give more conceptual clarity. If our new class is built on arrays, as in the `grid` example, we should be able to think of the new objects as arrays, when that makes sense. We should be able to do arithmetic, select subarrays, use `apply`, and so forth, easily and naturally. The chances are we will then come up with better ways of using the new objects.

Using attributes to define classes takes advantage of the behavior of functions in S when given such objects as their arguments. The table below reviews the general behavior of some commonly used functions in S when one or more arguments possess attributes. The rationale is that general attributes depend on the current order of the data, but not on the actual values. Special knowledge of the attributes in section 5.6 is sometimes used.

Functions	Examples	Behavior
Elementwise	`log, round`	Retain all attributes.
Binary Operators	`+, &, >`	Result has the attributes (possibly none) of *longer* operand. Special actions for arrays, time-series, categories.
Subscript	`x[i]`	Drop all attributes except `names`.
Array Subscript	`x[i,j]`	Compute and retain correct `dim` and `dimnames` for result, drop all other attributes.
Reordering	`sample`	Drop all attributes except `names`.

There are ways to override this behavior. However, life is much simpler if the behavior in the table corresponds to what we would want for the new class of objects. If so, or if the value of the inheritance to the new class is important, defining new classes by attributes is recommended.

We have been emphasizing in this chapter that S uses classes of objects in an informal way. How far you want to go in following the style we have illustrated is up to you. For S functions that are used very widely, there may be advantages in providing a general "inheritance" feature that lets the function adapt automatically to new classes, provided they follow a convention that makes them self-identifying.

This convention takes the form of an attribute and a corresponding function, `class`, that returns the class of an object, as a character string, analogous to the `mode` function to return the mode of the data in the object. Any object that does not conform to the convention will have a NULL class. Given this approach, a further convention would allow new classes to provide class-dependent versions of a function, say `print`, by appending the function name to the class name. For example, `lsfit.print` would be the function that printed `lsfit` objects in a nice form for people to read.

The `print` function could use the conventions as follows:

```
print <- function(x){
    xclass <- class(x)
    if(is.null(xclass)) old.print(x)
    else{
        fname <- paste(xclass,"print",sep="")
        if(exists(fname,mode="function"))
            do.call(fname,list(x))
        else old.print(x)
    }
}
```

Here `old.print` stands for the function that does printing without any special knowledge of the class convention. The technique here is quite similar to the way functions are allowed on the left side of assignments (section 7.3.4).

Is this sort of convention a good idea? You will have to decide for yourself in the context of your own applications. There is certainly some overhead in determining what function to use; in the case of printing this is unlikely to matter much, but if we had to do a similar amount of work in, for example, computing `x[i]`, the consequences would be more serious. Of course, the decision to pay attention to the convention can be made independently for each important function, so that there is no overhead forced on all functions. On the plus side, the mechanism is very general and can be implemented without using any new techniques or special built-in code. For applications with a rich structure of objects, and where users should be insulated from implementation, the approach is worth considering.

Answers to Selected Exercises

8.3   (page 248)
```
qqresid <- function(fit)
    qqnorm(fit$resid,ylab="Residuals from least-squares fit")
```
If you did nothing, `qqnorm` would label the y-axis as "`Sorted Data`".

8.4   (page 249) You want to call `identify` with the data plotted by `qqnorm`. An easy way to get that data is to call `qqnorm` again, with the argument `plot=F`. Labels can come from the names of the residuals, remembering that the points in the plot come from the *sorted* data.
```
qqresid <- function(lsfit) {
    res <- lsfit$resid
    qqnorm(res, ylab = "Residuals from lsfit")
    xy <- qqnorm(res, plot = F)
    lab <- dimnames(res)[[1]]
    if(is.null(lab))
        lab <- seq(along = res)
    identify(xy, labels = lab[order(res)])
}
```

8.5   (page 249) The Q matrix is (trivially) the result of applying the transformation to the identity matrix. We generally only want as many columns as there are linearly independent columns in x.

```
qr.qy(xqr,diag(xqr$rank))
```

8.8 (page 253) The point is that when one operand in a comparison has length zero, the value of the comparison is a logical vector of length zero, and the value of all(x) if x has length 0 is TRUE. *That* may seem bizarre, but in fact it is the standard definition in logic, and the right definition for most applications.

8.9 (page 253) Probably not. It's hard to imagine a useful set of default coordinates in four dimensions, even though S does provide an analogous default for time in time-series.

8.13 (page 256)

```
"doc<-" ← function(x, d){
    attr(x,"doc") <- d
    x
}
```

8.15 (page 256) There are two basically different ways to do this. You can reverse the process of designing the documentation structure, and write out a file that looks like the files in the .Help directories in $SHOME/s/.Functions. By creating such a file, with a non-standard name, in .Data/.Help, you could then use the help function itself to do the printing.

The other approach is to produce commands in your favorite typesetting system, directly from the documentation structure, and then use the unix function to invoke the typesetting command.

9
Examples and Case Studies

This chapter presents case studies and examples of the use of S, chosen to illustrate styles of computing with S that have proven to be effective. Each example tries to be fairly realistic and at the same time to feature one or more techniques. Many techniques, such as the "data cleaning" in section 9.1, are too heuristic and informal to come across well in an abstract discussion. This chapter illustrates such techniques by presenting examples and distilling from them some general lessons. You might want to read the introductory paragraphs to the individual sections to see whether the topics discussed fit in with what you currently want to do.

9.1 Data Input and Checking

In any data analysis, much time will be spent making sure the data have been correctly recorded and brought into S. This section illustrates methods for checking the validity of the data, turning the original data into S objects for analysis, and examining the data in S for further checking. These are important techniques for any data analysis; however, they are not easy to present in the abstract, which may be why they are rarely taught. We will present them in the context of some actual data, being as realistic as possible in the description. The general steps illustrated include:

- recording the data initially in the computer from an external source;
- examining this initial input file, as text, using a variety of tools;
- choosing a representation for the data in S, and doing the input;
- examining the S objects in various ways to continue the checking.

This process may be iterated; validity checks in S may suggest problems that lead to further checks on the original data.

We begin by describing the data in our case study. Records have been kept of the gasoline consumption for a family car owned by one of us. The automobile is a 1981 Honda Accord with automatic transmission, purchased new in April 1981. Each time gasoline was purchased, the tank was filled and the date, odometer reading, gallons, and price paid was recorded (by hand, naturally, in a notebook). Also, at each fillup, the trip odometer reading was recorded and then reset. There are records for the first 129,000 miles the car was driven.

The first task is to type the data into a computer file using a text editor. To match the way the data was collected, we type it with one line per fillup, giving our 5 items of information separated by spaces:

```
1/4/84 55261.8 10.8 13.00 236.2
1/9/84 55469.6 9.4 10.95 207.7
1/13/84 55731.7 11.4 13.30 262.2
1/17/84 55947.6 10.1 11.00 215.8
1/22/84 56143.9 9.4 10.9 196.3
1/24/84 56351.5 9.3 9.75 207.7
1/25/84 56624.7 12.0 13.50 273.2    ($1.12/gal)
1/27/84 56801.9 7.4 10.00 177.3
1/29/84 56951.6 7.5 9.50 149.7
1/31/84 57221.3 10.6 12.00 269.6
```

Notice that there is some redundant information in the data; for example, the value of the trip odometer should be the difference between successive odometer readings. Far from being a liability, however, having this redundancy available will help us to check the completeness and consistency of the data. Such data should be recorded whenever they provide a really independent check on the other data items. We also put a comment at the end of the few lines where special circumstances were noted in the original record. This information will be deleted when we bring the data into S, so it is important that some convention makes it easy to identify—it doesn't much matter what convention—in our case we parenthesized all comments.

The process of recording the data on a text file already requires making some important decisions: how to represent dates, how to handle inconsistencies and missing information. The important principle is: Keep it simple. We have used one line in the file for each entry in the notebook, making it easy to compare the two visually. Rather than doing any manual conversion of dates, they are recorded in the *month/day/year* form, assuming we will do conversions later.

The data are being typed in this case by someone who understands what they represent. As a result, some mistakes in the data can be found, and corrective actions can be taken that would otherwise have to wait for analysis. There were a few times when information was entered in the wrong order

(October data entered at the bottom of a partially empty July page, and even written 7/28 rather than 10/28). It was possible to discover this because the mileage reading gives a good sequence number. Also, even in a well-kept record like this, there are inevitably a few missing data values. These were entered in the file as "NA". More typically, problems should be noted but left to be fixed using the computer or by consulting with the person responsible for the collection of the data. In our data, for example, it was obvious that occasionally the trip odometer was not reset, leading to impossible readings (this automobile cannot go 400 miles between fillups). Also, a few stations measured their gasoline in liters rather than gallons. This could have been converted to gallons when the data was entered, but it was easier to leave unconverted, since the number of liters was always much greater than the possible number of gallons. There were a few instances where the number of gallons was omitted altogether. In several of those cases, the price had been noted in the original record, enabling calculation of the gallons.

Once the data has been typed in, we can use the computer to check it. Before making an initial attempt to read the data into S, we need to eliminate the comment information, since we chose not to read it into S. This can be done in a text editor; for example, via `sed`:

```
$ sed 's/\(.*$//' < auto.mileage > new.mileage
```

We can also do a preliminary check using tools in the UNIX system. The tools frequently used for such operations are `grep` and `awk`. The latter is more powerful, but also takes more learning. We will illustrate a check with `grep`, in the form

```
grep pattern new.mileage
```

where *pattern* is a regular expression. We know that only digits, periods, spaces, and slashes should appear in the file, so we use the pattern `[^ ./0-9]`, which matches any character other than the legal ones. We need to quote this pattern in the command:

```
$ grep '[^ ./0-9]' new.mileage
8/12/84 68034.5 NA 11.00 213.9
```

This only picked up a missing value that we put in intentionally; we can handle the NA later.

The S function suitable for input of numeric data like this is `scan`. Scan will read any number of fields per line, returning a list with one component per field; that is, all the values in the first field go into the first component of the list, and so forth. The arguments to `scan` include a template for the list, giving the name for each component and some data that indicates whether the component should be numeric or character. We will keep the dates as character for now; the other fields are all numeric.

```
> honda ← scan("new.mileage",
+   list(cd="", od=0, g=0, d=0, t=0))
```

One reason for using `scan` fairly early is that it will catch automatically many of the same problems we would have looked for in the text file. For example, if one or more fields are missing from a line, an error will occur.

The data are now in S as a list. However, we are likely to be dealing with the individual fields separately during the data cleaning and initial analysis phase. For this purpose, it will be simpler to break out the components into separate vectors: cdate, odometer, gallons, dollars, and trip.

```
> cdate ← honda$cd   # calendar form of date
> odometer ← honda$od
> gallons ← honda$g
> dollars ← honda$d
> trip ← honda$t
```

Notice that we did not convert the data into a matrix with one row per record. While some people, and some forms of statistical software, have a strong inclination to make any such data into a matrix, our experience suggests that such a "regular" form may be detrimental, at least during initial analysis, because you tend to waste time remembering what column represents what and then extracting the relevant columns. More insidious is the tendency to think that, because the data is a neat matrix, it should be suitable for an equally neat analysis, say regression or some multivariate reduction technique. It is better, we think, to keep closer to the original data, in its humbler form, until we begin to understand what is going on.

Now that the data are available, we can use interrelationships among the numbers in order to further verify the input. For example, we would like to believe that the odometer readings are always increasing:

```
> all(diff(odometer)>0)
[1] F
```

Whoops! Here's a problem. What are the dates where this problem occurs?

```
> cdate[diff(odometer)<=0]
[1] "3/24/82" "8/22/86"
```

When we look at the original data file, we find two typing mistakes: a 9 that should be an 8, and a 1005594.3 that should be 105594.3. We make the fixes and then reread the data file.

This is typical of the kind of data verification that can be done easily in S; another reason to read the data in early on. We use our knowledge of the real context of the data:

- to check reasonable ranges of the input data, and of the values computed from them;

- to check known relationships among the variables.

As another example, the differences in the `odometer` numbers should be less than 300; if they are not, it indicates a probable missing fillup.

```
> range(diff(odometer))
[1]   34.8 442.2
> cdate[diff(odometer)>300]
[1] "8/27/81" "3/31/87"
```

Sure enough, checking back with the original records indicates that these two times we must have missed a fillup. Later on, when we compute miles per gallon, we will have to remember these two dates and do something special.

The `trip` numbers, too, should be less than 300 (although in this case we know that the trip odometer was occasionally not reset).

```
> range(trip)
[1]   35.0 539.7
> trip[trip>300]
[1] 475.0 473.3 539.7 400.0 494.3 435.5 500.5 425.4
> cdate[trip>300]
[1] "6/8/82"   "3/25/83"  "5/14/83"  "12/2/83"
[5] "2/18/84"  "10/6/84"  "12/19/84" "4/6/87"
```

Once again, we can go back to the original record to check these out. Let's check consistency between `diff(odometer)` and `trip`.

```
> miles ← diff(c(0,odometer))
> diffs ← abs(trip-miles)
> stem(diffs[diffs>1])

N = 42   Median = 4.8
Quartiles = 1.8, 40.1

Decimal point is 1 place to the right of the colon

    0 : 1111111222223333344455789
    1 : 0017
    2 : 0
    3 :
    4 : 00
    5 :
    6 :
    7 :
    8 :
    9 :
   10 : 0

High: 192.50 199.30 199.70 200.00 202.70 223.10
High: 236.00 248.80 276.98
```

The stem-and-leaf display shows that very seldom (only 42 of the 558 fillups) are the differences more than 1 mile, and even then, the differences are very infrequently more than 5 miles. Perhaps the thing to do is to check out the large differences, but not where `trip>300`, since we already investigated those.

```
> cdate[diffs > 5 & trip < 300]
 [1]  "8/27/81"  "8/30/81"  "11/8/81"   "4/13/82"
 [5]  "10/13/83" "10/17/83" "8/6/85"    "11/24/85"
 [9]  "12/21/86" "6/1/87"   "6/6/87"    "8/11/87"
[13]  "8/29/87"
```

Better yet, let's show these discrepancies in a table (exercise 9.1 asks how to produce this output):

```
             [,1]   [,2]
  8/27/81   62.4 262.1
  8/30/81  442.2 242.2
  11/8/81  219.2 119.2
  4/13/82  244.0 224.0
 10/13/83  264.3 255.8
 10/17/83  217.2 226.2
   8/6/85  258.8 252.1
 11/24/85  274.4 257.5
 12/21/86  252.9 242.2
   6/1/87  248.0 208.0
   6/6/87  189.9 230.0
  8/11/87  235.4 245.4
  8/29/87  265.3 255.3
```

What caused these discrepancies? Look at the first one, 8/27/81. It is suspicious that the two values differ by almost exactly 200 miles. Looking back at the original record, we find that the odometer reading had been entered incorrectly into the original log. This also explains the "missing fillup" that we had noticed earlier at this date. For the remainder of the discrepancies, there were three typing errors in the odometer readings and three probable errors in the original entry of the trip mileage. By correcting the odometer readings, we find that only these last three cases stand out. Now, we can have some faith in using `miles` as our variable that records the miles between fillups.

A similar check can be made on the `gallons` variable; here we know the capacity of the car's tank (less than 13 gallons). The result is to pick out the cases where the fillup was measured in liters—now is the time to convert these to gallons:

```
> gallons[gallons>13] ← gallons[gallons>13]/3.78541
```

We also check that the `dollars` variable is reasonable:

```
> range(dollars)
[1]   4.0 15.3
```

Yes, that looks fine.

These have been some examples of the self-checking that characterizes good interactive data analysis. You're encouraged to play with the data on your own. The cleaned up data are available in S, as the list `honda`, once you attach the examples section of the library by

```
library("examples")
```

The expression

```
names(honda)
```

will show which variables are present.

Exercises

9.1   Notice our neat table for `miles` and `trip`, labelling the rows with the `cdate` values. How would you produce this?

9.2   We computed

```
miles ← diff(c(0,odometer))
```

rather than

```
miles ← diff(odometer)
```

Why?

9.3   Each line in the `auto.mileage` file has a date containing two slashes. The following `grep` command prints each line with fewer than two slashes:

```
$ grep -v '.*/.*/' auto.mileage
```

What `grep` command would you use to find lines that contain more than two slashes?

9.4*   The following simple `awk` command prints any line in the `auto.mileage` file that does not contain exactly 5 fields:

```
$ awk 'NF!=5' auto.mileage
```

Find out more about `awk` and suggest other ways it could be used to check input data.

9.2 Problem Solving: Algorithms

This section illustrates the use of S to solve problems. The emphasis is on coming up with general and *reusable* solutions. When successful, we will have produced a tool for solving a class of problems. Regardless of what language is used to implement the solution, the process usually involves understanding what basic computations are needed, and then finding a method, or *algorithm*, that produces those computations. Problem solving in S differs in several ways. Both the inputs to the problem and the results produced are best thought of in terms of how they can be naturally represented as S objects. The solution can use a variety of resources: existing S functions, the interface through the `unix` function to other tools, and the interfaces to algorithms implemented in C and Fortran.

9.2.1 *Working with Dates*

We often encounter data that is tagged with a date. In the example of section 9.1, the data was accompanied by a date recorded in the conventional American form `month/day/year`. In order to use dates numerically, it is convenient to change them from this form into the so-called *Julian* date, which gives the number of days since some particular fixed date. Having converted the dates to numbers, we can compute things like the average time between fillups.

To get the months, days, and years as separate numbers, rather than the character date used in the last section, the easiest procedure is to edit the file, changing all the "/" characters to a space or tab, and then read the file again with `scan`:

```
> z ← scan("mileage",list(m=0,d=0,y=0,NULL,NULL,NULL,NULL))
> month ← z$m; day ← z$d; year ← z$y + 1900
```

Notice that we gave `scan` four `NULL` fields to tell it to skip the other columns of data. Alternatively, we could have used

```
> z ← scan("mileage",list(m=0,d=0,y=0),flush=TRUE)
```

where the `flush=TRUE` argument causes the remainder of any line to be ignored.

From these standard dates we want to compute Julian dates. The difficulty is taking into account the leap years since the Julian start day. Fortunately, several papers have been written on the subject, so we can start with a known method and proceed to implement it.[†]

[†]See J. Douglas Robertson, "Remark on Algorithm 398", *Comm. ACM,* Vol 15, No. 10 (Oct. 1972), p. 918. This gives the algorithm for converting dates into day of the week and it references the other algorithms used here.

Here is a function that computes Julian dates from month, day, and year.

```
julian ← function(month, day, year){
    year ← year + ifelse(month > 2, 0, -1)
    month ← month + ifelse(month > 2, -3, 9)
    c ← year %/% 100
    ya ← year - 100 * c
    (146097 * c) %/% 4 + (1461 * ya) %/% 4 +
        (153 * month + 2) %/% 5 + day + 1721119
}
```

Notice the use of ifelse so that we can compute whole vectors of Julian dates at once; if we had used if we would only have been able to compute them one at a time. Now we can convert the fillup dates to numbers and plot a histogram to look at the spread of the dates:

```
> auto.days ← julian(month,day,year)
> range(diff(auto.days))
[1]   0 25
> hist(diff(auto.days), breaks = -0.5:25.5)
```

shown in Figure 9.1.

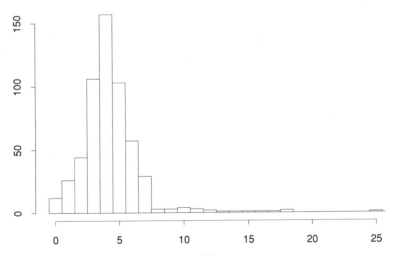

Figure 9.1. Distribution of days between fillups.

Sometimes it is convenient to convert Julian dates back into standard month/day/year form. For example, an equipment test is due to start April 20, 1995. On which day will it have been tested for 1000 days? We can do that with the following function. (This function is exceedingly ugly, but it is a literal translation of published Fortran code that we haven't tried to clean up. There are times when it is better to translate ugly code than to spend lots of energy making it aesthetically pleasing.)

```
month.day.year ← function(julian){
    j ← julian - 1721119
    y ← (4 * j - 1) %/% 146097
    j ← 4 * j - 1 - 146097 * y
    d ← j %/% 4
    j ← (4 * d + 3) %/% 1461
    d ← 4 * d + 3 - 1461 * j
    d ← (d + 4) %/% 4
    m ← (5 * d - 3) %/% 153
    d ← 5 * d - 3 - 153 * m
    d ← (d + 5) %/% 5
    y ← 100 * y + j
    y ← y + ifelse(m < 10, 0, 1)
    m ← m + ifelse(m < 10, 3, -9)
    list(month = m, day = d, year = y)
}
```

Now, to find out when the equipment test will end,

```
> month.day.year(julian(4,20,1995)+1000)
$month:
[1] 1
$day:
[1] 14
$year:
[1] 1998
```

Another problem is to determine the day of the week for a particular date. Again, others have blazed the trail, so we can just look up the relevant article and write the function.

```
day.of.week ← function(month, day, year){
    ix ← year + trunc((month - 14)/12)
    jx ← trunc((13 * (month + 10 - (month + 10) %/% 13 * 12)
        - 1)/5) + day + 77 + (5 * (ix - (ix %/% 100) *
        100)) %/% 4 + ix %/% 400 - (ix %/% 100) * 2
    jx %% 7
}
```

One other utility that we should have is a function that tells us today's Julian date. We can get today's date from the date function we used in section 6.3 to illustrate the unix interface, but we have to do a bit of manipulation in order to change it from the form that function gives back into a form we can compute with. The function, and the date command it uses, return a character string of the form:

```
> date()
[1] "Tue Jan 2 09:20:23 EST 2001"
```

There are several possible attacks, but perhaps the simplest is to replace the blanks in the string by newlines, using the editor sed. Then unix will read in the date as a character vector of length 6 (count the blanks), of which elements

2, 3, and 6 are month, day, year. So we can define the date function in this form as:

```
mdy ← function()
    unix("date|sed 's/  */\\n/g'")[c(2,3,6)]
```

(Note the two backslashes: we want the command to have "\n" in it, rather than an actual newline character.) Then, today's Julian date is given by:

```
jdate ← function(){
    months ← c("Jan", "Feb", "Mar", "Apr", "May",
        "Jun", "Jul", "Aug", "Sep", "Oct", "Nov", "Dec")
    now ← mdy()
    m ← match(now[1], months)
    d ← as.numeric(now[2])
    y ← as.numeric(now[3])
    julian(m, d, y)
}
```

Exercises

9.5   Write a function to take the output of `month.day.year` and produce a character string of the form: `"April 18, 1775"`.

9.6   Write a function `leap.year` that tells if the argument year is a leap year. Leap years are years that are divisible by 4. The exception is that centuries are not, but there is an exception to the exception that makes every fourth century, starting in 1600, a leap year.

9.7   Modify the `julian` function so that its first argument could be a character string giving a month name, rather than just a number.

9.8   Another form of date is "military Julian" which gives the year (of the 20th century) followed by the number of days into the year in the form "YYDDD". Thus, January 1, 1988 would be "88001". Write functions to compute military Julian dates from month, day, year.

9.9   Suppose you were given measurements of voltage along with the (irregularly-spaced) dates the measurements were taken. How would you produce a time-series plot of the voltage data in order to look for trends?

9.10   Another way of checking the dates for the automobile mileage is to use the S function `range` on the `month` and `day` vectors. The month numbers should be between 1 and 12 and the day numbers between 1 and 31. How could you use `range` to check that the day numbers within each month are valid, e.g., there is no February 31?

9.11   Was there any particular day of the week when gasoline was regularly purchased? Make a dot chart showing the number of gas purchases by day of the week.

9.12   Create a vector, `days`, giving the number of days the automobile has been operated, assuming it was delivered on April 29, 1981.

9.13   Compute miles per gallon and price per gallon vectors; plot each of them against days of operation.

9.14   The plot of miles per gallon against days of operation is hard to read because it contains outliers, has lots of variability, and lacks good date information. Produce a plot that omits the outliers and contains a fitted smooth line. Use the `axis` function to label the top of the plot at the beginning of each year from 1982 through 1987.

9.15*   Write a set of functions to compute with times expressed as hours/minutes/seconds. Try to integrate your functions with the date functions. You may find the notion of "seconds since midnight" an analogue to the Julian date. You may want to make use of the C-callable routine `time` described in section 2 of the UNIX system manual—it returns the number of seconds since the beginning of January 1, 1970.

9.2.2 *Sample Size from Percentages*

In a national computer magazine, an advertisement read[†] "If A and B tied for second, whose system was first? Ours." This was backed up by the following table:

Percent Considering Vendor for 1986		
1986 Rank		
1	Ours	14.6%
2	A	12.2%
3	B	12.2%
4	C	7.3%
5	D	7.3%

When reading this table, you may be struck by the exact duplication of the percentages for A and B, as well as for vendors C and D. Note, too that the 7.3% for C and D is exactly ½ of the 14.6% for Ours. These seem to imply a small sample size for the number of people in the survey. Can we figure out the sample size from this data?

     If there had been 1000 respondents, then we would know that 146 picked "Ours", 122 picked "A", and so on. But it is possible that the percentages in the table result from rounding the fractions based on a much smaller sample size. Also, we can't be sure of the exact size since there are many aliases—a fraction .1 could be generated by 1/10, by 2/20, by 3/30 ... , corresponding to sample sizes of 10, 20, and 30.

[†]Names have been disguised to protect everyone.

From this example, we can make an important generalization. What we really want to compute is the smallest sample size that could reasonably have generated the observed percentages or fractions. All we know is f, the published vector of fractions. We want to determine n, the denominator for those fractions, and i, the vector of numerators. Why do we expect we can do this? Each fraction gives some information about the possible denominator. If we use all of the fractions together, we can pool information and perhaps find a single denominator. Let us assume that the fractions f have been rounded to d decimal places; in our case $d = 3$. In other words, the fractions are accurate to $\pm\varepsilon = \frac{1}{2} \cdot 10^{-d} = 0.0005$, in our case. In symbols,

$$(f - \varepsilon) \le \frac{i}{n} \le (f+\varepsilon)$$

and it follows that

$$n(f - \varepsilon) \le i \le n(f+\varepsilon)$$

The following S function implements this idea.

```
find.denom ← function(f, eps){
    n ← 1
    repeat{
        i ← round(n * f)
        if(all((f-eps)*n <= i) && all((f+eps)*n >= i))
            return(n)
        n ← n + 1
    }
}
```

When we execute `find.denom`, we get:

```
> find.denom(c(.146,.122,.073),.0005)
[1]   41
```

Thus, we suspect that 41 people were involved in the survey and that 6 picked Ours, 5 picked A and B, and 3 picked C and D.[†]

Exercises

9.16   Will `find.denom` ever fail to stop?

9.17   How many people were involved if 38.5, 30.8, and 23.1% picked alternatives A, B, and C? What if the percentages were 14.2, 12.4, and 7.1?

[†]For further discussion of the ideas here, see W. Allen Wallis and Harry V. Roberts, *Statistics: A New Approach*, 1956, Free Press, New York, pp. 184-189.

9.18 Why would it be a good idea to have `find.denom` start with

```
n ← floor(1/min(f)+eps)
```

rather than `n ← 1`?

9.19* Find a better starting value for `n` than the one from the previous exercise. Hint: think of differences between values.

We have now solved the initial problem and produced a neat little method. If we were to apply this procedure widely, however, we might want to improve it by making it faster. As you may have guessed from looking at the previous solution, we are not being very efficient in our computations. Each time we try a new denominator, we execute

```
i ← round(n * f)
if(all((f-eps)*n <= i) && all((f+eps)*n >= i))
        return(n)
```

These computations take time proportional to the length of the `f` vector. Also, we expect that the number of iterations spent in the loop will be inversely proportional to the size of `eps`. This may mean lots of computation.

When we have a relatively simple algorithm that does not use any sophisticated S functions, one approach to speeding up the calculations is to look for something that could be fairly easily rewritten as a C or Fortran routine. This is a different rationale for using the C or Fortran interface than we discussed in chapter 7. There we emphasized being able to use existing, tested routines in those languages. Here, however, we are moving from an existing S function to a translation. In general, this is *not* as compelling a reason, but it may be advisable when the translation is straightforward and the potential time savings seem significant.

In our example, we anticipate some savings, because we can give up on a particular denominator as soon as a single fraction cannot be expressed with that denominator. At any rate, let's suppose we decide to implement the method as a C routine. Here is a working version:

```c
#include <math.h>

quantum(N, mm, DD, kk, dd)
long *N, *mm, *DD, *kk, *dd;
{
    int k = *kk, D = *DD, m = *mm, d, i, nout;

    for(i = 0; i <= k; i++)
        dd[i] = 0;
    for(d = 1; d <= D; d++) { /* count the outliers */
        nout = 0;
        for(i = 0; i < m; i++) {
            int n = round(N[i]*d, D);
            nout += 2*abs(n*D - N[i]*d) > d;
```

```
        if(nout > k) break;
    }
    if(nout > k || dd[nout] > 0) continue;
    k = nout;
    dd[k] = d;
    if(k == 0) break;
    }
}

round(n, d)
int n, d;
{
    double x = (double)n/d;
    return((int)(x+0.5));
}
```

We decided to call the function quantum because we are actually looking for the underlying size of the spacing between fractions, much as physicists looked for the finest-grained division in electrical charge. We also decided to add one other feature to the computations: the program will allow a certain number of "outliers"—fractions that are not representable with the particular denominator.

Let's look at the C routine for a moment: it represents the problem a little differently than before. Instead of accepting fractions as input, it takes the rational numbers N/D. (We will compute these from the fractions in the S function that calls this C routine.) It returns a vector of denominators, the first corresponding to 0 outliers, the second 1, etc. As before, the function loops through all possible denominators, but this time it stops considering a denominator as soon as more than the specified maximum number of outliers is detected.

Here is the S function that calls the C routine:

```
quantum ← function(f, outliers = 0){
    f ← unique(abs(f[!is.na(f)]))
    if(outliers > length(f)/2)
        stop("unusually large number of outliers")
    D ← 1
    repeat {
        N ← f * D
        if(all(abs(N - round(N)) < 1e-07)) break
        D ← D * 10
    }
    .C("quantum",
        as.integer(round(N)),
        as.integer(length(f)),
        as.integer(D),
        as.integer(outliers),
        d = integer(1 + outliers))$d
}
```

As usual when working with an interface to C or Fortran, it makes sense to clean up and check for anomalous data in the S function first. We get rid of missing data, take absolute values, and eliminate duplicates. We then test that the specified number of outliers is not too large. After that test, the function loops to find D and N, so that D*f is a vector of integers and D is a power of ten. Finally, the C routine is called and its results are returned.

Let's test the new function on a somewhat larger set of data. This data came from the newspaper *USA Today* in an article describing a forthcoming survey in which *US News and World Report* asked university presidents to list their choices for the best universities in the U.S. Here is the table of information, giving school name and the percent of the presidents who ranked that school in their top 10:

School	Percent	School	Percent
Stanford	65.0	Rice	23.6
Harvard	64.5	U. Va.	21.8
Yale	62.7	Johns Hopkins	19.1
Princeton	52.7	Northwestern	18.2
Berkeley	36.4	Columbia	17.3
Dartmouth	34.5	U. Pa.	16.4
Duke	32.7	U. Ill.	15.5
Chicago	30.0	Cal Tech	14.5
U. Mich	30.0	William & Mary	13.6
Brown	25.5	U. Wisc.	12.7
Cornell	24.5	Washington (Mo.)	12.7
MIT	24.5	Emory	10.9
U. N.C.	24.5	U. Texas	10.9

We may use `quantum` to answer the question, "How many university presidents appear to have responded to the survey?"

```
> quantum(university)
[1] 220
```

Thus, the fractions are perfectly consistent with responses from 220 university presidents. However, if we allow `quantum` to admit several outliers

```
> quantum(university,2)
[1] 220 110    0
```

This says that, if we are willing to accept a single outlier, the evidence points to 110 respondents. (The zero in the vector says that there is no denominator smaller than 110 that would work giving 2 outliers.) What is the outlying value? To answer this, we define a new function `quantum.out` that takes the fractions and the target denominator and returns the indices of the fractions that do not fit.

```
quantum.out ← function(f, d){
   D ← 1
   repeat {
      N ← f * D
      if(all(abs(N - round(N)) < 1e-07)) break
      D ← D * 10
   }
   seq(along = f)[abs(round(d * f)/d - f) > 1/(2 * D)]
}
```

```
> university.name[ quantum.out(university,110) ]
[1] "Stanford"
```

When the full details of the survey came out in the October 26, 1987 issue of *US News and World Report*, the value for Stanford was 65.5, not 65.0.

Exercises

9.20 Try running the `quantum` function for the university data, using `65.5` for Stanford.

9.21 The expression necessary to compute `D` is present in `quantum` and in `quantum.out`. Turn it into a separate function, `find.D`, then revise the other functions to use it.

9.22 How does the running time for this function vary with the length of the vector of fractions? with the number of outliers? Run a few tests to confirm your answer.

9.23 Modify `quantum.out` to allow it to take a vector of denominators and return a list, each element of which gives the subscripts of the outliers corresponding to one of the denominators.

9.24* Suppose you wanted to compute a rough "likelihood" measure corresponding to `quantum` output. You might think of using

```
quantum.prob ← function(f,d){
   D ← find.D(f)
   -(length(f)-seq(0,length=length(d))) * log10(d/D)
}
```

(Function `find.D` was introduced in exercise 9.21.) Try it on the university data. Explain what it does.

9.2.3 *Names from Phone Numbers*

Many businesses advertise catchy telephone numbers that are made up of letters rather than digits. "Want to sell your car? Dial C-A-R C-A-S-H." You have even seen it in this book; the AT&T Software Sales organization that distributes S has the phone number "800-828-UNIX".

Suppose someone has given you such a phone number and you'd like to find out what numbers to dial rather than letters. This is a character-transliteration operation, suitable for the *tr* command.

```
phone.number ← function(text)
    unix(
"tr abcdefghijklmnoprstuvwxy 22233344455566677788899",
        input=text)
```

The `phone.number` function uses `unix` to run a command that transliterates characters a, b, and c into 2, and so on, just mimicking the way that letters appear on the phone keys (in North America, at least). The modified character object then becomes the value of `phone.number`. For example:

```
> phone.number(c("car-cash","800-828-unix"))
[1] "227-2274"    "800-828-8649"
```

Of course, we would probably rather have one of the nifty phone numbers of our own, like "HOT-LINE" or "S-SYSTEM". Unfortunately, we are probably stuck with our present phone number, say 555-6789. The question is: are there any interesting words we can make out of it?

Let's start out with a somewhat simpler problem that will be important in the work we want to do: given an integer, how can we compute the individual digits? We want a function, `digits`, that will take a single multiple-digit number and produce a vector of the individual digits making it up. We already did this in section 6.2.3, using a recursive function. Let's try another approach here. The basic idea is to use the integer-divide operator, "`%/%`", to chop off trailing digits, and then use the modulus operator, "`%%`", to give us a single digit. For example

```
> 5556789 %/% 100
[1] 55567
> 55567 %% 10
[1] 7
```

Using this hint, can you write the function? Think about it for a minute or two before looking at our function. Try, as we have emphasized before, to think of the computation as a single operation using a vector of numbers, rather than iterating to get individual digits.

```
digits ← function(n){
    if(n == 0) return(0)
    n ← abs(n)
    powers ← round(10^(floor(log10(n)):0))
    (n %/% powers) %% 10
}
```

We generate a vector of powers of 10 as long as the number of digits of n. The function then divides the number by that vector (using integer division) and picks up the last digit of each of the quotients.

```
> digits(5556789)
[1] 5 5 5 6 7 8 9
```

Now that we have a mechanism for splitting the phone number into digits, we can think about the possible letters each digit can map into. Here's the idea: we create a list that gives the vectors of characters corresponding to each digit. Then, by subscripting that list, we pick up the letters corresponding to the digits in our phone number. Finally, we use the outer function in a loop, each time adding on one more letter to the set of words.

```
all.words ← function(n){
    dial ← list(
        "0",
        "1",
        c("a", "b", "c"),
        c("d", "e", "f"),
        c("g", "h", "i"),
        c("j", "k", "l"),
        c("m", "n", "o"),
        c("p", "r", "s"),
        c("t", "u", "v"),
        c("w", "x", "y")
    )
    d ← digits(n) + 1
    a ← dial[[d[1]]]
    for(letter in dial[d[-1]])
        a ← outer(a, letter, paste, sep = "")
    as.vector(a)
}
```

Let's try it on a short example (since a full phone number like 555-6789 can produce up to 3^7 candidate "words"):

```
> all.words(8649)
 [1] "tmgw" "umgw" "vmgw" "tngw" "ungw" "vngw"
 [7] "togw" "uogw" "vogw" "tmhw" "umhw" "vmhw"
[13] "tnhw" "unhw" "vnhw" "tohw" "uohw" "vohw"
[19] "tmiw" "umiw" "vmiw" "tniw" "uniw" "vniw"
[25] "toiw" "uoiw" "voiw" "tmgx" "umgx" "vmgx"
[31] "tngx" "ungx" "vngx" "togx" "uogx" "vogx"
[37] "tmhx" "umhx" "vmhx" "tnhx" "unhx" "vnhx"
[43] "tohx" "uohx" "vohx" "tmix" "umix" "vmix"
[49] "tnix" "unix" "vnix" "toix" "uoix" "voix"
[55] "tmgy" "umgy" "vmgy" "tngy" "ungy" "vngy"
[61] "togy" "uogy" "vogy" "tmhy" "umhy" "vmhy"
[67] "tnhy" "unhy" "vnhy" "tohy" "uohy" "vohy"
[73] "tmiy" "umiy" "vmiy" "tniy" "uniy" "vniy"
[79] "toiy" "uoiy" "voiy"
```

The function outer is the key to making all.words work. Make sure you understand how it works.

Exercises

9.25   Make `phone.number` recognize both upper-case and lower-case letters.

9.26   Extend `digits` to take a vector of numbers as input and produce a list, each element being the vector of digits in one of the input numbers.

9.27   Write an inverse of the `digits` function, that turns a vector of digits into a single integer.

9.28   Generalize digits and its inverse so that they take an optional `base` argument, with default value 10. Use these to write a function that converts an integer from one base to another.

9.29   Use the `all.words` function to determine what words you can make from your phone number.

9.30   Modify `all.words` to put out its answer in alphabetical order. Can you do it without using the `sort` function?

9.31*   The real problem with `all.words` is that it generates so much junk. Can you think of ways to determine the most interesting words in the output? You might consider letter combinations that occur frequently in English, etc.

9.3 Collections of Objects: Data Organization

Suppose we want to construct a function named `collection` to help collect objects into related groups. We would like to say

```
> collection("cars")
```

to announce that the objects we mention subsequently may belong to the "cars" collection. This would include newly created objects as well as existing objects in the "cars" collection. Objects in a collection are often related to a particular project—we want to keep these separate from objects in our other work. By putting, for example, the `days` object in the collection, we would be in no danger of overwriting another object with the same name but an entirely different purpose.

   The mechanism we will use to implement collections is the *search list* of data directories that S uses to find objects. See section 5.4 if you're not familiar with this topic. The `attach` function allows us to put something new on the search list, and in particular, attaching a new directory in position 1 causes the new directory to become the working directory. Attaching a new working directory has the effect that assignments will create objects there and all references to objects will be found there first.

   The next decision is where to put the new directory. To keep the collection mechanism reasonably hidden, and not likely to interfere with other work, we decide to put it in a *subdirectory* of the working directory, `.Data`.

Here's a simple implementation:

```
collection ← function(dir){
      realdir ← paste(".Data/.", dir, sep = "")
      attach(realdir, pos = 1)
}
```

This is an example of its use:

```
> x ← 1
> collection("cars")
> x ← 2   # this x is in the cars collection
> x
[1] 2
> q()        # quit from S
$ S          # back into S
> x          # will get the original x
[1] 1
```

Notice that we paste ".Data/." onto the front of the collection name in order to name the directory where the collection objects will go. We name the directory .cars rather than just cars so that there is a naming convention that will later enable us to recognize collections.

There are two problems with this implementation of collection:

- The search list grows with each call to collection. Since we want just one collection active at a time, we need to keep track of whether a collection was in effect so that the data directory corresponding to the previous collection can be taken off the search list.
- There is no way to say we want no active collection.

Let's remedy these problems now. We will change collection so that, if it is called without an argument, the name of the special data directory is taken off the search list. Also, if collection is executed while a collection is in effect, we will remove the old data directory from the search list before the new directory is added.

Let's create a permanent object, cur.collection, to hold the name of any current collection. We can also look at the argument to collection and operate differently if no argument was given:

```
collection ← function(dir){
    detach(1) # get rid of old collection directory
    if(missing(dir)) cur.collection <<- character(0)
    else {
        cur.collection <<- dir
        realdir ← paste(".Data/.", dir, sep = "")
        attach(realdir, pos = 1)
    }
}
```

In this version, we used the "`<<-`" assignment operator to force `cur.collection` to be assigned as a permanent object, rather than an object in the local frame of this call to `collection`.

Are there still problems with *this* version? Well, although we now save the name of the current collection in the object `cur.collection`, we did not check to see if `cur.collection` was defined before using `detach(1)` to remove the object in position 1 of the search list. This problem is easy to solve—we will use the `exists` function to see if `cur.collection` exists.

A more subtle problem is that the object `cur.collection` will be saved on a permanent data directory and hence will persist from one S session to the next. When you next start up S after a session using `collection`, the object `cur.collection` will still be around even though the corresponding directory will not be on the search list. What we need is to make the `cur.collection` object go away at the end of a session. To accomplish this, we use a *session object,* created by the `assign` function (see section 5.4). A session object is available only during a single session with S; when you quit from S, all session objects go away. To create a session object, use

```
assign("cur.collection", dir, frame=0)
```

instead of

```
cur.collection <<- dir
```

The `frame=0` argument to `assign` produces a session object. Now, here is the definition for our function:

```
collection ← function(dir){
    active ← exists("cur.collection") &&
        length(cur.collection)>0
    if(missing(dir)) {   # take off collection
        if(active){
            detach(1)
            assign("cur.collection", character(0), frame = 0)
        }
    }
    else {
        realdir ← paste(".Data/.", dir, sep = "")
        if(active) detach(1)
        attach(realdir, pos = 1)
        assign("cur.collection", dir, frame = 0)
    }
}
```

Notice the expression

```
exists("cur.collection") && length(cur.collection)>0
```

This works because of the "`&&`" operator.

The expression

```
length(cur.collection)
```

will only be evaluated if `cur.collection` exists.

This is better, but we can still improve on things. It would be nice to be reminded that we are using a particular collection. We can use the `options` function to change the S prompt to indicate that a collection is in effect. Also, we really ought to test whether the collection subdirectory exists and give the user the option to create it if it doesn't.

For now, assume that there exists a function `is.dir`, that checks to see if the specified directory exists (the definition of `is.dir` is presented below).

```
collection ← function(dir){
    active ← exists("cur.collection") &&
        length(cur.collection)>0
    result ← if(active) cur.collection else character(0)
    if(missing(dir)) {
        if(active) {
            detach(1)
            options(prompt = "> ")# restore prompt
            assign("cur.collection", character(0), frame = 0)
        }
    }
    else {
        realdir ← paste(".Data/.", dir, sep = "")
        if(!is.dir(realdir)) {
            cat(dir, "does not exist.  Create it? ")
            ans ← readline()
            if(!is.na(match(ans, c("n", "no", "N", "NO"))))
                return()
            if(unix(paste("mkdir", realdir), output = F))
                stop( )
        }
        if(active) detach(1)
        attach(realdir, pos = 1)
        assign("cur.collection", dir, frame = 0)
        options(prompt = paste(dir, "> "))
    }
    result
}
```

This version also returns the old value of the collection as its result.

Here is the promised definition for `is.dir`. It simply uses the `test` command to check to see if the directory exists. The `unix` function, when given `output=FALSE` as an argument, returns the status of the command as its (invisible) value. A status of zero means that the command worked.

```
is.dir ← function(dir)
    unix(paste("test -d", dir), output = F) == 0
```

Finally, let's put together a function `lscollection` to give us a listing of the existing collections. It just uses the command "`ls -aF .Data`" to get a list of all files and directories in `.Data`, with a "/" appended to any that are directories. Then `grep` is used to select all those that begin with "." and end with "/". Finally `sed` gets rid of the first two directory names, "." and "..", and strips off the trailing "/".

```
lscollection ← function()
    unix("ls -aF .Data|grep '^\\..*/'|sed -e '1,2d' -e 's/.$//'")
```

Now that we have written `collection` and `lscollection`, we can interact with S as follows:

```
> x ← 3    # creates x object
> collection("cars")
cars does not exist.  Create it? yes
cars >   # note that the S prompt is changed
cars >   # to reflect the new collection
cars >   x ← 7   # creates x in the collection directory
cars >   x
[1] 7
cars >   collection()  # take off the collection
> x  # now this refers to the original x
[1] 3
> lscollection()
[1] ".cars"
```

The exercises will help you enhance `collection` and `lscollection`.

Exercises

9.32   We implemented a collection, e.g. `cars`, by creating a directory `.Data/.cars` underneath the `.Data` directory. This means that S objects will all be contained at some depth within the `.Data` directory. What are the advantages and disadvantages of placing collection directories underneath the `.Data` directory? What alternatives can you think of?

9.33   The final version of `collection` printed a message for confirmation before creating a new collection directory. Is this a good idea?

9.34   What would happen if you had an S object named `.cars` and then tried to evaluate `collection("cars")`?

9.35   Modify `lscollection` to omit subdirectory `.Help` and to get rid of the leading "." on the subdirectory names.

9.36   Suppose you run S in a directory that does not contain a `.Data` directory. What happens if you try to use the `collection` and `lscollection` functions? What could be done about it?

9.37* The entire `collection` procedure can get confused if you decide to change the contents of the search list by calling `attach` or `detach` directly. Can you think of any way to avoid this situation while still allowing maximal freedom to adjust the search list?

9.38 Can you think of other features that might make `collection` more useful?

9.39 In the final version of `collection`, we had the line

```
if(unix(paste("mkdir", realdir), output = F))
    stop( )
```

Explain what it does (if you don't know, try it and figure out what it is trying to do).

9.40 The `collection` function returns the old value of the collection as its result. Why is this a good idea? Why might it be better to use `invisible(result)` as the last line of the function?

9.4 A Computer Game: Simulation

In this section, we will create a computer simulation of a card game, using interactive graphics. If this sounds too frivolous, console yourself that we are also illustrating principles for computer simulation of a model or system. We will see that the simulation can be organized effectively by designing a class of objects that represents the *state* of the system, and by writing the simulation as a simple process of updating the state of the system corresponding to an event. In our example, the simulation also involves interaction with a user, which we handle through graphical display and graphic input. The functions needed to do the simulation require a bit more programming discussion than the other sections of the chapter (although the implementation is much easier in S than in most other languages). The discussion is important, however, because it illustrates a style of top-down design that works well for many such problems.

We want to simulate a form of solitaire known as "golf". The game is simple, but with some strategy. Here are its rules:

- The player sorts the deck and lays out a board, face up, consisting of 7 columns and 5 rows. The remaining cards are then turned up, one at a time. The object of the game is to move cards from the board onto the current turn-up card.

- The bottom card of each column can move down if it is one more or one less than the current turn-up, except that nothing can be moved down onto a King. Cards are ordered Ace, 2, 3, ..., Jack, Queen, King, and a King may not be played on an Ace. The card moved down becomes the turn-up.

- When no more cards can be moved down, the next card from the hand is turned up.
- The game ends when the player has gone through the whole hand or has cleared the board.

Clearing the board occurs infrequently; a natural way of scoring the game is to count the number of cards left on the board at the end. Strategy comes in when there is a choice of card to be moved. The player wants to get as many moves in a row as possible, and also to leave the board in a state so that the next turn-up is likely to generate more moves. You might want to get a deck of cards and play a few times before reading on, to get a feel for the game.

We want to simulate this game. Specifically, we imagine a player sitting at a graphics display and typing:

```
> golf()
```

The function will then generate a new game, display it, and repeatedly interact with the user, who will point at the card to be moved down from the board, or at the turn-up card to take the next card from the hand. The displayed game, consisting of the board and the current turn-up, will be updated correspondingly. Moves will continue until the game ends, at which point the function will return the player's score. Turning this verbal description into an S function gives us:

```
golf ← function(){
    state ← generate.game()
    display.game(state)
    while(!finished(state))
        state ← next.move(state)
    score(state)
}
```

Here, `state` is some S object that represents the current state of the game. In our example, and in simulation generally, a clean design of this object makes the implementation easier and more effective. For `golf`, the state contains the game as visible to the player; namely, the board and the current turn-up card, and also the cards in the (turned-down) hand. Let's begin, then, by deciding to represent the state as an S list with components `board`, `turnup`, and `hand`. It is natural to think of `state$board` as a 5 by 7 matrix whose elements show the cards on the board. Then `state$turnup` is a single card and `state$hand` is the vector of the remaining cards.

To implement the state, we have to decide how to represent the cards themselves. The deck of 52 cards is identified by 4 suits with 13 cards, or "spots", in each suit. We will need to display the cards in this form, but let's use internally a simple representation of the deck as the numbers 1 to 52, with the understanding that `1:13` represent the clubs, `14:26` the diamonds, `27:39` the hearts and `40:52` the spades, each in increasing order from Ace to King.

With this choice for the state, generating a new game with a shuffled deck is simple. To shuffle the deck we use the function `sample`, and then make the board from the first 35 cards, the turn-up from the next card, and the hand from the remainder:

```
generate.game ← function(){
    deck ← sample(1:52, 52)
    list( board = matrix(deck[1:35],5,7),
        turnup = deck[36],
        hand = deck[37:52] )
}
```

Whenever a card is moved from the board, we also need some way to signal that this position is empty. A simple choice is to set the corresponding element of the board to 0.

With this design for the state of the game, the next step is to decide how to display it and interact to get the user's next move. We could just print out the board and the turn-up, and have the user type the move. However, this would be very different from the actual game, and so tedious for the user that no one would want to play. Instead we will use a graphical representation. The player will indicate his move by pointing (via graphic input) at the card to be moved. This will either be the bottom card in one of the columns, or else the turn-up card if the player has decided to turn up the next card in the hand. Figure 9.2 shows an initial configuration for the game.

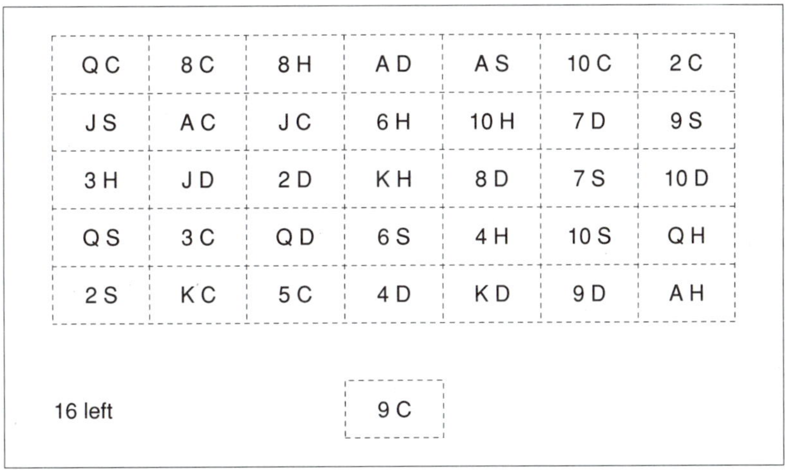

Q C	8 C	8 H	A D	A S	10 C	2 C
J S	A C	J C	6 H	10 H	7 D	9 S
3 H	J D	2 D	K H	8 D	7 S	10 D
Q S	3 C	Q D	6 S	4 H	10 S	Q H
2 S	K C	5 C	4 D	K D	9 D	A H

16 left   9 C

Figure 9.2. The card game "golf": a 5 by 7 board, a turn-up card to play onto, and an initial turned down deck of 16 cards.

To display the cards, we just need the 52 symbols (as character strings) in some object, say `deck.symbols`. In an elegant graphics display, this might actually contain the symbolic "pips" for the suits, but we'll settle for the letters "C", "D", "H", and "S" to denote the suits, and "A", "2", up to "K" to denote the spots. We will assume that there is an object of length 52, `deck.symbols`, containing character strings representing the cards. (See exercise 9.41 to generate `deck.symbols`.)

To display the current game, we need to choose a coordinate system. With the board represented as a matrix, it's natural to imagine the `[i,j]` element of the matrix displayed at x-coordinate `j` and y-coordinate `i`. The turn-up will be centered below the board, down a bit more so it is visibly not part of the board. A position of `(4, -1)` seems reasonable. Now we can write `display.game`: it will clear the display, set up the user coordinates, and plot the board and turn-up card:

```
display.game ← function(state){
    frame()
    par(usr=c(0,8,-2,6))
    board ← state$board
    text(col(board), row(board), deck.symbols[board])
    segments(0.5:7.5, 0.5, 0.5:7.5, 5.5, lty=3)
    segments(0.5, 0.5:5.5, 7.5, 0.5:5.5, lty=3)
    text(4, -1, deck.symbols[ state$turnup ])
}
```

(The functions `row` and `col` return matrices of the row and column numbers corresponding to `board`.)

Now to implement `next.move`. We need a function that calls the `locator` function to get the user's move, and decides whether the user has pointed to one of the columns, or to the turn-up card. Let's refer to the turn-up card as column 0, and encapsulate all this as the function `next.card`:

```
next.card ← function(){
    pos ← locator(1)
    if(pos$y < 0) 0
    else min(7, max( round(pos$x), 1) )
}
```

Using `next.card`, the definition of `next.move` function is then:

```
next.move ← function(state){
    repeat {
        which ← next.card()
        if(legal.move(state,which))break
        cat("The card in column", which,
            "is illegal; try again\n")
    }
    update.game(state,which)
}
```

Function `legal.move` returns TRUE or FALSE according to whether a move is legal. Remembering that we are setting elements of the board to 0 when they are moved, we just need to compare the first nonzero number in column `which` with the spot value of `state$turnup`.

```
legal.move ← function(state, which){
    if(which == 0)return(TRUE)  # next from hand
    row ← first.non.zero(state$board[,which])
    spot ← deck.spots(state$board[row,which])
    turnup.spot ← deck.spots(state$turnup)
    if(spot == 0) FALSE
    else if(turnup.spot == 13) FALSE    # King
    else if(turnup.spot == 1) spot == 2
    else abs(spot - turnup.spot) == 1
}

first.non.zero ← function(x)
    seq(along=x) [x!=0] [[1]]

deck.spots ← function(cards)
    ((cards - 1) %% 13) + 1
```

The last four lines of legal.move implement the rule we described at the beginning of the section. If there are no cards left in the column (spot == 0) or if the turn-up is a King, the move is illegal. If the turn-up is an ace, only a 2 is legal. Otherwise the spot must be one more or one less than the turn-up.

The function update.game updates the display for the corresponding move and returns the modified version of state. We need to erase the turn-up, replace it with the new card (either the next one from the hand or the first nonzero in the column) and, in the latter case, erase the card on the board. Erasing is done in S graphics by plotting in color 0 (the background color). At the same time, we will update the board, hand, and turn-up.

```
update.game ← function(state, which){
    text( 4, -1, deck.symbols[ state$turnup ], col = 0 )
    if(which>0) update.board(state,which)
    else update.hand(state)
}

update.board ← function(state, which){
    row ← first.non.zero(state$board[,which])
    new ← state$board[row,which]
    text( which, row, deck.symbols[new], col = 0)
    text( 4, -1, deck.symbols[new] )
    state$board[row, which] ← 0
    state$turnup ← new
    state
}

update.hand ← function(state){
    if(length(state$hand)>0){
        state$turnup ← new ← state$hand[1]
        text( 4, -1, deck.symbols[new] )
        state$hand ← state$hand[ -1 ]
    } else state$hand ← NULL
    state
}
```

Now we have everything except the rule for finishing the game and computing the score. The game is finished after the user picks the turn-up when there are no cards left in the hand—in this case `update.hand` has set the `hand` component to `NULL`. The game is also finished if all the cards on the board have been selected.

```
finished ← function(state)
    is.null(state$hand) || all(state$board == 0)

score ← function(state)
    sum( state$board > 0 )
```

That's it. A hundred lines of S to implement a nice little computer game. Try it out, if you have a suitable graphics device. As with the other examples in the book, you can attach the `golf` functions by

```
library("examples")
```

The exercises below mostly refine the user interface, examine some of the strategy of the implementation, and explore some extensions.

Exercises

9.41 Generate the object `deck.symbols`, containing the character strings "C A", "C 2", "C 3", and so on, up to "S K". Hint: think of the object as a 13 by 4 matrix:

```
"A C"   "A D"   "A H"   "A S"
"2 C"   "2 D"   "2 H"   "2 S"
"3 C"   "3 D"   "3 H"   "3 S"
"4 C"   "4 D"   "4 H"   "4 S"
"5 C"   "5 D"   "5 H"   "5 S"
"6 C"   "6 D"   "6 H"   "6 S"
"7 C"   "7 D"   "7 H"   "7 S"
"8 C"   "8 D"   "8 H"   "8 S"
"9 C"   "9 D"   "9 H"   "9 S"
"10 C" "10 D" "10 H" "10 S"
"J C"   "J D"   "J H"   "J S"
"Q C"   "Q D"   "Q H"   "Q S"
"K C"   "K D"   "K H"   "K S"
```

and use the `outer` function.

9.42 One user requested that the display show how many cards are left in the turned-down hand. Add this as a text display at the left, on the same level as the turn-up. Remember that you need to erase it as part of making each move, then redraw it.

9.43   The error message doesn't actually tell you what you did wrong. Change `legal.move` to print things like:

```
Can't play a 3 on a 7
Can't play anything on a K
```

9.44   It would be nice to keep track of the user's scores for all the games played. Add some code to `golf` that uses the `<<-` operator to create or add to a global object, say `Golf.score`, that contains the scores of past games.

9.45   Suppose several people wanted to play the same set of `golf` games in a tournament. How would you arrange that, without modifying `golf` itself?

9.46*   Add a feature that allows users to select a SAVE button on the screen, with the result that the current state of the game is saved in an object, say, `Golf.save`. To allow the user to restart the game, `golf` should take an optional argument that is the state saved from a previous game. If the argument is supplied, then `golf` will restart with that state, rather than generating a new game.

9.5 Presentation Graphics

The graphics facilities in S are most attuned to producing displays for analysis—presenting information in the best form for learning about the data. Sometimes, however, there is a desire for specific effects, pretty pictures, or what is often called "presentation graphics", characterized by areas of color, simulated 3-dimensional displays, extensive legends, etc. This section illustrates how the graphics primitives in S, along with its programming facilities, allow many of these displays to be created. We should say right away that nothing in this section will help particularly in analyzing data, and some of the displays are actually *less* insightful than simpler plots, because they add irrelevant material that can obscure what is really going on. Still, if the boss wants something striking, it's good to know how to produce it.

As an example, look at Figure 9.3, which adds drop shadows to a standard barplot. How did we arrive at this plot? First, let's see how we computed the data that was displayed on the plot.

```
> yearly.starts ← aggregate(hstart)
```

Since our housing start data, `hstart`, is monthly, we used the `aggregate` function that was introduced in 5.5.4 to add up the values in each year to create a yearly time-series.

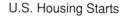

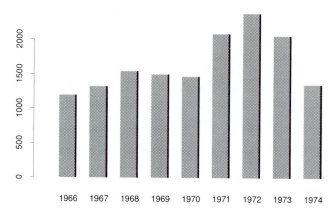

Figure 9.3. A barplot with drop shadows of United States housing starts.

Next, we constructed a slight modification of the `barplot` function that draws barplots with drop shadows.

```
backdrop ← function(x, names=NULL, ...){
    x ← rep(x,rep(2,length(x)))
    if(missing(names))
        barplot(x, space=c(1,-1.1), col=1:2, ...)
    else
        barplot(x, space=c(1,-1.1), col=1:2,
            names=c(rbind(names,""))), ...)
}
```

The idea is to lay down the drop shadow bar and then put another bar almost on top of it. We give two values as `barplot`'s `space=` argument. This argument tells how much space (in units of bar widths) should be put between adjacent bars. The `space` values are reused cyclically, so by giving two different values, the space between bars 1 and 2 is substantially different than the space between bars 2 and 3. Think of a pointer at the bar center. `Barplot` draws one bar, moves the pointer right by 1, adds in the spacing value of −1.1, thus moving leftward by .1 bar widths. The overlapping bar is drawn, and then the pointer moves rightward 1+1 bar widths to start the next set.

```
> backdrop(yearly.starts,
+    names=as.character(time(yearly.starts)))
> title("U.S. Housing Starts")
```

Finally, we invoked the function and put on an appropriate title. This function will only work on raster-based display devices that allow overplotting to wipe out what was previously plotted—not on pen plotters or other stroke-drawn graphics devices.

Exercises

9.47 Produce a drop-shaded plot showing housing starts aggregated by month. Your plot should contain 12 bars labelled "Jan", "Feb", etc.

9.48 Modify `backdrop` so that the drop shadows are on the left of the bar.

9.49 Can you think of other expressions that the `backdrop` function could use to replicate the x values?

9.50 Modify the `backdrop` function so that you can specify the colors of the bars and shadow. Make it possible for each bar to be a different color.

Another common habit in presentation graphics is to add numbers to barplots to tell the reader what actual data produced the results. Look at Figure 9.4.

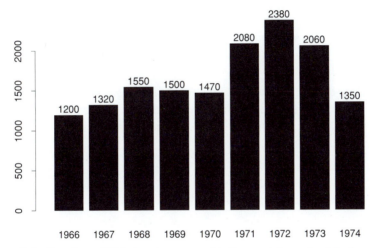

Figure 9.4. Bar chart of U.S. housing starts with figures at the ends of the bars.

Again, we wrote a function that wraps around `barplot`.

```
numbar ← function(x, ...){
    xmid ← barplot(x, ..., col=1)
    r ← diff(range(c(0,x)))
    text(xmid,x+.03*r,signif(x,3))
}
```

The `barplot` function returns a vector of the coordinates of the bar centers, and we use the `range` function to find the range spanned by the bars. Thus, it is easy to place counts, rounded to 3 significant digits, on the ends of the bars.

```
> numbar(yearly.starts,
+   names=as.character(time(yearly.starts)))
```

Exercises

9.51   Function `number` won't work right with negative values. Why not? Fix it.

9.52   Incorporate the features of `numbar` in the `backdrop` function.

Let us now leave the realm of barplots and look at another favorite pastime of presentation graphics—coloring or shading areas. How about jazzing up a standard time-series plot of our housing start data? Again, assume we have a raster-display device. Rather than plotting a simple line, we shade the area below the line, superimpose a title atop the shaded area, and omit the box. First, we construct a function to draw a shaded time-series plot.

```
shaded.ts ← function(x,color=1){
    plot(x,ylab="",type="n",bty="l")
    polygon( c(time(x),tsp(x)[2]),
        c(x,par("usr")[3]),
        col=color
        )
}
```

This function calls `plot` to set up the coordinate system and draw just the "L"-shaped box. It then draws a polygon that is topped by the data points, goes down to the *x*-axis, and then back to the left. We invoke the function as follows:

```
> shaded.ts(hstart,col=2)  # Figure 9.5
```

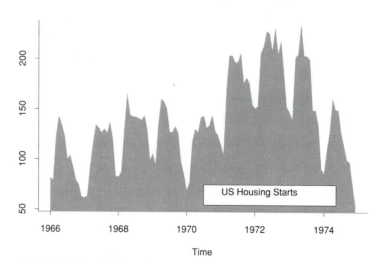

Figure 9.5. Monthly U.S. housing starts data drawn with the area under the curve shaded.

Now all that remains is to put the title on the plot. We could do this by using the `title` function, but this time we use `legend` to place the titling information atop the plot. `Legend` will blank out the area below the legend before drawing it by using `polygon` to draw a rectangle in color 0, the background color. All that we need to do is give the coordinates of the upper-left corner of the legend:

```
> legend(1970.5,75,"US Housing Starts")
```

Exercises

9.53 Should the `shaded.ts` function ensure that zero is the base for drawing the shaded area? Why or why not?

9.54 Construct a function that operates like `shaded.ts` but that shows two superimposed shaded time-series. This is another favorite style of graph for corporate reports, etc. Hint: draw the "largest" time-series in back and overlay the smaller one.

9.55 Extend your function from the previous exercise to accommodate an arbitrary number of time-series arguments.

Using function `shaded.ts` as a starting point, it is not very difficult to produce a function to shade in the area between two curves. Figure 9.6 shows a diagram much like the one that Playfair constructed to show the balance of trade in England from 1700 to 1780. We are given two time-series and want to fill in the area between them.

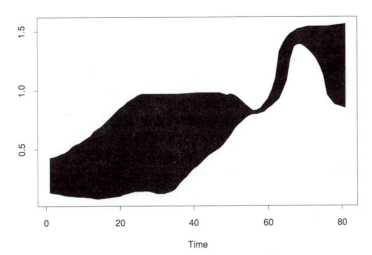

Figure 9.6. Plot of balance of trade in England, after Playfair.

```
balance.of.trade ← function(income,outgo,color=1){
    # adjust so income and outgo have same start and end
    income ← income+0*outgo
    outgo ← outgo+0*income
    plot(income,type="n",ylim=range(income,outgo),ylab="")
    lines(income)
    lines(outgo)
    polygon(
        c(time(income),rev(time(outgo))),
        c(income,rev(outgo)),
        col=color
        )
    }
```

What is special about this function? One feature is that it works when the two time-series have different time domains. Arithmetic operators in S, when given two time-series, always produce an output series that is the intersection of the two inputs. Hence, by adding `0*outgo` to `income`, we shorten income to the intersection of the time domains. The polygon drawing is practically identical to the polygon drawing done in the previous example. In this case, no over-plotting is done, so this plot can be done on any graphics device capable of shading in areas.

Anyway, now that the function is constructed, we need only invoke it

```
> balance.of.trade(imports,exports)
```

to produce our plot.

Exercises

9.56 Modify the `balance.of.trade` function to place labels on the plot identifying the two lines that bound the shaded region.

9.57 How would you superimpose the legend "Trade Imbalance" on top of the shaded area?

9.58 How effective is the `balance.of.trade` plot at showing the magnitude of the difference between imports and exports? What other plot would be more effective?

A new idea in business graphics was presented by Irwin W. Jarett in *Computer Graphics and Reporting Financial Data*, Ronald Press, John Wiley, 1983. The book shows graphical methods of displaying traditional business reports, for example, the income statement in Figure 9.7.

How do we construct such a plot? It is fairly easy given the tools already present in S. The plot looks basically like a horizontal barplot, and in fact, that is exactly how it was produced. Think of each line of the display as being composed of two bars—a background-colored bar (that may be of zero

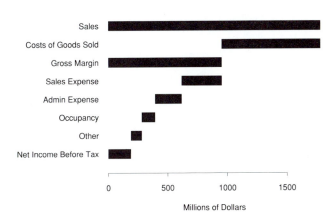

Figure 9.7. A graphical statement of income. Notice how the bars "add up" showing the relationships among the various lines of the report.

length) and a dark bar. The example of `barplot` in section 4.4 showed that it is capable of drawing several components per bar. Combine that information with the knowledge that color 0 is background color and the conceptual problems are solved.

Let us now fill in the details of our income statement function. Assume that the top 3 lines of the plot have fixed labels, as does the bottom line. We want the function to accept the total sales, cost of goods sold, a vector of other costs, and the names of these other costs.

```
income.statement ← function(
    sales, cost.of.goods.sold, other.costs, other.lab){
par(mar=c(6,10,4,2))
margin ← sales - cost.of.goods.sold
income ← margin - sum(other.costs)
m ← matrix(c(   # (invisible) bottoms of bars
    0,
    margin,
    0,
    income+rev(cumsum(c(0,rev(other.costs[-1])))),
    0,
    sales, # tops of bars
    cost.of.goods.sold,
    margin,
    other.costs,
    income), byrow=T, nrow=2)

bar.label ← c("Sales", "Costs of Goods Sold",
    "Gross Margin", other.lab, "Net Income Before Tax")
```

```
    o ← rev(1:ncol(m))
    barplot(m[,o], horiz=T, col=0:1, space=.9,
        names=bar.label[o])
    title("Statement of Income")
}
```

Read through the code to understand how the function works. Notice, in particular, that we construct the bars from top to bottom, but then reverse their order since `barplot` draws horizontal barplot from bottom to top. Now, given our vector of costs and their names, we produce the plot:

```
> costs ← c(336, 224, 112, 91)
> clab ← c("Sales Expense", "Admin Expense",
+   "Occupancy","Other")
> income.statement(1778, 825, costs, clab)
> title(xlab="Millions of Dollars")
```

One of the advantages of this plot is its ability to show the essence of the income statement in a unitless way. This makes it easy to compare income statements of companies who state their income in dollars, yen, marks, etc., without conversions.

Exercises

9.59   Does the function, as it stands, allow income statements that incorporate a net loss? If not, modify it so that it does.

9.6 Symbolic Computations: Derivatives

In this section, we will construct a function to take symbolic derivatives.[†] By this we mean taking an S expression and returning another S expression that is the derivative of the first with respect to a given variable. This expression can then be used, for example, to build a function that evaluates derivatives numerically. The symbolic derivative function illustrates two techniques: manipulating expressions symbolically and using recursive computations effectively. We will start out simply, and add functionality as we go.

First, we write a top-level function, `deriv`, that will accept arguments symbolically:

[†]The function illustrated in this section was originally written by Doug Bates.

```
deriv ← function(expr,name){
    expr ← substitute(expr)
    name ← substitute(name)
    D(expr,name)
}
```

The function will take the derivative of `expr` with respect to variable `name`. Actually, all of the work is going to be done in function `D`. The only reason that we wrote `deriv` as a separate routine is so that it could accept expressions as arguments and turn them into objects that could then be computed upon. The function `D`, that does all of the work, operates on an object that *contains* the expression.

```
D ← function(expr, name)
switch(mode(expr),
    logical = ,
    numeric = ,
    complex = 0,
    name = if(expr == name) 1 else 0,
    )
```

We decide what to do based on `mode(expr)`. If `expr` is a constant, then the derivative is `0`. If `expr` is a name, then the derivative is `1` if `expr` matches `name` and `0` otherwise.

Next, suppose that `expr` is a function call. In that case, `mode(expr)` will be `"call"`, and `expr[[1]]` will be the name of the function (see the table in section 7.5.3). For addition, subtraction and multiplication, the rules of differentiation are listed in the following table:

Operator	Derivative
+	$\dfrac{d}{dx}\,a{+}b = \dfrac{d}{dx}a + \dfrac{d}{dx}b$
−	$\dfrac{d}{dx}\,a{-}b = \dfrac{d}{dx}a - \dfrac{d}{dx}b$
*	$\dfrac{d}{dx}ab = \dfrac{da}{dx}b + \dfrac{db}{dx}a$

The following `switch` expression and recursive calls to `D` parallel the table.

```
switch(as.character(expr[[1]]),    # if mode(expr) is "call"
    "+" = call("+", D(expr[[2]],name), D(expr[[3]],name)),
    "-" = call("-", D(expr[[2]],name), D(expr[[3]],name)),
    "*" = call("+",
        call("*", D(expr[[2]],name), expr[[3]]),
        call("*", expr[[2]], D(expr[[3]],name))
        )
    )
```

The `call` function constructs, but does not evaluate, an expression representing a function call from the name of the function and the arguments. Recursive calls to `D` represent the derivatives naturally. Let's try our new function.

```
> deriv(a,a)
[1] 1
> deriv(1,a)
[1] 0
> deriv(6*a+3*b+a*b,a)
0 * a + 6 * 1 + (0 * b + 3 * 0) + (1 * b + a * 0)
```

The third example brings up a problem—the answer is needlessly complicated. We ought to be able to simplify the generated expressions. Let's write a simplifier that can be used in place of `call`.

```
simplify ← function(fname, arg1, arg2)
switch(fname,
    "+" = if(is.zero(arg1)) arg2
        else if(is.zero(arg2)) arg1
        else call("+", arg1, arg2),
    "*" = if(is.zero(arg1)) 0
        else if(is.zero(arg2)) 0
        else if(is.one(arg1)) arg2
        else if(is.one(arg2)) arg1
        else call("*", arg1, arg2)
)
```

The `simplify` function looks for arguments that are `0` or `1` and gets rid of them; if it cannot simplify, it uses `call` to build the function call. Here is `is.zero`:

```
is.zero ← function(x)
    is.numeric(x) && x==0
```

We change `D` to call `simplify` rather than `call`.

```
D ← function(expr, name)
switch(mode(expr),
    logical = ,
    numeric = ,
    complex = 0,
    name = if(expr == name) 1 else 0,
    call = switch(as.character(expr[[1]]),
        "+" = simplify("+",
            D(expr[[2]], name), D(expr[[3]], name)),
        "-" = simplify("-",
            D(expr[[2]], name), D(expr[[3]], name)),
        "*" = simplify("+",
            simplify("*", D(expr[[2]], name), expr[[3]]),
            simplify("*", expr[[2]], D(expr[[3]], name)))
    )
)
```

Now, repeating the previous example:

```
> deriv(6*a+3*b+a*b, a)
6 + b
```

That's much better. Now that we can compute symbolic derivatives, what can we do with them? One thing that we can do is save the symbolic derivative and evaluate it when we want:

```
> myderiv ← deriv(6*a+3*b+a*b, a)
...
> eval(myderiv)  # uses current value of b
```

We could also create a function to evaluate the derivative. See exercise 9.66.

Exercises

9.60 Unary minus appears in a parsed expression as a function named .Uminus. Extend `deriv` to handle unary minus. Try to provide appropriate simplification routines, too.

9.61 What happens when you try

```
deriv((a+b)*a,a)
```

Fix it.

9.62 Why did we need to write the function `deriv` when all it does is turn around and call `D`? What happens if you execute

```
D(ff+gg,ff)
```

Why?

9.63 Extend `deriv` to handle division and exponentiation "^".

9.64 Extend `deriv` to handle the `sin` and `cos` functions.

9.65 Extend `deriv` to handle `log` and `exp`.

9.66 Write a function `makederiv` that takes an expression and returns a function for the derivative of the expression. For example,

```
> makederiv(x^2+3*x+5)
function(x)
2 * x + 3
```

You can assume that the expression is a function of x.

It is often true that in a recursive computation, the same function may be called many times with the same inputs. How do we avoid recomputation? The solution, which is easy to implement in S, is to save the results the first time they are computed, and then to retrieve them whenever the same arguments appear again. We will use the function `assign` to assign derivatives during evaluation, the function `exists` to test whether they have already been computed, and the function `get` to retrieve them if they have.

Here's the idea. We write a new version of D, named `cache.D` that caches the value of each derivative as it is computed by `old.D`, the old version of D. We must put the cached values all in the same, known frame regardless of where we are in the recursive computation. At the same time, we don't want to clutter up a directory with the derivatives and we certainly don't want to expand the session data (frame 0) with them.

A simple solution is to put them in frame 1 under a name constructed from the deparsed form of the expression. Frame 1 belongs to the complete expression enclosing the call to `deriv`, and goes away when that complete expression is finished.

```
cache.D ← function(expr, name){
    which ← paste(deparse(expr),"::",deparse(name))
    if(exists(which,frame=1)){
        cat("Using cached value of",which,"\n")
        get(which,frame=1)
    } else {
        answer ← old.D(expr,name)
        cat("cached",which,"\n")
        assign(which,answer,frame=1)
        answer
    }
}
```

This version uses the `cat` function to tell us what is happening. After everything is working well, we'll take out the calls to `cat`. Now we have to construct a new version of `deriv` that will invoke `cache.D`. We would just as soon not mess around with the D function itself, since it is pretty large by now and calls itself recursively in many places. How can we accomplish this?

```
deriv ← function(expr,name){
    expr ← substitute(expr)
    name ← substitute(name)
    assign("old.D",D,frame=1)
    assign("D",cache.D,frame=1)
    D(expr,name)
}
```

Notice how we make a copy of D in frame 1, calling it `old.D`. We then made a copy of `cache.D`, calling it D. This effectively interposes `cache.D` into all of the calculations. Now we can try it:

```
> deriv((a+b)*(a+b), a)
cached a :: a
cached b :: a
cached a + b :: a
cached (a + b) :: a
Using cached value of (a + b) :: a
cached (a + b) * (a + b) :: a
(a + b) + (a + b)
```

In this example, we were only able to make use of the cached value once. However, be assured that there are many recursive calculations where caching can provide much more efficient computations.

Exercises

9.67 Implement caching for the recursive Fibonacci function `Fib` introduced in the last exercise of section 6.4. Does it improve performance?

9.68 Revise `deriv` to take partial derivatives of the expression with respect to a list of variable names.

9.69* In the previous exercise, the derivatives will often share many common subexpressions. Try to return an answer that evaluates the common subexpressions only once. Hint: use `deparse` to turn the various subexpressions into text strings.

9.70 What should `deriv` do if it encounters a function in `expr` that it doesn't know how to handle? Could you modify `deriv` to perform numerical differentiation in that case?

9.71* Write a function, `cache(f)` that takes a function `f` as its argument and returns another function that behaves just like `f` but caches intermediate results. Assume `f` has one argument named `x`.

9.72* Write a function

```
taylor(f,n,a=0)
```

that computes coefficients of the first `n` terms of the Taylor series of `f(x)` about the point `a`. Recall that the formula for the *i*th coefficient is $\dfrac{f^{(i)}(a)}{n!}$.

Answers to Selected Exercises

9.1 (page 267)
```
> bad ← diffs > 5 & trip < 300
> ttt ←cbind(miles[bad],trip[bad])
> dimnames(ttt) ← list(cdate[bad],NULL)
> ttt
```

9.3 (page 267)
```
$ grep '.*/.*/.*/' auto.mileage
```

9.6 (page 271)
```
leap.year ← function(y)
y %% 4 == 0 && (y %% 100!=0 || y %% 400 == 0)
```

9.8 (page 271) It's easy. Just compute the Julian date for the given day, subtract the date of January 1 of that year, and add 1 to give the day of the year. Then tack on the year number.

9.9 (page 271) Compute Julian dates for all of the data and subtract the Julian date for the first data point from all of these. This gives you a vector of "days since start of measurements" that you can use on the time axis of the plot.

9.10   (page 271)

```
lapply(split(day,month),range)
```

9.12   (page 271)

```
days ← julian(month,day,year) - julian(4,29,1981)
all(diff(days)>=0)  # are days in increasing order?
```

9.13   (page 272)

```
mpg ← miles/gallons
price ← dollars/gallons
plot(days,mpg)
plot(days,price)
```

9.14   (page 272)

```
ok ← mpg>19 & mpg<30
plot(days[ok], mpg[ok], pch=".")  # reduce clutter
lines(lowess(days[ok], mpg[ok], f=.2))  # smooth line
axis(side=3, 82:87,
     at=julian(1,1,1982:1987)-julian(4,29,1981))
```

9.15   (page 272)   Such a set of functions might include: get current time in seconds since midnight; turn seconds into days, hours, minutes, seconds; convert days into seconds.

9.16   (page 273)   Eventually the computations will be exact, when the denominator is large enough. Of course, it may take quite a while for the computations to succeed.

9.17   (page 273)   13 and 113.

9.18   (page 274)   Because the smallest percentage gives a lower bound on the size of the denominator. For example, if the smallest fraction were `.001`, then you would expect there were at least 1/(.001+eps) respondents in the survey.

9.19   (page 274)   Try the following:

```
n ← floor(1/(eps+min(diff(c(0,sort(uniq(f)))))))
```

This uses the minimum nonzero difference between the sorted values. In fact, for the example of this section, this formula almost gives the exact answer at the first iteration.

9.21   (page 277)

```
find.D ← function(f, eps=1e-7){
    D ← 1
    repeat {
        N ← f * D
        if(all(abs(N - round(N)) < eps)) break
        D ← D * 10
    }
    D
}
```

9.22   (page 277)   The running time should be independent of the length of the vector of fractions, since the inner loop should be exited as soon as the number of outliers is exceeded. Since most fractions and denominators will be incompatible, the inner loop should terminate very quickly. However, running time should go up linearly with the number of outliers.

9.24   (page 277)   We know that if we use D as a denominator, then we have a solution to the problem. However, our earlier computations found that the vector d gives solutions with 0, 1, ... outliers. Suppose that denominators for any particular fraction are uniformly distributed between 0 and D. What is the probability that all of the denominators are less than or equal to d? It is `(d/D)^length(f)`. The function computes the negative logarithm of this probability, adjusted for the number of outliers. Thus, the larger this value, the more "interesting" the denominator.

9.25 (page 280) You can easily do this by making the arguments to *tr* twice as long, including both upper-case and lower-case letters.

9.27 (page 280)
```
number ← function(digits)
    sum(rev(digits) * (10^(0:(length(digits)-1))))
```

9.28 (page 280)
```
digits ← function(n, base = 10){
    if(n == 0) return(0)
    n ← abs(n)
    powers ← round(base^(floor(log(n, base = base)):0))
    (n %/% powers) %% base
}

number ← function(digits, base=10)
    sum(rev(digits) * round(base^(0:(length(digits)-1))))

convert ← function(n, tobase=10, frombase=10)
    number(digits(n, tobase), frombase)
```

9.30 (page 280) By generating the words from last character to first character, the answer will be in alphabetical order.

9.32 (page 284) The primary advantage is that all of the S objects are located within a single place in the hierarchical file system. A disadvantage is, as we saw, that we need to use a funny name, such as `.cars`, for the collection in order to make sure we realize that it is not a simple data object. One alternative would be to use a directory parallel to `.Data` for each collection.

9.33 (page 284) For interactive use, this is probably a good idea, since it prevents the creation of extra directories when you accidentally misspell a collection name. On the other hand, it makes it difficult to create collections from inside functions. Suppose, for example, that you wanted to write a function that created a collection and put a few objects into it.

9.35 (page 284) The `.Help` subdirectory contains documentation for S functions and is not a collection, hence it should be omitted by `lscollection`. Simply add `-e '/.Help/d'` to the `sed` command. To get rid of the leading dot, add `-e 's/^.//'` to the `sed` command.

9.36 (page 284) The functions encounter errors since they cannot create nor access objects in subdirectory `.Data`. When you use S in a directory that has no `.Data` subdirectory, S uses `.Data` in your home directory for the working data. You might revise the functions to look in position 1 of the search list for the working directory name, using this name instead of `.Data` to create and list collections.

9.37 (page 285) It may be necessary to produce revised versions of `attach` and `detach` that know about collections. They could detect which directories are collections by their naming convention.

9.39 (page 285) The `unix` command with `output=FALSE` returns the status from executing the `mkdir` command. If the directory is constructed without error, the returned value will be 0, which is interpreted as FALSE by the `if` statement. If an error occurs, the UNIX system prints the message and the `stop()` function call aborts evaluation of the `collection` function.

9.40   (page 285)   Since `collection` returns its previous value, you can easily write a function that remembers the current collection, calls `collection` to set up a new collection temporarily, and then resets the collection back to its original value. Marking the result invisible means that the user is not bothered with a printed version of the old collection name.

9.41   (page 290)
```
deck.symbols ← outer(c("A", 2:10, "J", "Q", "K"),
    c("C", "D", "H", "S"), paste)
```

9.45   (page 291)   All you need to do is to make sure that everyone starts playing with the same `.Random.seed` value. You probably should set the seed prior to each game played, or else a player who used a random number generator between games would end up playing different games than the others.

9.49   (page 293)
```
c(rbind(x,x))
```
or
```
c(t(matrix(c(x,x),ncol=2)))
```

9.51   (page 294)   We need to drop the text *below* the bars for negative data. The simplest way is to refine the definition of `r`:
```
r ← diff(range(c(0,x))) * ifelse(x<0,-1,1)
```

9.58   (page 296)   Try the following:
```
plot(imports-exports,type="l")
```
Had you noticed the jump in trade imbalance following 1760?

9.61   (page 301)   The parenthesized expression is not recognized. We simply need a rule to strip off the parentheses.
```
# in the switch(mode(expr), ...
"(" = D(expr[[2]], name),
```

9.62   (page 301)   If, as is likely, you do not have objects named `ff` and `gg`, there will be an error message when `D` tries to evaluate the expression. The purpose of `deriv` is to make sure that we capture the expression before any function attempts to evaluate it.

9.66   (page 301)   The idea is to build the function with a null body and then insert the derivative into it. We know that the derivative will be a function of `x`. Then:
```
myfun ← function(x) NULL
myfun[[length(myfun)]] ← deriv(expr,x)
```
This would leave `myfun` as the desired derivative function.

9.69   (page 303)   Write a function that walks top-down over the expressions, deparses each subexpression, and makes a vector of all of these deparsed subexpressions. Only the duplicated values in this vector are common subexpressions. Make up a name for each common subexpression and then walk the expression tree again, replacing the common subexpressions by their names.

10

Advanced Graphics

High-level graphics functions, described in chapter 4, generate a complete plot from a description that says *what* to plot, without elaborate instructions about *how*. For looking at data, particularly at an exploratory stage, this is what we want: to get a picture with a minimum of effort, and then to get on with the process of learning from that picture. However, as we look more closely at the plot, or when we generate plots for communication with others as well as for learning, we will typically want to control the plot in more detail.

This chapter presents the information that you need in order to be able to exert precise control over the graphics produced by S. As such, it includes a number of low-level graphical operations that may at times seem confusing. The antidote for this confusion is to try to keep things simple and to refer back to the basic graphics routines described in chapter 4.

10.1 High-Level Plotting Functions

Chapter 4 introduced you to a number of *high-level* plotting functions; we use the term high-level to mean that the function produces a complete figure by itself. Most prominent of these functions is `plot`, which produces scatterplots.

For consistency and ease of remembering, `plot` and many of the other high-level plotting functions share a number of arguments. Foremost are the arguments x and y. Most commonly, they are two vectors, giving x- and y-coordinates for the points to be plotted. However, these arguments can be given in many different forms, and the y argument may even be omitted in the following circumstances:

1. The x argument is a list with components named x and y. In this case, the coordinates of the plotted points will be taken from these components.
2. The x argument is a 2-column matrix. The first column will be plotted on the *x*-axis, the second column on the *y*-axis.
3. The x argument has mode "complex". The plot will have Re(x) on the *x*-axis and Im(x) on the *y*-axis.
4. The x argument is a time-series. In this case, the actual data values of the time-series are plotted on the *y*-axis, and time(x) is plotted on the *x*-axis. This also takes care of the case where x is just a vector, with no special structure. It is coerced to a time-series, which causes time(x) to be the vector 1, 2, ..., length(x).

As you can see, there are many ways for the coordinates of the points to be given to plot. These same x and y arguments also apply to many of the low-level graphics functions presented in section 10.4.

Aside from the x and y arguments, high-level plot functions share these other arguments:

- xlab=, ylab= labels for the *x*- or *y*-axis. In the case of plot, these labels have default values which are the expressions given as the x and y arguments. For example, the expression

  ```
  plot(weight,1/mpg)
  ```

  would produce a plot with the *x*-axis labelled "weight" and the *y*-axis labelled "1/mpg". If you do not want the axes labelled, use xlab="" or ylab="".
- main= a main title plotted in enlarged characters (1.5 times standard size) above the plot.
- sub= a sub-title for the bottom of the plot, below the *x*-axis label.
- axes= logical flag. The specification axes=FALSE forces a high-level plotting function to omit drawing the axis lines, tick marks, and tick labels, as well as the box surrounding the plot. These features can be added to the plot at a later time by lower-level functions such as box and axis, which are described in section 10.5.
- xlim=, ylim= vectors giving the minimum and maximum values that should be accommodated on the *x*- and *y*-axes. The high-level functions guarantee that values in this range will actually fit on the axis, but may extend the axis further in order to produce "pretty" tick labels.
- log= character string giving the names of the axes to be logarithmic, e.g., log="yx". As the plotting function sets up the coordinate system, it makes the specified axes logarithmic, meaning that the coordinate system is set up on a log10 scale, but that the tick labels are in the original scale.

- type= the type of plot: "p" (points), "l" (lines), "b" (both), "o" (over-struck), or "h" (high-density). See Figure 10.1. It is also possible to use type="n", to set up the axes for a plot that will later be filled in by low-level graphics functions.

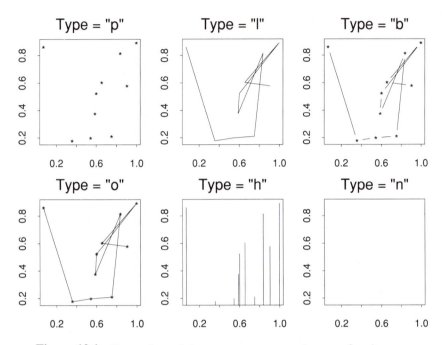

Figure 10.1. Six versions of the type= argument to the plot function.

Of course, not all high-level graphics functions share all of these arguments (a barplot can hardly have the type argument), but the arguments are shared amongst the high-level functions, whenever they make sense, to provide greater naturalness and uniformity.

10.2 Basic Notions

This section presents a number of notions basic to graphics in S. In particular, it describes the layout of figures, with plot regions, margins, and associated coordinate systems. Then it describes the difference between immediate plotting and the generation of graphics objects.

10.2.1 *Plots, Figures, and Coordinate Systems*

So far, we have said that high-level plot functions produce a complete "figure" without defining the term. A graphical display including titles and axes is called a *figure*. A figure is composed of a *plot* surrounded by *margins* as shown in Figure 10.2.

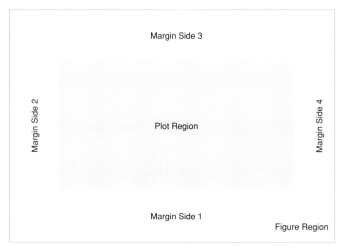

Figure 10.2. Graphical displays consist of a figure region, made up from a plot region (for points, lines, etc.) surrounded by margins which normally contain text.

The plot contains the graphical information (the plotted points of a scatterplot, the bars of a histogram, etc.) and is addressed by a *user coordinate system*; that is, by the coordinates determined by the user's data.

The *margins* surrounding the plot are used for tick labels, axis labels, titles, and other annotations. Locations within the margins are specified by a *margin coordinate system*. There are three parts to a margin coordinate: the *side* (1 for bottom, 2 for left, 3 for top, and 4 for right), the number of lines of text away from the edge of the plot, and the user coordinate along the edge of the plot. The mtext and axis functions, described in sections 10.4 and 10.5, are two of the functions that make use of the margin coordinate system.

Section 10.3 describes the graphical parameters that deal with the size and layout of plots, margins, and figures.

10.2.2 *Graphics Objects*

At this point, we should make a clear distinction between *immediate* graphics and the production of *graphics objects*. Suppose, for example, we are interested in creating a scatterplot with a fitted line. The following expressions will produce an immediate plot on the current graphics device.

```
> airflow ← stack.x[,1]
> plot(airflow, stack.loss)     # Figure 10.3
> abline(lsfit(airflow,stack.loss))
```

However, if `plot` and `abline` are arguments to the `graphics` function:

```
> fitted.plot ← graphics(
+    plot(airflow, stack.loss),
+    abline(lsfit(airflow,stack.loss))
+    )
```

we will have generated a graphics object, named `fitted.plot` that contains a description of the plot and fitted line. Typing

```
> fitted.plot     # Figure 10.3
```

causes the object to be displayed. In both instances, the plot looks like Figure 10.3.

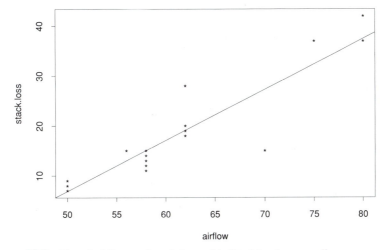

Figure 10.3. Plot of airflow and stack loss with fitted least-squares line.

This example illustrates that the S graphics system can operate in two distinct modes. If plotting functions are invoked inside a call to `graphics`, then no actual plotting is carried out. Instead, the `graphics` function returns a graphics object as its value. This object can be assigned, operated upon, or displayed. In fact, if the object is not assigned a name, it is "printed" by the function `gr.display`, which causes it to be displayed upon the current graphics device.

In general, there is no particular reason to construct and then display graphics objects if you have no desire to preserve them—use immediate graphics instead. The power of graphics objects is that you can keep them, operate on them, and display them at will without going back through the process that created them.

10.3 Graphical Parameters

The function `par` maintains a set of named graphical parameters, as part of the *graphics state*. A hidden object contains the parameters throughout an S session. Calls to `par` can set chosen parameters by name or retrieve the current parameter values. S graphics functions share conventions about the names and contents of the various parameters that are outlined in this section. Graphical parameters as set and returned by `par` are analogous to general S options as maintained by the `options` function.

Graphical parameters control many aspects of the appearance of plots. They can be used in two ways:

- as arguments to graphics functions, making *temporary* parameter settings for color, line type, plotting character, etc. The parameter settings stay in effect through the call to the function and are then reset to their previous value.
- as arguments to the `par` function. Parameters set in a call to `par` stay in effect throughout all plotting until reset in another call to `par` or until re-initialized to their default values when a new graphic device function is invoked.

As arguments either to graphics functions or to `par`, the parameters should be specified in the `name=value` form.

Graphical parameters can themselves be divided into two classes.

- primitive characteristics of graphical entities, such as line style, color, line width, coordinate system, etc.
- a characteristic that one or more graphics functions agree to make externally controlled. These include the algorithm by which plotting routines determine where to place tick marks, the size of the margins surrounding plots, the desired aspect ratio of plots, etc.

We will present here the most commonly used of the parameters; however, for the complete list of graphical parameters, see `par` in Appendix 1.

- `pch=` plotting character. The character given is used for scatterplots, for example in calls to `plot` or `points`. The default for this parameter is `pch="*"`, but for plots with many points, you might prefer `pch="."`, which makes the plotting character a centered dot. Numeric values can also be used for the `pch` parameter; they cause S to use one of a set of predefined plotting symbols (see Appendix 1 under `lines` for examples).
- `cex=` character expansion, relative to the standard character size for the graphical device. For example, `cex=0.5` gives half-size characters, `cex=1.5` gives characters `1.5` times normal size. Characters are

drawn using the capabilities of the device, so beware of the funny results that may happen if you specify a character expansion that the device doesn't know how to produce—positioning and centering of text will not be correct.

- `lty=` line type. A value of 1 gives solid lines. For devices that support multiple line types, values 2, 3, ... will select a non-solid line type.
- `lwd=` line width. The default width is 1, which corresponds to the standard width on the device. Larger values produce thicker lines; smaller values produce thinner lines. Many devices support only one line width.
- `col=` a numeric color specification. Devices which can automatically change color will change to one of a set of device-dependent colors. The default is color 1; 0 is background color.

Many of these parameters are device dependent. To learn how they are treated by any particular device, look up the device function, e.g., `postscript`, in Appendix 1.

Some examples of the use of the parameters we just described are shown in the following figure.

```
> plot(2:10,pch="X")     # Figure 10.4
> abline(0,1,lty=2,col=6)    # line with slope 1, intercept 0
> text(6,3,"This is text",cex=2.5)
```

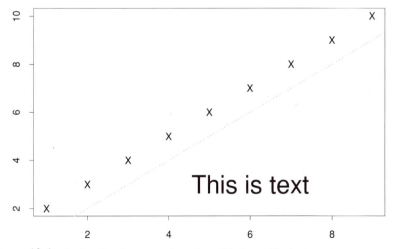

Figure 10.4. A plot showing a number of modified graphical parameters.

The low-level parameters that we introduced here are often useful with low-level functions that build up a plot (described more fully in section 10.4), since they allow different vectors of data on the plot to be distinguished.

A few high-level functions, notably `tsplot` and `matplot`, produce several lines or sets of points and hence take as arguments vectors of graphical parameters. The argument `type`, mentioned above in connection with high-level plotting functions, is dealt with similarly. For example, with `type` and `pch`, you can supply character strings with each character in turn taken as the parameter value for successive sets of data. Thus,

```
> tsplot(hstart, smooth(hstart),    # Figure 10.5
+   type="pl", col=c(1,3))
```

plots the series `hstart` as a set of points in color 1, and adds the series `smooth(hstart)` as a connected line in color 3 (see Figure 10.5).

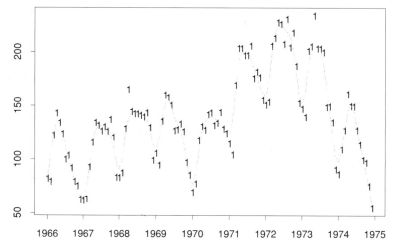

Figure 10.5. Time-series plot showing original points and smooth fit for housing start data.

To examine, without changing, the current values for some graphical parameters, call the function `par` with the character names of the parameter values you want returned. The function returns a list giving the values of those parameters whose (quoted) names are supplied as arguments. For example,

```
> par("pch","cex")
$pch:
[1] "*"

$cex:
[1] 1
```

returns a list containing the current plotting character and character size. When `par` is used to set some parameter values, it returns a similar list, this time containing the previous values. Calling `par` with this list as an argument restores the previous parameter values:

```
> oldpars ← par(pch="X",cex=1.5)
   ... do some plotting here with new plot character and size
> par(oldpars)   # reset old parameter values
```

As mentioned in section 10.2, `par` maintains a collection of graphical parameters that deal with the size and layout of plots, margins, and figures. For example, the parameter

```
mar=c(m1,m2,m3,m4)
```

controls the size of the margins that surround the plot. The margins by default are set large enough to accommodate 5, 4, 4, and 2 lines of text on the bottom, left, top, and right of the plot. These default settings are made in the function `Device.Default`; it is perfectly reasonable to write your own version of this function in order to provide default values that you like.

Suppose you wish to make the margins just large enough to accommodate tick labels. Looking at a plot shows that the numerical tick labels are spaced out 1 line from the edge of the plot. Since the labels themselves take 1 line, we need at least 2 lines of margin on the bottom and left for the tick labels generated by scatterplots. Therefore, assuming we won't generate any axis labels, we could use:

```
par(mar=c(2,2,0,0)+.1)
```

We added `.1` lines just to allow a bit of empty space around the plot. Of course, if we don't suppress axis labels in scatterplots, for example, by `xlab=""` and `ylab=""`, there will be warning messages from the plotting functions.

Another parameter, `pty`, is a character string that describes the plot shape. The default, `pty="m"`, sets up the maximum size plot possible on the device, after allowing for the margins. The other possibility is `pty="s"`, which will force the plot to be square, regardless of the shape of the device.

Exercises

10.1 Examine the function `Device.Default` and explain the graphical parameter settings made there.

10.2 What happens if you ask for more margin space than your device can accommodate? Try

```
par(mar=rep(40,4))
```

for example.

10.3 Suppose you want to produce a plot with large "S" characters as the plotting symbol. What happens if you execute the following expression?

```
plot(x,y,cex=3,pch="S")
```

10.4 Low-Level Plotting Functions

Section 10.1 described high-level plotting functions. Here, we will discuss
low-level plotting functions. The primary difference between the two is that
the low-level functions do not attempt to produce a complete figure; instead,
they operate on the existing plot, using the current coordinate system.
    These low-level functions include:

- `points(x,y)` to draw a set of plotting characters at specified coordinates;
- `lines(x,y)` to draw a set of lines connecting the specified coordinates;
- `polygon(x,y)` to fill the polygon outlined by the x and y values;
- `segments(x1,y1,x2,y2)` to draw a set of line segments from the (x1,y1) points to the (x2,y2) endpoints;
- `arrows(x1,y1,x2,y2)` to draw segments with arrowheads at the endpoints;
- `text(x,y,label)` to plot the character or numeric vector `label` at the specified positions;
- `abline(a,b)` to draw the line $y = a + b * x$;
- `locator(n)` to use graphic input to locate up to n points in user-coordinates;
- `identify(x,y,labels)` to use graphic input to place labels on selected points.

All of the low-level functions that take `x,y` arguments are able to
interpret them in the same manner as the high-level functions of section 10.1.
The functions that add points, lines, or text to a plot (with the exception of
`abline`) all recognize whether the previously set up plot had standard or logarithmic axes. If a logarithmic axis was set up, the data are transformed to the
log scale prior to plotting, and should be given in the normal, untransformed
scale. The functions `locator` and `identify` also work correctly in the presence of logarithmic axes.
    A number of high-level plotting functions can also operate in a low-
level way by using the `add=TRUE` argument. This specifies that they should
add to the current figure rather than create a new one. A particularly interesting function in this regard is `symbols`, since it can draw a number of different
parameterized symbols: circles, squares, rectangles, etc. For example,

```
symbols(x,y,circles=r,add=T)
```

draws circles of radius proportional to `r` at the specified points. (The constant
of proportionality is set so that the largest circle has radius 1 inch.) There are
several graphical parameters that affect text strings, whether plotted with `text`,
`identify`, or other text-plotting functions:

- `adj=` justification. The value `adj=0` will cause the string to be left-justified at the specified position, `adj=1` will right-justify, and `adj=.5` (the default) centers the string.
- `srt=` string rotation, measured in degrees counterclockwise from horizontal.
- `crt=` character rotation, measured in degrees counterclockwise from horizontal. By default, whenever `srt` is specified, `crt` is changed to the same value. However, it is possible to change `crt` afterwards. Thus,

```
text(x,y,"My Label",srt=-90,crt=0)
```

writes a vertical string from top to bottom, with characters oriented horizontally.

Graphics functions that deal with character strings have the added capability of utilizing embedded *newline* characters that may occur in strings. Whenever this character is encountered, the current plotting position is moved down one line (perpendicular to the string orientation), and the rest of the string is plotted there. In addition, each part of the string between newlines is adjusted independently according to the parameter `adj`. The newline character is entered into a string by using the two characters "\n":

```
title("This is the first line\nand this is the second")
```

A useful application of `text` is to label a curve or line on the plot. In interactive computing, it is often easiest to select the position for the text using `locator(1)` to point at the plot. An example of this process was given at the end of section 4.3. If we are not working interactively, or want to label a curve as part of the plot we are building, some systematic labelling is needed. Generally, we need some point (*x*, *y*) on the graph that is a good position to put a label (say, the mid-point of the curve). Given this, `text` can then be used to put on the label.

In addition to data-based information, we often want to add special explanatory information to graphs. S functions can be used to add text (`title`, `mtext`, `text`), to generate extra axis ticks and labels (`axis`), and to create legends with sample points and/or lines (`legend`).

The `title` function can plot a main title at the top, a subtitle at the bottom and text to label the x and y data. However, for more precise control of the location of information in the margins of a figure, the function

```
mtext(label, side, line)
```

can be used. The argument `side` specifies whether the text is to be on the bottom (1), left (2), top (3), or right (4) of the plot. The character string in `label` is plotted parallel to the specified side `line` lines of text out from the edge of the plot.

The optional argument `at` to the `mtext` function allows text in the margin to be associated with specific user coordinates. For example, if `side` is given as 1 or 3, the argument `at` is interpreted as a set of *x*-coordinates at which the vector of labels is to be plotted, with the *y*-coordinates of the text controlled by the `line` argument. This feature can be used to construct special user-defined axes, etc.; however, the `axis` function (section 10.5) is more flexible for this purpose.

Exercises

10.4   Use `tsplot` to plot manufacturing shipments (object `ship`) and a smoothed value of shipments. Use the function `legend` (look it up in Appendix 1) to annotate the plot.

10.5 Building Plots

Section 10.1 showed how to create plots using some of the high-level S functions, section 10.3 showed how to customize these plots by setting graphical parameters, and section 10.4 gave a set of low-level graphics functions that could add to plots. Let us now use these tools to make customized graphical displays by building up a plot and then adding text, lines, and other symbols. The paradigm for doing this consists of two steps:

1. set up the coordinate system and axes for the plot, typically by using the `plot` function to generate axes and labels (either plotting some data or with `type="n"`);
2. repeatedly invoke low-level graphics functions to add whatever kind of information you would like to the plot.

By using these two steps, and encapsulating the result in a function, you have a flexible way of creating new graphical displays.

10.5.1 *Building Graphs*

For a first example, suppose we want to make a scatterplot of `airflow` and `stack.loss` as we did in Figure 10.3, but instead of plotting the same character at each point, we want the points labelled by the observation number (`1:length(airflow)`) to show the pattern of recording the data. The `text` function can produce this (or any other sequence of numeric or character values). The first step of our paradigm is done by giving the argument `type="n"` to `plot`, to tell it to set up the plot, but not to plot any points. The expressions to generate our numbered scatterplot are:

```
> plot(airflow,stack.loss,type="n")   # Figure 10.6
> text(airflow,stack.loss,label=1:length(airflow))
```

However, since this seems like a useful type of plot in general, we would be better off creating a function `idplot` to produce such a plot:

```
idplot ← function(x,y) {
    plot(x,y,type="n")
    text(x,y,label=1:length(x))
}
```

We can then invoke `idplot`

```
> idplot(airflow,stack.loss)   # Figure 10.6
```

to produce the desired plot.

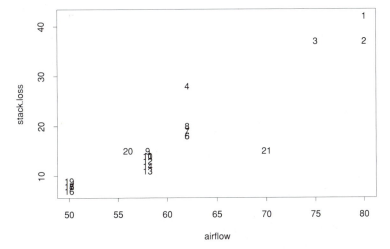

Figure 10.6. Plot of airflow and stack loss where each point is labelled by its observation number.

Next, suppose we want a plot containing a "+" where the residuals from the stack loss regression were positive and a "−" where the residuals were negative. Let's first write a function to produce this type of plot.

```
sign.plot ← function(x,y,r){
    plot(x, y, type="n")
    text(x[r>0], y[r>0],"+")
    text(x[r<0], y[r<0],"-")
    text(x[r==0], y[r==0], "o")
}
```

Now, we can compute residuals and invoke `sign.plot`:

```
> resids ← lsfit(stack.x, stack.loss)$resid
> sign.plot(airflow, stack.loss, resids)    # Figure 10.7
```

to produce the desired graph.

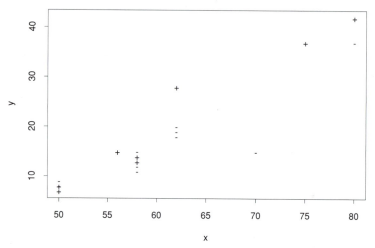

Figure 10.7. Plot of airflow and stack loss, with points labelled by the sign of the residual from a least-squares fit.

When we use S interactively, the `identify` function is probably the best way to label interesting points on a scatterplot. However, if the interesting points can be described by a logical expression, the `text` function is another way to do the job. Since `text` plots labels centered on the co-ordinates given, we will want to offset the labels when adding them to a scatterplot. One method is to put a couple of blanks on the front of the labels and include `adj=0` to left-justify the text. As an example, after producing Figure 10.7, we could describe the unusual points by the condition:

```
>   odd ← abs(resids)>4 | stack.loss>25
```

To label them:

```
> text(airflow[odd], stack.loss[odd], adj=0, "  odd")
```

The `label` argument to `text` can be numeric or character.

There are many functions that generate the data for a plot, but do no plotting. Instead, their result becomes the argument to one of the high-level or low-level plotting functions. For example, `lowess(x,y)` returns a smoothed version of two variables. Thus

```
> plot(airflow,stack.loss)    # Figure 10.8
> lines(lowess(airflow,stack.loss))
```

generates a smooth curve on the scatterplot of Figure 10.8.

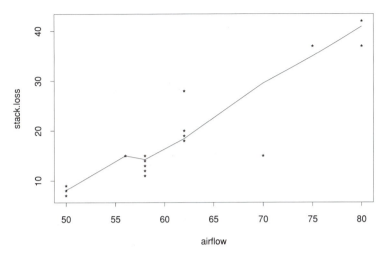

Figure 10.8. A smooth curve superimposed on the airflow and stack loss scatterplot.

(Here we wanted both the scatterplot and the curve, and so did not use the `type="n"` argument to `plot`.)

This use of `lowess` illustrates the power of the `x,y` argument matching in the `plot` function. As we have mentioned several times, objects with components named `x` and `y` can be given in place of the arguments `x` and `y`. This means that S functions can generate results that are easily plotted; plotting can be confined to the few graphics functions discussed in this chapter.

As another example of a function that computes an object suitable for plotting, `density` generates smoothed probability density estimates. We can construct an empirical density plot function by:

```
density.plot ← function(x){
    plot(density(x), type="l")
    points(x, x*0)    # 1-dim scatterplot below
    }
```

and use it to display the data in `resids`:

```
> density.plot(resids)    # Figure 10.9
> title("Empirical Density Plot",xlab="resids")
```

Some high-level plotting functions can be used with an argument `plot=FALSE`. In this form, they do no plotting, but instead return an object which may be used subsequently as an argument to other functions. For example, `qqplot` and `qqnorm` will return a list with `x` and `y` components representing the ordered quantiles and data values which they would have plotted. If `boxplot` is called with `plot=FALSE`, the object returned contains a matrix giving 5 statistics for each of the data sets given as arguments. (Function `bxp` produces a boxplot when given one of these objects.) The function `hist` will return an object suitable for input to the `barplot` function.

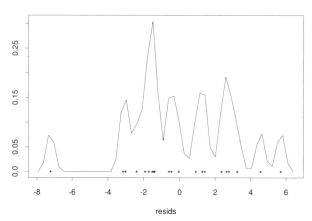

Figure 10.9. A smoothed probability density plot of the residuals from the linear fit to the stack loss data. A one-dimensional scatterplot appears at the bottom.

We can use the idea of building-up a plot to combine powerful computational facilities with graphics. For example, suppose we want to join selected cities into a network. We have dataset `city` (see `city` in Appendix 2) giving locations for various cities, so we will use those cities for the basis of the network. We draw a map of the United States by using the `usa` function introduced in section 2.6. We use the `mstree` function (see Appendix 1) to compute the *minimum spanning tree,* that is, the tree with the minimum total length that joins the cities. We then superimpose the tree on the map. The following S expressions produce Figure 10.10:

```
> usa(states=F,lty=2)    # dotted map - no state boundaries
> points(city.x,city.y,pch="o",col=2)   # plot the cities
> tree ← mstree( cbind(city.x,city.y*.8), plane=F )
>      # a degree of latitude is approximately
>      # 80% as large as a degree of longitude
> s ← seq(along=tree)
> segments(city.x[s],city.y[s],city.x[tree],city.y[tree])
```

Exercises

10.5 Generalize function `idplot` to take an optional vector of labels.

10.6 Using the objects listed in Appendix 2 under `state`, produce a plot of illiteracy vs. income, plotting the state abbreviation at the appropriate position on the scatterplot. The result of the previous exercise may be helpful.

10.7 In the example where we put the label "odd" next to the odd points, suppose instead we had wanted to display the observation number for each odd point.

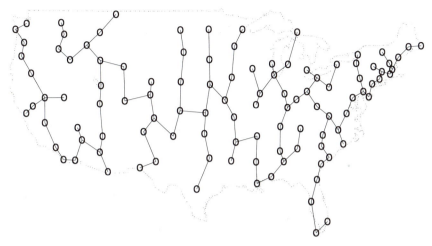

Figure 10.10. A minimal spanning tree connecting selected U.S. cities.

Produce such a plot. In the example, we put blank spaces on the front of the word " odd" to avoid overwriting the plotting symbol for the point. How would you ensure that the observation number does not overwrite the plotting symbol?

10.8 Using the function `arrows`, produce a plot showing the sequence of observations on the `airflow`, `stack.loss` scatterplot. That is, draw an arrow pointing from observation 1 to observation 2, another from observation 2 to observation 3, etc.

10.9 For a set of two-dimensional data of your own choosing (you can always make up data using random number generators), produce several scatterplots using different plotting characters. Try "*", "+", "o", and "." at least. Which plotting character do you like best?

10.10 The function `text` allows the arguments `col` and `cex` to give vectors of colors and character sizes. Use this to produce the airflow, stack.loss plot using one color for the "+" characters and another color for the "−" characters. Also try to make the character size proportional to the size of the residuals.

10.11 Look up the functions `matpoints`, `matlines`, `tspoints`, and `tslines` in Appendix 1. When might they be useful?

10.12 Create a function that will take as input the locations of a set of cities and generate a map showing the cities and the minimum spanning tree.

10.13 System datasets `corn.rain` and `corn.yield` give amounts of rainfall and corn yields for a number of years. Produce a scatterplot of this data, and draw the `lowess` fit on the plot.

10.14 Compute residuals from the fit in the previous exercise, and plot absolute residuals as a function of rainfall. Does the variance of the residuals appear to be constant? Hint: the function `approx` is useful for finding the fitted values based on `lowess` output.

10.5.2 *Control of Plotting Range*

So far, we have built up plots by using the high-level functions to generate the plotting range, axes and other paraphernalia, and then filling in with whatever we really wanted to plot. This is the preferred approach, since it leaves S to do the necessary calculations about ranges, pretty tick labelling, and so forth. Occasionally, we may be obliged to control the range for one of the coordinate axes to include some specific values. In this case, the range for plotting can be given by the optional arguments `xlim` and `ylim` to the `plot` function. For an example, let's turn to the `auto` data and suppose the 3 objects `price`, `mpg`, and `repair` have been created from the corresponding columns of `auto.stats` (from the S data directory, see Appendix 2). We want to plot a scatter of `price` and `mpg`, superimposing arrows that point to lower or higher prices for good or bad repair records (assuming $500 for each level of the 5-point repair scale above or below 3). We compute the adjusted price `p2` and draw the desired plot (shown in Figure 10.11):

```
> p2 ← price-500*(repair-3)
> plot(price,mpg,xlim=range(price,p2),type="n")
> arrows(price,mpg,p2,mpg)
> points(price[repair==3],mpg[repair==3],pch=0,mkh=.1)
```

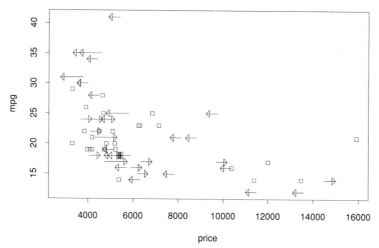

Figure 10.11. On a plot of price and miles-per-gallon, the arrows show price adjusted for repair record.

Because arrows of length zero disappear, we plotted a small symbol at the corresponding points, using `pch=0` and `mkh=.1`. See `lines` in Appendix 1 for pictures of the available plotting symbols.

A common requirement in plotting is to produce several plots that have an identical *y*-axis. This is quite easy to do. Simply compute the range of all of the *y* values, and then specify it as a `ylim` argument on all of the plots.

```
yrange ← range(y1,y2)
plot(x1,y1,ylim=yrange)
plot(x2,y2,ylim=yrange)
```

This simple use of `ylim` ensures that the two plots will have identical *y*-axes. Of course, the same trick works for *x*-axes. A related idea is the following:

```
par(pty="s")    # square plot
plot(x,y,xlim=range(x,y),ylim=range(x,y))
```

By setting up a square plot and insisting that each axis cover exactly the same range of values, the plot will have identical *x*- and *y*-axes.

10.5.3 *A Do-It-Yourself Plot Function*

Perhaps the best way to help you understand how the `plot` function works internally is to try to write one ourselves. Here's a first cut:

```
myplot ← function(x,y){
    frame()
    par(usr=c(range(x),range(y)))
    points(x,y)
    axis(side=1,at=seq(min(x),max(x),length=5))
    axis(side=2,at=seq(min(y),max(y),length=5))
    box()
}
```

This is a truly bare-bones function. It uses `frame` to advance to a new figure, sets up the user coordinate parameters based upon the ranges of the `x` and `y` values, plots a set of points, draws axes with 5 tick marks, and draws a box surrounding the plot. Let's try it:

```
> myplot(airflow,stack.loss)   # Figure 10.12
```

    The results are surprisingly good. Of course, we got lucky with the tick labels—they turned out to be relatively "pretty". However, notice how difficult it is to see the points that fall at the extremes of the *x*-axis. We can ensure that our tick labels are pretty by using the `pretty` function.

```
myplot ← function(x,y){
    frame()
    xticks ← pretty(x)
    yticks ← pretty(y)
    par(usr=c(range(xticks),range(yticks)))
    points(x,y)
    axis(side=1,at=xticks)
    axis(side=2,at=yticks)
    box()
}
```

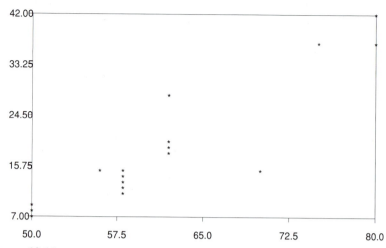

Figure 10.12. Scatterplot produced by the `myplot` function. This function is an attempt to use low-level graphics functions to produce something that works like `plot`.

This is actually a fairly satisfactory version. In the exercises below, we will add `xlim/ylim` and `xlab/ylab` arguments.

Nevertheless, `myplot` is missing many features of the standard S `plot` function. It does not accommodate the various alternative forms for the `x` and `y` arguments. It does not allow logarithmic axes. It is also simplistic in deciding how to generate a coordinate system and pretty tick marks. For example, the algorithm used by the S plotting function attempts to ensure that there is a standard amount of blank space between the extreme points in a plot and the surrounding box.[†]

As you can see, there are many decisions made when producing a plot. The graphics software in S uses some of the graphical parameters to provide a means of controlling these decisions without requiring you to rewrite the underlying graphics routines. For example, the axis set-up routines look at parameter `lab` in order to determine how many tick intervals there should be on the *x*- and *y*-axes. If you use

```
lab=c(7,10)
```

in a call to a high-level plot routine, it says that you want approximately 7 tick intervals on the *x*-axis and 10 on the *y*-axis.

Graphical parameters provide two way communication between you and graphics routines. High-level routines not only look at parameters to control how they should operate, but they also set some parameters that you can

---

[†]W. S. Cleveland, P. Diaconis, and R. McGill, "Variables on Scatterplots Look More Highly Correlated When the Scales are Increased," *Science*, June 4, 1982, Vol. 216, pp. 1138-1141.

examine. For example, any high-level function that sets up a plot sets the parameters `xaxp` and `yaxp` to indicate where tick marks will be placed on the axes, as well as `xaxt` and `yaxt` to indicate the type of axis. The `axt` parameter is a single character telling whether the axis is logarithmic "1", time "t", or standard "s". The `axp` values are vectors of length 3 that tell where the minimum and maximum tick marks should be placed and the number of tick intervals that have been set up. (They have slightly different values for logarithmic or time axes.)

These parameters that are set by high-level functions are also used to supply default values for certain low-level functions. For example, the `axis` function uses the `axp` parameter values to draw an axis, in the absence of other information. Thus:

```
plot(x,y)
axis(side=3)
```

produces a plot and adds an axis on the top.

A number of parameters affect the way axes are drawn after they have been set up. They influence the generation and plotting of numerical labels in the margins of scatterplots and similar displays.

- `las=` label style. If `las=1`, all axis labels will be horizontal. By default (`las=0`), they are oriented parallel to the axis on devices that have the ability to rotate characters.
- `tck=` tick mark length. Its default value is -0.02, i.e., 2% of the shorter side of the plotting region. This parameter, if positive, causes ticks to point into the plot. If `tck` is set to 1, grid lines are drawn instead of ticks.
- `xaxs=`, `yaxs=` axis style. This parameter specifies which algorithm a high-level plot function should use in setting up user coordinates and tick marks. The default, "r", ensures a constant amount of space between the extreme points on the plot and the surrounding box. Other styles are available—see `par` in Appendix 1 for details.
- `xaxt=`, `yaxt=` axis type. Ordinarily, the axis type is set by a high-level graphics function, and takes the values "s" (standard, linear), "1" (logarithmic), or "t" (time). However, if you set `xaxt="n"` when calling a high-level plot function, this will suppress the drawing of the x-axis. Thus, the expression

  ```
  > plot(x,y,xaxt="n")
  ```

  produces a scatterplot, but does not generate x-axis ticks or labels. You might want to suppress the axis in order to draw a specialized version with the `axis` function.

Another use of the axis style parameter is to specify an axis as "direct." The direct style allows an axis to be "locked in" so that it cannot be changed by later high-level plotting functions. For example

```
> plot(x,y,xlim=c(0,1),ylim=c(0,100))   # set up special axes
> par(xaxs="d",yaxs="d")        # lock the axes in
> plot(x2,y2)    # plot will have same axes as previous plot
```

will cause the special axes to be propagated to future plots. Another use of the par function is needed to "unlock" a direct axis, i.e.,

```
> par(xaxs="r",yaxs="r")    # set back to default style
```

If you know exactly what kind of axis you want, you can use the following function, `lock.axis`, to specify all of the critical parameters:

```
lock.axis ←function(which, umin, umax, tmin, tmax, tnint){
    usr ← par("usr")
    switch(which,
        x = par(usr = c(umin, umax, usr[3:4]), xaxs = "d",
            xaxp = c(tmin, tmax, tnint)),
        y = par(usr = c(usr[1:2], umin, umax), yaxs = "d",
            yaxp = c(tmin, tmax, tnint)),
        stop("Either x or y axis must be specified"))
}
```

The function takes as arguments which axis to lock ("x" or "y"), the minimum and maximum user coordinates to set up for that axis, and the position of the first and last tick marks as well as the number of intervals between ticks. Once these parameters have been set, the function locks them in by specifying a "direct" axis style. Since all high-level functions look at the axs parameters before setting up an axis, and since they do not set up an axis if the parameter is "d", this axis will stay in effect until the unlock.axis function is invoked:

```
unlock.axis ← function(which)
    switch(which,
        x = par(xaxs = "r"),
        y = par(yaxs = "r"),
        stop("Either x or y axis must be specified"))
```

This tells high-level plot routines that they should once again set up axes determined by the data.

Exercises

10.15 Why should plotting functions draw the axes and box last?

10.16 Using the first version of myplot, what would the axes have looked like if we had decided on 6 tick marks rather than 5? Try

```
myplot(runif(10),runif(10))
```

10.17 The function `pretty(x,nint)` takes a second argument `nint` that tells approximately how many intervals the range of `x` should be broken into. Add an argument to `myplot` that allows the user to control the number of tick intervals.

10.18 Add the arguments `xlim` and `ylim` to `myplot`.

10.19 Add the arguments `xlab` and `ylab` to `myplot`. Hint: the expression

```
as.character(substitute(x))
```

is useful.

10.20 A subtle problem with `myplot` is illustrated by the following example. Try

```
> x ← c(1,10,5,3,7)
> y ← c(NA,NA,4,2,1)
> myplot(x,y)
> plot(x,y)
```

How do you explain the differences? Can you fix `myplot`?

10.21 Fix the axis computation in `myplot` to ensure that points will not fall on axis lines.

10.6 Multiple Plots per Page

In section 10.2, we introduced the notion of a figure. Suppose we wish to position an array of figures on a single page of output as shown in Figure 10.13.

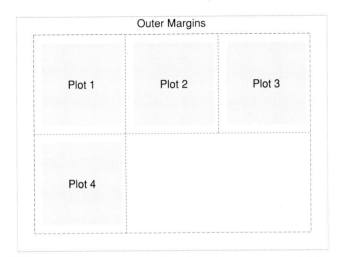

Figure 10.13. An array of figures positioned on the page, surrounded by outer margins.

In this case, each figure contains its own plot and margins, and the entire page has a set of *outer margins* surrounding the figures.

A parameter oma= specifies four values for the size of the outer margins, just as mar= does for margins. By default, there are no outer margins: par(oma=rep(0,4)).

Graphical parameters used with par provide the ability to set up an array of figures on an output device. For example, to have 6 plots appear on a page (2 rows of 3 plots each), use

```
par(mfrow=c(2,3))
```

Now, each successive high-level plotting function will automatically advance to the next available figure region on the page, in a row-first order (first the top row first column, then the top row second column, and so forth). When a page is exhausted, a new one is started, still in the 2 by 3 configuration. Similarly, the graphical parameter mfcol sets up an array of figures and accesses them in a column-first order. In addition, mfrow and mfcol automatically reduce character and margin size to half the standard size if there are more than two rows or columns.

Plotting can be returned to the normal one-per-page form by

```
par(mfrow=c(1,1))
```

This also restores standard character size.

Whenever using multiple figures on a page, it is important to make sure that you have trimmed-down the size of the margins to the minimum size you need, since each of the multiple figures on the page will have its own set of margins. If there is too much margin space allocated, there will be no room for the plots.

An option to mtext allows the overall labelling of a set of multiple figures. Remember the outer margins? The optional argument outer=TRUE allows the positioning of labelling information in the outer margins instead of in the normal figure margins. For example,

```
par(mfrow=c(3,2),oma=c(0,0,4,0))       # multiple figures
# with 4 lines of outer margin at top
plot(x,y,main="This is a Title for the First Figure")
mtext(side=3,line=0,cex=2,outer=TRUE,
"This is an Overall Title for the Page")
  ...
```

plots an array of figures with an overall title for the page as well as titles for each figure.

Exercises

10.22   Produce a plot that resembles Figure 10.1.

10.7 Advanced Graphics Applications

We conclude this chapter with some examples of graphics "tricks"—styles of plotting in S that may provide helpful paradigms.

It is common in time-series work to plot two sets of data on the same axes; the two series are normally related but may be measured on quite different scales, for example, a plot could be constructed with number of housing starts (in thousands) and manufacturing shipments (in millions of dollars). Given two time-series, `hstart` and `ship`, measured at identical times, the following will plot them on the same picture with a housing axis on the left and a shipment axis on the right (Figure 10.14):

```
> # allow 6 lines of margin information on each side of plot
> par(mar=rep(6,4))
> tsplot(hstart)   # plot with x and left y axis
> # say that current plot is new so that S will overplot
> par(new=TRUE)
> # dotted line, suppressing axes
> tsplot(ship,lty=2,axes=F)
> axis(side=4)   # draw y axis on right
```

Notice how we set another parameter, `new=`, to tell the high-level routine `tsplot` that it was already on a new frame and hence did not have to advance to another frame. Remember, the example here will only work if both time-series are measured at identical times.

There are times when the natural units for labelling an axis are not numbers—they might be months, or perhaps multiples of π. Consider the following:

```
> x ← seq(-1.1,1.1,len=200)*pi
> plot(x,sin(1/x),axes=F,type="l")     # Figure 10.15
> axis(2)
> axis(1,seq(-pi,pi,len=9),
+   c("-pi","-3pi/4","-pi/2","-pi/4","0",
+   "pi/4","pi/2","3pi/4","pi"))
```

Here, we used the `axis` function to allow us to put meaningful character labels on an axis.

There are also occasions when, although the tick labels are numeric, they come in an unusual order. Consider producing a map of the United States

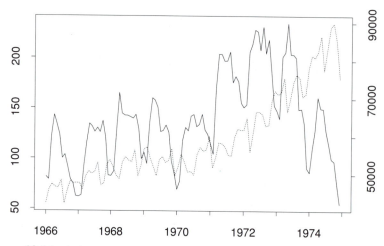

Figure 10.14. A time-series plot showing two sets of data with very different scales. The left axis is for the housing starts series, the right axis is for manufacturing shipments (dotted line).

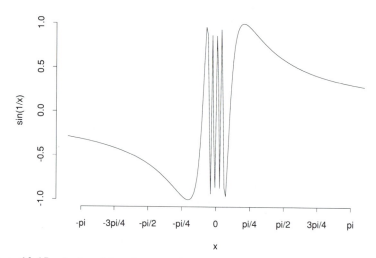

Figure 10.15. A plot of the trigonometric function `sin(1/x)` on the range $-\pi$ to π.

with latitude and longitude lines.

```
> usa(states=F)   # Figure 10.16
> usr ← par("usr")
> axis(2, pretty(usr[3:4]), tck=1, lty=2)
> xticks ← pretty(usr[1:2])
> axis(1, at=xticks, lab=-xticks, tck=1, lty=2)
> title(xlab="Longitude",ylab="Latitude")
```

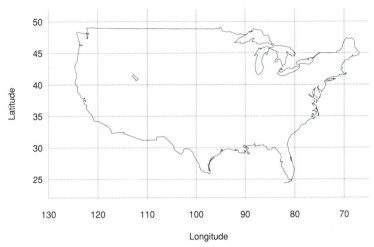

Figure 10.16. A map of the United States with latitude and longitude grid lines.

We allow the `usa` function to draw the map and set up the coordinate system. Afterward, we use `par` to find out the user coordinate system that was set up. We then use `pretty` to decide where to draw the tick labels. In using `axis` to draw the axes, we specify graphical parameter `tck=1` to draw grid lines using line style `lty=2`.

Exercises

10.23 As mentioned earlier, the iris data comes in three groups. Produce three separate plots, one for each group, of the sepal length and sepal width. Make the three plots appear on the same page. For ease of comparison, all three should have identical *x*- and *y*-axes.

10.24 Produce a scatterplot of your favorite *x*, *y* data. At the top and right edges, draw one-dimensional scatter plots of the *x* and *y* data. Next, produce a scatterplot with *jittered* one-dimensional scatter plots at the top and right. Jittering is accomplished by adding small amounts of random noise to the data to avoid exact overplotting. For one-dimensional scatterplots, jittering can be done perpendicular to the data axis.

10.25 Produce a normal Q-Q plot, and use the `axis` function to add an axis labelled with a probability scale.

10.26* Produce a figure like Figure 10.17 to display various device-dependent graphical parameters.

10.27 Produce your favorite scatterplot using the various axis styles `"s"`, `"i"`, `"e"`, and `"r"`. (Set parameters `xaxs` and `yaxs`.) Which style do you like best?

10.28 Produce your favorite scatterplot, with a *y*-axis, but no *x*-axis. Do this in two different ways, once using the `xaxt` parameter and once using the graphical parameter `axes` in the call to `plot`.

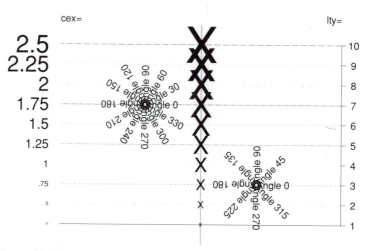

Figure 10.17. A figure that shows various device-dependent graphical parameters.

10.29   Produce an empty plot in which the *x*-axis has tick marks at `c(-15,-`
`5,5,15)` and the user coordinate system runs from `-17` to `17`.

10.30   Produce your favorite scatterplot overlaid with dotted grid lines.

10.31   If your plotting device has a surface 8 inches wide and 10 inches long, the
expression

```
par(usr=c(0,8,0,10))
```

will set up a coordinate system in inches. How could such a coordinate system be useful when trying to draw diagrams?

10.32   Use the `pos=0` argument to `axis` in order to draw a scatterplot with axes centered at the origin.

Answers to Selected Exercises

10.3   (page 315)   The parameter `cex` will affect not only the plotted points but also the tick and axis labels. To get the desired effect, you should use

```
plot(x,y,type="n")
points(x,y,cex=3,pch="S")
```

10.4   (page 318)

```
tsplot(ship,smooth(ship))   # type="pl" would be nice, too
legend(1967.3,85000,leg=c("Shipments","Smoothed Shipments"),
    lty=1:2, col=1:2)
```

10.7   (page 322)   The trick is to use the `paste` function to paste a couple of blank spaces onto the front of the sequence number. Hence:

```
> odd ← abs(resids)>4 | stack.loss>25
> text(airflow[odd], stack.loss[odd], adj=0,
+    paste("  ",seq(along=resids)[odd])
```

10.12   (page 323)

```
                city.connect ← function(city.x,city.y){
                    usa(states=F,lty=2)    # dotted map - no state boundaries
                    points(city.x,city.y,pch="o")   # plot the cities
                    tree ← mstree( cbind(city.x,city.y*.8), plane=F )
                      # a degree of latitude is approximately
                      # 80% as large as a degree of longitude
                    s ← seq(along=tree)
                    segments(city.x[s],city.y[s],city.x[tree],city.y[tree])
                }
```

10.13   (page 323)
```
            plot(corn.rain,corn.yield)
            lines(lowess(corn.rain,corn.yield))
```

10.14   (page 323)
```
            l ← lowess(corn.rain,corn.yield)
            fit ← approx(l,corn.rain)$y
            plot(corn.rain,abs(corn.yield-fit))
            # a smooth curve also helps show if variance is constant
            lines(lowess(corn.rain),abs(corn.yield-fit))
```

10.15   (page 328)   It gives the interactive user more time to look at the configuration of the data while the annotation is being put onto the plot.

10.19   (page 329)
```
        myplot ← function(x,y,
                xlim=NULL,ylim=NULL,
                xlab=as.character(substitute(x)),
                ylab=as.character(substitute(y))){
            frame()
            if(missing(xlim)) xlim ← range(x)
            if(missing(ylim)) ylim ← range(y)
            xticks ← pretty(xlim)
            yticks ← pretty(ylim)
            par(usr=c(range(xticks),range(yticks)))
            points(x,y)
            axis(side=1,at=xticks)
            axis(side=2,at=yticks)
            mtext(side=1,line=3,xlab)
            mtext(side=2,line=3,ylab)
            box()
        }
```

10.20   (page 329)   The x and y vectors are treated independently by myplot, but
plot realizes that missing values in either coordinate mean that the point will
not be plotted, hence it omits those points when setting up the axis limits.

10.21   (page 329)
```
            eps ← diff(range(x))*.05
            xticks ← pretty(range(x)+c(-eps,eps))
```

10.26   (page 333)
```
            frame()
            par(usr=c(0,10,0,11),mar=c(4,10,4,2))
            # line types and colors
            for(i in 1:10)
                abline(h=i,lty=i,col=i)
            # character sizes
            for(i in 1:10)
                mtext(side=2,at=i,line=1,adj=1,cex=i/4,as.character(i/4))
            axis(4,at=1:10)
```

```
            abline(v=5)
            for(i in 1:10)
                text(5,i,"X",cex=i/2)
            for(i in seq(0,330,len=12))
                text(3,7,encode("Angle",i),adj=0,srt=i)
            for(i in seq(0,315,len=8))
                text(7,3,encode("Angle",i),adj=0,srt=i)
            mtext(side=3,adj=0,"cex=")
            mtext(side=3,adj=1,"lty=")
```

10.30   (page 334)

```
            plot(x,y,axes=F)
            axis(1,lty=2,tck=1)
            axis(2,lty=2,tck=1)
            box()
```

10.32   (page 334)

```
            plot(x,y,axes=F)
            axis(1,pos=0)
            axis(2,pos=0)
```

11
How S Works

This chapter defines the S language, its evaluator, and some of the key S functions. The grammar used by the standard S parser is presented as a set of syntactic rules. The semantics of the S evaluator are discussed, using a model evaluator written in S. Two sets of functions are discussed: those that have special behavior during evaluation, such as `switch`, and some others that are evaluated in a standard way, but are important basic tools with special behavior for different kinds of arguments, such as subset and arithmetic operators.

The material in this chapter is not needed for ordinary use of S. It should be of interest to those who want to know more about the design of S, or who need to understand the language and its evaluation more precisely.

11.1 The Language

This section defines the rules for expressions in the S language, first for the grammar (the syntax) and second for the individual lexical tokens. The language described in this section is what the S user will ordinarily see. The rules specified here are not, however, fixed and unchangeable. They define only one interface, the `parse/deparse` interface, between the user and the internal objects representing the various kinds of expression, as summarized in section 7.5.3. The function `parse` converts from expressions typed, or contained in files or character vetors, to internal objects. The functions `deparse` and `dput` convert back to the printed form of the language. It is perfectly possible to implement a different grammar; for example, one based on a list-style representation of the language (see exercise 11.3 at the end of the chapter), or to modify the interface that the user sees, as was done in the `try.S` example of section 7.4.3. The operation of the evaluator, as we will discuss it in section 11.2, would be unchanged. The central identity of the language rests in the objects that represent it.

11.1.1 *The Grammar*

This section describes the syntax of the S language, as interpreted by the `parse` function. Table 11.1 gives the syntactic rules that define an S expression.

Literals	*number*	`"numeric"`
	string	`"character"`
	name	`"name"`
	comment	`"comment"`
	function (formals) expr	`"function"`
Calls	expr *infix* expr	`"call"`
	expr *%anything%* expr	
	unary expr	
	expr (arglist)	
	expr [arglist]	
	expr [[arglist]]	
	expr $ fname	
Assignment	expr ← expr	`"<-"`
	expr _ expr	
	expr -> expr	
	expr <<- expr	`"<<-"`
Conditional	*if* (expr) expr	`"if"`
	if (expr) expr *else* expr	
	for (name *in* expr) expr	`"for"`
Iteration	*repeat* expr	`"repeat"`
	while (expr) expr	`"while"`
Flow	*break*	`"break"`
	next	`"next"`
	return (expr)	`"return"`
	(expr)	`"("`
	{ exprlist }	`"{"`

Table 11.1. The patterns recognized by the S parser as valid instances of `expr`, an S expression. The first column is an informal categorization of the expressions. The third column is the mode of the corresponding object produced by the parser.

We have divided the rules into some categories, labelled in column one, although these categories are not themselves part of the grammar. The second column contains one or more lines of matching syntactic patterns, one alternative per line. The third column gives the mode of the object generated by the parser to match this pattern. Table 7.1 described the form that these special objects have. Terms appearing in `this font` in Table 11.1 are lexical objects; that is, strings recognized by the lexical analyzer and passed back as single objects to the parser. So also are all the special characters, like parentheses and commas, which stand for lexical objects containing themselves. Table 11.1 gives all the syntactic forms that are S expressions. Literals are unchanged by the evaluator. The remaining forms of expression are processed by the evaluator according to the semantic rules described in the next section. Operators are converted by the parser into calls to functions whose name is the name of the operator; for example `x[i]` is equivalent to

    "[" (x, i)

The lexical analyzer recognizes the following special strings as infix operators:

```
$    [    [[    ^    :
     *        /
     +        -
<    >    <=   >=   ==   !=
     &    |    &&   ||
←    _         →    <<-
```

Table 11.2. Special infix operators. Precedence goes from high to low down the table (see `Syntax` in appendix 1).

In addition, any string of characters bounded by "`%`" characters is an infix operator, with precedence just below "`:`". The operator "`**`" is a deprecated synonym for "`^`". The operators "`+`", "`–`", and "`!`" are also recognized as unary operators.

The following table defines the additional syntactic forms introduced in column two of Table 11.1. Included are three kinds of lists, the syntax for arguments in a call and for formal arguments in a function definition, and finally the rule that lets non-standard names appear quoted in function calls and assignments.

```
exprlist:    expr
             exprlist ; expr
arglist:     arg
             arglist , arg
formals:     empty
             formal
             formals , formal
arg:         empty
             expr
             fname =
             fname = expr
formal:      name
             name = expr
fname:       name
             string
```

A few constraints and properties in parsing are more easily expressed as actions than as syntactic rules:

1. The left side of assignments are required to be either an `fname` or one of the patterns that parses into an object of mode `"call"`.

2. Comments are included in the grammar: they are not thrown away, but become part of the object generated by the parse. They are attached to some, but not all, objects in the language. The result is an expression of mode `"comment.expression"`. The evaluator throws away the comments. The deparser, however, knows how to print out such expressions with the comments included. Because comments cannot be attached to all expressions, they may move around a little when some parsed text is deparsed again.

3. Some parsed function calls are given special treatment, for the sake of efficiency. Because the name "..." is treated specially in argument matching, calls containing that name are made the only element of an object of mode `"call(...)"`. The evaluator processes the element of this object as a call known to contain "...". A few special functions, for example `.Internal`, are given their own mode. These are intended to be built-in pieces of the language, not functions that might be redefined.

4. Some special names, like `TRUE` and `NULL`, are treated as symbolic constants. They can not be redefined by assignments, and the name is converted in the parse to the actual object it represents.

To see the semantics of the various kinds of expression, see section 11.2, which outlines a model for the S evaluator.

11.1.2 *Lexical Items*

The following table gives the lexical rules in S defining numeric and complex literals, and names.

numeric	integer
	float
complex	numeric "i"
	numeric [+-] numeric "i"
name	(.|letter) (.|letter|digit)*
integer	digit+
exponent	"e" [+-]? integer
float	integer exponent
	integer "." digit* exponent?
	"." integer exponent?

Table 11.3. Lexical rules. Names represent lexical types; "+" following means 1 or more instances; "*" means 0 or more instances; and "?" means 0 or 1 instances; "|" and new lines separate alternative patterns. Characters in quotes stand for themselves, and a list of characters in square brackets will match exactly one of those characters. "letter" matches any upper or lower case letter, and "digit" matches any decimal digit.

The notation is a simplified version of that used by the *lex* command. The following, while lexically names, are reserved in S for special purposes and cannot be used on the left of an assignment arrow to name an object:

if	else	
for	while	repeat
next	break	in
function	return	
TRUE	FALSE	T	F
NA	NULL	

The names above the line are allowed only in their special syntactic roles, as defined in Table 11.1. Those below the line are symbolic constants, and will be turned by the parser into the objects they represent. The evaluator will also print a warning if you make an assignment that masks one of the S system functions:

```
> c ← function(x) x+1
Warning messages:
  Assignment masks system function "c"
```

11.2 Semantics: A Model for Evaluation

This section describes a model for the S evaluator, in the form of an S function, `Eval`, which uses the same rules as the actual S evaluator (written in C). The closely related S function `eval` invokes the actual evaluator, and also has the property that, given an argument of mode "`expression`", it will evaluate all the elements of that object. `Eval` can be regarded as a model for `eval`. It serves as a convenient description of the semantic rules and internal objects used in evaluation.

The `Eval` function has the form:

```
Eval ← function(expr){
    if(is.language(expr)) switch(mode(expr),
        # the cases to be discussed below
        )
    else expr
}
```

The evaluator uses the mode of an expression to decide how to evaluate it. Evaluation is highly recursive, so that evaluating an expression will typically involve calling the evaluator again for elements of that expression. In the various subsections below, we define the semantics of evaluation for various modes. Each of these will be illustrated by corresponding expressions that would appear in `Eval` as cases in the `switch` call above. Some other functions will appear in these expressions. These will either be ordinary functions, like `is.language`, or else functions whose names have leading upper-case letters, like `Eval` itself. The latter together make up the semantic model; they often correspond to lower-case functions having an analogous role in "real" evaluation. If you attach the `semantics` section of the S library, by

```
library(semantics)
```

you will have available the full version of the `Eval` function.

11.2.1 *Function Calls: Mode* `call`

This is the most important language mode, and it drives the mechanism of the evaluator. It is evaluated as follows: the evaluator finds the definition of the function called, creates a new frame by matching the call and the definition, evaluates the body of the function by invoking `Eval` recursively, and returns the result.

A frame is a list whose components are the objects available locally by name during the evaluation of the call (see section 5.4). The frame initially is a list of expressions for all the arguments, with an attribute `"missing"`, such that

```
attr(Frame,"missing")[i]
```

is TRUE if the i-th argument was missing in the call. In the evaluation model, all the currently active frames are themselves elements of the global list Frames, with Nframe being the current frame number and Frames[[Nframe]] the corresponding frame.

The model for evaluating an expression, expr, of mode "call" is:

```
if(mode(expr[[1]] ==  "name"))
    definition ← Get(expr[[1]],mode="function")
else {
    definition ← Eval(expr[[1]])
    if(mode(definition)!="function")
        stop(paste(definition, "is not a function"))
}
New.frame(amatch(definition, expr), expr)
body ← definition[[length(definition)]]
value ← Eval(body)
if(Return.flag[[Nframe]])value ← Return[[Nframe]]
Pop.frame()
value
```

The first expression above finds the definition. Note that the Get call, including the mode argument, ensures that a local non-function with the same name does not hide the function definition. Also, the else branch allows the function definition to be the result of a computation, so that calls like

```
(myfuns[[which]]) (x, y)
```

will work.

The definition and the actual call are matched by the function amatch, which returns the initial frame containing the argument expressions and the missing information. See section 11.3.5 for a discussion of argument matching. The function New.frame puts this frame on the end of the Frames list, updates some other global objects used in the evaluation, and makes the new frame the current frame by setting Nframe:

```
New.frame ← function(frame, call){
    parent ← Nframe
    Nframe <<- length(Frames) + 1
    Frames[[Nframe]] <<- as.frame(frame)
    Calls[[Nframe]] <<- as.call(call)
    Nargs[[Nframe]] <<- length(frame)
    Parent[[Nframe]] <<- parent
    Return.flag[[Nframe]] <<- FALSE
}
```

After the new frame has been set up, the evaluator calls itself recursively to evaluate the body of the function. There may have been a return expression evaluated in the body somewhere; if so, Return.flag[[Nframe]] has been set and the return value has been saved in Return[[Nframe]]. This implements `return` expressions without explicit jumps (which don't exist in S).

The function `Pop.frame` sets the lengths of `Frames`, etc. to `Nframe-1` and sets `Nframe` to the parent of frame `Nframe`.

11.2.2 *Mode* name

Evaluating a name amounts to finding the corresponding object and, if the object is an unevaluated argument to the current frame, evaluating it.

```
Frame ← Frames[[Nframe]]; name ← as.character(expr)
n ← match(name, names(Frame), FALSE)
if(n) {   # local
    Temp ← Frame[[n]]
    if(is.language(Temp) &&
      n > length(Frame) - Nargs[Nframe]) { # argument
        if(attr(Frame, "missing")[n]) { # missing
            Insert(name,Bad.default,Nframe)
            value ← Eval(Temp[[2]])
            Assign(name, value, Nframe)
        } else {                      # actual argument
            i ← Nframe; Nframe <<- Parent[Nframe]
            value ← Eval(Temp[[1]])
            Nframe <<- i
            Insert(name, value, Nframe)
        }
    }
    Temp
}
else Get(name)   # non-local
```

If the name is found in the local frame, it may be an unevaluated argument; if so, then the expression for the argument, either the actual argument or the default, must be evaluated, and inserted into the frame. The default expression is evaluated in the current frame. Actual arguments are evaluated in the parent frame—the frame from which the current function was called.

With either default or actual arguments, the *evaluated* argument is inserted as the first element in the current frame. The next time the name gets evaluated in this frame, the call to `match` will get this new element. Therefore, arguments are evaluated at most once. The function `Insert` inserts the new item as the first element of `Frames[[Nframe]]`, with the appropriate name. That is why the test

```
n > length(Frame) - Nargs[Nframe]
```

determines whether the name is an unevaluated argument. The unevaluated expression for the argument is also retained in the frame, to be available for use by functions like `substitute` (see section 11.3.3).

The default expression for an argument can involve other arguments, which might also be missing. Therefore, we must watch for a loop in evaluating default expressions; for example, if the function

```
silly ← function( x = y-1, y = x+1)
        x+y
```

were called with no arguments. This check is implemented by inserting an assignment of the argument name before evaluating the default expression. The inserted definition is a special object with mode `"unknown"`. If this object is then encountered because of another reference to the same name before the evaluation of the default expression is complete, we know that a loop in default evaluation has occurred.

11.2.3 *Assignments*

Expressions of mode "<–" or "<<–" are evaluated with the intended side-effect of changing the contents of an object, accessible by name. Sticking for the moment to the usual assignment, "<–", the simple case has a name (or string) on the left and some expression on the right:

```
xx ← sample(1:1e6,10)
```

The assignment is a *replacement* if it has some function of the name on the left:

```
dim(m) ← c(r,c)
```

This case includes an operator expression involving the name, since these are parsed into ordinary function calls. For example, the left side of

```
z[[1]] ← new.value
```

is equivalent to `"[["(z,1)`. Finally, there can be arbitrary nesting of such function calls on the left side of the assignment.

```
dimnames(xm)[[1]] ← names(y)
```

meaning to extract the `dimnames` attribute of `xm`, replace its first element by the right side, and then replace the attribute by this modified expression.

The model for assignment reduces all these cases to a call to the `Assign` function:

```
Assign(name, replacement, frame)
```

with `name` the name for the object, `replacement` the new data to be assigned, and `frame` the number of the frame for the assignment. The frame number –1 stands for the working directory. For simple assignment, `replacement` is the value on the right side of the arrow. With a function on the left, the replacement is defined to be the result of calling the corresponding *replacement function*. The name of the replacement function is the name of the left-side function with "<−" pasted on the end. The arguments are the same as the arguments to the left-side function, plus one last argument for the replacement data, which will be the value of the right-side expression. For example, the assignment to the `dim` attribute above is equivalent to the expression

```
Assign("m", "dim<-"(m,c(r,c)), frame)
```

The replacement function's job is to return the new object that should replace the old one—it does not do any assignment itself. The power of this uniform approach is that users can have any left-side function they like, simply by defining the corresponding replacement function.

Assignments with nested functions on the left side are reduced to the preceding case by creating, and evaluating, an expanded form that does the replacement in steps (we will look at an example at the end of the subsection).

In the model evaluator, assignments work as follows:

```
perm ← mode(expr) == "<<-"
Temp ← Replace.expr(expr)
value ← Eval(expr[[2]]) # right-hand side
switch(mode(Temp),
    "<-" = ,
    "<<-" = {
        name ← as.character(expr[[1]])
        new.object ← value
        frame ← if(perm || Nframe==1) -1 else Nframe
    },
    call = {
        name ← as.character(Temp[[1]])
        Temp[[length(Temp)]] ← value
        new.object ← Eval(Temp)
        frame ← if(perm) -1 else Frame.of(name)
    }
    ,
    return(Eval(Temp))) # complicated case
Assign(name, new.object, frame=frame)
value
```

The function `Replace.expr` distinguishes the three kinds of left-side expression. For a name on the left side, it returns `expr`; for a simple function call, it creates and returns the call to the corresponding replacement function. For nested function calls, it generates a braced list of expressions that does the implied sequence of simpler assignments. The third case is done entirely by evaluating this alternative expression. In the other two cases, the new value for the assigned object is computed, along with the name to use, and these are given to `Assign`. The value of the assignment expression itself is always the right side, to give the correct semantics to expressions with multiple assignments:

```
nrow ← d[1] ← length(cases)
```

The correct frame for assignment is defined as follows. For simple assignments in frame 1, and for "<<–" in *any* frame, assignment is to the working directory. Replacements evaluated in frame 1 always put the result in the working directory if the object came from any permanent directory, and otherwise put the replacement back where the object came from. In all other frames, "←" always assigns to the local frame (to prevent functions from having side-effects).

The function `Replace.expr` works as follows:

```
Replace.expr ← function(expr){
    lhs ← expr[[1]]
    if(mode(lhs) == "name")return(expr)
    if(mode(lhs) != "call")
        stop(paste("Left side of assignment can't be of mode",
          mode(lhs)))
    object ← lhs[[2]]
    if(mode(object) == "name" ) { # make the replacement call
        fun.name ← lhs[[1]]
        lhs[[1]] ← paste(fun.name,"<-",sep="")
        lhs[[length(lhs)+1]] ← expr[[2]]
        lhs
    }
    else Expd.assign(expr, Nframe)
}
```

Simple assignments are returned unchanged. If the left side is a function call, with the object (the first argument) a name, a call to the corresponding replacement function is constructed. When several function calls are nested on the left side, an equivalent sequence of assignments is constructed by `Expd.assign`. For example, if `expr` contains the parsed expression:

```
z$a[1] ← 'Complete'
```

the expanded expression is:

```
{
    Assign("..0", z$a, frame = Nframe)
    ..0[1] ← 'Complete'
    z$a ← ..0
}
```

The frame argument to `Assign` is the frame in which the assignment is to be evaluated. Note that the call to `Assign`, even with `Nframe==1` is an assignment only for the duration of the expression. Otherwise, complicated replacements could create garbage in the working directory.

11.2.4 *Iteration*

The three kinds of iteration expressions in S, for, while, and repeat, have similar semantics, differing in how exiting is controlled. The evaluator repeatedly tests for completion of the loop, evaluates the body of the loop, and then tests for a break or next having occurred. The value of the whole iteration expression is the last evaluation of the body (not counting evaluations resulting in break or next).

Now we have to introduce the semantics of break and next. Global vectors Break.flag and Next.flag indicate whether a break or next is currently being processed in this frame. The evaluator sets both flags to FALSE when it starts evaluating an iterative expression. The corresponding flag is set to TRUE when a break or next expression is evaluated. Then the various recursive calls to the evaluator stop what they are doing and return, until we get back to the innermost iteration expression in this frame. The Eval call for the iteration resets the corresponding flag and either returns or continues.

Here is the semantic model for a repeat expression, which has no completion test and therefore is a little simpler than for or while:

```
Break.flag[Nframe] <<- FALSE
Next.flag[Nframe] <<- FALSE
Value ← NULL
repeat {
    Body ← Eval(expr[[1]])
    if(Break.flag[Nframe] || Return.flag[Nframe])break;
    if(Next.flag[Nframe]) Next.flag[Nframe] <<- FALSE
    else Value ← Body
}
Break.flag[Nframe] <<- FALSE
if(Return.flag[Nframe]) Return[[Nframe]]
else Value
```

The return expression behaves similarly to break and next. See section 11.2.1.

At this point, we admit that we have been describing a slightly simplified semantics. The return, break, and next expressions can in fact appear anywhere, so long as the evaluator checks the corresponding flag—Break.flag, Next.flag, or Return.flag, after all recursive calls to Eval. In particular, return, break, and next can all appear within arguments to functions or in conditional expressions. This can be of practical value; for example, one may want to put return expressions into arguments to the switch function. There are no new mechanisms involved in the more general form. However, to show all these checks in the illustrations in this section would add too much clutter, so we have omitted them in most examples.

The `while` semantics are the same as those of `repeat`, with the exception that a test is evaluated before evaluating the body:

```
Break.flag[Nframe] <<- FALSE
Next.flag[Nframe] <<- FALSE
Value <- NULL
repeat {
    if(!Eval(expr[[1]]))break
    Body <- Eval(expr[[2]])
    if(Break.flag[Nframe] || Return.flag[Nframe])break;
    if(Next.flag[Nframe]) Next.flag[Nframe] <<- FALSE
    else Value <- Body
}
Break.flag[Nframe] <<- FALSE
if(Return.flag[Nframe]) Return[[Nframe]]
else Value
```

Notice that here (and in the other iterations as well), the value of the iteration expression is NULL if there is an exit before the end of the first iteration.

The `for` expression does a little more work. The parsed form of the expression has three elements: the name to be used for the loop object, the expression for the values it should take, and the expression for the body of the loop. The evaluator first computes `counter`, the vector of values for the loop object. Then it saves the previous local assignment, if any, of the loop object. For each element of `counter`, it assigns the loop object and evaluates the body of the loop.

```
Break.flag[Nframe] <<- FALSE
Next.flag[Nframe] <<- FALSE
Value <- NULL
what <- as.character(expr[[1]])
counter <- Eval(expr[[2]])
old.what <- Frames[[Nframe]][[what]]
for(i in seq(along=counter) {
    Assign(what,counter[[i]],Nframe)
    Body <- Eval(expr[[3]])
    if(Break.flag[Nframe] || Return.flag[Nframe])break;
    if(Next.flag[Nframe]) Next.flag[Nframe] <<- FALSE
    else Value <- Body
}
if(!is.null(old.what))Assign(what,old.what,Nframe)
Break.flag[Nframe] <<- FALSE
if(Return.flag[Nframe]) Return[[Nframe]]
else Value
```

At the end of the iteration the previous assignment, if any, for the loop object is restored.

11.2.5 `return; break; next`

These expressions interrupt the flow of evaluation. The mechanism for this has been described in the previous subsection. The evaluation of the expressions themselves just sets the necessary flags. For `return`:

```
Return[[Nframe]] <<- Eval(expr[[1]])
Return.flag[Nframe] <<- T
Return[[Nframe]]
```

for `break`:

```
Break.flag[Nframe] <<- T
NULL
```

and for `next`:

```
Next.flag[Nframe] <<- T
NULL
```

11.2.6 *Braced Lists of Expressions*

The body of most function definitions and of most iterative loops consists of several subexpressions, enclosed between "`{`" and "`}`" and separated by semicolons or new lines. These braced expressions, which have mode "`{`", are evaluated by evaluating each subexpression in turn, but interrupting the evaluation if a `return`, `break`, or `next` is encountered. The value of the braced expressions is that of the last subexpression evaluated.

```
value <- NULL
for(subexpr in expr) {
    element <- Eval(subexpr)
    if(Return.flag[Nframe] || Break.flag[Nframe]
       || Next.flag[Nframe] ) break
    value <- element
}
value
```

In the case of a `return`, the value of the braced expression is irrelevant, since the value of the whole frame will be taken from the `Return` vector.

11.2.7 *Conditional Expressions:* `if`

The semantics are what one would expect: evaluate the test and, depending on its result, evaluate one of the branches.

```
if(Logical.value((expr[[1]]))) Eval(expr[[2]])
else if(length(expr)>2) Eval(expr[[3]])
else NULL
```

The expression will have length 2 if there was no `else` part to it. The function `Logical.value` evaluates its argument, coerces it to mode "`logical`", and does some checks on the result. It generates an error if there is no valid logical element and a warning if the length of the expression is greater than 1.

11.2.8 *Bound Function Calls: Mode* `frame`

These are generated by binding in current function definitions. They are evaluated like ordinary function calls, except that the search for the function definition has already been done and the matched arguments supplied in the `frame` expression.

```
New.frame(expr[[2]], expr[[3]])
value ← Eval(expr[[0]])
if(Return.flag[[Nframe]])value ← Return[[Nframe]]
Pop.frame()
value
```

Aside from being somewhat more efficient, bound calls have the property that they are semantically unaffected by redefining the functions called in the original expression. See the documentation for the function `bind` in Appendix 1.

11.2.9 *Internal Computations*

Functions written in S and the interfaces to the UNIX system, to C, and to Fortran provide very wide programming facilities. Some capabilities, however, have to be provided internally to "bootstrap" the rest of the language; for example, some basic functions to create vectors. Access to these facilities is provided by expressions of the form `.Internal(call,symbol)`, where `call` is an S function call expression and `symbol` is a character string giving the name of a C function. For example, evaluating

```
.Internal(parse(n, text, file, prompt), "S_parse")
```

invokes the internal code for the S parser and returns the expression resulting from the parse. The semantic definition of `.Internal` is that the S evaluator will evaluate the arguments in the call, and pass these in a standard way to the C routine corresponding to the symbol. The C code does the necessary computation and returns to the evaluator a pointer to an S object that is the value of the call. For the purposes of this book, the internal C routines are considered fixed: we do not suggest that users write new internal code.

The full form of the internal call is:

```
.Internal(call, symbol, evaluate, code)
```

where `evaluate` is a flag (true by default), saying whether the arguments in the call should be pre-evaluated before invoking the C routine, and `code` is a numeric code (zero by default) that is used to allow one C routine to implement several different internal functions. For example, one C routine implements several binary operators. The model for evaluating internals is as follows.

```
call ← as.call(expr[[1]])
args ← list()
code ← if(length(expr)<4)0 else expr[[4]]
if(length(expr)<3 || Eval(expr[[3]]))
    for(i in call[-1]) args ← c(args, Eval(i))
Do.internal(expr,call,args,code)
```

The call to `Do.internal` in the model corresponds to invoking the C routine in the actual evaluator.

11.3 Special Function Evaluation

The functions discussed in sections 11.3.1 to 11.3.4 are done by internal C implementations and do not have their arguments evaluated before invoking the C code. Therefore, their semantics cannot be inferred from the general discussion at the end of the previous section. We also discuss the matching of arguments in function calls, in section 11.3.5.

11.3.1 `switch`

The `switch` function evaluates its first argument. If the result is an object with mode "`character`", one of the following arguments is selected by matching against the names of the arguments. Otherwise, the result is interpreted as an integer and matched against `1:nargs()` - 1. If the match succeeds the corresponding argument is evaluated and the result returned; otherwise the value of the call is `NULL`. The following is a model for `switch`:

```
Switch ← function(EXPRESSION,...){
    branches ← expression(...,NULL)
    which ← EXPRESSION
    if(length(which)>1) warning(paste("switch value has",
        length(which),"elements: only the first used"))
    if(mode(which)=="character")
        n ← match(which,names(branches),length(branches))
    else {
```

```
                    n ← trunc(which)
                    if(n<1 || n>length(branches))n ← length(branches)
                }
            Eval(branches[[n]])
        }
```

The `switch` function uses a capitalized name for its first argument, to avoid conflicts with the names of other arguments.

11.3.2 *Missing Arguments*

If `abc` is a formal argument to the current function, `missing(abc)` is TRUE or FALSE according to whether there was no corresponding actual argument. Any other use of `missing` is an error.

```
        Missing ← function(what){
            argname ← substitute(what,Frames[[Nframe]])
            if(mode(argname)!="name")
                stop("The argument to missing() should be a name")
            call ← Calls[[Sys.parent(1)]]
            fundef ← Eval(call[[1]])
            formals ← names(fundef)[-length(fundef)]
            n ← match(argname,formals)
            if(is.na(n))
                stop(paste(argname,"should have been an argument name"))
            attr(amatch(fundef,call),"missing")[n]
        }
```

The `amatch` function mimics the argument matching process in the evaluation. See section 11.3.5.

11.3.3 *Substitution; Expressions*

The expression

```
        substitute(expr)
```

takes `expr` unevaluated, and tries to replace any name in the expression by the value of an object with the same name in the local frame. The search is done starting from the last element of the local frame and moving forward, with the result that arguments are matched in their unevaluated form. Names that are not matched in the local frame remain unsubstituted. It is possible to give `substitute`, as a second argument, an explicit list object in which to search instead of the local frame. In particular,

```
        substitute(x+y,list())
```

is a way to generate the parsed, but unevaluated, version of the expression "x+y".

Notice that `substitute` may return an object of mode "name", "call", "←", and so on. In contrast, functions `parse` and `expression` always return objects of mode "expression"—lists of one or more expressions. Function `substitute` always produces a single expression. Thus

```
expression(x+y)
```

returns an object of mode "expression", and length one; its single element is the same object as is returned by the last use of `substitute` above.

11.3.4 *Control:* `&&` *and* `||`

These functions evaluate their first argument as a logical condition. If it is FALSE in the case of `&&`, or TRUE in the case of `||`, the second operand is not needed and is not evaluated. Their simulation in the model is simple. Beware, however, that the model operators below have higher precedence than the operators they mimic.

```
"%&&%" ← function(e1,e2){
    if(Logical.value(e1))
        Logical.value(e2))
    else FALSE
}

"%||%" ← function(e1,e2){
    if(!Logical.value(e1))
        Logical.value(e2)
    else TRUE
}
```

The function `Logical.value` will ensure that the expressions evaluate to suitable logical objects; for example, it warns if its argument evaluates to an object of length > 1 (see the comments in section 11.2.7).

11.3.5 *Argument Matching*

The function `amatch` generates a local frame from a call to a function and the corresponding function definition. The central step in doing this is to match the actual arguments in the call to the formal arguments in the function definition. There are three steps in this matching process:

1. Arguments are matched if the name of the actual argument matches the name of the formal argument exactly;
2. Arguments are matched if the name of one actual argument matches a non-empty initial string of one formal argument;
3. Unnamed actuals are matched, in order, to remaining unmatched formals.

The following function, pmatch, models argument matching. It takes the two vectors of names, call.names and fun.names, and returns a vector of the indices in the second argument matching the elements of the first argument, with zero where there was no match.

```
pmatch ← function(call.names, fun.names){
    nargs ← length(fun.names)
    by.position ← nchar(call.names) == 0
    dot.pos ← match("...",fun.names,0)
    if(dot.pos) before ← 1:nargs < dot.pos
    else before ← rep(TRUE,nargs)
# step 1
    matched ← match(call.names, fun.names, 0)
# step 2
    partial ← !(matched | by.position)
    if(any(partial)){
        rows ← 1:length(call.names)
        cols ← (1:nargs)[before]
        xx ← first.match(call.names, fun.names[before])
        ok ← rows[partial & apply(xx, 1, sum) == 1]
        for(i in ok) matched[i] ← cols[xx[i,  ]]
        matched[duplicated(matched)] ← 0

    }
# step 3
    ok ← 1:nargs
    ok ← ok [ before & !match(ok,matched,0)]
    by.position ← (1:length(call.names))[by.position]
    length(by.position) ← length(ok) ←
        min(length(by.position), length(ok))
    if(length(by.position))
        matched[by.position] ← ok
    if(dot.pos)matched[!matched] ← dot.pos
    matched

}
```

Let's look at an example. Consider the function

```
get ← function(name, where, frame, mode = "any"){
    etc.
```

and a call to get of the form

```
get(mode="character",wh=1,"abcd")
```

The corresponding argument matching is described by the following computation:

```
> cn ← c("mode","wh","")
> fn ← c("name", "where", "frame", "mode")
> pmatch(cn,fn)
[1] 4 2 1
```

The three arguments in the call are matched at steps 1 through 3, respectively.

The implementation of `pmatch` takes account of the case that "..." was one of the formal arguments. In this case, step 1 remains unchanged, but step 2 and step 3 only apply to the formal arguments that came before "..." in the function definition. This is the semantic equivalent of the rule that arguments following "..." must be matched exactly by name (see section 6.1.3).

In our example, suppose the function had "..." inserted as the third formal argument, and let's add a few more actual arguments as well.

```
> fn2 ← c("name", "where", "...", "frame", "mode")
> cn2 ← c("mode", "wh", "f", "a", "", "nam", "")
> pmatch(cn2,fn2)
[1] 5 2 3 1 3 3 3
```

Note that the fourth actual argument matches the first formal argument by position, and that the actual argument named "f" is absorbed into "..." even though it partially matches the formal argument "frame".

Exercises

11.1   The function `pmatch` is one of the more concentrated examples of S programming in the book. Try to explain what is going on; e.g., say what happens on each line on which an assignment takes place to the `matched` vector.

11.2   The function `amatch` takes the result of the argument matching and makes a list of the corresponding actual or default expressions. The list also has a logical attribute "missing" that contains TRUE wherever the formal argument was not matched in the call. Write a model function `Amatch` that behaves like `amatch`, and uses `pmatch`.

11.4 Other Important Functions

The functions in this section do not have special behavior as far as their evaluation is concerned. Instead, they are discussed because they are important for many applications in S and because their behavior depends on the classes of objects they get as arguments.

In subsections 11.4.1 to 11.4.3, we define the semantics of expressions like

```
x[i]
x[[i]]
x[i,j,k]
x$a
attr(x,"origin")
```

and, by implication, of functions that are specialized applications of them, such as dim(x), which is equivalent to attr(x, "dim"). These are the *extraction* functions, returning some elements or properties of an object. They may also appear on the left of an assignment operation, to carry out *replacement* in an object. The corresponding replacement functions , such as "[<-", are built into the evaluator for efficiency.

We also define the semantics of all the infix operators, including arithmetic, comparison, and logical control. The issues for these functions involve the treatment of various special classes of objects, such as arrays and time-series.

11.4.1 *Vector Subscripts:* x[i]

The subscript function, "[", provides a basis for describing the other extraction and replacement functions, so we define it first. In the standard use of "[", one subscript expression, i, is supplied to extract or replace data from some object, x, to be treated as a vector.

The semantics are most easily defined in two stages. In the first, the subscript is interpreted to define a set of *indices*, numerical values that index which elements are being selected. The numbers in the indices are either positive, 0, or NA. In the second stage, the indices are used to select or replace elements in x. The function vec.index models the computations of the index values.

```
vec.index ← function(x,i,replace=F){
    all.i ← seq(along=x)
    if(missing(i))all.i
    else switch(mode(i),
    character = {
        n ← if(replace) match(i,as.character(names(x)))
            else pmatch(i,as.character(names(x)))
        nomatch ← is.na(n)
        n[nomatch] ← length(x) + seq(length=sum(nomatch))
        n},
    logical = {
        if(length(i) < length(x))
            i ←  rep(i,length=length(x))
        all.i[ i ] },
    numeric = {
        if(any(i<0)) {
            if(any(is.na(i) | i > 0))
            stop("only 0's with negative subscripts")
            all.i[i]
        }
        else i
    })
}
```

If the subscript expression is omitted; that is,

```
x[]
```

all possible indices are returned.

If `i` is not missing, the mode of `i` determines the computation of the indices. If `i` has mode "`logical`", the indices are produced by starting at 1 and selecting the numbers for which the corresponding element `i` is TRUE. If `i` is shorter than `length(x)`, it is extended by cyclic repetition. It can be longer than `length(x)` as well, with no change in the computation of indices.

If `i` has mode "`character`", indices are determined by matching the elements of `i` against `names(x)`. For those elements that do not match, the corresponding indices will be

```
length(x)+1, length(x)+2, ...
```

That is, the unmatched names correspond to indices beyond the current data. Name matching includes partial matching if the subscript expression is used in extracting data, but matching must be exact if the subscript expression appears on the left of an assignment.

If `i` is numeric, and `all(i<=0)` the indices consist of the elements of `seq(along=x)` that do not match any elements in `-i`. Otherwise, `i` itself is taken to be the indices. The indices can have any positive values, 0, or NA. Zeroes are now dropped before using the indices.

The indices as used by "`[`" will contain positive integer values, possibly larger than the current length of `x`. They may also contain NA's. The indices determine how elements are *extracted* from an object or how elements are *replaced* in an object by replacement data, when the subscript function appeared on the left of an assignment. Consider extraction first. The rule is that the value of

```
x[i]
```

has the same mode as `x`, and the same length as the number of indices. The elements of `x[i]` are the elements of `x` corresponding to the indices, except if the indices are greater than the length of `x` or are NA. In either of those exceptions the returned elements are "missing"; that is, NA for an atomic mode and NULL for a non-atomic mode. All the attributes of `x` will be discarded in the subset, except for the `names` attribute. The names attribute of `x[i]` will be

```
names(x)[i]
```

if `x` had a names attribute.

For replacements,

```
x[i] ← value
```

the rule is that the length of `x` will be set to the largest value in the indices, if that is bigger than the current length of `x`. If `x` and `value` do not have the same mode, then one or the other will be coerced to the common mode that can represent both without loss of information. Notice that this may mean that replacing elements of an object will change its mode; for example,

```
cols ← 0:p
cols[1] ← "()"
```

changes the mode of `cols` to "`character`". With the left side and right side now of the same mode, elements of x corresponding to the indices are replaced by successive elements of `value`, reusing the right side cyclically if necessary. Again, indices that are `NA` are exceptions: corresponding elements of `value` go "nowhere"; that is, replacement moves on to the next element of `value`, making no change in x.

11.4.2 *Array Subscripts*

We discuss now two special cases of subscripts that were omitted before:

1. the case that x is an array of k dimensions and there are k subscript expressions;
2. the case that x is an array of k dimensions and the single subscript expression is a matrix with k columns.

Consider the first case: there are k subscript arguments and x is a k-way array; that is,

```
length(dim(x)) == k
```

Extraction and replacement are done in this case by computing k separate vectors of indices, for each of the subscripts. The i-th vector is computed as it would be for indexing a vector of length `dim(x)[i]`. If the array has a dimnames attribute, the i-th indices are computed from character subscripts as for a vector whose names attribute is

```
dimnames(x)[[i]]
```

With these definitions, the indices are computed by the rules of the preceding subsection. The function `array.indices` models the computation:

```
array.indices ← function(a,...,replace=F){
    a ← as.array(a)
    d ← dim(a)
    k ← length(d)
    if(nargs()-1 != k)
        stop("Need",k,"subscripts for array")
    dn ← dimnames(a)
    z ← list(...)
```

```
for(i in 1:k){
    dummy ← 1:d[i]
    if(length(dn[[i]])>0)
        names(dummy) ← dn[[i]]
    z[[i]] ← vec.index(dummy,z[[i]],replace)
}
z
```
}

As an example, we compute some array indices for the 50 by 4 by 3 array, iris,

```
> from.iris ← array.indices(iris,1:10,-2,"Setosa")
> from.iris
[[1]]:
 [1]  1  2  3  4  5  6  7  8  9 10

[[2]]:
[1] 1 3 4

[[3]]:
[1] 1
```

The third subscript successfully matches the first element of dimnames(iris)[[3]].

Once the indices are computed, they imply a set of ordinary indices for the array treated as a vector, consisting of all combinations of elements from each of the k indices. The values of the ordinary indices depend on the way S interprets array subscripts. Multi-way arrays are stored with the first subscript varying most rapidly, then the second, and so on. Suppose i_1, i_2, $\cdots$, i_k are array index elements. The corresponding vector index is

$$i_1 + (i_2-1)d_1 + (i_3-1)d_1d_2 + \cdots + (i_k-1)\prod_{j=1}^{k-1}d_j$$

where the d_j are the elements of dim(x). The function a.to.vec.index models these computations:

```
a.to.vec.index ← function(all.i, dim){
    delta ← exp(cumsum(log(dim)))
    if(length(all.i)!=length(dim))
        stop("non-matching arguments")
    indices ← all.i[[1]]
    for(i in 2:length(dim)){
        ii ← (all.i[[i]] - 1) * delta[i-1]
        indices ← outer(indices, ii, "+")
    }
    as.vector(indices)
}
```

The data in `delta` are the cumulative products of the dimensions. The `for` loop computes the product of the `i`-th subscript with the corresponding product of dimensions, and then adds these in all combinations with the indices computed up to this point. As an example, we apply this to the array indices computed above for the `iris` data:

```
> a.to.vec.index(from.iris,dim(iris))
 [1]   1   2   3   4   5   6   7   8   9  10
[11] 101 102 103 104 105 106 107 108 109 110
[21] 151 152 153 154 155 156 157 158 159 160
```

The result is the first `10` elements of each of three selected indices for the second subscript, for the selected `"Setosa"` value of the third subscript.

Given the ordinary indices, extraction and replacement proceed as for vector subscripts, except that the extracted data continues to be a `k`-way array, with dimensions and `dimnames` determined by the `k` vectors of indices.

The second special subscript case comes about when `x` is a `k`-way array, and the single subscript `i` is a numeric matrix with `k` columns. As in the case of `k` subscripts, numbers in the `j`-th column of `i` are used to compute indices relative to `1:dim(x)[j]`. In this case, however, each row of `i` determines a single element to be extracted, following the rule above for defining vector indices. The result of the extraction is not an array. The following function models the computation of the vector indices from the single matrix subscript and the dimension of the array.

```
mat.index ← function(mat,dim){
    delta ← exp(cumsum(log(dim)))
    indices ← mat[,1]
    if(length(dim)>1)for(j in 2:length(dim))
        indices ← indices + (mat[,j]-1)*delta[j-1]
    indices
}
```

For example,

```
> xm ← matrix(nrow=4,ncol=3)
> xm[1,] ← c(1,1,3)
> xm[2,] ← c(1,2,3)
> xm[3,] ← c(2,1,1)
> xm[4,] ← c(2,3,1)
> mat.index(xm,dim(iris))
[1] 401 451   2 102
```

11.4.3 *Elements, Components, and Attributes*

The element or "`[[`" function computes indices in the same way as the "`[`" function. Once computed, however, the indices are required to determine a single element to be extracted or replaced.

If x is an atomic object, extraction or replacement then proceeds exactly as for "`[`". If x is recursive; for example, a list, then by definition the i-th element of x is itself an object. Then

```
x[[i]]
```

evaluates to that object, whereas by the rules of section 11.4.1,

```
x[i]
```

evaluates to an object of length 1 and the same mode as x, containing the element.

For replacement in recursive objects, such as lists, the expression

```
x[[i]] ← value
```

puts value into x as the i-th element. There is no coercing involved. The key distinction can be illustrated by three similar expressions. Suppose z is a list:

```
z[[1]] ← 101:102
z[1] ← list(101:102)
z[ 1:2 ] ← 101:102
```

The first two are equivalent in their effect: they both replace the first element of z by a numeric vector of length 2. The third expression replaces the first element of z by a vector of length 1, containing the value 101, and the second by a vector containing 102. Why? Because the right side is coerced to mode "`list`", producing a list of length 2 whose elements are numeric vectors of length 1. These elements are successively used to replace elements of z. A fourth expression

```
z[1] ← 101:102
```

was probably a mistake, meant to be the first expression. What it does, by the previous semantic rules, is to replace the first element of z by the first element of the right side, after coercing that to mode "`list`". It also issues a warning, since the length of the replacement vector is not a multiple of the number of replacement indices.

The `$` operator extracts and replaces components. The value of

```
x$a
```

is defined as the value of x[["a"]] if x is recursive, and NULL otherwise. When the `$` operator appears on the left side of an assignment, the object to which it is applied is coerced, if it is atomic, to mode "`list`". The replacement is then carried out as for x[["a"]]. For both `$` and `[[`, note that the matching against names(x) uses partial matching when extracting elements, but does *not* when replacing elements (otherwise it would be difficult to add an element named "a", for example, if there were already one named "ab").

The semantics of attributes follows from those of elements. Any object has an associated implicit list object containing its attributes. The value of

```
attributes(x)
```

is that list. If x is a vector (including recursive vectors such as lists), the attribute list has length 0. The expression

```
attr(x,"abc")
```

is equivalent to

```
attributes(x)[["abc"]]
```

whether for extraction or replacement. Some attributes are specially treated; namely, those that define arrays, time-series, and categories. Sections 5.5 and 5.6 discussed these attributes. The internal code for replacement will check that new values of the corresponding attributes are consistent and will generate an error if they are not.

11.4.4 *Binary (Infix) Operators*

This subsection discusses the behavior of the binary operators in S, including arithmetic (+, *, ^, etc.), comparison (==, <, etc.), and logical (&, etc.) operators. The focus is on their behavior with operands belonging to various classes of S objects. All the operators attempt in these cases to retain as much information in the value returned as possible, and also to use special knowledge about special classes of objects; namely, arrays, time-series, and categories. The behavior in these special cases was discussed in section 5.5. Now, we will give some general rules to supplement that discussion.

These operators require their arguments to be atomic vectors, possibly with attributes. The arithmetic operators will coerce their arguments to be numeric, and will generate an error if an argument has character data. Logical operators coerce their arguments to be logical, with the effect that any nonzero numeric or complex value, and any nonempty character string, maps into the logical value TRUE. Either argument may be of any length; the result will be the longer of the two arguments, with the shorter repeated cyclically. If the length of the longer is not a multiple of the length of the shorter, a warning is generated. There are some additional special rules for particular operators, such as ^ and %%; see the entries for arithmetic, comparison, and logical in Appendix 1.

If one or both of the arguments has attributes, *and* the lengths of the arguments are unequal, the result has the length and the attributes of the longer argument. This includes the case that the longer argument has no attributes: any attributes of the shorter argument will be dropped. If the arguments are of equal length, the result will have all the attributes of the first argument, *plus* any attributes of the second not present in the first. As noted, exceptions to this behavior are made for arrays, time-series, and categories. If both arguments are arrays, their dimensions must agree exactly or an error results. If both arguments are time-series, the intersection of the time domains is used for the value, and an error results if the time domains are non-intersecting or do not agree in frequency. Categories always lose their special structure.

Exercises

11.3* In section 11.1, we mentioned that the S language could be changed to another grammar, so long as the new language produced the same objects for the evaluator, as outlined in Table 7.1 and section 11.2. Write a parser that reads user expressions in a Lisp-like form, with tokens enclosed between left and right parentheses, and separated by white space. For example, in this language

```
y - 1
```

would be written

```
(- y 1)
```

and

```
x ← rnorm(10,mean(y))
```

would be

```
(<- x (rnorm 10 (mean y)))
```

Use the function `get.token` in `library(semantics)` to read individual tokens, one at a time, from standard input. It returns the parsed form of numeric values, names, strings and special tokens in the language, like `<-` or `if`. Read the online documentation of `get.token` for details.

Bibliography

The following books provide material that is suitable as an adjunct to using S. For each reference, we give a brief description of some of the material covered and the level of sophistication. For users who are new to the UNIX operating system, some introductory course or text, such as the book by McGilton and Morgan, is essential preparation.

John W. Tukey, *Exploratory Data Analysis,* Addison-Wesley, Reading, Massachusetts, 1977.

> Stem-and-Leaf Displays; Reexpression; Boxplots; Comparisons; Scatter Plots; Fitting Straight Lines; Smoothing; Median Polish; Two-way Fits; Counts; Shapes of Distributions.

> The "Bible" of EDA; probably the best place to read about the philosophy of data analysis. Numerous examples.

John M. Chambers, *Computational Methods for Data Analysis,* John Wiley & Sons, New York, 1977.

> Programming; Data Management and Manipulation; Numerical Computations; Linear Models; Nonlinear Models; Simulation; Computational Graphics.

> Intermediate book that describes modern methods of statistical computing. Concise descriptions of many of the algorithms used in S.

John M. Chambers, William S. Cleveland, Beat Kleiner, and Paul A. Tukey, *Graphical Methods for Data Analysis,* Wadsworth International Group, Belmont, California, 1983.

> Distribution of a Set of Data; Comparing Distributions; Two-Dimensional Data; Plots of Multivariate Data; Assessing Distributional Assumptions; Assessing Regression Models.

> Introductory text describing statistical graphics with emphasis on simple, practical methods; concentrates on graphical displays for analysis rather than presentation.

William S. Cleveland, *The Elements of Graphing Data,* Wadsworth Advanced Books and Software, Monterey, California, 1985.

> Principles of Graph Construction; Graphical Methods; Graphical Perception.

> Introductory text describing graphics for data analysis and for communicating with others. Excellent discussion of principles for constructing graphs as well as a description of the perceptual tasks involved in the visual decoding of graphs.

Henry McGilton and Rachel Morgan, *Introducing the UNIX System*, McGraw-Hill, New York, NY, 1983.

> Getting Started on the UNIX System; Directories and Files; Commands and Standard Files; Text Manipulation; The Ed and Sed Editors; The EX and VI Editors; Programming the UNIX shell.

> Introductory text describing the UNIX operating system. Particularly useful introduction to text editing and good hints about commonly encountered problems.

Brian W. Kernighan and Rob Pike, *The UNIX Programming Environment,* Prentice-Hall, Englewood Cliffs, New Jersey, 1984.

> UNIX For Beginners; The File System; Using the Shell; Filters; Shell Programming; Programming with Standard I/O; UNIX System Calls; Program Development; Document Preparation

> An intermediate discussion of tools, commands and programming in the UNIX system. A good place to look for ideas on what to put on the other side of the `unix` interface.

Appendix 1
S Function Documentation

This appendix contains detailed documentation in alphabetical order for the functions and commands supplied with S, plus detailed discussion of some general concepts. Where one description is provided for a group of functions, the description will appear under the most important name and the entries for the other functions will advise you to see the primary entry.

A convention for naming the entries in this appendix is intended to help make distinctions among different kinds of entries. Individual function names are nearly all lower case. Headings for general topics, like Syntax, have initial capital letters. UNIX system commands, like BATCH, are full upper-case names. These are invoked from the shell in the form S BATCH. You should *not* assume that these can be invoked from a running S session: they may conflict with the current S process.

This documentation reflects S as of the time this book was written. Your installation may have a version newer than that described here. The online documentation, available through the help function, is the definitive documentation for the version of S that you are running.

The functions described in this appendix are all available on the directory of S system functions, in position 2 of the default search list.

!	see Logic	!

!=	see Comparison	!=

%%	see Arithmetic	%%

%*%	see Matrix-product	%*%

%/%	see arithmetic	%/%

%c%	see crossprod	%c%

%m%	see Deprecated	%m%

%o%	see outer	%o%

[	see Subscript	[

[[	see Subscript	[[

^	see Arithmetic	^

_	see Assignment	_

{	see Syntax	{

|	see Logic	|

||	see if	||

$	see Subscript	$

| & | see Logic | & |

| && | see if | && |

| * | see Arithmetic | * |

| ** | see Deprecated | ** |

| + | see Arithmetic | + |

| − | see Arithmetic | − |

| -> | see Assignment | -> |

| / | see arithmetic | / |

| : | see seq | : |

| < | see Comparison | < |

| <- | see Assignment | <- |

| <<- | see Assignment | <<- |

| <= | see Comparison | <= |

| == | see Comparison | == |

| > | see Comparison | > |

| >= | see Comparison | >= |

| **abline** | Plot Line in Intercept-Slope Form | **abline** |

```
abline(coef)
abline(a, b)
abline(reg)
abline(h=)
abline(v=)
```

ARGUMENTS

coef vector containing the intercept `a` and slope `b` of the line y=a+b*x.

a,b intercept and slope as above.

reg a regression object, such as returned by `lsfit`. Specifically, `reg$coef`, if it is of length 2, will be used to define the intercept and slope of the line. If `reg$coef` is of length 1, it is treated as the slope of a fit through the origin.

h vector of y-coordinates for horizontal lines across plot.

v vector of x-coordinates for vertical lines across plot.

Graphical parameters may also be supplied as arguments to this function (see `par`).

SIDE EFFECTS

The effect of `abline` is that the line y=a+b*x or the specified horizontal and vertical lines are drawn across the current plot. A warning is given if an intercept/slope line does not intersect the plot.

EXAMPLES

```
        # line with 0 intercept and slope 1
abline(0,1)
        # line produced by least-squares fit
abline(lsfit(longley.x[,1],longley.y))
        # dotted vertical lines at x==0 and 10
abline(v=c(0,10),lty=2)
```

---

abs   Absolute Value   **abs**

```
abs(x)
```

ARGUMENTS
    x numeric. Missing values (NAs) are allowed.

VALUE
    vector like x, with absolute value taken of each data value.

---

acos   Inverse Trigonometric Functions   **acos**

```
acos(x)
asin(x)
atan(x)
atan(x, y)
```

ARGUMENTS
    x numeric or complex. Missing values (NAs) are allowed.
    y numeric, same length as x. Missing values (NAs) are allowed.

VALUE

data transformed by the specified inverse trigonometric function, with attributes preserved.

With two arguments, both arguments should be numeric. The return value satisfies `cos(atan(x,y))==y` and `sin(atan(x,y))==x`. This form should be used if y is near zero.

For numeric arguments, the domain of acos and asin is the interval $[-1,1]$, and the range is $0 <= acos(x) <= pi$ and $-pi/2 <= asin(x) <= pi/2$. The domain of atan is unrestricted and the range is $-pi/2 < atan(x) < pi/2$ or $-pi < atan(x,y) <= pi$. For values of the arguments outside of the appropriate domains, NA is returned and a warning is given. For further information on domains and branch cuts in the case of complex arguments, see section 5.1.5.

SEE ALSO
    Arg.

acosh	Inverse Hyperbolic Trigonometric Functions	acosh

```
acosh(x)
asinh(x)
atanh(x)
```

ARGUMENTS

x numeric or complex. Missing values (NAs) are allowed.

VALUE

data transformed by the specified inverse hyperbolic trigonometric function, with attributes preserved. Numeric arguments must be at least 1 for cosh and must be greater than 1 in absolute value for tanh, otherwise NA is returned and a warning is given. See section 5.1.5 for further details on domains and branch cuts in the case of complex arguments.

again	see history	again

aggregate	Decrease Periodicity of Time Series by Aggregation	aggregate

```
aggregate(x, nf=1, fun=sum)
```

ARGUMENTS

x time series.

nf desired frequency for aggregated time series; must be a divisor of the frequency of x.

fun function to be used in performing aggregation. Most commonly, fun is either mean, to give the mean level for rate-like series, or fun is sum in order to compute totals.

VALUE

new time-series with frequency nf. Each group of frequency(x)/nf observations is given to function fun to create the aggregate value.

EXAMPLES

```
aggregate(co2,1,mean)    # yearly co2 level
aggregate(ship,4,sum)    # quarterly manufacturing shipments
```

---

all   Logical Sum and Product   **all**

```
all(...)
any(...)
```

ARGUMENTS

     ...   any number of arguments, each coerced to mode logical. Missing values (NAs) are allowed.

VALUE

either TRUE or FALSE. all evaluates to TRUE if all the elements of all the arguments are TRUE. It is FALSE if there are any FALSEs. In all other cases (mixtures of NA and TRUE) the result is NA. If all the arguments are of length 0, all returns TRUE.

any evaluates to TRUE if any of the elements of any of the arguments is TRUE. It is FALSE if all the elements are FALSE. In all other cases (mixtures of NA and FALSE) the result is NA. If all the arguments are of length 0, any returns FALSE.

EXAMPLES

```
if(all(x>0)) x ← sqrt(x)
```

---

allocated   Memory Allocated in S Frames   **allocated**

```
allocated()
```

VALUE

vector showing the total amount of storage allocated in each frame. The names attribute gives the name of the function called in each frame.

EXAMPLES

```
# default allocations when called at top level, corresponding
# to the nesting of frames in .Program
```

```
allocated()
    Frame 1 switch assign eval
        20450    4090    4090 4090

function() {
        at.start ← allocated()
        # ... do some work ...
        now ← allocated()
        # changes in allocations
        now - at.start
}
```

amatch	Argument Matching	**amatch**

```
amatch(definition, call)
```

ARGUMENTS

definition an S function.

call an unevaluated call to the function given in `definition`.

VALUE

a list of the arguments, matched as they would be by the evaluator if the call were made to the function in `definition`. The list is in the order the arguments appear in `definition`. The value has attributes `names` and `missing` which give the formal names of the arguments and tell whether the corresponding argument was omitted from `call` (regardless of whether a default appears in the definition).

Aside from its role in the semantic model, `amatch` is chiefly used by functions that want to pre-match arguments in order to do something special about evaluation.

EXAMPLES

```
> amatch(get,expression(get("abc",w=2)))
$name:
[1] "abc"
$where:
[1] 2
$frame:
.Argument(, frame = NULL)
```

```
$mode:
.Argument(, mode = "any")

attr(, "missing"):
[1] F F T T
```

any	see all	any

aperm	Array Permutations	aperm

```
aperm(a, perm)
```

ARGUMENTS

  a array to be permuted. Missing values (NAs) are allowed.

  perm vector containing a permutation of the integers 1:n where n is the number of dimensions in the array a. The old dimension given by perm[j] becomes the new j-th dimension.

VALUE

  array like a, but with the observations permuted according to perm, e.g., if perm is c(2,1,3), the result will be an array in which the old second dimension is the new first dimension, etc.

  Attribute dimnames, if present, will be appropriately permuted.

SEE ALSO

  t for transpose of matrix.

EXAMPLES

```
        # turns 50 x 4 x 3 into 50 x 3 x 4
myiris ← aperm(iris,c(1,3,2))
        # make 150 x 4 matrix
myiris ← matrix(aperm(iris,c(1,3,2)),150,4)
```

append	Data Merging	**append**

```
append(x, values, after)
replace(x, list, values)
```

ARGUMENTS

      x vector of data to be edited. Missing values (NAs) are allowed.

   list indices of the elements in x to be replaced.

values vector of values to replace the list of elements, or to be appended after the element given. If values is shorter than list, it is reused cyclically. Missing values (NAs) are allowed.

 after index in x after which values are appended. after=0 puts values at the beginning.

VALUE

the edited vector, to be assigned back to x, or used in any other way. Remember, unless the result is assigned back to x, x will not be changed.

EXAMPLES

```
        # replace x[3] with 1.5
x ← replace(x,3,1.5)
        # alternative: replaces x[3] with 1.5
x[3]←1.5
        # append two values in x[7],x[8]
x ← append(x,c(3.4,5.7),6)
        # replace the four elements with 0
y ← replace(x,c(3,7,8,9),0)
```

apply	Apply a Function to Sections of an Array	**apply**

```
apply(X, MARGIN, FUN, ...)
```

ARGUMENTS

      X array. Missing values (NAs) are allowed if FUN accepts them.

MARGIN the subscripts over which the function is to be applied. For example, if X is a matrix, 1 indicates rows, and 2 indicates columns. For a more complex example of the use of MARGIN, see the last example below. In general, a subarray is extracted from X for each combination of the levels of the subscripts named in MARGIN. The function FUN is invoked for each of these subarrays, and the results, if any, concatenated into a new array. Note that MARGIN tells which dimensions of X are retained in the result.

FUN function (or character string giving the name of the function) to be applied to the specified array sections. The character form is necessary only for functions with unusual names, e.g., "%*%".

... optional, any arguments to FUN; they are passed unchanged to each call of FUN.

VALUE

If each call to FUN returns a vector of length N, and N>1, apply returns an array of dimension

```
c(N,dim(X)[MARGIN])
```

If N==1 and MARGIN has length > 1, the value is an array of dimension dim(X)[MARGIN] ; otherwise, it is a vector.

EXAMPLES

```
apply(x,2,mean,trim=.25)     # 25% trimmed column means
                 # The result is a vector of length ncol(x)

apply(x,2,sort)     # sort columns of x

t(apply(x,1,sort))     # transpose result of row sort

apply(z,c(1,3),sum)
```

The sorting examples show the difference between row and column operations when the results returned by FUN are vectors. The returned value becomes the *first* dimension of the result, hence the transpose is necessary with row sorts.

Suppose, in the last example, that z is a 4-way array with dimension vector (2,3,4,5). The expression computes the 2 by 4 matrix obtained by summing over the second and fourth extents of z (i.e., sum is called 8 times, each time on 15 values).

Each section of the input array is passed as the first argument to an invocation of FUN. It is passed without a keyword modifier, so, by keywords attached to argi, it should be possible to make the array section correspond to any argument to FUN.

SEE ALSO

Function `lapply` applies a function to each element of a list. Function `tapply` applies a function to a ragged array, defined by categories.

---

approx	Approximate Function from Discrete Values	**approx**

```
approx(x, y, xout, method="lines", n=50, rule=1)
```

ARGUMENTS

x, y coordinates of points. The coordinates can be given by two vector arguments or by a single argument x which is a time-series, a complex vector, a matrix with 2 columns, or a list containing components named x and y. The y values represent the surface to be approximated as a function of x.

xout optional set of x values for which function values are desired. If xout is not specified, the function will be approximated at n equally spaced data points, spanning the range of x.

method character describing the method to be used in approximating the function. Currently the only possible value is "linear" for linear interpolation (later may have "spline", etc).

n optional integer giving the number of points evenly spaced between the minimum and maximum values in x to be used in forming xout.

rule integer describing the rule to be used for values of xout that are outside the range of x. If rule is 1 NAs will be supplied for any such points. If rule is 2, the y values corresponding to the extreme x values will be used.

VALUE

list with components named x and y.

SEE ALSO

spline, lowess.

EXAMPLES

```
z ← approx(x,y,newx)      # linear interpolation at newx
quants ← approx(ppoints(x),sort(x),c(.1,.25,.5,.75,.9))$y
      # get the 10, 25, 50, 75 and 90 percentiles of x
```

Arg	see Complex	**Arg**

args	see help	**args**

Arithmetic	Arithmetic Operators	**Arithmetic**

```
e1 op e2
```

ARGUMENTS

e1,e2   numeric or complex. Missing values (NAs) are allowed.

op   one of +, -, *, /, ^, %/% or %%.

VALUE

numeric or complex result, with the shorter argument used cyclically, if necessary: +, -, * and / are the usual arithmetic operators and ^ is exponentiation. (** is a deprecated synonym for ^).

%/% is integer divide; the operands should be numeric and the result is floor(e1/e2) if e2!=0 and 0 otherwise.

%% is the modulo function; it also expects numeric operands and is defined as e1-floor(e1/e2)*e2 if e2!=0 and e1 otherwise (see Knuth). Thus %/% and %% always satisfy e1==(e2%/%e1)*e2+e1%%e2.

For ^ with numeric arguments, and negative elements in both e1 and e2: the values returned will be those of 1/(e1^(-e2)) if the element of e2 is judged to be exactly or nearly an integer, and NA otherwise. The integer test is machine-dependent and should not be counted on in doubtful cases.

Section 5.6.1 describes the rules for dealing with operands with attributes. Also see section 5.1.5 for details on domains and branch cuts in the case of complex arguments for exponentiation.

REFERENCE

D. E. Knuth, *The Art of Computer Programming, Fundamental Algorithms* Vol. 1, Section 1.2.4., Addison-Wesley, 1968.

EXAMPLES

```
x-mean(x)        # deviations from the mean; second argument used repeatedly
(1+(5:8)/1200)^12      # compound interest, 5:8 per annum monthly
```

---

array	Multi-way Arrays	**array**

```
array(data, dim=length(data), dimnames)
is.array(x)
as.array(x)
```

ARGUMENTS

data vector containing the data values for the array in the normal array order: the first subscript varies most rapidly. Missing values (NAs) are allowed.

dim vector giving the extent for each dimension—the dim attribute of the array.

dimnames list giving initial dimnames for the array.

x any S object.

VALUE

array returns an array with the same mode as data, dimensionality described by dim, and optional dimnames attribute. If data does not completely fill the array, it is repeated until the array is filled.

is.array returns TRUE if x is an array object, FALSE otherwise.

as.array returns x, if x is an array, otherwise a 1-dimensional array with data from x and dim attribute equal to length(x).

The array class of objects are those that have an attribute dim, a vector of integers whose product equals the length of data. An array may also have an attribute dimnames. If so, this is a list of length(dim) elements, each of which is either of length zero or else a character vector that gives the labels corresponding to the levels of the corresponding subscript in the array.

EXAMPLES

```
myiris ← array(scan("irisfile"),c(4,3,50))
        # creates a 4 by 3 by 50 array
```

arrows	see segments	**arrows**

as.array	see array	**as.array**

as.call	see call	**as.call**

as.category	see category	**as.category**

as.character	see character	**as.character**

as.complex	see complex	**as.complex**

as.double	see double	**as.double**

`as.expression`   see expression   **`as.expression`**

`as.function`   Function Objects   **`as.function`**

```
as.function(x)
is.function(x)
```

ARGUMENTS

    x an S object.

VALUE

    as.function merely changes the mode of x to "function". is.function tests whether x is a function.

`asin`   see acos   **`asin`**

`asinh`   see acosh   **`asinh`**

`as.integer`   see integer   **`as.integer`**

`as.list`   see list   **`as.list`**

`as.logical`	see `logical`	**`as.logical`**

`as.matrix`	see `matrix`	**`as.matrix`**

`as.name`	Name Objects	**`as.name`**

```
as.name(x)
is.name(x)
```

ARGUMENTS

    `x` an S object.

VALUE

    `as.name` coerces `x` to an object of mode `"name"`. This is most useful when `x` is of mode `"character"`. `is.name` tests whether `x` is a name object. Name objects are primarily used in the parsed form of expressions to represent names typed by the user.

`as.null`	Null Objects	**`as.null`**

```
as.null(x)
is.null(x)
```

ARGUMENTS

    `x` an S object.

VALUE

    `as.null` always returns `NULL`; `is.null` returns `TRUE` or `FALSE`, according as `x` is or is not `NULL`.

as.numeric	see numeric	**as.numeric**

as.qr	see qr	**as.qr**

assign	Assign Object to Directory or Frame	**assign**

```
assign(x, value, frame, where)
```

ARGUMENTS

x character vector giving the name of the object to be assigned.

value any S object; the value to be assigned to the name in x.

frame number specifying in which of the frames of the current evaluation the object is to be assigned. frame=0 assigns to the session frame; i.e., objects that will continue to be available throughout the current S session, but will disappear at the end of the session. Avoid creating many session objects—the space they occupy is not reclaimed in the present implementation. frame=1 means that the object is assigned to the expression frame. It will be available (from any frame) throughout the evaluation of the current expression, but will disappear when evaluation is complete. This is a useful way to create objects that are to be shared by several functions during the expression.

where directory in which the object is to be assigned. If where is supplied, it can either be a number or a character string. A number implies the corresponding element of the search list (.Search.list), so where=2, for example, assigns an object in the second directory. If where is a character string, this is taken as the path name for a directory in the file system. In this case, the directory must be an S data directory, but need not be on the search list.

SIDE EFFECTS

assign is executed entirely for its side effect of assignment. Unlike the assignment operators, such as ←, assign does not return a value. Assignments are committed when S finishes evaluating an entire expression. If an error occurs during evaluation of an expression, no assignments executed during that expression are committed.

If both `where` and `frame` are omitted, the `assign` function works exactly the same way as the operator ←; that is, it assigns (permanently) to the working data when used at top level (typed by the user, for example), and to the local frame of a function call when used from inside a function.

EXAMPLES

```
assign("abc", 1:3)  # assign "abc"
assign(".Options", options, frame=0)  # session dataset
assign(".Counts", counts, w=1)  # to working data (even in a function)
# make up variable names in a loop
for(i in 1:10) assign(paste("sample",i,sep="."),runif(10))
# save each column of matrix x under a different name
for(i in seq(ncol(x)))
      assign(colname[i], drop(x[,i]))
# save under a weird name !!
assign("a$b",1)
```

In the last example, note that this is distinctly not the way to create the component b of object a, as a$b ← 1 would do.

SEE ALSO

Assignment, remove, get, exists, attach, detach, search, synchronize.

Assignment   Assignment   **Assignment**

```
expression ← value
expression _ value
value → expression

expression <<- value
```

If `expression` is a name, the assignment operator, in any of its forms, causes the value of `value` to be saved under that name. Note that the arrow always points toward the name. The left-arrow is made up of the two characters < and -. An underscore, _, can also be used for left-arrow. Right-arrow is the two characters - and >. All three of these are equivalent semantically, and are referred to as ← throughout the book.

The `expression` can also specify a subset, element, or attribute of an object, or any combination of such expressions. Expressions of this form are called replacements, to distinguish them from simple assignments. Examples include:

```
x[-1] ← 0
length(mystuff) ← n
z$b ← 3
attr(obj,"myattr")[[1]] ← new.value
```

Once an assignment is made, the data can be retrieved (in the same frame) by mentioning the name used in the assignment. The value of the assignment (when used as an expression) is the value of the right-hand side. Notice that this is true for replacements as well; the value of a replacement is the substituted values, not the whole object in which the replacement occurs.

Assignments with ← take place in the frame of the function call in which they occur, or in the working directory if they occur in frame 1. Replacements taking place in frame 1 take place in the frame in which the object was found (the working directory, frame 1 or frame 0). They will create the corresponding object in the working directory if it was found somewhere else. For example, if there is no current object `iris` in the working directory,

```
dim(iris) ← c(50,12)
```

will create one. The `<<-` operator always does assignments and replacements on the working data directory, from any frame.

Assignments are committed when S finishes evaluating an entire expression. If an error occurs during evaluation of an expression, no assignments executed during that expression are committed.

SEE ALSO

`assign, remove, get, exists, attach, detach, search, synchronize.`

EXAMPLES

```
y ← sqrt( x←runif(100) )         # 100 uniforms saved as x
                # square root of sample saved under the name y
```

| **as.single** | see single | **as.single** |

| **as.ts** | see ts | **as.ts** |

| **as.vector** | see vector | **as.vector** |

| **atan** | see acos | **atan** |

| **atanh** | see acosh | **atanh** |

| **attach** | Attach a New Data Directory | **attach** |

```
attach(file, pos=2)
```

ARGUMENTS

file   character string giving the name of a new data directory to be accessed. The name must be a correct UNIX file-system pathname, specifying an S data directory. If file is omitted, attach has no effect on the search list, but it does return the current value of the search list.

pos   position in data directory search list that file should occupy. The data directories originally in position pos or beyond are moved down the list after file. If pos=1, file will be attached as the working directory (you must have write permission).

VALUE

a character vector giving the previous value of the search list of directories.

At the beginning of a session with S, three data directories are attached: working, system functions and system data, in that order. The working directory will be the subdirectory `.Data` of the current directory; if that does not exist it will be `.Data` in your home directory; and if that does not exist S will create `.Data` in your home directory.

The search list of data directories is valid only for the current session with S, i.e., it does not persist across S sessions. Only directories containing S datasets should be attached as S data directories; ordinary ASCII data files should be read by the `scan` function.

SEE ALSO

See `detach` for removing a data directory from the search list.

SIDE EFFECTS

The session object `.Search.list` is a character vector containing the current list of directories to be searched; this object is changed in frame 0 as a side effect of `attach`.

EXAMPLES

```
attach("/usr/joe/.Data")   # attach Joe's data directory
attach()   # what is current search list?
```

---

attr	Attribute of an Object	**attr**

```
attr(x, which)
```

ARGUMENTS

x any object

which character string specifying an attribute of x.

VALUE

the `which` attribute of `x`, if it exists; `NULL` otherwise. This function may be used on the left of an assignment to initialize or change attributes of objects. For the attributes like `dim` that are known internally to S, the assignment will only be accepted if it satisfies requirements for that attribute (for example, the length of `x` must equal the product of the dimensions). See the documentation for individual attributes. `attr` may also be used to set and get user-defined attributes. To explicitly delete the `which` attribute of x, use `attr(x, which)` ← NULL.

The semantics of `attr` are defined by saying that `attr(x,which)` is equivalent to `attributes(x)[[which]]` for either extracting or replacing attributes, with the restriction that `which` is interpreted as mode character. The value of `attributes(x)` is a list object (possibly of length 0) associated implicitly with any object x. See `Subscripts` for the semantics of "`[[`".

SIDE EFFECTS

An attribute of x will be changed as a result of the assignment version of this function.

SEE ALSO

For attributes known to S, see the documentation for `names`, `dim`, `dimnames`, `tsp`, and `levels`.

EXAMPLES

```
attr(m, "dimnames")      # equivalent to dimnames(x)
             # a possible way to store documentation with x
attr(x, "doc") ← doc
```

---

attributes	All Attributes of an Object	**attributes**

```
attributes(x)
attributes(x) ← value
```

ARGUMENTS

x any object.
value a recursive object, typically a list.

VALUE

a list of all the attributes of x: `names(attributes(x))` is the names of the attributes. Note that `length(x)` and `mode(x)` are not considered attributes for the purposes of this function.

As a replacement function, sets the attributes of x to the corresponding components of value; old attributes of x are deleted. If value has length 0, all attributes are deleted.

SIDE EFFECTS

The attributes of x will be changed as a result of the assignment version of this function.

SEE ALSO

For attributes known to S, see the documentation for `names`, `dim`, `dim-names`, `tsp`, and `levels`.

EXAMPLES

```
names(attributes(x))          # names of attributes of x
```

AUDIT	Audit the Data Analysis Process	**AUDIT**

```
S AUDIT [auditfile]
```

ARGUMENTS

`auditfile` the name (unquoted) of an audit file, by default, `.Data/.Audit`. This file must contain lines of the form

#˜get ...

#˜put ...

in order for the auditing procedure to work. This means that old-S diary files may not be auditable.

The `AUDIT` utility allows the user to review what has happened during a set of S sessions. When the `AUDIT` utility is invoked, it reads the file `auditfile` (`.Data/.Audit` by default), finding all top-level expressions, and which objects were read and written by each expression. It then allows the user (through an arcane syntax, see below) to inquire about which expressions read or wrote a specific object, to backtrack from a specific expression, or to create a source file that will recreate an expression.

The `AUDIT` utility can also be executed independently and in parallel with a copy of S that is writing the `auditfile`. `AUDIT` continuously attempts to read new information that may be written to the file by another process and updates its tables accordingly. It also numbers and displays each expression as it is executed by S. Thus, `AUDIT` is very useful on a multi-window workstation where one window can be used for running S and another for asking audit questions about the S session. The display of expressions can also be used with cut/paste operations to provide a means of re-executing or modifying previous expressions.

SEE ALSO

history.

EXAMPLES

```
$ S AUDIT diary    # audit the file "diary"
G x     # shows which statements "got" or read object x
S A     # show (in reverse order) all statements
E 100   # create script to recreate statement 100
```

COMMANDS TO AUDIT PROGRAM

E n1 n2 n3 n4 ... x

generates an Executable script on stdout that will incorporate all computations including statements n1 n2 ...

[L|G|P|B] name

will Lookup, show Gets, Puts, or will Backtrack

L will show the name from its symbol
table. The name can be the trailing portion of
a name, e.g. abc will match xyz.abc

G will show the statements in which it is used

P will show the statements in which it is assigned

B will backtrack, showing the statement
that most recently set a value for the name
and all statements that were predecessors of
that statement

[L|G|P|B] number

will Lookup, show Gets, Puts, or will Backtrack

L will lookup a particular statement

G will show the objects used (gotten) within the statement

P will show the objects assigned (put) within the statement

B will backtrack from the statement showing all predecessor
statements

N [N|G|P|A|GP]

will show names that were
- N not assigned or used
- G used but not assigned

- P assigned but not used
- GP assigned and used
- A All names

S [N|G|P|A|GP]

will show statements that contained various Gets or Puts
of objects, along with the object names that were
read or written

- N no assignments or use of objects
- G use of objects but no assignments
- P assignments but no use of objects
- GP assignments and use of objects
- A All statements

If you want all statements that created a object,
you need to use both S P and S GP.

q

quit

If you interrupt in the middle of a printout, you will be brought back to
the "Command: " prompt.

Processing of the user statements once the audit program has read the audit file is very fast. Interactive users notice no delay.

REFERENCE

Richard A. Becker and John M. Chambers, "Auditing of Data Analyses"
SIAM J. Sci. Stat. Comput. vol. 9 (no. 1), July, 1988.

| **axes** | see `title` | **axes** |

axis	Add an Axis to the Current Plot	**axis**

```
axis(side, at, labels=T, ticks=T,
     distn, line=0, pos, outer=F)
```

ARGUMENTS

  side side of plot for axis (1,2,3,4 for bottom, left, top, right).

  at optional vector of positions at which the ticks and tick labels will be plotted. If side is 1 or 3, at represents x-coordinates. If side is 2 or 4, at represents y-coordinates. If at is omitted, the current axis (as specified by the xaxp or yaxp parameters, see par) will be plotted.

  labels optional. If labels is logical, it specifies whether or not to plot tick labels. Otherwise, labels must be the same length as at, and label[i] is plotted at coordinate at[i].

  ticks if TRUE, tick marks and axis line will be plotted.

  distn optional character string describing the distribution used for transforming the axis labels. If dist is "normal", then values of at are assumed to be probability levels, and the labels are actually plotted at qnorm(at). This also implies a reasonable default set of values for argument at.

  line line (measured out from the plot in units of standard-sized character heights) at which the axis line will be plotted. Tick labels will be plotted relative to this position (as much as the tick labels and axis line differ in graphical parameter mgp).

  pos x- or y-coordinate position at which the axis line should be plotted. Labels will be on the side of the axis specified by side. If pos is omitted, argument line controls positioning of the axis.

  outer if TRUE, the axis will be drawn in the outer margin rather than the standard plot margin.

  Graphical parameters may also be supplied as arguments to this function (see par).

EXAMPLES

```
axis(3)   # add axis on top
axis(4,label=F)   # tick marks only on right

qqnorm(data)
axis(3,dist="normal")   # add normal probability axis at top
```

```
qqnorm(data,xaxt="n")      # normal prob plot, no x axis labels
probs ← c(.01,  .05,  .1,  .9,  .95,  .99)
axis(1,dist="norm",at=probs,
    lab=paste(probs*100,"%"))    # add user-defined probability axis

plot(x,y,axes=F)    # scatter plot with no box or axes
axis(1,pos=0); axis(2,pos=0)    # coordinate axes through origin

plot(fahrenheit)    # time-series record of temperatures
celsius ← pretty((range(fahrenheit)-32)*5/9)
axis(side=4, at=celsius*9/5+32,lab=celsius)    # celsius at right
mtext(side=4,line=4,"Celsius")
```

---

backsolve	Backsolve Upper-Triangular Equations	**backsolve**

```
backsolve(r, x, k=ncol(r))
```

ARGUMENTS

r square, upper triangular matrix.

x right-hand sides to equations.

k number of columns of r to use in solving the system.

VALUE

matrix like x of the solutions y to the equations r %*% y == x.

The lower triangle of r is not looked at (in particular, it does not need to be zero).

SEE ALSO

suitable r matrices can be obtained from chol and qr.

`barplot`	Bar Graph	**`barplot`**

```
barplot(height)    #simple form
barplot(height, width, names, space=.2, inside=TRUE,
        beside=FALSE, horiz=FALSE, legend,
        angle, density, col, blocks=TRUE)
```

ARGUMENTS

height matrix or vector giving the heights (positive or negative) of the bars. If
        height is a matrix, each column represents one bar; the values in the
        columns are treated as heights of blocks. Blocks of positive height are
        stacked above the zero line and those with negative height are stacked
        below the line. Matrix values in height can also be treated as the posi-
        tions of the dividing lines; see argument blocks.

width   optional vector of relative bar widths.

names   optional character vector of names for the bars.

space   how much space (as a fraction of the average bar width) should be left
        before each bar. This may be given as a single number or one number
        per bar. If beside is TRUE, space may be specified by 2 numbers
        where the first is the space between bars in a set, and the second is the
        space between sets.

inside if TRUE, the internal lines which divide adjacent bars will be drawn.

beside if TRUE and if height is a matrix, the bars for different rows will be
        plotted beside each other, not as a single divided bar. If width is given
        in the case beside=TRUE, there must be as many widths as the number
        of values in heights, not the number of columns. The same is true of
        names, if this is supplied.

horiz   if TRUE, the graph will be drawn horizontally, with the first bar at the
        bottom.

legend a vector of names to be correlated with the bar shading which should be
        plotted as a legend. The legend is put in the upper right of the plot by
        default; use the legend function if more control over legend positioning
        is required.

angle   optional vector giving the angle (degrees, counter-clockwise from horizon-
        tal) for shading each bar division. (Defaults to 45 if density is sup-
        plied.)

density optional vector for bar shading, giving the number of lines per inch for
        shading each bar division. (Defaults to 3 if angle is supplied.)

col   optional vector giving the colors in which the bars should be filled or
        shaded. If col is specified and neither angle nor density are given
        as arguments, bars will be filled solidly with the colors. If angle or
        density are given, col refers to the color of the shading lines.

blocks if TRUE, the `height` matrix is treated according to the "blocks" model in which each value in `height` is the height of a block to be stacked above or below the axis. If `blocks` is FALSE, values in `height` give the coordinates at which the bar dividing lines are to be drawn. In this case, the values in any column of `height` should be monotonically increasing.

Solid filling of bars is dependent on the area-filling capability of the device. For devices without explicit area-filling capability, solid filling can be simulated by specifying a very high density shading.

Graphical parameters may also be supplied as arguments to this function (see par).

VALUE

a vector, non-printing, which contains x-coordinates of centers of bars (y-coordinates if bars are horizontal). The returned value can be used if you want to add to the plot.

SEE ALSO

legend, dotchart, hist.

EXAMPLES

```
x ← barplot(height)    # do plot, save x coordinates of bar centers
text(x,height+1,height)    # label the tops of the bars

# The example plot was produced by
barplot(
        t(telsam.response[1:5,]),
        ylim=c(0,200),
        col=2:5,angle=c(5,40,80,125),density=(4:7)*3,
        legend=dimnames(telsam)[[2]],
        names=as.character(dimnames(telsam)[[1]][1:5]),
        xlab="Interviewer",
        ylab="Number of Responses",
        main="Response to Quality of Service Question"
        )
```

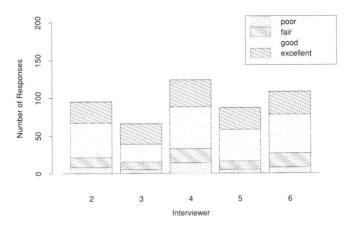

Response to Quality of Service Question

| **BATCH** | Batch (Non-Interactive) Execution of S | **BATCH** |

```
S BATCH in out
```

ARGUMENTS

 in the name of a file containing S expressions to be executed. The file may contain source and sink commands, etc. Interactive graphics functions (`tek4014()`, `hpgl()`, etc.) should specify a file name for their output in non-interactive mode.

 out the name of a file which will receive all of the output from the run. If supplied, `out` will contain a listing of each expression in `in`, followed by any printed output produced by the expression.

WARNING

Execution begins immediately after BATCH is invoked.

Beta	Beta Distribution	**Beta**

```
dbeta(q, shape1, shape2)
pbeta(q, shape1, shape2)
qbeta(p, shape1, shape2)
rbeta(n, shape1, shape2)
```

ARGUMENTS

q vector of quantiles. Missing values (NAs) are allowed.

p vector of probabilities. Missing values (NAs) are allowed.

n sample size. If `length(n)` is larger than 1, then `length(n)` random values are returned.

shape1 vector of (positive) shape parameters.

shape2 vector of (positive) shape parameters.

VALUE

density (dbeta), probability (pbeta), quantile (qbeta), or random sample (rbeta) for the standard beta distribution with parameters shape1 and shape2. Results are currently computed to single-precision accuracy only. The density function is given by

$$f_{s_1,s_2}(q) = \frac{\Gamma(s_1+s_2)}{\Gamma(s_1)\Gamma(s_2)}q^{s_1-1}(1-q)^{s_2-1}, \quad 0 \le q \le 1, \;\; s_1, s_2 > 0,$$

where s_1 and s_2 are the shape1 and shape2 parameters.

SIDE EFFECTS

The function rbeta causes creation of the dataset .Random.seed if it does not already exist, otherwise its value is updated.

EXAMPLES

rbeta(20,2,3) #sample of 20 with shape parameters 2 and 3

---

bind	Bind to Current Function Definitions	**bind**

```
bind(expr)
```

ARGUMENTS

expr any S expression, often a function definition.

VALUE

an expression equivalent to expr but with any calls to S functions matched to the current definitions of those functions. Specifically any subexpression of expr that is a function call is changed into an object of mode frame, containing the body of the corresponding function and a frame of matched arguments, representing the matching of the arguments in the call to the function definition. The result should run faster than the original. It will appear identical when printed, however. To see the gory detail of the bound code, print it with print.compiled (only to be done in case of dire need).

SEE ALSO

amatch, print.compiled.

EXAMPLES

```
myfun.fast ← bind(myfun)    # faster version of myfun
```

---

box	Add a Box Around a Plot	**box**

```
box(n=1)
```

ARGUMENTS

n number of times the box is drawn, surrounding the current plot (i.e., heaviness of line).

Graphical parameters may also be supplied as arguments to this function (see par).

EXAMPLES

```
box(5,col=2)     # draw a thick color 2 box around plot
```

| `boxplot` | Box Plots | `boxplot` |

```
boxplot(..., range, width varwidth=FALSE,
        notch=FALSE, names, plot=TRUE)
```

ARGUMENTS

    `...`   vectors or a list containing a number of numeric components (e.g., the output of `split`). Note that all other arguments must be specified by exact name. Missing values (`NA`s) are allowed.

  `range=` controls the strategy for the whiskers and the detached points beyond the whiskers. By default, whiskers are drawn to the nearest value not beyond a standard range from the quartiles; points beyond are drawn individually. Giving `range=0` forces whiskers to the full data range. Any positive value of `range` multiplies the standard range by this amount. The standard range is 1.5*(inter-quartile range).

  `width=` vector of relative box widths. See also argument `varwidth`.

`varwidth=` if `TRUE`, box widths will be proportional to the square-root of the number of observations for the box.

  `notch=` if `TRUE`, notched boxes are drawn, where non-overlapping of notches of boxes indicates a difference at a rough 5% significance level.

  `names=` optional character vector of names for the groups. If omitted, names used in labelling the plot will be taken from the names of the arguments and from the names attribute of lists.

  `plot=` if `TRUE`, the box plot will be produced; otherwise, the calculated summaries of the arguments are returned.

Graphical parameters may also be supplied as arguments to this function (see `par`).

VALUE

if `plot` is `FALSE`, a list with the components listed below. Otherwise function `bxp` is invoked with these components, plus optional `width`, `varwidth` and `notch`, to produce the plot. Note that `bxp` returns a vector of box centers.

  `stats` matrix (5 by number of boxes) giving the upper extreme, upper quartile, median, lower quartile, and lower extreme for each box.

  `n` the number of observations in each group.

  `conf` matrix (2 by number of boxes) giving confidence limits for median.

  `out` optional vector of outlying points.

group   vector giving the box to which each point in out belongs.
names   names for each box (see argument names above).

SEE ALSO

        bxp.

EXAMPLES

        boxplot(group1,group2,group3)

        boxplot(split(salary,age),varwidth=TRUE,notch=TRUE)

        # the example plot is produced by:
        boxplot(
                split(lottery.payoff,lottery.number%/%100),
                main=lottery.label,
                sub="Leading Digit of Winning Numbers",
                ylab="Payoff")

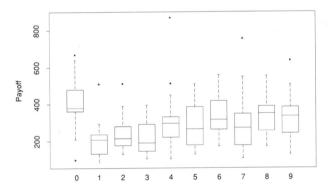

NJ Pick-it Lottery (5/22/75-3/16/76

Leading Digit of Winning Numbers

browser	Browse Interactively in a Function's Frame	**browser**

```
browser(frame, catch=TRUE)
```

ARGUMENTS

frame the frame in which the browser will look for information and will evaluate user expressions. By default this is the frame of the function calling browser. Therefore in its usual use, adding the expression browser() to a function allows you to see what the function has done so far.

catch logical; should errors and interrupts be caught in the browser? If TRUE, then the browser will be restarted after such errors, but see the quit signal comment below. If FALSE, any errors will return to the S prompt level.

VALUE

the value returned in a return expression typed by the user; if you return by giving a response 0 to the prompt, the value is NULL.

When the browser is invoked, you will be prompted for input. The input can be any expression; this will be evaluated in the frame. Three kinds of expressions are special. The response ? will get you a list of menu-selectable items (the elements of the frame). A numeric response is taken to be such a selection. A return expression returns from the browser with this value. The expression substitute(x) is useful to see the actual argument that was given, corresponding to the formal argument x.

The quit signal (usually the character control-backslash) will exit from the browser, and from the whole expression that generated the call to the browser, returning to the S prompt level. (Don't type two control-backslash characters, or one if catch=FALSE; either action will terminate your session with S!)

SEE ALSO

restart, debugger.

EXAMPLES

```
myfun ← function(x,y) {
        # lots of computing
        browser()  #now check things just before the moment of truth
        .C("myroutine",x,y,w)
    }
```

browser.trace	see trace.on	**browser.trace**

bxp	Boxplots From Processed Data	**bxp**

bxp(z, width, varwidth=FALSE, notch=FALSE)

ARGUMENTS

z list whose components define the boxplot statistics, normally the result of a call to boxplot (which see for the components of z), but can be built up in any other way.

width optional vector of box widths.

varwidth logical flag, if TRUE, variable width boxes are drawn based on z$n.

notch logical flag, if TRUE, use the z$conf to produce notched boxes.

Graphical parameters may also be supplied as arguments to this function (see par).

VALUE

invisible vector which contains x-coordinates of centers of the boxes. This vector is useful for adding to the plot.

SEE ALSO

boxplot.

.C	see .Fortran	**.C**

---

c	Combine Values	c

```
c(...)
```

ARGUMENTS

> ... any S objects. Missing values (NAs) are allowed.

VALUE

> vector which is the combination of all values from all arguments to the function. The mode of the result is the most general of all the modes in the arguments. In particular, list objects can be combined this way.

> Arguments that are NULL or length 0 do not contribute elements to the result. See the last example.

EXAMPLES

```
c(1:10, 1:5, 1:10)
c(1,2,3,5,7,11,13)

c(states, "Washington DC")

# build x, element by element
# useful if final length not known in advance
x ← numeric(0)
for(i in possibles)
    if(test(i))x ← c(x, fun(i))
```

---

call	Function Calls	call

```
call(NAME, ...)
is.call(x)
as.call(x)
```

ARGUMENTS

> NAME the character name of the function to be called.
> ... arguments to the function.
> x any object.

VALUE

> call creates a call to the named function, using the remaining arguments

as the arguments to the function call.   `is.call` checks whether `x` is a function call and `as.call` tries to coerce `x` to a function call.

SEE ALSO

`do.call` (to construct and evaluate a call).

EXAMPLES

```
funs ← c("sin", "cos")
my.call ← call(funs[which], as.name("x"))
# my.call ready to be evaluated or put into an expression
```

---

call_S	Call S from a C Routine	**call_S**

```
call_S(func, nargs, arguments, modes,
        lengths, names, nres, results)
char *func;
char **arguments, **modes, **names, **results;
long nargs, *lengths, nres;
```

ARGUMENTS

func   a pointer to an S function. This will have been passed through via an argument in a `.C` call; e.g.,

```
myfun ← function(x)x+1
.C("my_c_code",list(myfun),as.double(xx),
    as.integer(length(xx)))
```

The C code in `my_c_code` before the call to `call_S` should just pass this pointer around, not doing anything with it that might alter it.

nargs   the number of arguments to be passed to the S function.

arguments   an array of pointers to the data being passed to the S function. These can point to any type of data, but must be cast to type `char *` when put into arguments:

```
double *xarg;
    ...
arguments[0] = (char *)xarg;
```

modes   the modes of the arguments, as character strings containing the usual S modes (see the table in section 7.2.3).

lengths   the number of elements in each of the arguments to the S function.

names   the names for the arguments to the S function, to be matched against the argument names in the function definition.   names can be 0, as can any of names[i]. If names is not 0 and names[i] is not 0, then names[i] is a pointer to the character string in C to be used as the actual argument name corresponding in the call to the S function.

nres   the number of components of the value of the S function to be passed back to C. If nres is one and the function produces an atomic result (e.g., numeric), this is passed back. Otherwise, the S function is expected to produce a list whose elements provide the results passed back. If the actual number of results exceeds nres, the rest are ignored; if it is less than nres, null pointers are returned in the corresponding elements of results.

results   a vector in which the pointers to the data in the components of the results will be stuffed by call_S. The data may be of any mode, but will be cast to char * by call_S. The calling routine will want to cast them back to the desired type:

```
double *yresult;
  ...
yresult = (double *)results[0];
```

At the moment, the S function is responsible for assuring that the results are of the right mode and length expected by the C code.

Note that the calling routine is responsible for allocating space for all the arrays passed to call_S. See S_alloc for storage allocation.

EXAMPLES

```
/*
 * A C routine that gets S to call a
 * function that expects a "double" vector
 * and returns a "double" vector, together
 * with its "integer" length.  The routine
 * then replaces x with the return value
 * (which should be no longer than x) and
 * returns the new length of x.
 */
long rev_test(func, x, nx)
char *func;
double *x;
long nx;
{
        long lengths[2], count, i;
```

```
char *arguments[2], *values[2];
char *modes[2], *names[2];
double *xnew;

arguments[0] = (char *)x;
modes[0] = "double";
lengths[0] = *nx;
names[0] = "x";
call_S(*func, 2, arguments, modes,
        lengths, names, 2, values);
xnew = (double *)values[0];
count = *((long *)values[1]);
for(i = 0; i < count; i++)
        *x++ = *xnew++;
return(count);
}
```

cancor	Canonical Correlation Analysis	cancor

```
cancor(x, y)
```

ARGUMENTS

    x,y two matrices of data. The number of rows (number of observations) must be the same in each.

VALUE

    object representing the canonical correlation analysis; i.e., a set of pairs of linear combinations of the variables in x and in y such that the first pair has the largest possible correlation, the second pair has the largest correlation among variables uncorrelated with the first pair, and so on. The object is a list with the following components:

    cor the correlations between the pairs of variables.

    xcoef the matrix of linear combinations of the columns of x. The first column of xcoef is the linear combination of columns of x corresponding to the first canonical correlation, etc.

    ycoef the matrix of linear combinations of the columns of y. The first column of ycoef is the linear combination of columns of y corresponding to the first canonical correlation, etc.

cat	Print Anything	**cat**

```
cat(..., file="", sep=" ", fill=FALSE,
    labels=, append=FALSE)
```

ARGUMENTS

... any S objects. The objects will be coerced to character data and printed, using the other arguments to `cat` to control the output. All the elements of the first object will be printed, then all the elements of the second, and so on.

file character string naming the file to print on. If `file` is `""`, `cat` prints to the standard output.

sep character string to insert between successive data items of each object.

fill logical or numeric; should the output be automatically broken into successive lines, with new line characters added after each line? If numeric, the value of `fill` controls the width of the printing. If TRUE, the option `width` controls the width of the printing.

labels character vector of labels for successive lines. Only relevant if `fill` is TRUE.

append it TRUE, output will be appended to `file`; otherwise, output will overwrite the contents of `file`.

SEE ALSO

```
print, options, format.
```

EXAMPLES

```
cat("current x:", x, fill=T)
cat("Today's date is:",date(),"\n")
```

category	Create Category from Discrete Data	**category**

```
category(x, levels=unique(x),
         labels=as.character(levels))
is.category(x)
as.category(x)
```

ARGUMENTS

x data vector. Missing values (NAs) are allowed.

`levels` optional vector of levels for the category. Any data value that does not match a value in `levels` is coded in the output vector as NA. Missing values (NAs) are allowed.

`labels` optional vector of values to use as labels for the levels of the category.

VALUE

vector with `levels` attribute, indicating which level the category takes on for each data value. Think of the return value as a subscript into the `levels` attribute. NAs indicate places where a data value in x does not match any value in `levels`.

`is.category` returns TRUE if x is a category object, FALSE otherwise.

`as.category` returns x, if x is a category, `category(x)` otherwise.

SEE ALSO

`table` and `tapply` for common computations using categories.

EXAMPLES

```
category(occupation)    # "doctor", "lawyer", etc.

# make readable labels
occ ← category(occupation,level=c("d","l"),
    label=c("Doctor","Lawyer"))

# turn category into character vector
levels(occ)[occ]

colors ← category(color,c("red","green","blue"))
table(colors)    #table counting occurrences of colors
```

Cauchy	Cauchy Distribution	**Cauchy**

```
dcauchy(q, location=0, scale=1)
pcauchy(q, location=0, scale=1)
qcauchy(p, location=0, scale=1)
rcauchy(n, location=0, scale=1)
```

ARGUMENTS

q vector of quantiles. Missing values (NAs) are allowed.

p   vector of probabilities. Missing values (NAs) are allowed.

n   sample size. If `length(n)` is larger than 1, then `length(n)` random values are returned.

location   vector of location parameters.

scale   vector of (positive) scale parameters.

VALUE

density (dcauchy), probability (pcauchy), quantile (qcauchy), or random sample (rcauchy) for the cauchy distribution with parameters location and scale. Results are currently computed to single-precision accuracy only. The density function is given by

$$f_{l,s}(q) = \frac{1}{\pi s (1 + (q-l)/s)^2}, \quad s > 0,$$

where *l* and *s* are the location and scale parameters.

SIDE EFFECTS

The function rcauchy causes creation of the dataset .Random.seed if it does not already exist, otherwise its value is updated.

EXAMPLES

rcauchy(20,0,10)   #sample of 20, location 0, scale 10

---

cbind   Build Matrix from Columns or Rows   **cbind**

```
cbind(arg1, arg2, ...)
rbind(arg1, arg2, ...)
```

ARGUMENTS

argi   vector or matrix. Missing values (NAs) are allowed.

VALUE

matrix composed by adjoining columns (cbind) or rows (rbind). This matrix may have a dimnames attribute.

If several arguments are matrices, they must contain the same number of rows (cbind) or columns (rbind). In addition, all arguments that have names attributes must have the same length, which also must match the number of rows/columns of any matrix arguments.

Vector arguments are treated as row vectors by `rbind` and column vectors by `cbind`. If all arguments are vectors, the result will contain as many rows or columns as the length of the longest vector. Shorter vectors will be repeated.

The `dimnames` attribute of the returned matrix is constructed as follows: for any matrix argument, its `dimnames` attribute is carried over; for any vector argument with a `names` attribute, the `names` attribute becomes the row (column) component of `dimnames` for `cbind` (`rbind`); any vector argument may be given with a name that specifies its corresponding `dimname` entry.

If arguments are time-series, no attempt is made to relate their time parameters. See `tsmatrix` for this case. Arguments that are `NULL` are ignored.

SEE ALSO

`tsmatrix`.

EXAMPLES

```
# add column of ones
cbind(1,xmatr) %*% regr$coef

# add 2 new rows
rbind(matrix,newrow1,newrow2)

# 3 column matrix with column dimnames
cbind(gnp=gnp, income=income, unemployment=unemployment)

# build a matrix, one column at a time
# this is a common paradigm
x ← NULL
for(i in seq(5)) {
    ... # compute z
    x ← cbind(x,z)
}
```

ceiling	Integer Values	**ceiling**

```
ceiling(x)
floor(x)
trunc(x)
```

ARGUMENTS

x numeric. Missing values (NAs) are allowed.

VALUE

vector of same mode as x. ceiling(x) contains the smallest integers >= x. floor(x) contains the largest integers <= x. trunc(x) contains the closest integers to x between x and 0, inclusive, e.g., trunc(1.5) is 1, and trunc(-1.5) is -1.

SEE ALSO

round, signif.

chapter	see Defunct	**chapter**

character	Character Objects	**character**

```
character(length=0)
is.character(x)
as.character(x)
```

ARGUMENTS

length integer giving the length of the returned object.

x any S object.

VALUE

character returns a character vector of the length specified, containing null strings ("").

is.character returns TRUE if x is a simple object of mode "character", and FALSE otherwise.

as.character returns x if x is a simple object of mode "charac-ter", and otherwise a character vector of the same length as x and with data resulting from coercing the elements of x to mode "character".

Simple objects have no attributes. Data elements of objects of mode "character" are character strings. In most S expressions it is not necessary to explicitly ensure that data is of a particular mode. For example, the function paste does not need character arguments; it will coerce data to character as needed.

Note the difference between coercing to a simple object of mode "character" and setting the mode attribute:

```
mode(myobject) ← "character"
```

This changes the mode of myobject but leaves all other attributes unchanged (so a matrix stays a matrix, e.g.). On the other hand, the value of as.character(myobject) would have no attributes. Similarly, is.character would return FALSE for a matrix of character data.

EXAMPLES

```
character(length(zz))  # a character object the same length as zz
as.character(1:10)  # character representations of 1,2,...,10
```

Chisquare	Chi-Square Distribution	Chisquare

```
dchisq(q, df)
pchisq(q, df)
qchisq(p, df)
rchisq(n, df)
```

ARGUMENTS

    q vector of (positive) quantiles. Missing values (NAs) are allowed.

    p vector of probabilities. Missing values (NAs) are allowed.

    n sample size. If length(n) is larger than 1, then length(n) random values are returned.

   df degrees of freedom (>0).

VALUE

density (dchisq), probability (pchisq), quantile (qchisq), or random sample (rchisq) for the chi-square distribution with df degrees of freedom. Results are currently computed to single-precision accuracy only. The density function is given by

$$f_d(q) = \frac{1}{2\Gamma(\frac{d}{2})}\exp(-\frac{q}{2})(\frac{q}{2})^{\frac{1}{2}d-1}, \quad q > 0, \ d > 0,$$

where d is the `df` parameter.

SIDE EFFECTS

The function `rchisq` causes creation of the dataset `.Random.seed` if it does not already exist, otherwise its value is updated.

`chol`	Cholesky Decomposition of Symmetric Matrix	`chol`

```
chol(x, pivot=F)
```

ARGUMENTS

    `x` symmetric, positive definite matrix (e.g., correlation matrix or cross-product matrix).

`pivot` should pivoting be done?

VALUE

upper-triangular matrix, `y`, such that `t(y) %*% y` equals `x`. If `pivot` is `TRUE`, the result will contain attributes `rank` and `pivot` containing the computed rank and any pivoting of columns done by the algorithmic calculations. If `pivot` is `FALSE`, any singularities will result in an error.

`chull`	Convex Hull of a Planar Set of Points	`chull`

```
chull(x, y, peel=FALSE, maxpeel,
      onbdy=peel, tol=.0001)
```

ARGUMENTS

`x,y` coordinates of points. The coordinates can be given by two vector arguments or by a single argument `x` which is a time-series, a complex vector, a matrix with 2 columns, or a list containing components named `x` and `y`.

peel should successive convex hulls be peeled from the remaining points, generating a nested set of hulls?

maxpeel maximum number of hulls that should be peeled from the data, default is to peel until all points are assigned to a hull. If maxpeel is given, it implies peel=TRUE.

onbdy should points on the boundary of a convex hull (but not vertices of the hull) be included in the hull?

tol relative tolerance for determining inclusion on hull.

VALUE

vector giving the indices of the points on the hull. If peel is TRUE, returns a data structure with components depth, hull and count.

depth a vector which assigns a depth to each point, i.e., the number of hulls surrounding the point. Outliers will have small values of depth, interior points relatively large values.

hull vector giving indices of the points on the hull. Along with count, determines all of the hull peels. The first count[1] values of hull determine the outermost hull, the next count[2] are the second hull, etc.

count counts of the number of points on successive hulls.

EXAMPLES

```
hull ← chull(x,y)
plot(x,y)
polygon(x[hull],y[hull],space=0)   # draw hull

p ← chull(x, y, peel=T)    # all hulls
which ← rep(seq(p$count), p$count)    # which peel for each pt
s ← split(p$hull, which)
for(i in seq(s)) {    # plot all peels
        j ← s$[i]    # indices of points on ith peel
        polygon(x[j], y[j], space=0,lty=i)
}
```

clorder	Re-Order Leaves of a Cluster Tree	clorder

```
clorder(tree, x)
```

ARGUMENTS

tree list with components named merge, height, and order, typically a hierarchical clustering produced by function hclust.

x numeric vector with one value for each individual involved in the cluster tree.

VALUE

cluster tree structure with the merge and order components permuted so that at any merge, the cluster with the smaller average x value is on the left. This reorders tree so that the leaves are approximately in order by the associated x values.

SEE ALSO

hclust for the basic definition of the clustering method and structure.

EXAMPLES

```
h ← hclust(dist(votes.repub))
ave.repub ← apply(votes.repub, 1, mean)

# leaves ordered by average republican vote
h2 ← clorder(h, ave.repub)

plclust(h2, lab=state.abb)    #cluster plot
```

cmdscale	Classical Metric Multi-dimensional Scaling	cmdscale

```
cmdscale(d, k=2, eig=FALSE, add=FALSE)
```

ARGUMENTS

d distance matrix structure of the form returned by dist or a full, symmetric matrix. Data is assumed to be dissimilarities or relative distances.

k desired dimensionality of the output space.

eig if TRUE, return the eigenvalues computed by the algorithm. They can be used as an aid in determining the appropriate dimensionality of the solution.

add if TRUE, compute the additive constant (see component ac below).

VALUE

a structure potentially with three components named points, eig and ac. Results are currently computed to single-precision accuracy only.

points a matrix with k columns and as many rows as there were objects whose distances were given in d. Row i gives the coordinates in k-space of the i-th object.

eig vector of eigenvalues (as many as original data points), returned only if argument eig is TRUE.

ac constant added to all data values in d to transform dissimilarities (or relative distances) into absolute distances. The Unidimensional Subspace procedure, (Torgerson, 1958, p. 276) is used to determine the additive constant.

REFERENCE

Warren S. Torgerson, *Theory and Methods of Scaling,* pp. 247-297, Wiley, 1958.

EXAMPLES

```
x←cmdscale(dist)    #default 2-space
coord1←x[,1]; coord2←x[,2]
par( pty="s" )    #set up square plot
r←range(x)    #get overall max, min
plot(coord1,coord2,type="n",xlim=r,ylim=r)  #set up plot
    # note units per inch same on x and y axes
text(coord1,coord2,seq(coord1))    #plot integers
```

code	see Deprecated	code

coerce	see Deprecated	coerce

col	Column and Row Numbers For a Matrix	col

```
col(x)
row(x)
```

ARGUMENTS

x matrix. Missing values (NAs) are allowed.

VALUE

integer matrix, containing the row number or column number of each element. If z←row(x), z[i,j] is i; if z←col(x), z[i,j] is j.

SEE ALSO

diag for diagonal of matrix. (Do not confuse this function with the col parameter in graphics functions; see par for that use of col.)

EXAMPLES

```
x[row(x)>col(x)] ← 0        # zero the strict lower triangle of x
x[row(x)-col(x)==1]         # first sub-diagonal
```

Comparison	Comparison Operators	Comparison

```
e1 op e2
```

ARGUMENTS

e1, e2 numeric or complex objects. For complex data op orders first on the real part, then on the imaginary part if necessary. Missing values (NAs) are allowed.

op one of >, <, >=, <=, == or !=.

VALUE

logical vector with FALSE or TRUE in each element according to the truth of the element-wise comparison of the operands. See section 5.6 for the rules for dealing with operands with attributes.

SEE ALSO

match.

EXAMPLES

```
a > b          # true when a greater than b

x[x > 100]         # all x values larger than 100

state == "Wyoming"
```

Complex	Basic Complex Number Manipulation	**Complex**

```
Re(z)
Im(z)
Mod(z)
Arg(z)
Conj(z)
```

ARGUMENTS

z numeric or complex. Missing values (NAs) are allowed.

VALUE

vector of real parts (Re), imaginary parts (Im), modulii (Mod), arguments (Arg) or complex conjugates (Conj) of z. The value of Arg satisfies -pi < Arg(z) <= pi.

complex	Complex-valued Objects	**complex**

```
complex(length=0, real=0, imaginary=0,
        modulus=1, argument=0)
is.complex(x)
as.complex(x)
```

ARGUMENTS

length length of returned object.
real vector of real parts for use in construction of return value.
imaginary vector of imaginary parts for use in construction of return value.
modulus vector of moduli for use in construction of return value.
argument vector of arguments for use in construction of return value.
x any S object.

VALUE

complex returns a simple object of mode complex. If real and/or imaginary are specified, the real and/or imaginary parts of the result are set from them, using the defaults if necessary. If modulus and/or argument are specified, the modulus and/or argument of the result are set from them, using the defaults if necessary. If either of real or imaginary is specified, neither modulus nor argument may be specified, and vice versa.

is.complex returns TRUE if x is a simple object of mode complex, and FALSE otherwise.

as.complex returns x if x is a simple object of mode complex, and otherwise a complex object of the same length as x and with data resulting from coercing the elements of x to mode complex.

EXAMPLES

```
unit.disk ← complex(arg=runif(50,-pi,pi))
      #50 random complex numbers, uniform on the unit circle
```

compname	see Deprecated	**compname**

Conj	see Complex	**Conj**

contour	Contour Plot	**contour**

```
contour(x, y, z, v, nint=5, add=FALSE, labex)
```

ARGUMENTS

x vector containing *x* coordinates of grid over which z is evaluated.

y vector of grid *y* coordinates.

z matrix length(x) by length(y) giving surface height at grid points, i.e., z[i,j] is evaluated at x[i], y[j]. The rows of z are indexed by x, and the columns by y. Missing values (NAs) are allowed.

    v vector of heights of contour lines. By default, approximately `nint` lines are drawn which cover most of the range of `z`. See the function `pretty`.

  `nint=` the approximate number of contour intervals desired. Not needed if `v` is specified.

  `add=` flag which if `TRUE` causes contour lines to be added to the current plot. Useful for adding contours with different `labex` parameter, line type, etc.

  `labex=` the desired size of the labels on contour lines. By default the current character size is used. If `labex` is 0, no labels are plotted on contours.

The first argument may be a list, `xyz`, say. Components `xyz$x`, `xyz$y` and `xyz$z` will be used. In particular, the result of `interp` is suitable as an argument to `contour`.

Graphical parameters may also be supplied as arguments to this function (see `par`). Also, the arguments to the `title` function may be supplied to this function.

SEE ALSO

    `interp, persp.`

EXAMPLES

```
rx←range(ozone.xy$x)
ry←range(ozone.xy$y)
usa(xlim=rx,ylim=ry,lty=2,col=2)
i←interp(ozone.xy$x,ozone.xy$y,ozone.median)
contour(i,add=T,labex=0)
text(ozone.xy,ozone.median)
title(main="Median Ozone Concentrations in the North East")
```

Median Ozone Concentrations in the North East

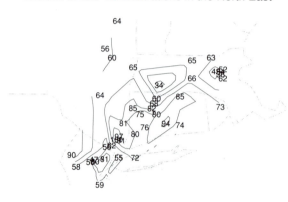

cor	see var	cor

cos	Trigonometric Functions	cos

```
cos(x)
sin(x)
tan(x)
```

ARGUMENTS

x numeric, in radians, or complex. Missing values (NAs) are allowed.

VALUE

data transformed by the specified trigonometric function, with attributes preserved. See section 5.1.5 for details on domains and branch cuts in the case of complex arguments.

| **cosh** | Hyperbolic Trigonometric Functions | **cosh** |

```
cosh(x)
sinh(x)
tanh(x)
```

ARGUMENTS

x numeric, in radians, or complex. Missing values (NAs) are allowed.

VALUE

data transformed by the specified hyperbolic trigonometric function, with attributes preserved. See section 5.1.5 for details on domains and branch cuts in the case of complex arguments.

| **count.trace** | see trace.on | **count.trace** |

| **crossprod** | Matrix Cross Product Operator | **crossprod** |

```
crossprod(mat1, mat2)
```

ARGUMENTS

mat1, mat2 matrix or vector, numeric or complex. If mat2 is omitted, it defaults to mat1.

VALUE

matrix representing the cross product of mat1 and mat2, defined as t(mat1) %*% mat2, where %*% is matrix multiplication and t is transposition. Thus the [i,j]th element of the result is sum(mat1[,i]*mat2[,j]).

`cstr`	see `Deprecated`	`cstr`

`cumsum`	Cumulative Sums	`cumsum`

```
cumsum(x)
```

ARGUMENTS

x numeric or complex. Missing values (NAs) are allowed.

VALUE

object like x whose i-th value is the sum of the first i values in x. If the first NA in x is x[j], the j-th and all following elements of the value will be NA.

EXAMPLES

```
cumprod ← function(x)
    exp(cumsum(log(x)))   # for positive numbers only
```

`cut`	Create Category by Cutting Continuous Data	`cut`

```
cut(x, breaks, labels)
```

ARGUMENTS

x data vector. Missing values (NAs) are allowed.

breaks either a vector of breakpoints, or the number of equal-width intervals into which the data in x should be cut. If a vector of breakpoints is given, the category will have `length(breaks)-1` groups, corresponding to data in the intervals between successive values in `breaks` (after `breaks` is sorted). Data less than or equal to the first breakpoint or greater than the last breakpoint is returned as NA.

labels character vector of labels for the intervals. Default is to encode the breakpoints to make up interval names (if `break` is a vector), or to use the names `Range 1`, etc., if `breaks` is a single integer.

VALUE

a category as long as x telling which group each point in x belongs to, along with an attribute, `levels`, which is a vector of character names for each group.

SEE ALSO

`category, table, tapply.`

EXAMPLES

```
cut (x, 3)     # cut into 3 groups
cut (x, breaks)    # cut based on given breakpoints
cut (x, pretty(x))     # approx 5 "pretty" intervals
```

---

cutree   Create Groups from Hierarchical Clustering   **cutree**

`cutree(tree, k, h)`

ARGUMENTS

`tree` hierarchical clustering tree structure, typically the output of `hclust`.

`k` optional, the desired number of groups.

`h` optional, the height at which to cut `tree` in order to produce the groups. Groups will be defined by the structure of the tree above the cut.

Exactly one of `k` or `h` must be supplied.

VALUE

vector with as many elements as there are leaves in the tree. The ith element of the vector gives the group number that individual i is assigned to. Individuals not in the current tree (if `tree` was a subtree from a larger original problem) are assigned group 0. Attribute `height` is a vector with as many values as there are resulting groups, the ith value gives the height of the last merge making up the group. Singleton clusters are given height 0.

EXAMPLES

`cutree(tr←hclust(dist),k=5)`   #produce 5 groups

---

cycle   see `time`   **cycle**

---

dataset	see Deprecated	**dataset**

date	Today's Date	**date**

date()

VALUE

a character string giving the current date and time.

SEE ALSO

stamp.

EXAMPLES

title(sub=date()) # add a date as a sub-title to a plot

dbeta	see Beta	**dbeta**

DBLEPR	Printing from a Fortran Routine	**DBLEPR**

```
SUBROUTINE DBLEPR(LABEL,NCHAR,DATA,NDATA)
SUBROUTINE  INTPR(LABEL,NCHAR,DATA,NDATA)
SUBROUTINE REALPR(LABEL,NCHAR,DATA,NDATA)
```

ARGUMENTS

LABEL quoted string label for the printout.

NCHAR number of characters in the label. Can be passed as -1 if you have a well-behaved Fortran compiler that inserts null bytes at the end of strings. To eliminate the label, pass 0 for NCHAR.

DATA the vector of data values (respectively double precision, integer, or real for the three subroutines).

NDATA the number of data values to be printed.

The specified data will be printed, using the same formatting procedures followed for automatic printing in S.

---

dcauchy   see Cauchy   **dcauchy**

---

dchisq   see Chisquare   **dchisq**

---

debugger   Computational State at the Time of an Error   **debugger**

```
debugger(data=last.dump)
```

ARGUMENTS

data list that describes the state of the computation at the time of the error. The names attribute of data gives the character form of the calls. Each element of data is one frame (itself a list) of the execution stack at the time of the error.

The debugger function allows you to browse among the frames associated with the various calls. See documentation for browser to learn more about the interactive interface presented by debugger.

SEE ALSO

dump.calls, dump.frames, traceback, browser.

---

define   see Defunct   **define**

Defunct	Defunct Functions	**Defunct**

```
chapter
define
edit
medit
prefix
```

These functions dealt old-S with concepts that are no longer part of S: they are not needed. See appendix 4 for more details.

density	Estimate Probability Density Function	**density**

```
density(x, n=50, window="g", width, from, to)
```

ARGUMENTS

x vector of observations from distribution whose density is to be estimated.

n the number of equally spaced points at which to estimate density.

window character string giving the type of window used in computation "cosine", "gaussian", "rectangular", "triangular" (one character is sufficient).

width width of the window. Default is width of histogram bar constructed by Doane's rule. The standard error of a Gaussian window is width/4.

from,to the n estimated values of density are equally spaced between from and to. Default is range of data extended by width*3/4 for gaussian window or width/2 for other windows.

VALUE

list with two components, x and y, suitable for giving as an argument to one of the plotting functions. Results are currently computed to single-precision accuracy only.

x vector of n points at which density is estimated.

y density estimate at each x point.

REFERENCE

Wegman, E. J. (1972), "Nonparametric Probability Density Estimation", *Technometrics,* Vol. 14, pp. 533-546.

EXAMPLES

```
plot(density(x),type="b")
```

---

deparse	Turn Parsed Expression into Character Form	**deparse**

```
deparse(expr, short=FALSE)
```

ARGUMENTS

    expr any S expression.

   short if TRUE, the deparsed character string may not be the full expression. Instead short forms are used, to keep the total length of the deparsed string within a constant limit. The short form is chiefly useful for trace printing and for labels in situations where space is at a premium.

VALUE

A character vector, containing the deparsed expression. There will be one element of the character vector for each line of output in dput(expr), unless short is TRUE, in which case only one character string is produced.

NOTE

It is typically not necessary to deparse expressions to print them. The process of coercing an expression to mode character usually achieves the same effect, more simply.

SEE ALSO

dput, parse.

EXAMPLES

z$model ← deparse(model) # save a symbolic form of an argument

---

Deprecated	Deprecated Functions	**Deprecated**

```
x %c% y          # use crossprod
x %m% mode       # use as.vector
code(...)         # use category
coerce(x, mode)   # use as.vector
compname         # use names
cstr             # use list
dataset          # use exists
encode           # use paste
fatal(message)   # use stop
gs(x)            # use qr
```

```
index(...)          # use list
len                 # use length
message(message)    # use cat
mstr                # see Subscript
na                  # use is.na
ncomp               # use length
nper                # use frequency
option              # use options
rdpen               # use locator
read                # use scan
reg, regress        # use lsfit
regprt              # use ls.summary
regsum              # use ls.summary
save                # see Assignment
search              # use attach
sys(command)        # use unix
tprint              # use print
uniq                # use unique
```

These functions are provided solely for compatibility with older versions of S. Use the suggested alternatives to achieve approximately the same effect.

cstr and mstr were used to make and modify both lists and objects with attributes. Now, use list to create lists and attr to set attributes. Lists can be modified by subscripting.

coerce and the %m% operators are better done by functions as.integer, as.double, etc., or by assigning to mode(x).

index is no longer needed, as its functionality was put into tapply. A list is used in place of the data object that index used to produce.

nper (and the associated argument to the ts function) are now named more appropriately frequency.

paste replaces encode. However, encode with one argument is nearly always redundant in current S: coercion to mode character happens automatically.

The name locator is a much better name than rdpen for a general graphic input operation.

No direct replacement is currently provided for `regprt`. Printing the components returned by `ls.summary` gives some of the same information.

The functionality of `tprint` is now incorporated into `print`.

.

detach	Detach a Data Directory from Search List	**detach**

```
detach(what=2)
```

ARGUMENTS

    `what` character string, logical vector, or numeric subscripts. If `what` is character, then it is the name of the directory to be taken out of the search list. If `what` is a logical vector, it should be the same length as the current search list; any `TRUE` values correspond to directories that are to be detached. If `what` is numeric, it gives the positions of directories in the search list to be detached.

VALUE

    old value of `.Search.list`.

SIDE EFFECTS

    changes the value of session object `.Search.list`.

SEE ALSO

    `attach, assign`.

EXAMPLES

```
detach("abc")
detach(what=3)  #detach shared data directory
```

`Device.Default`	Initialize Graphics Device	`Device.Default`

```
Device.Default (name)
```

ARGUMENTS

    `name` character string giving the name of the device.

This function is called by all device driver functions to set up default values for graphical parameters. At present, it sets axis styles to "r" and sets margin size.

The rationale for this function is that you can define your own version and thus control the default parameter values for the various devices you use.

SIDE EFFECTS

Session data object `.Device` is created, containing `name`. This can later be examined to determine if a device is currently active and what device it is.

`Devices`	List of Graphical Devices	`Devices`

`hp2623` Hewlett-Packard 2623 scope.

`hpgl`   Hewlett-Packard HP-GL plotters. (Including 7470, 7475, 7220).

`postscript` Produces Postscript™ output for various graphics printers.

`printer` Any printing terminal.

`tek4014` Tektronix 4014 scope.

`sun`   Sun workstation, using the *suntools* windowing system.

See the documentation under the individual device functions for details. New graphical devices are likely to be introduced after the book is printed; use `help("devices")` to get the most up-to-date list.

---

device.xy   Map Between World and Device Coordinates   **device.xy**

```
device.xy(dx, dy)
world.xy(wx, wy)
```

ARGUMENTS

    dx, dy vectors of *x*- and *y*-coordinates in the current device coordinate system.

    wx, wy vectors of *x*- and *y*-coordinates in the current world or user coordinate system.

VALUE

    a list with elements named x and y that give the mapped coordinates, i.e., world coordinates for device.xy and device coordinates for world.xy.

---

dexp   see Exponential   **dexp**

---

df   see F   **df**

---

dgamma   see Gamma   **dgamma**

---

dget   see dput   **dget**

diag	Diagonal Matrices	**diag**

```
diag(x, nrow, ncol)
```

ARGUMENTS

    x matrix or vector. Missing values (NAs) are allowed.

  nrow optional number of rows of output matrix.

  ncol optional number of columns of output matrix.

VALUE

if x is a matrix, the vector of diagonal elements of x; otherwise, a matrix with x on its diagonal and zeroes elsewhere. If x is a vector of length 1 and both nrow and ncol are missing, the value is an x by x identity matrix. By default, the matrix is square with zeros off the diagonal, but it can be made rectangular by specifying nrow and ncol.

EXAMPLES

```
diag(xmat)      # extract diagonal

diag(diag(xmat))     # square matrix with diagonal of xmat

diag(5)     # 5 by 5 identity matrix

diag(x,nrow=length(x))    # put x on the diagonal of a matrix
   # works even if length(x) is 1

x[ row(x)==col(x) ] ← diag(y)   # put diagonal of y
   # into diagonal of x
```

.Dictionary	Create a Dictionary	**.Dictionary**

```
.Dictionary(names, where)
```

ARGUMENTS

  names a list of object names identifying which objects should be included in the dictionary.

  where a character string giving the file to be created as the dfile (the concatenation of all the objects in the dictionary). By default, the file .dfile is created in the working directory.

VALUE

list, giving the names of the objects, their offsets in the dfile, and the prehashing of their names. In the standard use, the value is assigned to `.dictionary`, with the result that S will be able to use the dictionary as an efficient alternative way to access the objects named.

SIDE EFFECTS

The dfile is written.

EXAMPLES

```
.dictionary ← .Dictionary(list)  # the standard use
```

---

diff   Create a Differenced Series   **diff**

```
diff(x, k=1, n=1)
```

ARGUMENTS

  x a time-series or vector. Missing values (NAs) are allowed.

  k the lag of the difference to be computed.

  n the number of differences to be done.

VALUE

a time-series which is the nth difference of lag k for x. If $y \leftarrow$ `diff(x,k)`, $y[i]$ is $x[i]-x[i-k]$, and `length(y)` is `length(x)-k`. To construct an nth difference, this procedure is iterated n times. Any operation on an NA produces an NA.

EXAMPLES

```
# second difference of lag 1:
# the start date of d2x will be 2
# periods later than x
d2x ← diff(x,1,2)

diff(range(x))   # max(x) − min(x)
```

---

dim	Dim Attribute of an Object	**dim**

```
dim(x)
dim(x) ← value
```

ARGUMENTS

x any object.

value numeric vector suitable to be the dimensions of x, or NULL.

VALUE

if x has a dim attribute (i.e., x is an array) then this attribute is returned; otherwise NULL. The dim attribute is used for subset selection; see subset. It is an integer vector, with the property that prod(dim(x))==length(x). Assigning to dim(x) merely establishes or changes the dim attribute of x; no reordering of the elements of x is implied.

EXAMPLES

```
dim(iris)  # returns c(50,4,3)
length(dim(y))  # number of dimensions of y
if(!is.null(dim(z))) { .. z .. }  # do not operate on non-array data
if(is.array(z)) { .. z .. }  # better way to do the same thing
```

---

dimnames	Dimnames Attribute of an Object	**dimnames**

```
dimnames(x)
dimnames(x) ← value
```

ARGUMENTS

x any object.

value list of the same length as dim(x), or NULL.

VALUE

the dimnames attribute of x, if any; otherwise, NULL. Only arrays may have this attribute. It is a list whose length is length(dim(x)). The ith element of dimnames(x) is either of length 0 or is a character vector of length dim(x)[i], and in the latter case should be thought of as a set of labels for the ith dimension of x.

Assigning to `dimnames(x)` is permissible, provided x is an array, and the new value of the `dimnames` attribute is compatible with `dim(x)`. To explicitly delete the `dimnames` attribute, use `dimnames(x)`←NULL.

Array subscripts retain `dimnames`; see `Subscript`.

EXAMPLES

```
dimnames(iris)[[3]]  # iris species
```

`discr`	Discriminant Analysis	`discr`

```
discr(x, k)
```

ARGUMENTS

    x matrix of data. The rows of x must be ordered by groups.

    k either the number of groups (if groups are equal in size), or the vector of group sizes; i.e., first `k[1]` rows form group 1, next `k[2]` group 2, etc.

VALUE

    a list describing the discriminant analysis, with the following components:

    `cor` vector of discriminant correlations (correlations between linear combinations of variables and of groups)

    `groups` matrix of linear combinations of groups predicted.

    `vars` matrix of linear combinations of variables.

Columns of `vars` give discriminant variables; i.e., x `%*%` vars produces the matrix of discriminant variables.

EXAMPLES

```
# a function to do discrimination from a grouping variable
discr.group ← function(x,group) {
        size ← table(category(sort(group)))
        discr(x[order(group),],size)
}
```

dist	Distance Matrix Calculation	**dist**

```
dist(x, metric="euclidean")
```

ARGUMENTS

> x matrix (typically a data matrix). The distances computed will be among the rows of x. Missing values (NAs) are allowed.

> metric character string specifying the distance metric to be used. The currently available options are "euclidean", "maximum", "manhattan", and "binary". Euclidean distances are root sum-of-squares of differences, maximum is the maximum difference, manhattan is the sum of absolute differences, and binary is the proportion of nonzeroes that two vectors have in common.

VALUE

> the distances among the rows of x. Since there are many distances and since the result of dist is typically an argument to hclust, a vector is returned, rather than a symmetric matrix. The returned object has an attribute, size, giving the number of objects (that is, rows of x).

> Missing values in a row of x are not included in any distances involving that row. Such distances are then inflated to account for the missing values. If all values for a particular distance are excluded by this rule, the distance is NA.

EXAMPLES

```
dist(x,"max")  # distances among rows by maximum
dist(t(x))  # distances among cols in euclidean metric
```

dlnorm	see Lognormal	**dlnorm**

dlogis	see Logistic	**dlogis**

dnorm	see Normal	**dnorm**

do.call	Execute a Function Call	**do.call**

```
do.call(what, args)
```

ARGUMENTS

> what   character string, giving the name of the function to be called.
>
> args   list of the (evaluated) arguments to the called function.

VALUE

> the result of the evaluated call.

SEE ALSO

> call creates the call without doing the evaluation.

EXAMPLES

```
do.call("boxplot",split(x,group))
# equivalent to boxplot(split(x,group)) because
# boxplot takes any number of arguments
```

dotchart	Draw a Dot Chart	**dotchart**

```
dotchart(data, labels=NULL, groups=NULL,
         gdata=NULL, horiz=T, pch="o", lty=2)
```

ARGUMENTS

> data   vector of all data values.
>
> labels   optional vector of labels for data values.
>
> groups   categorical variable used for splitting data vector into groups and providing group labels.
>
> gdata   optional vector of group data, that is, an overall value for each group. This could be a sum or an average, for example.
>
> horiz   should data values be on horizontal or vertical axis?

`pch` optional character to be used as plot character.
`lty` line type used in drawing the dotted line.

Graphical parameters may also be supplied as arguments to this function
(see `par`).

EXAMPLES

```
perc.data ← c(5.4, 3.1, 3.5, 5.7, 8.6, 25.0, 20.4,
        26.0, 22.0, 36.3, 34.1, 28.0, 14.4, 11.4, 4.5)
percent ← matrix(perc.data,ncol=3,byrow=T)
community ← c("Old Suburb","Coast County","New Suburb")
service ← c("Child Care","Health Services",
        "Community Centers","Family & Youth", "Other")
com ← code(col(percent),label=community)
serv ← code(row(percent),label=service)

dotchart(percent,labels=levels(com)[com],group=serv)

dotchart(percent,labels=levels(serv)[serv],group=com,
    horiz=F)
```

\# now plot the same thing with the median percent for each service
\# the example plot was produced by:

```
gmed ← tapply(percent,index(com),median)
dotchart(percent,labels=levels(serv)[serv],group=com,
    gdata=gmed)
```

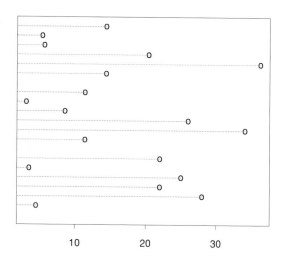

double	Double Precision Objects	**double**

```
double(length=0)
is.double(x)
as.double(x)
```

ARGUMENTS

length integer giving the length of the returned object.

x any S object.

VALUE

double returns a simple object of storage mode "double", and the length specified.

is.double returns TRUE if x is a simple object of storage mode "double", and FALSE otherwise.

as.double returns x if x is a simple object of storage mode "double", and otherwise a vector of the same length as x and with data resulting from coercing the elements of x to storage mode double.

These functions are needed when interfacing to Fortran or C algorithms, where it is important to emphasize the exact storage mode of data.

In most S expressions it is not necessary to explicitly ensure that data is of a particular storage mode. When testing for data suitable for arithmetic, for example, it is better to use is.numeric(x), which will return TRUE for any numeric object. Normally, S does numeric computations with double precision. Explicit reference to storage mode double is usually only relevant when passing arguments to Fortran or C routines that have arguments with double precision or float declarations.

Note the difference between coercing to a vector and setting the storage mode attribute:

```
storage.mode(myobject) ← "double"
```

This changes the storage mode of myobject but leaves all other attributes unchanged (so a matrix stays a matrix, e.g.). The value of as.double(myobject) would have no attributes.

SEE ALSO

.Fortran, .C.

EXAMPLES

z ← double(length(zz)) # double object same length as zz
.Fortran("mydsub",as.double(xm))

| **dput** | Write a Text Representation of an S Object | **dput** |

dput(x, file)
dget(file)

ARGUMENTS

   x any S object. Missing values (NAs) are allowed.

file character string giving the file name where the data structure is to be stored and later retrieved.

VALUE

the object x.

SIDE EFFECTS

dput writes an ASCII version of the object onto the file. In particular, this file is suitable for moving between computers. The function dget re-creates the object from file.

SEE ALSO

dump and restore.

WARNING

The exact format of the object on the file is subject to change. You should regard these files as ASCII versions of assignments.

Note also that exact equality of read-in numeric data cannot be guaranteed across machines.

EXAMPLES

dput(abc, "oldabc") # store abc on file oldabc
def ← dget("oldabc")   # read back in

dt	see T	**dt**

dump	Produce Text Representations of S Objects	**dump**

```
dump(list, fileout="dumpdata")
```

ARGUMENTS

list character vector giving the names of data objects.

fileout character name of a file on which the objects will be dumped.

VALUE

fileout is returned.

Currently, dump uses sink to direct its output to fileout. This means that any sink currently in effect will be lost.

SIDE EFFECTS

Text representations of the objects given in list are written to file fileout. The files are ASCII text, and can be shipped to another machine. The shipped file can then be used to restore the objects, either with source for small files, or with restore.

SEE ALSO

dput, restore.

EXAMPLES

```
dump(ls(), "all.files")
```

| **dump.calls** | Save All Calls or Frames on Errors | **dump.calls** |

```
dump.calls( )
dump.frames( )
```

These functions are typically used as an error action to save the current call stack or frames as an object that can later be examined by the `traceback` or `debugger` functions. When called, they write the message "Dumped" to the terminal.

Function `dump.calls` is the default error action in the `.Options` data object.

Function `dump.calls` dumps the current call stack; `dump.frames` dumps the call stack and all frames. Dumping the frames may take much more time than dumping calls, since the frames contain all intermediate data objects. However, the frames provide information that the `browser`-like function `debugger` can use to help you understand what state the computations were in when an error occurred.

SIDE EFFECTS

Object `last.dump` is created when either `dump.calls` or `dump.frames` is executed.

SEE ALSO

options, debugger, traceback.

EXAMPLES

```
options(error=dump.frames)
# after an error occurs
debugger()
```

| **dump.frames** | see dump.calls | **dump.frames** |

dunif	see Uniform	**dunif**

duplicated	see unique	**duplicated**

dyn.load	Dynamically Load an Object File	**dyn.load**

```
dyn.load(names)
```

ARGUMENTS

names character vector giving the names of object files. Here *object* does not mean *S object*; it is used in the sense of a relocatable object module from the compilation of a C or Fortran program, for example.

VALUE

(invisible) vector of the external symbol names that were defined by loading names.

When an object file is dynamically loaded, the machine allocates space for the executable code, reads the object file into the allocated space, relocates instructions, and resolves references to routines that are already part of the running version of S.

Because its implementation uses the object file format, the function dyn.load may not work on all machines on which S runs. As this book is written, there is a working dyn.load for Sun and Vax computers.

SEE ALSO

S LOAD does a static load.

EXAMPLES

```
# assuming there is source code for a C function named myfun()
# in file myfun.c
!cc -c myfun.c          # C compiler produces myfun.o
dyn.load("myfun.o")    # dynamically load myfun.o
.C("myfun",args)       # invoke the function
```

ed	Invoke ed Text Editor	**ed**

```
ed(data, file=tempfile("ed."))
```

ARGUMENTS

> data   any S object.
>
> file   the name of the file on which the object should be written while the editing is done.

VALUE

> the edited value of the object.

SIDE EFFECTS

> none. It is important to realize that ed does not change data; the returned value must be reassigned in order to save your editing changes, as in the example.
>
> If errors resulted during the evaluation of the expression containing the editing, the file is retained and calling ed with no arguments will allow re-editing the file. This is typically useful if editing a function definition produced a syntax error.

SEE ALSO

> vi.

EXAMPLES

```
ttt ← ed(ttt)
```

edit	see Defunct	**edit**

| **eigen** | Eigen Analysis of Symmetric Matrix | **eigen** |

```
eigen(x)
```

ARGUMENTS

   x matrix to be decomposed. Must be square and symmetric.

VALUE

a list containing the eigenvalues and eigenvectors of x.

   values vector of n eigenvalues in descending order.

   vectors matrix like x giving the eigenvectors corresponding to the eigenvalues in
   values.

SEE ALSO

   svd.

EXAMPLES

```
cors ← cor(x,y,trim=.1)
pprcom ← eigen(cors)
```

| **else** | see if | **else** |

| **encode** | see Deprecated | **encode** |

| **end** | see tsp | **end** |

| **eval** | Evaluate an Expression | **eval** |

```
eval(expression, local, parent)
```

ARGUMENTS

expression any S expression

local the frame in which to do the evaluation; by default, the frame of the caller of `eval`. If `local` is `FALSE`, evaluation is done in the global frame.
Otherwise, `local` can be either a numeric value, interpreted as one of the
frames of the evaluator, or it can be an explicit list, with the named elements of the list defining the bindings for the names occurring in the expression. A typical numeric choice of `local` would be
`sys.parent(1)`, meaning the routine that called the routine calling
`eval`.

parent the frame to use as the parent of the evaluation frame. Only needs to be
supplied when unevaluated arguments are to be handled by a special ar-
rangement (as required by `browser`).

VALUE

the value of `expression`.

EXAMPLES

```
# a function that can simulate the S program
# from inside a function: see section 7.4.3
try.S ← function()
        print(eval(parse(),F))
```

| **exists** | see get | **exists** |

---

exp   Exponential Functions   **exp**

```
exp(x)
log(x, base=exp(1))
log10(x)
sqrt(x)
```

ARGUMENTS

    x numeric or complex. Missing values (NAs) are allowed.

  base (positive) numeric or complex base for logarithms.

VALUE

data transformed by the specified function, with attributes preserved. By default, `log` computes natural logs. Numeric arguments must be positive for `log`, `log10` and `sqrt`, otherwise NA is returned and a warning message is generated. See section 5.1.5 for details on domains and branch cuts in the case of complex arguments.

Exponential   Exponential Distribution   **Exponential**

```
dexp(q)
pexp(q)
qexp(p)
rexp(n)
```

ARGUMENTS

    q vector of quantiles. Missing values (NAs) are allowed.

    p vector of probabilities. Missing values (NAs) are allowed.

    n sample size. If `length(n)` is larger than 1, then `length(n)` random values are returned.

VALUE

density (`dexp`), probability (`pexp`), quantile (`qexp`), or random sample (`rexp`) for the standard exponential distribution. The density function is given by

$$f(q) = e^{-q} \quad q > 0.$$

SIDE EFFECTS

The function `rexp` causes creation of the dataset `.Random.seed` if it does not already exist, otherwise its value is updated.

---

expression   Expression Objects   **expression**

```
expression(...)
as.expression(x)
is.expression(x)
```

ARGUMENTS

... any valid S expressions. They will *not* be evaluated by the call to `expression`.

x an S object.

VALUE

an expression, that is, an object of mode `"expression"`. Its elements are the arguments, unevaluated.

`as.expression` merely changes the mode of `x` to `"expression"`. `is.expression` tests whether `x` is a expression.

SEE ALSO

`eval, parse, substitute.`

EXAMPLES

```
methods ← expression(lsfit(x,y),l1fit(x,y))
eval(methods[[which]])
```

F   F Distribution   **F**

```
df(q, df1, df2)
pf(q, df1, df2)
qf(p, df1, df2)
rf(n, df1, df2)
```

ARGUMENTS

q vector of (positive) quantiles. Missing values (NAs) are allowed.

p vector of probabilities. Missing values (NAs) are allowed.

n sample size. If `length(n)` is larger than 1, then `length(n)` random values are returned.

df1 vector of degrees of freedom for numerator.

df2 vector of degrees of freedom for denominator.

VALUE

density (df), probability (pf), quantile (qf), or random sample (rf) for the F-distribution with degrees of freedom df1 and df2. Values are computed to single precision accuracy only. Results are currently computed to single-precision accuracy only. The density function is given by

$$f_{d_1,d_2}(q) = \frac{\Gamma(\frac{d_1+d_2}{2})}{\Gamma(\frac{d_1}{2})\Gamma(\frac{d_2}{2})} \frac{q^{d_1-1}}{(1+q)^{\frac{1}{2}(d_1+d_2)}} \quad q > 0, \;\; d_1, d_2 > 0,$$

where d_1 and d_2 are the df1 and df2 parameters.

SIDE EFFECTS

The function rf causes creation of the dataset `.Random.seed` if it does not already exist, otherwise its value is updated.

EXAMPLES

`rf(10,5,15)` #sample of 10 with 5 and 15 degrees of freedom

---

faces	Plot Symbolic Faces	**faces**

```
faces(x, which, labels, head, max, nrow, ncol,
      fill=TRUE, scale=TRUE, byrow=FALSE)
```

ARGUMENTS

x matrix of data values. Missing values (NAs) are allowed.

which the columns of x to be used as the first, second, etc. parameter in the symbolic face. Default `1:min(15,ncol(x))`. See NOTE below for meaning of parameters.

labels optional character vector of labels for the faces (i.e., for the rows of x).

head optional character vector to use as the heading for the plot.

max a suggested value for the number of rows and columns to go on each page. By default, all the faces will be fitted onto one page.

nrow

ncol optionally, may be given to specify exactly the number of rows and columns for the array of plots on each page.

fill if TRUE, all unused parameters of the face will be set to their nominal (midpoint) value. If FALSE, all features corresponding to unused parameters will not be plotted.

scale if TRUE, the columns of x will be independently scaled to (0,1). If FALSE no scaling will be done. The data values should then be scaled to the same overall range by some other means; e.g., by scaling the whole of x to the range (0,1).

byrow if TRUE, plots produced in row-wise order; if FALSE plots are produced in column-wise order.

NOTE

the feature parameters are: 1-area of face; 2-shape of face; 3-length of nose; 4-loc. of mouth; 5-curve of smile; 6-width of mouth; 7,8,9,10,11-loc., separation, angle, shape and width of eyes; 12-loc. of pupil; 13,14,15-loc., angle and width of eyebrow.

REFERENCE

H. Chernoff, "The use of Faces to Represent Points in k-Dimensional Space Graphically," *Journal of the American Statistical Association*, Vol. 68, pp. 361-368, 1973.

EXAMPLES

```
# the example plot is produced by:
faces(chernoff2[1:9,],
    head="Chernoff's Second Example (9 observations)")
```

Chernoff's Second Example (9 observations)

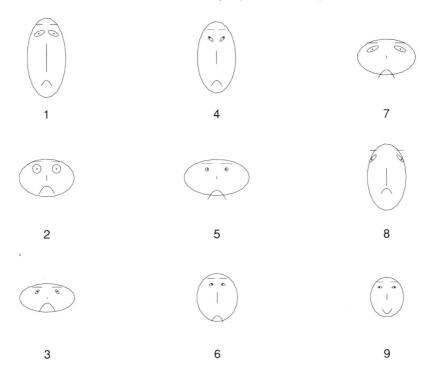

<table>
<tr><td>fatal</td><td>see Deprecated</td><td>fatal</td></tr>
</table>

<table>
<tr><td>fft</td><td>Fast Fourier Transform</td><td>fft</td></tr>
</table>

```
fft(z, inverse=FALSE)
```

ARGUMENTS

z numeric or complex.

inverse flag saying whether the inverse of the transform should be computed.

VALUE

the unnormalized discrete Fourier transform of the input data `z` (or the inverse transform if `inverse=TRUE`). The Fast Fourier Transform algorithm is used. No padding of the input data is done; `length(z)` is factored, if possible, and the factorization is used in the algorithm. Therefore, if `length(z)` is prime, there will be no advantage in using `fft` over computing the transform explicitly.

If `z` is an array, `fft` will return the multi-dimensional unnormalized discrete Fourier transform of `z`—a complex array with the same shape as `z`. If `z` is not an array, the definition of the transform `w ← fft(z)` is:

$$w_j = \sum_{t=1}^{n} z_t \exp(-i\omega_{j-1}(t-1)), \quad 1 \le j \le n,$$

where n is `length(z)` and ω_j is the jth Fourier frequency $2\pi j/n$. The initial sign in the exponential is reversed for the inverse transform. This formula is actually also valid when `z` is an array, by interpreting n as `dim(z)` and the subscripts j and t as vectors of subscripts. The formula for the jth Fourier frequency is to be taken componentwise and the product $\omega_{j-1}(t-1)$ as an inner product.

.First	Startup and Wrapup Actions	**.First**

```
.First()
.Last()
```

The `.First` function (or expression) is called (or evaluated) when S is started. It is used for its side effects: attaching directories, setting options and printing messages are examples. The `.Last` function (or expression) is called (or evaluated) when S is about to exit normally. It is not executed if S terminates abnormally. It should always be present, and should, at the very least, execute the C program `gr_wrap` to wrap up any graphics as illustrated in the example.

EXAMPLES

```
.First ← function() cat("Hello, Welcome to S\n")
.Last ← function(){
        if(exists(".Device")) .C("gr_wrap")
        cat("Bye bye.\n")
}
```

---

floor	see ceiling	**floor**

---

for	see Syntax	**for**

---

format	Formatted Character Data	**format**

---

format(x)

ARGUMENTS

x a vector of any atomic mode.

VALUE

character vector. The format function takes all elements of x and turns them into character form using a common format, just as they would be printed by the pratom function. This ensures that all elements of the value have the same number of characters and have decimal places aligned.

The function is useful for building custom output displays, and is often used in conjunction with cat to print such displays.

EXAMPLES

```
> format(2^seq(10))
 [1] "    2" "    4" "    8" "   16" "   32"
 [6] "   64" "  128" "  256" "  512" "1024"
```

.Fortran   Call a Fortran or C Routine   **.Fortran**

```
.Fortran(name, ...)
.C(name, ...)
```

ARGUMENTS

`name` a character string, giving the name of a subroutine. The name should be
as understood by Fortran or C; i.e., the same name you would use to call
the routine from Fortran or C (as opposed to the name the loader actually
puts in the symbol table).

`...` arguments to the subroutine. There must be exactly as many such arguments as the subroutine expects. They must agree in storage mode with
the corresponding argument to the Fortran or C subroutine: see Table 7.1
in section 7.2.3. Note in particular that all the arguments to the C subroutine *must* be pointers, and that character vectors in S correspond to
`char**` declarations in C. The length of the object passed in must be at
least what the subroutine expects; if not, expect memory faults and termination of the S session.

Arguments may have any name. The corresponding component of the
value will have the same name (see below). Arguments may have attributes; in particular, they can be matrices or multi-way arrays. The returned components will retain these attributes.

VALUE

a list with length equal to the number of `...` arguments; i.e., the list of
arguments to the subroutine. The values in the elements of the list will
be the values given to `.Fortran` or `.C`, unless the subroutine itself
overwrites some of the values, in which case the changed values will be
returned. Normally the subroutine *will* overwrite some of its arguments,
so that some computed results can be returned. Any attributes in the argument will be retained in the value; for example, arrays will still be arrays.

The names attribute of the list will be the names of the `...` arguments.

SEE ALSO

`S_alloc` for allocating storage in a C routine.

EXAMPLES

```
# a Fortran routine that takes a double precision array and its length
.Fortran("mycalc",as.double(x),as.integer(length(x)))
```

frame	Advance Graphics Device to Next Frame or Figure	**frame**

```
frame()
```

The current graphics device will eject to a new page, clear the screen, or do whatever is appropriate for the device.

In multiple figure mode, `frame` will advance to the next figure. It takes two calls to `frame` to skip a figure: the first goes to the next figure, and the second call skips to the next figure.

frequency	see `tsp`	**frequency**

Gamma	Gamma Distribution	**Gamma**

```
dgamma(q, shape)
pgamma(q, shape)
qgamma(p, shape)
rgamma(n, shape)
```

ARGUMENTS

    q vector of (positive) quantiles. Missing values (NAs) are allowed.

    p vector of probabilities. Missing values (NAs) are allowed.

    n sample size. If `length(n)` is larger than 1, then `length(n)` random values are returned.

shape vector of shape parameters (>0).

VALUE

    density (`dgamma`), probability (`pgamma`), quantile (`qgamma`), or random sample (`rgamma`) for the gamma distribution with shape `shape`. Results are currently computed to single-precision accuracy only. The density function is given by

$$f_s(q) = \frac{q^{s-1}\exp(-q)}{\Gamma(s)}, \quad q > 0, \ s > 0,$$

where s is the `shape` parameter.

SIDE EFFECTS

> The function `rgamma` causes creation of the dataset `.Random.seed` if it does not already exist, otherwise its value is updated.

EXAMPLES

> `rgamma(20,10)` #sample of 20 with shape parameter 10

---

gamma	Gamma Function (and its Natural Logarithm)	**gamma**

```
gamma(x)
lgamma(x)
```

ARGUMENTS

> x numeric. Missing values (NAs) are allowed.

VALUE

> gamma or natural log of gamma function evaluated for each value in `x`. For positive integral values, `gamma(x)` is `(x-1)!`. For negative integral values, `gamma(x)` is undefined. Function `lgamma` allows only positive arguments. NAs are returned when evaluation would cause numerical problems. Results are currently computed to single-precision accuracy only.

> Note that `gamma(x)` increases very rapidly with `x`. Use `lgamma` to avoid overflow.

EXAMPLES

> `gamma(6)`   # same as 5 factorial

---

get	Find an Object	**get**

```
get(name, where, frame, mode)
exists(name, where, frame, mode)
```

ARGUMENTS

> name character string giving the name of the object.
>
> where which directory should the object come from? If `which` is supplied, it can either be a number or a character string. A number implies the corresponding element of the search list, so `where=2`, for example, gets

an object from the second directory (typically the system function directory). If `where` is a character string, this is taken as the path name for a directory in the file system. In this case, the directory need not be on the search list. Use of `get` with a path name is a more efficient way to get a few objects from a known directory than using `attach`.

frame which of the current frames in the evaluation should be searched? Frame 0 is a legal argument, meaning to look in the session frame, which contains those objects created by `assign()` with `frame=0`. If both `where` and `frame` are omitted, the search is done as if `name` were an ordinary name in an expression. That is, the search is first in the local data frame, then in frame 1, then the session frame, and then in each of the permanent directories in the search list. It is an error to supply both `where` and `frame`.

mode character string giving the mode wanted for the object. By default, any mode is acceptable.

VALUE

In the case of `get`, the object is returned, if found subject to the constraints implied by arguments `mode`, `where`, or `frame`. Failure to find the object causes an error.

`exists` returns `TRUE` or `FALSE` according to whether the search succeeds.

Finding an object with `exists` that fails the `mode` test produces a warning message if the search otherwise succeeds. Finding a file `name` that does not contain an S object produces a warning message and returns `FALSE`.

EXAMPLES

```
get("[[")  # get an object of a non-standard name
get("abc",mode="function")  # get abc, but only if it is a function
joe.x ← get("x",w="/usr/joe/.Data")  # get joe's version of x
if(!exists("my.init",frame=0))  # look only in session frame
        do.initialize()
```

SEE ALSO

`assign, remove, ls.`

---

graphics   Create a Graphics Object   **graphics**

```
graphics(expr)
```

ARGUMENTS

expr any expression that would normally produce graphics output.

VALUE

a graphics object that describes the picture that would be produced by expr. This picture is not sent to the current device driver.

EXAMPLES

```
g.usa ← graphics(usa())
```

SEE ALSO

gr.display.

---

graphics.off   Turn Off Current Graphics Device   **graphics.off**

```
graphics.off()
```

This function executes the wrapup action for the currently defined graphics device. This is important for flushing buffers, etc. After execution, S is in the same state as when it is first started, i.e., there is no active graphics device.

---

gr.display   Display a Graphics Object   **gr.display**

```
gr.display(g)
```

ARGUMENTS

g a graphics object, i.e., an object of mode "graphics"

EFFECT

The picture described by the object g is displayed on the current graphics device. gr.display is called automatically by print, so that just typing g will cause it to be displayed.

SEE ALSO

> graphics.

EXAMPLES

> g ← graphics(plot(x,y)) #save a plot
> g #now display it

---

grep	Search for Pattern in Text	**grep**

> grep(pattern, text)

ARGUMENTS

> pattern character string giving a regular expression. Regular expressions are built
> up as for the egrep command.
>
> text character vector.

VALUE

> numeric vector telling which elements of text matched pattern.

EXAMPLES

> state.name[grep("ia$",state.name)]
> # find state names that end in "ia"

---

gs	see Deprecated	**gs**

---

hat	Hat Matrix Regression Diagnostic	**hat**

> hat(x, int=TRUE)

ARGUMENTS

> x matrix of independent variables in the regression model y=xb+e.
>
> int logical flag, if TRUE an intercept term is included in the regression
> model.

VALUE

vector with one value for each row of x. These values are the diagonal elements of the least-squares projection matrix H. (Fitted values for a regression of y on x are H %*% y.) Large values of these diagonal elements correspond to points with high leverage: see the reference for details.

REFERENCE

D. A. Belsley, E. Kuh, and R. E. Welsch, *Regression Diagnostics,* Section 2.1, Wiley, 1980.

EXAMPLES

```
h ← hat(longley.x)
```

---

hclust	Hierarchical Clustering	**hclust**

```
hclust(dist, method="compact", sim)
```

ARGUMENTS

dist a distance structure or distance matrix. Normally this will be the result of the function dist, but it can be any data of the form returned by dist, or a full, symmetric matrix.

method character string giving the clustering method. The three methods currently implemented are "average", "connected" (single linkage) and "compact" (complete linkage). (The first three characters of the method are sufficient.)

sim= optional structure replacing dist, but giving similarities rather than distances. Exactly one of sim or dist must be given.

VALUE

a "tree" representing the clustering, consisting of the following components:

merge an $(n - 1)$ by 2 matrix, if there were *n* objects in the original data. Row *i* of merge describes the merging of clusters at step *i* of the clustering. If an element *j* in the row is negative, then object $-j$ was merged at this stage. If *j* is positive then the merge was with the cluster formed at the (earlier) stage *j* of the algorithm.

height the clustering "height"; that is, the distance between clusters merged at the successive stages.

order a vector giving a permutation of the original objects suitable for plotting, in the sense that a cluster plot using this ordering will not have crossings of the branches.

In hierarchical cluster displays, a decision is needed at each merge to specify which subtree should go on the left and which on the right. Since, for n individuals, there are n-1 merges, there are 2^(n-1) possible orderings for the leaves in a cluster tree. The default algorithm in hclust is to order the subtrees so that the tighter cluster is on the left (the last merge of the left subtree is at a lower value than the last merge of the right subtree). Individuals are the tightest clusters possible, and merges involving two individuals place them in order by their observation number.

SEE ALSO

The functions plcust and labclust are used for plotting the result of a hierarchical clustering. dist computes distance matrices. Functions cutree, clorder, and subtree can be used to manipulate the tree data structure.

EXAMPLES

```
h ← hclust(dist(x))
plclust(h)

hclust(dist(x),"ave")
```

---

help   On-line Documentation   **help**

```
help(name="help", offline=F)
args(name="help")
```

ARGUMENTS

name a name or a character string giving the name of a function, operator, or other S object. If omitted, documentation on help is given (this documentation). The directories on the current search list are searched for documentation.

offline if TRUE, the requested documentation is run through the troff command and sent to an appropriate printer.

If information is found on `name`, the documentation will be printed. Documentation on S system functions corresponds to the contents of this appendix, possibly updated.

The function `args` prints only the title and usage portion of the documentation.

The `offline` argument is installation-dependent and must be set up appropriately by the administrator of S on each system. Preformatted versions of the help documentation may be set up by the administrator in directories named `.Cat.Help`, parallel to the `.Help` directories.

SEE ALSO

    `attach, prompt.`

EXAMPLES

```
help(stem)      # documentation for function stem()
help("+")       # addition (and other arithmetic)
help(state)     # state data
help(AUDIT)     # S audit utility

args(stem)    # describe arguments for stem
```

`hist`	Plot a Histogram	`hist`

```
hist(x, nclass, breaks, plot=TRUE,
        angle, density, col, inside)
```

ARGUMENTS

    `x` numeric vector of data for histogram.

  `nclass` optional recommendation for the number of classes (i.e., bars) the histogram should have. Default is of the order of log to the base 2 of length of x.

  `breaks` optional vector of the break points for the bars of the histogram. The count in the `i`-th bar is

```
sum( breaks[i] < x & x <= breaks[i+1] )
```

If omitted, evenly-spaced break points are determined from `nclass` and the extremes of the data.

plot   if TRUE, the histogram will be plotted; if FALSE, a list giving break-points and counts will be returned.

The hist function uses the function barplot to do the actual plotting. Consequently, arguments to the barplot function that control shading, etc., can also be given to hist. See barplot documentation for arguments angle, density, col, and inside.

Graphical parameters may also be supplied as arguments to this function (see par).

VALUE

if plot is FALSE, hist returns a list with components:

counts count or density in each bar of the histogram.
breaks break points between histogram classes.

EXAMPLES

```
# the example plot is produced by:
my.sample ←   rt(50,5)
lab ← "50 samples from a t distribution with 5 d. f."
hist(my.sample,main=lab)
```

50 samples from a t distribution with 5 d. f.

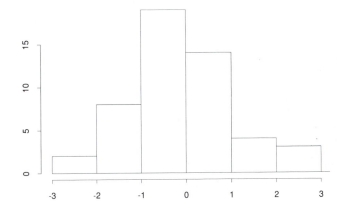

history	Display and Re-Execute S Expressions	**history**

```
history(pattern = ".",max = 1,
    evaluate=T, call, graphics=T)
again(pattern = ".")
```

ARGUMENTS

pattern pattern to select expressions. Previously evaluated expressions will be selected from the audit file if they match this pattern (as a regular expression in the sense of the awk language). See also argument call.

max maximum number of expressions to consider. Default 10.

evaluate logical flag: should the selected expression be evaluated?

call if this argument is given instead of pattern, the search is restricted to expressions containing calls(that is, to expressions containing this pattern followed by a left parenthesis). (In this case remember that other arguments, like max need to given in the name=value form, so they will not match pattern.)

graphics if TRUE, graphics menus will be used, if available. See function menu.

The history function looks backwards through the audit file, trying to find the most recent max expressions that match the pattern or call pattern. When these are found, if evaluate is TRUE, you will be requested, via the menu function, to select one of them. If you make a selection, the selected expression will then be evaluated by S.

The pattern is treated as a regular expression. This is important to know if your pattern includes parentheses, brackets, dollar signs, asterisks, etc. Each of these characters has a special meaning in a regular expression. In general, you will be safe if you use alphabetic and numeric characters, with periods (.) in the place of any other character. A period matches anything.

The function again re-evaluates the last matching expression. again() is equivalent to history(max=1).

VALUE

Either the value of the selected expression, or the parsed, but unevaluated version, if evaluate is FALSE.

SIDE EFFECTS

The selected expression is evaluated, if evaluate is TRUE.

EXAMPLES

```
history(max=20)  # the last 20 expressions
history("plot")  # recent references to plot
history(call=plot,max=1)  #re-evaluate the last call to plot
```

| **hp2623** | Hewlett-Packard 2623 Graphics Terminal | **hp2623** |

```
hp2623(ask=F, file="")
```

ARGUMENTS

ask should device driver print the message "GO?" to ask permission to clear the screen?

file character file name where output should be sent. This enables the characters that would have been sent to the terminal to be caught in a file for later plotting. By default, output is sent to the terminal.

If ask is TRUE, whenever a new plot is about to be produced the message "GO?" appears on the alpha screen. This allows further viewing, making a hard copy, etc., before the graphics screen is erased. When ready for plotting to proceed, simply hit carriage return.

When graphic input (identify, locator) is requested from this terminal, the graphic cursor appears. Use the arrow keys to position the cursor at the desired point, and then type any single character. A carriage return alone will terminate graphic input without transmitting the point.

There are eight character sizes (1 to 8) and characters can be rotated by multiples of 90 degrees. There are 7 line types (1 to 7) giving solid, dotted, short-dashed, long-dashed, dot-space-dash, dot-dot-dot and dot-dashed lines. These devices can fill rectangles (as generated by barplots) in eight patterns: solid, small checkerboard, large checkerboard, one white/3 black, very large checkerboard, spiral, diamond, and lattice.

A device must be specified before any graphics functions can be used.

hpgl	Hewlett-Packard HP-GL Plotters	**hpgl**

```
hpgl(width=10, height=7.25, ask=!auto, auto=F,
     color=2, speed=400, rotated=F, file="")
```

ARGUMENTS

width width of plotted surface in inches.

height height of plotted surface in inches.

ask should user be prompted by "GO?" prior to advancing to new frame?

auto logical, can device automatically advance the paper (H-P 7550)?

color integer reflecting the degree of color-plotting support provided by the device. 0=color changes ignored, 1=prompt user when color changes (to allow manual pen changes, etc), 2=device has automatic color changing capability.

speed maximum allowed axis pen velocity ranging from 1 to 400 mm/sec. Slower speeds are useful for high-quality work or for plotting on special paper or film.

rotated logical, tells whether the long dimension of 8.5 by 11 inch paper is oriented horizontally (not rotated) or vertically (rotated).

file file name for capturing HP-GL commands. Ordinarily, the HPGL characters are sent to the user's terminal.

This function works with plotters which accept the Hewlett-Packard HP-GL instruction set. This includes H-P pen plotter models 7220, 7470, 7475, 7550, and 7225. The plotters may be used with standard 8.5 by 11 inch paper with the long dimension horizontally or vertically, or with other paper sizes by means of arguments width and height.

If auto is FALSE, then whenever a new plot is about to be produced, the message "GO?" appears on the terminal. At this time, new paper may be loaded, pens changed, etc. When ready for plotting to proceed, simply hit carriage return.

When graphic input (identify, locator) is requested, the enter button will light. The pen should be positioned by means of the 4 directional buttons. When the desired pen position is reached, depress the enter button. To terminate the input, hit carriage return on the terminal. The coordinates of the terminating point are not transmitted.

Character sizes may be changed to any desired value. Color can be changed to any of the values 1 to 8, indicating the pens in stables 1 to 8. Characters can be rotated to any orientation. Different line styles (1, 2,

...) are available, with patterns becoming more spread-out as the line style is larger.

Always be sure that the pen is capped when you are done with the plotter.

NOTE

The switches on the back of the device should be set to reflect the correct speed and parity settings for the computer system. Incorrect parity settings may cause failures of digitizing functions, e.g., `locator` and `identify`.

A device must be specified before any graphics functions can be used.

`identify`	Identify Points on Plot	`identify`

```
identify(x, y, labels=seq(along=x), n=length(x),
         plot=T, atpen=T, offset=.5)
```

ARGUMENTS

  `x,y` coordinates of points. The coordinates can be given by two vector arguments or by a single argument `x` which is a time-series, a complex vector, a matrix with 2 columns, or a list containing components named `x` and `y`. Missing values (NAs) are allowed.

`labels` optional vector giving labels for each of the points. If supplied, must have the same length as `x` and `y`.

    `n` maximum number of points to identify.

 `plot` if TRUE, `identify` plots the labels of the points identified. In any case, the subscripts are returned.

`atpen` if TRUE, plotted identification is relative to locator position when point is identified; otherwise, plotting is relative to the identified `x,y` value. Useful for controlling position of labels when points are crowded.

`offset` identification is plotted as a text string, moved `offset` character widths from the point. If the locator was left (right) of the nearest point, the label will be offset to the left (right) of the point.

Graphical parameters may also be supplied as arguments to this function (see `par`).

VALUE

    indices (in `x` and `y`) corresponding to identified points.

See the documentation for the specific graphics device for details on graphical input techniques.

The nearest point to locator position is identified, but must be at most 0.5 inches away. In case of ties, the earliest point is identified.

EXAMPLES

```
identify(x,y,z)     # plot z values when x,y points identified

bad ← identify(x,y,plot=FALSE)
xgood ← x[-bad]          #eliminate identified "bad" points
ygood ← y[-bad]              #from x and y
```

`if`	Conditional Expressions and Operators	`if`

```
if(test) true.expr
if(test) true.expr else false.expr

e1 || e2
e1 && e2
```

ARGUMENTS

`test,`
`e1,e2` logical expressions of length 1.

VALUE

The `if` construct in the language evaluates `test`. If it is TRUE (i.e., if the first element of the result coerced to mode `logical` is TRUE), then `true.expr` is evaluated and returned as the value of the whole expression. Otherwise, the value of the expression is `false.expr` if present, or an empty value otherwise. An NA value for the test causes an error.

`&&` returns TRUE if both of its operands are TRUE (in the same sense as `test` above). If the left operand is not TRUE, the right operand is not evaluated.

`||` returns TRUE if one of its operands is TRUE (in the same sense as `test` above). If the left operand is TRUE, the right operand is not evaluated.

SEE ALSO

> Logical for element-wise logical operations (|, &, ! and xor); ifelse for parallel selection of values; and switch for multi-branch selections.

EXAMPLES

> if(mode(x)!="character" && min(x)>0) log(x)
>   # log(x) is an error if mode(x) is "character"

| **ifelse** | Conditional Data Selection | **ifelse** |

> ifelse(cond, true, false)

ARGUMENTS

> cond logical vector.
> true vector containing values to be returned if cond is TRUE.
> false vector containing values to be returned if cond is FALSE.

VALUE

> object with the attributes of cond and data values from the values of true or false depending on cond. If true or false are not as large as cond, they will be repeated cyclically. Missing values (NAs) are allowed. NA values in cond cause NAs in the result.

EXAMPLES

> log(ifelse(x>0,x,NA))   # compare the example in if.

> The above example avoids the warning message from taking logs of negative numbers.

SEE ALSO

> if, switch.

| **Im** | see Complex | **Im** |

index	see Deprecated	**index**

integer	Integer Objects	**integer**

```
integer(length=0)
is.integer(x)
as.integer(x)
```

ARGUMENTS

> length integer giving the length of the returned object.
>
> x any S object.

VALUE

> integer returns a simple object of storage mode "integer", and the length specified.
>
> is.integer returns TRUE if x is a simple object of storage mode "integer", and FALSE otherwise.
>
> as.integer returns x if x is a simple object of storage mode "integer", and otherwise an integer object of the same length as x and with data resulting from coercing the elements of x to storage mode "integer".
>
> In most S expressions it is not necessary to explicitly ensure that data is of a particular storage mode. For example, a numeric subscript vector need not be integer; it will be coerced to integer as needed. When testing for data suitable for arithmetic, for example, it is better to use is.numeric(x), which will return TRUE for any numeric object.
>
> Note the difference between coercing to a simple object of storage mode "integer" and setting the storage mode attribute:
>
> > storage.mode(myobject) ← "integer"
>
> This changes the storage mode of myobject but leaves all other attributes unchanged (so a matrix stays a matrix, e.g.). The value of as.integer(myobject) would have no attributes.

SEE ALSO

.Fortran, .C.

EXAMPLES

z ← integer(length(zz)) # integer object same length as zz
.Fortran("mysub",as.integer(xm))

.Internal	Call Internal C Code	**.Internal**

.Internal(call, entry, evaluate=T, code=0)

ARGUMENTS

call expression for the function call corresponding to the internal code. The C routine gets both the unevaluated and (optionally) the evaluated version of the argument list in the call expression.

entry character string name for the C routine being called.

evaluate if TRUE the argument expressions are evaluated before calling the C routine.

code numeric code (one number) used to combine several functions into one internal C routine.

VALUE

The value computed and returned by the specialized C routine.

This is the interface to the built-in C code in the S executive; that is, to the C routines that understand how S objects are stored internally and how to create and modify such objects. *It is not intended that users should write such code or use* .Internal *directly.*

---

interp	Bivariate Interpolation for Irregular Data	**interp**

interp(x, y, z, xo, yo, ncp=0, extrap=FALSE)

ARGUMENTS

x x-coordinates of data points.

y y-coordinates of data points.

z   z-coordinates of data points.

xo   vector of x-coordinates of output grid. Default, 40 points evenly spaced over the range of x.

yo   vector of y-coordinates of output grid. Default, 40 points evenly spaced over the range of y.

ncp   number of additional points to be used in computing partial derivatives at each data point. If ncp is zero, linear interpolation will be used in the triangles bounded by data points. Otherwise, ncp must be 2 or greater, but smaller than the number of data points. Cubic interpolation is done if partial derivatives are used.

extrap   logical flag, should extrapolation be used outside of the convex hull determined by the data points? No extrapolation can be performed if ncp is zero.

VALUE

list with 3 components:

x   vector of x-coordinates of output grid, the same as input argument xo.

y   vector of y-coordinates of output grid, the same as input argument yo.

z   matrix of fitted z-values. The value z[i,j] is computed at the x,y point x[i],y[j].

If extrap is FALSE, z-values for points outside the convex hull are returned as NA. The resulting structure is suitable for input to the function contour. Results are currently computed to single-precision accuracy only.

REFERENCE

Hiroshi Akima, "A Method of Bivariate Interpolation and Smooth Surface Fitting for Irregularly Distributed Data Points", *ACM Transactions on Mathematical Software,* Vol 4, No 2, June 1978, pp 148-164.

EXAMPLES

```
fit ← interp(x,y,z)        #fit to irregularly spaced data
contour(fit)      #contour plot
```

INTPR   see DBLEPR   **INTPR**

---

invisible   Mark Function as Non-Printing   **invisible**

```
invisible(x=NULL)
```

ARGUMENTS

x any S object.

VALUE

x.

SIDE EFFECTS

the function `invisible` reaches back 2 frames and sets a special flag, `.Auto.print`, to FALSE. This has the effect of preventing automatic printing, if the function calling `invisible` was called from the top level. Note that, if a function wants to transmit back such information from a function *it* calls, this can be done by checking `.Auto.print`, as in the example below.

EXAMPLES

```
checking ← function(fun,...) }{
    .Auto.print ← TRUE
    val ← fun(...)
    if(.Auto.print)val
    else invisible(val)
}
```

SEE ALSO

---

is.array   see array   **is.array**

---

is.atomic   see is.recursive   **is.atomic**

---

is.call	see call	is.call

is.category	see category	is.category

is.character	see character	is.character

is.complex	see complex	is.complex

is.double	see double	is.double

is.expression	see expression	is.expression

is.function	see as.function	is.function

is.integer	see integer	is.integer

is.language	see is.recursive	**is.language**

is.list	see list	**is.list**

is.logical	see logical	**is.logical**

is.matrix	see matrix	**is.matrix**

is.na	Test For Missing Values	**is.na**

```
is.na(x)
```

ARGUMENTS

x an S object, which should be logical, numeric, or complex.

VALUE

a logical object like x, with TRUE wherever there was an NA in x and FALSE elsewhere.

EXAMPLES

```
# if function transform(y) cannot take NAs:
y.ok ← !is.na(y)
y[y.ok] ← transform(y[y.ok])
```

`is.name`	see `as.name`	`is.name`

`is.null`	see `as.null`	`is.null`

`is.numeric`	see `numeric`	`is.numeric`

`is.qr`	see `qr`	`is.qr`

`is.recursive`	Test for Recursive or Atomic Objects	`is.recursive`

```
is.atomic(x)
is.language(x)
is.recursive(x)
```

ARGUMENTS

    `x` any S object.

VALUE

    `is.atomic` returns TRUE if the mode of `x` is numeric, logical, character, or complex. For example, an object of mode list is not atomic, while a matrix of mode numeric is atomic.

    `is.language` returns TRUE if `x` is some object that is part of the language (the value of a call to parse() or an object that has one of the special modes used by the S parser such as call, if, expression).

    `is.recursive` returns TRUE if the mode of `x` indicates that `x` is a recursive object; that is, an object that can contain other objects as elements; most commonly list, but also expression, graphics, and a

number of modes used in manipulating the language. Note that
is.recursive and is.atomic are not quite complementary, but they
do not overlap. For example, objects of mode name are neither recursive
nor atomic.

| **is.single** | see single | **is.single** |

| **is.ts** | see ts | **is.ts** |

| **is.vector** | see vector | **is.vector** |

| **l1fit** | Minimum Absolute Residual (L1) Regression | **l1fit** |

```
l1fit(x, y, int=TRUE)
```

ARGUMENTS

x *X* matrix for fitting $Y = Xb + e$ with variables in columns, observations
across rows. Should not contain column of 1's (see argument int).
Number of rows of x should equal the number of data values in y.
There should be fewer columns than rows.

y numeric vector with as many observations as the number of rows of x.

int flag for intercept; if TRUE an intercept term is included in regression
model.

VALUE

list defining the regression (compare function lsfit). Results are
currently computed to single-precision accuracy only.

coef vector of coefficients with constant term if int is TRUE.

resid residuals from the fit, i.e. resid is $Y - Xb$.

REFERENCE

Barrodale and Roberts, "Solution of an Overdetermined System of Equations in the L1 Norm", *CACM,* June 1974, pp. 319-320.

`labclust`	Label a Cluster Plot	**`labclust`**

```
labclust(x, y, labels)
```

ARGUMENTS

x,y coordinates of points. The coordinates can be given by two vector arguments or by a single argument x which is a time-series, a complex vector, a matrix with 2 columns, or a list containing components named x and y. Typically, these are the coordinates of the leaves of the tree, as produced by plclust. Missing values (NAs) are allowed.

labels optional control of labels on the cluster leaves. By default, leaves are labelled with object number. If labels is a character vector, it is used to label the leaves. Otherwise it is interpreted as a logical flag (in particular, the value FALSE suppresses any labelling of leaves, as is appropriate with large trees).

Graphical parameters may also be supplied as arguments to this function (see par).

EXAMPLES

```
xy ← plclust(tree,plot=FALSE)        # save coords of tree
plclust(tree,label=FALSE)       #plot it
labclust(xy,label=names)     #now label it
```

`lag`	Create a Lagged Time-Series	**`lag`**

```
lag(x, k=1)
```

ARGUMENTS

x a time-series. Missing values (NAs) are allowed.

k the number of positions the new series is to lag the input series; negative value will lead the series.

VALUE

a time-series of the same length as x but lagged by k positions. Only the start and end dates are changed; the series still has the same number of observations.

SEE ALSO

tsmatrix for aligning the time domains of several series.

EXAMPLES

l12gnp ← lag(gnp,12) # gnp lagged by 12 months

---

lapply	Apply a Function to Elements of a List	**lapply**

```
lapply(X, FUN, ...)
```

ARGUMENTS

X a list.

FUN function (or character string giving the name of the function) to be applied to the specified array sections. The character form is necessary only for functions with unusual names, e.g., "/".

... optional, any arguments to FUN; they are passed unchanged.

VALUE

a list like X where each element of the list has been replaced by the result of executing FUN on that element.

SEE ALSO

apply applies a function to specified subsets of an array. sapply is a more complex version of applying to a list. tapply is useful for ragged arrays.

EXAMPLES

```
#apply mean function to each element of list x
lapply(x,mean)

l ← as.list(1:5)
# generate a list with elements 1, 1:2, 1:3, ...
lapply(l,seq)

#generate a list with elements 1, c(2,2), c(3,3,3), ...
lapply(l,function(x)rep(x,x))   .
```

.Last	see .First	**.Last**

leaps	All-Subset Regressions by Leaps and Bounds	**leaps**

```
leaps(x, y, wt, int=TRUE, method="Cp",
      nbest=10, names, df=nrow(x))
```

ARGUMENTS

- x   matrix of independent variables. Each column of x is a variable, each row an observation. There should be a maximum of 31 columns and fewer columns than rows.
- y   vector of dependent variable with the same number of observations as the number of rows of x.
- wt   optional vector of weights for the observations.
- int   logical flag, should an intercept term be used in the regressions?
- method   character string describing the method used to evaluate a subset. Possible values are "Cp", "r2", and "adjr2" corresponding to Mallows Cp statistic, r-square, and adjusted r-square. Only the first character need be supplied.
- nbest   integer describing the number of "best" subsets to be found for each subset size. In the case of r2 or Cp methods, the nbest subsets (of any size) are guaranteed to be included in the output (but note that more subsets will also be included).
- names   optional character vector giving names for the independent variables. Default, the names are 1, 2, ... 9, A, B, ...
- df   degrees of freedom for y. Useful if, for example, x and y have already been adjusted for previous independent variables.

VALUE

list with four components:

- Cp   the first returned component will be named "Cp", "adjr2", or "r2" depending on the method used for evaluating the subsets. This component gives the values of the desired statistic.
- size   the number of independent variables (including the constant term if int is TRUE) in each subset.
- label   a character vector, each element giving the names of the variables in the subset.
- which   logical matrix with as many rows as there are returned subsets. Each row is a logical vector that can be used to select the columns of x in the subset.

REFERENCE

George M. Furnival and Robert W. Wilson, Jr., "Regressions by Leaps and Bounds", *Technometrics,* Vol. 16, No. 4, November 1974, pp. 499-511.

EXAMPLES

```
r ← leaps(x,y)
plot(r$size,r$Cp,type="n")
text(r$size,r$Cp,r$label)     # produces Cp plot
lsfit( x[,r$which[3,]], y )    #regression corresponding
                              # to third subset
```

legend	Put a Legend on a Plot	**legend**

```
legend(x, y, legend, angle, density, fill,
       col, lty, marks, pch)
```

ARGUMENTS

x,y   coordinates of two opposite corners of the rectangular area of the plot which is to contain the legend. A structure containing x and y values may be supplied.

legend   vector of text strings to be associated with shading patterns, line types, plotting characters or marks.

angle   optional vector giving the angle (degrees, counter-clockwise from horizontal) for shading each bar division. Defaults to 45 if density is supplied.

density   optional vector for bar shading, giving the number of lines per inch for shading each bar division. Defaults to 3 if angle is supplied.

fill   optional vector of colors for filled boxes.

col   optional vector giving the colors in which the points and lines should be drawn.

lty   vector of line types.

marks   vector of plotting symbol numbers (see documentation for function lines).

pch   character string of plotting characters. Single characters from pch will be used.

Graphical parameters may also be supplied as arguments to this function (see par).

legend draws a box at specified coordinates and puts inside examples of lines, points, marks, and/or shading, each identified with a user-specified text string.

SEE ALSO

documentation for `barplot` contains a sample legend.

EXAMPLES

```
# use locator to point at upper-left corner
# of area to contain the legend -- draw colored boxes
legend(locator(1),legend=c("IBM","AT&T","GM"),fill=2:4)

# draw legend with different line styles and plotting chars
legend(0,10,names,lty=1:5,pch="O+*")
```

---

len see Deprecated **len**

---

length Length of a Vector or List **length**

```
length(x)
length(x) ← value
```

ARGUMENTS

x any object.

VALUE

an integer that gives the length of the object, i.e., the number of elements in the object. Attributes of the object are ignored; `length` operates on the data portion of the object. This may result in inconsistent data objects, since the length and other attributes may not match.

EXAMPLES

```
> z ← list(a=1,b=letters,c=1:5)
> length(z)
[1] 3
```

`levels`	Levels Attribute	`levels`

```
levels(x)
levels(x) ← value
```

ARGUMENTS
> x any object, typically a category.

VALUE
> if x has a `levels` attribute then the value of this attribute is returned; otherwise NULL. To explicitly delete the `levels` attribute, use `levels(x) ← NULL`.

`lgamma`	see gamma	`lgamma`

`library`	Shared Functions and Datasets	`library`

```
library(section, first=FALSE, help)
library.dynam(section, file)
```

ARGUMENTS
> section character string or name giving the name of a section of the library.
>
> first if TRUE, the data directory for this section is attached before the system functions and data, in position 2 of the search list; otherwise it is attached at the end of the search list.
>
> help optional character string or name of a section on which help is desired. Help for a section gives (at least) a list of objects with brief descriptions. Once a section has been attached, the `help` function can be used to get detailed documentation on particular objects in the section.
>
> file character name of a file to be dynamically loaded.

If no arguments are given to `library`, a brief description of each available section is printed.

`library.dynam` is meant to be used by functions that are part of a library section to dynamically load object code. If the corresponding object code has not been loaded in this session, it constructs the correct path name for the code and calls `dyn.load`. Using `library.dynam` in functions in the library ensures that code is not loaded unnecessarily.

When S is shipped, the library always contains sections named `examples` and `semantics`. These correspond to many of the example functions used in the S book (see the index under `examples`). To try one of the functions given in this book that is not a standard part of S, do `library(examples)` and look for it there.

The functions and data objects accessed by `library` are often user-contributed and are not an official part of S. They should be used with caution.

A library section corresponds to a directory inside the `library` subdirectory of the S home directory. For example, if the S home directory is `/usr/s`, then the `examples` section corresponds to directory `/usr/s/library/examples`. Within each section, there must be a `.Data` directory with a `.Help` subdirectory containing, respectively, the objects and their documentation. There must be also a file named `README` that gives the overall description of the section. If there are C or Fortran routines whose object code is to be dynamically loaded by functions in the section, their source code and object files should also reside in the section directory. Any dynamic loading should be carried out through the `library.dynam` function. When source code is present, there should also be a `makefile` that makes the required object files. The library-level `README` file (`/usr/s/library/README`) contains the one-line descriptions of the sections of the library, and should be updated whenever a new section is added to the library. Library sections may be symbolic links to user-owned portions of the file system.

SIDE EFFECTS

These functions are used for their side effects: `library` prints documentation or attaches a data directory. The `library.dynam` function ensures that object code has been dynamically loaded. Objects `lib.loc` and `section.file` are created in frame 0.

SEE ALSO

`attach, dyn.load, help.`

EXAMPLES

```
library()      # print list of sections
library(help="examples")    # documentation on examples section
library(examples)   # attach examples data directory
```

library.dynam	see library	**library.dynam**

lines	Add Lines or Points to Current Plot	**lines**

```
lines(x, y, type="l")
points(x, y, type="p")
```

ARGUMENTS

x,y coordinates of points. The coordinates can be given by two vector arguments or by a single argument x which is a time-series, a complex vector, a matrix with 2 columns, or a list containing components named x and y. Missing values (NAs) are allowed.

type= values of "p", "l", "b", "o", "n", and "h" produce points, lines, both, both (overlaid), nothing, and high-density lines.

Graphical parameters may also be supplied as arguments to this function (see par). The graphical parameter pch= can be used to plot special symbols at the points. Basic marks are: square (0); octagon (1); triangle (2); cross (3); X (4); diamond (5) and inverted triangle (6). To get superimposed versions of the above use the following arithmetic(!): 7==0+4; 8==3+4; 9==3+5; 10==1+3; 11==2+6; 12==0+3; 13==1+4; 14==0+2. Filled marks are square (15), octagon (16), triangle (17), and diamond (18).

Data values with an NA in either x or y are not plotted by points. Also, lines does not draw to or from any such point, thus giving a break in the line segments.

If a log scale is currently in effect for either the x- or y-axis, points and lines will plot the corresponding values on a log scale.

SEE ALSO

segments, arrows, and symbols.

EXAMPLES

```
par(usr=c(-1,19,0,1))        # produce a plot of all the marks
for(i in 0:18) {
        points(i, .5, pch=i); text(i, .35, i) }
text(9, .75, 'Samples of "pch=" Parameter')
```

Samples of "pch=" Parameter

0	1	2	3	4	5	6	7	8	9	10	11	12	13	14	15	16	17	18

`list`	List Objects	`list`

```
list(...)
is.list(x)
as.list(x)
```

ARGUMENTS

> ... any arguments, with any names.
>
> x any S object.

VALUE

> `list` returns an object of mode list, with as many elements as there are arguments. The individual arguments become the elements of the list, and the argument names, if any, are the corresponding elements of the names attribute of the list.
>
> `is.list` returns TRUE if x is a simple object of mode list, and FALSE otherwise.
>
> `as.list` returns x if x is a simple object of mode list, and otherwise a list object of the same length as x. If x is an atomic object, the elements of the list will be objects of length 1, containing the individual elements of x. If x is a recursive object, its elements will be unchanged.

NOTE

> The constructor function for lists is different from those for atomic modes, which take the desired length as an argument. To generate a list of length 10, when you don't initially know what the elements should be:

```
vector("list", 10)
```

Lists are simple objects (see `vector`) when they have no attributes, other than `names`. It is possible, for example, to have a matrix, array or time-series of mode list.

EXAMPLES

```
list(original = x, square = x^2)
as.list(1:10)  # ten integer elements
```

LOAD	Create a Private Version of S	LOAD

```
S LOAD files ...
```

ARGUMENTS

`files`   names of source files that should be compiled and loaded into a private version of S. Loading these source files into a running copy of S means that the routines contained in `files` can be called by means of `.Fortran` and `.C` without dynamically loading.

The `LOAD` utility is of primary use for large collections of private routines that are loaded with S and for machines on which the `dyn.load` function does not operate.

SEE ALSO

`dyn.load`.

WARNING

A private version of S can occupy several megabytes of disk storage.

---

locator	Get Coordinates from Plot	**locator**

```
locator(n=500, type="n")
```

ARGUMENTS

n the maximum number of points to identify.

type character describing interactive drawing option. If type is "n", nothing is drawn. Values of "p", "l", "b", and "o" plot points at the digitized coordinates, lines connecting them, both points and lines, or overplotted points and lines.

VALUE

list containing vector components x and y which give coordinates for each point. The length of these vectors is at most n, but can be shorter if the user terminates graphic input after fewer than n points are given.

See the individual device documentation for the protocol on the device for identifying points and terminating graphic input.

EXAMPLES

```
# user points at outlier which is then labelled
text(locator(1),"outlier")

lines(locator( ))       # input a number of points, connect with line
locator(type="l")       # alternative
```

---

log	see exp	**log**

---

log10	see exp	**log10**

Logic	Logical Operators	**Logic**

```
e1 & e2
e1 | e2
! e1
xor(e1, e2)
```

ARGUMENTS
  e1,e2 logical vectors. Missing values (NAs) are allowed.

VALUE

logical result of and-ing, or-ing, negation or exclusive or-ing. For all but negation, the result is as long as the longer of the operands. Corresponding to NAs in the operands will be either a logical value or an NA, depending on whether the other operand uniquely determines the answer; for example, NA|TRUE must be TRUE, and NA&FALSE must be FALSE.

See section 5.1.5 for the rules for dealing with operands with attributes.

SEE ALSO

if for the || and && operators: sequential evaluation of expressions.

EXAMPLES

```
x[a>13 & b<2]       #elements of x corresp. to a>13 and b<2

a ← c(T,F,NA)
outer(a,a,"&")     # logic table for &
```

logical	Logical Objects	**logical**

```
logical(length=0)
is.logical(x)
as.logical(x)
```

ARGUMENTS
  length desired length for the resulting object.
       x any S object.

VALUE

logical returns a simple object of mode "logical", and the length specified.

is.logical returns TRUE if x is a simple object of mode "logical", and FALSE otherwise.

as.logical returns x if x is a simple object of mode "logical", and otherwise a logical object of the same length as x and with data resulting from coercing the elements of x to mode "logical".

Simple objects have no attributes. Logical objects will be coerced automatically to numeric for arithmetic and other numeric computations. In the coercion, TRUE becomes 1 and FALSE becomes 0. Conversely, numeric objects will be coerced to logical by setting all non-zero values to TRUE. Note that there is no allowance for rounding error in doing this, so it is not a good practice, except for computations known to have integer results.

Note the difference between coercing to a simple object of mode "logical" and setting the mode attribute:

```
mode(myobject) ← "logical"
```

This changes the mode of myobject but leaves all other attributes unchanged (so a matrix stays a matrix, e.g.). The value of as.logical(myobject) would have no attributes. Similarly, is.logical would return FALSE for a matrix of logical data.

EXAMPLES

```
logical(length(zz))  # logical object same length as zz
.Fortran("mysub",as.logical(xm))
```

Logistic	Logistic Distribution	**Logistic**

```
dlogis(q, location=0, scale=1)
plogis(q, location=0, scale=1)
qlogis(p, location=0, scale=1)
rlogis(n, location=0, scale=1)
```

ARGUMENTS

q vector of quantiles. Missing values (NAs) are allowed.

p vector of probabilities. Missing values (NAs) are allowed.

n sample size. If `length(n)` is larger than 1, then `length(n)` random values are returned.

location vector of location parameters.

scale vector of scale parameters.

VALUE

density (`dlogis`), probability (`plogis`), quantile (`qlogis`), or random sample (`rlogis`) for the logistic distribution with parameters `location` and `scale`. Results are currently computed to single-precision accuracy only. The density function is given by

$$f_{l,s}(q) = \frac{\exp\{-(q-l)/s\}}{s(1 + \exp\{-(q-l)/s\})^2}, \quad s > 0,$$

where *l* and *s* are the `location` and `scale` parameters.

SIDE EFFECTS

The function `rlogis` causes creation of the dataset `.Random.seed` if it does not already exist, otherwise its value is updated.

---

loglin	Contingency Table Analysis	**loglin**

```
loglin(table, margin, start, eps=.1,
       iter=20, print=TRUE)
```

ARGUMENTS

table contingency table (array) to be fit by log-linear model. Table values must be non-negative.

margins vector describing the marginal totals to be fit. A margin is described by the factors not summed over, and margins are separated by zeroes. Thus c(1,2,0,3,4) would indicate fitting the 1,2 margin (summing over variables 3 and 4) and the 3,4 margin in a four-way table.

start starting estimate for fitted table. If start is omitted, a start is used that will assure convergence. If structural zeroes appear in table, start should contain zeroes in corresponding entries, ones in other places. This assures that the fit will contain those zeroes.

eps maximum permissible deviation between observed and fitted margins.

iter maximum number of iterations.

print flag; if TRUE, the final deviation and number of iterations will be printed.

VALUE

array like table, but containing fitted values. Results are currently computed to single-precision accuracy only.

REFERENCE

S. J. Haberman, "Log-linear Fit for Contingency Tables—Algorithm AS51," *Applied Statistics,* Vol. 21, No. 2, pp. 218-225, 1972.

Lognormal	Lognormal Distribution	**Lognormal**

```
dlnorm(q, meanlog=0, sdlog=1)
plnorm(q, meanlog=0, sdlog=1)
qlnorm(p, meanlog=0, sdlog=1)
rlnorm(n, meanlog=0, sdlog=1)
```

ARGUMENTS

q vector of (positive) quantiles. Missing values (NAs) are allowed.

p vector of probabilities. Missing values (NAs) are allowed.

n sample size. If length(n) is larger than 1, then length(n) random values are returned.

meanlog

sdlog vectors of means and standard deviations of the distribution of the log of the random variable. Thus, exp(meanlog) is a scale parameter and sdlog is a shape parameter for the lognormal distribution.

VALUE

density (dlnorm), probability (plnorm), quantile (qlnorm), or random sample (rlnorm) for the log-normal distribution with parameters meanlog and sdlog. Results are currently computed to single-precision accuracy only. The density function is given by

$$f_{m,s}(q) = \frac{1}{\sqrt{2\pi}\,sq}\exp\{-\frac{1}{2s^2}(\log(q) - m)^2\}, \quad q > 0, \; s > 0,$$

where *m* and *s* are the `meanlog` and `sdlog` parameters.

SIDE EFFECTS

The function `rlnorm` causes creation of the dataset `.Random.seed` if it does not already exist, otherwise its value is updated.

EXAMPLES

```
log(rlnorm(50))  #hard way to generate a sample of normals
```

logo	Draw the S Logo	**logo**

```
logo(x, y, size=2.5)
```

ARGUMENTS

`x,y` optional coordinates for the center of the logo. By default, plotted in lower right of figure.

`size` optional size of logo relative to the height of a character.

Graphical parameters may also be supplied as arguments to this function (see `par`).

EXAMPLES

```
logo()
```

lowess	Scatter Plot Smoothing	**lowess**

```
lowess(x, y, f=2/3, iter=3, delta)
```

ARGUMENTS

`x,y` vectors of data for a scatter plot.

`f` fraction of data used for smoothing at each `x` point. The larger the `f` value, the smoother the fit.

     `iter` number of iterations used in computing robust estimates.

    `delta` interval size (in units corresponding to `x`). If `lowess` estimates at two `x` values within `delta` of one another, it fits any points between them by linear interpolation. Default 1% of the range of `x`. If `delta=0` all but identical `x` values are estimated independently.

VALUE

list containing components named `x` and `y` which are the x,y points of the smoothed scatter plot. Note that `x` is a sorted version of the input `x` vector, with duplicate points removed.

This function may be slow for large numbers of points; execution time is proportional to (`iter*f*n^2`). Increasing `delta` should speed things up, as will decreasing `f`.

REFERENCE

W. S. Cleveland, "Robust Locally Weighted Regression and Smoothing Scatterplots", *JASA*, Vol. 74, No. 368, pp. 829-836, December 1979.

EXAMPLES

```
plot(x,y)
lines( lowess( x,y ) )      #scatter plot with smooth

fit ← lowess(x,y)
resid ← y-approx(fit,x)$y #residual from smooth
```

`ls`	List of Datasets in Data Directory	`ls`

```
ls(pattern, pos=1)
```

ARGUMENTS

  `pattern` an optional character string describing the object names of interest. The syntax for `pattern` is that of the `ls` shell command. For example, `ls("abc")` matches the name of the object `abc`. The character "*" occurring in `pattern` matches any number (including zero) of characters. `ls("abc*")` returns the names of any objects whose names began with `abc`. The default pattern is "*", which matches all object names. The character "?" occurring in `pattern` matches any single character. A pattern consisting of characters between square brackets matches any one of the enclosed characters; a pair of characters separated by a "−" matches any character between the pair, in the ASCII ordering of characters.

    pos the position on the data directory search list of the data directory to be searched. Position 1 is the working directory. Normally, positions 2 and 3 are the function and system data directories. Position 0 refers to assignments to the session frame (see `assign`).

VALUE

a character vector containing the names of the objects that match the pattern on the specified data directory.

EXAMPLES

```
ls()        #list all working object names
ls("lottery*",pos=3)    #system database names
        # beginning in "lottery"
ls("???")   # 3-character object names
ls("[A-Z]*")   # starts with upper case letter
ls(".*")       # starts with "."
```

---

lsfit	Linear Least-Squares Fit	**lsfit**

```
lsfit(x, y, wt, intercept=T, tolerance=1.e-07,
      yname=NULL)
```

ARGUMENTS

    x X matrix for fitting $Y = Xb + e$ with variables in columns, observations across rows. Should not contain column of 1's, (see argument `intercept`). Number of rows of `x` should equal the number of rows of `y`. There should be fewer columns than rows.

    y y vector (or matrix with one column for each regression).

    wt vector of weights for weighted regression. Should have length equal to the number of rows of `y`. If the different observations have non-equal variances, `wt` should be inversely proportional to the variance. By default, an unweighted regression is carried out.

intercept if `TRUE` a constant (intercept) term is included in each regression.

tolerance numerical value used to test for singularity in the regression.

    yname optional name to be used for the `y` variate in the regression output. However, in the case that `y` is a matrix, its `dimnames` attribute should have the desired (column) names.

VALUE

a list representing the result of the regression, with the following components:

       `coef` matrix of coefficients with one column for each regression and (optional) constant terms in first row.

 `residuals` object like `y` containing residuals.

         `qr` object representing the numerical decomposition of the `x` matrix (plus a column of `1`s, if an intercept was included). If `wt` was specified, the `qr` object will represent the decomposition of the weighted `x` matrix. See function `qr` for the details of this object. It is used primarily with functions like `qr.qty`, that compute auxiliary results for the regression from the decomposition.

`intercept` records whether an intercept was used in this regression.

EXAMPLES

        `lsfit(cbind(a,b,c),y)`   `#regress y on a, b, and c with intercept`

---

ls.keep	Currently Hashed Functions	**ls.keep**

        `ls.keep()`

VALUE

        sorted character vector giving the names of all the functions and other S objects that are currently hashed internally for quick execution.

---

ls.summary	Summary Information from 'lsfit' Object	**ls.summary**

        `ls.summary(ls.out)`

ARGUMENTS

    `ls.out` output from `lsfit`

VALUE

        an object with components:

     `std.dev` residual standard deviation

         `hat` diagonal of the `hat-matrix` (see the `hat` function)

     `std.res` standardized residuals

`correlation` correlation matrix for the parameter estimates

     `std.err` standard errors of the parameter estimates

`match`	Match Items in Vector	`match`

```
match(x, table, nomatch=NA)
```

ARGUMENTS

    x vector of items that are to be looked for in `table`.

  table the possible values in `x`.

nomatch the value to be returned when an item in `x` does not match any item in `table`. A useful alternative to NA is `nomatch=0`, which has the effect that unmatched items are ignored when the matched indices are used in subscripts (see the last example below).

VALUE

    vector like `x` giving, for each element of `x`, the position in `table` of the first `table[i]` equal to that element.

SEE ALSO

    `amatch`.

EXAMPLES

```
match(data,primes)
state.abb[match(names,state.name)]   #change names to abbrevs
names[match(allnames,names,0)]   #those names also found in allnames
```

`matlines`	see `matplot`	`matlines`

`matplot`	Plot Columns of Matrices	`matplot`

```
matplot(x, y, type="p", lty=1:5, pch=, col=1:4)
matpoints(x, y, type="p", lty=1:5, pch=, col=1:4)
matlines(x, y, type="l", lty=1:5, pch=, col=1:4)
```

ARGUMENTS

  x,y vectors or matrices of data for plotting. The first column of `x` is plotted against the first column of `y`, the second column of `x` against the second column of y, etc. If one matrix has fewer columns, plotting will cycle back through the columns again. (In particular, either x or y may be a vector, against which all columns of the other argument will be plotted.) Missing values (NAs) are allowed.

type= an optional character string, telling which type of plot (points, lines, both, none or high-density) should be done for each plot. The first character of type defines the first plot, the second character the second, etc. Elements of type are cycled through; e.g., "pl" alternately plots points and lines.

lty= optional vector of line types. The first element is the hardware line type for the first line, etc. Line types will be used cyclically until all plots are drawn.

pch= optional character vector for plotting-characters (only the first element is used). The first character is the plotting-character for the first plot, the second for the second, etc. Default is the digits (1 through 9, 0) then the letters.

col= optional vector of colors. Colors are used cyclically.

Graphical parameters may also be supplied as arguments to this function (see par). Also, the arguments to the title function may be supplied to this function.

Function matplot generates a new plot; matpoints and matlines add to the current plot.

EXAMPLES

```
matplot(x,y,type="pl")  #points for 1st col, lines for 2nd
matpoints(x,y,pch="*")  # points with "*" for all plots
# the example plot is produced by:
matplot(iris[,3,],iris[,4,],xlab="Petal Length",
ylab="Petal Width",
sub="1=Setosa, 2=Versicolor, 3=Virginica",
main="Fisher's Iris Data", col=1)
```

Fisher's Iris Data

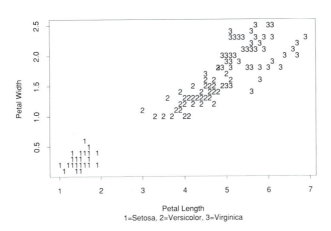

Petal Length
1=Setosa, 2=Versicolor, 3=Virginica

---

matpoints   see `matplot`   **matpoints**

---

matrix   Matrix Objects   **matrix**

```
matrix(data=NA, nrow, ncol, byrow=FALSE, dimnames)
is.matrix(x)
as.matrix(x)
```

ARGUMENTS

    `data`   vector containing the data values for the matrix in normal array order: the first subscript varies most rapidly. Missing values (NAs) are allowed.

    `nrow`   first subscript, number of rows.

    `ncol`   second subscript, number of columns

    `byrow`   flag, if TRUE the data values are assumed to be the first row, then the second row, etc. If FALSE the values are assumed to be the first column, then the second column, etc. (this is how the data is stored internally). Should be TRUE if the data values were read from a file, arranged by rows. If one of `nrow` or `ncol` is omitted, the dimensions of the matrix are determined by the other argument and the length of `data`.

dimnames   an optional list of length 2 giving a dimnames attribute for the matrix.

     x   any S object.

VALUE

an nrow by ncol matrix with the same mode as data. If the data does not fill the matrix, it is repeated until the matrix is filled.

is.matrix returns TRUE if x is a matrix object, FALSE otherwise.

as.matrix returns x, if x is a matrix; otherwise, a matrix with data from x and dimension c(length(x),1).

The matrix class of objects are those that have an attribute dim of length 2. The objects may also have an attribute dimnames. If so, this is a list of 2 character vectors, each of which is either of length zero or else gives the labels corresponding to the levels of the corresponding subscript in the matrix.

SEE ALSO

array.

EXAMPLES

m ← matrix(0,4,5)   #a 4 by 5 matrix of zeros

mm ← matrix(scan("mfile"), ncol=5, byrow=TRUE)
                           #read all rows from the file

Matrix-product   Matrix Multiplication Operator   **Matrix-product**

mat1 %*% mat2

ARGUMENTS

mati   matrix or vector.

VALUE

matrix product of mat1 and mat2.

The last extent of mat1 must be the same size as the first extent of mat2. Vectors are not oriented, therefore a vector of length n can multiply an n by n matrix on the left or right.

max	Extremes	**max**

```
max(...)
min(...)
```

ARGUMENTS
> ... any number of numeric arguments.

VALUE
> the single maximum or minimum value found in any of the args; any NAs in the data produce NA as a result.

SEE ALSO
> pmax and pmin for generating a vector of parallel extremes, and range for computing both max and min.

mean	Mean (Arithmetic Average) Value	**mean**

```
mean(x, trim=0)
```

ARGUMENTS
> x numeric. Missing values (NAs) are allowed.
> trim fraction of values to be trimmed off each end of the ordered data.

VALUE
> mean of x. If x contains any NAs, the result will be NA. If trim is nonzero, the computation is performed to single precision accuracy.

EXAMPLES
```
mean(scores)       # Computes the average
```

`median`	Median	`median`

```
median(x)
```

ARGUMENTS

    x numeric object. Missing values (NAs) are allowed.

VALUE

    median of data. If x contains any NAs, the result will be NA.

`medit`	see `Defunct`	`medit`

`menu`	Menu Interaction Function	`menu`

```
menu(choices, graphics=T)
```

ARGUMENTS

  choices character vector giving the menu choices to be presented to the user.

  graphics if TRUE, a graphics menu (for example, a pop-up menu) will be used if the current graphics device supports one.

    For non-graphics menus, the user must respond with either 0 or a number between 1 and `length(choices)`.

VALUE

    the number corresponding to the selected item. If no selection is made, 0 is returned.

EXAMPLES

```
items ← c("List Objects", "quit")
switch(menu(items)+1, cat("No Action\n"), ls(), q())
```

message	see Deprecated	**message**

min	see max	**min**

missing	Check for missing arguments	**missing**

```
missing(name)
```

ARGUMENTS

name the name of one of the arguments to the function from which the call to missing occurs.

VALUE

TRUE if the current call did not supply the argument named, FALSE if it did. It is an error if the argument to missing is not a name or not the name of an argument. Note that missing allows arguments to be omitted even though no default value is supplied (provided that some appropriate action is taken before the value of the argument is needed).

EXAMPLES

```
if(!missing(weight))y ← y * sqrt(weight)
```

Mod	see Complex	**Mod**

mode	Data Mode of the Values in a Vector	**mode**

```
mode(x)
mode(x) ← value

storage.mode(x)
storage.mode(x) ← value
```

ARGUMENTS

x any object. Missing values (NAs) are allowed.

VALUE

the mode of x, for example "null", "logical", "numeric", "list", or any of a number of modes used by the language.

storage.mode is relevant *only* when calling .Fortran or .C with numeric data. When mode(x) is "numeric", the data of x may be stored as integers, or as single-precision or double-precision floating point numbers: storage.mode(x) will be "integer", "single" or "double" correspondingly.

SIDE EFFECTS

When used on the left of an assignment, the mode of the object is changed to value, interpreted as a character string. Attributes of x are unchanged.

This function has nothing to do with the statistical concept of the mode of a distribution.

monthplot	Seasonal Subseries Plot	**monthplot**

```
monthplot(y, labels, prediction=1)
```

ARGUMENTS

y a time-series, typically the seasonal component of a seasonal adjustment procedure such as sabl. The series y is broken into frequency(y) subseries, e.g., the January subseries, the February subseries, *etc.* The plot shows variation about the midmean (25% trimmed mean) of each subseries.

labels   optional vector of labels for each subseries. Default values are: (1) month
names if frequency(y) is 12; (2) quarter number, if frequency(y) is
4; (3) digits from 1 to frequency(y), for all other cases.

prediction number of years at the end of the series which are predictions. These are
drawn as dotted lines (graphical parameter lty=2).

Graphical parameters may also be supplied as arguments to this function
(see par).

REFERENCE

William S. Cleveland and Irma J. Terpenning, "Graphical Methods for
Seasonal Adjustment", *Journal of the American Statistical Association*,
Vol. 77, No. 377, pp. 52-62, 1982.

EXAMPLES

```
fit ← sabl(ship)
monthplot(fit$seasonal,
      main="Seasonal Component of Manufacturing Shipments")
```

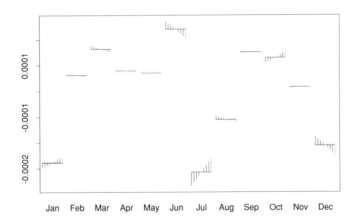

Seasonal Component of Manufacturing Shipments

| mstr | see Deprecated | mstr |

mstree	Minimal Spanning Tree and Multivariate Planing	**mstree**

```
mstree(x, plane=TRUE)
```

ARGUMENTS

   x   matrix of data where rows correspond to observations, columns to variables. Should be scaled so that values on all variables are roughly comparable (the algorithm computes Euclidean distances from one observation to another).

plane   logical, should multivariate planing and lining information be returned? If TRUE, all components listed below are returned; if FALSE, only the minimum spanning tree mst is returned.

VALUE

   list with components named x, y, mst, and order, describing the planing, minimal spanning tree, and two versions of lining. If plane is FALSE, only the mst vector is returned.

x,y   coordinates of the observations computed by the Friedman-Rafsky algorithm. Results are currently computed to single-precision accuracy only.

mst   vector of length nrow(x)-1 describing the edges in the minimal spanning tree. The ith value in this vector is an observation number, indicating that this observation and the ith observation should be linked in the minimal spanning tree.

order   matrix, nrow(x) by 2, giving two types of ordering: The first column presents the standard ordering from one extreme of the MST to the other. The second column presents the radial ordering, based on distance from the center of the MST.

REFERENCE

   J. H. Friedman and L. C. Rafsky, "Graphics for the Multivariate Two-Sample Problem", *J. Amer. Stat. Assoc.*, Vol. 76 (1981), pp. 277-287.

EXAMPLES

```
plot(x,y)     # plot original data
mst ← mstree(cbind(x,y),plane=F)      # minimal spanning tree
   # show tree on plot
segments(x[seq(mst)],y[seq(mst)],x[mst],y[mst])

i ← rbind(iris[,,1],iris[,,2],iris[,,3])
tree ← mstree(i)       # multivariate planing
plot(tree,type="n")    # plot data in plane
text(tree)             # identify points
```

---

mtext	Text in the Margins of a Plot	**mtext**

```
mtext(text, side, line, outer=FALSE, at)
```

ARGUMENTS
>   text character vector to be plotted.
>
>   side side (1,2,3,4 for bottom, left, top, or right).
>
>   line line (measured out from the plot in units of standard-sized character heights). By default, characters can be placed at values of line less than or equal to 4 on the bottom, 3 on left and top, and 1 on the right.
>
>   outer logical flag, should plotting be done in outer margin?
>
>   at optional vector of positions at which text is to be plotted. If side is 1 or 3, at will represent x-coordinates. If side is 2 or 4, at will represent y-coordinates. at can be used for constructing specialized axis labels, etc.

---

mulbar	Multiple Bar Plot	**mulbar**

```
mulbar(width, height, rowlab, collab, gap=.1)
```

ARGUMENTS
>   width matrix of bar widths. All values must be positive.
>
>   height matrix of bar heights. Values may be negative. width and height must have the same number of rows and columns.
>
>   rowlab optional character vector for row labels.
>
>   collab optional character vector for column labels.
>
>   gap fraction of plot used for gap between rows and columns.

>   Graphical parameters may also be supplied as arguments to this function (see par).

EXAMPLES

```
counts ← telsam.response[1:5,]
fit ← loglin(counts,c(1,0,2))   # fit independence model
resid ← counts - fit
par(mar=c(7,4.1,4.1,2))
mulbar(
        sqrt(fit),
        resid/sqrt(fit),
        collab=telsam.collab,
```

```
            rowlab=encode(telsam.rowlab[1:5]),
            ylab="Interviewer",
            main="Chi-Plot for Fit to Interviewer Data"
            )
    mtext(side=1,line=3,
      "Height prop. to Signed Contribution to Chi Statistic")
    mtext(side=1,line=4,
      "Width proportional to Root-Fitted Value")
    mtext(side=1,line=5,"Area proportional to Fitted Value")
```

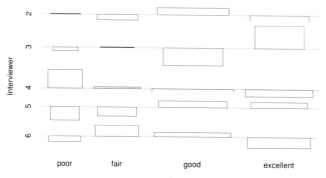

Chi-Plot for Fit to Interviewer Data

Height proportional to Signed Contribution to Chi Statistic
Width proportional to Root-Fitted Value
Area proportional to Fitted Value

na	see Deprecated	na

names	Names Attribute of an Object	names

```
    names(x)
    names(x) ← value
```

ARGUMENTS

    x any object.

VALUE

if `x` has a `names` attribute then this attribute is returned; otherwise `NULL`. The `names` attribute is used for subset and element selection; see `sub-set`. It is a character vector of the same length as `x`. To explicitly delete the `names` attribute, use `names(x)` ← `NULL`.

SIDE EFFECTS

On the left side of an assignment, sets the `names` attribute of `x` to `value`, which must have the same length length as `x`.

EXAMPLES

```
x.name ← x[names(x)!=""]
        # find the elements of x with non-null names
```

---

napsack   Solve Knapsack Problems   **napsack**

```
napsack(x, target, best=10)
```

ARGUMENTS

`x`   vector of generators for knapsack problem. The function attempts to find subsets of `x` whose sums are equal (or close to) `target`.

`target`   scalar target value.

`best`   the desired number of solutions (or approximate solutions) to the problem.

VALUE

matrix of logical values, of size `length(x)` by `best`. Each column tells which elements of `x` are contained in one of the `best` subsets. Thus, a column of the result can be used to subscript `x` to obtain a subset.

The knapsack problem is NP-complete, and the algorithm is exponential in time and space complexity. If `n` is the length of `x`, then the algorithm requires time $O(2^{(n/2)})$ and space $O(2^{(n/4)})$. Problems with `n<30` can be readily solved by this function. Remember that both time and space requirements increase very rapidly with problem size!

The solutions produced may not include all subsets that can generate solutions with a certain error. It is guaranteed to produce an exact solution if one is possible, but may not find all of a number of exact solutions. Results are currently computed to single-precision accuracy only.

REFERENCE

> Richard Schroeppel and Adi Shamir, "A T*S^2 = O(2^n) Time/Space
> Tradeoff for Certain NP-Complete Problems", *Twentieth Symposium in*
> *Foundations of Computer Science*, October 1979.

EXAMPLES

```
# given areas of counties of Nevada, find subsets of the
# counties with approximately 1/2 the total state area
subsets ← napsack(nevada,sum(nevada)/2)
crossprod(subsets, nevada)    # areas of the subsets
```

---

nargs	Number of Arguments to Function	**nargs**

```
nargs()
```

VALUE

> the number of actual arguments in the call to the function the called
> `nargs`.

EXAMPLES

---

nchar	Lengths of Character Strings	**nchar**

```
nchar(x)
```

ARGUMENTS

> x any S object.

VALUE

> a numeric vector the same length as x, containing the number of charac-
> ters in each of the elements of x. Note that x will be coerced to charac-
> ter, regardless of what it currently contains. Something will always hap-
> pen, but in the case of non-atomic data, the result may be somewhat
> surprising.

EXAMPLES

```
maxwid ← max(nchar(labels))  #max field needed
```

ncol	Extents of a Matrix	**ncol**

```
ncol(x)
nrow(x)
```

ARGUMENTS

x matrix. Missing values (NAs) are allowed.

VALUE

the number of rows or columns in x.

ncomp	see Deprecated	**ncomp**

next	see Syntax	**next**

Normal	Normal Distribution	**Normal**

```
dnorm(q, mean=0, sd=1)
pnorm(q, mean=0, sd=1)
qnorm(p, mean=0, sd=1)
rnorm(n, mean=0, sd=1)
```

ARGUMENTS

q vector of quantiles. Missing values (NAs) are allowed.

p vector of probabilities. Missing values (NAs) are allowed.

n sample size. If length(n) is larger than 1, then length(n) random values are returned.

mean vector of means.

sd vector of (positive) standard deviations.

VALUE

density (dnorm), probability (pnorm), quantile (qnorm), or random sample (rnorm) for the normal distribution with mean and standard deviation parameters mean and sd. Results are currently computed to single-precision accuracy only. The density function is given by

$$f_{m,s}(q) = \frac{1}{\sqrt{2\pi}\,s}\exp\{-\frac{1}{2s^2}(q-m)^2\}, \quad s > 0,$$

where m and s are the mean and sd parameters.

SIDE EFFECTS

The function rnorm causes creation of the dataset .Random.seed if it does not already exist, otherwise its value is updated.

EXAMPLES

rnorm(20,0,10) #sample of 20, mean 0, standard dev. 10

nper	see Deprecated	nper

nrow	see ncol	nrow

numeric	Numeric Objects	numeric

```
numeric(length=0)
is.numeric(x)
as.numeric(x)
```

ARGUMENTS

length integer giving the length of the returned object.
    x any S object.

VALUE

numeric returns a simple object of mode "numeric", and the length specified.

is.numeric returns TRUE if x is a simple object of mode "numeric", and FALSE otherwise.

as.numeric returns x if x is a simple object of mode "numeric", and otherwise a numeric object of the same length as x and with data resulting from coercing the elements of x to mode "numeric".

When x is of mode "numeric", the data of x may be stored as integers, or single or double precision floating point numbers and storage.mode(x) will be "integer", "single", or "double". Normally, all numeric constants that appear in expressions are read with mode numeric and storage mode double. This distinction is only relevant when using the interface to languages like C or Fortran.

The class of simple objects have no attributes. In most S expressions it is not necessary to explicitly ensure that data is of a particular mode.

Note the difference between coercing to a simple object of mode "numeric" and setting the mode attribute:

```
mode(myobject) ← "numeric"
```

This changes the mode of myobject but leaves all other attributes unchanged (so a matrix stays a matrix, e.g.). The value of as.numeric(myobject) would have no attributes. Similarly, is.numeric would return FALSE for a matrix of numeric data.

SEE ALSO

storage.mode, .Fortran.

EXAMPLES

```
z ← numeric(length(zz))  # double object same length as zz
.Fortran("mydsub",as.double(xm))
```

odometer   Multi-radix Counter   odometer

```
odometer(current, radix)
```

ARGUMENTS

current integer vector; the current value of the counter.

  radix integer vector; the values at which each "wheel" of the odometer "turns over".

On the first call to `odometer`, `current` should be all zeroes. `odometer` will return all zeroes when it has completed its cycle.

VALUE

the next value of the counter. The counter is a vector of integers; the ith element is always non-negative and less than `radix[i]`. The first element of `current` is incremented; if it reaches `radix[1]` it is reset to zero and the second element of `current` is incremented, and so on.

EXAMPLES

```
# a function that returns the next second
# in hours, minutes, seconds
next.second ← function(current.time)
        odometer(current.time, c(60, 60, 24))
```

on.exit   Exit Expression For a Function   on.exit

```
on.exit(expr)
```

ARGUMENTS

  expr S expression. If `expr` is omitted, the exit action is cancelled.

EFFECT

The *unevaluated* expression is stored away with the frame of the caller of `on.exit`. Just before this frame exits, exits (either an ordinary return or on an error or interrupt), `expr` will be evaluated in the frame. The expression is *not* evaluated at the time of the call to `on.exit`.

`on.exit` can be used, for example, to get rid of a temporary file created by the enclosing function—see the first example below. To use `on.exit` solely to trap errors, that is, not for normal return from the frame, call `on.exit(expression)` initially and then `on.exit()` just prior to returning from the function.

EXAMPLES

```
# Notice how on.exit is used to remove the temp file
foo← function(...){
        file ← tempfile("foo")
        on.exit(unlink(file))
        # now work with the temporary file
        # knowing that it will be removed when
        # the function exits
}

# Execute the expression only on error conditions
bar ← function(...){
        on.exit(cat("An error occurred\n"))
        # do the work
        on.exit()       # no more errors possible
        x       # return x as value of function
}
```

option	see Deprecated	**option**

options	Set or Print Options	**options**

`options(...)`

ARGUMENTS

`...` to set options, provide arguments in the `name=value` form. Options corresponding to these names will be set and remembered for the rest of the session, or until another call to `options` resets them. For example,

`options(digits=3, check=T)`

sets the `digits` option to `3` and the `check` option to TRUE. A list of the previous values of these options is returned. In the example, it would be a list of length 2, with components `digits` and `check`. This list can be used in a subsequent call to reset the options.

If an unnamed character vector is given as the only argument, a list will be returned, whose components contain the current values of the options named by the character vector. If no argument is given, options returns the entire current options list.

If an unnamed object of mode list is given as the only argument, its components will be copied in as the values for options with the corresponding names. This is what makes the resetting of options work as described above.

While any option names can be used, the following have special meaning.

echo   if TRUE, each complete expression will be echoed before it is evaluated.

width   the width (in print positions) of the user's terminal.

length   the length (in lines) of an output page.

prompt   the string to be printed by the S parser to prompt for an expression.

continue the string to be printed by the S parser to prompt for the continuation of an expression.

digits   number of significant digits to use in print (and therefore in automatic printing).

check   if TRUE S performs various internal checks during evaluation. This provides more information about warning messages and reloading, and may help track down mysterious bugs (such as S terminating abnormally). Evaluation will be somewhat slower with this option turned on.

memory   the maximum total size (in bytes) for all in-memory data. If this limit is exceeded, the session will be terminated (to avoid runaway computations that may slow down or crash the computing system). If total memory reaches half the allowed limit, S will automatically reload at the completion of the next expression, to get rid of garbage. See function reload.

object.size the maximum size (in bytes) for any single S object. If this limit is exceeded, an error is generated, but the sesion continues.

keep   determines what mode of objects are to be kept in an internal table once accessed in a session. Default strategy is keep="functions", so that future calls will be faster from not having to find the functions on the system database. The only likely other strategy is keep=NULL which turns off keeping, and might be a good idea if you were about to access a large number of functions sequentially.

error   function to be called when an error or interrupt occurs. Likely alternatives are dump.calls, dump.frames or NULL (no error action).

audit.size the maximum size (in characters) for the audit file. If this limit is exceeded at the beginning of a session, a warning message will be printed. You should then use the shell-level utility S TRUNC_AUDIT to reduce the size of the audit file.

show   should graphics be shown directly or returned as a graphics object?

The initial values for these options are as follows:

```
echo=F              width=80            length=48
prompt="> "         continue="+ "       digits=7
check=F             memory=5e7          object.size=5e6
keep="function"     error=dump.calls
audit.size=5e5      show=T
```

VALUE

options returns a list, whose components give either the previous or the current options, as determined by the arguments supplied. Thus, the expression

```
options()$show
```

gives the current value of the option show. Options that have never been set have the value NULL.

SIDE EFFECTS

A session object, named .Options, is modified.

EXAMPLES

```
options(width=50)     # 50-character wide line

temp ← options(prompt="Say something! ",continue="\t")
     # some computations, then
options(temp)  #restore prompt and continue
```

---

order	Ordering to Create Sorted Data	**order**

```
order(...)
```

ARGUMENTS

... any number of vectors. All arguments must have the same length.

VALUE

integer vector with same number of elements as data elements in the arguments. Contains the indices of the data elements in ascending order, i.e., the first integer is the subscript of the smallest data element, etc. For character vectors, sorting is based on the ASCII collating sequence.

Ordering is primarily based on the first argument. Values of the second argument break ties in the first, and so on. All sorting is done in ascending order.

This function is often used in conjunction with subscripting for sorting several parallel arrays. An implementation limitation causes numeric comparisons to currently be done in single precision, and does not allow the use of complex arguments. The function `sort.list` does not have these limitations, but only takes one argument. Otherwise, the two functions are identical.

SEE ALSO

`sort.list`, `rank` and `sort`.

EXAMPLES

```
# ordering by salary within age
ord ← order(age,salary)
cbind(x[ord],y[ord],z[ord])
```

outer	Generalized Outer Products	**outer**

```
X %o% Y  #operator form
outer(X, Y, FUN="*", ...)
```

ARGUMENTS

X, Y   first and second arguments to the function FUN. Missing values (NAs) are allowed if FUN accepts them.

FUN   in the general form, some S function that takes at least two vectors as arguments and returns a single value.

...   other arguments to FUN, if needed. The names of the arguments, if any, should be those meaningful to FUN.

VALUE

array, whose dimension vector is the concatenation of the dimension vectors of X and Y, and such that $FUN(X[i,j,k,...], Y[a,b,c,...])$ is the value of the $[i,j,k,...,a,b,c,...]$ element. outer forms two arrays corresponding to the data in X and Y, each of which has a dim attribute formed by concatenating the dim attributes of X and Y. It then calls FUN just once with these two arrays as arguments. Therefore, FUN should be a function that operates on vectors or arrays and expects (at least) two arguments.

EXAMPLES

```
z ← x %o% y      # The outer product array
   # dim(z) == c(dim(as.array(x)),dim(as.array(y)))


z ← outer(months,years,paste)  # All month, year combinations pasted.
```

pairs	Produce All Pair-wise Scatterplots	**pairs**

```
pairs(x, labels, type="p", head,
        full=FALSE, max, text, dataex)
```

ARGUMENTS

x matrix of data to be plotted. A scatter plot will be produced for each pair of columns of x. Missing values (NAs) are allowed.

labels optional character vector for labelling the x and y axes of the plots. The strings labels[1], labels[2], etc. are the labels for the 1st, 2nd, etc. columns of x. If supplied, the label vector must have length equal to ncol(x). If x has a dimnames attribute, the default labels are the column labels; otherwise, the default labels are "Var 1", "Var 2", etc.

type optional character string to define the type of the scatter plot. Possible values are "p", "l", "b" for points, lines or both. See also text below.

head optional character string for a running head. This is plotted as a title at the top of each page. By default, the name of the data is used. If there is more than one page, the page number is included in the title.

full should the full ncol(x)-1 by ncol(x)-1 array of plots be produced? By default, only the lower triangle is produced, saving space and plot time, but making interpretation harder.

max optional, suggested limit for the number of rows or columns of plots on a single page. Default forces all plots on 1 page. The algorithm tries to choose an array of plots which efficiently uses the available space on the display.

text optional vector of text to be plotted at each of the points. If the length of the vector is less than nrow(x), elements will be reused cyclically. If missing, the plotting is controlled by type.

dataex character size for the plotted data points. Default is the current value of parameter cex.

Graphical parameters may also be supplied as arguments to this function (see par).

EXAMPLES

```
pairs(longley.x,labels=longley.collab,head="Longley Data")
```

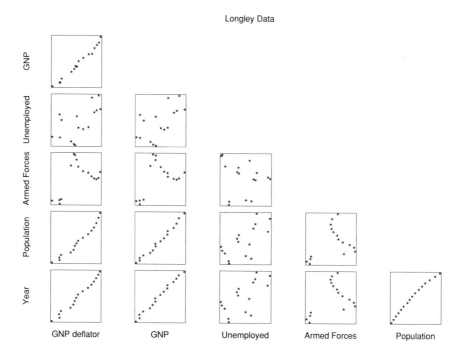

Longley Data

| **par** | Graphical Parameters | **par** |

```
par(...)
```

ARGUMENTS

... arguments that set parameters or query parameter values. Named arguments cause the parameters of the same name to be set to the specified value. Parameters can also be set by a single, unnamed argument that is a list containing components whose names match graphical parameter names given below.

Current values of graphical parameters may be queried by calling `par` with any number of character vectors as unnamed arguments. In this case, `par` returns a list of the corresponding parameter values. Then a later call to `par` with this list as argument resets the parameter values. If only a single character argument is given, `par` returns an atomic vector with the values of that parameter.

If `par` is given no argument, it returns a list of all current parameter values.

Graphical parameters may be set by the `par` function or by giving them as named arguments to other graphics functions. When given through `par`, the graphical parameters are set until changed or until the end of the session; otherwise, they are reset at the end of the function call in which they were specified.

VALUE

a list is returned giving the values of the parameters named in the arguments. The `names` attribute of the list gives the names of the parameters. Such a list may be given as input to a later invocation of `par`. An exception is that the returned value is an atomic vector if the only argument was a single character value. If parameter values were set, then the returned list is invisible.

EXAMPLES

```
par(mfrow=c(2,2),mar=rep(3,4))    # 2x2 array of figures
    # on the page, with 3 lines of margin around each
plot(x,y,col=3,pch=".")    # plot with specified color
    # and plotting character
par(col=3,pch=".")    # permanent change of color and
    # plotting character
usr ← par("usr")    # numeric vector of user coordinates

oldpar ← par(tck=.02,las=1)    # set new values, remember old
par(oldpar)    # set parms back to remembered values

par()    # returns all current parameter values
```

In the following lists of parameters, the notation `"c"` denotes one character, `i`, `j`, `m`, and `n` are integers, `L` is a logical value, and `x` is numeric.

GENERAL PARAMETERS

The following parameters can be used in any graphical functions, including `par`.

`adj=x` string justification. 0 = left justify, 1 = right justify, .5 = center.

`bty="c"` character representing the type of box. Characters o, 1 (ell), 7, c will produce boxes which resemble the corresponding upper-case letters. The value n will suppress boxes.

`cex=x` character expansion relative to device's standard size. For example, when cex = 2, characters are twice as big as normal for the device.

`col=x` color, device dependent. Default 1. Generally, small integers are used to specify pen numbers on pen plotters, color map indices on scope devices, etc. Color 0 is background.

`crt=x` character rotation in degrees measured counterclockwise from horizontal. When srt is set, crt is automatically set to the same value.

`csi=x` character height (interline space) in inches.

`err=x` error mode: −1 = do not print graphics error messages (points out of bounds, etc.), 0 = print messages (the default).

`font=i` font number, device dependent. Some devices allow this parameter to affect the font in which text is displayed.

`lab=c(x,y,llen)`
desired number of tick intervals on the *x* and *y* axes and the length of labels on both axes. Default c(5,5,7).

`las=x` style of axis labels. 0 = always parallel to axis (the default), 1 = always horizontal, 2 = always perpendicular to axis.

`lty=x` line type, device dependent. Normally type 1 is solid, 2 and up are dotted or dashed.

`mgp=c(x1,x2,x3)`
margin line for the axis title, axis labels, and axis line. Default is c(3,1,0).

`mkh=x` height in inches of mark symbols drawn when pch is given as a number.

`pch="c"` the character to be used for plotting points. If pch is a period, a centered plotting dot is used.

`pch=n` the number of a plotting symbol to be drawn when plotting points. See lines for a display of the plotting symbols.

smo=x   smoothness of circles and other curves. smo is the number of rasters that the straight-line approximation to the curve is allowed to differ from the exact position of the curve. Large values produce more crude approximations to curves, but allows the curves to be drawn with fewer line segments and hence speeds up output. The minimum number of line segments that will be used for a circle is 8, regardless of smo.

srt=x   string rotation in degrees measured counterclockwise from horizontal. When specified, sets crt to same value.

tck=x   the length of tick marks as a fraction of the smaller of the width or height of the plotting region. If tck is negative, ticks are drawn outside of the plot region. If tck = 1, grid lines are drawn. Default is −.02.

xaxp=c(ul,uh,n)

coordinates of lower tick mark ul, upper tick mark uh, and number of intervals n within the range from ul to uh.

xaxs="c"   style of axis interval calculation. The styles "s" and "e" set up standard and extended axes, where numeric axis labels are more extreme than any data values. Extended axes may be extended another character width so that no data points lie very near the axis limit. Style "i" creates an axis labelled internal to the data values. This style wastes no space, yet still gives pretty labels. Style "r" extends the data range by 4% on each end, and then labels the axis internally. This ensures that all plots take up a fixed percent of the plot region, yet keeps points away from the axes. Style "d" is a direct axis, and axis parameters will not be changed by further high-level plotting routines. This is used to "lock-in" an axis from one plot to the next. Default is "r".

xaxt="c"   axis type. Type "n" (null) can be used to cause an axis to be set up by a high-level routine, but then not plotted.

xpd=L   logical value controlling clipping. FALSE means no points or lines may be drawn outside of the plot region. TRUE means points, lines, and text may be plotted outside of the plot region as long as they are inside the figure region.

yaxp=c(ul,uh,n) see xaxp.

yaxs="c" see xaxs.

yaxt="c" see xaxt.

LAYOUT PARAMETERS

The following parameters may only be used in function `par`, because they change the overall layout of plots or figures.

`fig=c(x1,x2,y1,y2)`
> coordinates of figure region expressed as fraction of device surface.

`fin=c(w,h)`
> width and height of figure in inches.

`mai=c(xbot,xlef,xtop,xrig)`
> margin size specified in inches. Values given for bottom, left, top, and right margins in that order.

`mar=c(xbot,xlef,xtop,xrig)`
> lines of margin on each side of plot. Margin coordinates range from 0 at the edge of the box outward in units of `mex` sized characters. If the margin is respecified by `mai` or `mar`, the plot region is re-created to provide the appropriate sized margins within the figure. Default value is `c(5,4,4,2)+.1`.

`mex=x` the coordinate unit for addressing locations in the margin is expressed in terms of `mex`. `mex` is a character size relative to default character size (like `cex`) and margin coordinates are measured in terms of characters of this size.

`mfg=c(i,j,m,n)`
> multiple figure parameters which give the row and column number of the current multiple figure and the number of rows and columns in the current array of multiple figures.

`mfrow=c(m,n)`
> subsequent figures will be drawn row-by-row in an `m` by `n` matrix on the page.

`mfcol=c(m,n)`
> subsequent figures will be drawn column-by-column in an `m` by `n` matrix on the page.

`new=L` if TRUE, the current plot is assumed to have no previous plotting on it. Any points, lines, or text will set `new` to FALSE.

`oma=c(xbot,xlef,xtop,xrig)`
> outer margin lines of text. `oma` provides the maximum value for outer margin coordinates on each of the four sides of the multiple figure region. `oma` causes recreation of the current figure within the confines of the newly specified outer margins. Default is `rep(0,4)`.

`omd=c(x1,x2,y1,y2)`
> the region within the outer margins (which is to be used by multiple figure arrays) is specified by `omd` as a fraction of the entire device.

`omi=c(xbot,xlef,xtop,xrig)`
> size of outer margins in inches.

`pin=c(w,h)`
> width and height of plot, measured in inches.

`plt=c(x1,x2,y1,y2)`
> the coordinates of the plot region measured as a fraction of the figure region.

`pty="c"` the type of plotting region currently in effect. Values: `"s"` generates a square plotting region; `"m"` (the default) generates a maximal size plotting region, which, with the margins, completely fills the figure region.

`usr=c(x1,x2,y1,y2)`
> user coordinate min and max on *x*- and *y*-axes. Default, when device is initialized, is `c(0,1,0,1)`.

---

parse	Parse Expressions	**parse**

`parse(file="", n, text, file=, prompt, white=T)`

ARGUMENTS
> `file` optional character string, giving the file from which input to the parser should be read. If neither `text` nor `file` is provided, or if `file` is the empty string, the parser reads from standard input.
>
> `n` number of expressions to parse. If negative, parsing will continue to end of file. By default, `parse` reads to the end of the file or text, *except* when the file is the standard input, in which case `n=1`.

text optional character vector to use as input to parser.

prompt character string to use as prompt in interactive use of `parse`. Default is the value of the `option` named `prompt`.

white if `TRUE`, arbitrary white space can separate expressions; otherwise, only newlines or semicolons.

VALUE

an object of mode `expression`, containing the parsed version of the expression(s) read.

SEE ALSO

`options` for changing prompt and continue strings

EXAMPLES

```
parse(n= -1, file = "my.file")  # parse everything on my.file
```

paste	Glue Data Together to Make Character Data	**paste**

```
paste(..., sep=" " , collapse=)
```

ARGUMENTS

... vectors which may be either numeric, logical, or character. All arguments are coerced to mode character. Missing values (NAs) are allowed.

sep= the character string to be inserted between successive arguments. Can be "" for no space. Default is a single space.

collapse optional character string to use in collapsing the result. By default, no collapsing is done.

VALUE

character vector, with length equal to the maximum of the lengths of the arguments (unless `collapse` is given, in which case the length is 1). The i-th element of the result is the concatenation of the i-th elements of the arguments. If the length of any argument is less than the maximum, elements of that argument are repeated cyclically. In particular, an argument can be a single element, to appear in each element of the result. If `collapse` is given, all of the strings produced are finally collapsed into one long string with the `collapse` string inserted between elements.

EXAMPLES

```
paste("no.",1:10)      # gives "no. 1", "no. 2" ...

paste(1:10,collapse="")    # produces "12345678910"

paste(state.name,"pop=",pop)    # "Alabama pop= 12.345"...
```

pbeta	see Beta	**pbeta**

pcauchy	see Cauchy	**pcauchy**

pchisq	see Chisquare	**pchisq**

persp	Three-Dimensional Perspective Plots	**persp**

```
persp(z, eye=c(-6,-8,5), ar=1)
```

ARGUMENTS

z matrix of heights given over a regularly spaced grid of x and y values, i.e., z[i,j] is the height at x[i],y[j]. Although x and y are not input to persp, the algorithm plots as if x and y are in increasing order and equally spaced from −1 to 1.

eye vector giving the x,y,z coordinates for the viewpoint. Since the implied x,y grid ranges from −1 to 1, the x,y coordinates of eye should not both be in the range from −1 to 1.

ar aspect ratio of the actual x,y grid, i.e., (xmax-xmin)/(ymax-ymin).

persp sets up the plot under the assumption that a unit in the x, y, and z directions represents the same physical size. Thus the values in z should ordinarily be scaled to the range (0,1).

The algorithm attempts hidden-line elimination, but may be fooled on segments with both endpoints visible but the middle obscured.

EXAMPLES

```
persp(z)      #perspective plot of heights z
              #from default viewpoint
#the example plot is produced by:
i ← interp(ozone.xy$x,ozone.xy$y,ozone.median)
i$z ← ifelse(is.na(i$z),0,i$z)
persp(i$z/200)
title(main="Median Ozone Concentrations in the North East")
```

Median Ozone Concentrations in the North East

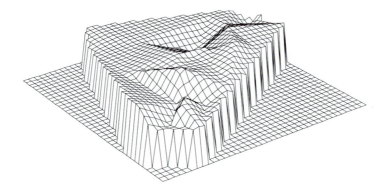

pexp	see Exponential	pexp

pf	see F	pf

pgamma	see Gamma	**pgamma**

pie	Pie Charts	**pie**

```
pie(x, names, size=.75, inner=.3, outer=1.1,
    explode, angle, density, col, rotate=TRUE)
```

ARGUMENTS

x vector of relative pie slice sizes. The ith slice will take the fraction `abs(x[i])/sum(abs(x))` of the pie. The slices start with a horizontal line to the right and go counter-clockwise.

names optional character vector of slice labels. Labels are positioned along the center-line of the slice, and are shifted as far in toward the center as possible without overlapping into adjacent slices (see arguments `inner`, `outer`, and `rotate`).

size optional fraction of the short dimension of the plot taken up by the circle.

inner optional fraction giving the innermost position that labels can occupy. The default value of .3 means that labels can go no further toward the center than .3 of the radius.

outer optional fraction giving the outer limit for starting the labels.

explode logical vector specifying slices of the pie which should be exploded (moved out from the center).

angle optional vector giving the angle (degrees, counter-clockwise from horizontal) for shading each slice. (Defaults to 45 if `density` is supplied.)

density optional vector for pie shading, giving the number of lines per inch for shading each slice. Defaults to 5 if `angle` is supplied. A density of 0 implies solid filling, and is the default if `col` is specified but angle is not. Negative values of density produce no shading.

col optional vector giving the colors in which the pie slices should be filled or shaded. If `col` is specified and neither `angle` nor `density` are given as arguments, slices will be filled solidly with the colors.

rotate logical flag controlling rotation of slice labels. If TRUE, names are drawn parallel to the center line of each slice. If FALSE, names are drawn horizontally. This is convenient if the graphics device has a limited capability for character rotation.

Solid filling of pie slices is dependent on the area-filling capability of the device driver. For devices without explicit area-filling capability, solid filling can be simulated by specifying a very high density shading.

Graphical parameters may also be supplied as arguments to this function
(see `par`).

EXAMPLES

```
pie(revenues,revenue.class)

pie(expenses,c("Interest","Materials","Payoffs"),inner=.5,
    outer=.5,size=1)    # force labels to start halfway out

pie(revenues, explode= revenues>.1*sum(revenues) )
    # explode any piece larger than 10% of the sum

pie(revenues, col=seq(revenues), inner=1.1, rotate=F,
        names=revenue.class)    # colored slices with external labels

# the example plot is produced by:
datatel←apply(telsam.response,2,sum)
pie(datatel,telsam.collab)
title(main="Response to Quality of Service Questions
concerning Telephone Service")
```

Response to Quality of Service Questions

concerning Telephone Service

plclust	Plot Trees From Hierarchical Clustering	plclust

```
plclust(tree, hang=.1, unit=FALSE, level=FALSE,
        hmin=0, square=TRUE, labels, plot=TRUE)
```

ARGUMENTS

tree   a hierarchical clustering tree, of the form returned by function `hclust`.

hang   the fraction of the height of the plot that any individual node will hang below the cluster that it joins. A value of -1 will cause all individuals to start at y-value 0.

unit   if TRUE, the heights of the merges will be ignored and instead merge i will occur at height i. Useful for spreading out the tree to see the sequence of merges.

level   if TRUE, plotted tree will be "leveled", where merges in different subtrees are arbitrarily assigned the same height in order to compress the vertical scale. Particularly useful with `unit=TRUE`.

hmin   optional minimum height at which merges will take place. Can be used to get rid of irrelevant detail at low levels.

square   if TRUE, the tree is plotted with "U" shaped branches, if FALSE, it has "V" shaped branches.

labels   optional character vector of labels for the leaves of the tree. If omitted, leaves will be labelled by number. To omit labels entirely, use `labels=FALSE`.

plot   logical flag. If TRUE, plotting takes place. If FALSE, no plotting is done (useful for returned value).

Graphical parameters may also be supplied as arguments to this function (see `par`).

VALUE

if `plot` is FALSE, an object containing the coordinates of the leaves of the tree and the interior nodes of the tree.

x,y   x and y coordinates of the leaves of the tree, i.e., `x[i]`,`y[i]` gives the coordinates of the leaf corresponding to the ith individual.

xn,yn   x and y coordinates of the interior nodes of the tree, i.e., `xn[i]`,`yn[i]` gives the coordinates of the node representing the ith merge.

SEE ALSO

hclust, dist, labclust, subtree, cutree.

EXAMPLES

```
plclust(hclust(distances))

plclust(tree,label=FALSE)       # plot without labels
xy ← plclust(tree,plot=FALSE)            # no plot, save structure
# allow user to point at leaf and have it identified
identify(xy)

# the example plot is produced by:
sums ← apply(author.count,1,sum)
adjusted ← sweep(author.count,1,sums,"/")
par(mar=c(18,4,4,1))
plclust(hclust(dist(adjusted)),label=author.rowlab)
title("Clustering of Books Based on Letter Frequency")
```

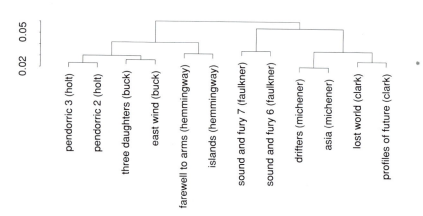

Clustering of Books Based on Letter Frequency

---

plnorm   see Lognormal   **plnorm**

---

plogis   see Logistic   **plogis**

`plot`	Scatter Plots	`plot`

$$\texttt{plot(x, y, type="p", log="")}$$

ARGUMENTS

x,y coordinates of points. The coordinates can be given by two vector arguments or by a single argument `x` which is a time-series, a complex vector, a matrix with 2 columns, or a list containing components named `x` and `y`. If a single numeric `x` is given, `time(x)` is plotted on the x-axis and `x` on the y-axis. If a single complex `x` is given, `Re(x)` is plotted on the x-axis and `Im(x)` on the y-axis. Missing values (NAs) are allowed. Any points containing missing values will be omitted from the plot.

type= values of "p", "l", "b", "o", "n", and "h" produce points, lines, both, both (overlaid), nothing, and high-density lines.

log= values of "x", "y", or "xy" specify which axes are to be plotted on a logarithmic scale. By default, logarithmic axes are not produced.

Graphical parameters may also be supplied as arguments to this function (see `par`). Also, the arguments to the `title` function may be supplied to this function.

EXAMPLES

```
plot(x,y)        #simple scatter plot
plot(x,y,type="l")   #connected lines
plot(x,y,log="xy")   #log-log plot
plot(x,y,type="n");text(x,y)      # do not plot, then
        # use text to label each point from 1 to n
plot(gnp,type="h")   #high-density plot of time-series
plot(density(x),type="l")   #plot of list xy
# the example plot is produced by:
plot(corn.rain,corn.yield)
```

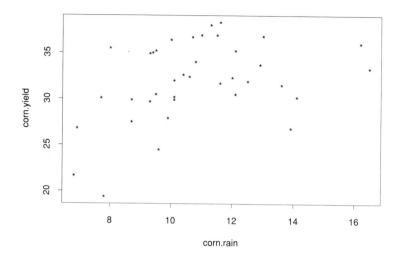

`plotfit` Two-way Plot of Fit `plotfit`

```
plotfit(fit, w=0, c=-1, rowlab, collab, grid=TRUE)
```

ARGUMENTS

fit object with components `row`, `col`, `grand`, and `resid`, reflecting a two-way fit to a matrix. See, for example, the output of function `two-way`. Missing values (NAs) are allowed in components of `fit`.

w interaction term, i.e., the coefficient of the row*col interaction. The residuals in `fit` should NOT reflect this term, i.e., `data[i,j]` equals `grand + row[i] + col[j] + resid[i,j]`.

c residuals larger in magnitude than `c` will be displayed. If `c<0`, no residuals will be displayed; if `c=0`, all residuals will be displayed.

rowlab character vector giving labels for the rows of the matrix. Defaults to "Row i". To omit labels, use `rowlab=""`.

collab character vector giving labels for the columns of the matrix. Defaults to "Col i". To omit labels, use `collab=""`.

grid should grid of fitted values be drawn?

Graphical parameters may also be supplied as arguments to this function (see `par`).

SEE ALSO

        twoway.

EXAMPLES

        plotfit(twoway(datamat))

        # the example plot is produced by:
        vy ← votes.year[27:31] #get last five election years
        vr ← twoway(votes.repub[1:10,27:31]) #first 10 states, last 5 years
        plotfit(vr,c=8,rowlab=state.name,collab=vy)
        title(main="Twoway Fit to Republican Votes",
                sub="10 States for 1964 - 1972")

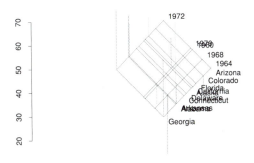

Twoway Fit to Republican Votes

10 States for 1964 - 1972

pmax	Parallel Maximum or Minimum	pmax

        pmax(...)
        pmin(...)

ARGUMENTS
        ... any number of numeric objects.

VALUE

        vector whose first element is the maximum (pmax) or minimum (pmin) of
        the first elements of the arguments, and similarly for the second element,

etc. The length of the vector is the length of the longest argument. Shorter vectors are reused cyclically. Missing values (NA) are allowed; if an element of any of the arguments is NA, the corresponding element of the result is also NA.

EXAMPLES

z ← pmax(x,y,5) # vector as long as larger of x and y
                 # where z[i] is max of x[i], y[i], and 5

SEE ALSO

Note the difference between pmax, pmin and max, min. The latter two give the single element which is the max or min of all the arguments. See also range.

| **pmin** | see pmax | **pmin** |

| **pnorm** | see Normal | **pnorm** |

| **points** | see lines | **points** |

| **polygon** | Shade in a Polygonal Figure | **polygon** |

polygon(x, y, density=-1, angle=45, border=T)

ARGUMENTS

x,y coordinates of the vertices of a polygon, listed in order, i.e., the ith point is connected to the i+1st. It is assumed the polygon closes by joining the last point to the first. A structure containing components x and y can also be given. Missing values (NAs) are allowed and signify breaks between polygons.

density density of shading lines in lines per inch. If `density` is zero, no shading will occur. If `density` is negative, the polygon will be filled solidly using the device-dependent polygon filling algorithm.

angle angle of shading lines in degrees measured counterclockwise from horizontal.

border should border of polygonal region be drawn?

Graphical parameters may also be supplied as arguments to this function (see `par`).

EXAMPLES

```
# read graphic input, draw and shade polygon
polygon(locator(type="l"))
    # shade the area between lines x1,y1 and x2,y2
polygon( c(x1,rev(x2)), c(y1,rev(y2)) )
    # two polygons px1,py1 and px2,py2 separated by NAs
polygon( c(px1,NA,px2), c(py1,NA,py2) )
```

---

postscript   Device Driver for PostScript Printers   **postscript**

```
postscript(file, command, horizontal=F,
        width, height, rasters, pointsize=14,
        font=1, preamble=ps.preamble, fonts=ps.fonts)
```

ARGUMENTS

file character string naming a file. If this argument is supplied, the output PostScript program is written to this file.

command character string naming a Unix command. If `file` is not supplied, the device driver output will be piped through `command`. The default value of `command` will be installation dependent, and might reasonably be a call to an appropriate line printer spooler.

horizontal specifies horizontal (landscape) orientation, default FALSE.

width width of plotting region in inches, defaults to 7.9 if `horizontal` is FALSE, 10.8 if `horizontal` is TRUE.

height height of plotting region in inches, defaults to 10.8 if `horizontal` is FALSE, 7.9 if `horizontal` is TRUE.

rasters number of plotting units per inch. Default is the typical laser printer device resolution of 300 units per inch.

`pointsize` base size of text, in points (one point = 1/72 inches). If the graphical
parameter `cex` is equal to 1, text will appear in this size.

`font` number giving default font for text (see argument `fonts`). A negative
number will select the font in its outline form.

`preamble` character object containing the postscript program that defines the driver.

`fonts` character object enumerating the fonts you want available with
`postscript`. Font number `i` will be the `i`-th font named in this vector.

This function is a device driver that produces a program in the
PostScript™ page description language. By default this program is sent
directly to a PostScript laser printer, via the `command` argument (which
will be installation dependent). When the `file` argument is given, the
program is collected on the named file (and not sent through the command). If `file` already exists, it will be truncated.

The `postscript` device driver supports variable character sizes, general
string and character rotations and ten line styles. Line width is specified
by the `lwd` parameter, and is interpreted in units of 1/36 inches, hence
the default `lwd=1` line is 2 points wide. A line width of 0 gives the thin-
nest possible line on the device. Colors may be specified in two ways:
`col` between 0 and 1 maps into a range from white to black; otherwise
`col` is truncated to an integer and indexes a table of gray levels. Fonts
that are normally filled (all but the Courier family) may be outlined by
specifying the font as a negative number. The `pch` graphical parameter
will select plotting characters from the Standard Encoding vector of
PostScript (see page 252 of Reference below). When plotted these characters are always centered. Setting `pch="."` gives a plotting dot;
`pch=183` gives a larger plotting dot. Using `pch=183` with a negative
`font` parameter gives a plotting circle.

REFERENCE

Adobe Systems, Inc., *PostScript Language Reference Manual,* Addison-
Wesley, Reading, Massachusetts, 1985.

SEE ALSO

`ps.fonts` and `ps.preamble` in Appendix 2.

EXAMPLES

```
postscript()   # send output directly to device
postscript("figure1.ps", font=-3)
               # save output on a file; text in outlined Times-Roman
```

ppoints	Plotting Points for Q-Q Plots	**ppoints**

```
ppoints(n,a)
```

ARGUMENTS

n sample size for which plotting points desired (if `n` has only 1 value) or data against which plot is to be made.

a Parameter that controls precise placement of plotting points, `0<=a<=1`. Default is `.5` if `n>10` or `.375` if `n<=10`.

VALUE

the vector of probabilities, `p`, such that `qdist(p)` plotted against `sort(y)` gives a probability (Q-Q) plot of `y` against the distribution of which `qdist` is the quantile function. Computes `p[i]=(i-a)/(n+1-2*a)`.

REFERENCE

G. Blom, *Statistical Estimates and Transformed Beta Variables*, Wiley, New York, 1958.

EXAMPLES

```
plot(qlnorm(ppoints(y)),sort(y))      #log normal q-q plot
```

prarray	Print a Multi-Dimensional Array	**prarray**

```
prarray(x)
```

ARGUMENTS

x an array (has a `dim` attribute).

VALUE

`x`, with the invisible flag set to prevent reprinting.

SIDE EFFECTS

`prarray` uses `prmatrix` to print successive slices from `x`. Both are called from the `print` function. If the `dimnames` attribute is present, it is used to title the matrix sections and to label their rows and columns. The `digits` option is honored in deciding how many significant digits to print.

SEE ALSO

```
print, options.
```

EXAMPLES

```
> iris[1:5,,1:2]

, , Setosa
      Sepal L. Sepal W. Petal L. Petal W.
[1,]     5.1      3.5      1.4      0.2
[2,]     4.9      3.0      1.4      0.2
[3,]     4.7      3.2      1.3      0.2
[4,]     4.6      3.1      1.5      0.2
[5,]     5.0      3.6      1.4      0.2

, , Versicolor
      Sepal L. Sepal W. Petal L. Petal W.
[1,]     7.0      3.2      4.7      1.4
[2,]     6.4      3.2      4.5      1.5
[3,]     6.9      3.1      4.9      1.5
[4,]     5.5      2.3      4.0      1.3
[5,]     6.5      2.8      4.6      1.5
```

pratom	Print Data with Atomic Modes	**pratom**

```
pratom(x)
```

ARGUMENTS

x a vector with an atomic mode.

The function `pratom` is normally called by the `print` function and not interactively. It computes a single format for the first page of output (determined by the current options; see `options`) and starts printing. It may change formats after each page of output. To cause it to print everything with one format, make the option `length` very large.

SEE ALSO

```
print, format, options.
```

prcomp	Principal Components Analysis	**prcomp**

```
prcomp(x, retx=TRUE)
```

ARGUMENTS

x   data matrix to be decomposed. Principal component analysis defines a rotation of the variables (columns) of x. The first derived direction is chosen to maximize the standard deviation of the derived variable, the second to maximize the standard deviation among directions uncorrelated with the first, etc.

retx   logical, if TRUE the rotated version of the data matrix is returned. Using retx=FALSE saves space in the returned data structure.

VALUE

list describing the principal component analysis:

sdev   standard deviations of the derived variables.

rotation   orthogonal matrix describing the rotation. The first column is the linear combination of columns of x defining the first principal component, etc. May have fewer columns than x.

x   if retx was TRUE, the rotated version of x; i.e., the first column is the nrow(x) values for the first derived variable, etc. May have fewer columns than x.

The analysis will work even if nrow(x)<ncol(x), but in this case only nrow(x) variables will be derived, and the returned x will have only nrow(x) columns. In general, if any of the derived variables has zero standard deviation, that variable is dropped from the returned result.

prefix	see Defunct	**prefix**

| **pretty** | Vector of Prettied Values | **pretty** |

```
pretty(x, nint=5)
```

ARGUMENTS

    x vector of data; prettied values will cover range of x. Missing values (NAs) are allowed.

    nint optional, approximate number of intervals desired.

VALUE

    vector of (ordered) values, defining approximately nint intervals covering the range of x. The individual values will differ by 1, 2 or 5 times a power of 10.

EXAMPLES

```
pretty(mydata,10)
```

| **print** | Print Data | **print** |

```
print(x, digits, quote=TRUE)
```

ARGUMENTS

    x any object. Missing values (NAs) are allowed.

    digits the number of significant digits that should be printed in numeric data. Since all numbers in any vector are printed in the same format, this may mean that some numbers will be printed with more than digits significant digits. If the argument is omitted, the digits option is used; see options.

    quote if TRUE, character strings are printed with surrounding quotes.

VALUE

    x, with the invisible flag set to prevent reprinting.

SIDE EFFECTS

    print attempts to print x in a form appropriate to the class of S objects it seems to belong to.

    The standard .Program of S calls print to print results of function calls, unless the invisible flag has been set (see invisible). The options `width` and `length` control line width and page length. When printing a vector a new format may be chosen for each page. When printing matrices, the column labels are repeated once per page.

SEE ALSO

`cat, format, invisible, prstructure, pratom, prlist, prarray, options.`

EXAMPLES

```
# in a loop, explicit printing is necessary
for(i in 1:10) print(i)
# compare this with the previous loop
for(i in 1:10) i
round(x,3)     #auto print of x rounded to 3 decimal places
print(x,3)     # x to 3-significant digits
```

---

printer	Printer Device Function	**printer**

```
printer(width=80, height=64, file="", command="")
show()
```

ARGUMENTS

width   the width, in characters, of the output device.

height   the height, in characters, of the output device.

file   optional file name. If specified, all graphical output will be sent to this file.

command   optional Unix command. If specified, the output of the `printer` driver will be piped into the command. This is most frequently used to pipe output directly into a line printer spooler.

Each plot is stored in an internal buffer. This enables functions to be given to add to the existing plot. When the next plot is started, the previous plot is printed. The function `show()` can be used to print the current plot. After using `show`, the plot can be further augmented.

The `printer` device is a primitive, low resolution device. It's primary justification is that it enables you to do some sort of graphics on arbitrary non-graphics terminals. It does not support line style changes, character size changes, character rotation or color.

Graphic input (`locator`, `identify`) done on this device will prompt for *x*- and *y*-coordinates. Type in the desired coordinates or hit carriage return to terminate graphic input.

If several plotted points (not lines) overwrite each other, the overwritten position is plotted as a "%" character.

EXAMPLES

```
printer(height=24)
plot(lottery.number,lottery.payoff)
show()   # look at the current plot
title("Lottery Data")        # now add title to it

printer(command="lp")        # pipe directly to line printer
```

---

prlist   Print a List   **prlist**

```
prlist(l)
```

ARGUMENTS

l any S object; typically recursive.

`prlist` treats l as an object of mode `"list"` and prints each of its elements, preceded by its name or element number.

SEE ALSO

`print`.

---

prmatrix   Print a Matrix   **prmatrix**

```
prmatrix(x, rowlab, collab)
```

ARGUMENTS

x a matrix, i.e., `length(dim(x))` is 2.
rowlab optional character vector of row labels.
collab optional character vector of column labels.

VALUE

x, with the invisible flag set to prevent reprinting.

SIDE EFFECTS

`prmatrix` prints `x` as a matrix. It is called as a result of automatically printing a matrix or a multi-way array. A format is chosen for each column, for each page, so that columns line up. Wide matrices are broken into blocks by choosing as many columns as fit on one line. If `x` has a `"dimnames"` attribute, `dimnames(x)[[1]]` provides row labels, if it has length > 0, and similarly `dimnames(x)[[2]]` provides column labels. If an explicit call to `prmatrix` supplies either `rowlab` or `collab`, these will be used instead. Otherwise, row labels are made up to look like row subscripts (`"[1,]"`, etc.) and column labels are made up to look like column subscripts (`"[,1]"`, etc).

After each page of output, the column labels are printed again, so that there should always be a copy of the column labels on the screen at any time. To avoid multiple copies of the column labels, execute

```
options(length=10000)
```

to specify a very long page. A new format may be chosen at the end of each page.

SEE ALSO

`print, prarray, options.`

EXAMPLES

```
> state.x77[, 1:4]
           Population Income Illiteracy Life Exp
  Alabama        3615   3624        2.1    69.05
   Alaska         365   6315        1.5    69.31
  Arizona        2212   4530        1.8    70.55
 Arkansas        2110   3378        1.9    70.66
  . . .
```

`proc.time`	Running Time of S	`proc.time`

```
proc.time()
```

VALUE

numeric vector, giving the user, system and elapsed times for the currently running S process, in units of seconds. If there have been any child processes spawned during the current session, the cumulative sums of the user and system times for them is also returned. This function is likely to be most useful in recording checkpoints for computations; particular expressions can be timed by computing the difference between such checkpoints.

SEE ALSO

```
unix.time.
```

EXAMPLES

```
now ← proc.time()[1:2]      # checkpoint
random ← runif(1000)        # or some other computation
speed ← proc.time()[1:2] - now    # time taken for computation
```

prod	see `sum`	**prod**

`.Program`	Control Execution of S	`.Program`

```
.Program
```

The `.Program` expression controls the operation of S. S repeatedly executes this expression, which generally calls `parse` to parse expressions and `eval` to evaluate the resulting expression. The standard `.Program` automatically prints the value of functions called at the top-level unless `.Auto.print` was set to `FALSE`.

SEE ALSO

```
invisible, parse, eval.
```

EXAMPLES

```
# a simplistic .Program
.Program ← expression(print(eval(parse(),0)))
```

prompt	Construct Documentation for Function or Data	**prompt**

```
prompt(name, filename)
```

ARGUMENTS

  name name or character string giving name of a function or data object.

 filename filename for resulting documentation; default is name.d.

SIDE EFFECTS

A file is written, containing an outline for documenting the function or object. The file will eventually be used by the `help` function to produce documentation for the function. As produced by `prompt`, the file will contain the call to the function and individual sections for each of the arguments. You will need to fill in the actual information about the arguments, a description of the value returned by the function, examples, and whatever other information appropriate. Lines in the file that contain "~" should be replaced with appropriate information.

Documentation for functions and data resides (as ordinary text files) in a subdirectory called `.Help` under the directory containing the S objects themselves. For example, if you are documenting a function `myfun` in the directory `/usr/me/.Data`, the completed documentation file should be moved into the `.Help` directory with the command

```
mv myfun.d /usr/me/.Data/.Help/myfun
```

To see more about how documentation files are organized, look at some examples. The documentation files for functions in this appendix are in the directory `s/.Functions/.Help` under the S home directory. Type

```
!echo $SHOME/s/.Functions/.Help
```

from inside S to see where this is on your machine.

EXAMPLES

```
prompt("grep")          # construct grep.d file
!vi grep.d   # fix up the documentation
!mkdir .Data/.Help   # if necessary, construct subdirectory
!mv grep.d .Data/.Help/grep          # install
```

---

prstructure　　　　　Print an Object with Attributes　　　**prstructure**

```
prstructure(x)
```

ARGUMENTS

x an object with attributes.

VALUE

x, with the invisible flag set to prevent reprinting.

SIDE EFFECTS

The function looks at the attributes of x and prints it as a matrix, array, or time-series, if the appropriate attributes (dim for the first two, or tsp for the third) are found. Other attributes are printed following the data in x. The print function calls prstructure if x has attributes.

SEE ALSO

print.

---

prts　　　　　　　　　　Print a Time Series　　　　　　　　**prts**

```
prts(x)
```

ARGUMENTS

x a time series, i.e., tsp(x) is not NULL.

VALUE

x, with the invisible flag set to prevent reprinting.

SIDE EFFECTS

prints x as a time-series; called by the print function if x appears to be a time-series. The time series parameters, tsp(x), are used to ensure that each line either contains a full cycle or that a full cycle occupies an integral number of lines. Month abbreviations are used for column labels if `frequency(x)` is 12, and quarter abbreviations are used if `frequency(x)` is 4. Otherwise the observation number within the current cycle is used.

After each page of output, the column labels are printed again, so that there should always be a copy of the column labels on the screen at any time. To avoid multiple copies of the column labels, execute

```
options(length=10000)
```

to specify a very long page. A new format may be chosen at the end of each page.

SEE ALSO

```
print, options.
```

EXAMPLES

```
> options(width=60)
> hstart
        Jan   Feb   Mar   Apr   May   Jun   Jul   Aug
1966:  81.9  79.0 122.4 143.0 133.9 123.5 100.0 103.7
1967:  61.7  63.2  92.9 115.9 134.2 131.6 126.1 130.2
1968:  82.7  87.2 128.6 164.9 144.5 142.5 142.3 141.0
...
        Sep   Oct   Nov   Dec
1966:  91.9  79.1  75.1  62.3
1967: 125.8 137.0 120.2  83.1
1968: 139.5 143.3 129.5  99.3
...
```

---

pt   see T   **pt**

---

punif   see Uniform   **punif**

q	Quit From S	q

```
q()
```

SIDE EFFECTS

Causes termination of the S session and returns to the operating system. If a graphics device is active, a device-dependent wrap-up routine will be executed. The function or expression `.Last` will be called or evaluated before quitting.

qbeta	see Beta	**qbeta**

qcauchy	see Cauchy	**qcauchy**

qchisq	see Chisquare	**qchisq**

qexp	see Exponential	**qexp**

qf	see F	**qf**

qgamma	see Gamma	qgamma

qlnorm	see Lognormal	qlnorm

qlogis	see Logistic	qlogis

qnorm	see Normal	qnorm

qqnorm	see qqplot	qqnorm

qqplot	Quantile-Quantile Plots	qqplot

```
qqplot(x, y, plot=TRUE)
qqnorm(x, datax=FALSE, plot=TRUE)
```

ARGUMENTS

x,y vectors (not necessarily of the same length). Each is taken as a sample, for the *x*- and *y*-axis values of an empirical probability plot. The function qqnorm takes a single vector of data for a normal probability plot.

datax if TRUE, data goes on the *x*-axis; if FALSE data goes on the *y*-axis.

plot if FALSE, qqplot and qqnorm return a list with components x and y, gving the coordinates of the points that would have been plotted.

Graphical parameters may also be supplied as arguments to this function (see par). These functions can also take arguments type and log to control plot type and logarithmic axes (see `plot`). Also, the arguments to the `title` function may be supplied to this function.

VALUE

if `plot` is FALSE, a list with components `x` and `y` are returned, giving coordinates of the points that would have been plotted.

EXAMPLES

```
zz ← qqplot(x,y,plot=F)          #save x and y coords of empirical qq
plot(zz)          #plot it
abline(rreg(zz$x,zz$y))    #fit robust line and draw it

# the example plot is produced by:
my.sample ← rt(50,5)
lab ← "50 samples from a t distribution with 5 d. f."
qqnorm(my.sample,main=lab,sub="QQ Plot with Normal")
```

50 samples from a t distribution with 5 d. f.

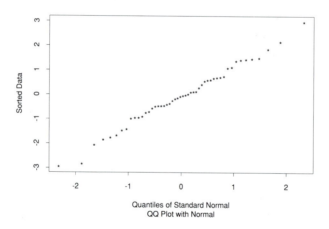

Quantiles of Standard Normal
QQ Plot with Normal

qr	QR Matrix Decomposition	**qr**

```
qr(x, tol = 1e-7)
is.qr(o)
as.qr(o)
```

ARGUMENTS

    x matrix of numeric data. Missing values are not allowed.

  tol tolerance for detecting linear dependencies among columns of x (see rank below).

    o any S object.

VALUE

qr returns an object representing the QR numerical decomposition of the matrix x. The method used is the Householder successive reflection procedure, adapted from the implementation used by the LINPACK library. The components of the returned object are as follows:

qr, qraux the numerical decomposition itself. qr is a matrix like x, while qraux is a vector of length ncol(x).

  rank the rank of x as computed by the decomposition. (If you really want to estimate the rank, the function svd is preferable.)

 pivot the pivoting of columns of x used to produce the decomposition.

is.qr returns TRUE if its argument has qr and qraux components, FALSE otherwise.

as.qr returns its argument if is.qr(x) is TRUE, and qr(x) otherwise.

NOTE

Unlike regression functions, qr does not add an intercept term. Bind on a column of 1s if you want an intercept. However, the results of qr.coef, etc., will reflect an intercept term, if used, when they take the decomposition as computed by a regression function.

SEE ALSO

qr.coef, qr.fitted, qr.resid, qr.qty, qr.qy, lsfit.

EXAMPLES

```
q ← qr(state.x77)
```

`qr.coef`   Use a QR Matrix Decomposition   **`qr.coef`**

```
qr.coef(qr, y)
qr.fitted(qr, y)
qr.resid(qr, y)
qr.qty(qr, y)
qr.qy(qr, y)
```

ARGUMENTS

  qr object representing a QR decomposition. This will typically have come from a previous call to the `qr` or `lsfit`.

  y vector or matrix of numeric data (the "dependent" data). The length of the vector or the number of rows of the matrix must correspond to the number of rows in the x matrix from which the decomposition was computed.

VALUE

  `qr.coef`, `qr.fitted` and `qr.resid` return the coefficients, the fitted values and the residuals that would be obtained by fitting y to the x matrix from which qr was obtained.

  `qr.qy` and `qr.qty` return the results of the matrix multiplications:

```
Q %*% y
t(Q) %*% y
```

  where Q is the order-`nrow(x)` orthogonal transformation represented by qr.

  The results of `qr.coef`, etc., will reflect an intercept term, if included, for example, in a call to `lsfit`.

  The QR decomposition used does not return an explicit orthogonal matrix. For reasons of accuracy and efficiency, an indirect representation of the decomposition is used. (See the LINPACK reference in section 8.2.)

SEE ALSO

  `qr`, `lsfit`.

EXAMPLES

```
reg0 ← lsfit(x,y)
coef1 ← qr.coef(reg0$qr, y1)  # different y, same x
```

qr.fitted	see qr.coef	**qr.fitted**

qr.qty	see qr.coef	**qr.qty**

qr.qy	see qr.coef	**qr.qy**

qr.resid	see qr.coef	**qr.resid**

qt	see T	**qt**

quantile	Empirical Quantiles	**quantile**

```
quantile(x, probs=seq(0,1,.25))
```

ARGUMENTS

    x vector of data.

  probs vector of desired probability levels. Values must be between 0 and 1 inclusive. The default produces a five number summary the minimum, lower quartile, median, upper quartile, and maximum of x.

VALUE

        vector of empirical quantiles corresponding to the probs levels in the sorted x data. Results are currently computed to single-precision accuracy only.

The algorithm linearly interpolates between order statistics of x, assuming that the ith order statistic is the $(i-.5)/\texttt{length(x)}$ quantile. The algorithm uses partial sorting, hence is quickly able to find a few quantiles even of large datasets.

EXAMPLES

```
quantile(mydata)      # five number summary
quantile(xxx,c(.33,.67))    # 33% and 67% points of xxx
```

---

quickvu	Make Slides with Simple Lists	**quickvu**

```
quickvu(head, listtype=".BL")
```

ARGUMENTS

head   optionally, the vu commands to start off the slide. By default, will color the title portion in color 1, embolden once and increase the size 20% over the remaining text.

listtype   The command defining the list type (".DL", ".NL", etc.) By default, bullet lists are produced.

VALUE

character vector implementing a slide suitably for an argument to the vu function. The slide consists by default of a multi-line title, left-justified and emboldened once, followed by a list of items. The quickvu function prompts for terminal input giving the title (terminated by an empty line). This is followed by input for the list items (one line per item by default) with an empty line signalling the end of the slide. Options are possible (see below).

The title, list marker and list text are generated in colors 1, 2 and 3 respectively. The limit of one line per item can be overridden by beginning the input line with "&". This character is thrown away and the rest of the line taken as a continuation of the previous line. (This allows also the input of vu control lines, but note that color, etc. are set at the beginning of each item; therefore, to change the color of an item make a .C line the first line of the item.)

SEE ALSO

vu.

EXAMPLES

```
> testvu ← quickvu( )
Title line: THE FIRST LINE OF THE TITLE
Title line: AND THE SECOND
Title line:
List item: I have a little list
List item: And they'd none of them be missed
List item: &  (which can be continued)
List item: And a third item.
List item:
```

qunif	see Uniform	qunif

range	Range of Data	range

```
range(...)
```

ARGUMENTS
>   ... numeric objects. Missing values (NAs) are allowed.

VALUE

vector of two elements, the first the minimum of all the elements of all arguments; the second the maximum. This function is useful as an argument to plotting when it is desired to specify the limits for the x- or y-axes. (See the example.) Any NAs in the input result in NAs in the output.

EXAMPLES

```
plot(x,y,ylim=range(y,0,1))  # force y-axis to include (0,1)
```

rank	Ranks of Data	**rank**

```
rank(x)
```

ARGUMENTS

  x numeric object.

VALUE

  the ranks; i.e., the i-th value is the rank of x[i]. In case of ties, the average rank is returned.

rbeta	see Beta	**rbeta**

rbind	see cbind	**rbind**

rbiwt	Robust Simple Regression by Biweight	**rbiwt**

```
rbiwt(x, y, start, k=6, tol=.001, iter=20)
```

ARGUMENTS

  x vector of observations on independent variable.
  y vector of observations on dependent variable.
  start vector giving starting values of intercept and slope. Default, use least-squares start.
  k biweight scale parameter.
  tol convergence criterion.
  iter maximum number of iterations.

VALUE

  list containing components coef, resid, and wt.

    `coef` vector giving intercept and slope.
  `resid` vector like `y` giving residuals from fit.
     `wt` vector giving weights used in final weighted least-squares step.

REFERENCE

Coleman, D., Holland, P., Kaden, N., Klema, V., and Peters, S. C., "A System of Subroutines for Iteratively Re-Weighted Least-Squares Computations", *ACM Trans. Math. Soft.*, Vol. 6, pp. 327-336, 1980.

SEE ALSO

Function `rreg` generalizes `rbiwt` to multiple regression.

EXAMPLES

```
plot(x,y)
abline(rbiwt(x,y))        #add line to plot
```

rcauchy	see Cauchy	**rcauchy**

rchisq	see Chisquare	**rchisq**

rdpen	see Deprecated	**rdpen**

Re	see Complex	**Re**

read	see Deprecated	**read**

readline	Read a Line from the Terminal	**readline**

```
readline( )
```

VALUE

character string giving the line read from the terminal.

EXAMPLES

```
cat("Do you want to continue? ")
ans ← readline()
if(ans=="n"|ans=="no") return()
```

REALPR	see DBLEPR	**REALPR**

reg	see Deprecated	**reg**

regprt	see Deprecated	**regprt**

regsum	see Deprecated	**regsum**

---

reload	Quit and Restart S	**reload**

```
reload()
```

SIDE EFFECTS

This function attempts to save the current context of S, quits from S, restarts and establishes the saved context. The purpose is to recover memory and reduce the size of an S process that has grown large because of a long period of computation. It should appear that nothing has changed as a result of the reloading; in particular, the contents of frame `0`, including options and search list, are preserved. One exception is that graphics devices are shut down and not restarted, since there is no way to guarantee that restarting the device would be harmless (for example, `postscript` might overwrite the output file).

This function will be called automatically whenever the memory usage exceeds one half of `options("memory")`. You can call it explicitly if you believe your process is slowing down because of accumulating memory.

---

remove	Remove Objects	**remove**

```
remove(names, where, frame)
```

ARGUMENTS

names character vector giving the names of objects to be removed.

where the S data directory from which the objects should be removed. It can either be a number or a character string. A number implies the corresponding element of the search list, so `where=2`, for example, removes an object from the second directory. If `where` is a character string, this is taken as the path name for a directory in the file system. The directory need not be on the search list.

frame the number of the frame, in the evaluation, from which the objects should be removed. Frame 0 is also a legal argument, meaning the session frame; i.e., those objects created by `assign()` with `frame=0`.

If both `where` and `frame` are omitted, removal is only permitted if the object came from the working directory. It is an error to supply both `where` and `frame`.

SEE ALSO

assign, get, ls.

EXAMPLES

remove ("abc") # remove "abc"

---

rep	Replicate Data Values	**rep**

rep(x, times, length)

ARGUMENTS

  x vector. Missing values (NAs) are allowed.

times how many times to replicate x. There are two ways to use times. If it is a single value, the whole of x is replicated that many times. If it is a vector of the same length as x, the result is a vector with times[1] replications of x[1], times[2] of x[2], etc.

length the desired length of the result. This argument may be given instead of times, in which case x is replicated as much as needed to produce a result with length data values.

VALUE

a vector of the same mode as x with the data values in x replicated according to the argument times or length.

EXAMPLES

```
rep(0,100)      # 100 zeroes
rep(1:10,10)       # 10 repetitions of 1:10
rep(1:10,1:10)  # 1, 2, 2, 3, 3, 3, ...
```

---

repeat	see Syntax	**repeat**

| **`rep.int`** | Replicate Integer Vector | **`rep.int`** |

```
rep.int(x, times)
```

ARGUMENTS

    `x` an object of storage mode "integer".

`times` number of times to replicate `x`.

This function is used internally in the `rep` function.

| **`replace`** | see append | **`replace`** |

| **`restart`** | Take Over Error Handling | **`restart`** |

```
restart(on=TRUE)
```

ARGUMENTS

    `on` if `TRUE`, cause errors to recall the function from which `restart` was called. If `FALSE` error control is returned to S (but see below).

This is a function to be used only by the adept and strong at heart. After it is called, and until a return from the function evaluation that contained the call to `restart`, all errors and interrupts, with one exception, will not get the user back to S prompt level. Instead, the function that called `restart` will be recalled, but with its local frame in the state that obtained when the error occurred. (Restart will have been cancelled at this point, but typically the restarted function will then call `restart` again.)

The one exception is that the quit signal (usually typed as control-backslash) will cancel unconditionally the restart and return the user to S prompt level. Keep in mind that a second quit signal will exit S entirely. (The quit signal has nothing to do with the S function `q`.)

Use of restart can be dangerous to your health and social standing. In particular, if the function calling `restart` has an error, an infinite loop of errors can easily result. Hence the use of quit as a loop-hole.

ALWAYS make sure that the calling function is bug-free before installing a call to `restart`.

EXAMPLES

```
# prompt for expressions & evaluate them
pause ← function() {
        restart(T)
        cat("Enter expressions, q to quit from pause\n")
        repeat {
                e ← parse(prompt = "<P> ")
                if(is.name(e[[1]]) && e[[1]]=="q")
                    return()
                print(eval(e, local = sys.parent(1)))
        }
}
# look at browser for another example
```

`restore`	Bring Back Dumped Objects	`restore`

```
restore(file)
```

ARGUMENTS

    `file` character string, interpreted as a file name.

SIDE EFFECTS

All data objects stored on `file` are placed in the local ".Data" directory. Normally, the file supplied to `restore` was previously created (maybe on another machine) by a call to `dump`. Note: this function is not affected by the current search list.

SEE ALSO

    `dget, dput, dump.`

EXAMPLES

```
dump(ls(),file="all.data")
restore("all.data")
```

return	see Syntax	**return**

rev	Reverse the Order of Elements in a Vector	**rev**

```
rev(x)
```

ARGUMENTS

     x   vector. Missing values (NAs) are allowed.

VALUE

vector like x but with the order of data values reversed (the last value in x is the first value in the result).

EXAMPLES

```
rev(sort(y))       # sort y in descending order
```

rexp	see Exponential	**rexp**

rf	see F	**rf**

rgamma	see Gamma	**rgamma**

rlnorm	see Lognormal	**rlnorm**

`rlogis`	see `Logistic`	`rlogis`

`rm`	Remove by Name	`rm`

```
rm(...)
```

ARGUMENTS

    ... names of objects to be removed. The arguments are not evaluated. The corresponding objects should either be on the working directory or be session objects.

SIDE EFFECTS

    the objects are removed.

SEE ALSO

    the function `remove`, which handles more general and more specific description of what objects to remove.

EXAMPLES

```
rm(x,y,z)  #remove objects x,y,z
```

`rnorm`	see `Normal`	`rnorm`

`round`	Rounding Functions	`round`

```
round(x, digits=0)
signif(x, digits=6)
```

ARGUMENTS

    x numeric object. Missing values (NAs) are allowed.

    digits number of decimal digits after the decimal point, in the case of `round` and total numer of digits, in the case of `signif`. For rounding, `digits` can be negative, for rounding large numbers to the nearest 10, 100, etc.

VALUE

object like x with data rounded to the specified number of places (round), or with the specified number of significant digits retained (signif).

SEE ALSO

ceiling, floor, trunc.

EXAMPLES

```
round(mydata, dig=2)      #round to 2 decimals
round(mydata, -1)         #round to nearest 10
x ← c(123456, .123456, .000123456)
round(x, 3)   # produces
[1] 123456.000      0.123      0.000
signif(x, 3)   # produces
[1] 1.23e+05 1.23e-01 1.23e-04
```

---

row   see col   **row**

---

rreg   Robust Regression   **rreg**

```
rreg(x, y, w, int=TRUE, init, method, wx,
        iter=20, k, acc, stop=1, conv=FALSE)
```

ARGUMENTS

　x matrix of independent variables for regression. Should not include a column of 1's for the intercept.

　y vector of dependent variable, to be regressed on x.

　w initial weights for robustness. w may be the weights computed from residuals in previous iterations of rreg. The argument wx should be used for weights that are to remain constant from iteration to iteration.

　int should intercept term be included in the regression?

　init optional vector of initial coefficient values (normally the result of some other regression, e.g., reg(x,y)$coef or l1fit(x,y)$coef). When omitted the initial value is computed as follows: if wx and/or w is supplied, it is the weighted least squares estimate, otherwise it is the ordinary least squares estimate.

method choice of method (see below). Default is the converged Huber estimate followed by two iterations of Bisquare.

wx optional weighting vector (for intrinsic weights, not the weights used in the iterative fit).

iter maximum number of iterations.

k constant in the weighting function. This constant is chosen to give the estimate a reasonable efficiency if the errors do come from a normal distribution. (See below for exact values.)

acc convergence tolerance; default 10*sqrt(machine precision).

stop method of testing convergence. Values 1, 2, 3, and 4 use relative change in residuals, coefficients and weights and an orthogonality test of residuals to x.

conv should component conv be returned as a result?

VALUE

list with the following components:

coef vector of coefficients in final fit.

resid vector of final residuals.

w vector of final weights in the iteration, excluding the influence of wx.

int flag telling whether intercept was used.

method name of robust weighting rule used.

k value of k used for method.

conv vector of the value of the convergence criterion at each iteration.

Results are currently computed to single-precision accuracy only.

METHOD

The routine uses iteratively reweighted least squares to approximate the robust fit, with residuals from the current fit passed through a weighting function to give weights for the next iteration. There are 8 possible weighting functions, all specified by character strings given as method: "andrews", "bisquare", "cauchy", "fair", "huber", "logistic", "talworth", and "welsch". The corresponding default values of k are 1.339, 4.685, 2.385, 1.4, 1.345, 1.205, 2.795, and 2.985. Method "huber" gives more least-squares-like fits usually; the proper choice of method, however, is still a research problem.

REFERENCE

Coleman, D., Holland, P., Kaden, N., Klema, V., and Peters, S. C., "A system of subroutines for iteratively re-weighted least-squares computations", *ACM Trans. Math. Soft.*, Vol. 6, pp. 327-336, 1980.

| rstab | see Stable | rstab |

| rt | see T | rt |

| runif | see Uniform | runif |

| .S | Call an Old S Function | .S |

```
.S(call, name)
```

ARGUMENTS

call expression calling the S function

name a character string, giving the name of the S function

VALUE

the value that the old-S function returns. Note that numeric arguments and numeric results are in single-precision.

Only users with old-S functions that are not to be rewritten in S have a reason to call .S (see appendix 4).

EXAMPLES

```
# Call an old
stem ← function(...)
.S(stem(...), "stem" )
```

`sabl`	Seasonal Decomposition	`sabl`

```
sabl(x, power, calendar=FALSE, trend=11,
     seasonal=15, revisions=FALSE)
```

ARGUMENTS

x   the time-series to be decomposed.

power   vector of powers for transforming `x`: `sabl` will pick the value from `power` that minimizes a measure of the interaction between trend and seasonal components. For a value `p` in `power`, `p>0` corresponds to the transformation `x^p`; `p==0` to `log(x)`; and `p<0` to `-x^p`. If `x` has any zero or negative values, no transformation is made and `power` defaults to 1. Otherwise, the default is `c(-1, -.5, -.25, 0, .25, .5, 1)`.

calendar   if `FALSE`, no calendar component is computed. Calendar computation can be done only for monthly data.

trend   number of points in the trend smoothing window, an odd integer greater than 2.

seasonal   number of points in the seasonal smoothing window, an odd integer greater than 2.

revisions   if `FALSE`, no revisions are calculated. The series must be at least 7 cycles long for revisions to be calculated. A maximum of 5 cycles of revisions are calculated.

VALUE

list with the following components:

trend   time-series giving the long term change in level.

seasonal   time-series giving the part of `x` that repeats or nearly repeats every `nper(x)` time units. This series contains predicted seasonal values for one additional cycle.

irregular   time-series giving the noisy variation not explained by `trend` or `seasonal` (or `calendar` if computed).

transformed   the series `x` after power transformation and month length correction, from which the components are extracted.

adjusted   time-series with the seasonal component and calendar component (if computed) removed, on the original (untransformed) scale.

calendar   time-series of variation due to day-of-the-week effect. Returned if argument `calendar` is `TRUE`. This series contains predicted calendar values for one additional cycle.

power   power that was actually used in transforming the time-series `x`.

tstat   vector of t statistics used to pick the power actually used to transform `x`. Only returned if length of the argument `power` is >1.

```
revisions
```
time-series of revisions, if computed.
```
weights
```
time-series of final robustness weights used in the decomposition.

The components returned by `sabl` are related as follows:

`transformed` **equals** `trend + seasonal + irregular`
    (if no calendar component was computed)

or

`transformed` **equals** `trend + seasonal + calendar + irregular`
    (if calendar component was computed)

REFERENCE

William S. Cleveland and Susan J. Devlin, "Calendar Effects in Monthly Time Series: Modeling and Adjustment", *Journal of the American Statistical Association,* Vol. 77, No. 379, pp. 520-528, September 1982.

SEE ALSO

`sablplot` and `monthplot`.

EXAMPLES

```
h ← sabl(hstart)     #decomposition of housing starts series
tsplot(hstart, h$adjusted, type="pl")
```

---

sablplot   Sabl Decomposition - Data and Components Plot   **sablplot**

```
sablplot(y, title="")
```

ARGUMENTS

y object containing components `trend`, `seasonal` and `irregular`, typically the result of a call to the function `sabl`. y may optionally contain the component `calendar`. The decomposed series may be in a component named `transformed` or `y`. If it is not present, it is computed as the sum of the `trend`, `seasonal`, `irregular`, and `calendar` (if present) components.

title main title for the page of plots.

EFFECT

This function produces one page of plots, showing in separate plots the decomposed series, and the trend, seasonal, calendar (if there is one), and irregular components. To the right of each plot is a bar which portrays the relative scaling of that plot.

REFERENCE

William S. Cleveland and Irma J. Terpenning, "Graphical Methods for Seasonal Adjustment", *Journal of the American Statistical Association,* Vol. 77, No. 377, pp. 52-62.

EXAMPLES

```
h ← sabl(hstart)
sablplot(h,"Housing Starts")
```

---

sample   Generate Random Samples or Permutations of Data   **sample**

```
sample(x, size, replace=FALSE)
```

ARGUMENTS

x   numeric or character vector of data (the population) to be sampled, or a positive integer giving the size of the population, which is then taken to be 1:x. Missing values (NAs) are allowed.

size   sample size. Default is the same as the population size, and thus (with replace=FALSE) will generate a random permutation.

replace   if TRUE, sampling will be done with replacement.

VALUE

if length(x)>1 a sample from x; otherwise, the result is a set of integers between 1 and x giving the indices of the selected elements.

EXAMPLES

```
sample(state.name,10)    # pick 10 states at random
sample(1e6,75)   # pick 75 numbers between 1 and one million
sample(50)       # random permutation of numbers 1:50
```

`sapply`   Apply a Function to Elements of a List   **`sapply`**

```
sapply(X, FUN, ...)
```

ARGUMENTS

     X   any S object; usually a list. Missing values (NAs) are allowed if FUN accepts them.

   FUN   function or character string giving the name of a function.

    ...   other arguments to FUN, if any.

VALUE

object whose first element is the result of FUN applied to the first element of X, and so on. If all the results are the same length, sapply returns a matrix with one column for each component. If all the results are scalars, a vector is returned. Otherwise a list of the results is returned.

SEE ALSO

lapply is a simplified version of sapply. lapply calls a function for each element of a list and returns a list. Function apply can be used to perform similar operations on the sections of a matrix or array, and tapply operates on data classified by categorical variables.

EXAMPLES

```
sapply(x,mean)  #vector of means of components of x
sapply(x,sort)  # sort the components
```

---

save   see Deprecated   **save**

`scale`	Scale Columns of a Matrix	`scale`

> `scale(x, center=TRUE, scale=TRUE)`

ARGUMENTS

x matrix to be scaled. Missing values (NAs) are allowed.

center control over the value subtracted from each column. If TRUE, the mean of (the non-missing data in) each column is subtracted from the column. If given as a vector of length `ncol(x)`, this vector is used; i.e., `center[j]` is subtracted from column j. If FALSE, no centering is done.

scale control over the value divided into each column to scale it. If TRUE each column (after centering) is divided by the square root of sum-of-squares over n−1, where n is the number of of non-missing values. If given as a vector of length `ncol(x)`, column j is divided by `scale[j]`. If FALSE, no scaling is done.

VALUE

matrix like x with optional centering and scaling.

The default values of `center` and `scale` produce columns with mean 0 and standard deviation 1.

SEE ALSO

`sweep`.

EXAMPLES

```
scale(x)   #scale to correlation (0 mean, 1 std dev)
scale(x, center=apply(x,2,median), scale=FALSE)
     #remove column medians, do not scale
```

scan	Input Data from a File	**scan**

```
scan(file="", what=numeric(), n, sep,
      multi.line = F, flush = F, append = F)
```

ARGUMENTS

file character string naming the file containing the data. If the string is empty (""), data will be read from standard input, scan will prompt with the index for the next data item, and data input can be terminated by a blank line. Otherwise, the end of input must be signalled by an end-of-file.

what a pattern for the data to be read, in the form of an S object. If what is a numeric, character, or complex vector, scan will interpret all fields on the file as data of the same mode as that object. So, what=character() causes scan to read data as character fields.

It is possible to read simultaneously data of more than one mode. For example, if fields were alternately numeric and character (e.g., two columns of data on the file),

```
scan(myfile,list(0,""))
```

would read them and return an object of mode list, with a numeric vector and a character vector as its two elements. The elements of what can be anything, so long as you have numbers where you want numeric fields, character data where you want character fields and complex numbers where you want complex fields. An element NULL in what causes the corresponding field to be skipped during input. The elements are used only to decide the kind of field, unless append is TRUE (see below). Notice that scan retains the names attribute, if any, of the list, so that

```
z ← scan(myfile,list(pop=0,city=""))
```

would let you refer to z$pop and z$city.

nmax maximum number of items to read from the file. If omitted, the function reads to the end of file (or to an empty line, if reading from standard input).

sep optional separator (single character). If omitted, any amount of white space (blanks or tabs) can separate fields. The main use for separators is to allow white space inside character fields. For example, suppose in the above the numeric field was to be followed by a tab with text filling out the rest of the line.

```
z ← scan(myfile,list(pop=0,city=""),sep="\t")
```

would allow blanks in the text. (The alternative would be to quote the text and omit the separator.)

multi.line   if FALSE, all the fields must appear on one line: if scan reaches the end of the line without reading all the fields, an error occurs. This is useful for checking that no fields have been omitted. If this argument is TRUE, reading will continue disregarding where new lines occur.

flush   if TRUE, scan will flush to the end of the line after reading the last of the fields requested. This allows putting comments after the last field that are not read by scan, but also prevents putting multiple sets of items on one line.

append   if TRUE, the returned object will include all the elements in the what argument, with the input data for the respective fields appended to each component. If FALSE (the default), the data in what is ignored, and only the modes matter.

VALUE

as described above, an object like that presented in the what argument.

Any field that cannot be interpreted according to the mode(s) supplied to scan will cause an error. The reading of numeric data in scan is done by means of C scan formats, rather than by the rules of the S parser (the function parse). This should not cause any serious inconsistencies between the two functions, but there is no guarantee that the same input read both ways would produce numeric results that are exactly equal.

Reading of large amounts of data is more efficiently done by scan than by parse, which on the other hand does not need to know in advance what type of data to expect in each field.

SEE ALSO

parse.

EXAMPLES

```
scan()  # read numeric values from standard input
# read a label & two numeric fields, make a matrix
z ← scan("myfile",list(n="",0,0))
mat ← cbind(z[[2]],z[[3]])
dimnames(mat)  ← list(z$n,c("X","Y"))
```

search	see Deprecated	**search**

segments	Plot Disconnected Line Segments or Arrows	**segments**

```
segments(x1, y1, x2, y2)
arrows(x1, y1, x2, y2, size=.02, open=F, rel=F)
```

ARGUMENTS

x1,y1,

x2,y2   coordinates of the end-points of the segments or arrows. Lines will be drawn from `(x1[i],y1[i])` to `(x2[i],y2[i])`. Missing values (NAs) are allowed. Any segments with any NAs as end-points will not be drawn.

size   width of the arrowhead as a fraction of the length of the arrow if `rel` is TRUE. If `rel` is FALSE, `size` is arrowhead width in inches.

open   logical, if TRUE the arrowhead is "v" shaped, if FALSE it is diamond shaped.

rel   logical, should arrowhead be sized relative to the length of the arrow?

Graphical parameters may also be supplied as arguments to this function (see `par`).

SEE ALSO

`lines` which draws a curve (connected line segments).

EXAMPLES

```
# draw arrows from ith to i+1st points
s ← seq(length(x)-1)    # sequence one shorter than x
arrows(x[s], y[s], x[s+1], y[s+1])
```

---

seq	Sequences	**seq**

```
from:to      # as operator
seq(from, to, by, length, along)   # as function
```

ARGUMENTS

from starting value of sequence.

to ending value of sequence.

by spacing between successive values in the sequence.

length number of values in the sequence.

along an object.

VALUE

a numeric vector with values (from, from+by, from+2*by, ... to). If arguments are omitted, an appropriate sequence is generated; for example, with seq(to=n) a sequence from 1 to the n is constructed. from may be larger or smaller than to. If by is specified, it must have the appropriate sign to generate a finite sequence.

To generate a sequence from 1 to length(x) to parallel an object x, use seq(along=x). This produces the desired result even if the length of x is 0 or 1. Except for these two cases, either seq(x) or 1:length(x) will produce the same result.

When used as an operator, : has a high precedence (see Syntax); for example, to create a sequence from 1 to n-1, parentheses are needed 1:(n-1).

EXAMPLES

```
seq(5)  #1,2,3,4,5
1:5 #same thing

5:1 #5,4,3,2,1

seq(0, 1, .01)  #0,.01,.02,.03,...,1.

seq(along=x)  # 1, 2, ..., length(x)

seq(-3.14,3.14,length=100)    # 100 values from -pi to pi
```

`set.seed`   Set Seed for Random Number Generators   **`set.seed`**

```
set.seed(i)
```

ARGUMENTS

    i numeric. Should be an integer between 0 and 1000.

Random number generators in S are all based upon a single uniform random number generator, that generates numbers in a very long, but ultimately periodic sequence. The position in the sequence is held in object `.Random.seed`. Function `set.seed` sets `.Random.seed` so that subsequent calls to random number generator functions (`runif`, `rnorm`, etc.) will generate numbers from a new portion of the overall cycle.

SIDE EFFECTS

    Sets value of object `.Random.seed` in the working directory.

SEE ALSO

    `.Random.seed` in Appendix 2.

EXAMPLES

```
set.seed(153)
```

---

show   see `printer`   **show**

---

signif   see `round`   **signif**

---

sin   see `cos`   **sin**

single	Single Precision Objects	**single**

```
single(length=0)
is.single(x)
as.single(x)
```

ARGUMENTS

length length desired for the resulting object.

   x any S object.

VALUE

single returns a simple object of storage mode single, and the length specified.

is.single returns TRUE if x is a simple object of storage mode single, and FALSE otherwise.

as.single returns x if x is a simple object of storage mode single, and otherwise a single object of the same length as x and with data resulting from coercing the elements of x to storage mode single.

In most S expressions it is not necessary to explicitly ensure that data is of a particular storage mode. When testing for data suitable for arithmetic, for example, it is better to use is.numeric(x), which will return TRUE for any numeric object. Normally, S does numeric computations with double precision. About the only need for storage mode single comes when using the interface to a Fortran subroutine with arguments that are declared REAL. (see .Fortran.)

Note the difference between coercing to a simple object of storage mode single and setting the storage mode attribute:

```
storage.mode(myobject) ← "single"
```

This changes the storage mode of myobject but leaves all other attributes unchanged (so a matrix stays a matrix, e.g.). The value of as.single(myobject) would have no attributes.

SEE ALSO

.Fortran, .C.

EXAMPLES

```
z ← single(length(zz))  # a single object same length as zz
.Fortran("mysub",as.single(x))
```

sinh	see cosh	**sinh**

sink	Send S Output to a File	**sink**

```
sink(file)
```

ARGUMENTS

file optional, character string giving the name of a file.

If file is given as a character string, output is diverted to a file named file. If file is omitted, diversion is ended.

SIDE EFFECTS

When output is being diverted to the sink file, nothing appears on the terminal except prompt characters and error messages. In particular, functions using the unix() interface will not put standard output on the user's terminal. This means that editor functions such as ed() and vi() can not be used when a sink is in effect.

Sink files cannot be nested, i.e., if sink is called when output is being diverted to a sink file, the previous diversion is terminated.

EXAMPLES

```
sink("my.output")        # divert output to file
... now do anything
sink( )   # revert output to the terminal
```

smooth	Non-linear Smoothing Using Running Medians	**smooth**

```
smooth(x, twice=TRUE)
```

ARGUMENTS

    x vector (at least 5 points) to be smoothed.

  twice logical flag, should twicing be done? Twicing is the process of smoothing, computing the residuals from the smooth, smoothing these and adding the two smoothed series together.

VALUE

smoothed vector using a method known as *4(3RSR)2H twice* (see the reference). Results are currently computed to single-precision accuracy only.

REFERENCE

J. W. Tukey, *Exploratory Data Analysis,* Chapters 7 and 16, Addison-Wesley, Reading, Massachusetts, 1977.

SEE ALSO

```
spline, lowess.
```

solve	Solve Linear Equations and Invert Matrices	**solve**

```
solve(a, b)
```

ARGUMENTS

  a matrix of coefficients. Must be square and non-singular.

  b optional matrix of coefficients. If b is missing, the inverse of matrix a is returned.

VALUE

the solution x to the system of equations a %*% x = b.

SEE ALSO

```
qr, qr.coef, chol.
```

EXAMPLES

```
ainv ← solve(a)       #invert a
```

| **sort** | Sort in Ascending Numeric or Alphabetic Order | **sort** |

```
sort(data)
```

ARGUMENTS

    data vector. Missing values (NAs) are allowed.

VALUE

vector with its data sorted in ascending order and any NAs omitted. Character data is sorted according to the ASCII collating sequence, where digits precede upper-case letters, which precede lower-case letters. The position of other characters is unintuitive.

Any attributes of x will be lost in the sorting; the result is always a vector.

Sorting of non-atomic data is allowed, but the definition of ordering is, inevitably, somewhat arbitrary. Its usefulness is mostly limited to special situations (like searching).

SEE ALSO

sort.list or order to do more flexible things.

| **sort.list** | List of Indices that Sort Data | **sort.list** |

```
sort.list(x)
```

ARGUMENTS

    x an object.

VALUE

permutation of the elements of x that would sort it in ascending order.

SEE ALSO

order, which does the job of sort.list on more than one object, and sort, which actually does the sorting.

EXAMPLES

```
# sort a matrix according to its 1st column
mat[ sort.list(mat[,1]), ]
```

---

source	Parse and Evaluate S Expressions from a File	**source**

```
source(file, local = F)
```

ARGUMENTS

`file` character string giving the name of a file. The entire contents of the file will be parsed and the resulting expressions evaluated. Assignments on the file will be global or local according to the optional second argument.

`local` if `FALSE`, the expressions on the file will be evaluated in the top (global) frame; otherwise, locally to the function calling `source`.

VALUE

the value of the last expression on the file (see `eval`). Automatic printing of this result is turned off, if `source` is called at the top level.

---

spline	Cubic Spline Approximation	**spline**

```
spline(x, y, n=100, periodic=FALSE, boundary=0,
       xmin=min(x), xmax=max(x))
```

ARGUMENTS

`x,y` x- and y-coordinates of points on a function to be approximated. This argument may be a list containing components named `x` and `y`.

`n` desired number of output points.

`periodic` logical, is the function periodic? If `TRUE`, the y-values at `min(x)` and `max(x)` should agree and the output will have derivatives matched at these end points.

`boundary` constant used in boundary value computation. The second derivative of the output function at the end points will be `boundary` times the second derivative at the adjacent point.

`xmin,xmax` output `x` values will be spaced in `n` equal increments from `xmin` to `xmax`.

VALUE

list containing components named `x` and `y` with the results of the cubic spline fitting. The spline output has two continuous derivatives and goes exactly through the input points.

REFERENCE

The function was derived from the UNIX system command "spline", which gives the following reference: R. W. Hamming, *Numerical Methods for Scientists and Engineers,* 2nd ed., pp. 349ff.

EXAMPLES

```
lines(spline(myx,myy))        # draw smooth curve through data
```

---

split   Split Data by Groups   **split**

```
split(data, group)
```

ARGUMENTS

data vector containing data values to be grouped. Missing values (NAs) are allowed.

group vector or category giving the group for each data value. For example, if the third value of `group` is 12, the third value in `data` will be placed in a group with all other data values whose group is 12.

VALUE

list in which each component contains all data values associated with a group. Within each group, data values are ordered as they originally appeared in `data`. The name of the component is the corresponding value in `group`, or the corresponding category name.

USAGE

The main use for `split` is to create a data structure to give to `boxplot`. A combination of `code` and `tapply` is usually preferred to using `split` followed by `sapply`.

EXAMPLES

```
boxplot(split(income,month))
split(people,age %/% 10)      # by decades
split(gnp,cycle(gnp))     #component for each month
split(student,grade)
```

sqrt	see exp	**sqrt**

Stable	Stable Family of Distributions	**Stable**

```
rstab(n, index, skewness=0)
```

ARGUMENTS

n sample size. If `length(n)` is larger than 1, then `length(n)` random values are returned.

index vector of indexes in the interval (0,2]. These are specified in the form given in the reference. An index of 2 corresponds to the normal, 1 to the Cauchy. Generally, smaller values mean longer tails.

skewness vector of modified skewnesses (see the reference). Negative and positive values correspond to skewness to the left and right.

VALUE

random sample from the specified stable distribution Results are currently computed to single-precision accuracy only.

Stable distributions are of considerable mathematical interest. Statistically, they are used mostly when an example of a very long-tailed distribution is required. For small values of `index`, the distribution degenerates to point mass at 0. See the reference and other works cited there.

Note that there are no density, probability or quantile functions supplied for this distribution. The efficient computation of such values is an open problem.

REFERENCE

J. M. Chambers, C. L. Mallows, and B. W. Stuck, "A Method for Simulating Stable Random Variables", *JASA,* Vol. 71, pp. 340-344, 1976.

EXAMPLES

`hist(rstab(200,1.5,1.5))` #fairly long tails, skewed right

| stamp | Time Stamp Output, Graph, and Audit File | stamp |

```
stamp(name=date(), print=TRUE, plot=TRUE)
```

ARGUMENTS

name character string to be printed, plotted, and put on audit file. Default is the current date and time in the form returned by the `date` function: `Tue Jun  1 14:00:16 EDT 1988`.

print should `name` be printed on the terminal? Default TRUE.

plot should `name` be plotted in the lower right corner of the current plot? Default TRUE if a graphical device has been specified.

Since the current date and time is plotted on the current graphical device as well as appearing on the terminal and in the audit file, the `stamp` function makes it easy to identify the functions used to create a plot or display.

EXAMPLES

```
plot(x,y)
stamp()    # an interesting plot
```

| stars | Star Plots of Multivariate Data | stars |

```
stars(x, full=TRUE, scale=TRUE, radius=TRUE,
      type="l", labels, head, max, byrow=FALSE,
      nrow, ncol)
```

ARGUMENTS

x matrix of data. One star symbol will be produced for each row of the matrix. Missing values (NAs) are allowed.

full logical; if TRUE, the symbols will occupy a full circle. Otherwise, they occupy the (upper) semi-circle only.

scale logical; if TRUE, the columns of the data matrix are scaled so that the maximum value in each column is 1 and the minimum 0. If FALSE, the presumption is that the data has been scaled by some other algorithm to the range $0<=x[i,j]<=1$.

radius logical, if TRUE, the radii corresponding to each variable in the data will be drawn (out to the point corresponding to $x[i,j]==1$).

      `type` optional character string, giving the type of star to draw. Reasonable values are `"l"`, `"p"`, `"b"` for lines, points and both.

    `labels` optional character vector for labelling the plots. If omitted, the first element of `dimnames(x)` is used, if available; otherwise, labels are `"1"`, `"2"`, etc. If supplied, the label vector must have length equal to `nrow(x)`.

      `head` optional character string for a running head. This is plotted as a title at the top of each page. By default, the name of the data is used. If there is more than one page, the page number is included in the title.

       `max` optional, suggested limit for the number of rows or columns of plots on a single page. Default forces all symbols to be on one page. The algorithm tries to choose an array of plots which efficiently uses the available space on the display.

   `byrow` logical; should the symbols be plotted row-by-row across the page, or column-by-column?

     `nrow`

     `ncol` optionally may be given to specify exactly the number of rows and columns for the array of plots on each page.

EXAMPLES

```
# the example plot is produced by:
stars(votes.repub[state.region==1,]/100,radius=T,scale=F,
      head="Republican Votes (Northeast) 1856 - 1976")
```

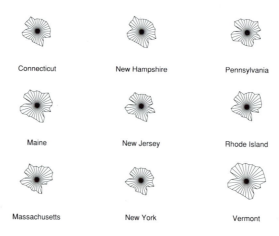

Republican Votes (Northeast) 1856 - 1976

Connecticut	New Hampshire	Pennsylvania
Maine	New Jersey	Rhode Island
Massachusetts	New York	Vermont

starsymb	Plot a Single Star Symbol	**starsymb**

```
starsymb(x, full=TRUE, scale=TRUE, radius=TRUE,
        type="l", collab, sample=1)
```

ARGUMENTS

- x   data matrix, as passed to stars. Missing values (NAs) are allowed.
- full   logical, TRUE if full 360 degree symbols wanted.
- scale   logical, TRUE, if the columns of the matrix should be scaled independently.
- radius   logical, if TRUE, radii corresponding to each variable will be drawn.
- type   the type of the plotted symbol (see stars).
- collab   vector of character string labels for the variables (columns of x). If available, the second element of dimnames(x) will be used as a default.
- sample   which of the star symbols for the data x (row of x) should be shown to illustrate the symbol?

EXAMPLES

```
# plot the republican votes from New Jersey
starsymb(votes.repub/100, sample=30, scale=F)
title(main=paste("Republican Votes for", state.name[30]))
```

Republican Votes for New Jersey

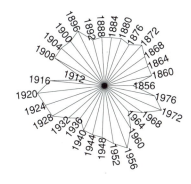

start	see `tsp`	**start**

std.trace	see `trace.on`	**std.trace**

stem	Stem-and-Leaf Display	**stem**

```
stem(x, nl, scale,
     twodig=1, fence, head=T, depth=F)
```

ARGUMENTS

- x   numeric vector to be displayed. Missing values (NAs) are allowed.
- nl   number of different leaf values on a stem. Allowed values are 2, 5, 10. Default is to determine an appropriate value automatically.
- scale   position at which break occurs between stem and leaf, counting to the right from the decimal point; e.g., −1 would break between the tens and the units digit. By default, a suitable position is chosen from the range of the data.
- twodig   number of leaf digits, 1 or 2.
- fence   the multiple of the inter-quartile range used to determine outliers. By default, any point further than 2 inter-quartile ranges from the nearest quartile is considered an outlier, and is printed separately from the body of the stem-and-leaf display. If the inter-quartile range is zero, the algorithm performs outlier detection by means of quartiles of the remainder of the data after exclusion of values equal to the median and quartiles.
- head   if TRUE, print a heading giving median, quartiles, and counts of data values and NAs.
- depth   if TRUE, precede each line with depth and count. The count is the number of data values on a line. The depth is the cumulative sum of the counts to the nearer extreme.

EXAMPLES

```
> stem(lottery.payoff)

N = 254    Median = 270.25
Quartiles = 194, 365

Decimal point is 2 places to the right of the colon

    0 : 8
    1 : 000011122233333333333344444
    1 : 5555556666667777777888888889999999999
    2 : 0000000111111111111222222223333333344444444
    2 : 555556666666666777778889999999999999999
    3 : 00000000111111222233333333333444
    3 : 555555556666677777777888888889999999
    4 : 0122234
    4 : 55555678888889
    5 : 111111134
    5 : 555667
    6 : 44
    6 : 7

High: 756.0 869.5
```

stop	Error and Warning Messages	**stop**

```
stop(message)
warning(message)
```

ARGUMENTS

message   character string. The function `stop` prints the name of the function calling `stop` and `message`, and then terminates execution of the current
expression. If `message` is omitted, the expression is terminated silently.
Function `warning` prints a similar warning message at the end of evaluation of the expression, but does not affect execution.

SIDE EFFECTS

If too many warning messages are generated in one expression (currently
more than five), the messages are stored together on a session object
named `last.warning`. Only the number of warnings is then printed.
The function `warnings` will print out the stored messages.

SEE ALSO

```
warnings, restart.
```

EXAMPLES

```
warning(paste("Rank is",n,"should be",ncol(x)))
if(any(is.na(x))) stop("NAs are not allowed in x")
```

---

storage	Show Memory Usage	**storage**

```
storage()
```

VALUE

object describing the current internal storage allocated by S. Internal storage in S is allocated in arenas (currently 4090 bytes) which are then divided to satisfy memory requests. Not all of the arena will be used up by current requests. Each arena is associated with one of the frames (function calls) currently being evaluated. Storage requests that would occupy more than half of a standard arena are given a separate individual arena.

The four components of the value of `storage` give the allocated and used sizes, the actual locations in memory, and the associated frame numbers.

`allocated` size (in bytes) of each allocated arena.
`used` number of bytes used in each arena.
`location` starting memory address for the arena.
`frame` frame (function call) associated with each arena.

EXAMPLES

```
# barplot (from a function) of local arenas
barplot(temp$allocated[temp$frame == sys.nframe()],
    xlab="Successive Arenas Allocated")
```

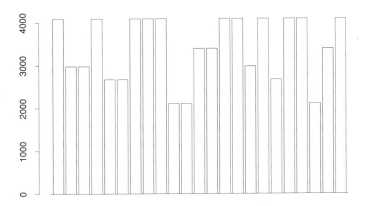

Successive Arenas Allocated

| `storage.mode` | see mode | `storage.mode` |

| `structure` | An Object with Given Attributes | `structure` |

```
structure(DATA,...)
```

ARGUMENTS

DATA any object.

... any number of named arguments, to become the attributes of the object.

VALUE

DATA, with attributes as specified by the remaining arguments.

This function is used to create an object and assign its attributes in one call; for example, the output of `dump` may contain calls to `structure`.

SEE ALSO

`attributes`.

EXAMPLES

```
structure(1:12,dim=c(3,4))
```

Subscript	Extract or Replace Parts of an Object	**Subscript**

```
x[i]
x[i, j, ...]
x[[i]]
x[[i, j, ...]]
x$name
```

ARGUMENTS

x any object.

i, j subscript expressions, used to identify which elements to extract or replace. The expressions may be empty (meaning all possible subscripts), logical, numeric, or character.

name an name or quoted string.

VALUE

These are the *extraction* functions, returning some elements or properties of an object. They may also appear on the left of an assignment operation, to carry out *replacement* in an object.

Vector subscripts are generated with x[i] when i and x are both vectors. The result of the expression is to extract or replace elements of x corresponding to a vector of positive *indices* computed according to the value of i.

If i is empty, all of x is extracted or replaced. If i is logical the indices are produced by starting at 1 and selecting the numbers for which the corresponding element i is TRUE. If i is shorter than length(x), it is extended by cyclic repetition. It can be longer than length(x) as well, with no change in the computation of indices. If i has mode "character", indices are determined by matching the elements of i against the attribute names(x). Unmatched names (including the case that there is no such attribute) index outside the current length of x. If i is numeric, and all(i<=0) the indices consist of the elements of seq(along=x) that do not match any elements in -i. Otherwise, i itself is taken to be the indices. The indices can have any positive values, 0, or NA. Zeroes are dropped before using the indices.

The computed indices are used for extraction or replacement. The rule for extraction is that the value of x[i] has the same mode as x, and the same length as the number of indices. The elements of x[i] are the elements of x corresponding to the indices, except if the indices are greater than the length of x or are NA. In either of those exceptions the returned elements are "missing"; that is, NA for an atomic mode and NULL for a non-atomic mode. All the attributes of x will be discarded in the subset, except for the names attribute. The names attribute of x[i] will be names(x)[i].

For replacements,

```
x[i] ← value
```

the rule is that the length of x will be set to the largest value in the indices, if that is bigger than the current length of x. If x and value do not have the same mode, then one or the other will be coerced to the common mode that can represent both without loss of information. This may mean that replacing elements of an object will change its mode.

If there are k subscripts and x is a k-way array, indices identifying a sub-array of x are computed from the i-th subscript with respect to (1:dim(x))[i]. Character subscripts in the i-th expression are used relative to the i-th element of dimnames(x). If x is a k-way array and the single subscript is a matrix with k columns, vector subscripts, one element per row of i, are computed in the same way.

The computations for x[[i]] are identical to the above except that the expression is required to identify a single element to be extracted or replaced. The value returned for extraction is the same as for x[i] if x is atomic (e.g., numeric). If x is recursive (e.g., a list) the single extracted element is returned, not the list of length 1 that x[i] would produce.

The expression x$name is the name *component* of x. It is equivalent to x[["name"]] if x is recursive and NULL otherwise. Replacement of the name component may coerce an object to be a list.

SEE ALSO

    attr.

EXAMPLES

```
x[x!=999.999]      # x values not equal to 999.999
x[order(y)]        # sort x by increasing values of y
x[-c(1,3)]         # all but the first and third
```

```
list(1:10,2:3)[2]        # value is list(2:3)
list(1:10,2:3)[[2]]      # value is 2:3
x[2,3] ← 8.4             # change the value of a matrix element
state.x77["Alabama",]    # print the row for Alabama
A ← array(1:30, c(5,3,2) )   # array with dimension 5 x 3 x 2
A[1,1,1]                 # a scalar, the first data value of A
A[1]                     # the same
A[,1:2,]                 # a (5,2,2) array
A[A>3]                   # the vector 4:30
lsfit(x,y)$coef          # coefficients from a fitted model
```

---

substitute   Substitute in an Expression   **substitute**

```
substitute(expr, frame)
```

ARGUMENTS

> `expr` an S expression.
>
> `frame` an object of mode `list`; if supplied, it is treated as the frame in which the substitution is done. More commonly, it is omitted and the local frame of the function calling `substitute` is used.

VALUE

> an object containing the unevaluated `expr`, with any names occurring in `expr` replaced by the corresponding component of `frame`. If the name was a formal argument to the function calling `substitute`, then the expression for that argument will be substituted—either the actual or the default expression. This substitution is unaffected by whether the argument has been evaluated yet. Any other names occurring in the frame will also be substituted with their local assigned values. Names that are not found in the frame will be left alone.
>
> If no name matches occur, `expr` is returned as a parsed, but unevaluated object. In this case the result is equivalent to
>
> > ```
> > expression(expr)[[1]]
> > ```

SEE ALSO

> `expression`.

EXAMPLES

```
# argument x as a character string label
label ← deparse(substitute(x))
```

subtree	Extract Part of a Cluster Tree	subtree

```
subtree(tree, leaves)
```

ARGUMENTS

    `tree` a cluster tree object, normally the result of a call to `hclust`.

    `leaves` vector of objects (i.e., row numbers of the original data matrix) which should be included in the extracted subtree.

VALUE

the smallest subtree of `tree` which includes all the `leaves`. The subtree includes the components `merge`, `height` and `order` described under `hclust`. It can be used in the various summaries of cluster results, such as `plclust`.

SEE ALSO

`hclust, cutree, plclust.`

EXAMPLES

```
z ← hclust(dismat)
subtree(z,c(1,10))    #subtree including 1st and 10th objects
```

sum	Sums and Products	sum

```
sum(...)
prod(...)
```

ARGUMENTS

    `...` numeric or complex objects. Missing values (NAs) are allowed, but will cause the value returned to be NA.

VALUE

the sum (product) of all the elements of all the arguments. If the total length of all the arguments is 0, `sum` returns 0 and `prod` returns 1.

EXAMPLES

```
mean(x) ← function(x) sum(x)/length(x)
```

| **sun** | Sun Device Driver | **sun** |

```
sun(ask=FALSE, color=FALSE)
```

ARGUMENTS

    `ask` should device driver print the message "GO?" to ask permission to clear the graphics window?

  `color` does this Sun workstation have color capability?

This device driver works by using the SunCore graphics routines to draw on the workstation screen. It works most naturally when using the Suntools window environment, although it will work in a non-window environment. When the driver is started, a new graphics window appears on the screen. This window can be repositioned and reshaped arbitrarily; whenever the window is changed, the current plot will be redrawn to fit in the new window.

When graphic input (`identify`, `locator`) is requested, use the mouse to position the cursor and hit button 1 to make a selection. Buttons 2 or 3 terminate graphic input.

Since characters are vector-drawn, character sizes and rotations are arbitrary. There are various line styles and colors.

A device must be specified before any graphics functions can be used.

| **svd** | Singular Value Decomposition | **svd** |

```
svd(x, nu, nv)
```

ARGUMENTS

    `x` matrix of arbitrary size.

  `nu` number of columns wanted in matrix `u`, possibly zero. Default is `min(nrow(x),ncol(x))`.

nv number of columns wanted in matrix v, possibly zero. Default is
min(nrow(x),ncol(x)).

VALUE

object containing the components of the singular value decomposition,
x=u %* d %*% t(v)

u if nu>0, an nrow(x) bx nu matrix of unit orthogonal columns. Missing
if nu=0.

d the vector of singular values (diagonal elements of matrix d).

v if nv>0, ncol(x) bx nv matrix of unit orthogonal columns. Missing if
nv=0.

---

sweep	Sweep Out Array Summaries	**sweep**

sweep(A, MARGIN, STATS, FUN="-', ...)

ARGUMENTS

A array. Missing values (NAs) are allowed.

MARGIN vector describing the dimensions of A that correspond to STATS.

STATS vector giving a summary statistic of array A that is to be swept out.
Missing values (NAs) are allowed.

FUN character string name of function to be used in sweep operation.

... additional arguments to FUN, if any.

VALUE

an array like A, but with marginal statistics swept out as defined by the
other arguments. In the most common cases, the function is "−" or "/" to
subtract or divide by statistics that result from using the apply function
on the array. For example: colmean ← apply(z,2,mean) computes
column means of array z. zcenter ← sweep(z,2,colmean) removes the column means.

More generally, based on MARGIN, there are one or more values of A that
would be used by apply to create STATS. sweep creates an array like
A where the corresponding value of STATS is used in place of each value
of A that would have been used to create STATS. The function FUN is
then used to operate element-by-element on each value in A and in the
constructed array.

SEE ALSO

> apply, scale.

EXAMPLES

> a ← sweep(a,2,apply(a,2,mean)) # subtract col means
> a ← sweep(a,1,apply(a,1,mean)) # subtract row means
> # a simple two-way analysis

---

switch	Evaluate One of Several Expressions	**switch**

> switch(EXPR, ...)

ARGUMENTS

> EXPR any S object; used to choose which of the remaining arguments to evaluate
>
> ... one of these arguments (at most) will be evaluated, and returned as the value of switch

VALUE

> switch evaluates its first argument. If the value is of mode character, the function looks among the names of the remaining arguments for one that exactly (not partially) matches the character string (only using the first element of the value). If there is a match, the corresponding argument is evaluated and returned as the value of switch; otherwise the first unnamed argument is evaluated and returned.
>
> If the first argument is not character, it is coerced to integer; if it is in the range 1 to nargs()-1, then the corresponding argument from the ... is evaluated and returned as the value of switch.
>
> If no selection is made, switch returns NULL.

symbols	Draw Symbols on a Plot	**symbols**

```
symbols(x, y, circles=, squares=, rectangles=,
        stars=, thermometers=, boxplots=,
        add=FALSE, inches=TRUE)
```

ARGUMENTS

x,y   coordinates of points. The coordinates can be given by two vector arguments or by a single argument x which is a time-series, a complex vector, a matrix with 2 columns, or a list containing components named x and y.

circles=   radii of circles.

squares=   lengths of the sides of squares.

rectangles=   matrix whose two columns give widths and heights of rectangles.

stars=   matrix with n columns, where n is the number of points to a star. The matrix should be scaled from 0 to 1.

thermometers=   matrix with 3 or 4 columns. The first two columns give the widths and heights of rectangular thermometer symbols. If the matrix has 3 columns, the third column gives the fraction of the symbol that is filled (from bottom up). If the matrix has 4 columns, the third and fourth columns give the fractions of the rectangle between which is filled.

boxplots=   matrix with 5 columns, giving the width and height of the box, the amount to extend on the top and bottom, and the fraction of the way up the box to draw the median line.

add   logical flag. If FALSE, a new plot is set up. If TRUE, symbols are added to the existing plot.

inches   if FALSE, the symbol parameters are interpreted as being in units of x and y. If TRUE, the symbols are scaled so that the largest symbol is one inch in size. If a number is given, the parameters are scaled so that inches is the size of the largest symbol in inches.

Only one of the arguments circles, squares, rectangles, stars, thermometers, or boxplots can be given.

Graphical parameters may also be supplied as arguments to this function (see par). Also, the arguments to the title function may be supplied to this function.

EXAMPLES

```
symbols(x,y,circle=radii,inches=5)
    # largest circle has radius  5 inches
```

```
p ← apply(parm,2,range)    #find min/max of each column of parm
pscale ← scale(p,center=p[1,],scale=p[2,]-p[1,])
symbols(x,y,stars=pscale)  # plot stars
```

synchronize	Synchronize Datasets	**synchronize**

```
synchronize(reset=FALSE, assign=TRUE, data=FALSE)
```

ARGUMENTS

reset should the current expression be terminated after synchronizing?

assign should pending assignments be committed?

data should the internal (frame 0 and other hashed) function definitions be thrown away?

SIDE EFFECTS

The internal contents of the evaluator are made consistent with the external databases, according to the arguments given. This takes place immediately, not at completion of the current expression. So, in particular, assignments are committed right away. An application of this function is to cases where another process wants to work with S as a co-process and both need to know that they are working with the same definition of the set of objects on the databases, even in the middle of an expression. The need may arise, for example, if the S expression is doing some interaction with the user. Another use of synchronize is in debugging, to ensure that objects are written to the working data.

EXAMPLES

```
# select datsets to remove, break to get out
cleandatabase ← function()
        repeat {
                cat(ls(), fill = T)
                name ← as.name(parse(prompt = "name? "))
                eval(substitute(rm(name)), local = F)
                synchronize()
        }
```

| **Syntax** | S Expressions | **Syntax** |

Expressions in S are typed by the user, parsed, and evaluated. The following rules define the expressions considered legal by the parser, and the mode of the corresponding object.

Literals

number	"numeric"
string	"character"
name	"name"
comment	"comment"
function (formals) expr	"function"

Calls

expr *infix* expr	"call"
expr *%anything%* expr	
unary expr	
expr (arglist)	
expr [arglist]	
expr [[arglist]]	
expr $ fname	

Assignment

expr ← expr	"<-"
expr _ expr	
expr → expr	
expr <<- expr	"<<-"

Conditional

if (expr) expr	"if"
if (expr) expr *else* expr	
for (*name in* expr) expr	"for"

Iteration

repeat expr	"repeat"
while (expr) expr	"while"

Flow

break	"break"
next	"next"
return (expr)	"return"
(expr)	"("
{ exprlist }	"{"

The additional syntactic forms introduced in the above rules are defined as follows:

exprlist:	expr
	exprlist ; expr
arglist:	arg
	arglist , arg
formals:	*empty*
	formal
	formals , formal
arg:	*empty*
	expr
	fname =
	fname = expr
formal:	*name*
	name = expr
fname:	*name*
	string

A typed expression may be continued on further lines by ending a line at a place where the line is obviously incomplete with a trailing comma, operator, or with more left parens than right parens (implying more rights will follow). The default prompt character is "> "; when continuation is expected the default prompt is "+ ".

Numeric literals (numbers) are defined by the following rules:

numeric:	integer
	float
complex:	numeric "i"
	numeric [+−] numeric "i"
name:	(.|letter) (.|letter|digit)*
integer:	digit+
exponent:	"e" [+−]? integer
float:	integer exponent
	integer "." digit* exponent?
	"." integer exponent?

String literals are contained between matching apostrophes or matching double quotes. Characters inside can be escaped by preceding them by the back-slash character: \n, \t, and \\ represent a new-line, tab and back-slash character. In addition, a back-slash followed by 1 to 3 octal digits represents the character with the corresponding octal representation.

The following *infix* operators are recognized by the parser. They are listed in decreasing precedence.

$	component selection	**HIGH**
[[[	subscripts, elements	
^	exponentiation	
-	unary minus	
:	sequence operator	
%*anything*%	special operator	
* /	multiply, divide	
+ -	add, subtract	
< > <= >=		
== !=	comparison	
!	not	
& | && ||	and, or	
<<-	assignment	
→		
← _		**LOW**

Any sequence of characters between matching "%" characters, not including a new line, is recognized as an infix operator.

A line whose first character is "!" is executed as a system command with no changes.

sys	see Deprecated	**sys**

sys.call	System Evaluator State	**sys.call**

```
sys.call()
sys.frame()
sys.nframe()
sys.parent(n=1)

sys.calls()
sys.frames()
sys.parents()
sys.on.exit()
```

```
sys.status()
```

VALUE

These functions all return various objects describing the current state of the S evaluator, in terms analogous to the model described in chapter 11. The first four functions describe the current frame (the function call from which, e.g., `sys.call` was called). `sys.call` returns the actual call; `sys.frame()` the list of objects in the current frame; `sys.nframe()` the numerical index of the current frame in the list of all frames; and `sys.parent` the index in the list of frames of the parent (i.e., the caller) of the current function. The argument to `sys.parent` says how many generations to go back (by default, to the caller of the caller of `sys.parent`).

The remaining functions describe the list of all frames that are currently open in the evaluator. `sys.calls` returns the list of the function calls that generated these frames; `sys.frames` is the list of the frames themselves (i.e., each element is a list giving the named objects in that frame, including the matched arguments in the call). `sys.parents` gives the indices of the parent frames of each of the frames. `sys.on.exit` is the list of expressions given to `on.exit` and currently still scheduled to be evaluated on exit from the corresponding frame. `sys.status` returns the complete internal evaluator status; that is, everything above.

SEE ALSO

`trace.on` for `sys.trace`.

EXAMPLES

```
# remove an object from my own local frame
        remove("xxx",frame = sys.nframe())
```

---

sys.calls   see `sys.call`   **sys.calls**

---

sys.frame   see `sys.call`   **sys.frame**

sys.frames	see sys.call	**sys.frames**

sys.nframe	see sys.call	**sys.nframe**

sys.on.exit	see sys.call	**sys.on.exit**

sys.parent	see sys.call	**sys.parent**

sys.parents	see sys.call	**sys.parents**

sys.status	see sys.call	**sys.status**

sys.trace	see trace.on	**sys.trace**

| **S_alloc** | Storage Allocation in C | **S_alloc** |

```
char *S_alloc(nelem, elsize)
unsigned nelem, elsize;
```

ARGUMENTS

    `nelem` how many elements of storage to allocate.

    `elsize` the size in bytes of each element; typically some C expression in involving `sizeof`; e.g., `sizeof(double)`.

VALUE

A (`char *`) pointer to a dynamically allocated block of memory suitable to hold the number of elements and type specified. This storage is associated with the S frame in which the `S_alloc` invocation occurred and disappears when that frame is completed.

In *any* C code being called from S, dynamic storage allocation should generally use `S_alloc`, instead of the standard C function `calloc`. It differs from `calloc` in that storage allocated this way is automatically freed by S at the appropriate time. You are free to use `calloc` as well, but it is only appropriate if you want the storage to last throughout the S session, or if you will free it yourself later on.

| **T** | Student's t-Distribution | **T** |

```
dt(q, df)
pt(q, df)
qt(p, df)
rt(n, df)
```

ARGUMENTS

    `q` vector of quantiles. Missing values (NAs) are allowed.

    `p` vector of probabilities. Missing values (NAs) are allowed.

    `n` sample size. If `length(n)` is larger than 1, then `length(n)` random values are returned.

    `df` vector of degrees of freedom.

VALUE

density (`dt`), probability (`pt`), quantile (`qt`), or random sample (`rt`) for Student's t-distribution on `df` degrees of freedom. Results are currently computed to single-precision accuracy only. The density function is given by

$$f_d(q) = \frac{\Gamma(\frac{d+1}{2})}{\Gamma(\frac{1}{2})\Gamma(\frac{d}{2})}(1+q^2)^{-\frac{1}{2}(d_1+1)}, \quad q > 0, \quad d > 0,$$

where d is the `df` parameter.

SIDE EFFECTS

The function `rt` causes creation of the dataset `.Random.seed` if it does not already exist, otherwise its value is updated.

---

t	Matrix Transpose	**t**

`t(x)`

ARGUMENTS

`x` matrix. Missing values (NAs) are allowed.

VALUE

transpose of `x` (rows of `x` are columns of result).

SEE ALSO

`aperm` for generalized transpose of arrays.

---

table	Create Contingency Table from Categories	**table**

`table(...)`

ARGUMENTS

`...` any number of objects, each to be interpreted as a category. All arguments must be of equal length. Together, they define a multi-way ragged array of as many dimensions as there are arguments. Missing values (NAs) are allowed.

VALUE

a multi-way array containing the number of observations in the cells defined by the arguments to `table`. For example, if

```
z ← table(arg1, arg2, arg3)
```

then `z[i,j,k]` is the number of times that the combination of the `i`-th level of the first category, the `j`-th level of the second, and the `k`-th level of the third appeared together in the data. A combination is not counted if missing values are present in the corresponding element of any of the arguments.

The `dimnames` attribute of the array contains the `levels` attribute of each of the individual.

SEE ALSO

Functions `cut` and `category` create categories; `tapply` can be used for applying functions to observations in table cells.

EXAMPLES

```
table(age,sex,race,income)
```

tan	see cos	**tan**

tanh	see cosh	**tanh**

| `tapply` | Apply a Function to a Ragged Array | `tapply` |

```
tapply(X, INDICES, FUN, ...)
```

ARGUMENTS

X vector of data to be grouped by `indices`. Missing values (NAs) are allowed if `FUN` accepts them.

INDICES list whose elements are interpreted as categories, each of the same length as `x`. The elements of the categories define the position in a multi-way array corresponding to each `x` observation. Missing values (NAs) are allowed.

FUN function or character string giving the name of the function to be applied to each cell. If `FUN` is omitted, `tapply` returns a vector that can be used to subscript the multi-way array that `tapply` normally produces. This vector is useful for computing residuals. See the example.

... optional arguments to be given to each invocation of `FUN`.

VALUE

`tapply` calls `FUN` for each cell that has any data in it. If `FUN` returns a single atomic value for each cell (e.g. functions `mean` or `var`), then `tapply` returns a multi-way array containing the values. Otherwise, `tapply` returns an array of mode `"list"`, whose elements are the values of the individual calls to `FUN`.

EXAMPLES

```
# generate mean republican votes for regions of the U.S.
# category that gives the region for each observation
region ← state.region[row(votes.repub)]
election ← category(votes.year)[col(votes.repub)]
mn ← tapply(votes.repub,list(region,election),mean)
round(mn,1)    # table of mean vote by region and election
positions ← tapply(votes.repub,list(region,election))
residuals ← votes.repub - mn[positions]
```

`tek4014`	Tektronix Storage Scope Device	`tek4014`

```
tek4014(ask=F, file)
```

ARGUMENTS

ask if TRUE, whenever a new plot is about to be produced the message "GO?" appears in the lower left corner of the screen. This allows further viewing, making a hard copy, etc., before the screen is erased. When ready for plotting to proceed, simply hit carriage return. If `ask=-1` is given, a hardcopy will be made of each frame prior to clearing the screen, and no user interaction is necessary.

file name of the file to which output should be sent. This enables the characters that would have been sent to the terminal to be caught in a file for later plotting. By default, output is sent to the terminal.

There are various models of Tektronix storage scope graphics devices which are slightly different from the 4014. Models 4006 and 4010 are upper-case only, 4012 has a smaller, lower-resolution screen than the 4014. Many personal computers and workstations have programs that can simulate a 4014.

The function `hardcopy`, given below in the examples section, can be used to automatically generate a copy of the information on the screen. To produce unattended plots, use `tek4014(ask=FALSE)` and then execute `hardcopy()` to make the copy.

When graphic input (`identify`, `locator`) is requested from these terminals, the cursor lines appear horizontally and vertically across the entire screen. The thumb wheels should be adjusted to position the intersection of the cursors at the desired point, and then any single character should be typed (may need carriage return on some terminals). A carriage return alone will terminate graphic input without transmitting the point.

Character sizes are .9, 1, 1.5, and 1.6. There are 5 line types (1 through 5) giving solid, dotted, dot dash, short dash, and long dash lines. Characters can not be rotated on this device.

A device must be specified before any graphics functions can be used.

EXAMPLES
```
hardcopy ← function(){
      cat("\033\027"); unix("sleep 30", out=F) }
```

`tempfile`	Create Unique Name for File	`tempfile`

```
tempfile(pattern="file")
```

ARGUMENTS

   `pattern` a character string that forms the start of a filename. The name is completed by some numbers.

VALUE

      a character string giving the name of a file that may be used as a temporary file. The names are essentially certain to be unique from one call to the next.

EXAMPLES

```
# an intermediate file for editing
my.ed ← function(x,file = tempfile("ed")) {
        if(missing(file)) on.exit(unlink(file))
        dput(x,file=file)
        unix(paste("ed",file), output=F)
        parse(file=file)[[1]]
}
```

text	Plot Text	**text**

```
text(x, y, labels=seq(along.with=x), cex, col)
```

ARGUMENTS

   `x,y` coordinates of points. The coordinates can be given by two vector arguments or by a single argument `x` which is a time-series, a complex vector, a matrix with 2 columns, or a list containing components named `x` and `y`. Missing values (NAs) are allowed. Labels are not plotted at any point with a missing *x* or *y* coordinate.

  `labels` normally, `labels[i]` is plotted at each point `(x[i],y[i])`. However, if `labels` is a logical vector of the same length as `x` and `y`, the value `i` is plotted at each `(x[i],y[i])` for which `labels[i]` is TRUE. Missing values (NAs) are allowed.

    `cex` character expansion parameter (see `par`) for each text string. May be a vector.

col   color parameter (see par) for each text string. May be a vector.

Graphical parameters may also be supplied as arguments to this function (see par).

If the lengths of x, y, labels, cex, and col are not identical, the shorter vectors are reused cyclically.

The text function can be used after plot(x,y,type="n") which draws axes and surrounding box without plotting the data.

EXAMPLES

```
plot(x,y,type="n")
text(x,y)    #plot i at (x[i],y[i])
```

---

time	Create Time Vector	**time**

```
time(x)
cycle(x)
```

ARGUMENTS

x   time-series. Missing values (NAs) are allowed.

VALUE

time-series with same start, end and frequency as x. time returns the time value at each point, e.g., the value at January, 1973 is 1973.0, and the value at July 1973 is 1973.5.

cycle returns the position of each observation within the cycle associated with the series. If x were monthly, this would be the month number: 1 for each January, etc.

EXAMPLES

```
cgrowth ← code(cycle(growth), 1:12, month.name)
tapply(growth, cgrowth, mean)    # mean growth for each month
```

`title`	Plot Titling Information and/or Axes	`title`

```
title(main, sub, xlab, ylab, axes=FALSE)
axes(main, sub, xlab, ylab, axes=TRUE)
```

ARGUMENTS

`main` optional character string for the main title, plotted on top in enlarged (`cex=1.5`) characters.

`sub` optional character string for the sub-title, plotted on the bottom below the x-axis label.

`xlab` optional character string to label the x-axis.

`ylab` optional character string to label the y-axis.

`axes` if `TRUE`, an enclosing box, tick marks and axis labels will be plotted.

Graphical parameters may also be supplied as arguments to this function (see `par`).

The two functions differ only in the default value for `axes`. Nothing is plotted for arguments not supplied.

EXAMPLES

```
title("residuals from final fit")  # main title only
axes(xlab="concentration",ylab="temperature")
```

`tprint`	see Deprecated	`tprint`

`trace`	Trace Calls to Functions	`trace`

```
trace(what, tracer = std.trace)
untrace(what)
```

ARGUMENTS

`what` character vector, giving the names of functions: `trace` adds the functions to the list of those whose calls are traced and `untrace` removes them from that list. There is no effect on the functions themselves.

`tracer` the name of a function, to do the tracing on `fun`. If omitted, a standard tracing function is used, which prints a line giving the function call itself before `fun` is called, and another giving the value of the call just before returning. See `trace.on` for other alternatives.

SIDE EFFECTS

The effect of putting a function, `fun`, on the trace list to be traced by the function `tracer` is exactly as if every call to `fun` were embedded in a call to `tracer`; i.e., `fun(...)` becomes `tracer(fun(...))`.

EXAMPLES

`trace("parse")` # record all calls to the parser

---

traceback	Print Call Stack After Error	**traceback**

`traceback(data=last.dump)`

ARGUMENTS

`data` list that describes the state of the computation at the time of the error. The "names" attribute of `data` gives the character form of the calls. This object is created is by a call to `dump.frames` or `dump.calls`, typically because one of them has been specified as option `error`.

The `traceback` function prints the call stack represented by this object, typically the calls that were in the process of being evaluated when an error occurred.

SEE ALSO

`dump.calls, debugger, options.`

trace.on	Control over Tracing	**trace.on**

```
trace.on(on = T)

std.trace(call)
count.trace(call)
browser.trace(call)

sys.trace()
```

ARGUMENTS

    on logical flag used to control whether tracing is activated or not. Most useful in trace print functions so that they, themselves, are not traced.

    call the actual function call that is about to be executed.

These functions are optional tracer functions to be used in the call to trace. The effect of putting a function, fun, on the trace list to be traced by the function tracer is exactly as if every call to fun were embedded in a call to tracer; i.e., fun(...) becomes tracer(fun(...)).

The tracer functions can do whatever they want, and are ordinary S functions, but they must end by returning the value of the call to fun. The standard minimal trace, std.tracer, just prints a message before and after the function call.

count.trace arranges to count the number of calls to the function being traced with it, leaving the counts in the object Trace.count. Trace.count should be initialized to an empty list before tracing begins.

browser.trace calls browser just before the call is executed.

trace.on controls an internal flag that causes tracing to be attempted; in particular, the three trace functions above use it to ensure that trace printing is not done during their own computations.

VALUE

Function sys.trace returns a list corresponding to functions currently being traced—the elements of the list are the tracing functions being used and the names of the elements are the names of the functions being traced.

WARNING

In principle, you can write your own trace functions as well, by using the three functions above as models. You are strongly warned to make sure the trace functions work well and obey the paradigm of using `trace.on` to set and unset tracing, BEFORE you try tracing with them. Having an error in a trace function causes much chaos.

The trace functions, like `std.trace` are useful only as arguments to `trace`. They should not be called directly.

---

trunc   see `ceiling`   **trunc**

TRUNC_AUDIT   Truncate the Audit File   **TRUNC_AUDIT**

```
S TRUNC_AUDIT size
```

ARGUMENTS

`size` desired size of the resulting `.Data/.Audit` file. Default is 100000 characters.

The `TRUNC_AUDIT` utility attempts to preserve the most recent `size` characters of the audit file. It does so by finding the first S expression in the audit file that is within `size` characters of the end of file.

If there is a problem in truncating the audit file, a message is produced and the audit file is not changed. If you get a warning, it may be an indication that the audit file has been corrupted.

Whenever S is started, one of the first things that it does is check the size of the audit file against the `audit_size` limit. If it is over the limit, a message is printed advising you to use the `TRUNC_AUDIT` utility. If your audit file contains important information, do not run `TRUNC_AUDIT`, but instead increase the `audit.size` option. Executing

```
.Options$audit.size ← x
```

will cause S to use `x` as the audit file size limit.

WARNING

The `TRUNC_AUDIT` utility cannot be run from inside S, since S normally has the audit file open for writing.

EXAMPLES

```
S TRUNC_AUDIT 0     # clear out the audit file
```

---

ts	Time-Series Objects	**ts**

```
ts(data, start, frequency=1, end)
is.ts(x)
as.ts(x)
```

ARGUMENTS

data   vector giving the data values for the time-series.

start   starting date for the series, in years, e.g., February, 1970 would be `1970+(1/12)` or `1970.083`. If `start` is a vector with at least two data values, the first is interpreted as the year, and the second as the number of positions into the year; e.g., February, 1970 could be `c(1970,2)`.

frequency   observations frequency; that is, how many observations per year. Monthly data has `frequency=12`; yearly has `frequency=1`.

end   ending date for the series.

x   any S object.

VALUE

`ts` returns a time-series containing the given `data`. Time-series attributes are assigned consistently with whichever of `start`, `end`, and `frequency` are supplied. If only two of the three are given, the other parameter will be computed based on the given values and `length(data)`. If both `start` and `end` are omitted, the series is started at 1. `ts` checks that the the arguments supplied are consistent.

The function has been described as if the unit of time were one year. However, any periodic data can be organized as a time-series. Hourly data might use days for `start` and `end` with `frequency=24`; daily data could use weeks with `frequency=7`. Internally, `frequency` is required to be a positive integer. There is also special printing for the cases of `frequency=1`, 4 or 12 (see `prts`).

is.ts returns TRUE if x is a time-series object, FALSE otherwise.

as.ts returns x, if x is a time-series, otherwise ts(x).

The time-series class of objects are those that have an attribute tsp, which must be numeric of length 3.

tslines	see tsplot	**tslines**

tsmatrix	Create Matrix with Time-Series as Columns	**tsmatrix**

tsmatrix(...)

ARGUMENTS

... any number of arguments, interpreted as time-series to form columns of the resulting matrix. The time window for the matrix will be the intersection of time windows for the arguments (i.e., the maximum of the start dates and the minimum of the end dates). All series must have the same periodicity. Missing values (NAs) are allowed.

VALUE

a matrix with one column for each argument and an attribute named tsp with the start date, end date, and frequency.

Note the distinction between tsmatrix and the related function cbind, which allows vectors or matrices as arguments as well, but makes no effort to make time parameters consistent. Frequently, the two functions can be used together (see example).

SEE ALSO

cbind, rbind.

EXAMPLES

```
tsmatrix(x,lag(x),diff(x))  #x, lag-1 of x and first diffs
cbind(tsmatrix(x,lag(x)),1)  #two series, column of 1s

yx ← tsmatrix(employment,gnp,lag(gnp), ...)
lsfit(yx[,1],yx[,-1])    # regression with x and y times aligned
```

tsp	Tsp Attribute of an Object	**tsp**

```
tsp(x)
start(x)
end(x)
frequency(x)
```

ARGUMENTS

    x any object.

VALUE

the `tsp` attribute of `x`, which will usually be NULL if `x` is not a time-series. The `tsp` attribute has three values giving the starting time, ending time, and observation frequency of the time-series. The `start` and `end` functions return their times as a pair of numbers: an integer number of time units, and the number of observations times after that integer. For example, for monthly series, with `frequency(x)` equal to 12, these are year and month.

To explicitly delete the `tsp` attribute, use `tsp(x) ← NULL`.

SEE ALSO

    `ts, tsmatrix.`

EXAMPLES

```
            # assume x is monthly from Jan. 1970 to Jul. 1975
tsp(x)        # is c(1970.0, 1975.5, 12)
start(x)      # is the vector c(1970,1)
end(x)        # is the vector c(1975,7)
frequency(x)      # is 12
xyz ← ts(data, start=start(gnp), frequency=frequency(gnp))
            # create a time-series beginning at same time as gnp
```

`tsplot`	Plot Multiple Time-Series	`tsplot`

```
tsplot(..., type="l", lty=1:5, pch, col=1:4)
tspoints(..., type="p", lty=1:5, pch, col=1:4)
tslines(..., type="l", lty=1:5, pch, col=1:4)
```

ARGUMENTS

...   any number of time-series to be plotted. The x-axis is set up as the union of the times spanned by the series. The y-axis includes the range of all the series. Missing values (NAs) are allowed.

type   an optional character string, telling which type of plot (points, lines, both, none or high-density) should be done for each plot. The first character of type defines the first plot, the second character the second, etc. Elements of type are used cyclically; e.g., "pl" alternately plots points and lines.

lty   optional vector of line types. The first element is the line type for the first line, etc. Line types will be used cyclically until all plots are drawn.

pch   optional character vector for plotting characters. The first character is the plotting character for the first plot of type "p", the second for the second, etc. Default is the digits (1 through 9, 0) then the lower case letters.

col   optional vector of colors. Colors are also used cyclically.

Function `tsplot` generates a new plot; `tspoints` and `tslines` add to the current plot.

Graphical parameters may also be supplied as arguments to this function (see `par`). Also, the arguments to the `title` function may be supplied to this function.

EXAMPLES

```
tsplot(gnp,smooth(gnp),type="pl")
tspoints(x,y,pch="*")  # points with "*" for both series
# the example plot is produced by:
tsplot(hstart,smooth(hstart),type="pl")
title(main="Housing Starts",sub="Data and Smoothed Values")
```

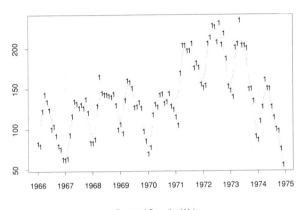

Data and Smoothed Values

---

tspoints   see `tsplot`   **tspoints**

---

twoway   Analysis of Two-way Table   **twoway**

```
twoway(x, trim=.5, iter=6, eps, print=F)
```

ARGUMENTS

     `x` matrix to be analyzed. Missing values (NAs) are allowed.

   `trim` optional trimming fraction for carrying out analysis. Default value corresponds to using medians. `trim=0` will cause analysis by means, .25 by midmeans, etc.

  `iter` maximum number of full (row and column) sweeps.

  `eps` error tolerance. If `eps` is given, the algorithm will iterate until the maximum change in row or column effects is < `eps`. Default is to iterate until the specified number of iterations or until converged to the accuracy of the machine arithmetic. It is not always possible to converge to a unique answer.

 `print` if TRUE, the maximum change in row/column effects in each iteration is printed.

VALUE

list with 4 components, `resid`, `row`, `col`, and `grand`, such that `x[i,j]` equals `grand + row[i] + col[j] + resid[i,j]`

grand   overall location estimate of the data.

row   vector of row effects.

col   vector of column effects.

resid   matrix of residuals from the fit.

Results are currently computed to single-precision accuracy only.

SEE ALSO

Function `plotfit` produces a graphical display of the fit generated by `twoway`.

EXAMPLES

```
twoway(temperature,trim=.25)  # analysis by midmeans
```

Uniform	Uniform Distribution	**Uniform**

```
dunif(q, min=0, max=1)
punif(q, min=0, max=1)
qunif(p, min=0, max=1)
runif(n, min=0, max=1)
```

ARGUMENTS

q   vector of quantiles. Missing values (NAs) are allowed.

p   vector of probabilities. Missing values (NAs) are allowed.

n   sample size. If `length(n)` is larger than 1, then `length(n)` random values are returned.

min   vector of lower limits.

max   vector of upper limits (greater than lower limits).

VALUE

density (`dunif`), probability (`punif`), quantile (`qunif`), or random sample (`runif`) for the uniform distribution on the range `min` to `max`. Results are currently computed to single-precision accuracy only. The density function is given by

$$f_{a,b}(q) = \frac{1}{b-a}, \quad a \leq q \leq b, \quad b > a$$

where a and b are the `min` and `max` parameters.

SIDE EFFECTS

The function `runif` causes creation of the dataset `.Random.seed` if it does not already exist, otherwise its value is updated.

EXAMPLES

```
x + runif(x)     # jitter the x data
runif(100,-1,1)  # 100 numbers uniform on −1 to 1
```

uniq	see Deprecated	**uniq**

unique	Unique or Duplicated Values in a Vector	**unique**

```
unique(x)
duplicated(x)
```

ARGUMENTS

x vector.

VALUE

Function `unique` returns an object like x but with no duplicate values. The values will be in the same order as x except that repeated values will be deleted. Function `duplicated` returns a logical vector as long as x that tells for each element of x whether that value has appeared before in x.

Function `unique` is actually implemented as `x[!duplicated(x)]`.

EXAMPLES

```
sort(unique(names))   #sorted list of names with no duplicates
```

unix	Execute a Command	**unix**

```
unix(command, input, output=TRUE)
```

ARGUMENTS

command any command suitable for execution by the shell.

input the data to be treated as the input to the command. If this argument is supplied, its elements are written out, one per line, to a file, and this file becomes the standard input to command. If input is missing, nothing special is done to provide input to the command.

output if TRUE, the standard output of the shell command will be returned as a character vector, with each line of output turned into one element of the vector. If FALSE, standard output for the command remains unchanged; typically, to the user's terminal.

Use output=FALSE when the executed command interacts with the user.

EXAMPLES

```
# get contents of a file, one element per line
unix("cat myfile")
```

unix.time	Execution Times	**unix.time**

```
unix.time(expr)
```

ARGUMENTS

expr any S expression.

VALUE

the time required to evaluate the expression. Times are returned as five numbers (in units of seconds) giving the user, system and elapsed times in S, plus user and system times taken in child processes, if any. The expression is evaluated in the frame of the function calling unix.time, so the semantics of the expression should be the same as if it had been evaluated directly, although the value of the expression (unless it is an assignment) will be lost.

SEE ALSO

```
proc.time
```

EXAMPLES

```
# time different sizes of a problem
time.mat ← matrix(ncol=5,nrow=3)
for(i in c(10,100,1000,5000,10000))
        time.mat[,i] ← unix.time(sort(runif(i)))
```

unlink	Remove a File	**unlink**

```
unlink(x)
```

ARGUMENTS

x character string giving the name of a file.

SIDE EFFECTS

The named file is removed.

EXAMPLES

```
# set up temp file and remove on exit
foo ← function() {
        file ← tempfile("junk")
        on.exit(unlink(file))
        . . .
}
```

unlist	Make Vector From a List	**unlist**

```
unlist(data)
```

ARGUMENTS

data an S object.

VALUE

a vector made up of by combining the leaf nodes of data.

EXAMPLES

```
unlist(as.list(1:10))
```

untrace	see trace	untrace

usa	United States Coastline and State Boundaries	usa

```
usa(states=TRUE, coast=TRUE, add=FALSE,
    xlim=c(65,135), ylim=c(24,50), fifty=FALSE)
```

ARGUMENTS

states logical flag to control whether state boundaries are plotted.

coast logical flag to control whether coast-line is plotted.

add logical flag. If TRUE, plot is superimposed on existing plot. Otherwise, a new plot is generated.

xlim optional limits for the *x*-axis (longitude).

ylim optional limits for the *y*-axis (latitude).

fifty logical flag. If TRUE, boxes are drawn in the Pacific Ocean to represent Alaska and Hawaii.

Graphical parameters may also be supplied as arguments to this function (see par).

The plot is done in correct physical proportion. The coordinate system set up for the plot uses negative longitude, so that *x*-values increase from left to right on the plot.

EXAMPLES

```
usa(states=F)  # the U.S. without state lines
usa(xlim=c(65,85),ylim=c(35,50))  #plot the north-east
# the example plot is produced by:
usa()
text(state.center,state.abb,cex=.5)
```

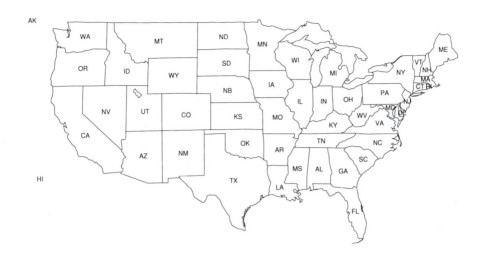

| **var** | Variance, Covariance, and Correlation | **var** |

```
var(x, y)
cor(x, y, trim=0)
```

ARGUMENTS

    x matrix or vector.
    y matrix or vector. If omitted, same as x.
 trim the proportion trimmed in the internal calculations for cor.

VALUE

correlations or variances (covariances). If x or y is a matrix, the result is a correlation or covariance matrix; the [i,j] element corresponds to the ith column of x and the jth column of y.

Variances are sample variances:

```
sum((x-mean(x))^2)/(length(x)-1)
```

Untrimmed correlations are computed from these variances. Trimmed correlations are computed by the standardized sums and differences method. Correlations are computed to single-precision accuracy.

EXAMPLES

```
cor(cbind(longley.x,longley.y))     # correlation matrix for longley data
std.dev ← sqrt(var(x))      # standard deviation of a vector
```

vector	Vectors (Simple Objects)	**vector**

```
vector(mode="logical", length=0)
is.vector(x, mode="any")
as.vector(x, mode="any")
```

ARGUMENTS

mode character string giving the mode wanted.
length integer value giving the length wanted.
x any S object.

VALUE

vector returns a simple object of the desired mode and length.

is.vector returns TRUE if x is a simple object of the mode specified, and FALSE otherwise. If the mode is "any", any simple object will match.

as.vector returns x if x is a simple object of the mode specified, and otherwise an object of the same length as x and with data resulting from coercing the elements of x to that mode. If the mode is "any", the effect is simply to remove any attributes of x in the result.

Note the difference between coercing to a simple object and setting the mode attribute:

```
mode(x) ← mode(y)
```

This changes the mode of x but leaves all other attributes unchanged (so a matrix stays a matrix). The value of as.vector(x,mode(y)) would have no attributes. Similarly, is.vector would return FALSE for a matrix.

EXAMPLES

```
vector("list", 10) # list of length 10, initialized to null elements.
as.vector(x,mode(y)) # make a simple object of same mode as y
```

vi	Invoke vi Text Editor	**vi**

```
vi(data, file)
```

ARGUMENTS

data any S object.

file the name of the file on which the object should be written.

VALUE

the edited value of the object.

SIDE EFFECTS

none. It is important to realize that vi does not change data; the returned value must be assigned in order to save your editing changes, as in the example.

If errors resulted during the evaluation of the expression containing the editing, the file is retained and calling vi with no arguments will allow re-editing the file. This is typically useful if editing a function definition produced a syntax error.

SEE ALSO

ed, source.

EXAMPLES

```
ttt ← vi(ttt)
```

vu	Create Vu-graphs (Slides)	**vu**

```
vu(text, indent=3, width=7, height=7,
   line=.015, csize, font)
```

ARGUMENTS

text character string vector, the elements of which are either lines of text to plot, or else commands to the vu function (see below). The text will be plotted, with character size as large as possible to fill the page.

For many purposes, the function quickvu will generate a dataset easily which vu can plot.

`indent` number of spaces to indent lists.

`width` width of the page in inches.

`height` height of the paper in inches.

`line` thickness of lines in inches (needed for bold face and for drawing bullets - see below). Default is .015 inches (the thickness of the thick pens for Hewlett-Packard plotters). Thin pens on the hp7221 are .01 inches.

`csize` vector of allowable character sizes for the plot, i.e., the values of graphical parameter `cex` that the device supports. This argument is important only for devices with a limited set of hardware-drawn character sizes when `font` is omitted. If `csize` is given as a scalar, any integer multiple of that size is allowed, otherwise `csize` is the vector of allowable sizes. Default is continuously variable sizes.

`font` optional character name of a font to be used in plotting the vugraph. If font is not specified, the hardware generated font of the plotting device will be used. Fonts can also be specified within `text` by the `.F` command.

Abbreviation	Font Name
`sr`	Simplex Roman
`cr`	Complex Roman
`dr`	Duplex Roman
`tr`	Triplex Roman
`ro`	Roman (Constant Width)
`ci`	Complex Italic
`ti`	Triplex Italic
`ss`	Simplex Script
`cs`	Complex Script
`sg`	Simplex Greek
`cg`	Complex Greek
`ge`	Gothic English
`gg`	Gothic German
`gi`	Gothic Italian
`cc`	Complex Cyrillic
`sp`	Special Symbols

SOURCE

Norman M. Wolcott and Joseph Hilsenrath, *A Contribution to Computer Typesetting Techniques,* "Tables of Coordinates for Hershey's Repertory of Occidental Type Fonts and Graphics Symbols", National Bureau of Standards Special Publication 424, April 1976.

The following are the commands recognized by `vu`. They are similar to commands in several `troff` macro systems, and they begin with a period (.) and one or two capital letters:

.C   Choose a color. This command takes an argument which is the color number, i.e., ".C 3" for color 3, etc.

.F   Choose a font. This command takes an argument which is the two-letter font name to be used for subsequent lines of text. If no font name is given, the font specified by the `font` argument is used. (To force use of the hardware font, give a nonexistent font name.) Note that fonts current-ly cannot be changed in the middle of a line. See also argument `font`.

.L   Make the text larger. Each time this command appears, the size is in-creased by 25%. This command may also take an argument, which is the desired character size relative to initial size 1, thus ".L 2" would be dou-ble the initial size, and ".L 1" would return to initial size. The argument to this command is *not* the same as the graphical parameter `cex`: vu al-ways adjusts the final value of `cex` so that all of the lines will fit on the final display. An argument to .L simply gives the size of the following text relative to the size of preceding text.

.S   Make the text size smaller, by the same amount that ".L" makes it larger. Thus, any number of ".S" commands cancel the same number of ".L" commands. This command may take an argument, in which case it behaves exactly as ".L".

.B   Embolden the text (done by replotting one line width to the right). The argument tells how many overstrikes to use, default 1.

.H   Highlight the text by plotting first in a highlighting color (given by the ar-gument) and then plotting the text in the current color. With no argu-ment, highlighting is turned off.

.R   Remove the emboldening.

.CE   The argument gives the number of following lines of text which are to be centered, default 1.

The next commands all create lists of items. The items in the list can be preceded by bullets, diamonds, numbers, or any character string (for example, "--"). Lists may be nested, but general or numbered lists may only appear once.

.BL   Start a bullet list.

.DL   Start a diamond list.

.GL   Start a general list with each item preceded by the character string given after the command. For long strings, the value of argument `indent` may need to be increased.

.NL   Start a numbered list, each item preceded by a sequential number and trailing dash.

.LI   List item. This command must precede **each** item in the list.

.LE   End of the list (causes the indenting of the list to be cancelled).

The following text illustrates four of the fonts described above.

EXAMPLES

```
.CE 4
.C 1
.F ro
.B
Slides Made With VU are
.R
.C 2
.S 1.5
.F ge
VERY SEXY
.S 1
.F cs
.C 3
And Also Simple To Make
.C 4
.F tr
QUICK and INEXPENSIVE
```

Slides Made With VU are

ℌ𝔈ℜℑ 𝔖𝔈𝔛ℑ

And Also Simple To Make

QUICK and INEXPENSIVE

warning	see stop	**warning**

warnings	Print Warning Messages	**warnings**

```
warnings()
```

This function is used if prior execution has produced multiple warning messages. S does not print more than five warnings from one expression. Instead it stores the messages in a session dataset named last.warning. Function warnings prints the contents of last.warning.

while	see Syntax	**while**

`window`	Window a Time-Series	`window`

```
window(x, start, end)
```

ARGUMENTS

     x time-series. Missing values (NAs) are allowed.

 start optional new starting date for the series; if earlier than start date of x, no change is made.

  end optional new ending date for the series; if later than end date of x, no change is made.

VALUE

    a time-series like x giving the data between the new start and end dates.

EXAMPLES

```
sgnp ← window(gnp,c(1970,1),c(1975,12))
    #subseries of gnp from Jan 1970 through Dec 1975
```

`world.xy`	see `device.xy`	`world.xy`

`write`	Write Data to File	`write`

```
write(data, file, ncolumns, append=FALSE)
```

ARGUMENTS

    data vector, missing values (NAs) are allowed.

    file optional character string naming the file on which to write the data.

ncolumns optional number of data items to put on each line of file. Default is 5 per line for numeric data, 1 per line for character data.

 append logical, should the data be appended to any information previously in file?

Because of the way matrix data is stored, matrices are written in column by column order.

SEE ALSO

`dput, dump, cat.`

EXAMPLES

```
write(x,"filex")
```

```
# write matrix row by row
write(t(x),file="byrows",ncol=ncol(x))
```

---

xor	see `Logic`	**xor**

---

xysort	Rearrange x-y Data for Fast Plotting	**xysort**

```
xysort(x, y, order=FALSE)
```

ARGUMENTS

`x,y`   coordinates of points. The coordinates can be given by two vector arguments or by a single argument `x` which is a time-series, a complex vector, a matrix with 2 columns, or a list containing components named `x` and `y`. Missing values (NAs) are allowed.

`order`   if `TRUE`, ordering vector is returned.

VALUE

list with components named `x` and `y`, giving a rearranged version of the input data points, plus an optional `order` component.

`x,y`   rearranged values of original `x` and `y` data. Points with NAs in either the original `x` or `y` coordinates are omitted.

`order`   a permutation vector is returned. This permutation can be used to rearrange the original `x`, `y`, or any other associated data.

Adjacent values in the returned `x` and `y` data are likely to be near one another in x-y space. The idea is that a mechanical plotter will be able to visit all of the points much faster when they are presented in the sorted order.

A greedy algorithm is used, finding the nearest neighbor to the first point, then the nearest neighbor to that point, etc. The algorithm has complexity `O(length(x)^2)`.

REFERENCES

Jon Louis Bentley, "A Case Study in Applied Algorithm Design", *IEEE Computer,* February, 1984, pp. 75-88.

Jon Louis Bentley, *Writing Efficient Programs,* Prentice-Hall, Englewood Cliffs, NJ, 1982.

EXAMPLES

```
plot( xysort(x,y) )

xyo ← xysort(x, y, order=T)
plot(xyo, type="n")
text(xyo, label[xyo$order])
```

Appendix 2
S Dataset Documentation

This appendix contains detailed documentation in alphabetical order for the datasets supplied with S. Where more than one name appears under a heading (e.g. `number` and `payoff` under the heading `lottery`), the actual dataset name consists of the heading, a period, and then the name (`lottery.payoff`).

This documentation reflects S as of the time this book was written. Your installation may have a version newer than that described here. The online documentation, available through the `help` function, is the definitive documentation for the version of S that you are running.

The datasets described in this appendix are all available on the data directory which appears in position 3 of the default search list.

---

akima   Waveform Distortion Data for Bivariate Interpolation   **akima**

---

x,y,z represents a smooth surface of z values at selected points irregularly distributed in the x–y plane.

SOURCE

Hiroshi Akima, "A Method of Bivariate Interpolation and Smooth Surface Fitting for Irregularly Distributed Data Points", *ACM Transactions on Mathematical Software,* Vol. 4, No. 2, June 1978, pp. 148-159. Copyright 1978, Association for Computing Machinery, Inc., reprinted by permission.

The data was taken from a study of waveform distortion in electronic circuits, described in: Hiroshi Akima, "A Method of Bivariate Interpolation and Smooth Surface Fitting Based on Local Procedures", *CACM,* Vol. 17, No. 1, January 1974, pp. 18-20.

---

author   Character Counts for Books by Various Authors   **author**

---

count matrix of 26 columns corresponding to letters of the alphabet. Each row contains data for one work, giving the counts of each letter. There are different total counts for each work, and proper nouns were removed prior to counting.

SOURCE

W. A. Larsen and R. McGill, unpublished data collected in 1973.

---

auto   Statistics of Automobile Models   **auto**

---

stats actual statistics corresponding to the variables and models. The matrix gives data on 74 models by 12 statistics. The variables are price in dollars, mileage in miles per gallon, repair records for 1977 and 1978 (coded on a 5-point scale, 5 is best, 1 is worst), headroom in inches, rear seat clearance (distance from front seat back to rear seat back) in inches, trunk space in cubic feet, weight in pounds, length in inches, turning diameter (clearance required to make a U turn) in feet, displacement in cubic inches, and gear ratio for high gear.

The data give statistics for automobiles of the 1979 model year as sold in the United States.

SOURCE

Fuel consumption figures from United States Government EPA statistics. All other data from "CU Judges the 1979 Cars", *Consumer Reports,* April 1979. Copyright 1979 by Consumers Union of United States, Inc., Mount Vernon, NY 10550. Reprinted by permission from *CONSUMER REPORTS,* April 1979.

bicoal	Bituminous Coal Production in USA	**bicoal**

tons   time-series giving production of bituminous coal in millions of net tons per year, 1920-1968.

SOURCE

U. S. Bureau of Mines, also in J. W. Tukey, *Exploratory Data Analysis,* 1977, Addison-Wesley Publishing Co., Massachusetts.

bonds	Daily Yields of 6 AT&T Bonds	**bonds**

yield   matrix of daily bond yields; rows represent 192 days from April 1975 to December 1975. Columns are one of 6 bonds, characterized by their coupon rate.

coupon   vector of 6 different coupon rates corresponding to columns of yield.

car	Fuel Consumption Data	**car**

time   number of days since initial car purchase.

miles   number of miles driven between this fill-up and previous fill-up.

gals   number of gallons required to fill tank.

This data pertains to an automobile new in 1974.

SOURCE

R. A. Becker, personal data.

cereal	Consumer Attitudes Towards Breakfast Cereals	**cereal**

attitude matrix giving percentage of people agreeing with 11 statements e.g., "Reasonably Priced", (rows) about 8 brands of cereals (columns).

SOURCE

T. K. Chakrapani and A. S. C. Ehrenberg, "An Alternative to Factor Analysis in Marketing Research—Part 2: Between Group Analysis", *PMRS Journal,* Vol. 1, Issue 2, October 1981, pp. 32-38. Republished by permission of the Professional Marketing Research Society.

chernoff2	Mineral Contents Data (used by Chernoff)	**chernoff2**

The data is a 53 by 12 matrix representing mineral analysis of a 4500 foot core drilled from a Colorado mountainside. Twelve variables (columns) represent assays of seven mineral contents by one method and repeated assays of five of these by a second method. Fifty-three equally spaced specimens (rows) along the core were assayed. Specimen ID numbers were 200 to 252.

SOURCE

H. Chernoff, "The Use of Faces to Represent Points in k-dimensional Space Graphically", *Journal of the American Statistical Association,* Vol. 68, No. 342, 1973, pp. 361-368. Republished by permission of the American Statistical Association.

city	Names and Location of Selected U.S. Cities	**city**

name character vector of city names.
state character vector giving state for each city.
x,y location of city: x is negative longitude to correspond to coordinate system set up by function usa. y is latitude (both measured in degrees).

These cities cover the geographical regions of the U.S., and were not chosen by population.

| co2 | Mauna Loa Carbon Dioxide Concentration | co2 |

This data represents monthly CO_2 concentrations in parts per million (ppm) from January 1958 to December 1975.

SOURCE

Data collected by Charles D. Keeling, Scripps Institute of Oceanography, La Jolla, California. An updated version of the data may be found in *Carbon Dioxide Review 1982*, Oxford University Press, New York, p. 378.

| corn | Corn Yields and Rainfall | corn |

yield yearly corn yield in bushels per acre, in six Corn Belt states (Iowa, Illinois, Nebraska, Missouri, Indiana, and Ohio).

rain rainfall measurements in inches, in the six states. from 1890 to 1927.

SOURCE

M. Ezekiel and K. A. Fox, *Methods of Correlation and Regression Analysis*, p. 212. Copyright 1959, John Wiley and Sons, Inc., New York. Data originally from E. G. Misner, "Studies of the Relationship of Weather to the Production and Price of Farm Products, I. Corn", mimeographed publication, Cornell University, March 1928.

| evap | Soil Evaporation Data | evap |

x matrix of independent variables: maximum, minimum, and average soil temperatures (integrated area under daily soil temperature curve), maximum, minimum, and average air temperature, maximum, minimum, and average relative humidity, and total wind (miles per day).

y daily amount of evaporation from the soil.

"It is desired to estimate the daily amount of evaporation from the soil as a function of air temperature, relative humidity, and wind. Since these factors vary considerably throughout the day it is not clear what function or aspect of these variables is most important. For this reason the following ten variables relating to these factors are recorded." (from Freund).

Observations represent 46 consecutive days from June 6 through July 21.

SOURCE

R. J. Freund, "Multicollinearity etc., Some "new" Examples", *American Statistical Association Proceedings of Statistical Computing Section,* 1979, pp. 111-112. Republished by permission of the American Statistical Association.

`font`	Vector Drawn Fonts	`font`

The font datasets describe vector drawn characters which make up sixteen different fonts. Each font is known by a 2-character name, e.g. `"sr"` for simplex roman. The corresponding font dataset is named `"font.sr"`.

Abbreviation	Font Name
cc	Complex Cyrillic
cg	Complex Greek
ci	Complex Italic
cr	Complex Roman
cs	Complex Script
dr	Duplex Roman
ge	Gothic English
gg	Gothic German
gi	Gothic Italian
ro	Roman (Constant Width)
sg	Simplex Greek
sp	Special Symbols
sr	Simplex Roman
ss	Simplex Script
ti	Triplex Italic
tr	Triplex Roman

These datasets are normally used by graphics functions which have vector font capability. The following information is not needed for the use of the fonts, but may be helpful for constructing new fonts.

Fonts are digitized on a coordinate system centered at (0,0) and ranging to at most 50 in all directions. An em is 32 units. Since the range of each coordinate is restricted, a single x- or y-coordinate can be represented in one ASCII character. Given an ASCII character, the coordinate value is found by taking the integer character number and subtracting 77 ("A" is 65 and thus represents coordinate -12).

Fonts contain information for drawing the 95 ASCII characters from space (32) to tilde (126). Each font is a character vector with one string for each of the 95 vector drawn characters in the font. Each string gives coordinate pairs used in drawing the character. A tab character appearing in the string indicates that the pen should be lifted at that point. The vector also has the following attributes:

left character vector containing a single string of 95 characters giving the leftmost coordinates of the characters in the font.

right character vector giving rightmost coordinates.

SOURCE

Norman M. Wolcott and Joseph Hilsenrath, *A Contribution to Computer Typesetting Techniques,* "Tables of Coordinates for Hershey's Repertory of Occidental Type Fonts and Graphics Symbols", National Bureau of Standards Special Publication 424, April 1976.

---

freeny	Revenue Data	**freeny**

y quarterly revenue, 39 observations from (1962,2Q) to (1971,4Q).

x matrix of independent variables. Columns are y lagged 1 quarter, price index, income level, and market potential.

SOURCE

A. E. Freeny, "A Portable Linear Regression Package with Test Programs", Bell Laboratories memorandum, 1977.

---

hstart	US Housing Starts	**hstart**

U. S. Housing Starts, monthly, January 1966 to December 1974.

SOURCE

U. S. Bureau of the Census, Construction Reports.

`iris`	Fisher's Iris Data	`iris`

Array giving 4 measurements on 50 flowers from each of 3 species of iris. Sepal length and width, and petal length and width are measured in centimeters. Species are Setosa, Versicolor, and Virginica.

SOURCE

R. A. Fisher, "The Use of Multiple Measurements in Taxonomic Problems", *Annals of Eugenics,* Vol. 7, Part II, 1936, pp. 179-188. Republished by permission of Cambridge University Press.

The data were collected by Edgar Anderson, "The irises of the Gaspe Peninsula", *Bulletin of the American Iris Society,* Vol. 59, 1935, pp. 2-5.

`letters`	The Alphabet	`letters`

`letters` character vector of the 26 lower-case letters
`LETTERS` character vector of the 26 upper-case letters.

`liver`	Carcinogeneity Studies of Rat Livers	`liver`

`cells` number of cells injected into each animal.
`exper` category for the three experiments (A, B, C) in the study.
`gt` matrix (52 by 4) for the 4 lobes (ARL, PRL, PPC, AC), with counts for each (observation,lobe) pair of the GT(+) colonies.
`section` category for the section (replication) for each observation. Successive observations are pairs of sections for the same specimen.

SOURCE

Data were collected by Brian Laishes, University of Wisconsin, Madison, Wisconsin.

The data were used in: B. A. Laishes and P. B. Rolfe, "Quantitative Assessment of Liver Colony Formation and Hepatocellular Carcinoma Incidence in Rats Receiving Intravenous Injections of Isogeneic Liver Cells Isolated during Hepatocarcinogenesis", *Cancer Research,* Vol. 40, pp. 4133-4143, November 1980. Republished by permission of Cancer Research Journal.

The data appear in: "Detection of Damaged Animals in Carcinogeneity Studies with Laboratory Animals", Camil Fuchs, 1980, University of Wisconsin Statistics Laboratory Report 80/3.

---

longley   Longley's Regression Data   **longley**

y   number of people employed, yearly from 1947 to 1962.

x   matrix with 6 columns, giving GNP implicit price deflator (1954=100), GNP, unemployed, armed forces, noninstitutionalized population 14 years of age and over, and year.

This regression is known to be highly collinear.

SOURCE

J. W. Longley, "An appraisal of least-squares programs from the point of view of the user", *Journal of the American Statistical Association,* Vol. 62, 1967, pp. 819-841. Republished by permission of the American Statistical Association.

---

lottery   New Jersey Pick-It Lottery Data   **lottery**

number   winning 3-digit number (from 000 to 999) for drawings from May 22, 1975 to Mar 16, 1976. (This was the beginning of the Pick-It lottery.)

payoff   payoff corresponding to each number (dollars).

Republished by permission of the New Jersey State Lottery Commission.

---

lottery2   New Jersey Pick-It Lottery Data (Second Set)   **lottery2**

number   winning 3-digit number (from 000 to 999) for drawings from Nov. 10, 1976 to Sep. 6, 1977.

payoff   payoff corresponding to each number (dollars).

| `lottery3` | New Jersey Pick-It Lottery Data (Third Set) | `lottery3` |

number   winning 3-digit number (from 000 to 999) for drawings from Dec. 1, 1980 to Sep. 22, 1981.

payoff   payoff corresponding to each number (dollars).

| `lynx` | Canadian Lynx Trappings | `lynx` |

The data give annual number of lynx trappings in the Mackenzie River District of North-West Canada for the period 1821 to 1934.

SOURCE

Elton and Nicholson, "The ten-year cycle in numbers of lynx in Canada", *Journal of Animal Ecology,* Vol. 11, 1942, pp. 215-244. Republished by permission of Blackwell Scientific Publications Ltd., Oxford, U. K., and the British Ecological Society, Reading, U. K.

Analyzed in: M. J. Campbell and A. M. Walker, "A Survey of Statistical Work on the Mackenzie River Series of Annual Canadian Lynx Trappings for the Years 1821-1934 and a New Analysis", *Journal of the Royal Statistical Society A,* Vol. 140, Part 4, 1977, pp. 411-431. Republished by permission of the Royal Statistical Society, London, U. K..

| `month` | Month Names and Abbreviations | `month` |

name, abb   character name and abbreviations for months of the year.

| `ozone` | Ozone Concentrations in North-East U.S. | `ozone` |

median   median of daily maxima ozone concentration for June-August, 1974. Concentrations in parts per billion (ppb).

quartile   upper quartile of daily maxima ozone concentration, in parts per billion (ppb).

city   character name of ozone monitoring site.

xy   list containing components named x and y, that give the negative longitude and latitude of the monitoring sites (in the coordinate system used by function usa).

SOURCE

> W. S. Cleveland, B. Kleiner, J. E. McRae, J. L. Warner, and R. E. Pasceri, "The Analysis of Ground-Level Ozone Data from New Jersey, New York, Connecticut, and Massachusetts: Data Quality Assessment and Temporal and Geographical Properties", Bell Laboratories Memorandum, July 17, 1975.

> Original data collected by New Jersey Department of Environmental Protection, New York State Department of Environmental Protection, Boyce Thompson Institute (Yonkers, NY data), Connecticut Department of Environmental Protection, and Massachusetts Department of Public Health.

`prim`	Particle Physics Data	`prim`

> `prim4` matrix of 500 experimental observations, with 4 parameters describing each.
>
> `prim9` matrix of 500 observations with 9 parameters describing each observation.

SOURCE

> Examples are believed to have been produced from work on the Prim-9 graphics system at Stanford Linear Accelerator. Probably related to the data cited in J. H. Friedman and J. W. Tukey, *IEEE Transactions on Computing*, Vol. C-23, 1974, pp. 881-889. If so, these are particle-scattering experiments, and the columns of the matrices represent some chosen set of parameters (energy, momentum, etc.) to describe the nuclear reactions.

`ps.fonts`	Available PostScript Fonts	`ps.fonts`

> This is a character vector containing the names of the available postscript fonts. The index of the font you want is the appropriate `font=` argument to a graphics function.

EXAMPLES

```
# which are the Times fonts?
> times.fonts <- grep("Times",ps.fonts)
> times.fonts
[1]   3 10 11 12
> ps.fonts[times.fonts]
[1] "Times-Roman"        "Times-Italic"
```

```
[3] "Times-Bold"          "Times-BoldItalic"
title("All the News",font=11) #Times-Bold
```

---

ps.preamble   Definitions for the Postscript Device Driver   **ps.preamble**

---

ps.preamble is a character vector, giving the fixed preamble for the S PostScript device driver—the code for the laser printer side of the driver. It contains only definitions.

Communication between the host and printer sides of the driver is through these variables (sent once when the driver is started):

Landscape	boolean indicating landscape or portrait orientation
Width	width of region to use
Height	height of region to use
RastersPerInch	number of S rasters per inch
PointSize	base text size—reference for cex

these procedures for drawing:

-	I	initialize
-	A	begin a page
-	B	begin a path
-	C	continue a path
-	E	end a path
x y	M	move to a point
x y	L	draw a line to a point
x1 y1 x2 y2	S	draw a segment between two points
-	F	close and fill the current path
c	P	plot a symbol at a point
str x y adj	T	show a text string at a point with given adjustment
-	Z	display the current page
-	X	interrupt and erase current page
-	W	wrapup

and these procedures for graphical parameter settings (first number is number of arguments expected):

1	St	line type
1	Sw	line width
1	Sc	color
1	Sp	plotting character

1	Sx	character expansion
4	So	plot region as proportion of figure region
4	Sg	figure region as proportion of page
1	Sr	string rotation
1	Sd	clipping flag: 0=clip to plot, 1=clip to figure
1	Sf	font for text

Other internal variables are:

Page	device driver's idea of imageable region
Figure	figure region as proportion of page
Plot	plot region as proportion of figure region
ClipToPlot	negation of clipping flag: false is clip to figure
Cex	holds current character expansion
Outline	is current font to be outlined?
Pch	string holding current plotting character
Pch-x,Pch-y	offset to get Pch centered
Texy-y	vertical offset to center text (per font)
LineTypes	array of line types
Fonts	font list is a convenient order
Adjust	adjustment for text
StringRot	srt graphical parameter

Other internal routines are:

x y	Rem z	z	floor(x%y)
-	RastersPerPoint x		rasters per point of text
a k	ScaleArray -		multiply array a by k
-	Coord -		initialize coordinate system
s	Show -		show a string
lx ly ux uy	Box -		add a box (lx,ly,ux,uy)
lx ly ux uy	BoxClip -		set clipping path
lx ly ux uy a	Subregion lx ly ux uy		subregion a (as in Plot) of box
-	SetPage -		fill Page (once)
-	SetFigure -		set clipping path to figure
-	SetPlot -		set clipping path to plot
-	SetClip -		clip as per ClipToPlot

Boxes are always given as llx, lly, urx, ury (ll is lower left and ur is upper right); this is not the order that the graphical parameters fig and plt are sent.

rain	New York City Precipitation	**rain**

nyc1 Yearly total New York City precipitation, in inches, 1869-1957; currently listed in World Weather Records.

nyc2 Yearly total New York City precipitation, in inches, 1869-1957; formerly listed in World Weather Records and found in some almanacs.

SOURCE

World Weather Records, U. S. Department of Commerce, Weather Bureau, Washington, D.C., 1959 (nyc1). Formerly published by Smithsonian Institution, Washington, D.C. (nyc2).

.Random.seed	Seeds for Random Number Generators	**.Random.seed**

The object .Random.seed is a vector of starting values for the various random number generators used in S. The generators (for all distributions) are organized so that successive random numbers are equivalent to a long sample from the underlying uniform distribution. This allows the long-term properties of the generator to be maintained. The first time a user generates some random numbers, the object .Random.seed is found on the system data directory. The values contained are the standard initial values of the underlying generator algorithm. After each random sample, the object .Random.seed is assigned on the users working database, to maintain consistent values on subsequent calls.

There is a useful technique for reproducing random samples in later work. Just copy .Random.seed before generating the sample for the first time, and then restore it when the sample is to be reproduced.

SOURCE

Adapted from G. Marsaglia, et al. *Random Number Package: "Super-Duper"*, School of Computer Science, McGill University, 1973.

EXAMPLES

```
oldseed ← .Random.seed #save it
y ← rnorm(1000)  # get sample, analyze, etc.
   . . .
yagain ← rnorm(1000)  # will be the same as y
```

| **saving** | Savings Rates for Countries | **saving** |

x matrix with 50 rows (countries) and 5 columns (variables)

SOURCE

David A. Belsley, Edwin Kuh, Roy E. Welsch, *Regression Diagnostics: Identifying Influential Data and Sources of Collinearity*, Wiley, 1980, pp. 39-42. Copyright 1980 by John Wiley and Sons, Inc., New York.

Originally from unpublished data of Arlie Sterling, these are averages over 1960-1970 (to remove business cycle or other short-term fluctuations). Income is per-capita disposable income in U.S. dollars; growth is the percent rate of change in per capita disposable income; savings rate is aggregate personal saving divided by disposable income.

| **ship** | Manufacturing Shipments | **ship** |

Value of shipments, in millions of dollars, monthly from January, 1967 to December, 1974. This represents manufacturers' receipts, billings, or the value of products shipped, less discounts, and allowances, and excluding freight charges and excise taxes. Shipments by foreign subsidiaries are excluded, but shipments to a foreign subsidiary by a domestic firm are included.

SOURCE

U. S. Bureau of the Census, Manufacturer's Shipments, Inventories and Orders.

| **stack** | Stack-loss Data | **stack** |

loss percent of ammonia lost (times 10).

x matrix with 21 rows and 3 columns representing air flow to the plant, cooling water inlet temperature, and acid concentration as a percentage (coded by subtracting 50 and then multiplying by 10).

The data is from operation of a plant for the oxidation of ammonia to nitric acid, measured on 21 consecutive days.

SOURCE

K. A. Brownlee, *Statistical Theory and Methodology in Science and Engineering,* Wiley, 1965, p. 454. Copyrigh⁺ 1965 by John Wiley & Sons, Inc., New York. Also in Draper and Smith, *Applied Regression Analysis,* Wiley, 1966, Ch. 6, and Daniel and Wood, *Fitting Equations to Data,* Wiley, 1971, p. 61.

---

state	States of the U.S.	**state**

`name, abb` character names and abbreviations for 50 U.S. states, sorted alphabetically by name.

`center` list with components named `x` and `y` giving the approximate geographic center of each state in negative longitude and latitude (as used by function `usa`). Alaska and Hawaii are placed just off the West Coast.

`region` category giving region (Northeast, South, North Central, West) that each state belongs to.

`division` category giving state divisions (New England, Middle Atlantic, South Atlantic, East South Central, West South Central, East North Central, West North Central, Mountain, and Pacific).

`x77` matrix giving statistics for the states. Columns are Population estimate as of July 1, 1975; Per capita Income (1974); Illiteracy (1970, percent of population); Life Expectancy in years (1969-71); Murder and non-negligent manslaughter rate per 100,000 population (1976); Percent High-school Graduates (1970); Mean Number of days with min temperature < 32 degrees (1931-1960) in capital or large city; and Land Area in square miles.

SOURCE

Statistical Abstract of the United States, 1977, and *County and City Data Book,* 1977, U.S. Department of Commerce, Bureau of the Census.

---

steam	Steam Usage Data	**steam**

`y` pounds of steam used monthly.

`x` matrix with 9 columns, giving pounds of real fatty acid in storage, pounds of crude glycerine made, average wind velocity (mph), calendar days per month, operating days per month, days below 32 degrees Fahrenheit, average atmospheric temperature, average wind velocity (squared), number of startups.

SOURCE

Norman Draper and Harry Smith, *Applied Regression Analysis,* Wiley, 1966, pp. 351-364. Copyright 1966 by John Wiley & Sons, Inc., New York.

---

sunspots   Monthly Mean Relative Sunspot Numbers   **sunspots**

Monthly means of daily relative sunspot numbers, which are based upon counts of spots and groups of spots.

SOURCE

D. F. Andrews and A. M. Herzberg, *Data: A Collection of Problems from Many Fields for the Student and Research Worker,* Springer-Verlag, New York, 1985.

The data was previously collected from different observers by the Swiss Federal Observatory, Zurich, Prof. M. Waldmeier, Director. M. Waldmeier, *The Sunspot Activity in the Years 1610-1960,* Schulthess, Zurich, 1961.

The data is currently collected by the Tokyo Astronomical Observatory, Tokyo, Japan.

---

swiss   Fertility Data for Switzerland in 1888   **swiss**

---

fertility standardized fertility measure I[g] for each of 47 French-speaking provinces of Switzerland at about 1888.

    x matrix whose columns give 5 socioeconomic indicators for the provinces: 1) percent of population involved in agriculture as an occupation. 2) percent of "draftees" receiving highest mark on army examination. 3) percent of population whose education is beyond primary school. 4) percent of population who are Catholic. 5) percent of live births who live less than 1 year: infant mortality.

SOURCE

Mosteller and Tukey, *Data Analysis and Regression,* Addison-Wesley, 1977, pp. 549-551.

Unpublished data used by permission of Francine van de Walle, Population Study Center, University of Pennsylvania, Philadelphia, PA.

---

switzerland   Heights of Switzerland on 12 by 12 Grid   **switzerland**

Height in 1000's of feet to nearest 1000 feet. Accuracy of the data is questionable.

SOURCE

Beat Kleiner, personal communication.

---

telsam   Interviewer Response Data   **telsam**

---

response table giving counts of number of answers poor, fair, good, and excellent (the columns) for a number of different interviewers (the rows).

---

tone   Bricker's Tone-Ringer Preference Data   **tone**

---

appeal matrix giving standardized ratings of 100 tones (rows) by 43 subjects (columns). Standardized so that each subject has mean 0 and biased variance 1.

SOURCE

P. J. Bricker, "Listener Evaluation of Simulated Telephone Calling Signals", *Bell System Technical Journal,* Vol. 50, No. 5, 1971, pp. 1559-1578.

---

util   Earnings and Market/Book Ratio for Utilities   **util**

---

earn earnings of 45 utilities.
mktbook market price to book value ratio for the utilities.

votes Votes for Republican Candidate in Presidential Elections **votes**	

repub   percent of votes given to republican candidate in presidential elections from 1856 to 1976. Rows represent the 50 states (See dataset state.), and columns the 31 elections.

year   year of each election (corresponds to columns of x).

Contains missing values (NAs) for years prior to statehood.

SOURCE

S. Peterson, *A Statistical History of the American Presidential Elections,* Frederick Ungar Publishing Co., New York, 1973. Republished by permission.

Data from 1964 to 1976 is from R. M. Scammon, *American Votes 12,* Congressional Quarterly. Republished by permission of Richard M. Scammon, Editor, Elections Research Center.

Appendix 3
Index to S Functions

This appendix is meant to aid you in finding S functions that perform specific tasks.

We define a number of groups under which functions are listed. The first section gives a brief description of the groups and what they refer to. Look in these descriptions for one or more groups that match your task. Then look in the following index of functions by groups for a function of interest, and look in Appendix 1 for that function.

Groups of S Functions

Categorical Data
> Create, tabulate, and analyze discrete data.

Classes of Objects
> The various classes of objects that S knows about, including functions to create such objects, check whether an object is in a class, and coerce it into an object from a certain class.

Complex Numbers
> Compute with complex numbers.

Data Attributes
> Information about the attributes of objects, both those known by S, such as dim and levels, and those created by the user.

Data Directories

Manipulate data directories and the directory search list; deposit or retrieve objects in specific directories.

Data Manipulation

Manipulate vectors by sorting, reversing, replicating, combining, selecting, changing modes.

Documentation

Finding online information about S, its functions and its datasets. Also, keep track of what has been done in an S session.

Graphics—Add to Existing Plot

Modify an existing plot.

Graphics—Computations Related to Plotting

Create data structures that can be used to augment or build up plots. Also includes graphical functions that return special data structures.

Graphics—High-Level Plots

Create a complete plot, including appropriate coordinate systems and axes.

Graphics—Interacting with Plots

Utilize the interactive capabilities of graphical devices.

Graphics—Specific Devices

Hardware (terminals and plotters) for graphics; also, functions specific to certain devices.

Input/Output—Files

Read or write UNIX system files.

Interfaces to Other Languages

Interface to other languages, such as C and Fortran.

Linear Algebra

Compute with matrices and arrays, including products and decompositions.

Logical Operations

Produce or operate on logical (TRUE/ FALSE) data.

Looping and Iteration

Facilities for iteration, including language constructs such as `repeat` and functions such as `apply`.

Mathematical Operations
Carry out basic mathematical operations on vectors; trigonometric functions, square root, sum, etc.

Matrices
Create, modify, or analyze matrix data; see also **Linear Algebra**.

Printing
Facilities for printing objects of various sorts and in various ways.

Programming
Facilities related to the S language itself, often useful in writing functions.

Programming—Error Handling
Deal with errors in the programming environment; tracing debugging, error messages

Statistics—Hierarchical Clustering
Compute and display clustering; operate on cluster trees and distance structures.

Statistics—Multivariate Techniques
Statistical techniques that operate on multivariate data, but not including hierarchical clustering or regression, which are listed separately.

Statistics—Probability Distributions and Random Numbers
Compute probabilities (begin with "p"), quantiles (begin with "q"), densities (begin with "d"), and generate random numbers (begin with "r") for many distributions. Also includes probability plots and sampling.

Statistics—Regression
Linear regression, including robust regression and non-linear smoothing.

Statistics—Robust/Resistant Techniques
Operations which provide resistance to outliers.

Time-Series
Operate on time-series objects: seasonal adjustment, smoothing, etc.

Utilities
Operate on external data files; execute S non-interactively; Computations which are carried out by programs running under the UNIX operating system rather than by S functions.

Index to S Functions by Group

In the remainder of this appendix, the left column gives the names of functions or utilities; the right hand side gives a brief description. For details on a particular routine, see Appendix 1 under the routine name—the first name on the line, if there are several.

Categorical Data

category is.category as.category	Create Category from Discrete Data
cut	Create Category by Cutting Continuous Data
levels	Levels Attribute
loglin	Contingency Table Analysis
split	Split Data by Groups
table	Create Contingency Table from Categories
tapply	Apply a Function to a Ragged Array

Classes of Objects

array is.array as.array	Multi-way Arrays
as.function is.function	Function Objects
as.name is.name	Name Objects
as.null is.null	Null Objects
category is.category as.category	Create Category from Discrete Data
character is.character as.character	Character Objects
complex is.complex as.complex	Complex-valued Objects
double is.double as.double	Double Precision Objects
graphics	Create a Graphics Object
integer is.integer as.integer	Integer Objects
is.recursive is.atomic is.language	Test for Recursive or Atomic Objects
list is.list as.list	List Objects
logical is.logical as.logical	Logical Objects
matrix is.matrix as.matrix	Matrix Objects
numeric is.numeric as.numeric	Numeric Objects
single is.single as.single	Single Precision Objects
ts is.ts as.ts	Time-Series Objects
vector is.vector as.vector	Vectors (Simple Objects)

Complex Numbers

Arithmetic + - * / ^ %/% %%	Arithmetic Operators
complex is.complex as.complex	Complex-valued Objects
Complex Re Im Mod Arg Conj	Basic Complex Number Manipulation
fft	Fast Fourier Transform

Data Attributes

attr	Attribute of an Object
attributes	All Attributes of an Object
col row	Column and Row Numbers For a Matrix
dim	Dim Attribute of an Object
dimnames	Dimnames Attribute of an Object
length	Length of a Vector or List
levels	Levels Attribute
mode storage.mode	Data Mode of the Values in a Vector
names	Names Attribute of an Object
ncol nrow	Extents of a Matrix
structure	An Object with Given Attributes
tsp start end frequency	Tsp Attribute of an Object

Data Directories

assign	Assign Object to Directory or Frame
Assignment _ -> <<- <-	Assignment
attach	Attach a New Data Directory
AUDIT	Audit the Data Analysis Process
detach	Detach a Data Directory from Search List
dput dget	Write a Text Representation of an S Object
dump	Produce Text Representations of S Objects
.First .Last	Startup and Wrapup Actions
get exists	Find an Object
library library.dynam	Shared Functions and Datasets
ls	List of Datasets in Data Directory
remove	Remove Objects
restore	Bring Back Dumped Objects
rm	Remove by Name

Data Manipulation

append replace	Data Merging
Assignment _ -> <<- <-	Assignment
c	Combine Values
cbind rbind	Build Matrix from Columns or Rows
ed	Invoke ed Text Editor
grep	Search for Pattern in Text
ifelse	Conditional Data Selection
match	Match Items in Vector
order	Ordering to Create Sorted Data
paste	Glue Data Together to Make Character Data
rep	Replicate Data Values
rep.int	Replicate Integer Vector
rev	Reverse the Order of Elements in a Vector
seq :	Sequences
sort	Sort in Ascending Numeric or Alphabetic Order
sort.list	List of Indices that Sort Data
split	Split Data by Groups

```
Subscript [ [[ $          Extract or Replace Parts of an Object
unique duplicated         Unique or Duplicated Values in a Vector
vi                        Invoke vi Text Editor
```

Documentation

```
AUDIT                     Audit the Data Analysis Process
help args                 On-line Documentation
history again             Display and Re-Execute S Expressions
prompt                    Construct Documentation for Function or Data
stamp                     Time Stamp Output, Graph, and Audit File
```

Graphics—Add to Existing Plot

```
abline                    Plot Line in Intercept-Slope Form
axis                      Add an Axis to the Current Plot
box                       Add a Box Around a Plot
contour                   Contour Plot
identify                  Identify Points on Plot
labclust                  Label a Cluster Plot
legend                    Put a Legend on a Plot
lines points              Add Lines or Points to Current Plot
logo                      Draw the S Logo
matplot matlines matpoints  Plot Columns of Matrices
mtext                     Text in the Margins of a Plot
polygon                   Shade in a Polygonal Figure
segments arrows           Plot Disconnected Line Segments or Arrows
stamp                     Time Stamp Output, Graph, and Audit File
symbols                   Draw Symbols on a Plot
text                      Plot Text
title axes                Plot Titling Information and/or Axes
tsplot tslines tspoints   Plot Multiple Time-Series
usa                       United States Coastline and State Boundaries
```

Graphics—Computations Related to Plotting

```
approx                    Approximate Function from Discrete Values
boxplot                   Box Plots
chull                     Convex Hull of a Planar Set of Points
density                   Estimate Probability Density Function
hist                      Plot a Histogram
identify                  Identify Points on Plot
interp                    Bivariate Interpolation for Irregular Data
lowess                    Scatter Plot Smoothing
mstree                    Minimal Spanning Tree and Multivariate Planing
par                       Graphical Parameters
plclust                   Plot Trees From Hierarchical Clustering
pretty                    Vector of Prettied Values
qqplot qqnorm             Quantile-Quantile Plots
quickvu                   Make Slides with Simple Lists
range                     Range of Data
```

Input/Output—Files

`AUDIT`	Audit the Data Analysis Process
`cat`	Print Anything
`dput dget`	Write a Text Representation of an S Object
`history again`	Display and Re-Execute S Expressions
`on.exit`	Exit Expression For a Function
`readline`	Read a Line from the Terminal
`scan`	Input Data from a File
`sink`	Send S Output to a File
`source`	Parse and Evaluate S Expressions from a File
`unix`	Execute a Command
`unlink`	Remove a File
`write`	Write Data to File

Interfaces to Other Languages

`.Fortran .C`	Call a Fortran or C Routine
`.Internal`	Call Internal C Code
`.S`	Call an Old S Function
`unix`	Execute a Command

Linear Algebra

`aperm`	Array Permutations
`apply`	Apply a Function to Sections of an Array
`backsolve`	Backsolve Upper-Triangular Equations
`chol`	Cholesky Decomposition of Symmetric Matrix
`crossprod %c%`	Matrix Cross Product Operator
`diag`	Diagonal Matrices
`eigen`	Eigen Analysis of Symmetric Matrix
`lapply`	Apply a Function to Elements of a List
`Matrix-product %*%`	Matrix Multiplication Operator
`napsack`	Solve Knapsack Problems
`outer %o%`	Generalized Outer Products
`prcomp`	Principal Components Analysis
`qr as.qr is.qr`	QR Matrix Decomposition
`qr.coef qr.fitted qr.resid qr.qty qr.qy`	
	Use a QR Matrix Decomposition
`scale`	Scale Columns of a Matrix
`solve`	Solve Linear Equations and Invert Matrices
`svd`	Singular Value Decomposition
`t`	Matrix Transpose

Logical Operations

`all any`	Logical Sum and Product
`Comparison != < <= == > >=`	Comparison Operators
`ifelse`	Conditional Data Selection
`Logic &	! xor`	Logical Operators

Looping and Iteration

apply	Apply a Function to Sections of an Array
lapply	Apply a Function to Elements of a List
sapply	Apply a Function to Elements of a List
sweep	Sweep Out Array Summaries
tapply	Apply a Function to a Ragged Array
unlist	Make Vector From a List

Mathematical Operations

abs	Absolute Value
acos asin atan	Inverse Trigonometric Functions
acosh asinh atanh	Inverse Hyperbolic Trigonometric Functions
approx	Approximate Function from Discrete Values
Arithmetic + - * / ^ %/% %%	Arithmetic Operators
ceiling floor trunc	Integer Values
Comparison != < <= == > >=	Comparison Operators
Complex Re Im Mod Arg Conj	Basic Complex Number Manipulation
cos sin tan	Trigonometric Functions
cosh sinh tanh	Hyperbolic Trigonometric Functions
cumsum	Cumulative Sums
diff	Create a Differenced Series
exp log log10 sqrt	Exponential Functions
gamma lgamma	Gamma Function (and its Natural Logarithm)
max min	Extremes
mean	Mean (Arithmetic Average) Value
median	Median
pmax pmin	Parallel Maximum or Minimum
quantile	Empirical Quantiles
range	Range of Data
rank	Ranks of Data
round signif	Rounding Functions
sum prod	Sums and Products
var cor	Variance, Covariance, and Correlation

Matrices

aperm	Array Permutations
apply	Apply a Function to Sections of an Array
array is.array as.array	Multi-way Arrays
backsolve	Backsolve Upper-Triangular Equations
cancor	Canonical Correlation Analysis
cbind rbind	Build Matrix from Columns or Rows
chol	Cholesky Decomposition of Symmetric Matrix
cmdscale	Classical Metric Multi-dimensional Scaling
col row	Column and Row Numbers For a Matrix
crossprod %c%	Matrix Cross Product Operator
cutree	Create Groups from Hierarchical Clustering
diag	Diagonal Matrices
dim	Dim Attribute of an Object

dimnames	Dimnames Attribute of an Object
discr	Discriminant Analysis
dist	Distance Matrix Calculation
eigen	Eigen Analysis of Symmetric Matrix
hclust	Hierarchical Clustering
l1fit	Minimum Absolute Residual (L1) Regression
leaps	All-Subset Regressions by Leaps and Bounds
loglin	Contingency Table Analysis
lsfit	Linear Least-Squares Fit
matplot matlines matpoints	Plot Columns of Matrices
matrix is.matrix as.matrix	Matrix Objects
Matrix-product %*%	Matrix Multiplication Operator
mstree	Minimal Spanning Tree and Multivariate Planing
mulbar	Multiple Bar Plot
ncol nrow	Extents of a Matrix
plclust	Plot Trees From Hierarchical Clustering
plotfit	Two-way Plot of Fit
prcomp	Principal Components Analysis
rbiwt	Robust Simple Regression by Biweight
rreg	Robust Regression
scale	Scale Columns of a Matrix
solve	Solve Linear Equations and Invert Matrices
Subscript [[[$	Extract or Replace Parts of an Object
subtree	Extract Part of a Cluster Tree
svd	Singular Value Decomposition
sweep	Sweep Out Array Summaries
t	Matrix Transpose
tapply	Apply a Function to a Ragged Array
tsmatrix	Create Matrix with Time-Series as Columns
twoway	Analysis of Two-way Table

Printing

cat	Print Anything
deparse	Turn Parsed Expression into Character Form
dput dget	Write a Text Representation of an S Object
format	Formatted Character Data
gr.display	Display a Graphics Object
prarray	Print a Multi-Dimensional Array
pratom	Print Data with Atomic Modes
print	Print Data
prlist	Print a List
prmatrix	Print a Matrix
prstructure	Print an Object with Attributes
prts	Print a Time Series

Programming

allocated	Memory Allocated in S Frames
amatch	Argument Matching
as.function is.function	Function Objects
as.name is.name	Name Objects
assign	Assign Object to Directory or Frame
bind	Bind to Current Function Definitions
call is.call as.call	Function Calls
call_S	Call S from a C Routine
DBLEPR INTPR REALPR	Printing from a Fortran Routine
.Dictionary	Create a Dictionary
do.call	Execute a Function Call
dyn.load	Dynamically Load an Object File
eval	Evaluate an Expression
expression as.expression is.expression	
	Expression Objects
.First .Last	Startup and Wrapup Actions
history again	Display and Re-Execute S Expressions
invisible	Mark Function as Non-Printing
missing	Check for missing arguments
nargs	Number of Arguments to Function
parse	Parse Expressions
.Program	Control Execution of S
restart	Take Over Error Handling
S_alloc	Storage Allocation in C
storage	Show Memory Usage
substitute	Substitute in an Expression
switch	Evaluate One of Several Expressions
synchronize	Synchronize Datasets
Syntax for repeat while break next { return	
	S Expressions
sys.call sys.calls sys.frame sys.frames sys.nframe sys.parent	
sys.parents sys.status sys.on.exit	
	System Evaluator State
trace untrace	Trace Calls to Functions
traceback	Print Call Stack After Error
trace.on std.trace count.trace browser.trace sys.trace	
	Control over Tracing
unlink	Remove a File

Programming—Error Handling

browser	Browse Interactively in a Function's Frame
debugger	Computational State at the Time of an Error
dump.calls dump.frames	Save All Calls or Frames on Errors
help args	On-line Documentation
on.exit	Exit Expression For a Function
options	Set or Print Options
stop warning	Error and Warning Messages
warnings	Print Warning Messages

Statistics—Hierarchical Clustering

clorder   Re-Order Leaves of a Cluster Tree
cutree   Create Groups from Hierarchical Clustering
dist   Distance Matrix Calculation
hclust   Hierarchical Clustering
labclust   Label a Cluster Plot
plclust   Plot Trees From Hierarchical Clustering
subtree   Extract Part of a Cluster Tree

Statistics—Multivariate Techniques

cancor   Canonical Correlation Analysis
cmdscale   Classical Metric Multi-dimensional Scaling
contour   Contour Plot
cutree   Create Groups from Hierarchical Clustering
discr   Discriminant Analysis
dist   Distance Matrix Calculation
faces   Plot Symbolic Faces
hclust   Hierarchical Clustering
labclust   Label a Cluster Plot
loglin   Contingency Table Analysis
mstree   Minimal Spanning Tree and Multivariate Planing
mulbar   Multiple Bar Plot
pairs   Produce All Pair-wise Scatterplots
persp   Three-Dimensional Perspective Plots
plclust   Plot Trees From Hierarchical Clustering
prcomp   Principal Components Analysis
stars   Star Plots of Multivariate Data
starsymb   Plot a Single Star Symbol
subtree   Extract Part of a Cluster Tree
twoway   Analysis of Two-way Table

Statistics—Probability Distributions and Random Numbers

Beta dbeta pbeta qbeta rbeta   Beta Distribution
Cauchy dcauchy pcauchy qcauchy rcauchy
                                    Cauchy Distribution
Chisquare dchisq pchisq qchisq rchisq Chi-Square Distribution
density   Estimate Probability Density Function
Exponential dexp pexp qexp rexp   Exponential Distribution
F df pf qf rf   F Distribution
Gamma dgamma pgamma qgamma rgamma   Gamma Distribution
Logistic dlogis plogis qlogis rlogis Logistic Distribution
Lognormal dlnorm plnorm qlnorm rlnorm Lognormal Distribution
Normal dnorm pnorm qnorm rnorm   Normal Distribution
ppoints   Plotting Points for Q-Q Plots
qqplot qqnorm   Quantile-Quantile Plots
sample   Generate Random Samples or Permutations of Data
set.seed   Set Seed for Random Number Generators
Stable rstab   Stable Family of Distributions

```
T dt pt qt rt                    Student's t-Distribution
Uniform dunif punif qunif runif  Uniform Distribution
```

Statistics—Regression

```
hat            Hat Matrix Regression Diagnostic
l1fit          Minimum Absolute Residual (L1) Regression
leaps          All-Subset Regressions by Leaps and Bounds
lowess         Scatter Plot Smoothing
lsfit          Linear Least-Squares Fit
ls.summary     Summary Information from 'lsfit' Object
rbiwt          Robust Simple Regression by Biweight
rreg           Robust Regression
```

Statistics—Robust/Resistant Techniques

```
lowess         Scatter Plot Smoothing
mean           Mean (Arithmetic Average) Value
median         Median
rbiwt          Robust Simple Regression by Biweight
rreg           Robust Regression
sabl           Seasonal Decomposition
smooth         Non-linear Smoothing Using Running Medians
twoway         Analysis of Two-way Table
```

Time-Series

```
aggregate        Decrease Periodicity of Time Series by Aggregation
diff             Create a Differenced Series
fft              Fast Fourier Transform
lag              Create a Lagged Time-Series
monthplot        Seasonal Subseries Plot
sabl             Seasonal Decomposition
sablplot         Sabl Decomposition - Data and Components Plot
time cycle       Create Time Vector
ts is.ts as.ts   Time-Series Objects
tsmatrix         Create Matrix with Time-Series as Columns
tsplot tslines tspoints  Plot Multiple Time-Series
window           Window a Time-Series
```

Utilities

```
AUDIT          Audit the Data Analysis Process
BATCH          Batch (Non-Interactive) Execution of S
DBCONVERT      Convert Old-S Datasets to S Objects
LOAD           Create a Private Version of S
MAC.to.FUN     Partial Conversion of Old-S Macros to Functions
TRUNC_AUDIT    Truncate the Audit File
```

Appendix 4
Old-S and S

This appendix describes S from the viewpoint of users of the previous S software, as described in the 1984 book, *S: An Interactive Environment for Data Analysis and Graphics*. It discusses some of the differences between the new and the old versions of S and outlines steps for converting from the old to the new.

This appendix is intended solely for those readers who have had contact with the old version of S. If this book was your introduction to S, you may (and should) ignore this appendix.

Why a New Version of S?

Since old-S was popular and widespread, why create a new version?

- The new function definition capability is much better than the old macro processor. It follows exactly the same semantic model as the rest of the language, and thus is much easier to learn and debug. Functions are much more powerful than macros and, since they are objects in the language, they can be printed, passed as arguments to other functions, etc., just like data objects.
- The new system makes writing S software simpler in many cases. For example, menu-driven interfaces are simpler and work better. S functions can use UNIX system commands more easily.
- There are new kinds of calculation that were not possible in old-S, such as symbol manipulation. There are new kinds of data structures, more general treatment of data, and the language itself can be treated as data.

- New features include complex arithmetic, double-precision computations, faster graphics, and more user control over the way the system operates. Internal changes make some computations more efficient, especially when explicit looping is involved.
- The algorithm and interface languages, described in *Extending the S System,* are no longer necessary. Instead, functions are able to call C and Fortran algorithms directly. Old-S interface routines can be called from functions, so that previous work will be reusable. In addition, UNIX commands can be called from S to do various operations.
- The integration of S into the operating system is much cleaner. The internal code forms a single process, essentially all written in C.

Conversion

Hopefully, the preceding section convinced you that you should convert from old-S to S. This section will give you the information on how to convert your existing old-S data so that it is available in S.

1. Since S uses a different internal form of data object than old-S, you need to convert any old-S data directories. They are UNIX directories, typically named `swork` or `sdata`. S combines these two into one directory named `.Data`. To do this conversion, first execute the UNIX command *cd* to get into the directory in which you will want to execute S. Typically, this will be the same directory where your `swork` and `sdata` directories reside. Execute the commands:

   ```
   $ S DBCONVERT swork
   $ S DBCONVERT sdata
   ```

   which create a `.Data` directory and convert all old-S data into the new form.

2. If you had macros in your `sdata` directory, you should convert them to S functions. Functions will run more quickly and can often be substantially simpler than macros. Calling a macro is possbile, but discouraged. You can *not* write new macros in S. The first step in conversion is to execute

   ```
   $ S MAC.to.FUN
   ```

   in the directory containing `.Data`. Any macros will undergo an automatic conversion process that gets them on the road to being functions. All of the converted macros will be placed together in a file named `mac.to.fun.out`. This is where the hard work begins; you must now modify these functions to work correctly in S. This may take a bit of work. Once you have modified the functions in the file `mac.fun.out`, execute

```
$ S <mac.to.fun.out
```

to define the new functions.

Use `help(DBCONVERT)`, and `help(MAC.to.FUN)` for more details.

One other S function that you might find useful is `.S`. This function allows an S function to invoke an old-S interface routine. (Interface routines were described in the book *Extending the S System*. If you don't know what an interface routine is, you probably don't have any, and you should skip ahead to the next section.)

Suppose you have an old-S interface routine that defines function `foo`. You can use `dyn.load` or `S LOAD` to incorporate the object code for `foo` into the running version of S. Then, you should write an S function:

```
foo <- function(...) .S(foo(...),"foo")
```

to invoke your object code from S. The `.S` function will automatically convert data objects from S form into old-S form, call the interface routine appropriately, and return the result.

Important Differences Between S and Old-S

The differences listed here are known incompatibilities between S and old-S. The reasons for these differ; in some cases the new version provides a substantial improvement over the old one. In other cases, there was no way to provide the functionality of the old version.

Terminology: Since the variety of data objects in S is much greater than that in old-S, we have dropped the term *dataset* in favor of the more general term *object*. Similarly, old-S *structures* are now typically *lists*.

Functions: Functions are now much more integrated into the language. In particular, each function is an object containing the function definition. This means that typing a function name by itself causes the function definition to be printed, while typing the function name followed by parentheses causes the function to be executed. For example:

```
> ls
function(pattern = "", pos = 1) {
    cmd <- paste("cd ", .Search.list[pos], "; ls 2>/dev/null")
    if(pattern!="") cmd <- paste(cmd, "-d", pattern)
    else cmd <- paste(cmd, "|sed '/^\./d'")
    unix(cmd)
}
```

```
> ls()
  [1] "x"   "y"   "z"
```

The old-S syntactic form that allowed you to omit parentheses in a top-level function call is now no longer available. Where you once could say

```
plot x,y
```

S now uses a single, uniform syntax for calls:

```
plot(x,y)
```

In particular, `plot` by itself means the function object, rather than a call with no arguments.

Because functions are ordinary objects, they can be hidden by objects of the same name. For example,

```
> matrix ←1:10
> matrix(1:12,3,4)
Warning messages:
Looking for object "matrix" of mode "function",
  ignored one of mode "numeric"
```

gets a warning message because the definition of the `matrix` function is hidden by the object named `matrix`.

The same situation may arise with arguments whose names are the same as functions. Suppose you want to define a function that will print something if an argument `print` is TRUE. The following will not work:

```
foo ← function(x,print=T) { if(print) print(x) }
```

because the function call `print(x)` is assumed to refer to the argument `print`. The solution is to name the argument something else:

```
foo ← function(x,printout=T) { if(printout) print(x) }
```

In this case, since argument names can be abbreviated, you can still use

```
foo(result,print=T)  .
```

Of course, there are benefits to this treatment of functions as objects. In particular, the functions `apply`, `tapply`, `sapply` and `help` no longer require function names to be quoted. Thus

```
help(stem)
```

gives information on the `stem` function.

Another feature of functions is that any objects created inside a function are *local* to that function—they go away when the function exits. Thus it is easy and efficient to create temporary objects inside functions. There is no need for a special naming convention to give unique names to temporary objects. If you must create a permanent object from inside a function, the permanent assignment operator, "<<–", can be used.

Macros: The macro facility is (barely) present in S and its use is discouraged. See `help(macro)` for details. In particular, there is no mechanism for defining new macros or modifying existing ones; functions `define` and `medit` no longer exist. Macros are created by the database conversion process, but the `MAC.to.FUN` macro-to-function converter should be run as soon as possible to turn any useful macros into functions.

Prefix: The `prefix` function is not supported. The UNIX system offers a good alternative, notably directories of various names to hold various related sets of data. See the `collection` example in section 9.3 for a facility similar to `prefix`.

Along with the demise of prefixes is the demise of the convention that objects can be named with a leading "$". (For those who do not know, in old-S, `$abc` meant the dataset named `abc`, regardless of any prefix in effect.)

Source: The semantics of the source function are changed. It is now evaluated in its entirety with no assignments happening until the source command exits normally. This means several things: source files that encounter errors will not affect any permanent objects; and large source files are somewhat inefficient. Also, the last expression evaluated in the source file is the value of the `source` function; this is the only value that will be auto-printed. A better way to evaluate a large source file, e.g., file `my.source`, is to execute the command

```
S <my.source
```

This evaluates the file one expression at a time and assignments happen as each expression is evaluated.

Extensions to S Functions

This section discusses old-S functions with new or extended capabilities.

Arithmetic: S now standardly uses double-precision computations, and it also incorporates a double-precision complex data mode. When double-precision data is passed to the (relatively few) functions that are still implemented by calls to the `.S` function, it is automatically converted to storage mode `single`. Complex data cannot be passed to such functions.

Other Operators: The comparison operators work on more kinds of data, including complex and recursive data modes. New rules provide uniform treatment of arrays and other special kinds of data when they are used as operands. There are new operators "`&&`" and "`||`" that provide conditional evaluation of "and" and "or".

Subscripts: Subscripting is also extended. The empty subscript, `x[]`, refers to all the data in the object. The subscript expressions on the left of an assignment can be more general than in old-S. There is an important new distinction between subscripts and single elements for lists, etc. See section 5.1 and 5.5 for other extensions.

Apply: The functions `apply`, `tapply`, and `sapply` are much more general. Any function, including user-written ones, can be applied. You also no longer have to quote the function name. Thus, you could write and apply a median-absolute-deviation function like this:

```
mad ← function(x) median(abs(x-median(x)))
m ← matrix(runif(20),4,5)
apply(m,1,mad)   # row mad's
```

These functions are no longer implemented specially. Therefore, there is no particular difference in efficiency between them and explicit iteration, such as `for` loops. A new function, `lappy`, is a simpler version of `sapply`, and is recommended for most applications.

Graphics: For all graphics devices, there is a function `Device.Default(name)` that takes care of setting up default values for the graphic parameters. Since user-written functions can override system functions, users can write their own version of `Device.Default` to do whatever device initialization they would like.

Also, many of the device driver functions have slightly changed arguments from the way they were in old-S. For example, `hpgl` has a new `file=` argument to allow the hpgl output characters to be sent to a file rather than just the UNIX standard output. The file can then be shipped to a batch plotter, for example an HP7550 plotter running as a spooled device.

Minor Differences

The following differences between S and old-S are minor and should cause at most minor inconvenience.

The precedence of arithmetic operators was changed slightly. In old-S, the precedence of unary minus was higher than that of exponentiation, and in S the situation has been reversed. The interpretation of

```
-x^2
```

is now

```
-(x^2)
```

which is more appropriate in typical computational situations.

The dataset `Random.seed` is now called `.Random.seed`.

The function `c` used to accept a structure and produce a vector of all data elements in the structure. It no longer does so; use `unlist` to perform this task.

The `options` function has several new arguments and has dropped some old ones.

The function `list`, which used to be identical to `ls`, now creates lists. If you want to know what is on a data directory, use `ls`.

Special operators, such as `%*` for matrix multiply, are now written with a leading and trailing percent, i.e. `%*%`, `%o%`, `%c%`. You can also define your own special operators; see section 7.3.

The `search` function now only lists data directories (since there are no longer any built-ins or chapters).

The `cstr` function no longer has an `stype=` argument. You probably never used it in old-S, anyway. In general, you should use the function `list` in place of the obsolete `cstr`.

The `rm` function no longer has `print=` or `value=` arguments.

The datasets `INT`, `REAL`, `LGL`, and `CHAR` are now of mode character rather than integer. However, they are still correct for the common use as in: `coerce(x,CHAR)`. The function `mode` returns a character string, not an integer.

The old-S function `NA(x)` is gone, although `na(x)` still works. The new primitive routine for testing for missing values is `is.na(x)`.

In old-S, when given a non-vector structure the `c` function would combine the values of all components into one vector. It no longer has this functionality.

The `menu` function has changed considerably. See section 6.2 for details of how to use the new menu facility.

Functions That Are Gone

This section describes old-S functions that are no longer provided and their replacements (if any). Look under `deprecated` in Appendix 1 for more details.

There are fewer device drivers for S than for old-S. If there is demand, it should be possible to resurrect (and even improve upon) old device driver functions. On the other hand, for some old devices, there are probably no users.

The `chapter` function is no more. Instead, use the `dyn.load` or S `LOAD` facility to put together your own version of S that incorporates your functions. Note that the `.S` function allows you to write functions that call the compiled versions of old-S functions.

The `save` function is gone. Since there are no longer two databases (`swork` and `sdata` are replaced by `.Data`) the `save` function is no longer needed.

The `diary` function is gone since there is a `.Audit` file always available. The function `history` uses `.Audit` to examine and re-evaluate past expressions. If you insist on not having an audit trail, you can create an unwritable `.Audit` file in the directory where you run S by typing

```
touch .Audit
chmod -w .Audit
```

A few functions have gone away due to lack of general usefulness: `hardcopy`, `mail`, `flood`, `hatch`, `polyfill`, `defer`, `replot`, `tprint`, `blitmenu`.

Functions designed specifically for the Teletype 5620 Dot Mapped Display terminal, specifically `blitid`, `scatmat`, and `spin`, have been moved to a section of the S library (see the detailed documentation for function `library`).

See the entries `Deprecated` and `Defunct` in Appendix 1 for a list of old-S functions in these two categories, with hints for what to do now.

Index

685